Sharing the Wealth

International union
for the scientific study
of population

The International Union for the Scientific Study of Population Problems was set up in 1928, with Dr Raymond Pearl as President. At that time the Union's main purpose was to promote international scientific co-operation to study the various aspects of population problems, through national committees and through its members themselves. In 1947 the International Union for the Scientific Study of Population (IUSSP) was reconstituted into its present form.

It expanded its activities to:

- stimulate research on population
- develop interest in demographic matters among governments, national and international organizations, scientific bodies, and the general public
- foster relations between people involved in population studies
- disseminate scientific knowledge on population.

The principal ways through which the IUSSP currently achieves its aims are:

- organization of worldwide or regional conferences
- operations of Scientific Committees under the auspices of the Council
- organization of training courses
- publication of conference proceedings and committee reports.

Demography can be defined by its field of study and its analytical methods. Accordingly, it can be regarded as the scientific study of human populations primarily with respect to their size, their structure, and their development. For reasons which are related to the history of the discipline, the demographic method is essentially inductive: progress in knowledge results from the improvement of observation, the sophistication of measurement methods, and the search for regularities and stable factors leading to the formulation of explanatory models. In conclusion, the three objectives of demographic analysis are to describe, measure, and analyse.

International Studies in Demography is the outcome of an agreement concluded by the IUSSP and the Oxford University Press. The joint series reflects the broad range of the Union's activities; it is based on the seminars organized by the Union and important international meetings in the field of population and development. The Editorial Board of the series is comprised of:

Sharing the Wealth

Demographic Change and Economic Transfers between Generations

Edited by

Andrew Mason and
Georges Tapinos

OXFORD
UNIVERSITY PRESS

This book has been printed digitally and produced in a standard specification in order to ensure its continuing availability

OXFORD
UNIVERSITY PRESS

Great Clarendon Street, Oxford OX2 6DP

Oxford University Press is a department of the University of Oxford.
It furthers the University's objective of excellence in research, scholarship,
and education by publishing worldwide in

Oxford New York

Auckland Bangkok Buenos Aires Cape Town Chennai
Dar es Salaam Delhi Hong Kong Istanbul Karachi Kolkata
Kuala Lumpur Madrid Melbourne Mexico City Mumbai Nairobi
São Paulo Shanghai Taipei Tokyo Toronto

Oxford is a registered trade mark of Oxford University Press
in the UK and in certain other countries

Published in the United States
by Oxford University Press Inc., New York

Reprinted 2003

ISBN 0-19- 829620-7

Editors' Preface

The papers in this volume are based on a conference on 'Intergenerational Economic Relations and Demographic Changes' held in Honolulu, Hawaii in September 1995. The conference was jointly sponsored by the International Union for the Scientific Study of Population (IUSSP) and the East-West Center Program on Population (EWCPOP).

Organization of the conference was initiated by the IUSSP Economic Demography Committee whose members included Georges Tapinos (Chair), Susan Jane, Jiang Zhenghua, Andras Uthoff, and Robert Willis. The Organizing and Editorial Committee for the conference was co-chaired by Andrew Mason and Georges Tapinos and its members included Andrew Foster, Susan Jane, Jiang Zhenghua, Ronald Lee, Andras Uthoff, and Robert Willis. Local arrangements were the responsibility of France Jans, on behalf of IUSSP, and Valerie Wong, on behalf of EWCPOP.

In addition to resources provided by IUSSP and the East-West Center, financial support for the conference was provided by the Unitied Nations Population Fund. Their contribution is greatfully acknowledged. We are deeply indebted to Sandra E. Ward, who directed copy-editing of the volume, and to Cynthia Nakachi, Ann Takeyasu, and Dolly Testa, who assisted with manuscript production. We also appreciate the effort and many useful suggestions of two anonymous reviewers.

Andrew Mason
Georges Tapinos

Honolulu and Paris

Contents

List of Figures

List of Tables

List of Contributors

Joseph G. Altonji is professor of economics at the Department of Economics and the Institute for Policy Research, Northwestern University, Evanston, Illinois.

Sumon K. Bhaumik is senior consultant at the Investment Information and Credit Rating Agency of India, Calcutta.

Didier Blanchet is director of the Ecole Nationale de la Statistique et de l'Administration Economique (ENSAE), Paris.

Jorge Bravo is expert in population, Latin American Demographic Centre (CELADE), Santiago, Chile.

Alessandro Cigno is professor of economics, Faculty of Political Science, University of Florence, Italy.

Andrew D. Foster is associate professor, Department of Economics, Brown University, Providence, Rhode Island.

Jagadeesh Gokhale is economic adviser to the Federal Reserve Bank of Cleveland.

Fumio Hayashi is professor of economics at Tokyo University, Tokyo, Japan.

Laurence J. Kotlikoff is professor of economics at Boston University, Boston, Massachusetts.

Anne Laferrère is head of the Housing division of the Institut National de la Statistique et des Etudes Economiques (INSEE), Paris.

Ronald D. Lee is professor of demography and economics at the University of California, Berkeley.

Yean-Ju Lee is assistant professor of sociology at the University of Hawaii, Manoa, and a fellow at the East-West Center, Honolulu.

Andrew Mason is professor of economics and chair at the University of Hawaii, Manoa, and a senior fellow at the East-West Center, Honolulu.

Tim Miller is a research analyst in the Department of Demography, University of California, Berkeley.

JEAN-ALAIN MONFORT is administrator at the Institut National de la Statistique et des Etudes Economiques (INSEE), Paris.

JEFFREY B. NUGENT is professor of economics at the University of Southern California, Los Angeles.

RAFAEL ROFMAN is a chief of the Economic Studies and Statistics Unit, Supervision of Pension Funds, and researcher at the Centro de Estudios de Población (CENEP), Buenos Aires.

MARK R. ROSENZWEIG is professor of economics, University of Pennsylvania, Philadelphia.

GEORGES TAPINOS is professor of economics and demography at the Institut d'Etudes Politiques de Paris.

SHRIPAD TULJAPURKAR is president of Mountain View Research, Los Altos, California, and consulting professor of biological sciences at the Morrison Institute for Population and Resource Studies, Stanford University, Stanford, California.

SALVADOR VALDÉS-PRIETO is professor of economics at the Institute of Economics, Pontificia Universidad Católica de Chile, Santiago.

1 Introduction

Andrew Mason and Georges Tapinos

The papers in this volume add to a growing literature on intergenerational transfers. The issues addressed are important ones. Roughly half of any population, children and elderly, depend on intergenerational transfers to fulfil their material needs. The transfers from the working population to these two dependent populations surely dominate all other transfers in any economy, modern or traditional. Thus the circumstances that govern the extent, timing, and magnitude of transfers have an enormous impact on the distribution of income, economic efficiency, and economic growth.

The welfare of future generations depends on the nature and extent of intergenerational transfers. Investment in physical plant, human capital, and research and development all involve, to some degree, transfers between the generations. The accumulation of human capital is determined largely by expenditures of parents on behalf of their children. The accumulation of physical capital is influenced by the extent of altruism that parents feel towards their children and by the extent to which parents upon reaching old age can rely on their children. More generally, the pace of economic development and the welfare of future generations depend on the sacrifices that current generations are prepared to make on their behalf.

Intergenerational transfers are a pervasive feature of all countries studied in this collection, but the function of transfers, their impact, and the means by which they are achieved vary greatly, depending on social, economic, demographic, and political circumstances. The demographic transition and accompanying changes in age structure have had a profound effect on the form of intergenerational transfers. High-fertility, rapidly growing populations are dominated by the young. Half or more of some populations are under the age of 15, and typically only 2 to 3 per cent are 65 or older. In such circumstances the dominant intergenerational resource flow is inevitably from workers to the young. As population growth slows and population ageing begins, the demographic balance changes inexorably. In Western Europe the percentage of the population under age 15 has dropped to 18 per cent or less and the percentage 65 or older has reached 15 per cent. Given current fertility and mortality patterns, it is only a matter of time before the proportion of elderly exceeds the proportion under age 15. What are the implications of these demographic changes for the direction and magnitude of transfers? For the institutional arrangements that affect transfers? And for economic growth and the broader macroeconomy?

Economic conditions vary as widely as demographic circumstances. Differences in living standards, in economic stability, and in rates of economic growth all have implications for intergenerational transfers. For example, differences in rates of economic growth produce intergenerational differences in income. Simple calculations illustrate this point. Between 1950 and 1990, real output per worker grew at 5.4 per cent per annum in Japan, 1.5 per cent in the United States, and 0.9 per cent in Kenya (Summers and Heston 1991). Given such rates of growth, reckoning 25 years as a generation length, and abstracting from details, we calculate that each successive generation in Japan can expect to earn 3.9 times the amount of the preceding generation. US growth rates yield an income for members of one generation equal to 1.44 times the income of the previous generation. In Kenya the ratio is 1.26. To what extent do these differences in income and economic growth reflect differences in behaviour, institutions, and policies towards intergenerational transfers? And how, in turn, will differences in intergenerational income affect transfers in the future?

Intergenerational transfers are achieved by three types of institutions: the family, the financial market, and the state. The effectiveness with which these institutions function varies enormously. An overly simple generalization is that in traditional settings, financial markets, and political institutions are poorly developed. A safer generalization is that informal credit markets give way to formal, centralized markets as development proceeds, and that local, village-level political institutions may erode and centralized, national political systems develop as communications and transportation systems improve and mobility increases. With changes in the institutional setting come changes in the ways and possibly the effectiveness with which intergenerational transfers achieve the objectives that motivate such transfers.

The chapters in Part I of this volume describe the intergenerational features of the macroeconomy and analyse how the 'intergenerational economy' interacts with other features of the economy or population. Analysis of the macroeconomy requires a standard set of tools for measuring economic activity. The development of national income and product accounts has allowed us to track the features of economies over time and to compare one economy with another. Likewise, the analysis of populations is greatly facilitated by agreed-upon tools for describing populations. By comparison, the development of standard tools for describing the intergenerational features of an economy is in its infancy. What features of the intergenerational economy are important? What are the respective roles of the household sector, the business sector, and the government? What are the accounting relationships? How can 'intergenerational accounts' be constructed and how sensitive are they to the alternative assumptions that inevitably must be made? The potential pay-off to understanding the workings of the intergenerational economy is clearly evident in the variety of issues addressed in these chapters. Those issues include fertility decline, the distribution of income, and saving rates.

Part II addresses the prominent role the public sector has attempted to play as a guarantor of economic security for the elderly. In no area is the interaction between population and intergenerational economic issues more apparent than in the development and maintenance of programmes for the elderly. The programmes currently in place were developed during an era when the elderly represented a small fraction of the population. Pay-as-you-go (PAYGO) systems, in which current retirees were supported by current workers, were irresistible to many governments. As the demographic balance has shifted, the same systems have become increasingly burdensome for workers and calls for reform increasingly vocal. How the current systems evolved, how they should be reformed, and how efforts to reform them will interact with political realities are issues that will engage researchers for a long time to come.

The 'intergenerational behaviour' of the family and its interaction with the public and private sectors are the common themes of the chapters presented in the final section of this volume. Understanding the behaviour of the family is the key issue addressed here, as in many studies published elsewhere, because decisions by the family have an important bearing on efficiency, equity, and economic security. Understanding the behaviour of the family, and how it varies from setting to setting, is central to understanding human capital formation, economic growth, and the distribution of income. The role of the family is far from static, however. In traditional societies, the young and the elderly depend almost exclusively on other family members to fulfil their material needs. The development of financial and political institutions supplements and, to some extent, supplants the family. What factors determine the ways in which these alternative institutional arrangements evolve and interact with one another? What are the implications of the alternative arrangements for economic security, equity, and growth?

Chapters contained throughout this volume are noteworthy for their efforts to deal with difficult theoretical and empirical issues. Intergenerational transfers and the conditions believed to govern them are notoriously difficult to measure. Intergenerational transfers often occur within households and, thus, are not captured by surveys which take the household as the decision-making unit. Monetary transfers are a small portion of the goods and services exchanged between generations in traditional and industrial societies alike. Transfers in kind are difficult to value. When time is exchanged even the direction of the resource flow is in question. Only rarely are data collected with the study of intergenerational transfers in mind. Altonji *et al.*'s analysis of the PIDS demonstrates the rich returns possible when such data are collected. However, analysis of intergenerational transfers outside the USA, especially, in traditional settings, will continue to rely heavily on the ability of the researcher to tease out results through the use of sound theory and appropriate statistical method. Despite the obstacles, the papers presented in this volume and research reported elsewhere is providing a better understanding of the extent of intergenerational transfers, the motivations behind them, and their economic impact.

Part I: Intergenerational Accounting

The existence and significance of intergenerational or inter-age transfers for the macroeconomy have been recognized for some time. Such transfers have played a prominent role in life-cycle saving models (Modigliani and Brumberg 1954; Modigliani 1966, 1988*b*). Samuelson's classic (1958) article on intergenerational transfers and the biological rate of interest has spurred a mini-industry of overlapping generation models. Barro (1974) has demonstrated the importance of these transfers for understanding the central workings of the macroeconomy.

The contribution to this volume by Ronald Lee in Chapter 2 is part of his path-breaking and continuing effort to provide a comprehensive framework for understanding and analysing inter-age transfers. Four elements of Lee's work are present to varying degrees in this contribution. First, he develops measures and tools for describing the reallocation system. Second, he presents a set of principles that govern the reallocation system. Third, he applies those methods to a variety of contexts describing how reallocation systems vary across time and place. And, fourth, he uses the methods and empirical work to examine some of the important macro-level implications of real allocation systems.

Lee and his colleagues have examined the US reallocation system in some detail in previous studies. In the current study he marshals evidence needed to describe reallocation systems in developing economies and pre-agricultural societies. In each setting the reallocation system has been dominated by transfers from older to younger generations. By contrast, the US reallocation system and, according to Ermisch (1989), the reallocation systems of Japan and England transfer resources from the young to the old. Thus available cross-sectional evidence indicates that the direction of intergenerational resource flows is reversed during the demographic transition and development process.

This finding is contrary to the Caldwell's (1976) hypothesis that fertility decline is a consequence of the reversal of intergenerational resource flows from children to parents. Lee finds that family transfers are from parents to children in both the traditional and the modern societies he has analysed. Lee finds that the direction of total, as opposed to family, transfers reverse direction as part of the development process, but in the opposite direction hypothesized by Caldwell.

That resources flow downward in pre-industrial societies reflects the resource requirements of children and the fact that over the life cycle consumption on average precedes earning. Equivalently, societies, taken as a whole, hold negative total (life-cycle) wealth. Of the mechanisms available for reallocating resources across age groups (investment, credit transactions, and transfers), only transfers will support a reallocation system characterized by negative life-cycle wealth. Historically in pre-industrial societies and today in developing countries, transfers are effected primarily by families, with the public sector playing a secondary role. Even in the United States, family transfers are overwhelmingly in a downward direction, from parents to children. In industrial societies studied to date the reversal in the flow of resources does not reflect a change in family behaviour but rather the increased importance of investment and public-sector programmes that transfer resources upward and dominate family-based transfers.

An analysis by Andrew Mason and Tim Miller in Chapter 3 shares Lee's focus on macro-level aspects of intergenerational transfers, but the analysis is directed exclusively at family transfers. Intergenerational accounting methods are described that provide estimates of the income of the extended families of members of each age cohort. The authors apply the methods to Taiwan and examine the capacity of the extended family to smooth consumption over the life cycle by redistributing income among its members. The full sharing of resources by family members would purge most of the life-cycle variation in income. However, systematic variation in the age structure of extended families produces a Chayanov-type cycle of income that cannot be modulated by within-family transfers (Chayanov 1966). As a consequence, either consumption must be characterized by a similar cycle or the other reallocation mechanisms identified by Lee must be employed to smooth life-cycle income further.

Analysis of household income data available annually from Taiwan for 1976 to 1991 shows that until 1988 income was fully shared across generations through co-residence within extended families. Per capita household income was independent of age save for variation imparted by the Chayanov cycle. Since 1988, however, the per capita household income of the elderly has declined in relation to the per capita income of the extended families to which they belong. Declining co-residence of the elderly within extended families is responsible for the relative decline in their income. Although interhousehold family transfers have increased during the same period, they have only partially offset the effect of the increase in independent living.

In Chapter 4 Jagadeesh Gokhale reviews generational accounts developed by him and his colleagues (Auerbach, Gokhale, and Kotlikoff 1991, 1994; Kotlikoff 1992) and uses wealth measures that incorporate generational accounts to describe the possible impact on US national saving of demographic change between 1960 and 2030. He uses generational accounts to assess the current intergenerational stance of fiscal policy by estimating the present value of taxes net of transfers for members of any age group, including the combined group of all those not yet born. Gokhale's analysis of current US policy implies that current generations have increased their own wealth by imposing obligations on future generations. In 1993 the largest net lifetime tax obligation was borne by a 25-year-old male, who owed nearly $200,000. The largest surplus was enjoyed by those aged 70, $108,000 for men and $140,000 for women, who received large health-care and retirement benefits. Net tax payments, or the generational account, are 150 per cent higher for future generations than for current generations.

In Ronald Lee's terminology, the government has created, through Social Security, Medicare, and Medicaid, positive transfer wealth. The effect of those programmes on saving is an issue of considerable importance to continued US economic growth. Current generations can maintain their life-cycle wealth in the face of a rise in transfer wealth generated by public programmes by reducing their family transfer wealth (that is, by increasing bequests or gifts to younger generations). If they do so, neither saving nor real wealth will be affected (Barro 1974). If, however, current generations maintain their life-cycle wealth by reducing their real wealth, i.e. saving less, economic growth will be adversely affected (Feldstein 1974).

Gokhale considers another aspect of saving. Using a definition of wealth that includes generational account wealth, he constructs new estimates of age profiles of the average propensity to consume out of wealth. He then employs those estimates to assess the effect of the US baby boom and subsequent population ageing on aggregate saving, assuming no change in the average propensity to consume. His analysis suggests that changes in age structure may be primarily responsible for the decline in US net national saving rates during the last two decades.

Part II: Government-funded Pension Programmes

Pension reform is increasingly a global issue. In some parts of the world, notably Asia and Africa, public pension programmes are relatively new or underdeveloped. This situation is in direct contrast to Europe and the Americas, where large public pension programmes were established at least four decades ago. In most instances the programmes are PAYGO systems that, at the time they were established, exploited the favourable rates of return implicit in the high ratio of workers to retirees in rapidly growing populations. As growth rates have slowed and populations have aged, the flaws in seemingly attractive retirement systems have become much more apparent. The authors of this section of the volume address several important issues associated with the evaluation and reform of public pension programmes. Should we abandon PAYGO programmes in favour of fully funded retirement systems? What are the appropriate roles of the public and private sectors? How do we assess programmes with regard to their equity, both in a cross-section and intergenerationally? How do we frame appropriate policies in the face of uncertainty and the long time horizons that characterize pension programmes?

In Chapter 5 Jorge Bravo extends the analytical tools available for application to PAYGO pension systems by deriving the relationship between the rate of return and the features of defined-benefit pension systems. In general, the rate of return depends on features that affect the contribution by workers, the benefit to retirees, and the number of years by which benefits lag contributions. In Bravo's analytic approach, contributions are determined by ages at workforce entry and retirement and the tax rate imposed on participants. Benefits are defined by a base-year salary—that is, the average salary received over the x years immediately preceding retirement—the fraction of that salary replaced, the extent to which benefits are indexed to productivity increases, and the ages of retirement and death. Bravo applies the analytic model to three Latin American countries to demonstrate how pension reforms have influenced rates of return. He also considers the effect of imposing fiscal balance on pension systems, showing that his analytic model is consistent with Samuelson's consumption-loan model in that PAYGO pension systems cannot sustain a rate of return different from the rate of population growth plus the rate of growth of labour productivity.

Next, Rafael Rofman (Chapter 6) addresses an important issue in Latin America: the costs of transition from PAYGO to fully funded public pension programmes. In the early 1980s, public pension programmes in Latin America faced a crisis caused in part by overly generous payments and excessively young ages at retirement. As pension systems matured and Latin American populations began to age, deficits rose. Efforts to increase revenues through higher tax rates were frustrated by widespread evasion. During the 1970s and 1980s it became increasingly apparent that workers were burdened by unsustainable pension payments.

Reform has relied on multi-pillar systems that seek to fulfil commitments both to current retirees and to workers who have contributed to PAYGO systems while moving new workers to defined-contribution programmes that are financially viable. Rofman details the enormous costs of abandoning a PAYGO system. Revenues decline much more rapidly than expenditures as younger workers shift from the system and prior commitments are fulfilled to retirees who have contributed to the system. Rofman observes that 'Argentina's reform reduced the national system's revenues by almost 20 per cent, without having in place an explicit financing mechanism'. Whether increased public debt or general tax revenues are used to fund such deficits, the costs of transition, or what are essentially the costs of previous excesses, are borne primarily by future retirees.

Salvador Valdes-Prieto provides a fascinating, in-depth look at the emergence of PAYGO pension programmes in Chile and the political forces that governed their development and eventually led to their demise (Chapter 7). Mandatory programmes, established in the 1920s, generated huge cash surpluses while they were maturing. Eventually, however, 'the Chilean social security system became, in reality, an aggregation of diverse pension systems negotiated between those in political power and various groups with electoral influence.... [who] managed to obtain heavily subsidized credit, premature retirement without actuarial adjustment, and pensions with privileged inflation adjustments'. By 1975, contribution rates ranged from 51 to 59 per cent of earnings. Evasion had become such a problem that tax-rate increases were causing a decline in total revenues.

In 1973 the Chilean system underwent a complete reform. The PAYGO system was replaced by a defined-contribution programme with individual accounts owned by workers. Today pension funds are managed by private firms selected by individual workers, who have the option of changing funds every four months. The role of the government has been reduced to two principal functions: setting the minimum contribution and monitoring and regulating the companies that manage the pension funds.

Several features of the reformed system directly address the problems of a state-run PAYGO system. First, individual ownership confers to workers property rights, which traditionally enjoy greater protection than pension rights. Second, tighter linkages between contributions and benefits substantially reduce incentives to evade. Third, relying on a defined-contribution plan rather than on a defined-benefit plan frames the policy debate in a manner that is more likely to lead to an efficient and equitable outcome. Fourth, privatizing the administration of the programme and allowing workers to choose from several competing funds has created a political constituency (fund-management firms, or AFPs) whose interests largely converge with those of the beneficiaries rather with those of employers or political parties.

Every system is vulnerable to rent-seeking and to the political process, of course. The government can intervene in many ways to promote its own interests rather than those of participants in the system. It can do so, for example, by regulating fees, restricting investments, or taxing retirement accounts or the AFPs. There is always a danger that the regulators and the AFPs can collude.

In Chapter 8 Didier Blanchet and Jean-Alain Monfort examine pension reform issues in France—a very different setting, politically, economically, and demographically, from Latin America. Nonetheless, many of the issues confronting the French are similar to those in Latin America. The current French retirement programme was established in 1946 and, like other PAYGO systems in ageing countries, is now struggling to maintain benefits for current and future retirees without unduly burdening working populations. Among the changes adopted in the 1993 pension reform, Blanchet and Monfort examine two: a modification of the rules used to index pension benefits on productivity increases, and a redefinition of the reference wage as the average of the best twenty-five, rather than the best ten, years.

Their evaluation of the reforms shares some similarity to generational accounts, discussed by Gokhale in Chapter 4, in that the focus of their analysis is the lifetime experience of successive cohorts. In addition, Blanchet and Monfort propose innovative ways of assessing each cohort's experience, emphasizing net wages relative to those of other members of the population at each time point.

In the absence of reforms, the PAYGO system receives relatively good marks on intergenerational equity grounds. Those who entered the system while it was maturing, particularly those born during the early 1920s, were somewhat favoured. However, particular cohorts of future retirees are neither widely rewarded nor punished. Maintaining the pre-reform system, however, would have resulted in a contribution rate nearly double the current rate of 15 per cent of wages.

Reforms will reduce the contribution rate by up to 10 percentage points, with disindexation having the greatest impact. In a steady state, net wages of those working would increase by about 10 per cent. Higher wages are achieved at the expense of both current and future pensioners. Those who are currently retired are less affected by the reforms and particularly by disindexation.

In Chapter 9 Shripad Tuljapurkar and Ronald Lee address a problem that permeates all assessments of social security programmes and reforms: uncertainty. They describe and apply a stochastic method for forecasting the US population and age structure, and, when supplemented with appropriate economic assumptions, the financial viability of Old Age and Survivors Disability Insurance (OASDI), the principal US public pension programme. Conventional population projections rely on alternative low, medium, and high scenarios based on alternative a priori assumptions about fertility and mortality. Stochastic forecasts provide an expected path for the population and age distribution and, importantly, confidence intervals around the expected path.

Tuljapurkar and Lee compare their own (TL) forecast with two official US population projections, the Census Bureau (CB) projection and the Social Security Administration (SSA) projection. The range between the CB's high and low population projections is similar to that of the TL forecast, but the range for the dependency ratio is much narrower for the CB projection. By contrast, the range for the SSA population projection is much narrower than that of the TL forecast, but the dependency ratio is very similar to that of the TL projection.

The reason for this disparity between the two official projections is that the Census Bureau has chosen to provide alternative assumptions about population size, and so its projections combine high fertility with low mortality; whereas the Social Security Administration is interested in the possible ranges in age structure and therefore combines high fertility with high mortality. This is one respect in which the TL forecasts are a considerable improvement over conventional approaches to population projections.

Using economic assumptions employed by OASDI, Tuljapurkar and Lee employ their population forecasts to assess the effect of population ageing in the United States on the combined OASDI Trust Fund. Their point estimate forecast is for the fund to increase to about 1 trillion (1994) US dollars in 2015 but to drop to zero dollars around 2025. They also provide a 95 per cent confidence interval for the date of 'bankruptcy'—2020 to 2030.

Part III: The Family and Intergenerational Transfers

The six chapters presented in Part III are concerned with transfers and the extended family. Among recurrent themes, both in these chapters and in the literature as a whole, are the diverse functions of family transfers and the effects on transfers of the evolution of modern institutions. Perhaps the most prominent theme is the search for a parsimonious model that explains family transfer behaviour and its evolution during the development process. That this is an elusive goal is apparent in the varied conclusions the authors reach with regard to which model—one-way or mutual altruism, exchange, a corporate model, some combination of these, or 'none of the above'—is most consistent with observed behaviour. The chapters are drawn from diverse settings, including some of the world's poorest and wealthiest societies, and some of the most stagnant and most dynamic economies. As a consequence, the rich complexity that characterizes the family and its diverse roles is well represented.

Addressing the question of whether banks crowd out private (informal or family) insurance arrangements in low-income rural areas, Andrew Foster and Mark Rosenzweig in Chapter 10 present a theoretical model in which alternative mechanisms are available to a household for protecting itself from fluctuations in its income. The household can accumulate a financial asset, relying on a bank for that purpose, or it can enter into a risk-sharing agreement with another household. Two types of contracts are also considered. Those 'without commitment' are enforceable only to the extent that a household that breaks the contract is excluded from entering into any future risk-sharing agreements. Contracts 'with commitment' are fully enforced.

Foster and Rosenzweig's simulations show that relying on a combination of financial assets and enforceable risk-sharing contracts is nearly equivalent to full insurance. Financial assets and enforceable contracts provide similar levels of insurance. Contracts without full commitment are somewhat inferior to enforceable contracts, particularly when used in concert with the accumulation of financial assets. The implication of the theoretical model for the question originally posed is that the development of financial institutions does not fully undermine informal, usually family-based, support networks. However, financial institutions do yield insurance value well beyond what can be provided by risk sharing between two parties.

In an empirical analysis, Foster and Rosenzweig examine transfer and saving behaviour in India and Pakistan and how proximity to a bank affects that behaviour. They find in both India and Pakistan that only in villages near banks is saving used to smooth consumption; that is, positive income shocks generate saving, and saving is inversely related to assets. Likewise, in both countries net transfers smooth consumption in villages far from banks; positive income shocks generate net transfers, and net transfers are inversely related to transfer assets (previous transfers). As the authors anticipate in their theoretical model, in India net transfers play an even more important role in villages near banks. (The estimates from Pakistan are too imprecise to shed any light on the issue.) Thus the analysis provides partial support for the hypothesis that the development of modern financial institutions is partly responsible for the erosion of traditional ones.

In Chapter 11 Alessandro Cigno considers a world in which old-age security is provided by three means: the extended family, participation in government-sponsored PAYGO pension systems, and the accumulation of wealth during the working years. Couples engage in one of two strategies. Either they act alone, bearing no children and relying on saving to supplement their PAYGO pension, or they bear children, rely on them for old-age support, and accumulate no wealth during their working years.

Cigno's theoretical model exhibits several important features. First, unlike models with descending or ascending altruism, in his model intergenerational transfers flow in both upward and downward directions among those who rely on extended families as a means of providing for their old-age support. Second, his model demonstrates how a self-enforcing family constitution can 'guarantee' to working generations that their children will provide a level of transfers that is economically efficient.

Cigno uses his model to show how saving and fertility are affected by feasible government policies—that is, policies that are consistent with the government's budget constraint. The policies he considers are an increase in child benefits funded by a tax increase; increases in public pension payments funded either by a PAYGO or a fully funded approach; and a reduction in current taxes funded by an increase in future taxes. The implications of Cigno's model for saving are quite distinctive. He finds that under some circumstances an increase in public pensions may lead to higher saving. In contrast, life-cycle models imply that saving will be crowded out and altruism models imply that saving will be unaffected. A more conventional implication of his model is that an increase in public pensions has an anti-natalist effect, but surprisingly an increase in childrearing subsidies has an ambiguous effect on childbearing.

The subject of Sumon Kumar Bhaumik and Jeffrey Nugent's study (Chapter 12) is Peru in the mid-1980s, where, as in many traditional societies, co-resident adult children are a major source of support for elderly parents. Their analysis of co-residence is, in general, consistent with exchange and altruism motives for intergenerational transfers. Parents with higher income or who own a business are more likely than others to have adult children living with them, as are those who are married or who have more living children. The latter finding is, of course, important in light of the substantial decline in fertility during the last two decades.

Support by non-co-resident children is heavily influenced by whether or not their parents are living independently. In households with no co-resident children present, social security partially 'crowds out' transfers; in households with co-resident children, social security has no significant effect. In general, urbanized households, female-headed households, and households with married heads receive more transfers from adult children than do other households. Bhaumik and Nugent find little evidence to support the altruism model of transfers. Household heads with especially great need are unable to attract more support from their children than are better-off heads.

Yean-Ju Lee (Chapter 13) investigates intergenerational transfers in the extraordinarily dynamic context of South Korea. She uses a unique set of survey data to examine transfers from migrant adult children to elderly parents residing in rural Korea. The children in question were key participants in Korea's transformation from a rural, agricultural society to an urban, industrial one.

That transformation was accomplished in large part because parents invested in their children. Lee notes two important forms of investment that characterize the adult children in her sample: education and support for their migration.

She addresses several questions in this chapter. First, to what extent do adult children transfer resources to their elderly parents in reciprocity for the support they received while growing up? In particular, have economic development, industrialization, and Western cultural influences undermined the close interdependence that characterized traditional Korean society? Second, what factors influence whether adult children choose to provide economic support to their parents? Which of the behavioural models used to describe intergenerational transfers is most consistent with the Korean experience—altruism, exchange, or some alternative?

Despite the country's rapid changes, transfers from children to elderly parents are still an important feature of Korean society. Lee shows that about 60 per cent of adult children provided some financial support to their parents during the twelve months preceding the survey. More than 80 per cent of elderly parents received financial assistance from at least one adult migrant child.

Lee's analysis emphasizes the effects of income, education, and migration decision-making on transfers from children to their parents. Children's own income had a positive effect on their giving, and so did the average educational level of all the children in a family, but their own education did not. Parents' income had an inverse effect on transfers from children. However, better-educated parents and those less disabled were more likely than others to receive transfers from their children. Parents who were involved in the decision of their children to migrate were also more likely to receive transfers.

Lee believes that the survey evidence supports her view that migration is governed by a corporate group model, much like the model presented by Cigno in Chapter 11. Exchange is undertaken so as to maximize family welfare and to distribute resources equitably across generations. To accomplish these goals requires intergenerational transfers that flow in both directions.

Joseph Altonji, Fumio Hayashi, and Laurence Kotlikoff (Chapter 14) use a rich set of US survey data, the Panel Survey of Income Dynamics (PSID), to analyse the effects of income and, to a lesser extent, wealth on transfers between parents and children. In this path-breaking and innovative study, the authors match households of parents and children and exploit the longitudinal nature of the data to construct reliable estimates of permanent income and the incomes of all parties directly relevant to the intergenerational transaction. They are also able to assess how transfers are affected by the incomes of siblings, by the incomes of wives' versus husbands' parents, and by the incomes of ex-husbands and ex-wives.

In contrast with the studies of Yean-Ju Lee and, to some extent, Bhaumik and Nugent, Altonji and his co-authors find the effects of income on transfers to be generally consistent with two-sided altruism models but less so with exchange models of transfers. However, the size of transfers elicited by changes in income and wealth are far smaller than predicted by the altruism models governing current research.

Money transfers, especially from adult children to parents, are small in the United States. About one-quarter of surveyed parents gave money to their adult children. Of those who gave, the median transfer per year was about $500 and the mean nearly $2,000. In contrast, fewer than 5 per cent of parents received any transfer from their children. Transfers made were of similar magnitude to those flowing in the opposite direction. Money transfers generally flowed from rich to poor households within the extended family. The transfers were insufficiently responsive to income to mitigate changes in permanent or transitory income. The largest effect of a change in permanent income was the effect of a change in parents' income on transfers to their children. A child received only one additional dollar for every 100 dollars in additional income earned by his or her parents.

Time transfers are common and flow in both directions. Twenty-seven per cent of surveyed children reported providing substantial help to their parents. Among those who gave, the mean and median amounts of time per year were 242 and 100 hours, respectively. Thirty per cent of children reported receiving time transfers from their parents. The mean and median hours per year for those who received some time were 281 and 100 hours, respectively. Economic circumstances appear to have little systematic effect on time transfers from parents to their children. Lower-income children were more likely than higher-income children to provide time to their parents, and lower-income parents were more likely than higher-income parents to receive time from their children—a finding that is more consistent with altruism than with exchange motives.

Among the empirical studies of transfers in this volume, Anne Laferrère's (Chapter 15) is alone in its focus on inheritance rather than *inter vivos* transfers. At least among the industrialized countries, available evidence indicates that bequests dominate interhousehold transfers. In the United States, for example, bequests are nearly five times as important as other interhousehold transfers (according to Ronald Lee, in Chapter 2). Housing, the focus of Laferrère's study, is typically a major component of bequests in France, accounting for more than 40 per cent of the total value, on average.

Laferrère's study draws on a 1991–2 survey of housing inheritance conducted by the Institut National de la Statistique et des Etudes Economiques (INSEE). Respondents were from households in which the reference person was at least 30 years old and had at least one parent or parent-in-law who was deceased. Laferrère examines the experience of a sub-sample consisting of those whose parent or parents had owned a home at the time of their death. She addresses two questions: What factors influenced the likelihood that the reference household would inherit the parents' home? And to what use was an inherited home put by the children who inherited it?

Laferrère finds that a number of demographic factors had an important bearing on whether a child inherited a home. Inheritance was more likely if the child had a few siblings, if he or she had ever married, and if both parents were deceased. Interestingly, income had no significant effect on the probability of inheriting, suggesting that the intergenerational transmission of housing wealth does not serve to equalize wealth among children as suggested by altruism models. Laferrère also finds that inherited housing was typically held as housing wealth by the recipient, in contrast with Great Britain, where the wealth was more frequently converted into financial wealth. The implications of her findings for capital accumulation are potentially quite interesting.

Conclusions

The growing interest in intergenerational transfers reflects an increased appreciation for their importance in both modern and traditional economies. Intergenerational transfers arise, in part, as an essential response to one key feature of the human species: our extended childhood. The human race's continued existence requires that productive, adult members of the population transfer a large share of their output to society's next generation. The size of the transfer to children, the impact of development on the size and direction of the flow of resources between parents and children, and the implications for childbearing and human capital is one of the important issues addressed here and, in a vast literature, elsewhere.

The exchange between parents and their 'dependent' children is neither unidirectional nor driven only by childrearing costs. Families enter into a variety of intergenerational arrangements that involve transfers, especially in traditional settings. They establish productive enterprises. They enter into risk-sharing arrangements. They engage in joint consumption. They exchange goods and services, some of which are uniquely available only within the family.

In industrial societies, transfers from productive adults to the elderly loom large. The rise in life expectancies, the decline in retirement ages, and changes in age structure all have served to increase the number of dependent elderly and the portion of current output they consume.

Despite the diverse nature of intergenerational transfers, the research presented below examines a coherent set of issues. How do intergenerational transfers influence economic efficiency, equity, and growth? What principles govern decisions by economic agents to engage in intergenerational exchange? What is the role of public policy with respect to intergenerational transfers?

In addressing these questions, the following chapters tackle many difficult conceptual and empirical problems. They provide new insights about intergenerational behaviour and its consequences. They examine the complexity of and demonstrate the importance of public policy. We hope, as well, that they will inspire new research into this fascinating and important area.

Part I

Intergenerational Accounting

2 Intergenerational Transfers and the Economic Life Cycle: A Cross-cultural Perspective

Ronald D. Lee

Reallocations of resources across age and time take place in many ways and for many reasons. Positive interest rates encourage people to defer consumption. This incentive is reinforced by a biocultural-institutional-behavioural need to provide for consumption in old age when productivity falls or retirement occurs, by a desire to leave bequests for children, and by a desire to hedge against future risk. Furthermore, in some settings parents may be able to capture the surplus production of their young children, or their adult children may support them in old age. All these factors tend to make labour earnings exceed consumption at younger ages and for consumption to exceed earnings at older ages, which requires a net upward reallocation of income from younger to older ages. At the same time, however, impatience and uncertainty about survival encourage consumption in advance of earnings. This tendency is reinforced by the costs of rearing children and perhaps by the receipt of bequests. These factors tend to make consumption exceed labour earnings at younger ages, and the reverse at older ages, requiring a downward reallocation of income from older to younger ages.

We can imagine that each person, even a child, accumulates wealth when consumption is less than earnings, and draws down wealth or goes into debt when consumption exceeds earnings. With suitable discounting, we can then associate a level of wealth with a person at each age. This is called *life-cycle wealth*; it is the wealth necessary to achieve the desired path of consumption over the life cycle. I shall later show that when net reallocations of income are on average upward in the population, the average person will hold positive life-cycle wealth; and when net reallocations are on average downward in the population, the average person will hold negative life-cycle wealth. The direction in which income is reallocated in a population and the sign of average life-cycle wealth are fundamental features of an economy.

Reallocations take place in many ways. Some are enforced by law and flow through the public sector. In the United States examples include Social Security, Medicare, Medicaid, public education, and a host of smaller programmes and their associated taxes. Others reflect individual decisions about fertility, investment in children, bequests, private provision for old age, purchases of houses, cars, or lesser durables, and so on. In this case, the vehicles range from credit-card debt, car loans, and mortgages to the stock and bond markets and private pensions and annuities, to stuffing money under the mattress.

In this chapter, I first develop an analytic framework for addressing these issues and then attempt to measure the direction of reallocations in societies ranging from hunter-gatherer horticulturists of the Amazon Basin to the United States. Where possible, I go beyond examining the direction of these reallocations to say something about the mechanisms and institutions through which the reallocations are achieved. I shall show that there are three broad kinds of mechanisms through which resources can be reallocated: (1) the accumulation and decumulation of real wealth, or *capital*; (2) borrowing and lending, or *credit transactions*; and (3) outright gifts with no quid pro quo, or *transfers*. Throughout the chapter the main emphasis will be on transfers, which will be seen to have some special properties that give them a unique role in the macroeconomy.

Why Care about Transfers?

The study of transfers may appear to be an esoteric and narrow topic of little general interest or importance. Before proceeding, therefore, it is useful to mention the ways in which transfers matter, and at the same time to introduce briefly some of the literature in this area.

Age- and generation-related transfers may be substitutes for wealth and may therefore affect life-cycle saving (Feldstein 1974); conversely, the desire to make transfers in the form of bequests may motivate saving and capital formation (Kotlikoff and Summers 1981). Thus intergenerational transfers are closely related to the process of wealth accumulation.

The desire or necessity to make such transfers acts as a kind of price effect for certain decisions, such as childbearing. If children transfer income, on net, to their parents, then there is an incentive for adults to bear many children, as Caldwell (1976) has argued. If, on the other hand, parents seek to nullify the effects on their children of public-sector pension programmes by increasing familial transfers to their children (Barro 1974), then children become more costly, and there is an incentive to reduce fertility (Becker 1988; Willis 1994). As suggested by the previous point, intergenerational transfers through the public sector may lead to externalities to childbearing, such that private fertility decisions are not socially optimal (Willis 1987; R. D. Lee and Miller 1990).

Public-sector transfers, such as the massive transfers to the elderly in the United States through Social Security, Medicare, and Medicaid, raise questions of intergenerational equity, particularly in the context of either demographic change or programme change (Auerbach, Gokhale, and Kotlikoff 1991). Government debt can also be viewed as an important kind of intergenerational transfer from the young to the old, raising issues of generational equity—although debt can also be used to achieve an efficient amount of capital per worker (Diamond 1965).

Because many transfers, both familial and public, are so age-specific, they are strongly affected by changes in a population's age distribution, and in particular by population ageing. Thus the study of inter-age transfers sheds light on the consequences of population ageing.

Society, through its institutions and mores, can create *transfer wealth*. Transfer wealth (the present value of expected future net transfers) is worthless from the point of view of production, but from the point of view of consumption spreading it is a close substitute for physical wealth. Transfer wealth can therefore enable people to attain life-cycle consumption paths that are preferable to those attainable through market mechanisms alone (Samuelson 1958; R. D. Lee 1994*b*).

A major aspect of an economy is whether, on net, resources in it flow upward or downward across age (Gale 1973; Willis 1988; R. D. Lee 1994*a*, 1994*b*). Economists often assume that resources flow upward as workers attempt to provide for retirement years, but whether that is the case is an empirical question.

The net direction of transfers across ages is directly related to the effect on welfare of a marginal increase or decrease in the population growth rate, and therefore to the issue of optimal population growth rates (Samuelson 1975; Arthur and McNicoll 1978; Willis 1988; R. D. Lee 1994*a*, 1994*b*).

Behavioural ecologists have questioned how upward transfers could be consistent with evolutionary theory, which stresses that reproductive fitness requires parental investment in offspring (see Turke 1989; Fricke 1990; Kaplan 1994).

The effect of demographic change on aggregate savings rates (Mason 1987) will depend on the extent to which transfers, rather than saving, are used to smooth consumption over the life cycle.

Many important and influential publications have contributed to the literature on inter-age transfers, some of which I have just cited. Yet the possibilities for systematic integration of work on these topics have not been fully realized, and the time is ripe for synthesis and for progress on some new fronts. The theoretical literature, starting with Samuelson's (1958) seminal article, has analysed mainly the case of a hypothetical population with two age groups, in which there is 100 per cent survival until the end of the second age group, at which point all die.[1] The assumption of two age groups means that one cannot consider together the three stages of the human economic life cycle—childhood, working years, and retirement—and severely limits the problems that can be examined. The rectangular survival assumption means that one cannot consider the effects of declining mortality on the life cycle, nor distinguish between changes in population growth rates originating in fertility or morality. This too is a severe limitation. Finally, the highly schematic and abstract nature of both assumptions means that there is no possibility at all of implementing the models empirically.[2]

Empirical studies typically look in detail at specific transfer systems, but the results are not placed in the framework of the overlapping generations model. Although this chapter does not develop much explicit theory, the framework employed here has elsewhere been used to derive formal results of the classic overlapping-generations literature in a more general demographic context (Bommier and Lee 1995).

Conceptual Background

This section sets out the conceptual framework that underlies the subsequent discussion. The nature of reallocation systems is described in detail and important properties are identified. Examples are from the United States.

Reallocation systems

As mentioned earlier, there are many ways in which reallocations take place. Despite this great variety of market and non-market mechanisms, there is a simple, suggestive, and analytically useful way to categorize what I shall call these 'reallocation systems'. By reallocation system, I mean, loosely speaking, a self-contained collection of flows by age. For example, the Social Security reallocation system includes both the benefits and the related pay-roll taxes, as does Medicare. Only the portion of pay-roll taxes needed to offset the benefits and meet administrative costs is part of the Social Security transfer system; that portion of pay-roll taxes that is, in principle, used to accumulate a reserve fund is counted as part of some other system—possibly the federal debt system, possibly public-sector capital accumulation. Childrearing is a familial transfer system, consisting of the support parents give to their children and the support children receive from their parents; these constitute a closed system. Similarly, the age profiles of people making bequests and receiving bequests together constitute a system.

There is no particular level at which disaggregation should stop; different levels are appropriate for different questions. In one context, we might work with a system of government transfers; in another context, we might restrict attention to the federal transfer system; and in still another context, we might examine the Aid to Families with Dependent Children (AFDC) transfer system, which has cut across federal and state governments. However, the discussion that follows establishes a minimum level of disaggregation that is necessary to achieve analytically appropriate categories. The approach could also be extended to include time inputs (R. D. Lee and Lapkoff 1988), but that will not be done here.

A net reallocation schedule, $g(x)$, derives from gross schedules, $g^{+}(x)$ and $g^{-}(x)$, describing flows into (+) and out of (−) the household or individual budget of surviving members or the population. For example, $g^{+}(x)$ might be Social Security benefits received, and $g^{-}(x)$ might be pay-roll taxes. At any age x, the sum of labour earnings plus all net reallocations minus consumption equals zero (where the reallocations must be defined in an exclusive, that is non-redundant, way).

These concepts can be illustrated by the example of the US Social Security system, which is mainly a public-sector pension system. Figure 2.1 plots the relevant age schedules. Panel A shows $g^{+}(x)$ and $g^{-}(x)$, the gross inflows and outflows corresponding to benefits received by age and taxes paid by age into the system. The schedule of benefits includes some payments for disability and for benefits to survivors of the primary insured, in addition to pensions; but pensions dominate the picture. Panel B shows the net reallocation system, $g(x)$, which is just the sum of these two. Panel C shows the transfer wealth, $W(x)$, generated by the system for the average person at each age, calculated as the survival-weighted present value of expected future receipts of benefits from the system minus the expected future payment of taxes, on the assumption that these age profiles will remain fixed in the future. This plotted $W(x)$ schedule assumes that the market rate of interest, r, exceeds the sum of the population growth rate and the growth rate of the productivity of labour by 0.04, which is probably an unrealistically high amount.

Much of the discussion that follows does not need to assume a stable population or an economic steady state (see Bommier and Lee 1995, for example), but for the most part I shall make these assumptions here to simplify the exposition.[3] Thus I shall assume that the age profiles of reallocation systems are fixed over time, which is of course unrealistic. In most cases neither the analytic framework nor the empirical results are altered if it is instead assumed that the cross-sectional shape of the reallocation profile remains fixed while the level shifts upward at a constant rate equal to the growth rate of labour productivity. However, in many cases this kind of assumption will be violated: pension systems may be extended to cover an increasing share of the population, housing prices and the value of housing services may rise much more rapidly than the general price level, and in general the problem of capital gains and losses may be significant—to mention only a few of the many difficulties. In principle, the analysis can also be carried out on changing age schedules for reallocation systems, as is done, for example, in empirical implementations of generational accounting (see Auerbach *et al.* 1991).

It should be noted that this analysis of reallocation systems does not yet take account of collective goods and resources. For example, it is not clear how the environment, or commonly held land, should be treated. Nor is it clear how to treat the institutions that are passed down from generation to generation. These are important topics to address in future work.

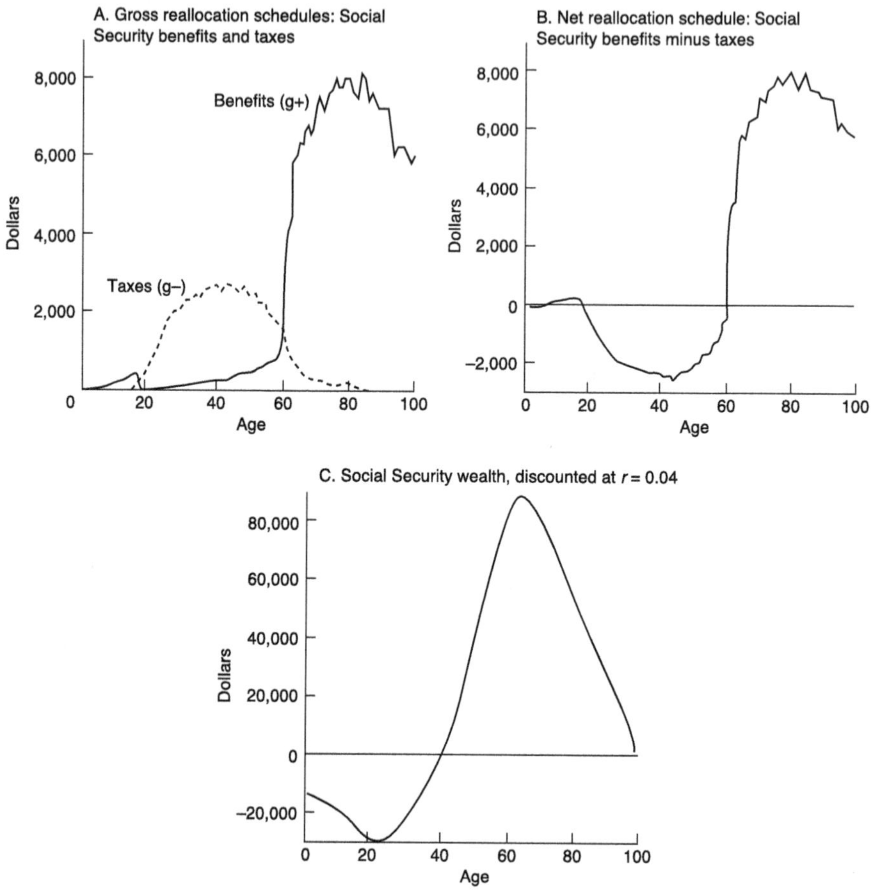

Note: The data on Social Security benefits (Old Age, Survivors, and Disability Insurance, or OASDI), including pensions, survivors' benefits, and disability benefits, but excluding Medicare) by single years of age are taken from the *Social Security Bulletin, Annual Statistical Supplement* (US, Social Security Administration 1994). The data on taxes by single years of age are calculated from data on taxable labour earnings taken from the 1993 Current Population Survey of the United States. Both age profiles were multiplicatively adjusted by a small amount so that when multiplied by the population age distribution and summed, they total the aggregate amounts for benefits and taxes reported in official sources.

Source: R. D. Lee and Miller (1995, fig. 2).

Fig. 2.1. An example of a reallocation system: Social Security in the United States, 1993

Classification of reallocation systems: transfers, credit, and capital

For any system of reallocation g, the gross flow schedules g^+ and g^- can each have any shape, sign, and magnitude. However, their sum, the net allocation schedule $g = g^+ + g^-$, may be subject to certain constraints. Suppose we weight a schedule g by the stable age distribution and then sum over all ages; call this operation *Pop*(g):

$$Pop(g) = b\int_0^{\omega} e^{-nx}p(x)g(x)dx,$$

where b is the crude birth rate and n the growth rate in the stable population, and $p(x)$ is the survival schedule. For any reallocation schedule g, this sum either equals zero or does not equal zero. Alternatively, suppose we calculate the survival-weighted present value of g at birth discounted at rate r; call this operation *PV*(g):

$$PV(g) = \int_0^{\omega} e^{-rx}p(x)g(x)dx.$$

PV(g) also either equals zero or it does not.

We can define a four-way classification of reallocation systems g, depending on whether or not $Pop(g) = 0$, and whether or not $PV(g) = 0$. *Competitive reallocations* are those obeying the *PV* constraint, since they can be supported by selfish maximizing behaviour over the life cycle, subject to a life-cycle budget constraint. *Conservative reallocations* are those satisfying the n constraint, because in this case the set of age-specific flows neither augments nor depletes the societal stock of goods, but rather conserves its level. If r happens to equal n, then any conservative system is also competitive, and vice versa.

For transfer systems such as social security or childrearing, *Pop*(g) must be zero because transfer systems simply reshuffle the existing output of a given time period among individuals and age groups, and are therefore conservative. In general, however, *PV*(g) does not equal zero for transfers, and so transfers are not competitive. For example, the implicit real rate of return on participation in a mature social security system equals n, the population growth rate, which typically is less than the real market interest rate, r, so that *PV* (social security) is less than zero. For all transfers, *Pop*(transfers) equals zero and *PV*(transfers) does not equal zero. This is true for both public-sector and familial transfers. (Actually, the rate of return on a transfer system equals the population growth rate plus the rate of growth of labour productivity.)

Now consider credit transactions. Like transfers, they involve a reshuffling of resources among age groups in any time period, and therefore *Pop*(credit) equals zero (if we ignore foreign participation in credit markets and government debt). In this case, however, *PV*(credit) equals zero as well, since in competitive economies, borrowing and lending take place at market interest rates. (Familial or public-sector credit transactions will be viewed as partial transfers when the terms diverge from market interest rates.) Thus credit transactions are both competitive and conservative.

Finally, for saving and net investment (capital formation) in competitive steady-state economies, *PV*(investment) equals zero because credit markets are an alternative repository for savings from the point of view of individuals, and therefore the expected rate of interest should equal the rate of return on capital. But in a steady state, the stock of capital grows at the same rate as the population (plus labour-augmenting technical progress, which I ignore here), so that *Pop*(investment) equals nK, which is more than zero. This, of course, is the standard result for growth of capital in a steady state. Therefore investment in real capital or equity instruments is competitive but not conservative.

There is a fourth category, in which neither $Pop(g)$ nor $PV(g)$ is zero. In this case some stock grows at the population growth rate, but the discounted value of the age-specific flows into the stock is not zero over the life cycle. This category is occupied by sums of members of other categories, such as investment plus transfers. It is also occupied by what we might call the total reallocation, given by $g^{+}(x)$ = consumption and $g^{-}(x)$ = labour earnings.

	$PV(g) = 0$	$PV(g) \neq 0$
$Pop(g) = 0$	Credit	Transfers
$Pop(g) \neq 0$	Capital	Mixed

Every reallocation system must fall into one of these four categories; the classification system is exhaustive. This is important because it ensures that the analysis sketched below is general and encompasses any means of reallocating resources across age in steady states. I shall continue to name each type after presenting the leading example of category member, but in fact there are other important members as well.[4]

Consider the budget constraint of the individual at age x. The gap between labour earning, $yl(x)$, and consumption, $c(x)$, must equal the net inflows from transfers from family and government, plus the net inflows from credit transactions, plus net inflows from capital (see R. D. Lee 1994*a*). This decomposition of the gap between labour earnings and consumption is shown for the United States in Figure 2.2, which plots, by age of the household reference person (who is similar to the household head), the net flows into the household for each of the three kinds of reallocation system based on the 1991 Consumer Expenditure Survey. The patterns are easy to see above age 60: there is an enormous gap between consumption and labour earnings, and this gap is made up by the sum of transfers (largely from public-sector pensions and health care), credit (largely returns to bonds and money-market holdings of the household and its private-sector pension funds), and returns to capital (a combination of household capital, principally services from an owned home and consumer durables, plus household investments in the stock market, plus payments from private-sector pensions holding investments in stocks and physical assets). In the middle years the household makes major transfers to others through the public sector and also makes major net payments into credit systems (paying a home mortgage and buying credit instruments). On the positive side, the household receives a net inflow of returns to capital, probably mainly in the form of housing services that offset its outflows of investments. Young households are both net recipients of transfers and net recipients of funds through credit (borrowing), while funds flow out to acquire capital (housing and consumer durables).

Here I have classified reallocation systems according to properties that have deep implications, as we shall see in a moment. But reallocations can also be cross-classified by institution, since reallocations take place within the family, the market, or the public sector (see R. D. Lee 1994*a* or 1994*b*). (There may be additional institutions through which reallocations take place, such as charitable institutions or clans.) These institutional channels also have important implications. Later in this chapter I shall describe in some detail public-sector transfers in some Third World nations and the United States, and also familial transfers in the United States (more detail can be found in R. D. Lee 1994*b* and R. D. Lee and Miller 1995).

Derived properties of reallocation systems

From the various combinations of these two aggregate (or overall per capita) constraints, we can derive important formal properties of each of the four kinds of transfer system, under steady-state assumptions, as follows (proofs omitted):

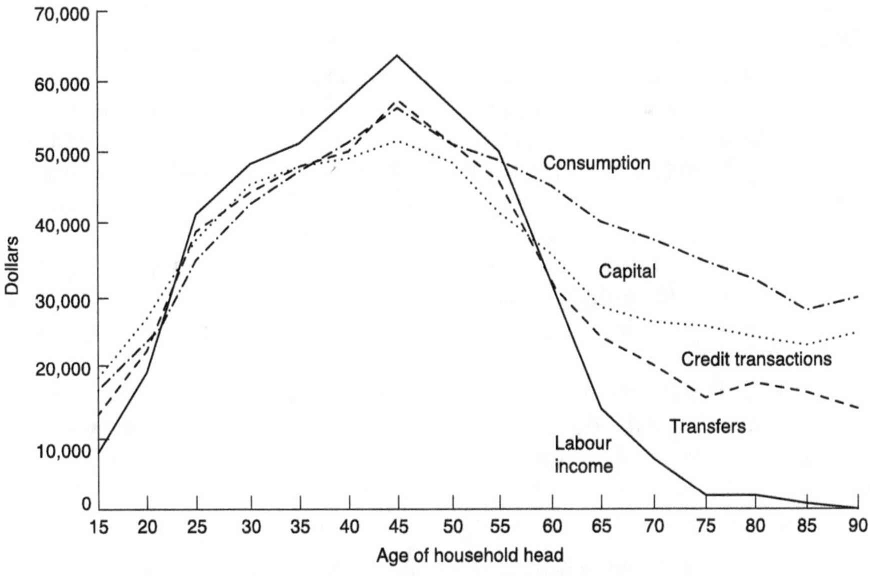

Note: For details, see note to Fig. 2.7 and R. D. Lee and Miller (1995).

Source: Based on the 1991 Consumer Expenditure Survey and reproduced from R. D. Lee and Miller (1995, fig. 7).

Fig. 2.2. How the three kinds of reallocation system make up the gap between consumption and labour earnings for US households, 1991

1. *The implicit rate of return earned through any transfer system equals the population growth rate*. This result must apply to any transfer system, including familial ones such as bequests or childrearing. For example, if n is greater than zero, then a couple will pay out more in childrearing costs than it received as children, and it can be shown to pay 'interest' at rate n on what it received. The result follows immediately from inspection of the equation for $Pop(g) = 0$.

2. *The* g(x) *function for credit must cross the zero line at least twice, while for transfers and for investment it must cross the zero line at least once.* In other words, for a credit system there must be at least two age intervals of net borrowing (lending) separated by a period of net lending (borrowing). This Bommier and Lee (1995) have proved formally, but it should be intuitively clear from the fact that a credit system must be both competitive and conservative. In any model with two age groups, no credit transactions can take place between generations because at most one cross-over is possible. The economic interpretation is simply that if generations overlap for only one period, then repayment is impossible, so that no intergenerational credit transactions can take place. In a population with three age groups there can be two cross-over points, making intergenerational borrowing and lending possible.[5]

At this point it will be useful to consider the stocks that are generated by the age-specific flows that I have analysed thus far. Let us define $G(x)$ to be the present value at age x of survival-weighted expected future $g(x)$; it is the wealth held at age x through system g. Let G be the population-weighted average of $G(x)$. G is the measure of aggregate wealth held in system g. For example, if $g(x)$ describes a social security system, then $G(x)$ is the difference between the present value of survival-weighted expected future benefits and expected future payroll taxes, and is therefore social security wealth at age x. G is social security wealth per capita in the whole population. $G(x)$ was plotted in Panel C of Figure 2.1.

In the remainder of the chapter, $G(x)$ will be used for the general concept; but life-cycle wealth will be denoted by $W(x)$, transfer wealth by $T(x)$, wealth held in real capital by $K(x)$, and wealth held as credit by $M(x)$. $T(x)$ is the sum of familial transfer wealth and governmental transfer wealth: $T(x) = T^F(x) + T^G(x)$. Governmental transfer wealth, $T^G(x)$, is closely related to the generational accounting approach described by Gokhale in Chapter 4 of this volume; the main difference is that the taxes included in generational accounts include not only those taxes that pay for public transfers, but also the taxes used to pay for other government expenditures such as defence, research, or investment in infrastructure, which are not age-specific.

3. *In the population at any instant, for any dollar of debt that one person owes, there must also be a corresponding dollar of credit that is due to someone else, so that aggregate credit wealth must be equal to zero:* $G^C = 0$. This can be shown to follow from the property of a credit system that $PV(g) = 0$ and $Pop(g) = 0$. For transfers, G^T will typically be non-zero, so that transfer systems can support positive or negative wealth in a society as a whole. This is so because transfer

systems can obligate people who do not yet exist: my Social Security wealth is based in part on the obligation of children not yet born to pay taxes when they become adults. It is because of this fundamental property of transfers, in contrast to credit, that they can enable an economy to achieve an efficient outcome when purely market mechanisms may fail, as in Samuelson's (1958) classic example.

4. *If the market interest rate equals the population growth rate—that is, in the golden-rule case—then* $G = g(A_{g+} - A_{g-})$, *where* g *is the average gross reallocation in the population* [$g = Pop(g^+) = Pop(g^-)$] *and* A *is the average age in the population at which a gross flow takes place.* For example, $A_{g+} = Pop[xg^+(x)]/Pop[g^+(x)]$. This accounting identity states that the wealth held through a reallocation system equals the size of the per capita flow in the population multiplied by the difference between the average age at which people receive inflows or benefits from the system and the average age at which they make payments into the system. For example, in the case of the US Social Security system, the average age of receiving a pension benefit is 71 years, and the average age of paying taxes into the system is 43 years (both for households by age of the reference person), so that the difference is 28 years. This figure, multiplied by the average annual flow per household of about $2,500, gives an estimated Social Security wealth per household of $70,000. This tells us that the average household, looking forward, expects to receive $70,000 more in benefits in the future than it expects to pay in taxes. This accounting identity also suggests the graphic device of drawing an arrow with the tail at the average age of paying into a system, the head at the average age of receiving from the system, and the width equal to the average flow, as a way of portraying a reallocation system and the wealth it generates, which is then indicated by the area of the arrow and signed by the direction of the arrow.

5. *In steady states with capital,* Pop(*investing*) = nK, *where* K *is the level of capital per capita in the population.* This simply states that if a reallocation does not average out to zero in the population, then the stocks to which it gives rise must grow at rate *n*, as does capital in neoclassical growth theory.

6. Life-cycle wealth, $W(x)$, is the amount of generalized wealth (or debt) accumulated up to age x, given the consumption age profile $c(x)$ and the labour-earnings profile $y_l(x)$. This is a standard definition (see, for example, Kotlikoff and Summers 1981). Averaged across the whole population, this gives W, average life-cycle wealth in the population. *When the interest rate equals the population growth rate, then* $W = c(A_c - A_y)$ *as in proposition 4. In any event, there is a fundamental result:* $W = K + T$. Life-cycle wealth can be held in the form of transfer wealth or capital. Capital, of course, is productive and raises output, while transfer wealth has no such effect, and so it is a matter of great concern to society in which of these forms life-cycle wealth is held.

Additional results can be derived along these lines, including expressions for wealth when the interest rate does not equal the population growth rate, and also when the population and the economy are not in a steady state (see Bommier and Lee 1995). The following expression for the change in wealth held through a reallocation system for non-golden-rule, non-steady-state economies is due to Bommier and is proven and discussed in Bommier and Lee (1995):

$$dW(g,t)/dt = [r(t) - n(t)]W(g,t) + b(t)PV(g,t) + Pop(g,t).$$

From this equation a number of useful dynamic properties can be derived, and in addition the expressions for average wealth held through reallocation systems of each kind can be inferred for the non-golden-rule, steady-state case.

Let us return to the equation $W = K + T$, which is an accounting identity. Because an infinite variety of behaviours can satisfy it, it cannot tell us how people behave. Nevertheless, we can gain some insights from interpreting it. Consider two identical stable populations with identical life-cycle profiles of earning and consumption, and therefore identical $W(x)$ functions and the same per capita wealth, W. Their identity tells us that the sums of transfer wealth and capital wealth must be equal. But one population could hold more of its life-cycle wealth in the form of capital, and the other could hold more in the form of transfer wealth. In some sense, then, transfer wealth and capital can be thought of as substituting for each other as vehicles for satisfying individuals' demand for life-cycle wealth. From the point of view of production in the macroeconomy, however, they are not substitutes at all; transfers are useless. Feldstein (1974) and many others have argued that the enormous increase in transfer wealth resulting from the establishment of the Social Security system in the United States and the dramatic extension of its coverage and benefits have substituted for private life-cycle savings, and have therefore reduced capital formation. Barro (1974) has countered that the public-sector transfer wealth through Social Security should merely have substituted for familial transfer wealth: elderly parents compensate for their increased wealth due to public-sector transfers by increasing their gifts or bequests to their children, thereby creating offsetting negative transfer wealth and leaving T and K unchanged.

Alternatively, consider the financing of higher education for two societies with the same life-cycle profiles, the same population age distribution, and therefore the same life-cycle wealth. In one, children must borrow the funds from the market, their parents, or the government to pay for their higher education. In the other, the parents transfer the necessary funds to their children. When education is funded by transfers, which are necessarily downward in this case, overall transfer wealth is less. To maintain the equality of transfer wealth plus capital to life-cycle wealth, capital must be increased (which means, of course, that labour productivity would be higher, and the assumption of identical life-cycle wealth in the two societies would be violated—but the point should be nonetheless clear). What has happened? Suppose education is funded by parental loans. In that case the parents can count on repayment later as part of their provision for old age. If instead they transfer the funds, then they will have to do additional saving and capital formation to provide for their old age.

Inference from life-cycle profiles

For most of the societies considered in the next section, the only information currently available is the age profiles of labour earning and consumption. The gap between these two can in principle be decomposed into familial and public-sector transfers, credit transactions, and real capital transactions; but in practice the data needed to do this are not yet available except for the United States. Nonetheless, consideration of the analytic framework developed earlier shows that it is possible to draw useful inferences about familial transfers from these simple life-cycle profiles in the case of the pre-agricultural and agricultural societies with very limited public sectors, to be considered in the next section. First, note that K must by definition be non-negative. Second, for these societies either public-sector transfers are almost entirely absent, or they are not reflected in the life-cycle age profiles we use. Third, for credit transactions, whether within the family or between families, the average ages of borrowing and lending in the population must be equal and the stock of net credit in the population must be zero (if we assume the population does not hold government debt or foreign net credit). From these considerations, it follows that life-cycle wealth, W, must exceed familial transfer wealth, T^F. It also follows that the net direction and distance of familial transfer flows, given by the difference between the average age of receiving a gross transfer and the average age of making one, must satisfy the condition of

$$A_{\tau+} - A_{\tau-} \leq (c/\tau)(A_c - A_{yl}),$$

where τ is the per capita flow of gross familial transfers and c is per capita income.

From this we can infer that if the net reallocation of resources over the life cycle is downward, then so is the net direction of familial transfers; and if the net direction of reallocations is upward, it is still possible that familial transfers may be, on net, downward if the per capita capital stock is sufficiently large. If τ is no larger than c, then the familial transfers will be at least as downward in years as is net reallocation over the life cycle. I shall use these results as the basis of inference about familial transfers in the next section.

Inter-age Resource Flows and Life-Cycle Wealth across Economic and Cultural Systems

Whereas the needs and dependency of childhood have always been with us, it appears that the quantitative significance of the dependency of old age may be a relatively new phenomenon—both because old age was rarely achieved in the past and because those who did achieve it often remained quite productive. Old-age dependence as a general phenomenon has resulted from changes in both the demographic life cycle and the economic life cycle. These same changes have altered childhood dependency as well, both weakening it demographically, as declining fertility and lengthening life have reduced the preponderance of children in the population, and strengthening it, as the industrial economy has limited the economic contribution of children by rewarding extended training. Within each population, these first and third stages of life dominate the flows of resources from those who produce a surplus to those whose consumption exceeds their output. Beyond these great tidal flows up and down the age scale there are, of course, eddies and cross-currents as well, which largely cancel one another.

As the demography and economics of the life cycle change, it appears that the net direction of transversal resource flows changes as well. It is likely—and the evidence will be considered later—that in many, if not most, pre-agricultural societies, the direction of net flows was strongly downward, from older to younger. In agricultural societies, before the demographic transition commenced, the flow was still, very likely, downward. Although the third stage of the economic life cycle had begun to emerge in the sense that elderly people may have consumed more than they produced, the third stage of the demographic life cycle remained undeveloped. During the initial stages of the demographic transition, mortality declines made old age loom larger in the individual life cycle, but the same mortality declines caused a dramatic acceleration of population growth and actually made populations somewhat younger rather than older. Consequently, from a demographic point of view, the first stage of the demographic transition made the third stage of the life cycle less, not more, important. When the modern industrial state *cum* welfare state is in full flower, however, the direction of resource flows is strongly reversed, becoming distinctly upward. This reversal is due in part to the changing demography, as both mortality and fertility reach low levels and the population ages, and in part to the emergence of thoroughgoing retirement. Paralleling these changes are massive institutional changes: the rise of the state and the emergence of its transfer functions, the emergence of property rights, and the emergence of financial institutions and capital markets, and of insurance.

Caldwell's theory

In Caldwell's (1976) classic article on demographic transition theory, he states his views on the direction of inter-age resource flows unambiguously:

> The key issue here, and, I shall argue, the fundamental issue in demographic transition, is the *direction and magnitude of intergenerational wealth flows* or the net balance of the two flows—one from parents to children and the other from children to parents—over the period from when people become parents until they die. . . . It may even be closer to the truth in the older traditional village to speak of the flow being from the younger to the older in the community as a whole with the parent-child relationships in each family playing only a secondary role. . . . In all primitive societies and nearly all traditional societies the net flow is from child to parent. (Caldwell 1976:140)

The anthropological literature, when it addresses the issue, is more cautious on this point. According to an old but still much-cited synthetic study by Leo Simmons (1945), who reviewed a large collection of qualitative ethnographic studies on the role of the elderly, the elderly tend to receive a share of general food production beyond their own contribution when there is general food sharing. General food sharing is more likely in harsh and variable environments, and less likely where food sources are more abundant, such as in agricultural settings, and where property rights are better established. In particular, a survey of data from fifty to 100 groups suggests that food sharing in general, and net food contributions to the elderly in particular, are most common in gathering and fishing groups, next most likely in hunting and horticultural groups, and least likely in agricultural groups. From Simmons's discussion, it appears that there may be systematic differences among cultural and economic groups in whether the elderly are net producers or net consumers in pre-agricultural societies. However, Simmons's sources did not attempt to quantify the productive contributions of children or the elderly in relation to their consumption.

Caldwell (1976: 141) argues forcefully that the qualitative assessments of informants cannot be taken at face value in this regard. He suggests that it would be difficult to evaluate the net direction of wealth flows by examining the interactions of parents and children because some of the transfers of resources might take place through institutional channels above the family, such as the village. One straightforward way to avoid this difficulty in evaluating the direction of resource flows is simply to estimate what the average person produces and consumes at each age. The difference must be some sort of reallocation across ages and, as discussed earlier, must be either a transfer, or a credit transaction, or capital accumulation. In many contexts, capital accumulation can be ruled out as a possibility (see Kaplan 1994), just as Samuelson (1958) ruled it out by assumption. As already shown, credit cannot be used to reallocate resources either upward or downward in the aggregate within a closed population, and so it cannot alter the net direction of resource flows. For many societies, particularly those in which market financial institutions do not exist and the state is an irrelevancy, any discrepancy between producing and consuming, or at least any net upward or downward reallocation, can be safely attributed to familial transfers. In these circumstances the inequality given earlier, linking familial transfers and the average ages of consuming and producing, will be close to an equality.

Hunter-gatherer horticulturist groups in the Amazon Basin

Anthropologists have gathered detailed information on the economic activities of many small groups that live by either hunting and gathering, forest horticulture, or extensive agriculture (swidden). Some of those studies provide data on time use by age and sex; others provide estimates of the caloric content of food gathered or grown and food consumed. Such studies must confront many difficulties, including the ascertainment of age, the determination of whether time is being used productively,[6] the measurement of consumption when food is eaten from a common pot, the extreme scarcity of people at advanced ages, and varying degrees of exposure to a wider market (see Dodds, Friou, and Mason 1996).

Kaplan (1994) has carried out one such study of three groups of forest horticulturists in the Amazon Basin that is unusually careful and detailed, and that directly addresses the question of intergenerational transfers. The groups produce food through swidden agriculture supplemented by some hunting and gathering. Kaplan's data include measures of the caloric yield of the productive activities of each individual sampled. He has found that in each of the groups, transfers pass wealth strongly from adults and elderly down to children, so that the net direction is downward, contrary to Caldwell's assertions. Kaplan has generously provided me with his basic aggregated data in tabular form, and I have reanalysed it using the analytic framework and methods described earlier. Because the age profiles are quite similar for all three groups and the groups are all small, I grouped them together into a single population of 430.

Figure 2.3 presents the results. Panel A, which plots the age distribution for both sexes combined, indicates that this population is very young, with a median age of 15 and 59 per cent under the age of 20. (Persons 60 and older are assumed to be equally distributed between the age groups 60–4 and 65–9.) In Panel B, which plots the age profiles of consumption and production, the level of the consumption profile has been proportionally adjusted so that given the population age distribution, total production equals total consumption. This is consistent with Kaplan's assertion that all output is consumed within a few days and there is no store of value. In Panel B we note that children do not begin producing as much as they consume until age 20, echoing a conclusion of Kaplan's. Once people become net producers, they remain so, on average, for the remainder of their lives; at no point in these data do we observe the older members of the population reducing their productive output below their consumption needs.[7] Indeed, Kaplan reports that the more children or grandchildren an older person has, the harder he or she works, and the more wealth that person transfers downward.

From these data can be computed the average ages of production and consumption.[8] They are, respectively, 34 years and 23 years. In other words, the net direction of transfers in this pooled group is strongly downward from older to younger; the average calorie of food is consumed by someone 11 years younger than the person who produced it.

We would also like to be able to compute transfer wealth, $W(x)$, at each age x and as an average in the population. To do this, we need a survivorship schedule and a discount rate. We have neither. However, when all reallocations are transfers, the appropriate discount rate is the implicit rate of return earned on transfers.[9] In a stable population, that would equal the population growth rate, as noted earlier. Let us suppose for a moment that we already know the

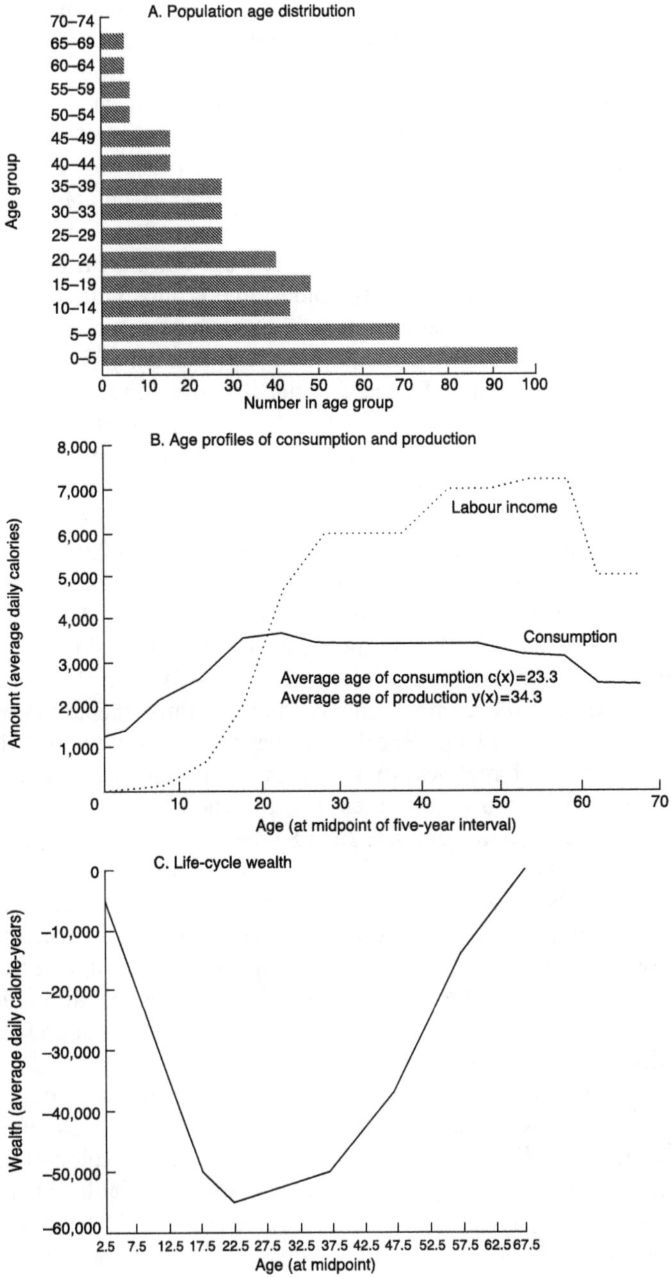

Note: A general description of the means of calculation and the data source is given in the text. For further details, see Kaplan (1994).

Fig. 2.3. Inter-age resource reallocations for Kaplan's horticulturists (pooled)

survivorship schedule, $p(x)$. In that case there are two routes by which we can find an appropriate discount rate. First, armed with $p(x)$ we can estimate the rate of population growth from the cross-sectional age distribution and use it as the discount rate.[10] Second, again armed with $p(x)$, we can calculate the internal rate of return to the transfer system,[11] and use the solution r as the discount rate. In practice, the two methods give a similar result, as they ought.[12] Panel C of Figure 2.3 plots $W(x)$ per surviving cohort member calculated by using the internal rate of return. Transfer wealth becomes more and more negative as children age, reaching its minimum at just after age 20; thereafter, it rises more slowly than it fell, reaching zero at the oldest age group. Thus people at every age owe transfer debt—that is, have negative transfer wealth.

I made these estimates on the assumption that mortality corresponded to a life expectancy of 52.5 years. To see whether it matters much which mortality level we choose, I recalculated all the estimates assuming that life expectancy at birth was 35 instead of 52.5. Fortunately, the results are hardly altered at all, and certainly they do not change in the least qualitatively. With higher mortality, the estimated rate of natural increase is lower, dropping from 0.037 to 0.029, and the internal rate of return is also lower, dropping from 0.035 to 0.028. The lower probability of surviving to advanced ages is almost exactly offset by the lower discount rate or rate of population growth.[13]

This life-cycle pattern of consumption and production could not possibly be supported by credit transactions. Adults reallocate food to their children for many years, and the children never 'repay' them, because the adults remain net producers even in their old age. Recalling a theoretical result from earlier in this chapter, we know that a reallocation system $g(x)$ must change sign at least twice if it is supported by borrowing and lending; but the $g(x) = y(x) - c(x)$ crosses the zero line only once, at around age 20 in Kaplan's data. Nor could the pattern of consumption and production be supported by capital accumulation followed by disinvestment, because according to Kaplan there are no durable stores of value in these groups. Even if there were, investment and disinvestment could reallocate resources upward to a later stage in the life cycle, but never downward to an earlier stage. In societies like those studied by Kaplan, capital accumulation could occur only if downward transfers were increased enough to sustain it, as I shall discuss later.

Using a large collection of data sets called the Human Resources Area Files (HRAF), we can get a broader view of these patterns, for other Amazon Basin groups and beyond. HRAF contains monographs and time-allocation data for a large number of societies, largely hunters and gatherers but also horticulturists and intensive agriculturists, and even urban dwellers in industrial nations. The data were collected by various anthropologists for a variety of purposes and were then coded according to a uniform scheme so that a certain degree of comparability has been attained. The time-allocation studies rely mostly on the spot-check technique developed by Allen Johnson (1975). (For further details, see Dodds *et al.* 1995.)

The most commonly available kind of study provides data on the age and sex distribution of a population and on the use of time in a variety of activities, of which those classified as 'productive' and 'housework' (see Sackett 1989) are of interest in the present context. A research group at the University of California, Berkeley, led by anthropologist David Dodds, has begun to analyse data for a selection of the societies in the HRAF. For the purpose of analysis, I grouped together data from five Amazonian societies based on work by Dodds *et al.* (1996). I conducted my analysis exactly like the analysis of the Kaplan data just described, except that in this case it was necessary to use profiles of consumption by age compiled by Mueller (1976) and productivity per hour of work by age. Use of Mueller's profiles can be justified only as a temporary expedient until more appropriate age profiles become available. Figure 2.4 presents the results of this analysis.

Panel A plots the population age distribution, which is even younger than that in Kaplan's pooled data. Here the median age is 14, and 63 per cent of the inhabitants are under the age of 20. Panel B, which plots the age profiles of consumption and production, shows that children become net producers earlier in their lives, perhaps at 14 or 15, and remain net producers for a very long time. Nonetheless, there is a clear decline in productivity after the mid-forties, and at some point in their mid-sixties people become net consumers. The decline in production in old age is due almost entirely to Mueller's (1976) efficiency weights rather than to reduced hours of work. These profiles indicate less clearly the absence of old-age dependency. Nevertheless, the average ages of producing and consuming show that the average good produced is consumed by someone seven years younger than its producer. Once again, there is compelling evidence that resources flow downward, at least in this kind of group in this part of the world. Panel C, which plots life-cycle transfer wealth discounted at the internal rate of return and assuming a life expectancy of 52.5 years, shows a pattern very similar to that in Kaplan's data.

It would be premature to conclude that resources typically flow downward from older to younger members of pre-agricultural societies, because the groups we have examined are economically and geographically similar. I should mention, however, that such a conclusion is sustained not only in these pooled data, but also for every group in the pool individually. It is my hope to extend this analysis, drawing upon the file of anthropological time-use studies, to other continents and to other groups producing food more exclusively through hunting and gathering. Nonetheless, the results for these populations are so strong that they may well be found more generally.

The strength of the results derives in good part from the extremely young age structure of these populations. Of course, the data on age may be unreliable, but it is hard to imagine how this could matter much to the qualitative results. If all ages were on average overstated by 50 per cent, for example, no conclusions would be changed. All that is needed for the results to be qualitatively right is that the ranking by age in the populations be correctly reported; absolute age

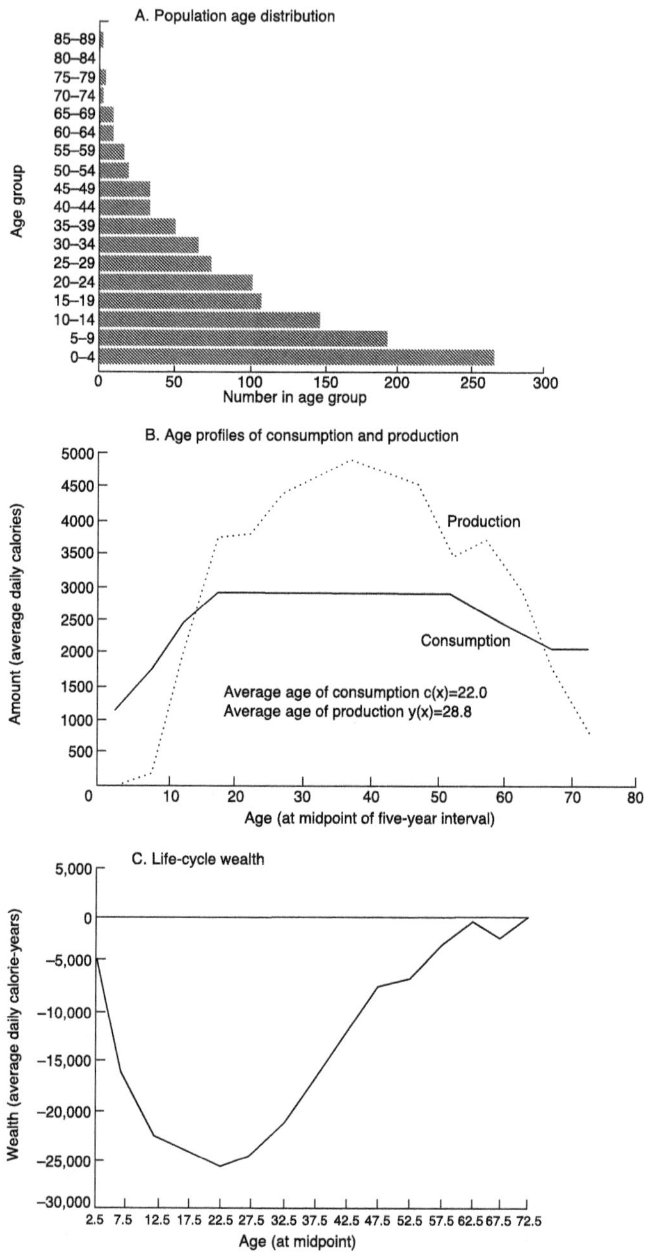

Note: A general description of the means of calculation and data source is given in the text. For details, see Dodds *et al.* (1996).

Fig. 2.4. Inter-age resource reallocations for other Amazonian horticulturists (pooled)

does not matter much. If we continue to take the age data literally, then only about 5 per cent of each of these populations is above age 50, while at least 50 per cent is below age 15. Children below 15 are net consumers in both pooled data sets; and even if those above age 50 were net consumers as well, those over 50 would have to consume enormous amounts to cause a reversal of the downward direction of resource flows.

Sackett (1989) provides relevant evidence covering a much wider range of societies. He has compiled a set of 105 time-use studies by anthropologists for groups of hunters and gatherers, forest horticulturists (like those in the Kaplan and Amazonian data sets), extensive and intensive cultivators, and urban dwellers from areas in Latin America, Africa, and Asia. His general description of the age profiles of work activity is that they reach a plateau at ages 15 to 20, continuing steady into the forties, then declining slightly, and reaching a level of about two-thirds of the prime-age adult work time at about age 65 (ibid. 6). When he groups together what he calls 'extensive' groups (hunters and gatherers, forest horticulturists, and extensive cultivators), he finds that children in those groups tend to reach adult levels of work time later than do those in the intensive groups, and that the elderly tend to begin to do less work earlier than do their counterparts in the intensive groups (ibid. 8). This description of the contributions of children appears to be quite consistent with Kaplan's data and that for the other groups in Amazonia. The description of the labour of the elderly is also consistent with the Amazonian data collected by Dodds and his colleagues, which show a substantial reduction already by the late forties. The description is less consistent with Kaplan's data on the elderly, but the point is that even with the Amazonian profiles of Dodds *et al.*, which on the basis of Sackett's work appear to be more generally characteristic of groups before the advent of intensive agriculture, the direction of transfers is strongly downward.

An extensive agriculturist society: Côte d'Ivoire

Guy Stecklov (1995) has analysed data from the World Bank's Living Standards Measurement Survey for Côte d'Ivoire to examine the direction of inter-age resource flows in that population. This is the first such study of a Third World national population using actual survey data specific to that country. The data include information on hours of work of various kinds for members of households in both rural and urban areas, and total labour income for the household. Stecklov used the Mueller (1976) indices of productivity per hour of work in a calculation that allocated the total household labour income to individual household members based on their hours of work. In this way he developed age profiles of output by age. He estimated consumption by using weights developed by Deaton and Muelbauer (1986) to allocate total household consumption to individual members by age and sex, on a household-by-household basis. Then he calculated consumption by age for both sexes combined by averaging the consumption by all individuals in the sample.

Figure 2.5, from Stecklov (1995), shows the age profiles of consumption and production calculated separately for the urban and rural households in his sample. From these data and from data on the population, which was very young and growing at 3.5 per cent annually, the average ages of consumption and production can be calculated. In rural areas they are 36.8 and 33.0, respectively, for a difference of almost four years. Thus once again, the direction of flows is decisively downward, although less strongly so than in the societies previously considered.

For individuals in urban areas, the results are even more striking: the corresponding average ages are 38.1 and 27.2, for a difference of 11 years. This results from the exceptionally late break-even age for urban youth in Côte d'Ivoire. If the rural and urban data are pooled, then the overall average ages are 37.5 and 29.8, for a difference of 7.7 years.

Other data in Stecklov show that in contrast to the Amazonian groups discussed above, in Côte d'Ivoire the hours worked fall off rapidly after the late forties, so that even before weighting by productivity per hour, it is clear that the elderly are much less productive than younger adult workers. This is true in both rural and urban areas.

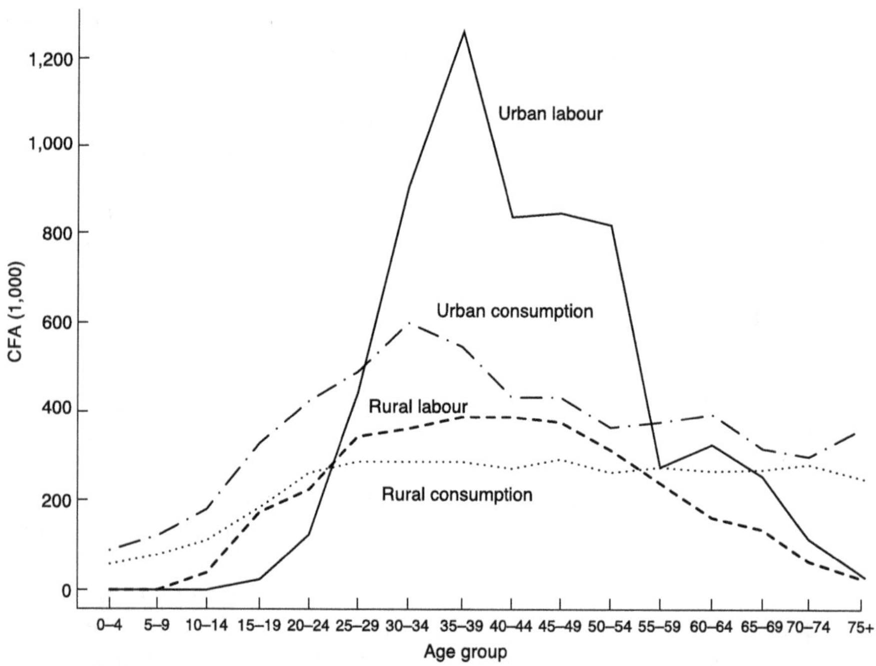

Note: A general description of the methods and data source is given in the text. For details, see Stecklov (1995).

Source: Reproduced from Stecklov (1995, fig. 3).

Fig. 2.5. Age profiles of consumption and labour earnings in Côte d'Ivoire

Intensive agricultural societies

Mueller's (1976) synthetic study of production and consumption by age in peasant agriculture provides a basis for assessing the direction of transfers in a generic Third World context. Drawing upon a survey of nine sets of profiles in the literature, Mueller has distilled consumption profiles that she believes to be appropriate for poor agricultural populations in which food is the dominant item consumed. Most of her production data, and those data she draws upon most strongly, refer to such societies as India and Egypt, where intensive rather than extensive agriculture is practised.

Her labour-supply data are based on a review of international overview studies by Durand (1975) and the UN, DESA (1962), as well as on her examination of census and survey data for specific countries such as India and Egypt. Those data are supplemented by data on hours worked by participants and by a careful examination of data on the productivity of an hour worked, tabulated by age and sex, based on wage data and other sources. From this information Mueller constructs her overall production profiles for males and females (1976: 118). These profiles apply to only the kinds of work that contribute to the gross national product as conventionally measured and therefore exclude most kinds of home production. She evaluates these profiles as follows (ibid. 119): 'In contrast to the consumption profiles, the work-input data show a considerable degree of consistency. Despite the many weaknesses cited earlier, the work-input estimates from many countries and diverse sources have important similarities. This consistency justifies some confidence in the production profiles.' For our purposes and for hers, it is not the absolute levels of these profiles that matter. For a given population's age distribution, one profile is raised or lowered in relation to the other until some targeted aggregate balance is achieved, such as an aggregate saving rate of 10 per cent. In our case, the consumption profile will be adjusted so that total consumption equals total agricultural output.

Following Mueller (1976), we take the population to be stable, with mortality for both sexes set at the Model West Female (MWF) level of fourteen deaths per 1,000 population ($e_0 = 52.5$) and a gross reproduction rate (GRR) of 3.0 daughters per woman, leading to an annual population growth rate of 2.9 per cent. The resulting population age distribution is very young, but not so young as either of the Amazonian populations studied above. Median age is 18, with 55 per cent of the population under the age of 20.

Panel A of Figure 2.6 plots the age profiles. It clearly reveals a life-cycle stage in which the elderly consume somewhat more than they produce, but because of the young age distribution it receives little weight. After age 65 the average person produces only about two-thirds of what he or she consumes. Unfortunately, a more detailed breakdown by age is not available. The average age of production is 32 years and of consumption, 26 years, so that the direction of transfers is once again very strongly downward from older to younger. Panel B

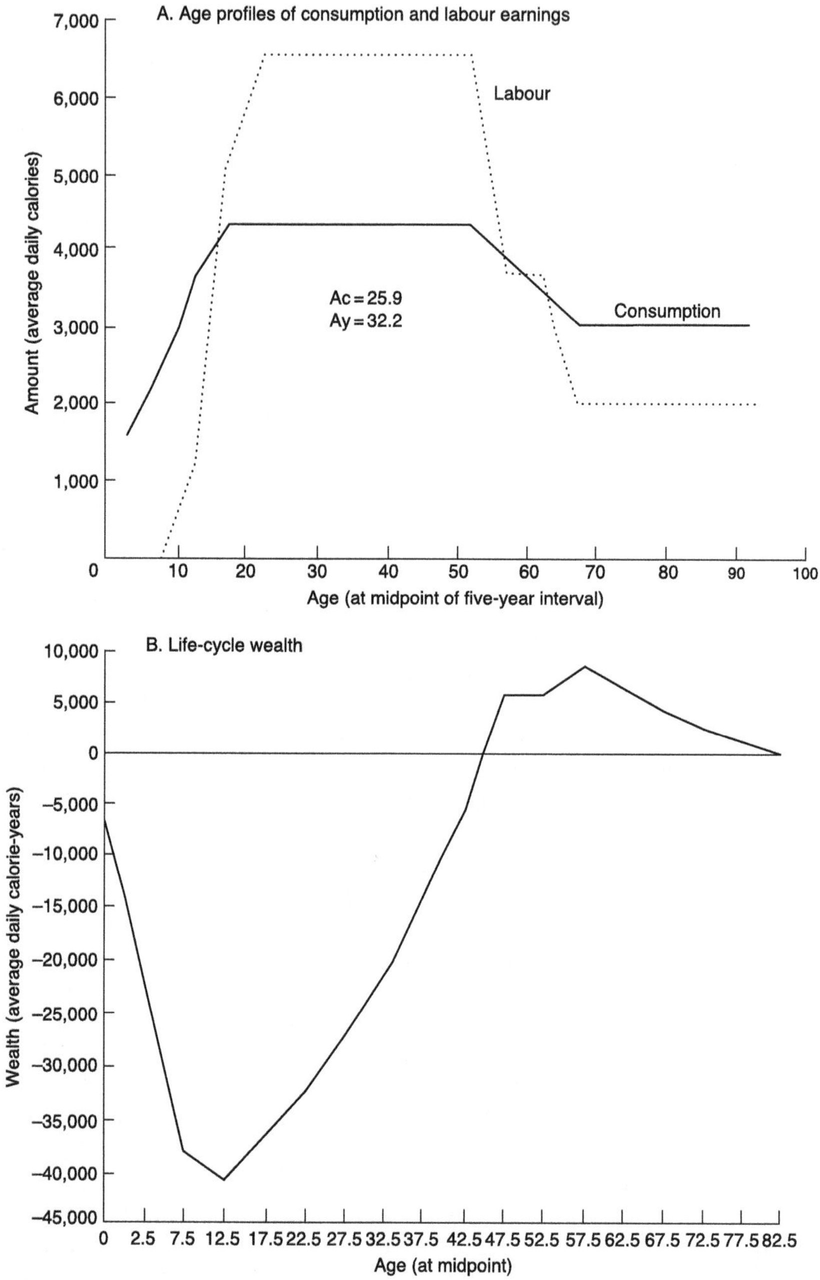

Note: For a description of the data and method, see text and Mueller (1976).

Fig. 2.6. Inter-age resource reallocations for a typical rural population practising intensive agriculture (after Mueller)

plots life-cycle wealth per original member of the birth cohort. In contrast to the data for pre-extensive agricultural societies, the third life-cycle stage, in which consumption falls more substantially short of production, now leads to a substantial segment of the $W(x)$ schedule in which life-cycle wealth is positive; that is, after age 45 or so, the average person would expect to consume more than he or she produced in survival-weighted present value for the rest of his or her life. Nonetheless, the overall average wealth in the population (the population-weighted average of $W(x)$) is overwhelmingly negative.

How much are these results for Mueller's data altered if we alter the demographic assumptions? When we use a stable population with the same mortality, but with a GRR of 2 instead of 3, the growth rate drops to 1.5 per cent per year and the population becomes older. Nevertheless, the direction of transfers remains strongly downward, with the average age of production being 35 years and of consumption, 30 years. When we use a stable population with a life expectancy of 35 (MWF 7) and a GRR of 3, the growth rate drops to .004 and again the population is older, but the direction of transfers remains the same: the average age of production is 36 years and of consumption, 32 years. In other words, given the Mueller profiles and the assumption that aggregate consumption equals aggregate production among the rural peasant population, the conclusion of strong downward transfers is robust to plausible variations in demographic assumptions across steady states.

Contemporary United States

In other studies (R. D. Lee 1994*a*, 1994*b*), I have used mainly a household rather than an individual framework for doing the accounting for the United States, but here I shall express results in the individual framework for sake of comparability. For the United States, labour income includes pre-tax wages and salaries, self-employment income, fringe benefits, and the employer's share of the Social Security pay-roll tax. Consumption includes the kinds of expenditures usually included in a household survey, except that expenditures for owner-occupied housing, automobiles, and other consumer durables are treated not as current consumption but as investment, and the imputed services flowing from these capital goods are counted as consumption in the years following the purchase. In addition, in-kind government transfers, particularly public education and publicly provided health services (Medicare and Medicaid) are included as consumption. My data come from the 1991 Consumer Expenditure Survey (CES) and from other standard government sources. Expenditures are available only for households, not for individuals. I used the Lazear-Michael (1988) weights to estimate the share of household consumption going to each member of a household, and then I averaged those amounts across age groups to derive a profile of consumption by age for individuals. There are many difficulties in such an allocation of consumption to individuals; these are discussed in R. D. Lee (1988, 1994*a*). The resulting profiles differ from the earlier ones in that in-kind government transfers and services from capital goods, such as housing or cars, were explicitly included.

Using the actual age distribution for the US population, I calculated the average ages of consuming and producing to be 43 and 41, respectively, so that reallocations are upward rather than downward. In the stationary population the direction remains upward and the age gap grows to four years.

Figure 2.7, Panel A, shows the age profiles that result from these calculations. The young do not become net producers until their early twenties, and the elderly become net consumers in their early sixties. Consumption rises slowly but steadily from the early twenties through the mid-sixties, after which it becomes flat.

Two points should be borne in mind in relation to this profile. First, about a quarter of consumption at advanced ages is in the form of in-kind health-service transfers from the government; in the absence of the health transfers, the profile would slope strongly downward. Second, the profile is cross-sectional; if labour productivity grows over time, as it has throughout most of the twentieth century, then an individual will experience more strongly rising consumption over the life cycle.

For reasons that remain unclear, it was not possible to solve for the internal rate of return when I balanced the profiles using the actual US population age distribution, and so I assumed a stationary age distribution instead, corresponding to a life expectancy of 75. The wealth profile, $W(x)$, is plotted in Panel B. It can be seen that there is now a substantial period of the life cycle in which life-cycle wealth is positive, with a cross-over at around age 37 or 38. Life-cycle wealth peaks at about $275,000 at age 62 or 63. The population-weighted average of life-cycle wealth, W, is now positive.

When the calculations are done on a household basis, using the age of the household reference person instead of the age of an individual household

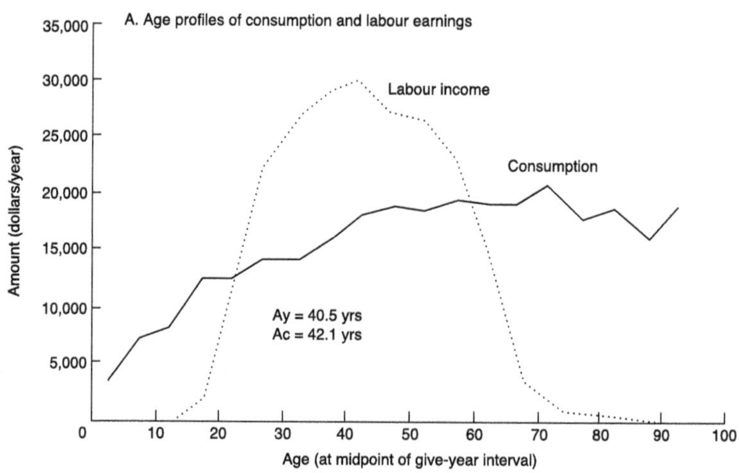

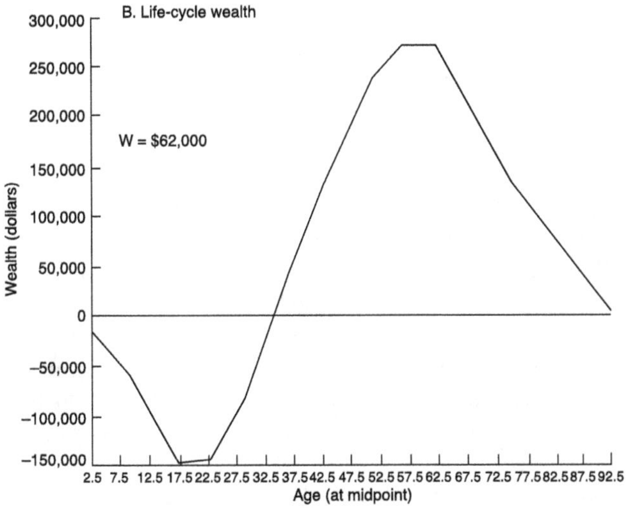

Note: Labour earnings are pre-tax and include the employer's contribution to pay-roll tax and benefits, as well as self-employment income. Consumption includes conventional household expenditures, less expenditures on purchases of homes, cars, and consumer durables, plus the imputed flow of services from these. The resulting household consumption is then allocated to individuals in the household using Lazear and Michael's (1988) method and estimated coefficients. In-kind government transfers of education and health care are added to each age as appropriate. Next, the age profile of labour earnings is inflated by a factor calculated to equate the population-weighted total of labour earnings and consumption. The population used for equalizing generalized consumption and labour earnings is the stationary (life table) population for the United States with e0 = 75 because when the actual population was used, the calculation produced no economically reasonable internal rate of return.

Sources: Data come from the 1987 Consumer Expenditure Survey, supplemented by data on public education from the *Statistical Abstract of the United States* (US, Bureau of the Census 1990) and from the Survey of Health Expenditures.

Fig. 2.7. Inter-age resource reallocations for individuals in the United States, 1987

member, the difference in average ages of consumption and production is larger because reallocations downward to children within the family are submerged. Using data for 1991, Miller and I report an average age of consumption of 48.9, and of earning, 43.2, for a difference of 5.6 years, based on the actual age distribution of households (R. D. Lee and Miller 1995: 11). Ermisch (1989), replicating a study of mine (R. D. Lee 1985) and using household data for Japan and England, found that reallocations were upward by about seven and five years, respectively.

Summary of directional flows

Figure 2.8 summarizes these data by plotting, for each group, an arrow with its tail at the mean age of producing and its head at the mean age of consuming. Ordinarily in this kind of diagram, used for comparisons within a given population, the thickness of the arrow would indicate the size of the annual per capita flow in the population; and the area of the arrow, the product of its length and its thickness, would equal the per capita wealth averaged across all ages. In these cross-cultural comparisons, however, nothing would be gained by depicting the thickness of the arrows, which would depend only on differences in per capita consumption between the societies and on the monetary units used. It might be argued that the absolute size of the directional flows is significant in itself and, in particular, that the vast increase in the net flows from parents to children in the industrial populations is an important cause of the fertility decline. This is indeed an important hypothesis to consider, and it is an important aspect of economic theories of fertility decline such as that of Becker (1981). What matters here, though, is the expenditure per child multiplied by the marginal utility of consumption. This marginal utility should be much lower in industrial countries with their extremely high levels of consumption than in traditional societies with their low levels of consumption. This does not mean to say that the hypothesis is wrong, but rather that testing it would not be a simple matter and cannot be attempted here.

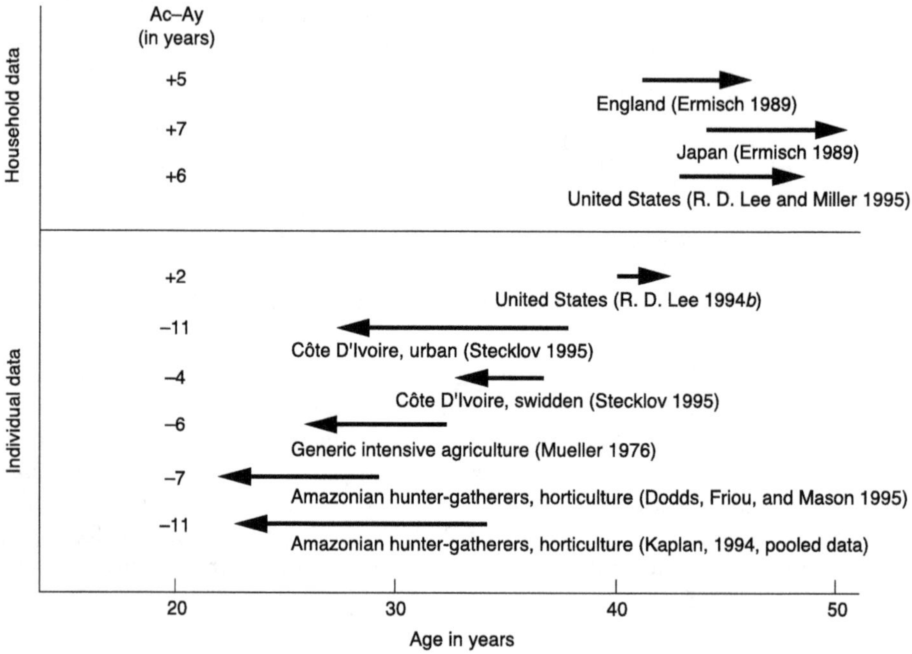

Note: The figure plots estimated average ages from the data used in Figures 2.3 to 2.7, where further information on data and methods can be obtained. The tail of each arrow is placed at the average age of producing (labour earnings), and the head of the arrow is placed at the average age of consuming.

Fig. 2.8. Summary of inter-age reallocations in various contexts

Figure 2.8 tells a clear story: for every pre-industrial society examined, the direction of net transfers is downward, usually strongly so. It remains to be seen whether studies of other societies confirm this pattern, but it appears quite likely that they will. For the United States, which is the sole industrial society examined with individual data, the net direction of reallocation is upward. The upper panel of Figure 2.8 plots Ermisch's (1989) household-based estimates of the direction of flows for England and Japan, which are upward by five and seven years, respectively, and are similar to the 5.6 years that Miller and I (1995) find for the United States. It appears, then, that as Caldwell suggested, there has been a reversal in the direction of wealth flows; but contrary to Caldwell's assertion, wealth flows have been downward from older to younger generations in traditional societies, and upward from younger to older generations in modern societies.

So far we have considered neither the mechanisms nor the institutional channels through which these reallocations are channelled. At the end of the theoretical section of this chapter, however, I showed that for the pre-industrial data sets we could conclude that downward reallocations implied in general that familial transfers were correspondingly downward. For industrial societies, the situation is rather different because of the importance of both capital and public-sector transfers. Separating familial transfers, T^f, and governmental transfers, both financial and in-kind, T^g, we have $T^f = W - K - T^g$. We have seen that W is positive, and that reallocations in general are upward by about four years. As we shall see in the next section, however, both K and T^g are very substantial positive values, so that in fact familial transfers in the United States are strongly downward, just as in the other societies examined. The reversal of the direction of net reallocations does not correspond to a reversal of the direction of transfers within the family. Regarding Caldwell's assertion, it is these familial flows that are most relevant, for they reflect the net costs of children and childbearing incentives. Although the pre-transitional downward familial flows are inconsistent with Caldwell's claims, the flows in industrial, post-transitional United States are consistent with them. I shall examine the structure of these downward familial transfers in the United States in more detail later in this chapter.

Direction of familial transfers and the costs and benefits of children

So far I have shown that the direction of net reallocations is strongly downward in all the pre-industrial settings I have examined. Perhaps it is not clear that this concept of the direction of wealth flows is directly relevant for the fertility decision, and so I shall also do a rough calculation that bears more directly on Caldwell's theory of incentives for childbearing in relation to the direction of flows.

Consider a young parent deciding whether to have an additional child. The mean age at childbearing can be taken to be 30, so that for concreteness we will imagine a 30–year-old facing this decision. Lacking data on the costs and returns from an incremental child, the calculation will assume that this child consumes the same amounts and makes the same transfers at each age as the average pre-existing child.

Under the assumption that all transfers are familial, we can take the net cost of a child to both parents to be the integral under the $[y_l(x) - c(x)]$ curve, weighted by survival $p(x)$, over the range in which consumption exceeds output. We can take the return to all childbearing, from the point of view of the two parents, to be the transfers received at older ages that permit consumption to exceed earnings; this will be given by twice the integral under the $[y_l(x) - c(x)]$ curve, weighted by survival $p(x)$, over the range in which it is negative at old ages. However, since the adult will not be in a position to make a fertility decision unless he or she is alive, we can assume that age 30 was attained, and condition our calculations on survival to this point. The returns to childbearing should then be as just described, but divided by $p(30)$.

Taking these various factors into consideration, we conclude that the costs and benefits of bearing an additional child should be related to the age profiles of consumption and production as follows:

$$\text{Net cost of child } (NCC)\text{: } NCC = \int_0^{\alpha} [y_l(x) - c(x)]p(x)dx \text{ and}$$

$$\text{Return per child } (RPC)\text{: } RPC = 2\int_{\beta}^{\omega} [y_l(x) - c(x)]p(x)dx/[TFR \times p(30)],$$

where α is the age at which a child breaks even, with earnings equal to consumption, and β is the age at which an older person again just breaks even, with falling earnings intersecting the consumption curve.

For the groups studied by Kaplan (1994) this whole line of analysis is irrelevant because there is no period in the life cycle in which adults are consuming more, on average, than they are producing. For the Mueller profiles with $e_0 = 52.5$ and GRR $= 3.0$, the calculations come out as follows: $NCC = 2.63$ units, $RPC = 0.25$ units, and the ratio of RPC to $NCC = 0.1$. In other words, parents can expect to get back in old-age support from an incremental birth about one-tenth of what they spend to rear the child of that birth. One might argue that it is wrong to weight this amount by the probability of surviving to the age at which the support would be received, for it is a kind of insurance against the contingency of survival. If we condition the return on surviving from age 30 to age 65, it becomes larger by a factor of $[p(30)/p(65)]$, which in the present case is about 1.6. In this case, a parent *who survived to age 65* would receive from each child about one-sixth of what had been invested in that child.

I have also calculated the implicit rate of return that is earned on the expenditure on children in this example, which is -0.067 per year. This figure is based on the calculated return of one-tenth of what has been invested, and taking account of the gap between the average age of investing in a child, which is 30 + 8, or 38, and the average age of receiving a return transfer, which is 73, for a gap of 35 years. If there is economic progress such that the age schedules for consumption and production shift upward at some annual rate, then that rate would be added to the calculated rate of return. For example, if there were progress at 3 per cent per year, then the average annual rate of return would rise from −0.067 to −0.037. In sum, bearing children is an extremely costly way of providing for old age, yielding far less in old-age transfers than it costs, so that the rate of return is strongly negative.[14]

Questions may be raised about this calculation. What about transfers by older children, say those of ages 15 to 25, to their parents before they leave the parental home? What about possible transfers from parents to their children when their children are in the years of heaviest childrearing pressures? In preliminary related work I have developed a method for estimating the age schedule $\delta(a)$ of transfers to a person of age a from his or her parent, based on only the gap between consumption and labour earning at each age, and the survival and fertility age schedules.[15] When this is done using the Mueller profiles, the result is qualitatively the same, but not quite so strong, as in the calculation reported above: a child costs four or five times as much as his or her expected return over the life cycle.

I believe that these data and calculations demonstrate that wealth does not flow upward in the traditional societies examined here. I believe that Caldwell's assertion that it does so is mistaken. Yet Caldwell's main point, that high fertility is economically rational for one or both parents in traditional societies, in my view does not require that wealth flow upward. In the absence of institutions that provide various kinds of insurance and permit the reallocation through savings of resources to old age, children may still be the best deal around, although the extent to which such assets as land or livestock fulfil the same functions in agricultural societies is unclear. Didier Blanchet, in his comments on an earlier draft of this chapter, illustrated this point formally with a model in which risk-averse parents improve their welfare by having children who provide insurance, even though the direction of wealth flows is strongly downward. Yean-Ju Lee and Bhaumik and Nugent (in this volume) provide evidence of gross upward transfers from older children outside the parental home to their parents in a number of Third World countries; but it is highly doubtful that these transfers would be large enough to offset the costs of childrearing incurred by their parents earlier.

Capital accumulation with negative life-cycle wealth

Capital accumulation has two effects of interest here. First, capital is productive, and its presence raises both the productivity of labour and total output. Second, the accumulation of capital defers consumption, since it is necessary to forgo consumption of some output today in order to create the capital; and it raises consumption in the future when the returns to capital are received. Thus capital has both a productive function and a reallocative function. Yet one may want to accumulate capital (in the form of farm animals, farm machinery, land, and so on) for efficiency in production but not want to defer consumption, or one may want to defer some consumption until old age but have no need for productive capital. For an individual, the link between deferring consumption on the one hand and acquiring productive capital on the other can be broken by borrowing the money necessary to pay for the capital. But for a society as a whole this is not possible because the stock of debt must equal the stock of credit (unless the society borrows from foreigners or the government issues debt). For a society as a whole, if it is limited to purely market mechanisms, the stock of capital must equal life-cycle wealth, W; and life-cycle wealth, as it must necessarily equal the value of the capital stock, which must be non-negative, must itself be non-negative. In reality, however, no society is limited to purely market mechanisms; and transfers, at least to children, are always present. At the societal level, transfer wealth, T, breaks the link between capital accumulation and waiting. K no longer needs to equal W.

The theory of life-cycle saving asserts that the desire to provide for net consumption in old age is the main motivation for saving and capital formation, and therefore it is the underlying explanation for the accumulation of wealth (Modigliani 1988*a*). Nevertheless, we have seen that in all the pre-industrial societies we examined, life-cycle wealth is actually negative—that is, the average person in the population desires to hold negative wealth, or debt, to achieve consumption-smoothing over the life cycle. How, then, is it possible for such societies to have any capital stock at all, and can these circumstances be reconciled with the life-cycle saving theory? (It should be noted that there is considerable doubt that saving in poor agricultural societies is motivated by life-cycle needs rather than by precaution.)

First, it is important to recall that in every society there are strong familial transfers to children. When a household framework is used for the accounting of inter-age resource flows, then the transfers to children do not enter into the total because they are mostly intra-household transfers. To some degree the downward transfers we find in these societies simply reflect the downward transfers to children. If the downward transfers to children are sufficiently large, then we might well have $T < W$, so that $W - T = K > 0$. But even if transfers to young children are not sufficiently large to offset negative W, capital accumulation may still be achieved in the ways discussed below, which often involve transfers from older parents to adult children.

In the case of the Amazon Basin horticulturists, we are told by Kaplan (1994) that $K = 0$ and can infer that $W = T \ll 0$, where $\ll$ is used to denote 'substantially less than'. Here there is nothing to discuss about the substitution of K and T. In the agricultural societies, we also appear to have $W \ll 0$, $T \ll 0$. K, however, is held in the form of land, livestock, and gold jewellery, for example, so that $K > 0$ and we can infer that $T < W \ll 0$. How are we to think of the substitution of K and T in this kind of setting? How does there come to be capital at all when life-cycle wealth is negative? There are several possibilities.

First, adults may accumulate some assets during their years of net production, planning to draw upon them during their older years. This would be life-cycle saving. In this case, they are using capital to support consumption in excess of production in their later years, and this is clearly an alternative to achieving the same result through transfers. This strategy of life-cycle saving would therefore reduce or eliminate some older years that would otherwise necessarily have $T(x) > 0$, given the assumption that production and consumption profiles are held fixed. In this way, K substitutes for T. Second, older people may avoid drawing down their assets and instead pass them on as bequests to their children when they die. In this case the positive K is exactly offset by a decrease in T (T becomes more negative) because of the downward flow of bequests, and again K and T substitute for one another. Third, older people may make greater transfers to young adults, in excess of the net consumption needs of young adults, permitting them to accumulate capital of their own (as in the case of a dowry or help to acquire a farm, a house, or livestock). Once again, K increases and T decreases (becomes more negative).

Of course, in most forms K not only serves as a store of value (as with gold jewellery that is not worn), but also is a productive asset that raises the productivity of labour (as with land or livestock). This makes the assumption of fixed production and consumption profiles unrealistic, which is of course the reason for Feldstein's concern about the effects of social security to begin with.

Institutional Channels and Mechanisms for Reallocations

Except for some age profiles for the United States that I used earlier to illustrate the main concepts of reallocation systems, the empirical work reported in this chapter has been limited to examining the age patterns of labour earnings and consumption, and the difference between them. Figure 2.2 decomposed the gap between these two age profiles into net flows through each of the major kinds of reallocation system: transfers, credit, and investment in capital. Unfortunately, nothing similar has yet been done for countries other than the United States, so that comparative results cannot be reported in any general way. However, there are two specific kinds of transfer systems for which some comparison is possible. First, I shall present comparative results on public-sector transfers in some Third World countries and the United States. Second, I shall present some results on familial transfers in the United States that may be roughly compared to the earlier results on production and consumption profiles in pre-industrial societies, which I argued must reflect almost exclusively familial transfers.

Public-sector transfers in the United States and selected Third World nations

Not surprisingly, the industrial welfare states devote a substantially greater proportion of national income to public-sector transfers, both in cash and in kind, than do typical Third World countries. For example, whereas India in recent years has devoted about 4 per cent of its GNP to public expenditures on health, education, and pensions, of which nearly two-thirds has gone for education and only 10 per cent for pensions, the United States has spent about 15 per cent of its GNP, or four times India's share, on such transfers, of which 36 per cent was for education and about 35 per cent was for pensions.

The difference is not just in the scale of public-sector transfers, but also in their allocation by age. The industrial nations have far higher proportions of elderly in their populations than do the Third World nations. In the United States, for example, at current vital rates, the stable population would have a ratio of children to the elderly about *one-twentieth* as high as Kenya's. This purely demographic difference would tend to make the economic burden of supporting the elderly more important in industrial nations. However, this is only half the story. In most Third World countries, care and support for both children and the elderly are largely family matters. In industrial nations, by contrast, although the rearing of children remains primarily a family obligation, the elderly are increasingly supported by the public-sector through income transfers (pensions) and in-kind transfers of health services. In the United States an average elderly person receives net public transfers costing roughly 3.7 times as much as does an average child. In India, Bangladesh, Kenya, and Saudi Arabia, the same ratio is between 0.6 and 0.8 (see R. D. Lee, 1990). Given these differences in age distribution and in the scale of transfers, in the United States an elderly person receives annual transfers equal to 59 per cent of per capita GNP, while in Bangladesh the corresponding percentage is 1.8. In the hypothetical US stable population, more than 10.6 per cent of GNP would be transferred to the elderly, whereas in none of the four Third World countries in Africa and Asia that I examined would this be more than 0.5 per cent; and in Kenya and Bangladesh it would be less than 0.2 per cent (ibid. 1990). The situation is doubtless quite different for some Latin American countries with strong public-sector pension programmes, such as Brazil. It appears that in Brazil the average elderly person receives perhaps fifteen times as much as the average child from the public sector, a ratio that is many times higher than prevails even in the industrial nations (R. D. Lee and Miller 1990). Throughout Latin America there is growing interest in converting the pay-as-you-go public pension programmes to funded public programmes (see Chapter 6 by Rofman and Chapter 7 by Valdés-Prieto in this volume).

It is instructive to consider the population-weighted age profiles of public-sector transfers for India *circa* 1981, which appears to be fairly typical of Third World nations in this regard. The profiles, plotted in Figure 2.9, show that transfers are, on average, received at a younger age than are the taxes paid that support them, and calculations reveal that the gap in average ages is 11 years downward. Similar calculations for a number of other Third World nations show a similar pattern; for example, public-sector transfers were downward by 11, 13, and 14 years, respectively, in Bangladesh, Saudi Arabia, and Kenya. For

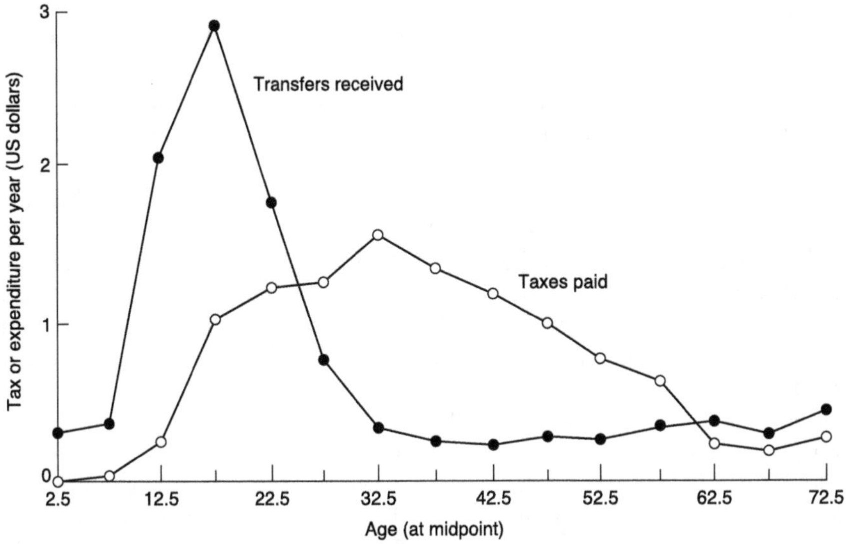

Note: For details on methods, assumptions, and sources, see R. D. Lee (1991).

Fig. 2.9. Public-sector transfers in India (health, pensions, and education in 1981)

Brazil, however, the net direction of transfers was upward, despite a relatively young population age distribution, owing to the importance of pensions (ibid.). In the United States the net direction of public-sector transfers is strongly upward, by 10 years, and most likely the situation is similar in all industrial nations.

The downward direction of public transfers in most Third World nations is a source of negative externalities to childbearing, for the reason that a younger age distribution is costly to the public but those costs are not borne directly by the individual parents who decide to have a child (R. D. Lee and Miller 1990). Similarly, the upward direction of public transfers in the United States and probably in other industrial nations is a source of positive externalities to childbearing, because a younger age distribution is beneficial to the public, reducing the per worker costs of supporting the elderly; but this benefit does not accrue to the individual parent. In most Third World nations, the size of the negative externality arising in this way is fairly small relative to per capita GNP. For example, in India, Bangladesh, Saudi Arabia, Kenya, and Mexico the fraction is −0.1, −0.04, −0.2, −0.2, and −0.1, respectively. In Brazil, however, it is positive, at +0.25, and in the United States it is more than 2! (see ibid.).

Familial transfers in the United States

I have reported that the overall direction of reallocated wealth over the life cycle is downward in all the pre-industrial populations I have examined, and upward in all the industrial populations I have examined. But this generalization is somewhat misleading, particularly when considered in conjunction with fertility theory. The fact is that in the United States reallocations are strongly upward through capital accumulation and through public-sector transfers, but they are strongly downward through the family, just as they are in every other society examined in this chapter. Not only do parents in the United States make downward transfers to their young children, as appears generally to be the case, but also the elderly make downward familial transfers, on net, to their adult children. It should be noted, however, that this net downward direction of transfers from the elderly might look different if the value of the time spent by adult children in caring for their elderly parents, and parental time investments in their children, were taken into consideration.

Figure 2.10, which is based on US data, uses an arrow diagram to portray four kinds of net transfers within the family and between families. In Panel B, child costs are a measure of the average direct costs of rearing a child through age 17, net of the child's labour earnings. The flows to children are calculated as described earlier for the consumption profile. The tail of each arrow is located at the average age of the parent making the transfer, and the head of the arrow is located at the average age of the child receiving the transfer. The thickness of the arrow represents the average flow to children per member of the total population, and the area of the arrow is therefore the average total cost of a child (discounted at the population growth rate, here taken to be zero). This total cost was $80,000 in 1987 and constitutes negative transfer wealth. The arrow for private expenditures on higher education is similarly constructed and indicates negative transfer wealth of $6,000. Together they indicate a net transfer to children while they are young of $86,000 per birth; that amount also measures the direct cost of a child. Note that if we assumed that costs of a child were rising at, say, 3 per cent per year, and we also discounted at 3 per cent per year, the result would remain exactly the same.

Panel A shows familial transfers between households. Those include *inter vivos* gifts and transfers, which generate negative wealth of $5,500 per household, or about $2,000 per individual. Such transfers are doubtless seriously under-reported in the Consumer Expenditure Survey and should be considerably larger. Finally, bequests constitute an important downward flow at the end of life. Their measurement has been highly controversial (Kotlikoff and Summers 1988; Modigliani 1988*a*), but I believe that the arrow in the diagram reflects a reasonable interpretation of the data (see R. D. Lee 1994*b*, for further details). The arrow indicates a downward flow generating negative bequest wealth of about $44,000 per household, or $17,000 per person in the population. For some purposes one may want to consider these transfers to adult children as a portion of the total cost of children.

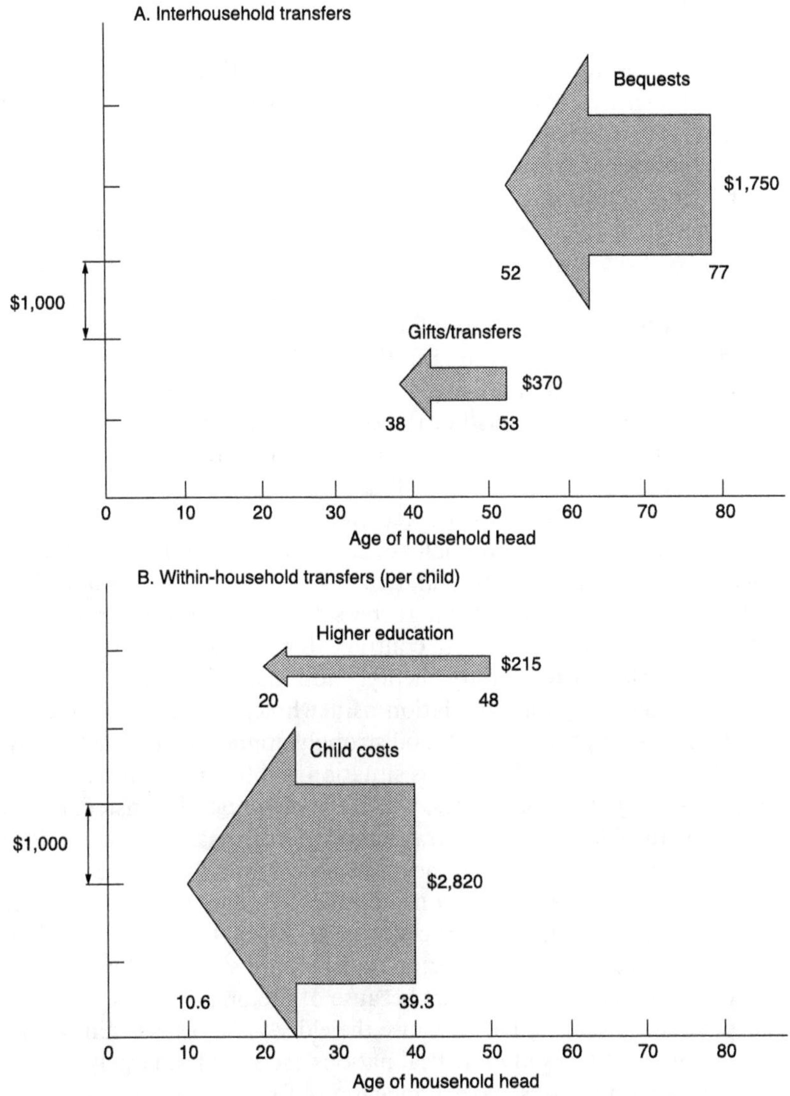

Note: Net familial transfers to children are calculated as described in the note to Figure 2.5, based on the profiles for consumption and labour earning for ages 0 to 17 (the age interval 15–19 was weighted by 0.6). Transfers for costs of college are estimated from data in the *Statistical Abstract of the United States* (US, Bureau of the Census 1990). Bequest flows are estimated from data discussed in Modigliani (1988*a*). Other inter-household familial transfers are estimated from data in the Consumer Expenditure Survey and are surely substantially underestimated. For further details on methods, assumptions, and sources, see R. D. Lee (1994*b*).

Fig. 2.10. Familial transfers in the United States

Conclusions

Reallocation of resources from one age group to another is a pervasive phenomenon in all societies. Patterns of reallocation have a number of important implications—for example, for an understanding of the societal accumulation of wealth, for theories of fertility, and for the consequences of population ageing. Although many important studies have focused on one or another specific reallocation system, such as bequests, savings, or government transfers, there seems to have been little systematic attempt to understand the underlying patterns of reallocations as a whole, either theoretically or empirically. Theoretical work has been profound and influential, but its demographic foundations have been so highly stylized as to limit the problems that can be examined and the empirical applications that might be made. This chapter has sketched a conceptual framework that has been developed in more detail elsewhere, and then explored the patterns of transfers in several societies with diverse kinds of economic bases, to the extent that the limited data permit.

Although the empirical basis for generalization is still very restricted, the findings are consistent so far. In small horticulturist and hunter-gatherer groups and societies practising extensive and intensive agriculture, reallocations of resources over the life cycle appear to be strongly downward from older to younger members of the population, contrary to what has often been suggested, particularly in relation to fertility theory. Notional life-cycle wealth in these societies, averaged over the population as a whole, is negative: the need for providing for consumption in childhood strongly dominates the need, if any, for providing for dependent old age. This situation is different for industrial societies, or at least for the United States, where the direction of transfers is upward from younger to older. Although transfers within the family remain strongly downward as in other societies, they are now more than offset by capital accumulation, which reallocates consumption to older ages, and by strong upward transfers through the public sector. It appears that in most, but not all, Third World nations, public-sector transfers are strongly downward from older to younger generations, in part because of the preponderance of children in those populations and in part because the elderly are still sustained through familial transfers, whereas in industrial nations the state has largely taken over that role. These differences have implications for capital accumulation, for fertility theory, for externalities to childbearing, and for the consequences of population ageing.

Notes

Hillard Kaplan generously made available the tabulated data for the Amazonian groups he has studied. Participants in the Seminar on Intergenerational Transfers made many helpful suggestions, and comments from Didier Blanchet were particularly helpful. I am grateful to David Dodds, Carl Mason, Diana Friou, Guy Stecklov, Tim Miller, and Antoine Bommier for many helpful discussions and for permission to borrow from the results of their ongoing research. The research on which this chapter was based was funded by a grant from the National Institute on Ageing, No. AG11761-01A1.

1. Other theoretical studies, such as those by Gale (1973) and Willis (1988), consider an n age-group population. Neither of these articles includes non-trivial mortality, however. Arthur and McNicoll (1978) develop and analyse a model with continuous age distribution and realistic mortality; the analytic framework for this chapter owes a good deal to their analysis, and to Willis (1988).
2. A handful of computable general-equilibrium models with overlapping generations consider the n age-group case, sometimes with non-trivial mortality, as in Auerbach and Kotlikoff (1987).
3. The accounting system can handle situations in which the age patterns of transfers or other forms of reallocation change over time. An equation describing the evolution of the various forms of wealth under these circumstances appears later in the chapter. However, the changing age profiles must be given. It is very difficult to deal with non-stability in a model of optimizing behaviour rather than in a purely descriptive and accounting model.
4. e.g. government debt in a steady-state economy falls into the category of transfer, although this is not immediately obvious, because debt grows in proportion to the population and also because the government must pay the market rate of interest to those who hold it. However, we must include the taxes levied to pay interest on the debt as a part of the reallocation system and on the new debt that is issued, so that total debt grows at rate n. Once we do, we can see that taxes must equal the difference between the population growth rate and the interest rate, multiplied by the value of outstanding debt. Viewed as a whole, the system of issuing debt, and taxing to pay interest to its holders, can be seen to fall within the category of transfers: *Pop*(taxes, interest) $= 0$; *PV*(taxes, interest) $\neq 0$. Fiat money also has transfer-like properties, as shown in Samuelson (1958).
5. Without children, the credit market can clear only if some working age group, probably the youngest, is induced by negative interest rates to consume in excess of earnings. See Samuelson's (1958) three age-group example.
6. e.g are teenage boys, accompanying women and girls on a gathering expedition and providing some protection by their presence as they play games, engaged in productive activity? (This example has been suggested in a personal communication by E. A. Hammel.)
7. It is puzzling that per capita output rises from around age 40 to around age 60 in these data, given that other data show hours of work actually to decline somewhat at those ages. I do not have an explanation for this aspect of the data.
8. If $N(x)$ is the population at age x, then the average age of production, for example, is $\sum xN(x)y(x)/\sum N(x)y(x)$.
9. The discounting actually has a demographic role and interpretation. It expresses the fact that any net consumption in old age does not result from transfers from a single birth, but rather from all children combined. It must be set against the costs incurred in raising all children born, including both survivors and those who die before attaining the age of making transfers to their parents. (The consumption of the children should be divided in two, if we consider the return to the average individual parent.)

10. In a stable population, $N(x)$ is proportional to $\exp(-nx)p(x)$, where n is the stable population growth rate. Dividing both sides by $p(x)$ and taking the natural logarithm yields $ln[N(x)/p(x)] = k - nx$. In a stable population, this would be an identity. In a non-stable population we may first plot the dependent variable against age to see if the relation is roughly linear; and if so, we can then estimate n through a regression. The estimated value of n can then be used as the discount rate. In the pooled data from Kaplan, the plotted relationship does appear linear for assumed mortality of Model West Female (MFW) 7 and 14 ($e_0 = 35$ and 52.5), and therefore I have computed the regression estimates as reported below.
11. The internal rate of return solves for r in the equation $\sum p(x)[y(x) - c(x)] \exp(-rx) = 0$.
12. e.g. if life expectancy at birth is assumed to be 35 years, the estimated rate of natural increase is 0.0292 and the estimated internal rate of return is 0.0283. For $e_0 = 52.5$ years, the corresponding estimates are 0.0372 and 0.0349.
13. If we knew the fertility level, and if we were willing to assume that the populations were closed and stable, then we could estimate the mortality level and the population growth rate. For example, with $e_0 = 52.5$ and $n = 0.0372$ as estimated, the implied level of total fertility would be 7.75 children per woman (based on Coale and Demeny's [1983] MWF 7 stable population). Kaplan (1994) estimates the TFR to be somewhat higher than this, at 8.2 or so, for the groups he studies. At $e_0 = 35$ and $n = 0.0292$, the implied TFR would be 8.6. Kaplan reports (ibid. 786, n. 9) that 28% of the Ache reached age 60, and that about twice that fraction reached age 20. These figures are in close agreement with MWF 7, $e_0 = 35$, in the Coale–Demeny tables, which gives 0.29 reaching 60 and 0.60 reaching 20. Thus the scenario with $e_0 = 35, n = 0.0292$, and TFR $= 8.6$ agrees very well with the data Kaplan reports.
14. I am unable to relate these expressions and results explicitly to the calculated direction of reallocations, although I believe the two to be closely connected.
15. $\delta(a)$ describes flows conditional on the survival of both parent and child, and those may be positive or negative. The solution is not exact because there are ω age-specific balancing equations to be satisfied, but the number of deltas is only ω minus the earliest age of childbearing, say 15 years.

3 Dynasties, Intergenerational Transfers, and Life-Cycle Income: A Case Study of Taiwan

Andrew Mason and Tim Miller

The life cycle of income is a prominent feature of all economies. The young experience extended periods of time during which they are dependent upon their parents or other adults for their very survival. The personal incomes of the elderly are typically well below the levels achieved during their prime earning years. Because of these sustained periods of dependency, intergenerational or inter-age transfers are a pervasive aspect of all economies.

Three institutions have evolved that effect the transfer of economic resources from working generations to the young and the elderly: the state, financial markets, and the family (R. D. Lee in this volume). The state uses its taxing and spending authority to transfer resources between generations. Financial markets enable individuals to save during some periods in their lives and dissave during others. Families redistribute income among their members by living together and pooling their individual incomes or by making interhousehold transfers.

Perhaps in all societies the family is the paramount institution for solving the life-cycle problems of the young. In traditional societies the family has played an equally important role in providing for the elderly. In modern Asia, many individuals live in extended families from birth to death. Those who are able to provide for others support the consumption of all.

The life-cycle problem is by no means peculiar to developing countries. In fact, the life cycle is a more prominent feature of industrialized, high-income countries. The period of child dependency is extended by the increased investment in education. An extended period of retirement becomes a realistic possibility with improved standards of living. Moreover, as mortality conditions improve, the expected numbers of years beyond traditional retirement ages increase.

Even though the importance of the redistributive function does not decline with development, the importance of the family as an agent for intergenerational redistribution has eroded in many countries. Increased nuclearization of the family has been a prominent feature of many societies, with more and more elderly living independently from their adult children. Tasks that were once the sole province of the family are taken on by the state, which provides education, health care, retirement programmes, and other social programmes that transfer enormous amounts of resources from one generation to another. Economic development has also brought the development of financial markets and an increase in private saving.

This chapter examines the role of the family as an agent for redistributing resources across generations, focusing on Taiwan as a case study and on two mechanisms employed by families for effecting intergenerational transfers: pooling of resources through co-residence and shifting of resources through interhousehold transfers. In all societies, co-residence is the primary means by which resources are transferred from working-age parents to dependent children. Both co-residence and interhousehold transfers play prominent roles in transfers to the elderly. In Taiwan, as in other Confucian cultures, co-residence has been a particularly important means by which resources are pooled even across generations of adults. We do not consider the intrahousehold distribution of income here. The outcome of the redistributive process we examine is per capita household income by age of household member.

In a simple overlapping generation model, the distribution of income between adults and children, as addressed here, would not be an issue. Consider a three-period, one-sex model in which all individuals are children in the first period of life, parents during the second period, and retirees during the third. If parents bear n children, live with their children, and earn y household income, then all parents and all children will have per capita household incomes of $y/(1+n)$. From the perspective of the analysis presented here, parents always transfer $y/(1+n)$ to each child, ensuring that resources are completely shared across the two generations.

Outside the world of the simple overlapping generation model, other outcomes are possible for at least two reasons. First, in childrearing households both household income and the number of dependent children vary over time (or by age in a cross-section). The number of dependent children increases as parents approach the end of their childbearing and declines as the dependent children reach adulthood. Likewise, household income initially increases and then declines as working adults age. Thus per capita household income and the amount transferred varies with the age of household members. Second, heterogeneity in childbearing means that, at the aggregate level, children may not fully share the income of adults. If, for example, fertility is inversely related to income, the per capita household income of children will be lower than that of adults, creating generational inequality.

Although we rely on a unified analytic framework for examining the distribution of income among all generations, the outcomes for prime-age adults and elderly parents involve somewhat different issues from those related to children. In a strictly patrilocal society, where all elderly parents live with their adult children, the expected outcome of a simple intergenerational model would be intergenerational equality. In other words, the per capita household incomes of adult children and elderly parents would be identical. As with children, however, the observed outcome will deviate from equality for several reasons. One is that elderly parents may have several children with whom they can live. By choosing to live with higher-income children, they can increase the intergenerational transfer. Another reason is that survival among the elderly may depend upon family resources. If higher income leads to greater survival, the intergenerational transfer will be increased because surviving elderly will be pooling with higher-income children.

If the elderly live independently of their children, the differences in personal income between the elderly and their adult children may have a more substantial effect on the gap between the household incomes of the elderly and their children. The magnitude of the gap will depend upon a couple of factors: the extent to which interhousehold transfers increase as co-residence declines and the extent to which altruism governs transfer decisions, whether they be decisions to co-reside or decisions to provide interhousehold transfers.

The outcomes of these redistributive processes are readily observable in countries with basic economic survey data. In this chapter we use household surveys of family income and expenditure to estimate age profiles of personal income by single years of age for males and females. These data provide estimates of the income of individuals in the absence of any current intergenerational transfers.[1] Per capita household income, excluding interhousehold transfers, documents the effect of co-residence on income. Private interhousehold transfers document the effect of interhousehold, intergenerational transfers on household income. We assume that all private interhousehold transfers are intergenerational transfers.

Although the outcomes of redistributive processes can be observed directly, developing and estimating even a simple model of intergenerational transfers is difficult. Many of the changes that affect intergenerational transfers cannot be readily observed. In particular, there are no data on the existence, income, and other characteristics of non-co-resident family members.[2] One cannot readily ascertain, for example, the extent to which members of different generations are pooling their incomes or whether the emergence of intergenerational differences in income reflects behavioural changes or changes in the underlying demographic structure of the population. Answering even a simple question, such as why the average household income of older women declines in Taiwan, is impossible in the absence of information about the income of the non-co-resident family members.

The analysis presented here is based on a modelling effort used to describe, at the aggregate level, key demographic and economic features of extended families, or what we call 'dynasties'. We use indirect methods and historical data on fertility, mortality, marriage, and migration to estimate the intergenerational links between the members of each single-year age group and their family members, such as grandparents, parents, children. The demographic data enable us to estimate the number and demographic composition of dynasties, defined to conform to the patrilineal, extended family. We combine our estimates with age-income profiles to estimate the incomes of dynasties and to determine, for each year of the analysis, how the average income per dynasty member varies over the life cycle of individuals.

We have chosen Taiwan as the setting for our study of intergenerational transfers both because enormous economic and demographic changes occurred there in recent decades and because the data documenting those changes are extensive and of high quality. Real gross domestic product grew by an average annual rate of 9.7 per cent during the 1970s and 8.5 per cent during the 1980s. The only other Asian country to manage such rapid economic growth during the last two decades was South Korea (ADB 1991). The speed of Taiwan's demographic change has also been extraordinary. Over a thirty-year period, between 1956 and 1986, the total fertility rate dropped from 6.5 to 1.7 births per woman. Only mainland China has had such a rapid fertility decline. An annual household survey of personal income and expenditure allows us to examine a sixteen-year period (1976–91) during which economic relations among the generations underwent a fundamental transformation.

Taiwan's cultural context, particularly the way families organize themselves and carry out their diverse functions, has an important influence on how economic and demographic change is transforming that society. Confucian ideals emphasizing filial piety have a considerable influence on marriage, living arrangements, and in general the relations within and between the generations. Marriage has been nearly universal and divorce rates low, although recent evidence suggests this may be changing. Extended, multi-generational households are much more common there than in the West, in accordance with the Confucian teaching that sons and their wives should live with or near their fathers. (Cho and Yada 1994 and Thornton and Lin 1994 provide recent detailed discussions of Asian families.)

The capacity of the dynasty, or extended family, to purge for its members the variation in income over the life cycle is the first issue we consider. Families are dynamic entities that are subject to a range of demographic events affecting their capacity to provide for their members. The number of dependants varies as children are born and the elderly die. The earning capacity of the family increases as young adults complete their schooling and enter the workforce; it declines as older members retire. Depending upon the social conventions that define the family, new families are formed and old ones are dissolved with, for example, the death of the patriarch. These phenomena take on great significance for individual families, but how important are they in the aggregate? How does the demographic transition affect the life cycle of the family? In particular, does it reduce the effectiveness of the family as an agent for transferring resources across generations?

We find that the patrilineal, extended family in Taiwan has the capacity to serve as an extraordinarily effective institution for dealing with life-cycle variation in income. By redistributing income among its members, the extended family can achieve an age profile of per capita income that exhibits a small fraction of the age variation characteristic of personal income. Rapid economic growth and demographic change have neither substantially eroded nor enhanced the capacity of the family to smooth life-cycle income.

Nevertheless, the extended family cannot purge all of the age variation from per capita income by redistributing income among family members. Income per dynasty member exhibits a distinctive generation-length cycle—an aggregate Chayanov cycle (Chayanov 1966). The cycle in income is transmitted by a cycle in the age composition of the dynasty. Roughly speaking, income per dynasty member peaks when the proportion of dynasty members of working age peaks.

Using estimates of dynastic income as a benchmark, we assess the extent to which extended families in Taiwan pool their incomes, making transfers to eliminate intergenerational differences in income. During the first decade examined, more specifically from 1976 until 1987, family members were fully sharing the incomes of their dynasties. Being a member of an age group with low or high personal income had little discernible effect on the age group's household income. The per capita household incomes of the young and the elderly were nearly identical to the per capita incomes of the dynasties to which they belonged. To the extent possible, therefore, extended families were purging personal income of its inherent life cycle. However, after 1987 the extent of intergenerational income pooling among family members declined. The household income of both young and elderly males and females deteriorated in relation to dynastic household income or, in effect, the income of those of prime working age.

Co-residence is the overwhelmingly important mechanism used to effect intergenerational transfers in Taiwan. Private interhousehold transfers are far less important, and in many years they have served to increase rather than to reduce the life-cycle variation in income. Even so, they have provided significant support to the elderly, particularly in the last few years.

The decline in intergenerational transfers to both the young and the old can be traced directly to a decrease in co-residence. The elderly are particularly affected. Prior to 1988, intergenerational transfers were more than sufficient to close the gap between their own income and that of other members of their dynasties. From 1988 to 1991, however, transfers to the elderly achieved through co-residence closed only about three-quarters of the gap. Private interhousehold transfers to the elderly increased during the period, but the rise was insufficient to offset the decline associated with decreased co-residence.

Methodology Used to Study Dynasties

Identifying families and their generations is a relatively straightforward task at the microlevel. Family links between any individual and the members of his or her family can be readily identified. The members of a family can be divided into mutually exclusive generations consisting of a husband and wife, their parents, their children, their grandchildren, etc. In some Western societies, such as the United States, family connections have become more complex as divorce and multiple marriages have become more common, but these are unusual phenomena in Taiwan.

Defining families and generations at the aggregate level is a more vexing problem. Indeed, much of the literature treats generations and age groups as equivalent concepts, studying the younger or the older generation. In a similar vein, a vast literature identifies generations as members of a birth cohort. The baby-boom generation, consisting of persons born between 1946 and 1964, is the most famous. 'Generation X' is the most vague. Generational accounts operationalize generations as single-year cohorts and all future generations as a single group consisting of those yet to be born (Auerbach, Gokhale, and Kotlifkoff 1991, 1994; Gokhale, in this volume).

The utility of using the terms 'age' or 'cohort' as the equivalent of 'generation' is demonstrated by the wide usage. Moreover, inter-age transfers, as distinct from intergenerational transfers, are an exceedingly important and understudied aspect of the macroeconomy. There are, however, some unsatisfactory aspects of treating age and generation as equivalent concepts. (Ronald Lee, in this volume, is careful not to do this.) First, any age cut-off has an arbitrary aspect to it that does violence to the meaning of the term 'generation' as employed at the microlevel. Persons who are 65 and older have spouses and siblings who are under 65, and to assign them to different generations is clearly at variance with what is meant by the term 'generation'. Second, as operationalized at the aggregate level, 'generation' loses the family connections that are so important at the microlevel. Our interest is not just in the common experience of members of a single age group, but also in their relationships to their parents, their children, and members of other generations.

The methods used here identify and construct demographic and economic measures based upon the family links that exist within any population. We estimate the numbers of males and females at each age who have links to parents or to offspring, the number and demographic characteristics of the persons with whom they have intergenerational family links, and the income of those family members (see also Mason and Martin 1982). Chain rules are used to estimate links to other family members, such as grandparents and grandchildren. A full description of the methodology used to quantify the intergenerational features of a population and an economy are beyond the scope of this chapter. The interested reader is referred to Mason and Miller (1995) for a full documentation of the data and procedures used; historical and contemporary demographic information were drawn from a variety of sources also documented there. Our source of economic data was the Survey of Personal Income Distribution in the Taiwan Area, frequently referred to as the Family Income and Expenditure Survey, available annually starting in 1976 (Taiwan, DGBAS, various years).

Families and dynasties

Estimates of the family links that exist within a population can be used to define and to estimate the demographic and economic characteristics of the population's families. To do this requires that we define the term 'family'. In reality, the family is a fluid concept, although probably less so in Taiwan than in many other societies. In a heterogeneous society, various segments of the population conceptualize the family in different ways. Moreover, the concept of the family may vary according to the task or problem at hand. In short, a fuzzy and movable border divides a population into families. Implementing a model, however, requires precisely defined boundaries. Our use of the term 'dynasties' in our model is a way of recognizing the difficulty of defining extended families as equivalent to a particular kinship group.

The definition of a dynasty is based on the patrilineal, Han Chinese family system, which is dominant in Taiwan. The system was established by waves of immigrants from the Chinese mainland in the seventeenth to nineteenth centuries and again around 1950, when the Nationalist Army and its supporters fled to Taiwan at the conclusion of China's Civil War. The backbone of the dynasty is the patriarch and his male descendants. Daughters become members of their husbands' dynasties when they marry, and marriage has been nearly universal in Taiwan (Fricke, Chang, and Yang 1994).

Taiwan's population is divided into exhaustive, mutually exclusive dynasties. Each dynasty is headed by a patriarch, any adult male who has no surviving father. (This definition admittedly overstates the number of patriarchs because some adult males have deceased fathers but surviving grandfathers.) The male members of the dynasty consist of the patriarch and all surviving male descendants—sons, grandsons, and great-grandsons. The female members include the patriarch's wife, the wives of any male descendants, the widowed or divorced mothers of the patriarch or his male descendants, and any never-married female descendants. Never-married women without surviving fathers are assigned to the dynasties of their siblings (Figure 3.1).

The number of patriarchs, and hence the number of dynasties, is equal to the number of males without surviving fathers. To estimate the number of such males, we have used survival data for Taiwan and estimates of the age distribution of their fathers. Owing to the particular historical circumstances of Taiwan, there is a second group of patriarchs whose fathers—although they may still be alive—are not living in Taiwan. A significant group of adult men living in Taiwan emigrated from the mainland in the aftermath of China's Civil War. Until recently ties with family members on the mainland were essentially severed. Those who emigrated without their fathers make up a sizeable portion of Taiwan's patriarchs.

We have estimated the numbers of surviving sons, grandsons, and great-grandsons of patriarchs using historical data on the distribution of births by age of father. Numbers of surviving daughters, granddaughters, and

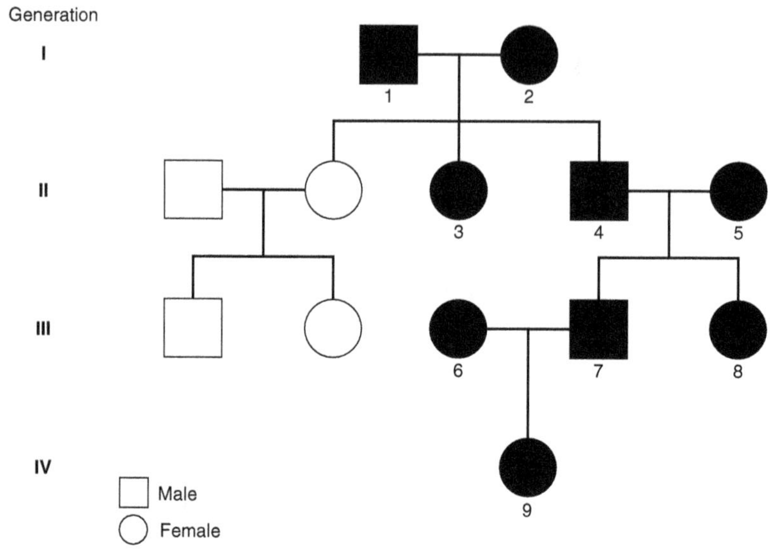

Fig. 3.1. Genealogy of a hypothetical dynasty

great-granddaughters have been estimated in similar fashion, and only those who have never married are members of the dynasties to which their fathers belong. Married women have been assigned to the dynasties of their husbands. We have done this by using estimates of the joint age distribution of husbands and wives. Widowed and divorced women we have assigned to the dynasties of their sons, using estimates of the joint age distribution of women and their offspring. The procedures have yielded estimates of the average number of members of sex s, age a, and relationship to patriarch r per dynasty with a patriarch aged z, designated as M_{sarz}. All values are estimated for single years of age of both members and patriarchs ranging from zero to 100.

Taiwan's dynasties

We estimate that in 1990 Taiwan had 3.4 million dynasties averaging 6.0 members each (Table 3.1). Nearly 700,000 of the dynasties were headed by patriarchs who had produced no heirs. Of the 10.5 million males living in Taiwan in 1990, 32 per cent were patriarchs, 46 per cent were sons of patriarchs, 21 per cent were grandsons, and 0.7 per cent were great-grandsons. Of the 9.8 million women living in Taiwan, 6 per cent were mothers of patriarchs, 26 per cent were patriarchs' wives, 43 per cent were daughters or daughters-in-law, 21 per cent were granddaughters or granddaughters-in-law, 0.7 per cent were great-granddaughters, and 4 per cent were unwed sisters of other dynasty members (data not shown). Although the average age of patriarchs rose only moderately, from 43.7 to 49.9 between 1970 and 1991, the percentage of dynasties headed by

Table 3.1. Characteristics of dynasties: Taiwan, 1970–91

Year	No. of dynasties	Total population	Average dynasty size	Average age of patriarch	Percentage of dynasties headed by patriarchs aged > 65
1970	2,502,617	14,676,460	5.86	43.7	7.7
1971	2,542,654	14,994,018	5.90	44.1	8.1
1972	2,579,299	15,287,687	5.93	44.4	8.5
1973	2,614,804	15,563,574	5.95	44.8	8.9
1974	2,652,366	15,850,604	5.98	45.1	9.4
1975	2,691,120	16,147,995	6.00	45.5	9.8
1976	2,733,190	16,506,209	6.04	45.8	10.3
1977	2,770,816	16,811,181	6.07	46.1	11.1
1978	2,811,274	17,133,906	6.09	46.4	11.8
1979	2,856,283	17,477,413	6.12	46.7	12.4
1980	2,905,239	17,802,972	6.13	47.0	13.0
1981	2,949,566	18,133,323	6.15	47.3	13.5
1982	2,995,258	18,455,757	6.16	47.6	14.1
1983	3,036,518	18,730,955	6.17	47.8	14.6
1984	3,090,607	19,009,812	6.15	48.1	15.2
1985	3,142,316	19,254,211	6.13	48.4	15.9
1986	3,185,022	19,451,803	6.11	48.6	16.7
1987	3,244,022	19,669,291	6.06	48.9	17.5
1988	3,292,676	19,900,586	6.04	49.2	18.2
1989	3,340,224	20,104,173	6.02	49.4	18.9
1990	3,396,667	20,350,321	5.99	49.6	19.8
1991	3,453,085	20,553,060	5.95	49.9	20.8

patriarchs over age 65 rose dramatically, from 8 to 21 per cent. The change is undoubtedly due to Taiwan's secular rise in longevity over the past quarter-century.

By age 41, half of all males were patriarchs. The average ages of patriarchs, sons, grandsons, and great-grandsons were 49.6, 25.0, 10.5, and 4.6, respectively. The average ages of mothers, matriarchs, daughters, granddaughters, great-granddaughters, and unwed sisters were 64.6, 47.2, 23.7, 10.1, 4.6, and 30.3, respectively. The complete age distributions are provided in Figures 3.2 and 3.3).

The average size of a dynasty increases with the patriarch's age. In 1990, dynasties with patriarchs under the age of 25 averaged fewer than two members and consisted primarily of a son and his widowed mother. As patriarchs age, additional members are added to their dynasties (Figure 3.4). First, wives, sons, and daughters are added, raising the average size of a dynasty to about five members before a patriarch reaches age 50. Next, daughters and daughters-in-law exchange places and grandchildren are added to the dynasty, raising the

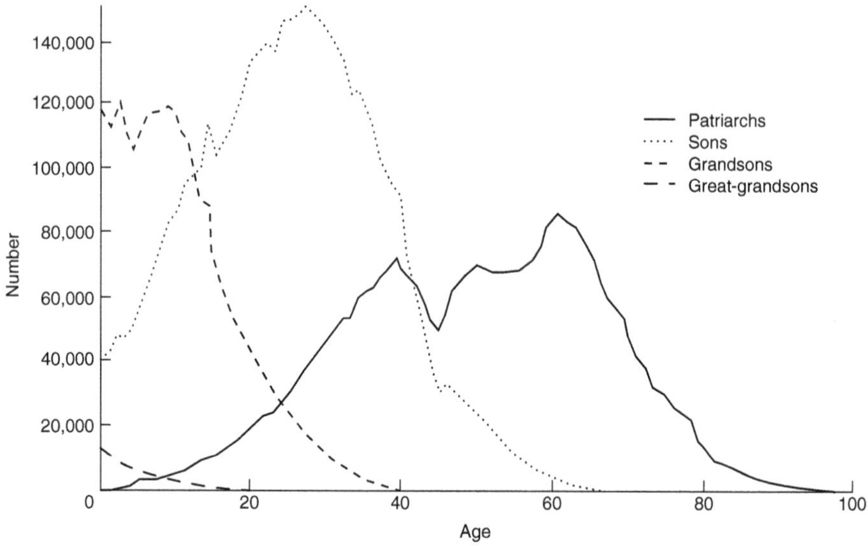

Fig. 3.2. Age profiles of males, by relationship to patriarch: Taiwan, 1990

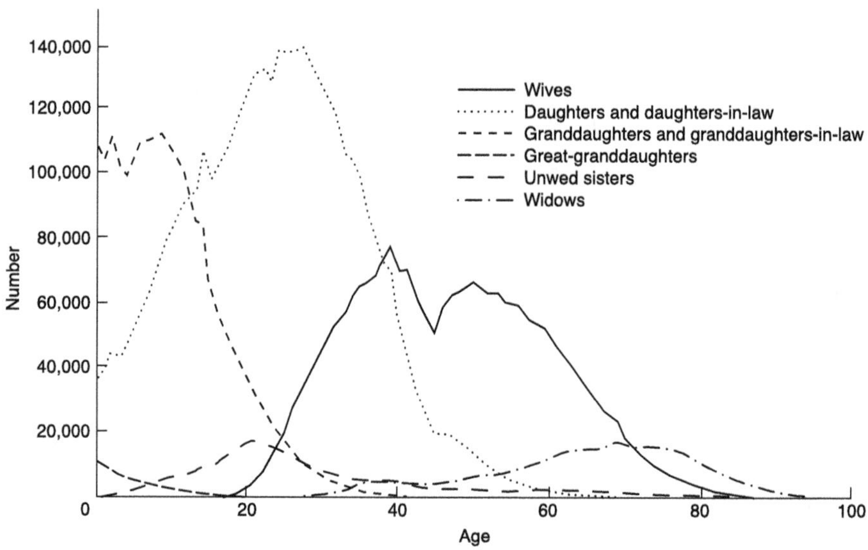

Fig. 3.3. Age profiles of females, by relationship to patriarch: Taiwan, 1990

average dynasty's size to about eleven members for patriarchs who are still surviving at age 75. Finally, a fourth generation, of great-grandchildren, is added to the dynasty. Average dynasty size peaks at about fifteen members for patriarchs who are in their early nineties.

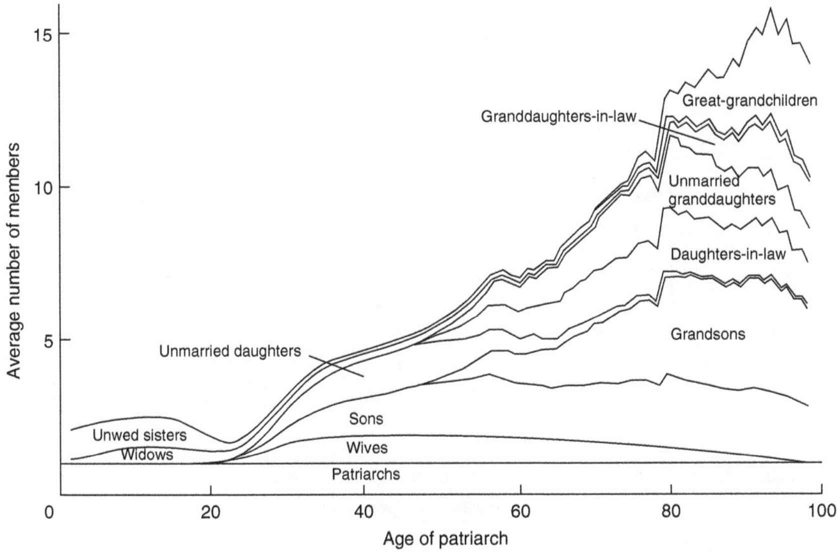

Fig. 3.4. Membership of Taiwan's dynasties, 1990

Our principal interest is in how the demographic characteristics of dynasties vary with the ages of dynasty members rather than the ages of patriarchs. To determine this, we use (1) the joint age distributions of individuals and their patriarchs and (2) the demographic composition of the dynasty by age of the patriarch. Figure 3.5 illustrates the joint age distribution for selected ages in 1990. Most newborn males belonged to dynasties headed by their grandfathers, whose ages varied around 60. A substantially smaller proportion belonged to dynasties headed by their fathers, whose ages varied around 30. By the time men reached age 30, almost 25 per cent of them were patriarchs; but most belonged to dynasties headed by their fathers. Few were members of dynasties headed by their grandfathers. At higher ages, men were increasingly likely to be the patriarch of their own dynasty and less likely to be a member of their father's dynasty.

For young women the age distribution of patriarchs is similar to that for young men. As women begin to marry, however, a different pattern emerges. Adult women become members of the dynasties of their husbands or fathers-in-law; older women are members of the dynasties of their husbands or sons.

We use the age distributions of patriarchs in combination with the demographic characteristics of dynasties to estimate dynastic characteristics by the age of dynasty members (including patriarchs). Letting M_{sarz} be the average number of members of dynasties with patriarchs aged z, and d_{gxz} the proportion of males or females (g) aged x belonging to a dynasty with a patriarch aged z, we calculate the average number of members aged a, sex s, and relationship r belonging to dynasties of persons of age x and sex g as

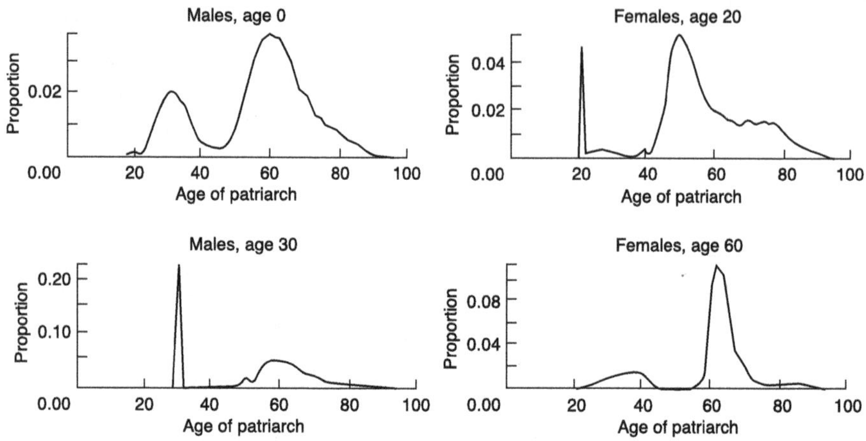

Fig. 3.5. Age distribution of patriarchs, by sex and selected ages of dynasty members: Taiwan, 1990

$$M_{gxsar} = \sum_z d_{gxz} M_{sarz}. \tag{3.1}$$

The reliability of the procedure depends upon the extent to which, given the age of the patriarch, the variable in question is independent of the age of individual dynasty members.

Calculating dynastic income

We estimate dynastic income by the age of the patriarch using the following procedures. Designating the number of members aged a and sex s who belong to a dynasty with a patriarch aged z by M_{saz} and the average income of persons aged a of sex s by Y_{sa}, we calculate the total income of all dynasties with a patriarch aged z as

$$Y_z^D = \sum_s \sum_a M_{saz} Y_{sa}. \tag{3.2}$$

The average income of dynasties with a patriarch aged z is calculated by dividing Y_z^D by the number of dynasties with a patriarch aged z. The average per capita income of dynasties with patriarchs aged z, y_z^D, is calculated by dividing Y_z^D by the number of persons belonging to dynasties with patriarchs aged z.

Per capita dynastic income of persons aged x and gender g, y_{xg}^D, is calculated as a weighted average of the per capita income of dynasties by the age of the patriarch. The weights are the proportion of persons aged a who are members of dynasties with patriarchs aged z, d_{gxz}:

$$y_{gx}^D = \sum_z d_{gxz} y_z^D. \tag{3.3}$$

Before presenting additional results and using dynastic income to analyse intergenerational transfers, we should address the reliability of the constructed variables. The calculation procedures used to estimate the number and demographic and economic characteristics of dynasties are much more involved than the cursory description provided here suggests, and are based on a number of simplifying assumptions that are violated to one extent or another. Moreover, implementing the procedures requires a substantial amount of detailed economic and demographic data that are subject to error.

In general, Taiwan's demographic data are of good quality. They include censuses and vital statistics collected under the Japanese administration during the first part of the twentieth century (Chen and Tuan 1951; Barclay 1954; Chang 1959; Teng 1964; T. Lee 1968). Nonetheless, Taiwan experienced major upheavals during World War II and its aftermath, which affected the availability and quality of data for the 1940s and early 1950s.

No independent sources of information are available that can be used to validate (or invalidate) our demographic estimates with certainty. Some available data do allow a partial assessment of the reliability of our estimates. The most useful data for that purpose are those on surviving number of children ever born, collected as part of the 1980 census. The reported values closely match our independent estimates of surviving offspring for 1980 (Mason and Miller 1995). Because such a high percentage of young children live with their parents, data on the number of young children per household provides another, though somewhat flawed, means of validating our estimates.[3] Tabulations from the household roster for the 1990 Personal Income Distribution Survey are quite consistent with our estimates of surviving offspring per mother, but they indicate that estimates of surviving offspring per father are somewhat less reliable. A possible source of error is that historical fertility data specific to the ages of fathers are reported only in five-year age groups as compared with single-year age groups for mothers. There are no reliable procedures for interpolating single-year estimates from five-year data, especially in the tails of the distribution.

Except for data on household income, no data are available for Taiwan that can be used to validate our estimates of the economic characteristics of dynasties. If co-residence conforms to the patrilineal family system as characterized by our model, the age profiles of household income and dynastic income should be identical. Not all members of dynasties co-resided in 1976, but multigeneration extended families were common in Taiwan. In 1973 more than 80 per cent of the parents of offspring in the 20–39 age group lived with a married son. Almost 80 per cent of persons aged 20–39 and married during the previous five years had lived with their parents for at least one month after their marriage (Weinstein *et al.* 1994). For 1976 the age profiles of per capita household income and per capita dynastic income are nearly identical. (In the upper age ranges, household income is subject to large fluctuations due to the small number of observations.) Given that data quality has improved over time, this result provides reassuring, though indirect, evidence that the assumptions underlying the estimates and any errors in the data have not unduly affected our estimates of dynastic income.

The Dynasty and the Life Cycle

Applying the methods described above to the data for Taiwan provides estimates of how family resources have varied over the life cycle of individuals. Here we briefly present those results, examining how the size, age composition, and per capita income of the dynasty have varied with the age of individuals.

Demographic features of dynasties

Average dynasty size varied remarkably little with age for females in 1990 (Figure 3.6). Newborns belonged to dynasties with an average size of 6.7 members. Average size rose gradually with age, peaking at 6.9 members for women aged 24; and until age 64 it varied from a high of 7.1 to a low of 6.9 members. For elderly women, average dynasty size increased gradually with their age, reaching 7.5 members by age 90.[4]

Average dynasty size was essentially flat for males younger than 55, but it increased substantially with age among elderly males, peaking at slightly more than fourteen members for men in their nineties. The difference in dynasty size between older men and women is a reflection of the patrilineal definition of a dynasty. As mentioned earlier, nearly all older men are patriarchs, whose

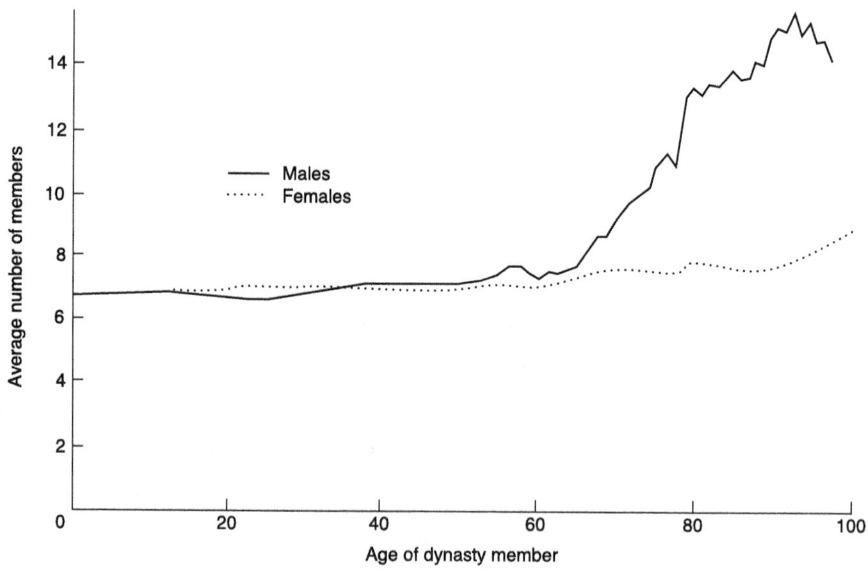

Fig. 3.6. Average size of Taiwan's dynasties, by ages of males and females, 1990

dynasties increase in size as long as they survive. Older women maintain their membership in a dynasty only so long as their husbands survive. Upon the death of a woman's husband, she becomes a member of a smaller dynasty headed by one of her sons.

Average dynasty size was invariant with respect to age in 1990 because all but older men were subject to two distinctive and offsetting processes. For those whose dynasty remained intact, average dynasty size increased. For those who experienced the death of their patriarch, average dynasty size declined. The decline in average dynasty size for those individuals offset the increase in the size of dynasties for individuals whose dynasties remained intact. The result was a fairly constant dynasty size over a wide portion of the age span.

Explaining how such a seemingly unlikely outcome could occur makes it no less surprising that average dynasty size varies so little with age, especially given the rapid decline in fertility in Taiwan during the last four decades. A comparison of average dynasty size in 1990 with 1970 and 1980 is instructive (Figures 3.7 and 3.8). In some respects the mystery deepens. The average size of dynasties headed by men 60 and older has declined during the last two decades, from 11.3 members in 1970 to 10.1 members in 1980 and to 8.7 in 1990. However, for men under the age of 60 and for women at all ages, average dynasty size has varied little over the last two decades—fluctuating around seven members.

We find a pronounced cyclical pattern in average dynasty size in 1970 and 1980 that reflects family-building processes among dynastic members of child-bearing age. In 1970, average dynasty size rose steadily for women in their late teens, twenties, and early thirties. The children they were bearing outnumbered

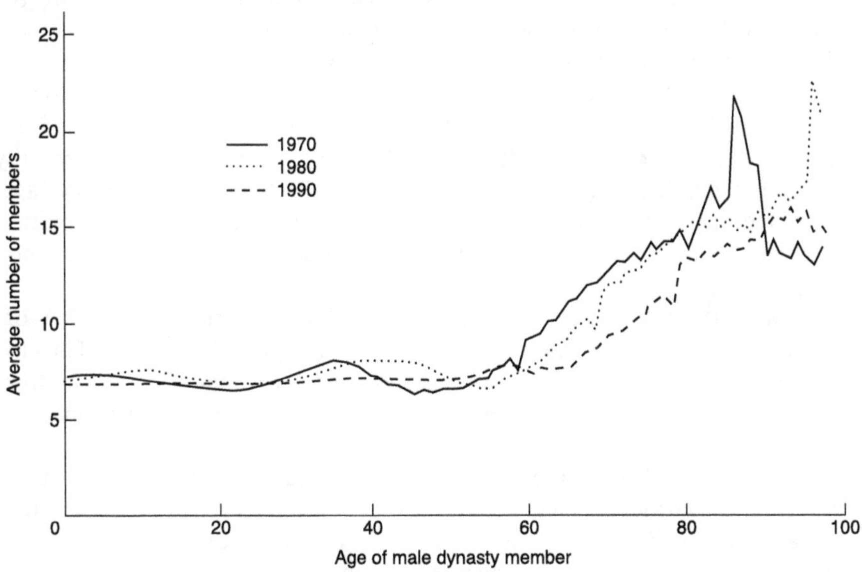

Fig. 3.7. Average size of Taiwan's dynasties, by age of males, 1970, 1980, and 1990

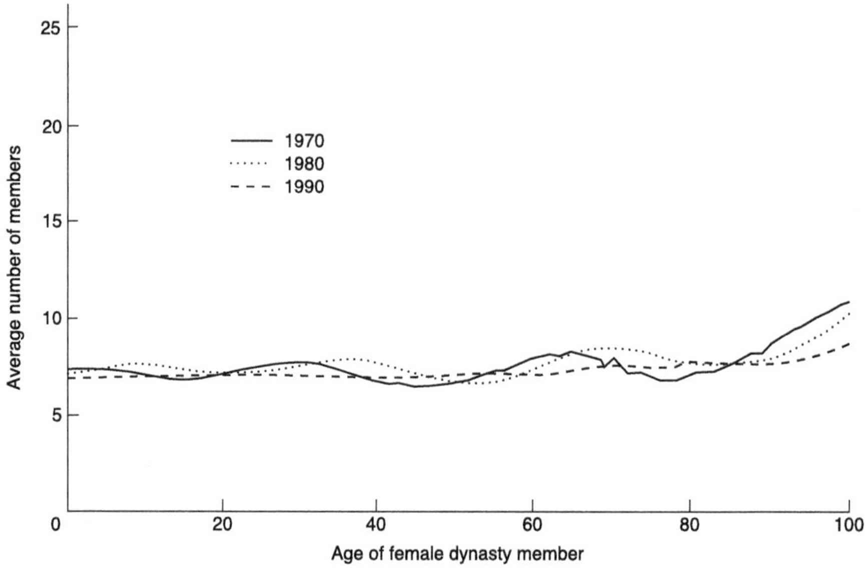

Fig. 3.8. Average size of Taiwan's dynasties, by age of females, 1970, 1980, and 1990

losses to the dynasty through mortality. As their rates of childbearing slowed, the mortality of dynasty members began to dominate and average dynasty size declined. The cycle is repeating itself because women in their sixties are the mothers of the women just described; young girls are their daughters.

The cyclical variation in the age composition of the dynasty is much more pronounced than the variation in average size. In 1990 the proportion of dynasty members under age 15 varied in cyclical fashion from a low of less than 0.15 to a high of nearly 0.36 (Figure 3.9). The cycle length was essentially equal to the length of a generation. Males who were 9, 38, and 67 years of age, on average, lived in households with the greatest childrearing responsibilities. The cycle of dependency is essentially an aggregate Chayanov cycle (Chayanov 1966).

The proportion of elderly also exhibits a cyclical pattern at ages below 65, but the amplitude is much more modest than in the cycle for children. Thus for those under 65 the variation in overall dependency is dominated by children. The proportion of members aged 15–64 essentially mirrors the proportion below age 15.

For those 65 and older the age profile of dependency is quite different. Of course, the proportion of dependants who are elderly is much larger at other ages, although still not so large as the proportion of dependants who are children. The overall level of dependency is quite high for those in their late sixties but declines as they age.

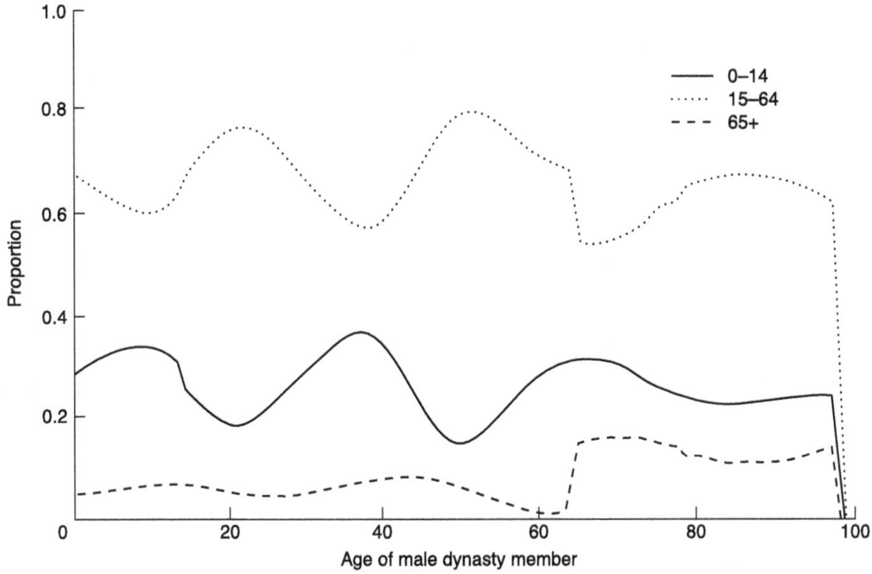

Fig. 3.9. Proportions of dynasty members in three broad age groups: Taiwan, 1990

The demographic features of Taiwan's dynasties described in this section dominate their ability to smooth income over the life cycle. As will be seen in the next section, the average per capita income of a dynasty is, at the gross level, relatively independent of age: the average per capita incomes of dynasties to which children belong and to which the elderly belong are close to the average per capita income of dynasties to which prime age adults belong. In other words, the dynasty has the capacity to smooth individual life-cycle variation in income. Nevertheless, the variation in dependency, or Chayanov, cycles affects the incomes of dynasties and constrains intergenerational transfers by the family.

Does dynastic income have a life cycle?

The patrilineal, extended family in Taiwan has the capacity to eliminate a large portion of the life-cycle variation in income. Figure 3.10 compares the personal income of men and women by age with the per capita income of the dynasties to which individuals belonged in 1990. The weighted coefficient of variation of the pre-transfer, age-income profile was 0.858. Were income equally shared among all dynasty members, the weighted coefficient of variation would decline to 0.036. In other words, the sharing of incomes among dynasty members could have eliminated 96 per cent of the life-cycle variation in income. Although gender inequality is not a central issue in this chapter, the patrilineal family also has the capacity to eliminate gender differences in income.

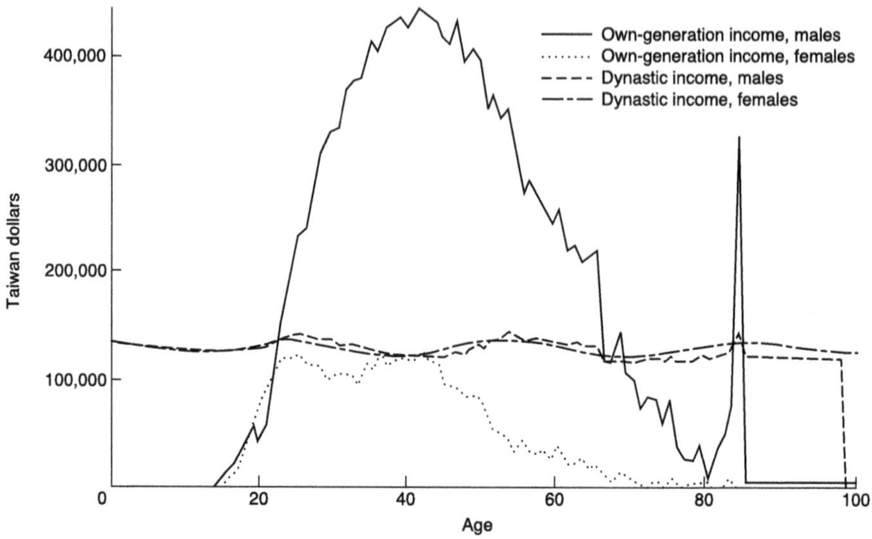

Fig. 3.10. Own income and dynastic income: Taiwan, 1990

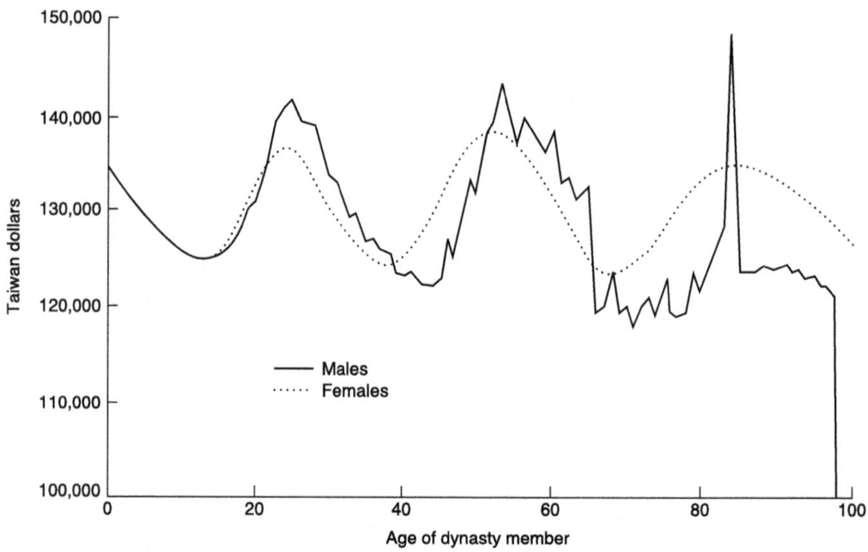

Fig. 3.11. Dynastic income per capita: Taiwan, 1990

A second feature of the dynasty in Taiwan is that its income is characterized by a Chayanov cycle, rising and falling in a distinctive pattern that mirrors the variation in the percentage of the population aged 15–64 (Figure 3.11). The pattern is particularly regular for females. Dynastic per capita income in 1990 reached peaks for newborns and women of ages 24, 52, and 84. Troughs occurred at ages 12, 38, and 67. The pattern for men is somewhat different. Dynastic income per capita varies more widely, the peaks and troughs occur at somewhat later ages, and the cycle is dampened or non-existent for elderly men, who have depressed levels of per capita dynastic income.

What causes the cycle in per capita dynastic income? Individuals are disadvantaged if their dynasty has only one generation that is economically active but advantaged if their dynasty has two generations whose members have significant personal incomes. For example, personal income peaked at about age 40 in 1990, but the children of 40–year-olds were too young and the parents too old to contribute to the dynasty's income. Consequently the per capita dynastic income of a 40–year-old was in a trough.

The length of the cycle is determined entirely by demographics. If a 50–year-old has a high dynastic income, then the parents, children, and grandchildren will be similarly advantaged. Peaks in dynastic income will occur at the ages at which the members of each generation are concentrated. In other words, the cycles will come at generation-length intervals. In 1990 the second peak followed the first by 28 years of age; the third followed after an additional 31 years of age. The amplitude of each cycle depends upon both the characteristics of the age distribution of personal income and the demographic features of dynasties. If personal income is distributed more or less uniformly across ages, the amplitude of per capita dynastic income will be low. If the age difference between parents and offspring has a high variance, the amplitude of the cycle will also be low.

Dynastic per capita income is an estimate of the capacity of the extended family to redistribute per capita income across generations and, consequently, across ages. The actual distribution of income across age groups varies from estimated per capita dynastic income for two reasons. First, family members with higher incomes may not choose to share their incomes fully with lower-income members through co-residence or interhousehold transfers. Second, the construction of dynasties and dynastic-income abstracts from many sources of co-variation between the income of the dynasty and the membership of the dynasty. If, for example, fertility and dynastic wealth are inversely related, the per capita family income of children will be less than per capita dynastic income. Both decisions about transfers and co-variation between income and dynastic membership limit the extent to which the family can equalize income across generations or age groups.

Age inequality and intergenerational transfers

If intergenerational transfers were not common in Taiwan, the extent of income inequality by age would be very substantial. Equalizing income across all ages in 1991 would have required that 40 per cent of national income be redistributed. About 35 per cent would have gone to increasing the incomes of children and 4.4 per cent to increasing the incomes of the elderly (Table 3.2).

Table 3.2. Total income gap before and after transfers: Taiwan, selected years, 1976–91

Year	Own-generation income	Household income	Proportion due to		
			Co-residence	Private transfers	Public transfers
All household members					
1976	0.451	0.014	1.012	0.0033	−0.0153
1981	0.423	0.028	1.017	0.0053	−0.0225
1986	0.410	0.024	1.016	0.0127	−0.0285
1991	0.397	0.035	1.007	0.0075	−0.0149
Young dependants					
1976	0.427	0.016	1.020	−0.0027	−0.0168
1981	0.392	0.029	1.027	−0.0041	−0.0226
1986	0.374	0.028	1.033	−0.0039	−0.0294
1991	0.353	0.031	1.036	−0.0127	−0.0233
Old dependants					
1976	0.023	−0.002	0.890	0.1009	0.0088
1981	0.030	−0.001	0.907	0.1151	−0.0218
1986	0.036	−0.004	0.864	0.1573	−0.0212
1991	0.044	0.003	0.783	0.1665	0.0505

The three main transfer mechanisms used to reduce the age inequality in income—co-residence, private interhousehold transfers, and public-sector transfers—in combination have eliminated 90 per cent of the gap between the initial distribution of income by age and a completely uniform distribution. After taking them into account, we estimate that complete equalization of income across age groups would have required only 3.5 per cent of total income in 1991. Co-residence has been responsible for most of this redistribution, dwarfing the contributions of private and public transfers. In 1991, for example, private interhousehold transfers constituted less than 1 per cent of the transfers generated through co-residence. Public transfers were about equal to private interhousehold transfers, but they increased rather than reduced the age inequality in income.[5]

The importance of co-residence, private transfers, and public transfers varies with the age of the transfer recipients. Co-residence is, of course, the dominant mechanism for transferring resources to the young. It is less important, though still the primary mechanism, for transfers to the elderly. In 1991, co-residence accounted for 78 per cent of the transfers to the elderly, whereas private interhousehold transfers accounted for 17 per cent and public transfers for only 5.1 per cent of transfers.

Some noteworthy changes can be observed in age inequality and intergenerational transfers during the sixteen years analysed. The percentage of total income required to eliminate income inequality by age declined overall (from

45 to 40 per cent) and even more so for young dependants (from 43 to 35 per cent), while rising for older dependants (from 2.3 to 4.4 per cent). Although we have not formally investigated those changes, they were undoubtedly largely a by-product of three changes in Taiwan's age distribution: an overall decline in dependency, a large decline in the percentage of young dependants, and a rise in the number of elderly dependants.

During this decline in pre-transfer income inequality, intergenerational transfers also fell. In 1976, intergenerational transfers through co-residence, private transfers, and public transfers amounted to 44 per cent of national income. By 1991, they had declined to 36 per cent of national income. The decline in resources transferred was so substantial that post-transfer intergenerational income inequality increased—from an income gap requiring 1.4 per cent of national income to close to one requiring 3.5 per cent.

The post-transfer household income of both the young and the elderly shrank relative to that of prime-age adults between 1976 and 1991. The percentage of national income required to bring the young to parity nearly doubled, from 1.6 to 3.1 per cent of national income. The elderly moved from a position of advantage to one of disadvantage. In 1976 their 'claim' on national income exceeded their pro rata share by 0.2 per cent. By 1991 they were experiencing a shortfall of 0.3 per cent.[6]

Co-residence continues to be the dominant transfer mechanism for the young, and there is no evidence that either interhousehold private transfers or public transfers increased the relative per capita income of households containing young members. By contrast, the change for the elderly was quite substantial between 1976 and 1991. Co-residence declined significantly while private interhousehold and public transfers increased in importance.

Modelling the effects of private intergenerational transfers

We turn next to a formal analysis of intergenerational transfers achieved through co-residence and interhousehold exchanges. We exclude public transfers from the analysis for the reason that, because they are not made within a dynasty, they are not constrained by the resources of the dynasty. Figure 3.12 sets the stage for this analysis by presenting four alternative income measures for men in 1990.

The first is own-generation income, which is the per capita income available to men or women if they share their resources equally with their spouses, in the absence of any intergenerational transfers. (More specifically, own-generation income is the personal income of individuals plus the personal income of any marital partners, divided by the number of individuals plus the number of marital partners.) The age profile of own-generation income varies enormously, dominated by the life cycle of individuals. The second income measure is per capita dynastic income, which is our estimate of the age profile of per capita household income for males (or females) if dynasties fully pool the income of all

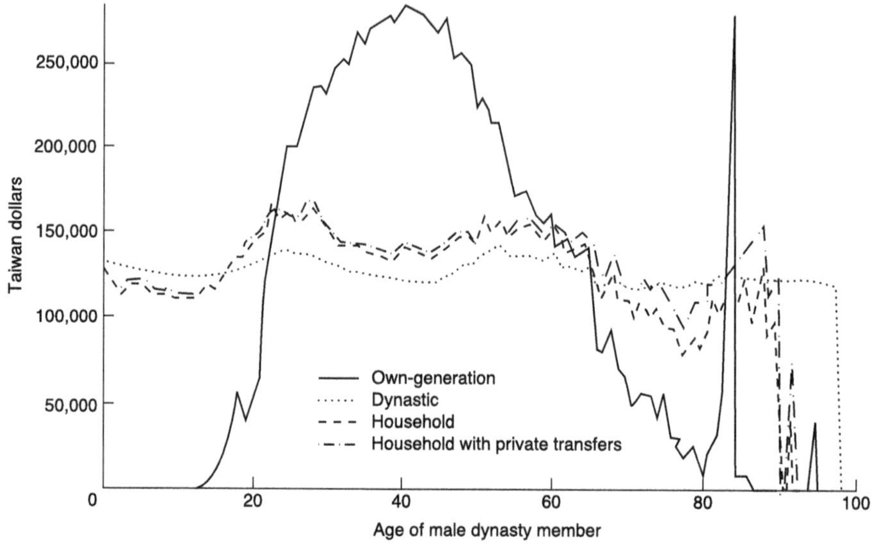

Fig. 3.12. Four measures of income, by age of male dynasty members: Taiwan, 1990

dynasty members, through either co-residence or interhousehold transfers. The final two curves in Figure 3.10 represent observed profiles of per capita household income tabulated from the 1990 Personal Income Distribution Survey. Household income, excluding all transfers, represents the age profile achieved in 1990 through co-residence alone. A cursory inspection shows that, in 1990, co-residence eliminated a large percentage of the variation in own-generation income. However, household income clearly depends, to some extent, on own-generation income. Dynasties were not fully pooling the incomes of their members in 1990.

The incremental effect of interhousehold transfers is captured by the final age profile, household income including interhousehold transfers. Interhousehold transfers served to reduce further the gap between own-generation income and dynastic income for the elderly. The effect on children, however, was to increase the gap by a small amount.[7] Interhousehold transfers reduce the household income of children because such transfers originate in the households of the children's parents.

We employ a simple statistical model to summarize, for each year, the extent to which dynasties rely upon co-residence and interhousehold transfers:

$$T^i_{sa} = \alpha^i_s GAP_{sa} + \varepsilon_{sa}, \tag{3.4}$$

where T^i_{sa} is net per capita intergenerational transfer received by males or females, s, aged a. Intergenerational transfers are measured as the difference between per capita own-generation income, y^0_{sa}, and the average per capita income of the households to which males or females aged a belong $(y^i_{sa} - y^0_{sa})$. For each year, total private transfers, $y^{h+p}_{sa} - y^0_{sa}$, and transfers realized through co-residence only, $y^h_{sa} - y^0_{sa}$, are estimated, where y^{h+p} is per capita household income including private transfers and y^h is per capita household income excluding private transfers.

GAP_{sa} is the difference between per capita own-generation and per capita dynastic income $(y^d_{sa} - y^0_{sa})$ and measures the income transfer that would be realized if income were shared equally among all dynasty members. The coefficient, then, is an estimate of the proportion of the gap between own-generation income and income available through sharing that is eliminated through transfers. If dynasty members engage in full income sharing, α will equal 1; in the absence of sharing, α will equal zero.

Substituting for T and rearranging terms yields an alternative interpretation of Equation 3.4. Per capita household income can be represented as a weighted average of own-generation and dynastic incomes, where α is the weight afforded to dynastic income.

$$y^i_{sa} = \alpha^i_s y^d_a + (1 - \alpha^i_s) y^0_a. \tag{3.5}$$

If α is equal to 1, the age profile of household income is determined solely by the income of the dynasties to which individuals belong and is independent of own-generation income. If α is equal to zero, the converse holds.

The final form used to estimate intergenerational transfers allows the transfer, i.e. α, to vary with age. Three groups are distinguished: young dependants, those who are under age 40 and for whom GAP is greater than zero; old dependants, those who are 40 or older and for whom GAP is greater than zero; and, non-dependants, those for whom GAP is greater than zero. Essentially non-dependants are prime-age adults.[8] The equation estimated is:

$$\begin{aligned} T^i_{sa} = {} & \alpha^i_{s1} GAP_{sa}(a.le.40)(GAP_{sa}.gt.0) + \alpha^i_{s2} GAP_{sa}(GAP_{sa}.le.0) \\ & + \alpha^i_{s3} GAP_{sa}(a.ge.40)(GAP_{sa}.gt.0). \end{aligned} \tag{3.6}$$

We estimated the model separately for males and females in each year (1976–91), using weighted least squares regression and the population at each age as weights. The model explained between 98 and 99 per cent of the variance in the age profile of intergenerational transfers—that is, the difference between household and own-generation income. Coefficient estimates for young dependants were estimated with a high degree of reliability; standard errors varied from 0.019 to 0.010 for both males and females. Coefficients were somewhat less reliably estimated for elderly dependants, especially males. For early years, estimated standard errors are as high as 0.15 for elderly male recipients and 0.05 for elderly females. For later years, standard errors are around 0.06 for elderly males and 0.03 to 0.04 for elderly females.

The results for the early years of the analysis (prior to 1988) are consistent with a high degree of income pooling. Intergenerational transfers were sufficient

Table 3.3. Estimated proportion of income eliminated by intergenerational transfers: Taiwan, 1976–91

Year	$\alpha^{(h+p)}$		α^{h}		$\alpha^{(h+p)} - \alpha^{h}$	
	Males	Females	Males	Females	Males	Females
Young dependants						
1976–87	0.979	0.939	0.983	0.942	−0.004	−0.003
1988–91	0.926	0.896	0.937	0.906	−0.011	−0.010
Elderly dependants						
1976–87	1.120	1.033	0.948	0.943	0.171	0.090
1988–91	0.953	0.865	0.772	0.739	0.181	0.126

to raise the per capita household incomes of young male dependants to nearly the per capita incomes of the dynasties to which they belonged. During that period, private transfers closed 98 per cent of the gap between own and dynastic per capita income. The coefficients dropped modestly during the period and were 0.96, and significantly less than one, in 1986 and 1987 (Table 3.3).[9]

Estimated coefficients for young dependent females are also consistent with a high degree of intergenerational income pooling, but they are distinctly smaller than the estimates for males. Prior to 1988, about 94 per cent of the gap between own-generation income and dynastic income was closed through private transfers. For each year analysed, we can reject full intergenerational income sharing with young female dependants.

There is a notable shift in the estimated coefficients for both young males and young females during the last few years analysed. For the period 1988–91, the per capita household income of young male dependants dropped to 92.6 per cent of dynastic income; young female dependants averaged 89.6 per cent. In the absence of comparable analyses of other countries, we are not in a position to declare this a large shift nor to say that youth in Taiwan are in a markedly disadvantaged position relative to adults of prime ages. Taiwan's youth are possibly in a favourable position compared with those in Western countries. Nonetheless, the change does appear to be part of a qualitatively important departure for a society in which generations traditionally engaged in a remarkably high degree of income pooling.

Estimated intergenerational transfers to the elderly prior to 1988 are also consistent with full pooling of income. Indeed, intergenerational transfers to elderly men and women exceeded their intergenerational income gap in every year between 1976 and 1987, although in no single year can we reject the hypothesis that α was equal to 1 for the elderly. Beginning in 1988, however, the estimated intergenerational transfer ratio dropped quite markedly, averaging 0.95 and 0.86, respectively, for males and females over the 1988–91 period. For females, the estimated coefficients are significantly less than 1 after 1987; for males, however, coefficients are estimated with insufficient accuracy to rule out full income sharing. The gender difference for transfers to the elderly is even greater than was the case for transfers to the young.

To separate the effects of the two mechanisms for achieving intergenerational transfers, we decided to estimate the proportion of the intergenerational gap in income eliminated in the absence of interhousehold transfers and to compare the resulting estimates with those obtained when interhousehold transfers were included (i.e. the values reported above). We found that the intergenerational redistribution of income to the young was accomplished entirely through co-residence. Interhousehold transfers have a slightly negative effect on the young because the dominant flow is from households headed by prime-age adults, which contain children, to households of the elderly. The negative effect on children was somewhat larger after 1987 than before, for two reasons. First, the transfers received by the elderly increased over those remitted between 1976 and 1987. Second, the elderly constituted a larger share of the population in later years, thus requiring greater sacrifices on the part of young households in order to achieve a given transfer to the elderly.

Although co-residence has been the exclusive vehicle for making intergenerational transfers to the young, interhousehold transfers have been quite significant for the elderly. During the period 1976–87 the elderly nearly achieved parity with other members of their dynasties even in the absence of interhousehold transfers. Interhousehold transfers, particularly to the households of men, were sufficient to raise the per capita income of elderly households to levels well above those of their dynasties.

The effect of the increase in independent living by the elderly can be seen clearly in the latter years of the analysis. For elderly women, declining co-residence reduced their intergenerational transfer by 20 percentage points. The drop for elderly men was almost as high. Interhousehold transfers increased somewhat but incompletely compensated the elderly for the loss resulting from changing co-residence patterns.

Discussion

Several inferences can be drawn from this analysis of intergenerational transfers in Taiwan. Despite rapid social and economic change, the extended family is still the primary economic institution for transferring resources from high- to low-income generations, whether they be the young or the elderly. This will come as no surprise to those who have studied the family from a demographic perspective. Although co-residence among adult children and their elderly parents has declined in recent years, it remains an important feature of Taiwan's social arrangements.

Change is clearly beginning to come to Taiwan's families. Prior to 1988, Taiwan's generations were fully sharing their incomes. Since 1988, this has no longer been true. The per capita incomes of the households with children and the households of the elderly, in particular, fall short of dynastic income.

On the basis of this evidence alone, one cannot argue that the standard of living for the elderly has declined relative to that of their offspring. We know nothing about the intergenerational distribution of resources within the household. By living apart from their adult children, the elderly are giving up a small piece of a big pie to have a large piece of a smaller pie. Exactly how they are faring in this process cannot be judged from the evidence presented here. A further complication is that co-residence involves more than the sharing of economic resources. It also affects the exchange of time and the extent of companionship and privacy.

The analysis presented above documents the decline in intergenerational transfers, but we have not addressed the reasons for the decline. The enormous rise in living standards in Taiwan offers a ready explanation for the increase in independent living by the elderly that underlies their declining claim on dynastic income. The fertility decline has not yet affected the availability of surviving offspring with whom elderly parents could live. In fact, the average number of surviving offspring of the elderly increased during the 1970s and 1980s. The decline in intergenerational sharing between the elderly and their families may be in part a consequence of an increase in the number of elderly with severed links. This problem, however, is confined primarily to elderly men, whereas the decline in transfers to the elderly has been greater for women.

The decline in the extent to which children share the incomes of older generations is smaller than the decline for the elderly. Nonetheless, the change is startling. Obviously, this is not a case of dependent children living separately from their parents. As shown in the detailed income profiles for 1990, the per capita household income of young children is below their per capita dynastic income. One possibility is that the decline in the proportion of three-generation families is adversely affecting intergenerational transfers to the young. If, however, intergenerational transfers to the elderly are declining because of the decline in three-generation households, it seems that children should benefit, rather than be disadvantaged (because their parents are transferring less to the children's grandparents). A second possibility is that the relative economic decline of children reflects changes in the economic situation of parents as compared with non-parents. If childbearing becomes the province of lower-income families, the economic status of children relative to older generations will obviously suffer.

One of the important features of intergenerational transfers documented by this analysis is that interhousehold transfers have played a much less important role than co-residence. Total private interhousehold transfers are small as a percentage of total income. In 1991, for example, private interhousehold transfers represented only 0.3 per cent of total income. The impact of private interhousehold transfers on intergenerational inequality is further reduced because of the high degree of co-residence. Transfers to old or young individuals become the income of the households to which those individuals belong and thus have an attenuated effect on the income of the individuals receiving the transfers. Of course, given the effectiveness of co-residence and the relatively small percentages of older dependants, there is little need for private interhousehold transfers. As the number of elderly increase and independent living becomes more established, private interhousehold transfers can be expected to increase.

The significant gender issues noted above represent an area that warrants considerably more attention than could be provided here. We find the differences to be large and persistent, and to affect both young and elderly dependants. In the absence of further analysis interpreting these differences would be premature.

Conclusions

Our analysis has found that the family remains the major vehicle for transferring resources between generations in Taiwan. Of the two private forms of intergenerational transfers, co-residence plays a much more important role than interhousehold transfers. The analysis has also documented a decline in transfers through co-residence in recent years. Although interhousehold transfers have risen, the increase has been insufficient to maintain the economic position of the young and, especially, the elderly. In addition to these findings, several broader conclusions can be drawn from our results.

First, the extended family can be an extraordinarily effective institution for equalizing income across generations. This is a modestly surprising result for Taiwan, given its unusual demographic history. Because of the large-scale immigration by Nationalist forces at the end of China's Civil War, many men in Taiwan never married. The high prevalence of severed intergenerational links, however, does not appear to have had a noticeable aggregate impact on the family's intergenerational-support capacity. Among other things, this finding provides indirect support to Barro's (1974) position that the family is capable of neutralizing fiscal policies.

Second, the analysis sheds light on whether economic or demographic change impinges on the ability of extended families to solve the life-cycle problems of their members. The period analysed is one of extraordinarily rapid economic growth and fertility decline in Taiwan. Not only have income levels risen rapidly, but also the structure of earnings has shifted noticeably in favour of the young. Yet we find no evidence that the capacity of the family to smooth income has been affected to any significant degree. Consequently, the decline in the importance of the family relative to other mechanisms for redistributing income across generations cannot have been caused by a decline in the family's capacity to serve as a vehicle for achieving intergenerational equity.

Third, the research demonstrates the existence of a cycle in income at the aggregate level that is quite different from the traditional life cycle that has played such a prominent role in research on saving. The life-cycle saving model has been frequently criticized for its nuclear-family roots, but little work has been done to establish whether or not the extended family experiences a life cycle and what the macroeconomic implications of such a life cycle might be. The analysis of Taiwan provides clear evidence of a persistent life cycle among extended families.

Notes

We thank Frances Tsung, Noreen Tanouye, and Dolly Testa for their assistance.

1. Transfers prior to the period of observation will affect personal income. Property income will depend upon intergenerational transfers of wealth, whereas labour income will depend upon human capital investments in children by their parents.
2. One notable exception is the Panel Survey of Income Dynamics, which collects information about non-co-resident family members. See Ch. 14, by Altonji, Hayashi, and Kotlikoff, in this volume.
3. The probability of establishing a household is undoubtedly influenced by the number of children. Thus the number of children per household is an upwardly biased estimate of the number of children per mother or father, especially for younger parents.
4. As we have reported above, the mean size of a dynasty is slightly less than six members because of the variation in dynasty size. Most persons, however, belong to dynasties that have seven or more members. In the calculations for individuals, one dynasty of fifteen members has fifteen times the weight of a one-person dynasty.
5. The effect of public transfers is not independent of co-residence because transfers to one age group 'leak' to other age groups sharing the same household income.
6. The magnitudes of the numbers for the elderly are small because the elderly made up only 6% of Taiwan's population 1991. Thus a smaller portion of national income is required to raise their income.
7. That such a small sacrifice on the part of younger generations can support a more substantial increase in the income of older generations reflects, of course, the small percentage of the population 65 and older.
8. Defining groups in this way avoids an arbitrary definition of the ages of dependency. It also accommodates the possibility that the ages of dependency vary over time if, for example, educational attainment rises or the age of retirement declines.
9. We report only the average coefficients for 1965–87 and 1988–91. Detailed estimates are available from the first author upon request.

4 Demographic Change, Generational Accounts, and National Saving in the United States

Jagadeesh Gokhale

In recent years the role of fiscal policy in redistributing resources across generations has been subjected to intense scrutiny. That is not surprising because fiscal policy has played an increasingly important role in transferring resources between generations, especially in developed economies.[1] Until recently, however, no technique was available for measuring the extent of intergenerational wealth redistribution via the public channel. This gap has now been filled by 'generational accounting', a method for keeping track of prospective and lifetime resource flows towards or away from specific generations as a result of a government's tax and spending policies (Auerbach, Gokhale, and Kotlikoff 1991, 1994; Kotlikoff 1992).[2]

A generational account is the present value of taxes (net of transfers) per capita that members of a given generation may expect to pay to the government during their remaining lifetime if current fiscal policy is maintained. Generational accounting studies of the United States reveal a sizeable imbalance in US fiscal policy: the continuation of current policy for those now alive will entail the imposition of enormously larger fiscal burdens on generations to come. Similar conclusions emerge from generational accounting analyses for Italy, Germany, Norway, and Canada. (See Gokhale, Raffelhüschen, and Walliser 1995 for the case of Germany; Auerbach *et al.* 1992 for Norway; Oreopoulos 1995 for Canada; and Franco, *et al.* 1994 for Italy.)

A critical element in the calculation of the accounts is long-range population projections. Population projections are usually fairly reliable over the short term, but long-term trends in mortality, fertility, and immigration cannot be estimated precisely beyond a couple of decades. Despite the important role that population projections play in generational accounting, the sensitivity of its conclusions to alternative population projections has not been investigated to date. One goal of this chapter is to perform such an analysis.

A second goal is to analyse the effect of changes in the age structure of a population on national saving. According to the life-cycle hypothesis with certainty (Ando and Modigliani 1963), the current consumption of an individual depends upon his or her age-specific propensity to consume out of lifetime resources. If this hypothesis is valid, the age structure of a population could be a potentially important determinant of national saving. Understanding the trend in national saving would, then, require the measurement of the total resources available to each generation (the amount of which would be affected by its generational account), generation-specific propensities to consume out of those resources, and the current and projected age structure of the population.

Studies of the United States that use the framework for data organization suggested by the life-cycle hypothesis have found that the ongoing resource transfers away from young and future generations, and towards older generations, are capable of explaining a sizeable fraction of the recent decline in US saving (Gokhale, Kotlikoff, and Sabelhaus 1996). Nevertheless, the role of a changing population age structure in the United States on US aggregate saving has not been explored in much detail. This chapter asks and answers two questions about the effect of a change in population age structure on national saving: first, to what extent has the evolving age structure contributed to the decline in US saving since the late 1970s, and, second, what likely role will the ongoing demographic transition play in determining future US national saving?

The chapter first describes the methodology of generational accounting, presents the accounts for the United States, and describes the sensitivity of the results under alternative interest-rate and growth-rate assumptions and under alternative projections of federal health-care expenditures. Next, it describes the demographic transition currently under way in the United States and performs sensitivity tests on US generational accounts under various assumptions about future mortality, fertility, and immigration rates. Finally, it uses a framework based on the life-cycle hypothesis to examine the role of demographic change in influencing national saving in the United States.

The Method of Generational Accounting

The method of generational accounting takes the government's present-value budget constraint (also known as its intertemporal budget constraint) as a starting point. That constraint may be written as

$$PVG_t = NWG_t + PVL_t + PVF_t. \tag{4.1}$$

Equation 4.1 states that at time t (the current period), the present value of government purchases of goods and services, PVG_t, must be paid for by the sum of three items: the net wealth of the government, NWG_t; the present value of *net tax payments* by living generations at time t, PVL_t; and the present value of net tax payments by future generations, PVF_t. The term 'net tax payments' refers to taxes paid to the government net of transfers received from it. The 'generational account' of a generation is a dollar amount and is defined as the *actuarially discounted present value of net tax payments per capita* over the generation's remaining lifetime. Note that Equation 4.1 can be viewed as a financing constraint. Under a given policy for government purchases and given the government's current net worth, future generations must assume the burden of paying for government purchases that are not covered by the net tax payments made by living generations. The focus of generational accounting is the trade-off between PVL_t and PVF_t. The following describes the method of estimating the components of Equation 4.1.

The sum of generational accounts over all members of living generations, PVL_t can be written as

$$PVL_t = \sum_{jt=0}^{D} \left[\eta^m_{jt,t} \, p^m_{jt,t} + \eta^f_{jt,t} \, p^f_{jt,t} \right], \tag{4.2}$$

where D is the maximum age of life. A distinction is made between male and female generations, whose populations are represented by $p^m_{jt,t}$ and $p^f_{jt,t}$; and the terms $\eta^m_{jt,t}$ and $\eta^f_{jt,t}$ represent the generational accounts in year t of male and female generations aged j in year t (indexed by $_{jt}$).

The generational accounts, $\eta^x_{jt,t}$ where the superscript x stands for male or female, is defined by Equation 4.3:

$$\eta^x_{jt,t} = \frac{1}{p^x_{jt,t}} \sum_{s=t}^{t+D-jt} p^x_{jt,s} \left[\sum_{i=1}^{m} q^x_{i,jt,s} \right] R^{s-t}. \tag{4.3}$$

Here, $R = 1/(1+r)$ and r is the discount rate. In Equation 4.3, $q^x_{i,jt,s}$ stands for the per capita payment (or receipt, when q is negative) of type i in a future period s by a member of the generation of sex x aged j in year t. The sum within square brackets over the m types of per capita payments in period s provides the net payment per capita in that period. This term, multiplied by the population of such persons in period s, $p^x_{jt,s}$, provides the total net payment that individuals of sex x aged j in year t make in year s. For the United States, estimates of $p^x_{jt,s}$ are those of the Social Security Administration. Summing over such discounted values for each period s over the remaining lifetime of individuals aged j in year t provides their total discounted value of net payments. Division by $p^x_{jt,t}$, the population of such persons in year t, converts this discounted sum to a per capita amount and represents the generational account of the generation aged j in year t. Note that multiplying the sum of net payments in each period s by the number of surviving members in period s of the generation aged j in year t, and finally dividing by their population in period t, amounts to actuarially discounting their future net payments.

For future years, the per capita payments of each type are estimated either by distributing projected aggregate payments of that type in future years using relative profiles by age and sex or, if projections of aggregate payments are not available, by applying a growth factor to similarly estimated per capita payments for the base year t for which the aggregate payment is available. In the latter case,

$$q^x_{i,jt,s} = q^x_{i,jt,t}(1+g)^{s-t}. \tag{4.4}$$

The relative profiles used for distributing base-year (or future-year) aggregate payments by age and sex are obtained from household surveys that contain the pertinent information.[3] These empirically determined relative profiles and the associated aggregate payments and receipts collectively constitute an element of the time-t intergenerational stance of fiscal policy in that they specify the pattern of payments and receipts imposed on living generations at time t. The relative profiles are normalized to 1 for males aged 40 in year t (or s). Hence the per capita payment for 40–year-old males can be expressed as

$$q^{x}_{i,40t,t} = \frac{Q_{i,t}}{\sum_{jt=0}^{D}\left[r^{m}_{i,jt,t}\, p^{m}_{jt,t} + r^{f}_{i,jt,t}\, p^{f}_{jt,t}\right]}, \tag{4.5}$$

where $r^{x}_{i,jt,t}$ represents the amount of payment (receipt, if negative) of type i that a person aged j in year t makes relative to the payment of a 40–year-old male in year t, and $Q_{i,t}$ is the aggregate payment of type i made in year t. Of course,

$$q^{x}_{i,jt,t} = q^{x}_{i,40t,t}\, r^{x}_{i,jt,t}, \quad \text{for } x = m,f;\ jt = 0 \ldots D. \tag{4.6}$$

This completes the description of the method for estimating the generational accounts and the aggregate net tax payments, PVL_t, of living generations. The term PVG_t is estimated by discounting future projections of aggregate purchases back to period t. If projections of aggregate future government purchases are not available, it is possible to estimate PVG_t by dividing government purchases at time t into several age-specific categories, assuming that the relative age-specific purchases per capita for each category will remain constant in the future, and using population projections and productivity growth to project the path of aggregate purchases in the future.[4] Government purchases include not only purchases of goods and services but also outlays for federal, state, and local civilian and military retirement, disability, and life insurance programmes and expenditures for workers' compensation.[5] The division of government purchases into several age-specific categories is determined empirically, and it represents an element of the current intergenerational stance of fiscal policy.

Government net wealth, NWG_t, can be estimated by computing the cumulative sum of past government deficits. It should be noted that existing physical assets of the government, such as parks and infrastructure, are a part of its net wealth. However, they also represent the consumption of public goods, the present value of which has to be included in PVG_t if their asset value is included in NWG_t. Because the value of government assets must, by definition, equal the present value of their consumption flow, the exclusion of physical assets from both sides of Equation 4.1 leaves the constraint unchanged. That is, the trade-off between PVL_t and PVF_t, which is the focus of generational accounting, remains unaffected by the omission of the value of government assets from NWG_t.

Because Equation 4.1 must hold at time t, and because we have estimated three of the four elements in that equation, we can calculate the fourth term,

PVF_t, as a residual. How this residual net payment that must be imposed on unborn generations will actually be distributed among those generations is not clear from the vantage point of time t. As an illustrative device, let us assume an equal, growth-adjusted distribution of the residual, PVF_t, among members of all future generations. In so distributing the residual burden, we assume that the net payment by unborn males relative to unborn females is maintained equal to that between newborn male and female generations (who are treated as members of living generations) under current policy. Hence

$$PVG_t - NWG_t - PVL_t = \sum_{s=t+1}^{\infty} \left[\eta^m_{0s,s}\, p^m_{0s,s} + \eta^f_{0s,s}\, p^f_{0s,s} \right] R^{s-t}, \tag{4.7}$$

where $\eta^x_{0s,s}$ is the present value as of period s of the net payment of the generation of sex x aged 0 in period s, and $p^x_{0s,s}$ is the population of such individuals in period s. Each future generation's aggregate net payment is discounted back to period t. Let (ϕ^m be 1 and $\phi^f = \eta^f_{0s,s}/\eta^m_{0s,s}$ $s = t+1, \ldots \infty$, the net payment of future female generations relative to future male generations. Further, let $\eta^m_{0s+1,\,s+1}/\eta^m_{0s,s} = (1+g)$, $s = t, \ldots \infty$. Thus each future generation is assumed to pay $(1+g)$ times the net payment of the immediately preceding generation, where $(1+g)$ is the gross rate of growth of labour productivity. Dividing and multiplying the right-hand side of Equation 4.7 by $\eta^m_{0t+1,\,t+1}$ and manipulating the expression within square brackets yields

$$\eta^m_{0t+1,\,t+1} = \frac{PVG_t - NWG_t - PVL_t}{\sum_{s=t+1}^{\infty} \left[\phi^m p^m_{0s,s} + \phi^f p^f_{0s,s} \right] R^{s-t} (1+g)^{s-(t+1)}}. \tag{4.8}$$

The term on the left-hand side of Equation 4.8 represents the net payment (as of period t) of the generation born in period $t+1$.[6] Because period-t newborns and future generations have their entire lifetimes ahead of them, it is possible to compare the net payment of the generation born in period t to that of the average net payment of those born in period $t+1$. Note, again, that the latter net payment represents the growth-adjusted burden on all future generations because it is computed under the assumption of an equal distribution of the residual burden, PVL_t, across all future generations. The difference between the two measures, computed as a percentage, or

$$P = \left[\frac{\eta^m_{0t+1,\,t+1}}{\eta^m_{0t,\,t}(1+g)} - 1 \right] \times 100, \tag{4.9}$$

provides a measure of the degree of inequality between newborns and future generations embedded in current fiscal policy.

An alternative measure of the fiscal burden on a generation is the *lifetime net tax rate* that a generation faces under current policy. That rate is computed as the ratio of the generational account *at birth* to the present value of per capita labour income over the generation's entire lifetime. Thus we can express the lifetime net tax rate, τ, as

$$\tau^{x}_{jt,t-j} = \frac{\eta^{x}_{jt,t-jt}}{\sum_{s=t-jt}^{t+D-jt} \varepsilon^{x}_{jt,s} R^{s-(t-jt)}}, \tag{4.10}$$

where $\tau^{x}_{jt,t-jt}$ is the lifetime net tax rate of the generation of sex x aged j in year t, and $\varepsilon^{x}_{jt,s}$ is the average labour earnings in year s of this generation.[7] Note that the summation is over the entire lifetime of the generation and the present values for both the numerator and the denominator are computed as of the generation's year of birth, $t - jt$. The lifetime net tax rate represents the fraction of the present value at birth of lifetime labour earnings that will be paid to the government. Hence, in computing lifetime net tax rates for living generations, it is necessary to include past as well as future projected labour earnings in the denominator, and past as well as future projected annual net tax payments in the numerator.

Generational Accounts for the United States

Table 4.1 shows generational accounts for selected male and female generations in the United States, with 1993 as the base year (year t). The computations use data on aggregate taxes, transfers, and projections of government purchases through 2030 provided by the United States Office of Management and Budget. Projections of taxes, transfers, and spending after 2030 assume that per capita amounts will grow at an annual rate of productivity growth of 1.2 per cent. Present values are calculated with a 6 per cent rate of discount in all cases.[8]

The generational accounts for living generations (shown under the 'net payment' column) exhibit significant differences among individuals at various stages of their lives. Younger generations' net payments are positive, reflecting their active working and earning stage of life, while older generations' net payments are negative because they are retired and receive large amounts in the form of Social Security and health benefits.[9] The generational accounts for very young living generations are much smaller than for those in their middle ages because the former are far removed in time from their working, earning, and prime tax-paying years.

The generational account for future generations is much larger than that for living newborns (those aged 0 in 1993). The value of P in Equation 4.9 turns out to be 146.1 per cent. That is, future generations must, on average, make net payments one and a half times larger than those of current newborns if current fiscal treatment is extended to those future generations throughout their lifetimes. Thus, under the illustrative assumption that the residual burden is allocated equally among future generations, generational accounting reveals a substantial imbalance in the intergenerational stance of current US fiscal policy.

Table 4.1. Composition of male and female generational accounts ($r=0.06$, $g=0.012$): United States (present values in 1993 US$000s)

Generation's age in 1993	Net payment	Tax payments, by type				Transfer receipts, by type		
		Labour income	Capital income	Pay-roll	Excise	OASDI	Health	Welfare
Males								
90	−57.6	0.5	0.0	0.5	6.2	32.8	30.6	1.4
85	−75.3	0.6	0.0	0.7	7.9	41.8	40.9	1.8
80	−85.8	0.9	9.9	0.9	11.9	54.3	52.5	2.7
75	−100.6	1.6	19.8	1.6	17.1	71.5	65.4	3.7
70	−108.4	3.1	29.5	3.2	22.6	85.7	76.6	4.5
65	−105.2	7.2	37.3	7.2	28.2	93.6	86.3	5.1
60	−57.2	18.1	42.5	18.9	34.1	83.8	81.0	5.9
55	6.9	34.0	46.2	35.5	40.2	67.4	75.1	6.6
50	67.7	50.6	48.2	52.5	45.7	54.2	67.8	7.3
45	119.4	65.8	47.7	67.6	50.1	43.8	60.1	7.9
40	158.4	78.0	45.0	79.8	53.3	35.7	53.4	8.6
35	182.5	86.1	39.9	88.0	54.6	28.9	48.0	9.2
30	195.4	90.7	33.7	92.9	55.9	23.7	44.3	9.9
25	199.5	92.1	28.5	94.4	57.1	19.8	42.5	10.3
20	188.6	86.6	24.1	88.1	57.0	16.7	40.8	9.7
15	160.0	73.7	19.2	73.7	52.7	14.9	36.4	8.0
10	130.2	60.0	15.2	59.0	46.2	12.9	31.0	6.3
5	106.9	49.1	12.1	47.7	40.1	10.9	26.3	5.0
0	86.8	39.8	9.6	38.2	34.4	8.8	22.5	3.9
Future generations	213.6							
Difference (%)	146.1							
Females								
90	−64.4	0.1	0.0	0.1	7.1	32.4	38.1	1.3
85	−88.3	0.1	0.0	0.1	9.4	42.8	53.4	1.7
80	−111.3	0.3	4.7	0.3	12.6	57.0	69.9	2.2
75	−131.1	0.5	12.4	0.5	17.3	72.0	87.1	2.6
70	−140.5	1.0	22.6	1.2	22.8	84.9	100.0	3.1
65	−139.5	2.6	32.1	3.0	28.0	92.2	109.6	3.5
60	−101.5	7.3	38.2	8.5	33.7	83.2	102.0	3.9
55	−50.4	14.7	41.8	16.9	39.3	66.0	92.5	4.6
50	−0.8	23.4	44.1	26.7	44.3	52.3	81.2	5.7
45	42.4	31.8	45.3	35.8	48.5	41.8	70.0	7.3
40	76.0	39.1	44.5	43.6	51.4	33.8	59.1	9.7
35	97.3	44.3	41.2	49.0	52.8	27.4	50.1	12.5
30	109.2	48.4	35.8	53.1	53.3	22.4	43.2	15.8
25	114.7	51.1	30.7	55.7	53.8	18.8	38.5	19.4
20	109.2	49.4	25.5	53.2	53.2	15.7	34.6	21.7
15	93.1	42.3	20.4	44.7	49.4	14.0	30.4	19.2
10	77.2	34.6	16.1	35.9	43.9	12.2	25.6	15.4
5	64.3	28.3	12.8	29.0	38.5	10.3	21.6	12.3
0	53.0	23.0	10.2	23.2	33.1	8.4	18.4	9.8
Future generations	130.4							
Difference (%):	146.1							
Lifetime net tax rates (%)								
on future generations 82.80								
on age 0 generations 33.64								

OASDI: Old age, survivor's, and disability insurance.

Note: Lifetime net tax rates are population-weighted averages over rates for male and female generations.

Source: Author's calculations.

The bottom section of Table 4.1 shows that the lifetime net tax rate facing current newborns is 33.6 per cent whereas the average rate facing future generations is 82.8 per cent.[10] The net tax rate for future generations represents the average rate that each member of all future generations will have to pay to balance the government's intertemporal budget, shown in Equation 4.1. Such a policy, involving a lifetime net tax rate on current newborns that is less than the average net tax rate that all future generations must bear in order to satisfy constraint (1), is clearly unsustainable. If such a policy were maintained for a period of time, each successive newborn generation would contribute less than this average net tax rate, thereby increasing the average net tax rate that all remaining future generations would have to pay. Thus, at some future date, the average net tax rate on all remaining future generations would exceed 100 per cent—which is not feasible. Levying such an enormously high average rate on future generations is obviously *in*feasible.

Sensitivity of generational accounts to alternative interest rates and growth rates

Table 4.2, which presents the lifetime net tax rates on current newborn and future generations under alternative interest-rate and growth-rate assumptions, shows that increasing the rate of interest increases the net tax rates on living

Table 4.2. Lifetime net tax rates for 1993 newborns and future generations under alternative interest-rate and growth-rate assumptions: United States

Generation	Alternative assumptions		
1993 newborns			
Interest rate (%)	3.0	6.0	9.0
Growth rates (%)			
0.7	29.5	40.4	46.5
1.2	22.7	33.6	39.7
1.7	16.9	27.9	33.8
Future generations			
Interest rate (%)	3.0	6.0	9.0
Growth rates (%)			
0.7	65.1	103.8	175.8
1.2	49.9	82.8	142.5
1.7	37.7	65.7	115.2
Percentage difference in net tax burdens			
Interest rate (%)	3.0	6.0	9.0
Growth rates (%)			
0.7	120.3	157.2	277.8
1.2	119.7	146.1	259.1
1.7	122.4	135.8	241.0

Source: Author's calculations.

newborns. This is so because in present value calculations, a higher interest rate implies that payments further out in the future receive lower weights. Labour earnings and tax payments occur at roughly the same time during the lifetime, but benefit receipts occur later. Hence higher interest rates reduce the present value of future benefits by more than they reduce the present values of taxes and labour income. Lifetime net tax rates are therefore larger when the assumed discount rate is higher. The net tax rates are lower for higher assumed rates of productivity growth.

The average lifetime net tax rate on future generations is significantly higher than that on living newborns, exceeding 100 per cent for some interest- and growth-rate combinations. The third panel of Table 4.2 shows the values of P for the alternative cases. In none of the cases is P less than 100 per cent; rather, future generations may be expected to pay, on average, at least twice as much as current newborns under current fiscal policy.

Sensitivity of Generational Accounts to Alternative Assumptions about Health-Care Outlays

An important and rapidly growing share of government outlays in the United States is devoted to providing health-care insurance and services to the elderly through Medicare and the poor through Medicaid. Because recent and projected growth in those two programmes is extremely high relative to the rest of the economy, they play a significant role in generating the imbalance between the accounts of newborn and future generations. The high growth rates in Medicare and Medicaid are expected to continue under current policies, but legislation may be enacted to reduce the rate of outlay growth in these items.

The first two columns of Table 4.3 are the same as the 'net payment' columns of Table 4.1: they show generational accounts for males and females under a continuation of current fiscal policy. The second pair of columns shows the accounts under a highly optimistic assumption—that the growth of federal health-care outlays will be 'stabilized' beginning in 1996. Stabilization is taken to mean that the growth in outlays equals the growth rate of the recipient population plus the rate of productivity growth. For example, total health-care outlays on 70–year-old males in year $t+1$ would equal the per capita outlays on 70–year-old males in period t times the productivity growth factor, $1+g$, times the number of 70–year-old males alive in period $t+1$. In this case, the lifetime net tax rate on living newborns increases from 33.6 per cent to 38.1 per cent and that on future generations declines from 82.8 per cent to 50.5 per cent. This implies an imbalance of 33 per cent compared with 146 per cent under the base case. Thus the rapid projected growth in federal health-care outlays goes a long way towards explaining the sizeable generational imbalance in current US fiscal policy. The last two columns in Table 4.3 show the results of assuming, more realistically, that the growth in health-care outlays will not be

Table 4.3. Generational accounts under alternative federal health-care outlay projections: United States (present values in 1993 US$000s)

Age	No change in outlays		Stabilization in 1996		Stabilization in 2003	
	Male	Female	Male	Female	Male	Female
90	−57.6	−64.4	−55.4	−61.0	−57.5	−64.3
85	−75.3	−88.3	−70.8	−80.9	−74.9	−87.4
80	−85.8	−111.3	−77.5	−97.5	−84.6	−108.7
75	−100.6	−131.1	−86.8	−109.0	−97.6	−125.2
70	−108.4	−140.5	−88.0	−109.7	−102.6	−130.2
65	−105.2	−139.5	−78.1	−101.1	−95.7	−124.5
60	−57.2	−101.5	−24.6	−58.0	−44.0	−82.6
55	6.9	−50.4	40.8	−6.9	23.2	−28.8
50	67.7	−0.8	99.3	38.5	84.2	20.2
45	119.4	42.4	147.0	75.8	133.7	60.2
40	158.4	76.0	182.1	104.1	170.2	90.5
35	182.5	97.3	203.1	120.9	192.3	109.2
30	195.4	109.2	213.9	129.2	203.9	119.2
25	199.5	114.7	216.8	132.4	207.3	123.5
20	188.6	109.2	205.2	125.0	195.9	117.0
15	160.0	93.1	175.5	106.9	166.8	99.9
10	130.2	77.2	143.8	88.9	136.3	82.9
5	106.9	64.3	118.6	74.3	112.3	69.2
0	86.8	53.0	96.8	61.4	91.5	57.1
Future generations	213.6	130.4	128.5	81.5	173.7	108.4
Difference (%)	146.1		32.8		89.8	
Lifetime net tax rates (%)						
on newborn generation		33.6		38.1		35.8
on future generations		82.8		50.5		67.9

Source: Author's calculations.

stabilized until the year 2003.[11] Delaying the stabilization of health-care outlays until the year 2003 will result in a substantial increase in the lifetime net tax rates of future generations and a substantial increase in the imbalance relative to the optimistic scenario—to 90 per cent.

Sensitivity of generational accounts to alternative population projections

Figure 4.1 shows actual growth in the US population between 1960 and 1995 and three alternative projections of the population to 2200 made by the Social Security Administration.[12] The alternative II projections are used in the estimates of generational accounts shown in Table 4.1. As is clear from Figure 4.1,

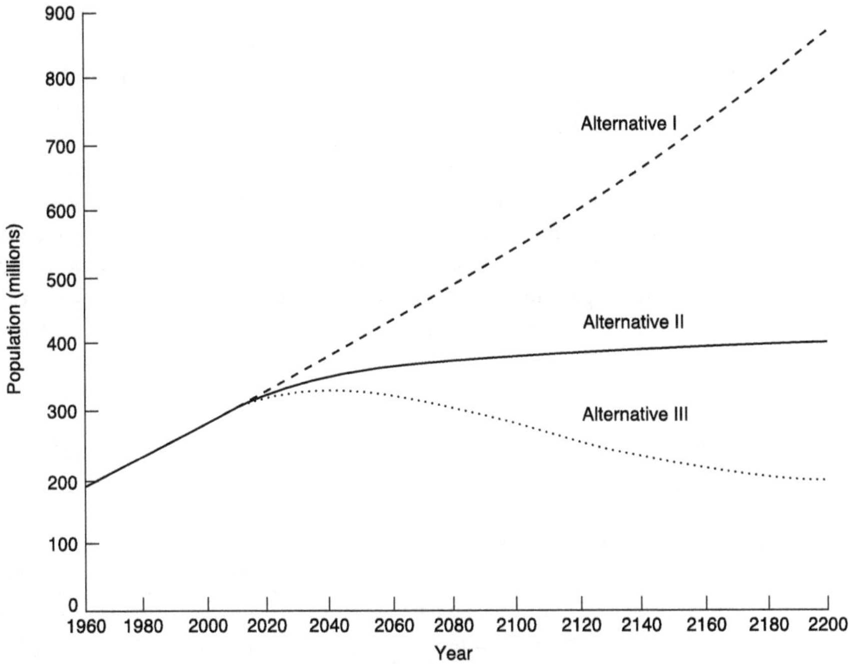

Sources: Social Security Administration and author's calculations.

Fig. 4.1. Actual population of the United States, 1960–95, and projections to 2200

Alternative I represents more than a doubling of the population projected by Alternative II in the year 2200. Under Alternative III the projected population in the year 2200 is half as large as that under Alternative II in that year. Another way of comparing the three alternatives is to compare their population counts in 2200 to the actual size of the population in 1993. Under Alternative I, the population grows to more than three times its 1993 size by 2200. Under Alternative II it increases by about 50 per cent. Under Alternative III, however, it declines to about 70 per cent of its 1993 level. Thus these three alternatives encompass a reasonably wide range of future population-growth possibilities.

The three alternative projections are designed by the Social Security Administration to represent low-cost (Alternative I), intermediate-cost (Alternative II), and high-cost (Alternative III) assumptions for purposes of computing the long-range actuarial balance of the Social Security system. Alternative I embodies high fertility, mortality, and immigration rates. Under this scenario, the high fertility and immigration rates imply that there will be a large number of young cohorts who will pay taxes. The high mortality rates, on the other hand, imply that current and future generations of elderly will die off quickly, thus receiving a smaller present value of Social Security benefits. Alternative III embodies the opposite assumptions of low fertility, mortality, and immigration rates. This high-cost scenario implies that there will be fewer younger people in the future to pay taxes and larger numbers of older people to receive benefits.

Table 4.4 projects net payments under the three demographic alternatives. A well-known feature of the mortality rates is that they are extremely low at ages below 50 and rise rapidly with age thereafter. Hence most of the difference in mortality rates between the three alternatives occurs at older ages. As expected, then, net payments of living generations are higher under Alternative I than under Alternative II. The reasons are that at each age a higher mortality implies a lower present value of benefits when old; but because mortality rates do not differ much at young ages, tax burdens of the young are not much affected. Under Alternative III, in contrast, net payments are smaller for the opposite reasons.[13]

Table 4.4. Generational accounts under alternative population projections ($r = 0.06$, $g = 0.012$): United States (present values in 1993 US$000s)

Generation's age in 1993	Alternative I		Alternative II		Alternative III	
	Males	Females	Males	Females	Males	Females
90	−56.9	−63.6	−57.6	−64.4	−58.2	−65.2
85	−74.2	−86.8	−75.3	−88.3	−76.4	−89.8
80	−84.2	−109.0	−85.8	−111.3	−87.4	−113.6
75	−98.5	−128.1	−100.6	−131.1	−102.6	−133.9
70	−106.2	−137.4	−108.4	−140.5	−110.5	−143.4
65	−103.3	−136.9	−105.2	−139.5	−107.0	−141.8
60	−55.9	−99.9	−57.2	−101.5	−58.4	−103.1
55	7.4	−49.8	6.9	−50.4	6.3	−51.2
50	67.6	−0.7	67.7	−0.8	67.7	−1.0
45	118.9	42.0	119.4	42.4	119.7	42.4
40	157.7	75.4	158.4	76.0	158.6	76.2
35	181.7	96.5	182.5	97.3	182.3	97.6
30	194.8	108.4	195.4	109.2	194.8	109.4
25	199.7	114.3	199.5	114.7	198.6	114.6
20	190.4	109.5	188.6	109.2	186.9	108.8
15	161.9	93.5	160.0	93.1	158.7	92.7
10	131.0	77.2	130.2	77.2	129.8	77.0
5	107.2	64.1	106.9	64.3	106.7	64.3
0	86.8	52.7	86.8	53.0	86.8	53.0
Future generations	191.2	116.1	213.6	130.4	239.4	146.2
Difference (%)	120.3		146.1		175.7	
Lifetime net tax rates (%)						
on newborn generation	32.3		33.6		34.5	
on future generations	71.1		82.8		95.0	

Source: Author's calculations.

The generational account of future generations under Alternative I is smaller than that under Alternative II because higher fertility rates assumed under the former imply larger future cohorts among whom the residual burden can be distributed. In contrast, the average net payment burden on future generations is larger under Alternative III because of the lower fertility rates embodied in it.

Among the three alternatives, the percentage difference between newborn and future generations ranges from 120 per cent under Alternative I to 176 per cent under Alternative III. Future generations' lifetime net tax rates range from 71 per cent under Alternative I to 95 per cent under Alternative III. Thus even under Alternative I's assumptions of high fertility, mortality, and immigration—that is, its 'optimistic' assumptions from the perspective of generational accounting—the conclusion that current US fiscal policy contains a sizeable imbalance and is placed on an unsustainable course remains valid.

Generational accounts and private budgets

The generational accounts of living generations represent a net drain on their total resources under current US fiscal policy. Generational accounts are, therefore, an element of the prospective lifetime budget constraints for living

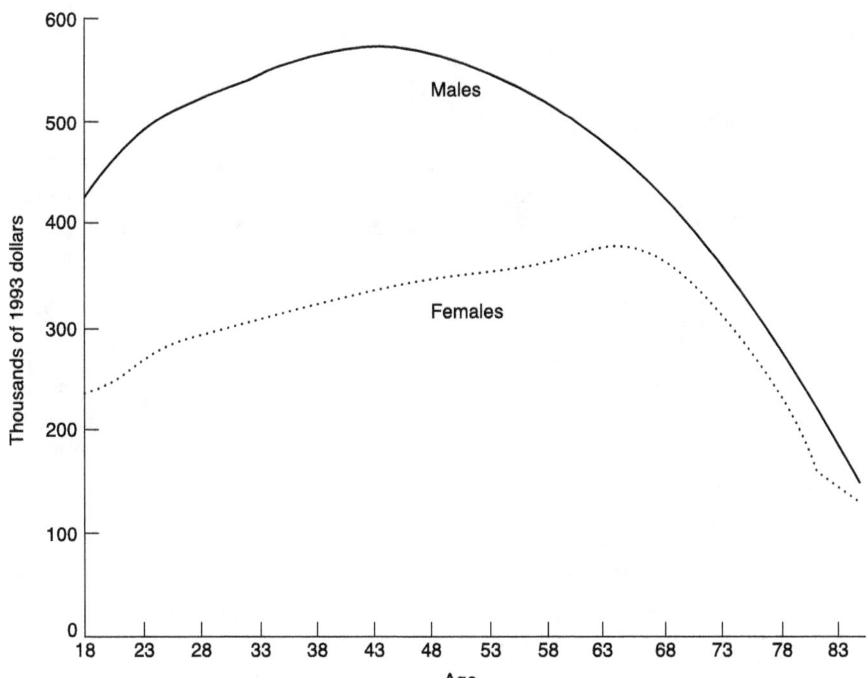

Source: Author's calculations.

Fig. 4.2. Resources per capita, by age and sex: United States

generations. The total resources in year t of an individual aged j in year t can be expressed as

$$\rho^x_{jt,t} = \omega^x_{jt,t} + \sum_{s=t}^{t+D-jt} \left[\varepsilon^x_{jt,s} + \pi^x_{jt,s}\right] R^{s-t} - \eta^x_{jt,t}, \tag{4.11}$$

where $\rho^x_{jt,s}$ represents resources per capita, $\varepsilon^x_{jt,s}$ the average labour earnings, $\pi^x_{jt,s}$ the average pension earnings, and $\omega^x_{jt,s}$ the total net worth, in year s, of a member of the generation of sex x aged j in year t. Thus a generation's per capita resources are the sum of its per capita non-human, human, and pension wealth, less its generational account.[14] Here I use relative profiles by age and sex of labour earnings and of public and private pension benefits to distribute aggregate labour and pension incomes in order to obtain the human-wealth and pension-wealth components of total resources. The procedure for distributing the aggregates is similar to that given in Equations 4.5 and 4.6 earlier. The non-human-wealth component is obtained by distributing aggregate private net worth by age-sex relative profiles of net worth from microdata surveys.[15]

Figure 4.2 shows the age-sex distribution of resources per capita. As would be expected, resources of younger women are much lower than those of men, primarily because of their lower rates of labour force participation and earnings.

Population age structure and national saving

According to the life-cycle hypothesis, consumption in year t of an individual aged jt depends upon the *average* propensity to consume out of lifetime resources at that age. Thus aggregate consumption in period t can be expressed as

$$C_t = \sum_x \sum_{jt=0}^{D} c^x_{jt,t}\, p^x_{jt,t} = \sum_x \sum_{jt=0}^{D} \alpha^x_{jt,t}\, \rho^x_{jt,t}\, p^x_{jt,t} \tag{4.12}$$

where c is consumption per capita and α is the average propensity to consume out of lifetime resources.[16] Generation-specific estimates of $\alpha_{jt,t}$ are obtained by distributing aggregate personal consumption expenditures in period t according to age-sex profiles of consumption and dividing the per capita amounts by total resources per capita.[17]

Figure 4.3 depicts average propensities to consume by age and sex for the United States as of 1993 (year t for this analysis). Consistent with the predictions based upon the life-cycle hypothesis, the propensity to consume increases with age. For males it increases from 2 per cent at age 18 to nearly 15 per cent by age 85. For females it increases from just under 4 per cent for 18–year-olds to over 17 per cent for 85–year-olds. The consumption propensities of women are much higher than those of men, especially at younger ages. Women's consumption does not adequately reflect their lower total resources, due to their lower lifetime

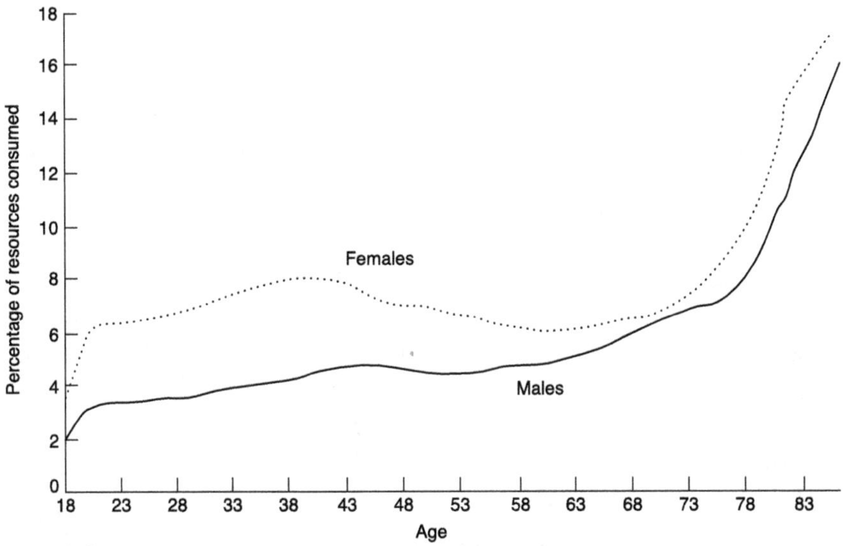

Source: Author's calculations.

Fig. 4.3. Average propensities to consume out of total resources: United States

labour earnings, for the reason that substantial amounts of goods and services are consumed jointly within families.

The net national saving rate can be expressed as

$$\frac{S_t}{NNP_t} = 1 - \frac{C_t}{NNP_t} - \frac{G_t}{NNP_t}. \tag{4.13}$$

Here, S_t stands for aggregate saving, C_t for aggregate personal consumption expenditures, G_t for government purchases, and NNP_t for the net national product in period t. Equations 4.12 and 4.13, and the fact that the propensity to consume increases with age, imply that the age structure of the population may be potentially important in determining the aggregate saving rate. Figure 4.4 shows male and female populations (actual and projected) for every twentieth year between 1900 and 2080. Clearly visible in the charts is the significant baby boom that begins in the 1940s and traverses through the age profile over time. As is well known, the occurrence of the baby boom, together with a lengthening of the average lifespan, is expected to increase the fraction of the elderly in the population.

Given that the elderly consume more out of lifetime resources than do the young, a significant change in the relative size of the elderly population may be expected to boost aggregate consumption and reduce aggregate saving. How large is this effect? To investigate this question, let us replace the population counts for year t, $p^x_{jt,t}$ in Equation 4.12 with those that are consistent with the population's age profile for year s, $s \neq t$, while maintaining the total population

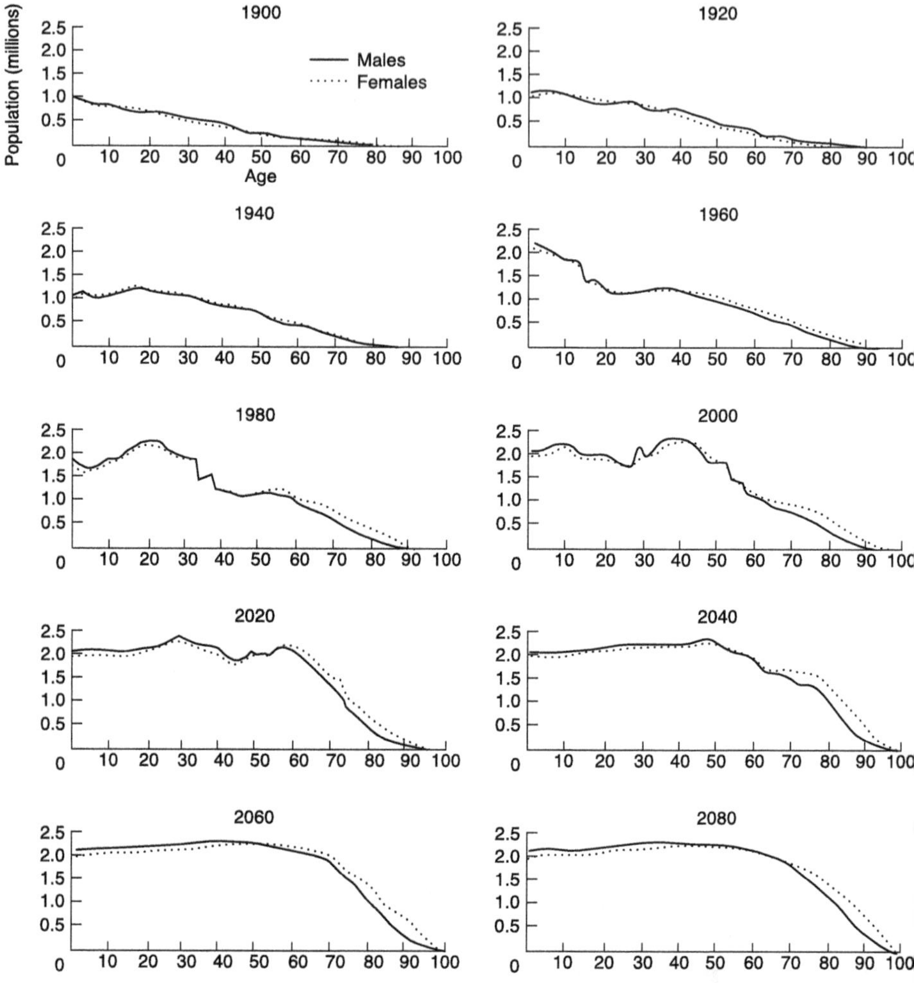

Sources: US censuses (1900–80), population projections of the US Social Security Administration, and author's calculations.

Fig. 4.4. Actual (1900–80) and projected (2000–80) population profiles of the United States, by age and sex

at its year-t level. This experiment isolates the effect of changes in the total population's age structure on the net national saving rate, provided that propensities to consume and per capita resources remain at their year-t (1993) age-specific levels.

Figure 4.5 depicts saving rates resulting from substituting the year-s age structure of the population in Equation 4.12 for s ranging from 1960 to 2030. This time span is shown because the oldest baby boomers entered adulthood during the early 1960s and the youngest boomers will have retired by 2030.

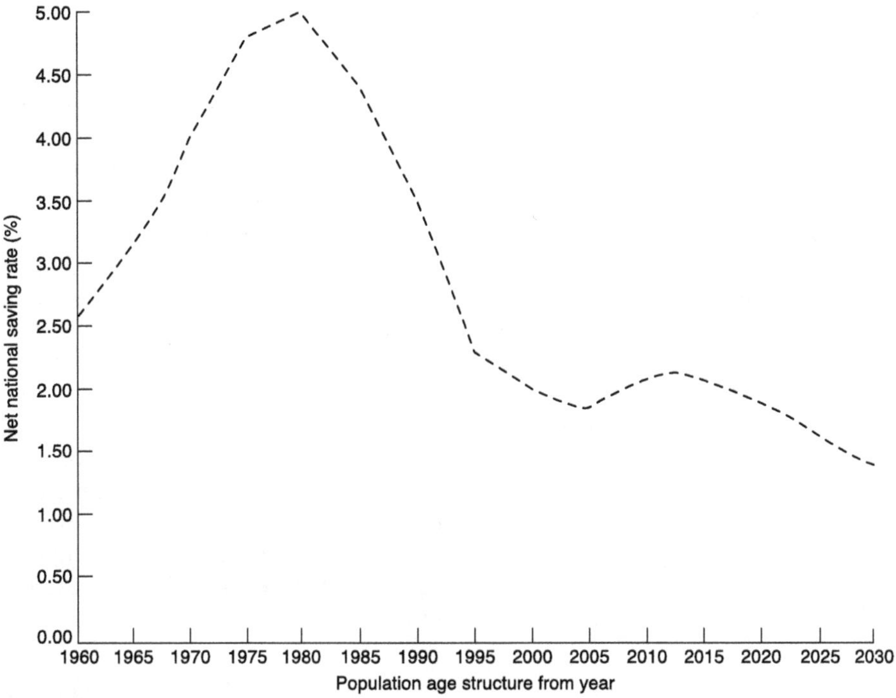

Source: Author's calculations.

Fig. 4.5. Effect of a changing population age structure on aggregate saving

The figure suggests that the effect of population age structure on national saving can be quite substantial. It also shows that the ageing of the US population may have significantly contributed to the decline in US national saving rates that began in the late 1970s and continued through the 1980s and early 1990s.[18]

In 1993 the US aggregate saving rate was 2.7 per cent. Given the population age structure that existed in the late 1970s, when a significant fraction of the population (the baby-boom generations) was in the age groups associated with low consumption, the 1993 saving rate might have been at least 85 per cent higher than its actual level. Figure 4.5 indicates that the US population structure of the twenty-first century is not likely to provide a fillip to national saving. Just after the turn of the century, members of the 1970s baby-boomlet are expected to enter the ages of low consumption propensities while the post-war baby boomers will not yet have entered the ages of significantly higher consumption propensities. Using the population age structure for the year 2010 produces only a slight uptick in the saving rate. Substituting the age structure projected after 2010, however, produces a decline in saving, reflecting a predominant increase in the number of baby boomers in ages with high consumption propensities.

Conclusion

The technique of generational accounting enables the measurement of intergenerational resource transfers that occur through fiscal policy. A generational accounting analysis of the United States shows that current US fiscal policy is unsustainable because its continuation would place immense fiscal burdens on future generations. This conclusion remains robust over a reasonably wide range of assumptions about future discount rates and economic growth rates and over projections of large federal health-care outlays and sizeable population growth: Under an optimistic assumption about health-care provision, about half of future generations' lifetime labour earnings would have to be taxed away, on average. Under an assumption of rapid population growth, the fraction that would have to be taxed away would be 70 per cent.

Prior to 1980 the ongoing demographic transition in the United States probably provided a boost to national saving. Thereafter it probably accounted for a sizeable part of the decline in US national saving rates. In the future any increase in the number of young individuals with low consumption propensities will be offset by the entry of the baby boomers into ages with high consumption propensities. As a result, future demographic changes are likely to exert a further downward pressure on national saving.

Notes

Thanks are due to Felicitie Bell for providing critical data on US population projections and to Laurence Kotlikoff and Robert Willis for their helpful comments. The opinions expressed herein are my own and not necessarily those of the Federal Reserve Bank of Cleveland or of the Federal Reserve System.

1. Resources are, of course, redistributed across generations through a variety of channels, of which public policy is but one. Markets and families are the other two important institutions that redistribute wealth across generations. Markets play a role as young savers and new enterpreneurs purchase housing and capital stocks from older generations and firms. The family plays a role as the elderly provide *inter vivos* transfers and bequeath wealth to their offspring. Intrafamily intergenerational transfers also occur in the form of time and care provided by the young to the old. For a broader discussion and framework, see Ch. 2 in this volume.
2. Fehr and Kotlikoff (1995) use a simulation model to measure the relative sizes of direct and indirect wealth redistribution induced by fiscal policy changes. In many of the cases they analyse, they find that the direct redistribution accounts for most of the total redistribution.
3. In the case of the United States, these data are taken from the Federal Reserve System's *Survey of Consumer Finances,* the Census Bureau's *Current Population Survey,* the Social Security Administration's *Annual Statistical Supplement to the Social Security Bulletin,* the Health Care Financing Administration, and the US Bureau of Economic Analysis's *Survey of Current Business.* For a discussion of the

treatment of individual taxes and transfers, see Auerbach, Gokhale, and Kotlikoff (1991 and 1994).

4. A large chunk of government purchases, such as those for defence and general administration, cannot be attributed to specific age groups. They are attributed equally to all individuals alive at time *t*.
5. Although classified as transfers under National Income and Product Accounts, the latter outlays are treated as government purchases of services because they represent deferred compensation on past services of government employees and military personnel.
6. Note that the summation in the denominator goes to infinity. The population projections extend only through the year 2200. The calculations are adjusted to account for payments by generations born after the year 2200.
7. Lifetime labour income rather than total income is used because income from a normal rate of return on saving out of labour income reflects only an intertemporal reallocation of lifetime resources, not an increase in those resources. Extranormal returns on saving and receipts from intergenerational transfers should be included in the denominator in computations of lifetime net tax rates. This I have not done because of the lack of reliable data.
8. The choice of the productivity growth rate is close to that actually experienced over the last four decades. The discount rate is chosen to reflect the assumption that although future transactions with the government (payment of taxes and receipts of benefits) are not likely to be as risky as the long-term return on private capital (about 9%), they are not entirely risk-free.
9. Generational accounts for other countries have similar age profiles. See, e.g. Gokhale, Raffelhüschen, and Walliser (1995) for the case of Germany; Auerbach *et al.* (1992) for Norway; Franco *et al.* (1994) for Italy; and Oreopoulos (1995) for Canada.
10. To calculate lifetime net tax rates on newborn and future generations, I have assumed that future real labour earnings by age and sex will be the same as those for living generations except for productivity growth. The latter is assumed to be 1.2% per year, which roughly corresponds to that experienced during the period since World War II.
11. In 1995, when I conducted these experiments, the US Congress and the Administration were negotiating a budget package to balance the federal budget by the year 2002. As the new budget agreement is likely to have year-by-year projections of health-care outlays through that year, I have selected 2003 as the year for beginning a policy of stabilizing health-care outlays.
12. The Social Security Administration projects the US population through 2070 for making long-range actuarial projections for the US Social Security system. In my generational accounting calculations, I have used these projections after extending them through 2200. The extended projection uses the Social Security Administration's assumptions about mortality, fertility, and immigration that it has applied to its projections to 2070.
13. The future evolution of fertility, mortality, and immigration rates is uncertain. Even small changes in all three could completely alter the population shares of different generations. This point is exemplified by Ronald Lee in Ch. 2 of this volume. An alternative procedure would be to conduct a similar exercise and estimate the distribution of generational accounts, computing confidence intervals around the point estimates presented in the earlier sections of the current chapter. Such an

analysis is not attempted here, but the procedure I have followed may be viewed as a close substitute.

14. The argument in this section follows that in Gokhale *et al.* (1995).
15. Labour earning and pension profiles for the United States are based on the Census Bureau's *Current Population Surveys*. The relative profiles for private net worth are from the Federal Reserve System's *Survey of Consumer Finances*. The aggregates distributed according to these profiles are from the National Income and Product Accounts, published in the July 1994 *Survey of Current Business*, and from the Federal Reserve System's *Balance Sheets of the U.S. Economy*.
16. I assume that average and marginal propensities to consume out of lifetime resources are equal and depend only on age—a result that emerges when lifetime utility is maximized, subject to the lifetime budget constraint under the life-cycle hypothesis with certainty.
17. Aggregate personal consumption expenditures are those from the National Income and Product Accounts, and the relative profiles for distributing the aggregate are based on the Census Bureau's Consumer Expenditure Surveys of 1987–90. For a detailed description of the method of allocating consumption within households, see Gokhale *et al.* (1995).
18. Changes in the age structure prior to 1975 should have increased US saving rates. Other factors, however, such as shifting age-resource profiles in favour of older generations, may have helped to maintain saving rates. See Gokhale *et al.* (1995) for a description of the evolution of US saving rates during the post-war period and for an analysis of other factors affecting national saving.

Part II

Government-Funded Pension Programmes

5 On the Rate of Return of Unfunded Pension Systems

Jorge Bravo

It has been long recognized that demographic growth is a key factor in rates of return of such transfers as unfunded pension systems. In his seminal paper, Samuelson (1958) showed that in a stationary consumption-loan economy the implicit rate of return (ρ) of a 'pay-as-you-go' transfer system is equal to the population growth rate (n). A new research field, now well developed, sprang from Samuelson's work and that of Diamond (1965) on the basis of overlapping generations models and the study of the associated intergenerational transfers. (See Chapter 2 by R. D. Lee in this volume for a broad, up-to-date assessment of the field.) It is now well known from that research that any upward transfer system, in which resources flow from the young to the older members of a population, benefits from greater demographic growth. In expanding economies, the rate of return of this kind of transfer system should increase in direct proportion to the rate of productivity growth; in fact, it is straightforward to show that, in the context of an equilibrium consumption-loan economy or transfer system, ρ is equal to n plus the annual earnings growth rate.

These insights are simple and useful. However, when one asks more generally about the rate of return of real pension systems, important qualifications to this result must be made. First, and most obviously, not all pensions are financed on a pay-as-you-go basis. The rate of return of fully funded (i.e. capitalization) systems reflects the economic yield of the pension-fund investments. Under some theoretical conditions, demographic and earnings growth can be closely associated with the capital market rate of return, although these associations need not hold in real economies that may not be in general equilibrium or growing along dynamically efficient paths.[1] Second, pay-as-you-go systems can be contribution-defined or benefit-defined and in reality experience temporary disequilibria. In contribution-defined systems, the benefits are calculated as the annuity that corresponds to the present value of lifetime pension taxes (or 'contributions'), and the rate of return is whatever discount rate is used to bring past contributions into present value. In steady-state financial equilibrium, this discount rate must equal n plus the earnings growth rate; but again, this result may not hold in real systems that experience financial disequilibria. The same is true of benefit-defined systems. As this chapter shows, these features imply that the implicit rate of return of the system depends upon the benefit formulas and the financial balance of the system, and in turn condition the effect of demographic and earnings growth.

Analytical Framework

Specific analyses of the role of demographic trends in the rates of return of unfunded pension systems have been carried out by Keyfitz (1985) and Lapkoff (1985, 1991), who developed theoretical models and empirical analyses to study intergenerational inequities in rates of return brought about by unstable age distributions in the United States. Rofman (1993) has examined intragenerational differentials induced by varying mortality patterns, and R. D. Lee (1994*c*) has analysed interethnic income transfers and differences in the system rate of return due to differential demographic patterns in the United States. This chapter draws from some aspects of those studies, but it concentrates on the role played by earnings growth, benefit formulas, and the financial balance of the system in the intergenerational differences in ρ, which previous research has not explored systematically. It is important to note, however, that intragenerational inequities in rates of return can be as large or greater than inequalities across generations.

Most of the analyses of the rate of return have relied on several simplifying assumptions about the value of pensions and the financial stance of the system. In the present discussion I lift some of those assumptions and set out to work within a still simple theoretical framework, which is nonetheless closer to real-world conditions of productivity growth and the institutional rules of the pension systems. As stated above and to be shown in what follows, all of these factors affect the rate of return that people receive from participating in these transfer systems. Nevertheless, my own approach is much more limited and partial in scope than much of the literature on intergenerational transfers. In particular, I restrict my attention to unfunded pensions, ignoring other transfers, capital dilution effects, fertility and mortality distinctions, and general equilibrium issues.

This last restriction is an important one and thus merits a special comment. On the one hand, ignoring the issues of macro-efficiency and general equilibrium may be seen as a severe limitation, as in fact it strongly narrows the kinds of questions that may be posed in relation to the macroeconomy, which are clearly outside the scope of this chapter. On the other hand, the decision to concentrate on the basic accounting relations that describe the unfunded systems has the advantage of providing a sharper focus on the workings of the fundamental elements of such systems, which, as I suggest below, give a reasonable approximation to the first-order effects of the considered exogenous variables. The 'expanded' basic accounting of unfunded systems developed in this chapter could be incorporated into more refined general equilibrium models in future work.

One simplifying assumption I shall keep in the present discussion is that the 'typical' individual life cycle is fixed, characterized by birth at time (and age) 0, entry into the labour force at age a, retirement at age z, and death at age ω. Full age schedules of survivorship and labour-force participation could be introduced without essentially changing the conclusions obtained. The approach of incorporating earnings growth, benefit formulas, and the financial balance in the analysis requires a brief explanation, to which I turn next.

Earnings growth

Medium-and long-term growth in labour productivity and earnings is a distinctive feature of modern economic development. It has been observed during the twentieth century in most countries with available data, despite temporary setbacks, such as those associated with short-term economic cycles. As will be shown next, earnings growth may or may not have consequences on ρ, depending upon the formula used for the calculation of pensions and the policies affecting the financial balance of the pension system in each country. Earnings at age x and time t are denoted by $y(x, t)$. I assume a constant rate of earnings growth of σ per year, so that for any age x and time $t, y(x, t) = y(x, 0)e^{\sigma t}$.

Pension formulas

Pension taxes in most benefit-defined pension systems are set to be a constant fraction (τ) of earnings for all workers. Pension formulas differ from country to country, although most systems define the value of the individual's pension (p) as a product of the individual's 'base salary' (s) and a replacement rate (r); that is, $p = r \times s$. This amount is sometimes added on to a uniform pension not related to the workers' past earnings (see, for example, Bengtsson and Kruse 1992 and Chapter 8 by Blanchet in this volume, on the cases of Sweden and France, respectively). The replacement rate can be the same for all retirees or vary among individuals within a pre-specified scale. For the present purposes, I shall take r to be a fixed percentage representing the average replacement rate in a given country.

The definition of 'base salary' varies more substantially from one country to another. In most Latin American countries, the base salary is calculated as the average of earnings over the last k years prior to retirement (age z), with k equalling one to five or more years. In the United States, s is called the average index of monthly earnings and is obtained as the average of monthly earnings over most or all of the working life, adjusted by overall wage growth. Using the present terminology, one can regard the US index of average monthly earnings as a special case, in which $k = z - a$. Several European countries (e.g. Sweden, France, and Poland) stand somewhere between Latin America and the United States in this regard, with k equal to ten to twenty years. Finally, depending upon the legislation in each country, the base salary may or may not be indexed by overall wage growth. As I shall show next, the specific formula used determines not only the value of pensions but also the effect that other factors have on ρ.

Financial equilibrium and disequilibrium

Pay-as-you-go pension systems are not designed to accumulate substantial funds or debt, but in reality they are rarely, if ever, exactly balanced. Incipient systems tend to show a surplus, given their low retiree/contributor ratio, whereas mature systems tend to display deficits. In Latin America during the 1980s some systems experienced large deficits, due to recessionary economic conditions; and the US Social Security Trust Fund is now starting to build up reserves in anticipation of the retirement of the large baby-boom cohorts in the 2020s. All these examples support the notion that the equilibrium condition that most analyses use is rarely followed in practice. More important, as will be shown below, financial disequilibria and therefore policies regarding the financial balance of the system (F) are key determinants of ρ.

Many other factors can, at least potentially, affect the rate of return that individuals obtain from participating in unfunded pension systems. Among them, special mention must be made of demographic non-stability. Keyfitz (1985) and Lapkoff (1985, 1991) have shown, theoretically and for the case of the United States, that non-stability can have significant consequences on the rate of return obtained by various birth cohorts. This conclusion is reached under the premiss that the pension system's budget is held in balance over time, and that temporary demographic fluctuations are compensated by adjustments in taxes or benefits. Here I adopt the view that the financial balance can often be the *result* of defined benefits and labour market and demographic trends as well as a pivot around which taxes, benefits, and eligibility requirements are modified.

The present analysis applies mainly to steady states. I do not consider demographic non-stability explicitly, although some of my conclusions apply to systems with non-stable populations as well. I abstract from other factors, such as inflation-adjustment mechanisms and special legislation or rules affecting population sub-groups, by assuming that *real* taxes and benefits (i.e. fully adjusted by inflation) and average cohort conditions (those of 'typical' individuals) obtain throughout.

Of the elements analysed in this chapter, two are macrolevel and largely exogenous from the point of view of the social security administrations: demographic trends and productivity growth. The other two, on the other hand—benefit rules and the system's financial balance—can be and are used in practice as policy variables. The former, together with eligibility requirements, are usually used as instruments to achieve given goals affecting the latter. It is often overlooked, however, that changes in both these sets of policy variables modify the rate of return that different generational groups obtain from participating in the system. The remainder of this chapter shows how changes in the pension formulas and in the financial balance affect the degree to which demographic and earnings growth influence ρ.

Analysis

The notation referred to so far can be summarized as follows:

a = age at entry to labour force
z = age at retirement from labour force
ω = age at death
ρ = the (implicit) rate of return that individuals obtain by participating in a pay-as-you-go pension system
n = (stable) population growth rate
$y(x,t)$ = labour earnings per worker aged x at time t
σ = earnings growth rate
τ = pension tax rate
r = replacement rate
s = base salary; calculated as s = mean y over k years prior to z, with $0 \leq k \leq z - a$
p = value of pension ($p = r \times s$)
F = financial balance of the pension system, expressed as a fraction of total pension taxes

ρ under various pension formulas

Remember that, in most unfunded systems that are benefit-defined, the value of pensions is the product of the replacement rate and the base salary. Letting X be the age interval that corresponds to the base salary defined in the pension formula, we can denote base earnings by $y(X, X)$. More precisely stated, $y(X, X)$ is the average of earnings over $x \in X$ and $t \in X$, where the second argument of the y function, time, is measured with respect to the individual's or cohort's birth. Figure 5.1 provides a graphical image of the age-earnings profiles and related notation. $W = (a, z)$ denotes the working-age interval, $X = (z - k, z)$ the age interval of base earnings, $R = (\omega, z)$ the retirement age interval, and A_W, A_X, and A_R their respective means.

In some cases, such as in the US pension system, base earnings are adjusted for overall wage growth. To allow for this possibility, I express the value of the annual pension as

$$p = ry(X, X)e^{i(A_R - A_X)\sigma}, \qquad (5.1)$$

where i equals 1 if the base salary is fully adjusted by overall wage growth and zero if not.

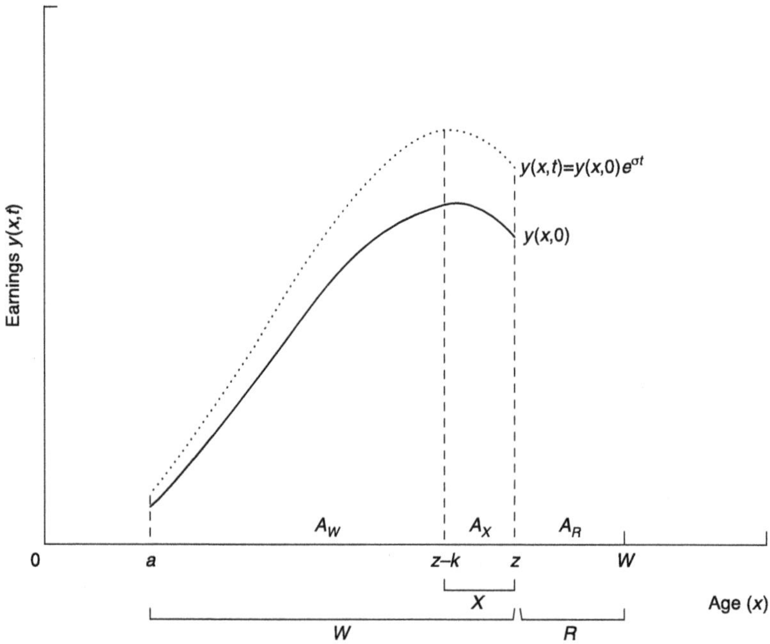

Fig. 5.1. Age-earnings profiles

The implicit rate of return of participating in the system ρ must satisfy the life-cycle constraint, whereby the discounted value of lifetime contributions equals the discounted value of lifetime benefits:

$$\int_a^z \tau y(x,x)e^{-\rho x}dx = \int_z^\omega ry(X,X)e^{i(A_R-A_X)\sigma}e^{-\rho x}dx. \tag{5.2}$$

The length of working life, $z-a$, will be abbreviated by LW and the length of retirement life, $w-z$, by LR. Using an approximation for the e^{-rx} terms in both sides of Equation 5.2 yields, approximately,

$$e^{(A_R-A_w)\rho} = \frac{r}{\tau}\left(\frac{LR}{LW}\right)\frac{y(X,X)}{y(W,W)}e^{i(A_R-A_X)\sigma}. \tag{5.3}$$

Because earnings grow at an annual rate σ, $y(X,X)/y(W,W)$ may be written as

$$\frac{y(X,X)}{y(W,W)} = \frac{y(X,X}{y(W,X)}\frac{y(W,X)}{y(W,W)} = \frac{y(X,X)}{y(W,X)}e^{(A_X-A_W)^\sigma}. \tag{5.4}$$

Substituting Equation 5.4 in Equation 5.3 and taking logs, I obtain a general expression for the rate of return of the system:

$$\rho = \frac{1}{(A_R-A_W)}\left[\ln\left(\frac{r}{\tau}\right)+\ln\left(\frac{LR}{LW}\right)+\ln\left(\frac{y(X,X)}{y(W,X)}\right)+(A_X-A_W)\sigma+i(A_R-A_X)\sigma\right]. \tag{5.5}$$

ρ is seen to depend, in direct proportion, on (1) the ratio of the replacement rate to the tax rate of the system (r/τ); (2) the relative length of life in retirement LR with respect to working life LW; (3) the age profile of earnings $y(x, t)$ and the legal norms regarding X; (4) the interaction between the rate of growth of earnings and the difference between the mean timing of base earnings (A_X) instituted in the pension formula and the timing of tax payments (A_W) within the life cycle; and (5) the adjustment for overall wage growth. In particular, Equation 5.5 shows that there are a couple of ways to capture productivity growth into ρ. This can be achieved either by an explicit adjustment for overall growth (last term in Equation 5.5) or, implicitly, by setting the timing of base earnings close to the time of retirement (third and fourth terms). The above expressions hold for any benefit-defined system regardless of the population age structure and growth, be it stable or not, as long as the set parameters are held at their fixed values over the individual's (or cohort's) adult lifetime.

Next, we examine a few special cases. First, let us take a benchmark case in which base earnings are lifetime earnings (so that $k = z - a$, $X = W$ and $A_X = A_W$), with no indexing for overall wage increases ($i = 0$). The last three terms of Equation 5.5 vanish, resulting in a rate of return equal to

$$\rho_1 = \frac{1}{(A_R - A_W)} \left[\ln\left(\frac{r}{\tau}\right) + \ln\left(\frac{LR}{LW}\right) \right] = \rho_{bench}. \tag{5.6}$$

I shall refer to this rate of return as the benchmark ρ, or ρ_{bench}. Now let us take a second case, such as the United States, where base earnings are lifetime earnings ($X = W$ and $A_X = A_W$) with full wage growth indexing ($I = 1$). The third and fourth terms of Equation 5.5 vanish again, but the last term becomes $(A_R - A_W)\sigma$, which implies that an amount equal to σ gets added to the benchmark ρ:

$$\rho_2 = \rho_{bench} + \sigma. \tag{5.7}$$

Finally, let us take the third case of some European and many Latin American countries, where no such indexing takes place ($I = 0$) but where k is small compared with $z - a$, and thus A_X is near z. One may take $a = 20$, $z = 60$, $\omega = 80$, and, at the limit, $A_X = 60$. In this case, $(A_X - A_W)/(A_R - A_W) = (60 - 40)/(70 - 40) = \frac{2}{3}$, so that ρ is

$$\rho_3 = \rho_{bench} + \frac{\ln\left(\frac{y(X, X)}{y(W, X)}\right)}{30} + \frac{2}{3}\sigma, \tag{5.8}$$

—that is to say, more than two-thirds of σ greater than ρ without productivity growth. This implies that instituting the period of base earnings (X) close to the time of retirement (z) in the pension formula captures most of the overall productivity growth in the value of pensions, even with no explicit indexing.

Figure 5.2 shows how ρ varies with σ according to which type of benefit formula is in place. A base $y(x, t)$ of 1 per cent per year is obtained in this figure,

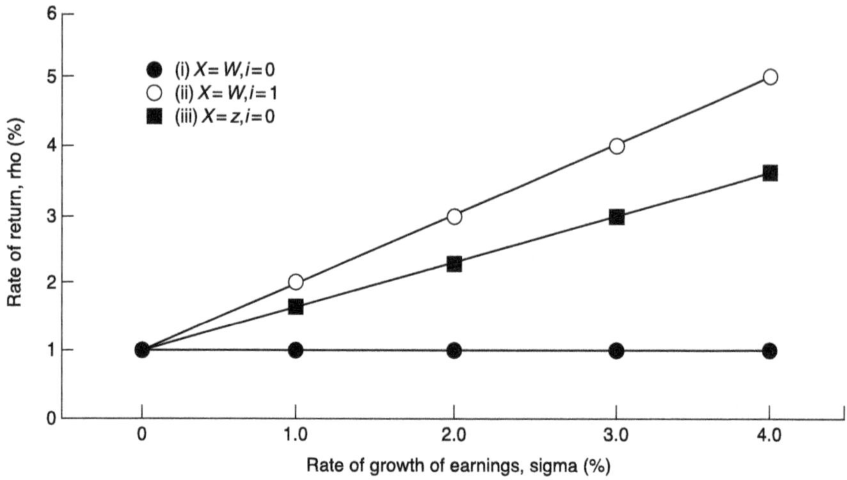

Assumptions: $r/\tau = 4$, $a = 20$, $z = 60$, $\omega = 80$, $y(X, X) = y(W, X)$.
Sources: Equations 5.6 to 5.8

Fig. 5.2. Rho under alternative pension formulas and earnings growth rates

if we assume that $r/\tau = 4$, $a = 20$, $z = 60$, $\omega = 80$, and $y(X,X) = y(W,X)$. It is noteworthy that in neither of these cases does population growth have an effect on ρ; the link between n and ρ is broken by the dominance of benefit formulas (over financial balance rules) in benefit-defined systems. Figure 5.2 also illustrates the extent to which the link between σ and ρ is conditioned by the kind of pension formula that is in force. When the first formula (base earnings equal lifetime earnings, no indexing) is in place, productivity growth does not affect the rate of return. The discrepancy between the base ρ and the rates obtained under the alternative pension formulas increases with ρ and can be quite substantial for high wage-growth economies. It is important to note that the analysis thus far has proceeded under the general premiss that all key parameters, including r/τ, remain constant over time.

ρ and the financial balance

So far I have not explicitly considered the financial side of the system. Nonetheless, if the system is equilibrated in a stationary economy, adding productivity growth (and, let us assume, also earnings growth) will enlarge the tax base and, for fixed r and τ, will lead to a surplus. The government of the country where this happens may decide to spend this extra income in some arbitrary fashion, to save it by placing it into a reserve fund, or to transfer it back to wage earners through tax cuts. Alternatively, it may decide to distribute it among retirees by inflating the value of pensions up to the point where the system is equilibrated again.

These alternative policies will have different effects on the return that individuals obtain from the system. I now introduce some equations that will help to make explicit the role of financial factors. First, note that currently retired persons have, approximately, average age A_R, and they receive a pension proportional to a base salary that corresponds to their earnings $A_R - A_X$ years ago. For brevity's sake, I denote the lag between the present (time t) and the timing of the base earnings by $\lambda_t = t - (A_R - A_X)$. The financial balance of the system at any time t, expressed as a fraction of total taxes, can be written as

$$F_t = 1 - \frac{r\, y(X, \lambda_t)}{\tau\, y(W, t)} e^{i(A_R - A_X)\sigma} D_t, \tag{5.9}$$

where D_t is the system's dependency ratio—i.e. the ratio of the retired to the economically active population (this is basically the same as equation 2 in Bravo (1994), except for a change in notation and the adjustment factor). This equation, unlike those of Tuljapurkar and Lee (Chapter 9 in this volume), does not take into account interest receipts or payments arising from the cumulated balance of the reserve fund. There is some justification for this omission, aside from mathematical simplicity, because in many cases system imbalances are absorbed by the general government budget, so that the associated interest income or payments are treated exogenously to the system accounts.[2] As

$$\frac{y(X, \lambda_t)}{y(W, t)} = \frac{y(X, \lambda_t)}{y(W, \lambda_t)} e^{-(A_R - A_X)\sigma},$$

then

$$F_t = 1 - \frac{r\, y(X, \lambda_t)}{\tau\, y(W, \lambda_t)} e^{-(1-i)(A_R - A_X)\sigma} D_t \tag{5.10}$$

and

$$\frac{r}{\tau} = \left(\frac{1 - F_t}{D_t}\right) \frac{y(W, \lambda_t)}{y(X, \lambda_t)} e^{(1-i)(A_R - A_X)\sigma}. \tag{5.11}$$

Equation 5.11 gives the replacement/tax ratio compatible with given benefit rules, earnings growth rate, adjustment mechanisms, demographic structure, and financial balance. For the comparative static analysis that follows, I shall employ the fiction of a representative individual or cohort. For this 'typical' individual, what matters are the F_t and D_t to which he is subject over his lifetime, the averages of which I shall denote by F and D, respectively. According to the assumptions made, the (proportional) *shape* of the earnings curve by age is constant over time. This implies that substitution of Equation 5.11 in Equation 5.5 leads to the cancellation of the y terms, and it follows that

$$\rho = \frac{1}{(A_R - A_W)} \left[\ln\left(\frac{1 - F}{D}\right) + \ln\left(\frac{LR}{LW}\right)\right] + \sigma. \tag{5.12}$$

This gives a simple quantitative relationship between ρ and the system's financial balance and the dependency ratio, in addition to other factors already discussed (fraction of life in retirement and σ). Caution should be taken when making welfare comparisons on the basis of this equation. A strict welfare interpretation of ρ in this context holds only when the system imbalances are not compensated by other direct or indirect taxes or transfers over the lifetime of the cohort in question. (This would be the case, for example, of a system that experienced temporary imbalances but was nonetheless actuarially equilibrated.) If, for example, a pension system deficit was totally financed with general taxes levied on the reference generation, ρ would in fact be equivalent to the rate of return under financial equilibrium; the same would be true if the money amount of a surplus was returned in full to the reference cohort in the form of public transfers. A general treatment of the many different possibilities in this regard would require a much lengthier discussion than this chapter allows. For two good studies that examine different financing mechanisms in the Chilean case, see Arrau (1991) and Cifuentes (1995).

With these precautions in mind, Equation 5.12 shows that if the government runs a deficit to finance a given level of pension outlays, individuals receive a higher rate of return than in the scenario in which the value of pensions is deflated or taxes are inflated to equilibrate the system's budget. Likewise, the rate of return is smaller when the government runs a surplus, instead of inflating pensions or reducing taxes to achieve financial equilibrium. Seen from a slightly different perspective, it is apparent that governments can—and should, from an intergenerational welfare standpoint—use temporary surpluses and deficits for the purpose of minimizing inequalities in rates of return of different cohorts. Chronic financial disequilibria that lead to actuarial deficits are another matter, for they eventually require some kind of adjustment in the system's parameters. The point stressed here is simply that policy analyses and definitions should take into account both intergenerational equity and financial aspects because they are closely interrelated. All too frequently, the greater public visibility of financial problems leads to policy measures that ignore and often damage intergenerational equity.

A number of special cases can be hypothesized. Let us next examine several important ones.

First, let us consider the 'pure' equilibrium pay-as-you-go case, in which F_t is set at zero for all relevant t. After the substitution of $F = 0$ in Equation 5.12, ρ becomes

$$\rho_{F=0} = \eta + \sigma,$$

where

$$\eta = \frac{\ln(\frac{LR}{LW}) - \ln(D)}{(A_R - A_W)} \tag{5.13}$$

may be interpreted as the average implicit period population growth rate, measured in terms of the economically active population with respect to the

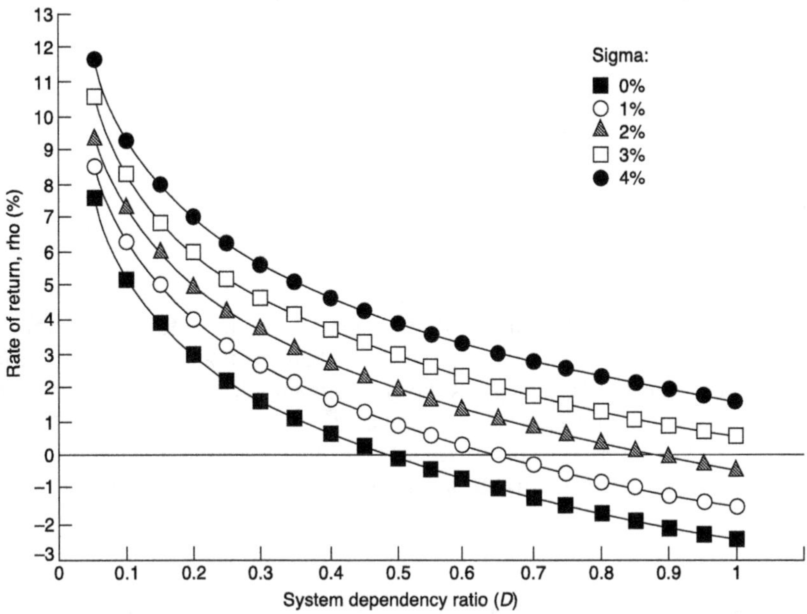

Assumptions: $r/\tau = 4$, $a = 20$, $z = 60$, $\omega = 80$, $y(X, X) = y(W, X)$.
Source: Equation 5.13.

Fig. 5.3. Balanced-budget rho

retired. When the population is stable, η coincides with the stable population growth rate, n, so that ρ becomes $n + \sigma$, as expected. Note that both the stable and the non-stable results are valid regardless of the pension formula.

Figure 5.3 shows levels of balanced-budget (under various levels of the dependency ratio and earning growth rate. The values are obtained under the same set of assumptions for age of entry, retirement, and death as in Figure 5.2. The gradient is clearly non-linear: very high rates of return can be sustained in countries in the early stages of the demographic transition or with incipient systems, or both. The return falls rapidly as the system approaches maturity, but falls off more gradually after dependency ratios of 0.4 to 0.5 are achieved. Positive rates of return appear to be possible for economies growing at 2 per cent per year or more, even in countries with older populations and high dependency ratios. In stagnating economies ($\sigma = 0$), negative rates of return would set in for dependency ratios above 0.5, a level being approached by the countries with the most aged populations in Latin America, such as Argentina and Uruguay.

Second, let us consider the case of population stability. Because in this case

$$D = \left(\frac{LR}{LW}\right)e^{-(A_R - A_W)n}, \tag{5.14}$$

it can be shown that Equation 5.12 reduces to

$$\rho_{N\ stable} = \frac{\ln(1-F)}{(A_R - A_W)} + (n+\sigma) \tag{5.15}$$

This confirms my earlier observations about the inverse relationship between the financial balance and ρ. If F = 0, it is also confirmed that, in a stable-population, equilibrium pay-as-you-go system,

$$\rho_{F=0,\ N\ stable} = n + \sigma, \tag{5.16}$$

which is basically the 'biological' rate-of-return result, adding the effect of earnings growth. Note that these results are independent of the benefit formula and even of the *type* of unfunded system (benefit-defined or contribution-defined). In other words, as long as the government sticks to a balanced-budget policy, it does not matter how it enunciates the rules of the system because participants will in any case pay taxes and receive benefits in flows equivalent to an implicit rate of return equal to $\eta + \sigma$, or $n + \sigma$ if the population is stable.[3]

Three examples

To illustrate the effects of changes in eligibility requirements and pension formulas on intergenerational equity and the financial balance, I next make a rough assessment of some policy changes in three Latin American countries on the basis of the derived formulas. In all of the following examples, I assume that a = 20, ω = 80, σ = 0.01, and $y(X,X) = y(W,X)$. All other parameters are derived from specific country data. For simplicity, the legal retirement age for men is adopted in the calculations because men comprise a large proportion of the labour force in the three countries.

The ρ estimates presented are conservative, as I use the 'basic' (i.e. minimal) replacement rate of each country and assume that contributions are made over the whole working-age range. That is not always the case in practice.

Colombia

Until recently, the Colombian pension system had a basic replacement rate of $r = 0.45$, a pension tax rate of $\tau = 0.065$, and a legal retirement age of $z = 60$ years. Base earnings were calculated as the average of earnings over the last $k = 3$ years before retirement. A recent government reform proposal increases the tax rate to about 0.135, among other measures. Substituting these values in Equation 5.5, I obtain a value of ρ of 4.76 per cent for the conditions before 1995 and a ρ of 2.32 per cent after the tax increase. Thus an apparently modest change in the pension tax rate has reduced to one-half the rate or return of all those entering the labour force from 1995 onward. For those previously in the labour force the reduction will be smaller: it will be lower for the generations that were, by 1995, closer to the time of retirement and greater for the younger workers. As per Equation 5.10, the tax increase translates into a 38 per cent improvement in the system's balance.

Uruguay

Until 1980 Uruguay had $r = 0.60$, $\tau = 0.27$, $z = 60$, and $k = 3$. From that year onward, new legislation established adjustments of the value of pensions by economy-wide wage growth. In terms of Equation 5.5, this means that $i = 1$ starting in 1980. These conditions yield $\rho = 0.97$ per cent before 1980 and a rise of ρ to 1.35 per cent for all those workers who retired after the legislation became effective. Those generations that had retired prior to the new indexing law have benefited by only a small fraction of that change, the benefit being lower for the older retired generations. The reason why the effect of wage indexation is so small in this case is that (as per Equations 5.5 and 5.8) most of the effect of earnings growth was already being captured by the benefit formula, which puts base earnings very close to the moment of retirement. (Equation 5.5 makes clear that the effect of earnings growth cannot be greater than ρ.) The indexing benefit has been obtained at the cost of raising the deficit by about 8 per cent of the system's receipts.

Chile

Prior to 1979 the Chilean pension system was financed through pay-as-you-go principles, with $r = 0.50$, $\tau = 0.19$, $z = 60$, and $k = 5$. In that year a new retirement age of 65 years was established, and two years later a reform of the system created a new individual-capitalization system. Subscription to the new system has been obligatory for all new entrants to the labour force since 1981 but was voluntary for those who were already working at the time of the reform. For those who remained in the unfunded regime, the increase in the legal retirement age meant that they would spend a smaller proportion of their adult lives in retirement, thus lowering their implicit rate of return. Specifically, the basic ρ was about 1.50 per cent until 1981 and fell to about 0.71 per cent for the generations retiring after that year.

This result, like the foregoing ones, can also be expressed in terms of contribution rates or lifetime projected pension-system wealth by means of a simple function of ρ and a given discount rate. The effects, estimated in terms of those variables, are similar to those obtained by Arrau (1991) and Cifuentes (1994 and 1995) by means of general equilibrium models (see note 5). In particular, Arrau's observation that the only significant impact of the change in the retirement age is on the pension system variables (Arrau 1991: 13) is consistent with the present analysis.[4]

It is also important to note that raising the retirement age need not lead to intergenerational inequities if the retirement life span is increasing in an appropriate proportion. In the case of Chile, for the increase in retirement age to be neutral in terms of intergenerational equity, an increase in life expectancy at age 60 of some eight years would have been required for all those affected by the five-year increase in the age at retirement.

These results seem significant because they measure only single-policy, marginal effects. In many Latin American countries, more comprehensive policy packages, including increases in retirement age, tax increases, and more stringent eligibility requirements, are considered in current reform discussions.

Conclusions

The main ideas of this chapter can be summarized as follows. Earnings growth, benefit formulas, the pension system's financial balance, and demographic trends can affect the rate of return (ρ) of the system. In benefit-defined systems, when pension formulas dominate, the first two factors interact in their effects on ρ; but population growth (n) plays no direct role in its determination. When a given financial policy dominates (for example, the rule of balanced budget), the benefit formula and whether the system is benefit- or contribution-defined are irrelevant (Equations 5.13, 5.15, and 5.16). More specifically:

1. In benefit-defined systems, pension formulas condition the degree to which earnings growth (σ) influences ρ. Indexing base earnings by overall wage growth and setting the timing of base earnings in the pension formula close to the moment of retirement are two ways of capturing productivity growth in the value of pensions and, in that way, in ρ (Equations 5.5 to 5.8).
2. The system's financial balance, and what the government does about it, has important consequences for the value of ρ (Equations 5.12 to 5.16). The government can—and should, from an intergenerational welfare standpoint—use temporary surpluses and deficits to reduce intergenerational inequity in rates of return. Certain policies, such as increasing the legal retirement age, can, if properly implemented, help to improve both the financial stance and the equity of the system.
3. If the system maintains financial equilibrium over time, eligibility requirements, benefit formulas, and even whether the system is benefit-or contribution-defined do not affect ρ, as participants in fact pay taxes and receive benefits in amounts that correspond to an implicit rate of return equal to $\eta + \sigma$, or to $n + \sigma$ if the population is stable (Equations 5.13 and 5.16). In many empirical cases, however, where the system is not in financial equilibrium all the time, the rules defining base earnings, tax and benefit rates, the legal retirement age, and indexing are key determinants of the system's rate of return. Normally, changes in these variables are induced solely by financial considerations; this analysis shows that these changes have significant intergenerational distributive consequences that should also be taken into account when policies are defined in this area.

The analysis developed here provides the direct, first-order effects of certain perturbations in the variables considered. It is not clear whether these first-order effects could be dominated or overwhelmed by higher-order, general equilibrium forces, in spite of the fact that the rough estimates made for the case of Chile suggest that they tend not to. This is an open question that remains to be explored more carefully in future research.

Notes

I thank Ronald D. Lee and Antoine Bommier for useful comments on the initial notes that led to this chapter.

1. In standard (Phelps-type) economic growth models, the capital/labour ratio is maximized when the rate of return of capital equals the population growth rate, whereas in dynamically efficient settings the steady-state rate of return to financial market investments should be larger than the growth rate of the wage mass. The partial equilibrium analysis in this chapter makes no assumptions about whether these conditions are met or not.
2. Omitting interest from this analysis does not make much quantitative difference if financial imbalances are temporary and relatively small, but it could be important where substantial reserves are accumulated, such as in the United States in the 1990s and coming decades.
3. Contribution-defined systems may differ from benefit-defined ones in other respects, such as in the incentives to contribute over the entire lifetime, which is less clear in benefit-defined systems that specify base earnings over the last few years before retirement. If individuals evaded contributions during the earlier (non-base salary) period as a consequence, then a benefit-defined system would find it more difficult to achieve financial equilibrium.
4. Changes in ρ can also be expressed in terms of changes in the contribution rate τ or the expected pension system lifetime wealth. Arrau (1991) assesses the effect of the change in retirement age (z) in Chile by means of a general equilibrium (Auerbach-type) model, estimating that the equilibrium contribution rate decreases by about 9.9% (0.148 – 0.049) when z changes from 55 to 65 years. Using Equation 5.11 of this chapter, with the same empirical parameters as in Arrau, I estimate the change to be about 9.1% (0.148 – 0.057). When the change in retirement age is the only perturbation considered, Arrau shows that the macroeconomic variables other than those of the pension system are not significantly affected, which provides some validation of the partial equilibrium analysis done here. Whether this result holds more generally, however, is an open question.

   Cifuentes (1994 and 1995) estimates the welfare effect of the change of z from 60 to 65 years, with a general equilibrium model similar to that of Arrau. In the 1994 paper, the largest reduction in welfare falls on those who were around 55 years by the time of the reform and is estimated to vary from 9.4 to 11.4%, depending upon the method used to finance the transition to the fully funded regime. Using the same empirical parameters as in that paper, I estimate a reduction in pension lifetime wealth of 7 to 10%, for discount rates of 0.10 and 0.09, respectively. In Cifuentes's 1995 paper, he estimates the welfare reduction to range between 13 and 17% for the aforementioned cohort. Using the same parameters as in that paper (including a discount rate of 0.08) and the equations in this chapter, I estimate the wealth reduction to be about 13%. Thus, at least in the particular case of the change in retirement age in Chile, the bulk of the pension system effects produced in the general equilibrium economy seem to be captured reasonably well by the much more parsimonious accounting framework developed here.

6 Moving Social Security towards Fully Funded Schemes: Who Pays the Cost?

Rafael P. Rofman

Analysing the costs involved in social security reforms is not an easy task. In theory, assessing the cost of closing down a balanced pay-as-you-go system and replacing it with a pure fully funded one should be simple because it requires only an estimation of the expenditures necessary to continue paying benefits to older retirees and eventually to compensate those workers who contributed to the pay-as-you-go system. Most reforms, however, aim to replace pay-as-you-go schemes made seriously unstable by deficits and other problems with multi-pillar systems, which include elements of both pay-as-you-go and fully funded schemes. In addition, most reforms include some measures that improve the performance of the systems, such as increasing contribution tax rates or raising minimum ages for retirement. These changes should not be confused with introducing a fully funded scheme, for they could be applied without modifying the basic pay-as-you-go scheme of the old systems. In that sense, it is necessary to disentangle the effects of these corrective measures from those of creating a new, fully funded system.

This chapter first describes the background of the social security reforms in Latin America, then discusses the most important causes of the systems' crises and presents the main characteristics of the new, reformed systems. Next, it reviews a few basic concepts necessary to organize the discussion of the transition costs, taking into consideration the problems of the time frame used for analysis and the need to compare normative with real-world systems. A simple model is presented that, by formalizing the basic equations of pay-as-you-go and multi-pillar systems, makes it possible to frame the problem of transition costs. A final section describes the social security system of Argentina, including its main characteristics before 1994 and the main changes introduced by that year's reform. An estimate of the transition cost is presented, as well as a description of the main mechanisms used to finance it.

Social Security Systems in Latin America

Throughout most of Latin America social security systems have been facing growing financial difficulties in recent decades as a result of population ageing, poor administration and planning, and unexpected side effects of economic processes. These problems thus have three dimensions: demographic, institutional, and socio-economic.

As a result of the demographic transition, most Latin American countries are experiencing a sustained ageing process that started in the 1960s and is increasing its pace. The region's old-age dependency ratio—that is, the number of individuals 65 years old and older per 100 individuals aged 15 to 64—rose from 6 to 8.4 per cent between 1950 and 1995 and is expected to reach a level of 26 per cent by the year 2050 (UN, Population Division 1994). The population ageing process did not begin at the same time in every Latin American country and has not developed at a uniform pace. For example, in 1950 Uruguay's dependency ratio was more than twice the Latin American average and 66 per cent higher than in any other major country of the region, and it will continue to be the highest until 2030. The evolution of the dependency ratio for the region and several countries that have reformed, or are in the process of reforming, their social security systems can be seen in Figure 6.1. The pace of the ageing process varies, mostly because of short-term variations in fertility.

The ageing process is reflected in the basic relations of a pay-as-you-go scheme. On the assumption that all individuals between ages 15 and 64 are active workers and all those 65 and over are retired, a contribution tax of 10 per cent of salaries would generate an average replacement rate that would decline from slightly more than 160 per cent in 1950 to less than 40 per cent in 2050 for the region as a whole (Figure 6.2). The replacement rate is defined as the percentage of current active workers' average wage received by current retirees as an average benefit. The evolution of the potential replacement rate varies

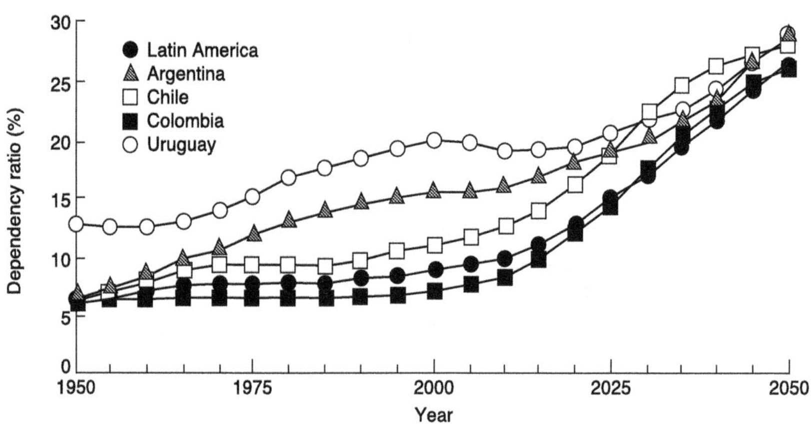

Note: Ratios for 1950–90 are actual ratios based on population estimates. Ratios for 1995–2050 are based on population projections.

Fig. 6.1. Old-age dependency ratios: Latin America and selected countries: 1950–2050

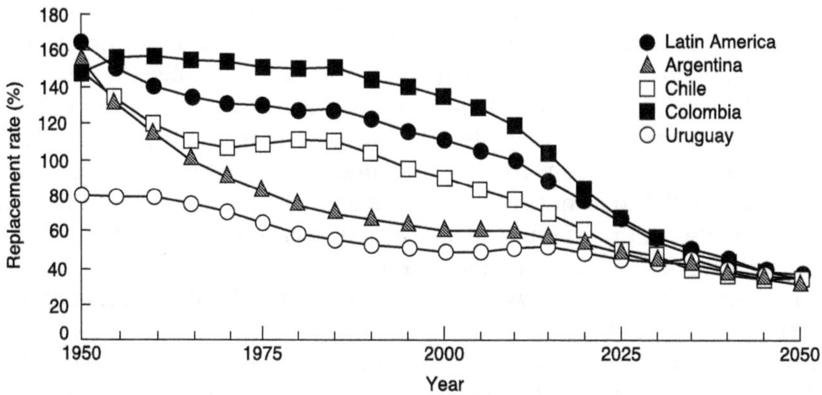

Fig. 6.2. Replacement rate in a pay-as-you-go scheme, assuming a constant contribution tax rate of 10 per cent and full coverage: Latin America and selected countries: 1950–2050

among the countries considered. Again, Uruguay has the least ability to offer generous benefits to its retirees, and Argentina appears to be in the second most difficult position during most of the period considered. The effects of short-term variations in fertility can be seen clearly in the non-linear trends of the replacement rates.

Latin America's social security systems were created, in most cases, in response to pressure from groups interested in gaining benefits for themselves. In his studies of those systems, Mesa-Lago (1978, 1989, 1994) has shown how the fragmentary and uncoordinated characteristics of the systems led to serious inequities in benefits, the minimum age for retirement, and the minimum number of contributions. Those differences were slowly eliminated in most countries, and by the 1980s the more mature systems had common rules that applied to most workers. In all cases the institutional and socio-economic settings of the systems can be assessed according to five characteristics: whether affiliation is compulsory, minimum ages for retirement, the minimum number of years of contributions for retirement, the average contribution tax rate, and the average replacement rate.

Affiliation with pay-as-you-go schemes has traditionally been compulsory in most countries, as a mechanism to reduce the negative effects of myopia and self-selection. In some cases, self-employed workers were not obliged to participate and civil servants had their own closed system, but the national systems were compulsory for most of the labour force. Nevertheless, compliance has not always been as complete as expected. Several socio-economic problems, including the widespread informality in Latin America's developing economies, have reduced the number of contributors to about 50 per cent of the labour force, while the relaxed enforcement of rules for obtaining retirement benefits have made coverage in old age much broader.

Minimum ages for retirement in the old pay-as-you-go programmes were, in most cases, 60 years for men and 55 for women. This low retirement age generated a high dependency ratio in the system, seriously affecting their financial equilibrium. In addition, the minimal number of years that workers were required to contribute to a system before becoming eligible for retirement benefits varied widely from country to country—from as little as five years in Brazil (until 1991) to as much as thirty years in Uruguay. Because of the weak regulatory system, these minimum ages were sometimes ignored, worsening the financial situation. As an example, data for 1995 show that approximately 25,000 retirees in Argentina were younger than the official minimum ages for retirement (ANSeS 1995*b*).

Finally, contribution tax rates and replacement rates in the old systems varied widely. In general, contribution rates were a fixed proportion of wages (being as high as 26 to 30 per cent in Uruguay and Argentina and as low as 6.5 per cent in Colombia). Replacement rates were determined by workers' reference incomes (usually the average for the last few years in the labour force), the number of years of contributions, and the age at retirement. The resulting replacement rates were around 70 to 90 per cent of the reference income.

The combination of ageing populations, widespread evasion of contributions, low requirements on age at retirement, and generosity in benefits led, unavoidably, to crises in the systems. Combined with a political climate favourable to privatization, the crises prompted efforts to reform the systems.

Beginning with Chile in 1981, several retirement systems in Latin America were redesigned, becoming mixed models, with some fully funded and others having pay-as-you-go characteristics. In most cases the new systems were designed as multi-pillar schemes, following a model that has had strong support from international agencies and has been officially supported by them since the mid-1990s (World Bank 1994). In no case did the reforms modify the rules applied to workers already retired (henceforth called 'old retirees'). Those persons continued to receive benefits according to the rules current at the time of their retirement, although the mechanism used to maintain real values of benefits was changed in several cases. Moreover, workers in the labour force at the time of the reform ('old workers') were given the choice of joining the new, fully funded scheme or remaining in the pay-as-you-go scheme, which was, in most cases, modified somewhat. This choice was open to all workers in some countries, whereas in others it was limited to certain age groups.

For workers who would enter the labour force after the reform ('new workers') two distinct approaches were followed. Several countries, including Chile and Peru (which reformed their systems in 1993), made affiliation with the fully funded system compulsory for new workers. Others, such as Colombia in 1993 and Argentina in 1994, permitted new workers to choose between pay-as-you-go and fully funded schemes. The reforms included mechanisms for both contributions and benefits.

On the contribution side, the employees' tax rates were increased in most cases, although in Peru the increase was offset by a mandatory increase in salaries. Chile and Peru eliminated employers' contributions, but elsewhere those contributions were maintained and applied to finance the new pay-as-you-go schemes.

As for benefits, within a fully funded scheme the contributions of workers who join it are deposited in individual accounts that are managed by an investment company, which may be privately owned. Contributions made during a worker's active life are accumulated until the worker reaches the minimum age and number of years of contributions for retirement. At that point the funds in the individual account are used to finance an annuity-like benefit. Of course, the magnitude of the benefit depends upon several factors, including the amounts contributed, the conditions of financial markets, and the life expectancy of the retiring worker. In several programmes, workers must also cover the cost of life and disability insurance. Some programmes, such as Argentina's, deduct this cost (approximately 2 to 2.5 per cent of covered wages) from the workers' contributions, whereas others, such as those in Chile and Peru, cover it with an additional contribution. An administrative fee (usually around 1 to 1.5 per cent of wages) is also charged.

The contributions of workers who have stayed in the pay-as-you-go scheme will continue to finance current benefits. In turn, their future benefits will be calculated as a proportion of the last few years of their wages before retirement (as in the old system) or as a function of their ages and the number of years of contributions, as in the case of Argentina.

Most of the reforms have raised the minimum age for retirement to 65, although in several cases they have maintained a lower age (60) for women. They also have increased the minimum number of contributions required to retire if the state partially finances the benefits.

A significant aspect of the reforms is a provision giving special benefits to workers who contributed to the old system but did not retire before the reform and now are contributing to the fully funded scheme. When analysing this issue, one must consider both the size and timing of the compensation. The amount to be paid to each worker can be estimated by considering either the total contributions the worker made to the old system or the expected benefits the worker is losing because of the reform. The first option should yield a lower compensation if, as in many pay-as-you-go schemes, the implicit rate of return is higher than the market rates. Three approaches to the timing of compensations are possible. The first is for the state to make a one-time transfer to the worker's account, giving him a starting fund. The second is a variation of the first, in which the 'debt' to the worker is estimated and documented but not paid. In this case, a 'recognition bond' is issued and the state promises to pay its value, plus interest, to the worker when he retires, so that the state's contribution increases the total amount of funds used to acquire the retirement annuity. The third option consists in promising that, after retirement, the worker will receive a supplemental monthly benefit from the state that is somehow proportional to the 'debt'. This benefit is based upon the size and number of past contributions.

As for the timing of compensation, the first approach is unfeasible because the old social security systems cannot afford to make transfers of the magnitude that would be required over the short term. The second approach has been used in Chile, Peru, and Colombia, where the value of the bonds was estimated as a function of the number of past contributions and recent salaries. The third approach has been used in Argentina, where the state pays a benefit proportional to the number of past contributions and the salary before retirement to all workers who contributed to the old system.

A final aspect to consider is the existence of a multi-pillar structure, including the fully funded scheme. Chile, Peru, and Colombia chose a one-pillar model, in which the fully funded scheme pays all benefits. In Chile and Colombia the state guarantees a minimum benefit, creating a de facto second pillar financed with general revenue taxes. Argentina and Colombia, however, maintain an explicit two-pillar model, according to which a basic, universal benefit, financed as a standard pay-as-you-go scheme, is paid to all retirees in addition to their annuity benefits.

Assessing the Costs of the Transition

Analysing the costs generated when a social security programme is modified can be complicated because several factors are usually involved. If we consider social security from a broad perspective, it is reasonable to argue that a retirement system does not have a cost, and that any change introduced in the system will not have a cost either, except for administrative costs. This argument goes as follows: Given that a retirement programme is a transfer scheme (with both inter- and intra-generational aspects), there are no 'costs' involved in running it to anyone outside the programme, but only transfers among the groups involved. In this sense, a traditional pay-as-you-go scheme is a huge transfer scheme in which those who started the system receive large benefits whereas those still contributing when the system is terminated will have a significant loss, thus producing a long-term intergenerational transfer. Something similar happens in a fully funded scheme as well. In that case, however, the intergenerational transfers are less obvious because each generation (or person, if the capitalization model is based upon individuals) owns the funds and no explicit intergenerational transfers are made. Nevertheless, changes in long-term interest rates result in involuntary transfers. All mature retirement systems, whether pay-as-you-go or fully funded, consist in continuous financial transfers from younger to older generations and between members of each generation, either through a social security institution (as in a pay-as-you-go scheme) or through the financial markets (as in a fully funded scheme). In both cases, the basic rule of the scheme is the promise, implicit or explicit, to members of each generation that the transfers they make while in the labour force will be repaid, when they retire, by younger generations.

These considerations imply that, in strict terms, one should not refer to 'reform costs' but instead to 'redistribution'. The system and any reform in its rules do not involve a cost but rather a modification of distributive flows, as long as the perspective is broad enough to include all potential actors. Of course, the effects of a reform can be regarded as a cost to one specific generation or group. The approach I take here attempts to measure the 'costs' of a reform in this context; if a change in a system's rules affects inter- and intra-generational transfers, then some groups will find that the transfers they had expected to receive will not materialize, resulting in a cost for them, whereas other members will receive larger transfers than expected. Along the same line, if some workers are required to finance a system that will not pay benefits to them in the future, those workers will also have to sustain the cost originated in the reform.

In a 'pure' context, in which a fully funded scheme simply replaces a mature and balanced pay-as-you-go scheme that pays no more benefits, the evaluation of costs is simple. In that case, a few calculations will yield the amount of benefits lost by workers who contributed to the pay-as-you-go system—that is, the cost and who paid it. If the termination of the pay-as-you-go scheme implies stopping the collection of contributions but maintaining all promised benefits, the total cost will be the same, although in this case it will be sustained by whoever in the society has to generate the financial resources to pay those benefits.

Real-world reforms do not simply terminate balanced pay-as-you-go schemes while creating single-pillar, fully funded schemes. In most cases the reforms are enacted to deal with pay-as-you-go schemes suffering from serious financial and institutional problems, including large deficits and non-compliance with rules by many participants. Analysing the redistributive effects of such reforms is not simple. First, it is necessary to decide whether one should compare how the old system should have worked, according to its formal rules, with the expected behaviour of the new system or whether one should compare the actual performance of the old system with the expected actual performance of the new one. In addition, most reforms include rules that, while changing the dynamics of the system, are not necessarily connected with a change from pay-as-you-go to full funding. For example, increases in the minimum age for retirement or in workers' contribution tax rates can be enacted without introducing fully funded elements into a system. Thus it is necessary to disentangle the various elements involved in a reform in order to assess its effects.

In formulating a model to measure the costs and benefits generated by a transition and to estimate their distribution among the various social groups and generations, it is important first to identify the main players in this process and to define the role they play. Ideally the model should simulate the behaviour of the social security system. The model must incorporate many variables. This type of approach has been used (e.g. by Valdes-Prieto 1994*a*) to evaluate theoretical systems, with interesting results. Unfortunately, the poor quality of data in most countries makes it difficult to apply this approach to real-world cases.

From a theoretical viewpoint, the system should affect only those directly involved in it—that is, the contributors and beneficiaries. In a real-world situation, however, where deficits and surpluses are present and the possibility exists of using general revenue resources to finance benefits, many other players appear on scene.

The first group of actors in the model consists of the institutions that manage the system. It includes the state, represented by the agency responsible for administering the public pay-as-you-go scheme. In a fully funded scheme it includes the companies that manage the pension funds and the insurance companies that cover life and disability insurance in the private sector and administer the annuities. In the event of a reform, these groups will see their economic situation improve or deteriorate.

Two alternative criteria can be used to classify the individuals affected by the reform. The first is a generational division of the participants into three age groups: those over the age of retirement at the time of the reform (old retirees); those in active ages at the time of the reform (old workers); and those who have not entered the labour force age by the time of the reform (new workers). Each group will be affected by the reform in a different manner and should be considered separately. The second is a differentiation based upon the relationship each group has to the system. In this classification the groups include individuals in the labour force who contribute regularly to the system, individuals in the labour force who evade their contributions, individuals who are retired and receiving social security benefits (including secondary beneficiaries, such as spouses), and individuals who are not in the labour force and not receiving any social security benefits (this includes all types of economically inactive individuals under the age for retirement and older individuals who do not qualify to receive benefits). The two proposed criteria for classifying the population overlap in several cases, but they are not equivalent.

To assess the effect of the reform upon the financial status of the social security system, it is necessary to compare the financial situation prior to the reform with the situation that exists after the reform. In theory, traditional pay-as-you-go pension systems' resources come from employees and employers' contribution taxes, with a usually constant rate for all wage levels. The total revenue of the system (C_t) at any time (t) depends upon the number of active workers (A) and their average wage (w_t):

$$C_t = A_t * w_t * (c^{\omega} + c^e), \tag{6.1}$$

where c^w is the tax rate for employees and c^e is the tax rate for employers. Similarly, the total expenditures (B_t) of the system depend upon the number of retired workers (R_t), the average wage (w_t), and the replacement rate (b):

$$B_t = R_t * w_t * b. \tag{6.2}$$

As in any stable pay-as-you-go system, current revenue must be equal to current expenditures, resulting in the relation

$$C_t = B_t \Rightarrow A_t{*}w_t{*}(c^w + c^e) = R_t{*}w_t{*}b. \tag{6.3}$$

In Latin America, because of diverse institutional, demographic, and socio-economic circumstances, several social security systems gradually abandoned the basic equilibrium of Equation 6.3, mainly for two reasons. One was that evasion became significant, reducing the number of active workers contributing to the system by a proportion (e). The other was that the administrators of the systems began, in several cases, to manipulate the inflation-adjustment indexes, producing an erosion of the replacement rate, symbolized by i. In several cases the resulting reduction in expenditures was not enough to equilibrate the financial situation of the systems, forcing the governments to use general revenue funds (G_t) to cover the deficits. Thus the real situation of the retirement systems before the reforms is expressed by

$$R_t{*}w_t{*}[b{*}(1 - i)] - [A_t{*}(1 - e)]{*}w_t{*}(c^w + c^e) = G_t. \tag{6.4}$$

Once reforms are enacted, the financial equation of the public pay-as-you-go systems is modified. On the revenue side, the changes can affect the contribution tax rates, the size of the potentially contributing population (if there is any change in coverage), the evasion levels, and the amounts supplied by the state. Tax rates can be increased (as in the case of Argentina) or decreased (as in the case of employers' contributions tax rates in Peru, where they were eliminated). For workers switching from the old pay-as-you-go scheme to a fully funded one, the contribution tax rates are reduced to zero, although a partial contribution to the pay-as-you-go scheme may be maintained in some cases. The size of the potentially contributing population can change with the inclusion of new groups (in Chile self-employed workers were given the choice of joining the new system) or as the national system absorbs smaller local or industry-specific retirement programmes (in Argentina several provincial funds were merged with the national system). Evasion levels should decline as a result of the reform. In fact, a strong argument offered in favour of introducing Latin America's reforms was that the possibility of having some control over their accumulated funds would encourage workers to contribute to the new systems. The resulting revenues of the pay-as-you-go scheme after the reform becomes

$$C_t = A_t^P{*}w_t{*}(cp^{P,w} + cp^{P,e}) + A_t^F{*}w_t{*}(cp^{F,w} + cp^{F,e}), \tag{6.5}$$

where the superscript P represents workers who choose to remain in the pay-as-you-go scheme, superscript F represents workers who choose to switch to the fully funded scheme, and cp represents the tax rate corresponding to contributions to the pay-as-you-go scheme.

The reform also affects the expenditures equation. Benefits paid to old retirees should not be significantly affected and will continue to be calculated as a proportion of current contributors' wages, resulting in a replacement rate of

b^r. In some cases a modification of inflation-adjustment factors may produce a change in i. Instead, benefits paid to old and new workers will be clearly affected. As mentioned before, old workers may receive a special benefit, designed to compensate them for their years of contributing to the old system. Both old and new workers may receive a benefit from the pay-as-you-go scheme if the new system follows a multi-pillar model. Finally, workers who choose to stay in the pay-as-you-go scheme will receive a new regular benefit. The four components of expenditures can be presented separately. Equation 6.6 indicates the magnitude of total expenditures (B_t^r) directed to old retirees R_t^r :

$$B_t^r = R_t^r * w_t * (b^r * i). \tag{6.6}$$

The expenditures to finance the compensatory benefit (B_t^c) for old workers (A_t^o) will depend upon the method of compensation chosen. Three alternative methods are possible: (1) a lump-sum payment at the time of the reform, (2) a bond that matures when the worker retires, or (3) a monthly benefit that is paid to the worker when he or she retires, in addition to other benefits. The total expenditures can be expressed as in Equation 6.7, which presents the specification for each option:

$$\begin{aligned} &\text{if option (1) then} \quad B_t^c = A_t^0 * w_t * o_t, \\ &\text{if option (2) then} \quad B_t^c = Re_t^0 * w_t * o_t, \\ &\text{if option (3) then} \quad B_t^c = R_t^0 * w_t * o_t, \\ &\quad \text{where} \qquad\qquad\quad o_t = f(T_o). \end{aligned} \tag{6.7}$$

In this case the total amount will depend upon the number of old workers, the current average wages, and a factor (o_t), a function of the average number of years of contributions to the old system, which determines the replacement rate of this benefit.

If the compensation is made through a lump-sum payment at the time of the reform, the value of o_t will be very large for $t = \textit{year of the reform}$ and zero for any other t. If, instead, the second or the third option is adopted, o_t will be large immediately after the reform and then will decline slowly over time (because T_o will decline when younger generations start to retire). The expected evolution of B_t^c will also depend upon the option adopted. In the first case there will be a unique large expenditure. In the second case the expenditures should be high after the reform (when both the number of retiring workers, Re_t^o, and the value of o_t are high) and slowly decline later. If the third option is chosen, the expenditures curve should assume an inverted U-shape with a long right tail. This shape will result from an initial low number of retired old workers, which will increase rapidly and then (as a result of mortality) decrease, combined with an ever-decreasing value of o_t.

Both old and new workers may receive some additional benefits from the state if the new system includes a multi-pillar scheme. These benefits, B_t^m, are either a flat amount paid to all retirees or the result of a minimum pension value, guaranteed by the state. In the first case the total expenditures will depend upon the number of retired old and new workers, $R^o + R^n$, receiving it and the amount of the flat benefit, usually a proportion, m, of average current wages. If the multi-pillar component consists of a minimum guaranteed pension, mp_t (in most cases a proportion, μ of average wages), then the total expenditures will be a function of the number of retired old and new workers receiving a pension under the minimum and the difference between their average benefits, p_t, and the minimum benefit. Then, if u_t is the proportion of retired old and new workers receiving a benefit below the minimum and p_t the value of their average benefit, the value of the multi-pillar benefit, B_t^m, can be estimated as follows:

$$\begin{aligned} &\text{if option (1), then} \quad B_t^m = \left(R_t^o + R_t^n\right) * w_t * m; \\ &\text{if option (2), then} \quad B_t^m = \left(R_t^o + R_t^n\right) * u_t * (\mu - p_t). \end{aligned} \tag{6.8}$$

Finally, in some cases old and new workers are allowed to continue participating in a pay-as-you-go scheme instead of moving to the fully funded scheme. In countries were this is an option, an additional expenditure of the public retirement system is the payment of benefits to those workers. If the benefit is still calculated as a replacement rate of current wages, then the total expenditures in this programme, B_t^p , will be a function of the number of retired old and new workers who remain in the pay-as-you-go scheme, R_t^p, the current average wage, w_t, and the new replacement rate, b^p:

$$B_t^p = R_t^p * w_t * b^p. \tag{6.9}$$

The total expenditures of the public system after the reform will be the sum of the four types of expenditures already mentioned: expenditures on old retirees' benefits, those on compensatory benefits, those on multi-pillar benefits, and those on old and new workers' benefits if they remain in the public system. Equation 6.10 shows the total expenditures, B_t, equation.

$$B_t = B_t^r + B_t^c + B_t^m + B_t^p. \tag{6.10}$$

The final balance of the system will then be determined by the difference between revenues, C_t, and expenditures, B_t. If expenditures exceed revenues, once again the state will have to apply general revenue resources to equilibrate the system.

$$B_t - C_t = G_t. \tag{6.11}$$

By comparing the financial situation of the public scheme before and after the reform, it is possible to assess the effect of the reform upon the public finances. Of course, an increase or decrease in the financial deficits does not reflect the distributive effect by itself. On the one hand, it is reasonable to expect that even if the reform does not affect G_t, there may still be some redistribution, with the different flows cancelling each other. The analysis should not stop at the verification of an increased or decreased deficit, but instead should also consider how this deficit will be financed.

Although the total redistribution may be difficult to measure, it seems reasonable to assess what can be called 'transition cost'. By considering the effect of the reform in the short, medium, and long term, it should be possible to determine the cost of switching from a traditional pay-as-you-go model to a fully funded or multi-pillar one, and which groups will pay it.

A Real Case: Argentina

Argentina's reform followed, in broad lines, the model supported by international agencies. Coming from a traditional pay-as-you-go model, with both contributions and benefits defined and large deficits present, the new system is a multi-pillar scheme containing both pay-as-you-go and fully funded elements. According to the old rules, workers had to contribute for at least twenty years before retiring (men's minimum age was 60 years, women's was 55). The contribution tax rate was 26 per cent of gross salaries, shared by employees (10 per cent) and employers (16 per cent). Contributions were mandatory for all active workers, including the self-employed, who were responsible for the full 26 per cent, applied on an estimated income level. Once the minimum requirements were met, workers could retire with a benefit equivalent to 70 per cent of their pre-retirement salary. If they chose to stay in the labour force longer, their benefits were increased to as much as 82 per cent of their previous salaries. In both cases, an inflation-adjustment procedure was established, which should have maintained the real value of benefits. Because the government manipulated the indexes, however, the actual value of benefits averaged no more than 50 per cent of current average wages.

High levels of evasion (estimated at 57 per cent in 1990) prevailed, creating serious financial difficulties. Official figures indicate that, by 1993, the retirement system had a surplus of $4.760 billion dollars, or almost 42 per cent of expenditures (ANSeS 1994). This figure is highly inflated by the use of general revenue taxes to finance social security and the unlawful reduction of benefits. As shown in Table 6.1, if these factors are taken into account, the actual performance of the system produced a deficit of 33 per cent of expenditures, about 2 per cent of the gross domestic product.

The reform aimed to stop the continuous increase in deficits and the decline in real benefits by modifying some basic rules. First, employees' contribution tax rate was increased from 10 to 11 per cent of gross wages. The minimum age for retirement was increased by five years, and the minimum number of years of making contributions was increased by ten years. More importantly, the government enacted a major overhaul of the benefits system. Since 1994, all workers have had to choose between remaining in a state-run, pay-as-you-go scheme or moving into a privately managed, fully funded scheme. In all cases, workers will receive, after retirement, a universal flat benefit, equivalent to 27.5 per cent of average wages. If workers choose the new pay-as-you-go scheme, they will

Table 6.1. Financial status of Argentina's social security system: 1993 (1993 US$ millions)

	Official figures (a)	External resources (b)	Savings due to benefit reduction (c)	Real balance (d = a − b + c) (d)
Revenues (i)	16,170	6,653	0	9,517
Expenditures (ii)	11,410	0	6,120	17,530
Balance (iii = i − ii)	4,760	6,653	−6,120	−8,013
Balance, as % of expenditures (iv = iii/ii)	41.7			−46.2

Notes: The figures in column (b) represent the revenue generated by general revenue taxes and privatizations. Those in column (c) are an estimation of the difference between benefits actually paid and benefits that should have been paid if retirees had received an average of 75% of their active workers' wages.

Sources: Columns (a) and (b): ANSeS (1994); columns (c) and (d): author's calculations.

receive a 'permanence benefit' (*Prestación por Permanencia*), calculated as a proportion of their pre-retirement salaries and number of contributions to the system (0.85 per cent of base salary times the number of years of contributing to the new system). If, instead, they choose the fully funded scheme, the benefit will result from an annuity acquired with the funds accumulated by the time the workers retire. In addition, workers who contributed to the old system will receive a compensatory benefit, calculated as a proportion of pre-retirement salaries and the number of contributions to the old system. The formula used for the calculation is slightly more generous than the one used for the permanence benefit (1.5 per cent of their pre-retirement salary times the number of years of contributing to the old system). Various simulations indicate that, under reasonable assumptions about long-term wage increases and interest rates, substitution rates—that is, the percentage of pre-retirement salaries received by retirees as a benefit—should be similar for workers choosing either scheme. The new system introduced some differences between workers with similar contribution histories, especially in the benefits of men and women (annuities paying smaller benefits to women because they retire earlier and survive longer) and those of married and single retirees (because annuities must cover survivors' benefits).

The reform's distributive effects are rather complex. Table 6.2 presents the most relevant measures in the reform and their effects upon public finances. It is clear that the first six measures in the table are not linked directly to the introduction of a fully funded scheme; all six could have been applied within a pay-as-you-go model. The seventh measure directly reflects the cost of switching from the old pay-as-you-go system to the new multi-pillar model. The first five measures should help to finance the transition cost.

Table 6.2. Main measures in Argentina's social security reform of 1994 and their consequences

Measure	Effect on public pay-as-you-go system	Comments
1. Increased employees' contribution, from 10 to 11%.	Positive: improved revenue; will be even higher if most workers in the pay-as-you-go scheme remain there.	The cost of this change is paid directly by active workers.
2. Progressively increased the minimum age for retirement.	Positive: decreased expenditures on benefits in the short and long term.	The cost is sustained by active workers, who must delay retirement.
3. Increased the minimum number of years of contributions.	Positive: decreased expenditures on benefits in the short term by excluding workers from the system.	The cost is paid by workers with irregular contribution histories. In some cases they will not be able to retire with benefits.
4. Eliminated inflexible defined benefits for workers choosing capitalization.	Positive: reduced the potential cost of defined benefits in many cases.	If interest rates are low, workers in the fully funded scheme may receive very low benefits.
5. Linked increases in benefit levels to increases in revenue.	Positive: created a safeguard against disequilibria between revenues and expenditures.	May reduce real value of benefits if revenues are reduced.
6. Created a new pay-as-you-go scheme as part of a multi-pillar model.	Neutral in the short term: employees' contributions continue to flow towards the public system.	The contributions help to finance the transition.
	Potentially negative in the long term: under reasonable assumptions the new pay-as-you-go scheme may generate a deficit.	A long-term deficit would produce a new financial crisis.
7. Employees' contributions for workers choosing the fully funded scheme are deposited in the pension funds.	Negative: revenues are greatly reduced. The larger the proportion of the labour force switching to the fully funded scheme, the larger the loss.	This is the main component of the transition cost. A policy to finance it must be developed.

Applying the model

Applying the model developed in the previous section is not an easy task, given the limited availability of data. The financial situation before the reform can be presented using Equation 6.4 and the data in Table 6.1. The resulting figures are presented in Table 6.3.

Table 6.3. Financial status of the social security system before the reform: Argentina, 1993

Variable	No./amount
Active workers (A_{1994})	10,000,000
Average annual wage (w_{1994})($s)	8,300
Employee contribution rate (c^w) (%)	10
Employer contribution rate (c^e) (%)	16
Total potential revenue ($s)	21,580,000
Evasion rate (e) (%)	56
Actual revenue ($s)	9,517,000
Retired workers (R_{1994})	2,000,000
Survivors' beneficiaries	1,200,000
Total beneficiaries	3,200,000
Replacement rate (b)	
Retired workers (%)	75
Survivors' beneficiaries (%)	50
Total (%)	66
Total potential expenditures	17,530,000
Inflation erosion (i)	35
Total actual expenditures	11,410,000
General revenue funds	6,653,000
Surplus (deficit) of the system	
Under hypothetical assumptions*	4,050,000
Under actual circumstances**	4,760,000
Under actual circumstances without general revenue funds†	(1,893,000)
Under actual circumstances for revenues and hypothetical assumptions about expenditures‡	(8,013,000)

* Assumes the evasion rate and inflation-erosion rate are equal to zero and no general revenue funds are used.

** Assumes the evasion rate and inflation-erosion rate are those observed and general revenue funds are used.

† Assumes the evasion rate and inflation-erosion rate are those observed and no general revenue funds are used.

‡ Assumes the evasion rate is that observed and the inflation *h* erosion rate is equal to zero and no general revenue funds are used.

Notes: Monetary values expressed in 1993 US dollars. Some calculations appear to differ from the equations because of rounding errors.

Source: Author's estimates, based upon INDEC (1994) and ANSeS (1994).

The financial equation after the reform can be built by using Equations 6.5 to 6.11. In the model, total revenues will now depend upon the number of workers who remained on the public system, the new contribution tax rates, and average wages. Of course, the contributions will change over time if the number of contributors and average wages change. Table 6.4 presents the values of the

Table 6.4. Estimated revenues in the public social security system immediately after the reform: Argentina, 1995

Variable	No./amount
Active workers (A_{1995})	10,302,250
in the new pay-as-you-go scheme (A^{P}_{1995})	5,151,125
in the new fully funded scheme (A^{P}_{1995})	5,151,125
Average annual wage (w_{1994}) ($s)	8,750
Employee contribution rate to pay-as-you-go scheme	
Employees choosing pay-as-you-go scheme ($cp^{P,w}$) (%)	11
Employees choosing fully funded scheme ($cp^{F,w}$) (%)	0
Employer contribution rate to pay-as-you-go scheme	
Employees choosing pay-as-you-go scheme ($cp^{P,e}$) (%)	16
Employees choosing fully funded scheme ($cp^{F,e}$) (%)	16
Total potential revenue	19,381,000
Evasion rate (e) (%)	60.0
Actual revenue	7,752,000

Notes: Monetary values expressed in 1995 US dollars. Total population of active workers is an estimate based upon a 1.5% annual growth since 1993. The proportion of workers choosing the new, fully funded scheme is assumed to be 50%, according to official estimates in early 1995. Average annual wage is estimated from the average monthly compulsory contribution, which should be about 11% of average wages. The evasion rate is estimated to be close to 60%, based upon the number of actual contributors to the system in mid-1995. Some calculations appear to differ from the equations because of rounding errors.

relevant variables for estimating the revenues of the system immediately after the reform.

The system's total expenses can be calculated by using Equations 6.6 to 6.10. The public system will have to continue paying benefits to old retirees (Equation 6.6), a compensatory benefit to old workers (option (3) of Equation 6.7), a flat benefit to all retirees (option (1) of Equation 6.8), and benefits from the new pay-as-you-go scheme (Equation 6.9). Table 6.5 presents the composition of expenditures in 1995.

Because of the progressive increase in minimum ages for retirement, the number of new retirees in 1995–8 and 2001 can be expected to be negligible, if not zero. As shown for male workers in Table 6.6, if all workers retire at the minimum age, there should not be any new retirees during those years.

As a consequence, the expenditures on new retirees will be very low during the first few years after the reform but will start to grow thereafter. Thus the new balance of Equation 6.11, should be, for 1995 to 2000, approximately that presented in Table 6.7.

On the basis of these estimations, the actual deficit of the public social security system (without the application of general revenue funds) could be expected to grow from $1,893 million in 1993 to $3,976 million in 1995, almost exactly a 100

Table 6.5. Expenditures of the social security system immediately after the reform: Argentina, 1995

Variable	Amount
Old retirees (R_{1995})	
Retired workers	1,960,200
Survivors' beneficiaries	1,188,060
Total	3,148,260
Replacement rate (b^r)	
Retired workers (%)	75
Survivors' beneficiaries (%)	50
Total (%)	65.5
Potential expenditures on old retirees	$18,043,000
Inflation erosion (i) (%)	35
Actual expenditures on old retirees	$11,728,000
Workers retired after the reform	0
Potential and actual expenditures on new retirees ($)	0

Notes: Monetary values expressed in 1995 US dollars. The estimated number of old retirees assumes a mortality rate of 1% a year since 1993. The estimated number of survivors' beneficiaries assumes that 30% of deceased old retirees generate survivors' benefits. Some calculations appear to differ from the equations because of rounding errors.

Table 6.6. Age and year of retirement for male workers born between 1934 and 1938: Argentina

Year of birth	Age in 1994	Year and age of retirement				Actual year of retirement
		Under old system		Under new system		
1934	60	1994	60	—	—	1994
1935	59	1995	60	1999	64	1999
1936	58	1996	60	2000	64	2000
1937	57	1997	60	2002	65	2002
1938	56	1998	60	2003	65	2003

per cent increase. This deficit should start to decline almost immediately as a result of mortality among old retirees and the change in minimum age for retirement for new retirees. Thus by 2000, the total deficit should be around $2,660 million, a reduction of 33 per cent from the 1995 level, but still 40 per cent higher than in 1993.

Estimating the financial situation after the year 2000 requires a number of assumptions that go beyond the scope of this chapter. In particular, it is difficult to estimate the number of new retirees because that depends not only upon the demographics of the population but also upon the proportion of workers who can satisfy the required thirty years of contributions. Nevertheless, the total

Table 6.7. Financial balance of the public social security system after the reform: Argentina (US$000s)

Year	Expenditures			Revenue	Expected deficit[a]
	Old retirees	New retirees	Total		
1995	11,728,250	—	11,728,250	7,752,000	(3,976,250)
1996	11,727,080	—	11,727,080	7,946,960	(3,780,120)
1997	11,702,220	—	11,702,220	8,146,830	(3,555,390)
1998	11,630,130	—	11,630,130	8,351,720	(3,278,410)
1999	11,488,010	182,110	11,670,120	8,561,770	(3,108,350)
2000	11,254,810	182,090	11,436,890	8,777,100	(2,659,800)

[a] Expected deficit under actual circumstances, with no general revenue funds considered.
Notes: The following assumptions were used to estimate these figures: (1) the mortality of retirees was 1% in 1995 and is growing at a steady rate, (2) average wages are growing at 1% per annum, and (3) there will be 40,000 new retirees in 1999, receiving, on average, a 50% substitution rate, from the public social security system.

deficit of the public system should decline during the next few decades, although at a much slower pace than prior to 2000.

The transition cost and who pays it

The total transition cost of the reform must be assessed over a long period of time. As long as any person—whether an old retiree or an old worker—is receiving any type of benefit linked to the old system, the transition is not completed and the cost of the benefit must be computed. This situation will continue for many decades, until the last old worker dies, which will happen around the year 2070. Over the short term, the transition cost can be assessed by using Equations 6.4, 6.5, and 6.6.

If we consider only the effect of introducing the fully funded scheme, the main consequences of the reform will be the loss of revenue suffered by the public system and the progressive reduction in expenditures, resulting in figures like those just estimated for years before 1999. We know, however, that new benefits will be paid by the public system, and they should be taken into account.

The transition cost of Argentina's social security reform is the difference between the reductions in revenues produced by the transfer of contributions to the fully funded scheme and the reduction in expenses, produced by mortality among old retirees. Of course, part of this reduction is offset by the cost of compensatory benefits and the basic flat benefit, which must be financed from the same resources. Thus the transition cost (TC_t) at any time t can be represented as follows:

$$TC_t = (C_0 - C_t) - \left(B_0 - B_t^o\right) + B_t^m + B_t^c. \tag{6.13}$$

The total cost of the transition will be equal to the sum of TC_t for t between 1 (immediately after the reform) and approximately 80 (when the last recipient of a compensatory benefit dies). As mentioned before, a complete estimation of the transition cost is not feasible because not enough data are available to estimate B_t for years after 2000. Clearly, the highest cost will be in the first years, when revenues are reduced but savings due to old retirees' mortality are very small; but it will be reduced afterwards.

Although we do not know the exact figure for the transition cost, it is possible to assess which social groups will pay it and through which mechanisms. For a first approach, it seems reasonable to consider the measures defined by the reform, as described in measures 1 to 5 of Table 6.2. The increase in employees' contribution tax rate of one percentage point is increasing the public system's revenues, although the effect is minuscule. If all workers had stayed in the pay-as-you-go scheme, this change would have increased the total contribution tax rate from 26 to 27 per cent, a mere 3.8 per cent. Approximately 50 per cent of workers chose to join the fully funded scheme, however, reducing the positive effect to about 1.8 per cent of revenues, which means that active workers will sustain almost 10 per cent of the transition cost.

The second and third measures of Table 6.2, the progressive increases in minimum ages and contributions for retirement, are also helping to finance the transition cost, by delaying the retirement of currently active workers. In particular, the cost will be higher for workers who are closer to retirement. The effect will depend upon the age distribution of retiring workers. If all workers retired at the minimum age, these measures could reduce expenditures by as much as 15 per cent. If instead all workers retired five years after reaching the minimum age, having contributed during their entire active life, these measures would have no effect at all. Of course, reality is somewhere between these two extremes, and it is probable that the effect will be around 7–8 per cent of previous expenditures. This cost will be paid by active workers, in particular those who were close to minimum age for retirement prior to the reform and planned to retired immediately.

The fourth measure, which has linked all benefit increases to increases in revenues, may or may not have an effect. Benefits will now be a function of previous contributions by the workers and current revenues. If the basic macroeconomic variables (e.g. wage growth, inflation, evasion) behave under reasonable assumptions, substitution rates are likely to be similar to those paid to old retirees before the reform. That being the case, the measure will have no role in financing the transition cost. If, instead, real wages decline or evasion grows, the measure will produce a reduction in real benefits, facilitating the transition. In that event, the cost will be borne entirely by retirees. It is not possible to measure the potential magnitude of this mechanism because it depends upon the variations in macroeconomic variables.

Besides the formal measures included in the new system to finance the transition, two other implicit mechanisms may have a role. First, the government expected a strong reduction in evasion, which involved as many as 60 per cent of the labour force before the reform. If that proves to be the case, part of the transition cost will be paid by active workers who were not paying their contributions before the reform. This strategy seems to have had some success during the affiliation period, for many workers joined either a pension fund or the National Administration of Social Security. Nevertheless, a few months after the new system began, official figures indicated that many of the newly registered workers were not making their contributions. As of March 1995, evasion was close to pre-reform levels (ANSeS 1995*a*), indicating that reducing evasion will not be a simple task. The government's second strategy was to increase the public debt to finance the new deficits of the social security system. In doing so, it decided to transfer part of the transition cost to future generations. According to official figures, slightly more than 50 per cent of all pension funds are invested in government bonds, implying that approximately one-third of the funds that were lost by the public system return to it through national debt. (A second third is invested in other financial assets, and the last third is used to pay insurance and fees.)

Conclusions

Empirically assessing the transition costs can be a difficult exercise when a multi-pillar scheme replaces a pay-as-you-go system. The many complexities include the need to define a time frame and to decide whether the purpose is to compare the real-world situation with theoretical models. There is no unique 'technical' answer to these questions; several answers are reasonable, depending upon the type of approach chosen to conduct the analysis.

I have proposed a model in which the main financial equation of the public systems is the basic framework used in empirical analysis. The model includes a number of variables that may be affected by a social security reform, and in this chapter I have commented on the various forms that the combined effect can take. Although the model is not detailed enough to assess fully the distributive effects of a reform, I believe that it is a first step in gaining an understanding of this complex issue.

Argentina's social security reform, enacted in 1994, offers one of the most interesting cases for study because of the large coverage rate of the system and the multi-pillar characteristics of the new system. The old social security system shared many problems experienced by other developing countries undergoing the ageing process: a high dependency ratio, a high level of evasion, and poor administration. In addition, the quality of data is poor, as in most other countries with similar problems, limiting the possibility of preparing a detailed assessment of the transition costs. Nevertheless, the basic framework presented here can be used to gain an understanding of the significance of the transition costs and to identify the social groups most affected by them. I estimate that

Argentina's reform reduced the national system's revenues by almost 20 per cent, without having in place an explicit financing mechanism. According to the law, an increase in the contribution tax rate and in the minimum age for retirement will help to finance the transition, but I have estimated that, at most, this will cover half of the cost. The rest, which the government hoped would be financed by a reduction in evasion, will most likely be paid with an increase in public debt.

This difficult issue deserves careful study. Its relevance goes beyond the academic appeal of an interesting methodological problem because understanding it is critical to the policy-design process. Many Latin American and former Soviet governments are discussing the possibility of reforming their traditional pay-as-you-go systems to include fully funded elements. In too many cases, the potential costs of the transition between the two systems are not being carefully assessed, thereby risking a failure in the reform process. One can only hope that further research on this topic will help to improve the reform proposals being contemplated or implemented.

7 The Political Economy of Two Chilean Pension Systems

Salvador Valdés-Prieto

The latest wave of reforms of mandatory pension systems has included shifts away from the pay-as-you-go financing method towards partial or full funding. This is not the first time that funding has been attempted. Many pension systems started in the first quarter of this century were partially or fully funded. The provident funds created in ex-British colonies in the 1950s and 1960s also attempted funding. One new aspect of the most recent wave of reforms is that they have privatized pension provision. Examples are found in Chile (1981), Switzerland (1985), the United Kingdom (1988), Australia (1986 and 1992), Peru (1993), and Argentina (1994). In this chapter I link privatization to the political economy of pension systems.

Pension policy is a creation of the state, not a market phenomenon. In addition, I argue that political analysis is more important in pension economics than in other areas of economic policy. The reason is that pension institutions must function suitably over a time horizon that spans six or more decades, a period long enough for the state itself to experience profound changes. Therefore, the optimal pension policy appears to be a function, first and foremost, of the stability of a country's political regime.

Both economists and political scientists have studied pension policy. In the welfare economics literature, pension policy is analysed as if it were a response to market failure or as the least costly way to pursue a non-economic aim such as income distribution. Examples of this approach are Diamond (1977) and Kotlikoff (1987). In the political science literature, pension policy is considered to evolve in response to the process of state formation, marked by the emergence of a patronage-free civil service, the democratization of the electorate, and other national characteristics such as constitutional constraints. An example of this approach is Orloff (1992).

This chapter offers an analysis of the politics of Chilean pensions. In it I first analyse the experience in the 1950s and 1960s with the old pension system and then describe and compare the two pension systems that currently coexist in Chile. These are the new privatized and funded system created in 1981 and the state-run, pay-as-you-go financed system that succeeded the old system in 1981. (For a full description of the regulations that govern the new Chilean pension system, see Diamond and Valdés-Prieto 1994.)

Many factors have had important effects on the evolution of the Chilean pension systems since 1924. They include the demographic transition, fluctuations in the rate of growth rate of real wages, and fluctuations in the relative size of the independent, informal sector, which is not covered by the pension system. The two latter factors have been governed by the forces and events that shaped economic development in Chile, including the Great Depression, the closing of the economy to international trade between 1930 and 1974, the Frei and Allende regimes' attempts to redistribute the ownership of productive assets by non-compensated expropriation, the market-oriented reforms of the 1970s, their failure in the early 1980s, and their subsequent success. Within this wide panorama, this chapter focuses on the political aspects of the Chilean pension systems.

It begins with a review of the political ideals on which the old pension system was based, which were the social democratic ideals that sustain welfare states. The significant power of politicians and bureaucrats found in welfare states is usually justified as a necessary means to achieve an increase in equality—in this case redistributive pensions. However, because the Chilean political regime was characterized by heavy patronage, the pension system actually delivered a reduction of equality and an increase of the power wielded by the political cliques over the ordinary citizen. As their power reduced the legitimacy of democratic decisions, this process ultimately hampered the development of democracy in Chile. In other words, the overall design of the old Chilean pension system encouraged certain relationships between voters and politicians, in particular patronage and populism, which retarded Chile's political development.

Of course, the relationship between politics and economics in pension systems runs both ways. I provide evidence that the intervention of politicians did not lead to adequate and secure pensions. Inflation was allowed to erode the real value of pensions for many decades, even though contributions grew in line with inflation. The initial value of pensions depended too much upon the nominal salaries earned just before retirement, and the contribution rates were allowed to rise to levels above 50 per cent, encouraging a reduction of coverage for the poorest. The electoral push for improving the benefits of the currently voting generation was allowed to jeopardize the security of the pension promise for the future, as seen from the fact that the backing of the pension promises offered by the judicious investment of pension reserves was allowed to dwindle through inattention to the investment management function.

Until the late 1960s the intervention of politicians led to large non-pension benefits, such as generous family allowances and the rapid expansion of free health services to the participants of social security. For the most part, non-pension benefits appear to have been distributed progressively. However, the massive intergenerational redistribution associated with the start-up of a pension system financed by means of the pay-as-you-go method led to miserable pensions from the 1970s to the present, and to a serious drag on economic development, because the resources spent in family allowances and health benefits in 1940–60 were not saved to secure decent pensions for the future.

The chapter next describes how the two current pension systems (the privatized funded one and the pay-as-you-go, state-managed one) were designed and reformed in 1979–80 with the aim of preventing patronage and populism. A visible identification of the income-redistribution tools that are used within the pension system and a constitutional provision that prevents parliamentarians from initiating law in pension matters were the means used by those who wrote the 1980 Constitution to insulate the two new pension systems from patronage and populism. The degree of insulation between politics and the two pension systems increased dramatically. In the case of the new privatized system, additional measures were adopted that included the privatization of provision, individual freedom to choose the provider, and the defined-contribution design. As a result, the influence of the political regime was reduced substantially. The evidence suggests that the old pension system continues to have some influence on political development, even though it was reformed by the unification of the benefit and contribution conditions and is now subject to stricter constitutional controls. I conclude that the character and capacity of the national political institutions and the type of politics (both electoral and that relating to pressure groups) dominating pension policy should form the basis of choice between the basic design options of pension systems.

Political History of the Old Chilean Social Security System

The emergence of social security in Chile corresponds to a crisis period of classical liberalism. Like other social policies, social security was an answer to social problems associated with the expansion of industrial capitalism during the nineteenth century. Those problems were perceived as impossible to solve through voluntary exchange but could be mitigated through an extension of the state's agenda. By 1920 the formulas offered by the capitalist approach to preventing future contingencies, such as voluntary savings and private insurance plans, appeared too unreliable and expensive either to meet the demands of the large masses of industrial workers who had quit their support networks in the rural regions or to respond to the political challenges put forth by critics of capitalism. The dozen pension institutions (*Cajas*) established voluntarily before World War I provided defined-benefit pensions for government employees in the armed forces, railroads, and public service and for some private employees (those in banks and some large firms); but overall coverage was small.

In 1924 the Chilean government made contributing to social security mandatory for all employees in the private sector; and for that purpose it created two new institutions, one for white-collar workers (Caja de Empleador Particulares, or EMPART), and the other for blue-collar workers (Servicio del Seguro Social, or SSS). These new *Cajas* kept individual accounts, but workers could not choose their pension institution. Lack of choice was a serious limitation because there were substantial differences between the various *Cajas*, both in their contribution rates and in the types and level of benefits they offered, which ranged from old-age and disability pensions to health care and family allowances. The *Cajas* served workers of disparate socio-economic levels. EMPART included 450,000 members, who received 59 per cent of covered wage income, whereas the SSS had 1.2 million members, who received 33 per cent of covered wage income (Prat 1962: 60). The governing boards of the *Cajas* were formed by representatives of labour unions, the employers' association, and the government, so that they appeared to be somewhat insulated from electoral and pressure-group politics. The *Cajas* had a huge cash surplus during the first thirty years of the system, and it was used to finance large new legislated benefits (e.g. free health coverage and family allowances).

At its inception in 1924, the old system was designed to finance old-age benefits by capitalization. Later, investment was discredited as a use of funds, for several reasons. One was general ignorance of financial indexation methods, which are needed to protect the real value of debt securities from large swings in inflation rates. Others were the deterioration of domestic debt markets (due to interest-rate regulation) and of domestic equity markets (due to punitive taxation) and the losses experienced in many investments during the Great Depression. Pension benefits, however, were defined in nominal terms, and so the *Cajas* were able to pass along to their pensioners the investment losses caused by inflation.

Social democratic ideas about social security exerted great influence on the reforms of the Chilean pension system that took place from 1942 to 1952. The proposals of William Beveridge (1942) were broadly seen as postulates for a democratic social security system. The social democratic welfare state was conceived as a response to the 'failure' of unbridled capitalism. That response was seen as better than communism because it retained democracy and the rule of law. The idea was to expand the scope of state activities to include social welfare, which included both insurance aims and redistribution. The state would nationalize the essential saving and insurance functions that the financial market failed to provide, assuring wide availability, and in addition redistribution would be performed.

As one of the main aims was egalitarian, the juridical statute of the services rendered by social security included a duty of the state towards the inhabitants of the national territory. A right to social security would be the expression of the principle of solidarity of the entire community towards members who were in need. Designers of this system assumed that social security not only should be carried out with the concurrence of the state, but also was one of the state's functions. They did not even consider the alternative of creating a private system that would be subject to government regulation, or limiting the government's role in redistribution to design and financing.

The ideal welfare state offered a guarantee of egalitarian consumption of a few composite goods, which it conventionally identified as eight or nine 'states of need'. Financing was to be based on taxes, mostly on labour income, which were called contributions. A single fund fed from the contributions of the workers, the contributions of employers, and the state (through other taxes) would finance consumption of this basket of goods (health care, family allowances) and services (insurance of several types, savings for old age) of equal value for everyone. After World War II, this rapidly became the prevalent formula for democratic societies.

In contrast to this model, in Chile in 1942–52 various pension systems were operating, inherited from the previous periods. The segmentation of benefits and contributions was in conflict with the principle of equality espoused by the social democratic ideology. The Chilean pension reforms of 1942–52 attempted to eliminate those differences by increasing benefits and contribution rates. In EMPART, contribution rates rose during 1942–47 from 24.5 to 41.8 per cent. (In 1937 they had risen from 10.0 to 23.3 per cent when health and other benefits were first added.) In the SSS, contribution rates jumped from 10.2 to 30.2 per cent of wages between 1952 and 1954.[1] The increased resources were spent immediately on the provision of massive amounts of benefits, especially on free health services and large family allowances.

In addition, the original funding strategy was abandoned during the 1940s. When invested, the initial surpluses obtained negative real rates of return, owing to the regulatory and economic factors mentioned above. In 1952 a major legislative reform explicitly transformed the financing method from funding to pay-as-you-go. It should be recalled that at the time most developed countries were implementing the same reform, for similar reasons. It has also been argued that Chile's modest life expectancy at age 60 during that period (see Table 7.1) played a role in the decision to spend the pension reserves to finance benefits for

Table 7.1. Actual and projected life expectancies: Chile, 1920–2020

Year	Years of life remaining	
	Men	Women
At age 60		
1920	11.8	12.6
1930	13.4	15.3
1940	13.5	15.2
1950	14.6	16.9
1960	15.2	17.7
1970	15.7	18.4
At age 65		
1980	13.6	16.4
1990	14.4	17.8
—	—	—
2020	16.3	20.2

Sources: 1920–40: Cabello *et al.* (1946); 1950–2020: CELADE (1994).

the current contributors and their families. However, that short expected payout period was not managed by reducing the contribution rate, as it might have been. Instead, both benefits and contributions were expanded, and that fact seems to require a political argument, not a demographic one.

The political foundation of the diversity of pension regimes and the nature of Chilean politics was not considered seriously at the time. The main way to obtain support in political competition, which was increasingly transformed by the enlargement of the franchise, was to distribute economic benefits to party activists and their relations, a phenomenon called patronage. Patronage manifested itself in many areas of state activities. Tariff protection became ever more complex and discriminatory, the price controls created in the Great Depression were captured by the producer cartels, and some tax laws suffered a similar capture process. Consequently the political effect of the massive infusion of resources to the *Cajas* over 1942–54 was to fund patronage at a scale never before seen in Chile. Those reforms failed to take into account the actual stage of political development of the Chilean state and its real capacities.

Patronage expressed itself in a growing number of pension laws. The Prat Report (Prat Commission 1962: 41) indicates that 515 legal texts, including laws, decrees, and regulations, controlled the operations of this complex system. This legal overabundance reflected the action of groups with economic capacity and political power to obtain pension legislation that would protect them in a privileged manner. Thus each group acquired a level of benefits proportional to its social and political power. Accordingly, during the 1940s and even more so in the 1950s, the Chilean social security system became, in reality, an aggregation of diverse pension systems negotiated between those in political power and various groups with electoral influence. By this route, some groups managed to obtain heavily subsidized credit, premature retirement without actuarial adjustment, and pensions with privileged inflation adjustments.

Board positions in the *Cajas* and higher management of the main social security institutions turned into the most coveted political parcels. Increasingly they came to be distributed among members of the governing coalition of parties, with nominal regard to the members' technical qualifications. Those in charge achieved this result without altering the tripartite composition of the boards—consisting of organized labour, employers, and the ministries. For example, at EMPART in 1960, after a streamlining reform, the board included six labour representatives who were chosen by the Chilean president—not elected—from all short lists of three candidates proposed by white-collar unions with more than 100 members. By law, those short lists had to represent the three largest pluralities in a secret ballot among the directors, not the members, of each union. The two employers' representatives in EMPART's board were also chosen by the president from four short lists of three candidates each, proposed by the industrialists' association (SOFOFA), the merchants' association, the mining employers' association, and the main farmers' association. In addition, five other board members were either government officials or directly designated by the president. Appointment to the board was for a period of three years (Prat 1962: 966). At the SSS the governing coalition of parties had still more influence (ibid. 987–8).

It was easy to organize a group of 100 workers to create a union, and the group would be automatically entitled to designate three candidates to the board of EMPART. Receiving the nomination required being on good terms with the governing political coalition because the president could choose among many candidates. Still, unions with electoral influence in some districts could trade electoral support for approval of their demands for special legislation. It is clear that the boards of the main *Cajas* were subject to coalition politics.

The assumptions upon which the pension system had been established in 1924 were also overly optimistic about the administrative capacities of the Chilean state. The system provided for individual records, and some of the *Cajas* actually issued individual savings passbooks to members; but then they ceased to keep the records current. This was due in part to the take-over of *Cajas* by politicians that occurred between 1942 and 1970, which seriously affected the continuity of the institutions and the cost of their administration. It was also due to a lack of trained personnel and weak administrative controls. The risk to individual members of being unable to document their contributions when they reached retirement age was also large, especially at the SSS, where workers were required to take their passbook annually to an SSS office for registration of the previous year's contributions. If a worker left his job on bad terms with the employer or lost his passbook, his contributions failed to increase his benefit.

The number of social security institutions grew over time, reaching eighteen in the early 1960s, when they administered almost sixty regimes, not counting those of the armed forces and of the police (Thayer and Fernández 1981: 31). By 1979 there were thirty-two institutions, which managed more than 100 social security regimes (Cheyre 1991: 36, 170). The legal and institutional profusion increased the administrative costs of pensions and the rate of return on investments.

In 1957 the Klein-Saks Mission, formed by American economists, issued the first critical report on the pension system. The report identified a number of ailments afflicting Chile's social security system: as total contribution rates had reached the 40–9 per cent of wages range,[2] the system had become an onerous burden on wages and salaries and on the capital of companies; it inhibited savings; and the proliferation of *Cajas* increased the expense of their administration and reduced the quality of service. In reference to the accumulated funds, the report added that only small investments had been made on development projects; and that, on the contrary, loans had been granted and homes built that benefited only a minority, not safeguarding the value of the capital invested or loaned (Klein-Saks 1957: 25). However, the mission failed to report on the political foundations for this state of affairs.

In response to the Klein-Saks Mission's warnings, President Jorge Alessandri (1959–64) created a special commission headed by a respected lawyer and politician, Jorge Prat, to issue a definitive report. A social democrat, Prat argued that legislation should ensure that the redistribution of the social security funds 'does not benefit groups or oligarchies, but rather is distributed under that healthy concept of redistribution in favour of the weakest and more numerous sectors of society' (Prat 1962: 53). He was shocked to find that Chilean social security promoted discrimination rather than equality.

The Prat Report (Prat Mission 1961) provides sobering data about the rate of return of pension reserves: 35 per cent of the surplus intended for capitalization was invested in loans and bonds in nominal terms, in a setting where, between 1940 and 1954, the instruments suffered the effects of an accumulated inflation of 322 per cent; that is, they lost around 80 per cent of their real value (Prat 1962: 61). This was due not simply to the fact that the increasingly regulated and taxed Chilean financial market yielded low and variable real returns for all investors, including the *Cajas*. A study by Wallich (1983) provides evidence that the politically managed *Cajas* performed much worse than the *Cajas* established before 1924, which were privately managed. This is not surprising, given that 'the involvement of the Chilean Congress went far beyond simply the investment guidelines of the portfolio.... Congress set the interest rates which could be charged on each type of loan, their maturities and amortization rates. Rent controls were also established in the buildings owned by the *Cajas* for let to members' (ibid.: 66).

According to Prat the solution to the problem of social security was to have 'a single and egalitarian system of social security, but our system is differentiated by groups and is discriminatory' (Prat 1962: 54). Unified systems had been adopted in many member countries of the Organization for Economic Cooperation and Development (OECD); but hindsight suggests that their success elsewhere may have been due more to the higher degree of political development in those countries, which limited patronage and populism, than to unification *per se*. However, the Chilean Congress did not approve unification during the 1960s despite the fact that, beginning in 1952 (and continuing throughout the 1960s), all the presidents of the Republic characterized the social security system as being in a state of crisis. At the end of his mandate, President Eduardo Frei Jr. (1964–70) virtually repeated the criticism of the system that he had made in 1964. All the presidents acknowledged that they had been unable to overcome the opposition of the political parties or pressure groups to reform. By then those groups had become entrenched. Even so, the commission headed by Prat established as a political fact that the system was regressive and inefficient, and accordingly its findings (Prat Commission 1962) had widespread respect.

During the three years that President Salvador Allende (1970–3) was able to govern, his administration attempted pension reform in the direction of revolutionary socialism. The objective ceased to be insurance coverage for all workers of the formal sector. Instead, it was to achieve solidarity for all by extending social security to population groups in urgent need of coverage—that is, regardless of their contribution record. Social insurance was to be merged with social assistance and the tax system. The means were radical, as the cause of this poverty was considered to be 'the socio-economic structure of a capitalist nature that existed when the current government took over' (Allende 1972: 871). In his last message to the nation, before the collapse of his government, Allende asserted that his pension policy in this area was oriented towards the replacement of social security 'for the purpose of correcting its deficiencies, a product of a scheme of typical capitalist nature' (Allende 1973: 800). Allende's reform initiatives were part of his drive to achieve a socialist welfare state modelled after the Soviet Union and Cuba. They required the break-up of liberal democracy and the rule of law. Those initiatives were aborted by the military intervention of September 1973.

The only study available shows that, except for the effect of family allowances, by 1970 the Chilean pension system had become regressive (Foxley, Aninat, and Arellano 1977). Debate has been hampered by the authors' decision to include the large family allowances (a flat benefit) in their summary of results, maybe because this allowed them to report that the total package turned out to be slightly progressive. Their figures show, however, that pensions were regressive. Other authors (e.g. Arellano 1985) have also made much about the fact that the first participating generations obtained a high personal rate of return from the Chilean pension system, suggesting that the rate establishes the superiority of pay-as-you-go financing. In reality there is no such implication because that high personal rate of return is just another way of presenting the well-known intergenerational transfer brought about by shifting from funding to pay-as-you-go financing.

By 1970 the Chilean pension system had made a promise to millions of workers—around 70 per cent of the labour force—to provide them a pension close to 70 per cent of their final earnings. Those workers did not have effective alternative options, for they had lost contact with their rural communities and the financial market had been prevented from providing the required services. The level of old-age security that the system actually delivered proved to be quite modest: in 1995 more than 70 per cent of its pensioners were receiving a minimum pension, and over the period between 1960 and 1979 the real value of the minimum pension (subsidized by the government) had a standard deviation of 24 per cent (Wagner 1991).

The real achievement of the Chilean pension system over 1924–70 was that it financed large levels of non-pension benefits for three decades, mainly in the form of free health coverage and large family allowances. Why politicians did not finance those progressive benefits with a separate and transparent pay-roll tax is a question that can be answered with the observation that it is generally harder to obtain approval for contemporaneous redistribution from upper-middle-income voters to lower-middle-income groups than to obtain their approval of intergenerational redistribution mixed with contemporaneous redistribution.

In the meantime the mechanics of pension-system maturity and the unfavourable effects of the demographic transition were beginning to reduce pensions.

Real pensions continued to fall during the 1970s because real wages, contributions, and coverage declined dramatically in response to various domestic and external shocks. The number of pensioners almost doubled, rising from 581,000 in 1970 to more than 1 million in 1979. However, the number of contributors grew by only 200,000, from 2.2 million to 2.4 million. Thus each pensioner came to be supported by just 2.4 active workers on average (Thayer and Fernández 1981: 51). In the early 1970s the government accommodated pressure on the system by increasing contribution rates, which reached the range of 51–9 per cent in 1975 (including health). By 1976 this solution had proven unfeasible for the same reason that is apparent in Western Europe now: high contribution rates encourage evasion and independent work to such an extent that they reduce revenue. System maturity, coupled with economic and demographic shocks that are quite likely to last six to eight decades (that is, the length of time that any individual participant remains in a pension system), and the exclusive reliance on financing by current contributions, introduced financial pressures for radical reform at the same time that the pension system had become politically discredited.

The Old Social Security System and Political Freedom

The old Chilean social security system failed to meet the goal of equality. It also failed to meet political goals related to freedom. The Prat Report (Prat Commission 1962) provides overwhelming evidence that the various social security regimes emerged as the effects of political patronage, or clientelism. The successive appearance of groups protected by social security regimes was the result of negotiations and transactions of social security benefits for political favours, which the groups considered 'social conquests'. In this manner, the beneficiaries, segmented in groups, became the clients of political leaders whom they supported and with whom exchanges of mutual favours were established. As the political parties were the stronger part of this bargaining pair, clientelism had the general effect of eroding the freedom of its beneficiaries, who became exposed to manipulation by the political class.

Patronage also had specific effects on political freedom. In this clientelistic setting, the groups with the most power and influence exercised their influence to the disadvantage of less organized groups. Thus most Chileans in the system had only minimal social security, the amount of which was extraordinarily dependent upon the state, and therefore the governing coalition could manipulate them more easily than the average covered worker. The system was configured in such a way that the largest group of members was subject to the greatest number of mechanisms for controlling them politically, and this prevented them from exercising their freedom.

Populism, a political process in which a leader buys the support of the electorate, was also prevalent. In line with international literature on this topic, recent empirical evidence shows that during election periods the Chilean regimes and the political class intervened in the economic cycle.[3] Surveying the fifty years of the political-economic cycle from 1939 to 1989, Assael (1993) investigates whether, in order to achieve favourable electoral results for those in power, the political authorities in charge of the economic sector manipulated the monetary, fiscal, and foreign-exchange-rate variables. She concludes that the regimes from 1945 to 1970 did manipulate the monetary and fiscal variables in a significant way during electoral cycles.

The Prat Commission (1962) also alleged the existence of populism. A periodic legislative discussion was needed to revalue pensions because a mechanism for automatically adjusting pensions to inflation did not exist. From 1924 to 1951 Chile had no laws regarding revaluation, but inflation had always been below 10 per cent except in 1932. In 1952 legislation was enacted prescribing periodic revaluation of pensions, but the revaluations were fixed at between 25 and 90 per cent of the increase in the cost of living during the previous year, favouring the smaller pensions with the highest percentages. However, as inflation rates rose to nearly 30 per cent per year, pensioners' purchasing power fell by between 3 and 23 per cent (Prat Commission 1961: 1153–67). In addition, the fixed time period between revaluations exposed pensioners to massive losses in the short run if the inflation rate accelerated before the next revaluation came due.

As a result, specially legislated inflation adjustments became much more important than the prescribed minimum revaluation. Pensioners became dependent upon social legislation, which tended to occur just before elections. Inflation adjustments to current pensions offered a valuable opportunity for populism to prosper, further weakening Chilean political development.

A final issue is the freedom of the privileged groups. Many of them were net losers in social security because of the extent of inefficiency induced by clientelistic competition. For that reason they wanted to work out alternatives, but their privileged status was also dependent upon the favouritism of the political class, and so they had little freedom to question the overall social security system.

The 1970s' Reform to the Old System

During the 1970s the demand for an economy capable of generating growth in consumption and economic well-being was very strong, and the military regime attempted to create one by adopting an economic policy that favoured markets, competition, and capital accumulation. Strong underlying forces also supported a return to democracy. For those reasons the social security reforms carried out in Chile during that period had two characteristics: they were tailored to a market economy and to capitalist institutions, and they were tacitly functional conducive to liberal democracy, under its constitutional and representative form, because they relied heavily upon the rule of law. Other reforms were the liberalization of international trade, the liberalization of financial contracts, including interest rates, and the privatization of many state-owned enterprises. The regime pursued the traditional redistributive goals of public policy in a different way, directing redistribution towards the middle class, which participated in formal social security, but excluding independent workers, most of whom were mired in extreme poverty.

The unification reforms

The first pension reform of the authoritarian regime affected the old system and occurred between 1974 and 1979. Its purpose was to impose uniformity upon most of the benefits; but in contrast to previous reforms, the uniformity imposed was highly restrictive. The reasons were that the pension system's maturation was pinching government finances and the extremely high total contribution rates already reached in 1976 made a 1952-style solution, of making the benefits of all Chileans equally generous, impossible.

The first subject of the unification process was a cost-of-living adjustment. In the old pension system, the inflation adjustments for the four main groups—blue-collar workers, white-collar workers, public employees, and the armed forces—were governed by separate laws and mechanisms. Diversity was widespread within those groups (Prat Commission 1961). In 1974 a decree law unified the first three revaluation systems (Decree Law 670, *Diario Oficial*, 2 Oct. 1974).

Nevertheless, retired military officers adjusted their pensions according to changes in the nominal salaries of the current occupants of the last posts they had held just prior to retirement. This implied adjustment with an index of nominal wages, which over the long term grew faster than nominal prices. The regime eliminated this provision in 1979, and all pensions became entitled to a uniform cost-of-living adjustment (Decree Law 2448, *Diario Oficial,* 9 Feb. 1979). This particular reform is noteworthy because the military regime took away its own privilege, which had substantially benefited its own retirees.[4] Between 1979 and 1995 revaluations in the old system were uniform, with few exceptions, to be discussed later in this chapter.

What, precisely, was the unified inflation adjustment? Starting in December 1974, the government legislated full adjustment to past inflation of the consumer price index, or CPI (Decree Law 670). However, the timing was fixed for specific months of 1975, without establishing a permanent timing formula. It was not until 1979 that both the timing and the magnitude of revaluations were fixed in a permanent law (Decree Law 2448). The law established a cost-of-living adjustment (revaluation) for the full change in the CPI since the previous revaluation. Its timing was fixed either in 30 June of each year or when the cumulative CPI change since the previous revaluation surpassed 15 per cent, which made timing endogenous to the level of inflation. As worded, the law had a technical imperfection: it was interpreted by the *Contraloría* (General Accounting Office) and later ratified (by Law 18,549 of 1986) as implying that only one of the two mechanisms could be used in a given calendar year. For example, if a revaluation occurred in June, then no other revaluation could be granted until 1 January of the next year, even if cumulative inflation after June was above 15 per cent.

In the absence of other reforms, an especially important unifying reform for long-term financial stability of the old pension system was an increase of the pensioning age for men, to 65 years for all the *Cajas*. Sixty-five had always been the pensioning age at the blue-collar *Caja*, the SSS.

In 1981 a third unifying reform took place with the merging of the administration of the old *Cajas* into a single institution, the Instituto de Normalización Previsional, or INP. The legal regimes, however, were maintained, so that the INP was left in charge of more than 100 separate social security regimes.

The unification reforms were politically important because they reduced the likelihood of future patronage legislation: any benefit increase would have to be granted to everyone and therefore would be more expensive and less likely to occur. Moreover, reforms of the political regime itself were taking place at the constitutional level, and they also reduced the scope of populism and patronage to influence pensions.

The constitutional reforms

In 1980 the Chilean electorate approved a new constitution by referendum. This constitution, which became fully effective in 1980 (except for transitory articles that ceased to be effective in 1989), emphasizes the rule of law and equality before the law. It contains an article stating that 'there are no privileged persons or groups; neither the Law nor any authority whatsoever may establish arbitrary differences' (Chile 1993, Article 19, No. 2), and that article has helped to prevent both patronage and the creation of special pension regimes for pressure groups.

The new constitution has special provisions regarding pensions, which have contributed to an improvement in the performance of the old pension system since 1980. In the first place, it establishes the basis of social security in an article that is protected by a quorum of two-thirds (Article 116). By stipulating that 'the laws that regulate' the exercise of the right to social security 'shall require qualified quorum' to be approved—that is, absolute majority of all members, not merely of those present (Article 17)—it prevents simple coalition-building by individual parliamentarians, who traditionally traded their approval of other parliamentarians' initiatives for approval of reforms to obscure pension legislation that favoured their own political clientele.

The new constitution also limits the initiative on laws affecting social security to the presidency, preventing parliamentarians from initiating pension legislation by themselves. Similarly, the constitution denies Congress the power to initiate law on matters that involve public spending, which include the pension benefits of the old pension system, minimum pensions (partially non-contributory), and assistance pensions (non-contributory).

These reforms indicate that the forces behind state formation and political development began to evolve defences against the vices that had led to the destruction of democracy during 1970–3. Among those defences were ones designed to limit the influence of the pension system on politics, as it was widely recognized as being a mainstay of patronage and populism.

The new politics of redistribution

From 1974 onwards the Chilean government pursued traditional redistributive goals of public policy with new policy tools, which attempted to address the needs of the large class of workers in extreme poverty who did not participate in formal social security. The new approach produced much larger and better targeted social-assistance programmes, a streamlined value-added tax with fewer loopholes, and progressive income taxes, property taxes, and car-purchase taxes. Other policies sought to increase the growth rate of the gross domestic product and the volume of efficient employment.

During this period redistribution through the pension system came to be increasingly linked in the political arena to so-called minimum and assistance pensions, rather than to formulas for redistributing benefits that are characteristic of many OECD countries. A minimum pension is an expenditure programme that supplements the pension amount an individual would receive if the usual rules for determining benefits were applied to him. An assistance pension is a non-contributory programme designed to benefit the elderly and the disabled who live below a poverty line.

From 1975 to 1980 several reforms perfected the social-assistance network for the poor working in the independent and informal sectors. A non-contributory family allowance for poor children was created in 1975 and began to reach them through the municipalities. An assistance pension had existed since 1961, but in 1975 it was expanded to cover all eligible Chileans who had not contributed to the formal social security institutions. This sector was large because the poorest Chileans usually work independently in the informal sector or in subsistence farming. Those eligible were elderly (over age 65) and the disabled above age 18 who met two tests: they were not receiving another pension, and they had passed a needs test based on an interview at home with a social worker from the municipality. The CASEN survey, conducted in 1987, found that 65 per cent of the recipients of the assistance pension's recipients were women, and 82 per cent had never contributed to any pension system. According to the survey, the benefits from the programme reached 35.3 per cent of lowest income decile, 50.4 per cent of the lowest quintile, and 73.8 per cent of the lowest 40 per cent (Haindl, Budinich, and Irarrázabal 1989: 71, 75). The inflation adjustment for the assistance pension was pegged at the same level as the adjustment for the minimum pension.

Since 1952 the government has paid the minimum pension to those who have contributed their share to a mandatory pension system. The amount of the minimum pension is about double the assistance pension. For example, the amount paid in June 1992 was 25.2 per cent of average taxable income after contributions. The minimum pension covers old age, disability, and survivorship. The requirement for eligibility is approximately twenty years of contributions, but the exact requirement varies according to the pension regime.

The minimum pension applies to both the old and the new pension systems and is financed out of general revenue. This arrangement is explicit in the new system and implicit in the old system, which has been in deficit since the creation of the new system in 1981. In the tradition of conventional pension systems, the commitment to pay minimum pensions is not contractual but legislated. Because it is defined in nominal terms, and adjustment for inflation requires specific legislation, the real value of minimum pensions varies substantially.

Wagner (1991) projects the minimum pension for a steady state of demographics and pension-system maturity, but with the same per capita capital stock and education levels that were present in the late 1980s. He finds that, for a level of minimum pension equal to the historical average of the last thirty-five years in real terms, the proportion of each age group receiving it in the long term will range between 10.7 and 33.7 per cent, depending upon whether the average rate of return is 5 per cent or 3.5 per cent per year. The number is large because the level of the minimum pension is a high proportion of the average reported taxable income, and because many workers spend only part of their careers in covered employment. The uncovered sector is large and there is substantial mobility between the covered and uncovered sectors.

From a political standpoint, the growth and improvement of the assistance and the minimum pensions signals a change in priorities that favours the poorest old rather than those lower-middle-income old who would have benefited from egalitarian redistribution in the formal sector, as proposed by Prat. This change was important because it provided an alternative to the traditional linkage between redistributive aims and the pension system. That is why the new system could be presented as a strictly actuarial system that did not attempt to redistribute income or wealth—apart from the minimum pension, which was funded separately. As I shall show, however, those new priorities began to lose importance after the return to democracy in 1989.

The outcome of the reforms to the old system

Analysing the inflation adjustment of pensions in the old system over the period 1985–93, Godoy and I have found that the old pension system continues to have some influence on political developments but has much less influence than in the past (Godoy and Valdés-Prieto 1995). It is not used for patronage purposes, and the manipulation of its benefits for electoral purposes has been much moderated. Our analysis indicates that the promise of full CPI indexation issued in

1979 was kept, despite increasing unemployment and a 20 per cent fall in real wages until mid-1985. At that point the government legislated that a 10.6 per cent adjustment would be skipped. The political uproar was such that over the next few years the military government provided extra real increases in pensions for the lowest pensions in the old system. When the Aylwin government took office in 1990, one of its priorities was to 'return' the 10.6 per cent, and it achieved this by enacting special laws that took effect from July 1991 to December 1992.

Some of the increases had a clear electoral purpose, such as the real increase favouring the lowest pensions, granted in 1988 just five months before the referendum in which General Pinochet was refused continuation in power. In June 1989, five months before a presidential election, a 5 per cent real increase was granted to the lower half of pensions of the old system. During the democratic presidency of Patricio Aylwin, the formula for indexation was changed in a way that increased real pensions a few weeks before the presidential election in which Eduardo Frei Jr. was elected, in late 1993.

Although real increases in the pensions of the old system have not been large and may be explained as a simple attempt to catch up with the real increase in average wages, the timing of those increases creates the suspicion of populism. The unification and constitutional reforms seem unable to counteract the political forces that impinge on traditional defined-benefit, state-managed pension systems.

In May 1995, without any election in sight, the government proposed a 10 per cent real increase in assistance pensions, minimum pensions, and pensions from the old system that were below 100,000 pesos a month—which is close to 50 per cent of average reported taxable wages. The proposal excluded pensions in the new system that were above the minimum pension but below 100,000 pesos a month. This initiative was approved by Congress with little discussion. From the political perspective, it marks a turning point because it extends redistribution to the lower-middle classes (i.e. the income classes between the minimum pension and twice the minimum pension). Moreover, the initiative limits redistribution to the old system by excluding those pensioners in the new system who belong to the same income class (above the minimum pension). This action suggests that the new system is strongly insulated from the political process but that the lower-middle-income classes are being stimulated to request a return to the old system. The coexistence of the two systems may be fraught with political problems.

The political basis of the new pension system

The second pension reform introduced by Chile's authoritarian regime was the one that created a new pension system alongside the old one. The workers who had contributed to the old system were allowed to choose between the old and the new pension systems. Obviously, the new Chilean pension system is ideologically consistent with the economic and political reforms of the authoritarian regime. This reform was first proposed in 1973 by a group of free-market Chilean economists trained at the University of Chicago (Méndez 1992: 129–36).

In this period (1974–88), the vacillation between ideological trends that had blocked pension reform until 1970 disappeared, for several reasons. First, the authoritarian regime did not allow other expressions and dislodged established pressure groups. Second, the development of the capital markets enabled them, by the 1970s, to offer better saving and insurance vehicles than during the 1930s. This change allowed privately managed solutions to several of the problems that had characterized social security. Third, a technically qualified elite had emerged in Chile, which was available for significantly improving the state's administrative and regulatory capacities. In practical terms, the state was now able to put into practice laws that allowed for the private provision of social security services, subject to strong public regulation. The advancing process of state formation permitted the creation of organizations that were less state-oriented.

The basis of the new pension system is the accumulation, in individual accounts, of the mandatory contributions periodically deposited in them, plus interest, for the purpose of financing the old-age pensions.[5] The old-age pension funds, owned by the holders of the individual accounts, are administered by private pension-fund management firms called *Administradoras de Fondos de Pensiones,* or AFPs. During a worker's economically active life, his old-age pension functions as a standard defined-contribution regime, but at retirement it becomes a defined-benefit regime if the worker has chosen the annuity option. This financial arrangement contrasts with the standard defined-benefit systems for the active life seen in both occupational and state-managed pensions in most countries of the OECD except Australia.[6] The full return is allocated to individual returns during active life, so that the system provides stability only by diversification across investments and over time during that phase of life.

Individuals entering the system have a number of options, which have important political implications. The first is to choose and change their AFP. Individuals may also make voluntary contributions in excess of the mandatory 10 per cent to increase their capitalization fund, which allows them to finance an early retirement. In addition, once the accumulation cycle is completed, individuals are allowed to choose between assuming the financial risk of their own longevity by receiving pensions with a programmed withdrawal formula, or insuring against the financial cost of longevity by acquiring an annuity from one of a number of private life insurance companies, which they choose themselves. These annuities are indexed to the CPI and offer options such as bequests. Competition between AFPs provides for the maximization of returns on investment. The state has a supplementary but significant role, mandating contributions and regulating the private firms that manage the pension funds to prevent fraud and, more generally, to ensure that they fulfil their obligations.

Individual ownership

Laws governing property rights protect the private ownership of contributions and of the return earned. Chilean property rights were weakened during the 1960s as a result of the constitutional reforms allowing uncompensated nationalization of the large copper-mining establishments and medium-sized and large agricultural estates. In addition, during the regime of President Allende, the executive branch used previously unenforced laws inherited from a brief socialist period in 1932 to move the political system towards socialism, weakening property rights even further. The 1980 constitution restored the protections of property rights and the juridical certainty they had lost. In this new setting, the owners of individual accounts today have full juridical protection for the decisions they are allowed to make about the use of their funds.

Although individuals in welfare states also have rights that apply to pension benefits promised in their countries' pension systems and can defend their rights in court, those rights have substantially less protection than private ownership, as shown by the history of legislative changes to the present value of pension benefits that many democratic countries have adopted. In the Chilean case, the courts protect only the nominal value of a pension granted by the old system; there is no entitlement to a cost-of-living adjustment. This is a serious disadvantage in a country having an average annual inflation rate of 15 per cent.

In Chile individual ownership of contributions is enhanced because all contributions are made in the name of the worker, and none in the name of the employer. Of course, the employer withholds and pays all contributions to the pension fund. This is true in both the new and the old systems. However, the lack of contributions in the name of the employer causes some workers to believe that they are losing a subsidy from the employer, and that misperception can be a political issue. Their concern is groundless because the law that reset the size of contributions also required the gross wage to be raised to the initial wage plus the employer's contributions, so that take-home wages would not be affected.

The linkage between contributions and benefits

Citizens are likely to feel they have a stake in the pension system if they perceive that a sacrifice (contribution to a pension fund) they make today will produce a reward (an asset that is juridically certain) in the future. Each member of the new system knows that the level of his pension is directly proportional to the balance accumulated in his own account. Such a system is very different from a pension system in which citizens know, or suspect, that their benefits are subject to group pressure, political mobilization, or electoral impact.

The benefit formula of Chile's defined-contribution systems is transparent. It would be politically unthinkable for a pressure group to seek lump-sum transfers of tens of thousands of dollars from the state to the individual accounts of members who are about to retire, or for the state to issue bonds in the financial market to pay for those transfers. The discrimination would be so egregious that it would not obtain political approval. However, it is quite easy to obtain legislative approval for a 10 per cent increase in pensions for a pressure group that offers critical electoral support to weak incumbents. Economically, both subsidies are the same, but politically they are very different.

The reason is that the new pension system fosters the perception that a balance exists in the individual accumulation account, and the linkage of that balance to contributions is evident. This emphasis is due in part to the use of the defined-contribution approach, which offers the account's owner a visible account balance to check at any time. The result is that most discussions about the Chilean pension system focus on how to increase benefits, given fixed contributions and the fact that there are no subsidies.

Compare this situation with the political debate prompted by a system in which one law defines benefits, another law sets contribution rates, and the two are not linked at the individual level. There, the analysis focuses on comparing benefits: Who obtained better pensions and who did not? Why should the government grant unequal pensions? The government grants equal police protection to everybody, so why should pension benefits be earnings-related if police protection is not ?

The most dramatic political impact of the defined-benefit approach occurs in the initial stages when mandatory pensions are introduced. People want to know why those who are age 55 at the introduction date should not obtain pensions similar to those of workers who are age 40 or 30. Politicians are sensitive to charges of unequal treatment between politically equal citizens, and so they tend to grant similar pensions to both groups, even though one of them contributes for only ten years and the other contributes for thirty-five. Diamond (1996) has called this political phenomenon the 'framing effect' of defined-benefit systems, which is particularly damaging in the initial stages of mandatory social security. Its absence in defined-contribution systems is an important political advantage.

The same situation arises during a demographic transition. In any pension system subject to an increase in the dependency ratio, pensions must fall. The fall is smaller in a funded system than in a pay-as-you-go system because the liquidation of assets by the aggregate pension fund is spread out over many years and the induced rise in interest rates stimulates all cohorts to increase their savings voluntarily and reduce investment. This reduction compensates for the aggregate negative impact on the consumption of retirees to some extent. In a defined-contribution system the fall in pensions occurs over many years and shows up as a secular fall in asset prices that is masked by short-term fluctuations. In such setting it is hard to build up a pressure group to obtain state aid for those generations. In a funded defined-benefit system, however, pressure groups can simply claim that legislated benefit promises must be honoured. This forces the political system to choose between reducing benefits—which risks losing the next election—or increasing taxes—which has the same risks. From a constitutional standpoint, the framing effect of legislated defined-benefit pensions is dangerous for fiscal stability and opens the field to pressure groups in a socially inefficient manner.

The role of the state in the new Chilean system

The new Chilean system has been characterized as a government system in which some functions have been contracted out to private providers. This description is not exact, but it is a useful reminder of the enormous role played by the state in the new system. The state acts as a supervisor so that the AFPs can duly administer the funds, the AFPs' use in the capital markets can be transparent, and the funds can be subject to the least possible risk for a given return. The regulatory activity of the state is greater than its role in standard public systems, in which the functions of supervision and operation are not separated explicitly.

Most importantly, the state forces the working population (its employers) to make contributions to individual accounts. In response, the individuals exercise rights of ownership in the use of their accumulated resources, but with tight limitations. Each person is free to change AFP (after a minimum stay of four months), but only among licensed AFPs. He cannot dispose freely of the accumulated contributions. Moreover, the use of retirement savings is limited to financing certain types of need in the future.

The Chilean constitution includes the 'right to social security' in the chapter on constitutional duties and rights. There, after establishing that social security is a right, it states that 'the Law may establish mandatory contributions' (Article 18). This approach may be contrasted with the radical libertarian thesis of the minimal state, which places the obligation to meet individual needs on the individual. According to that perspective, private ownership of social security accounts is appropriate, but compulsory contributions and limitations on their use are not. Stated in a different way, the libertarian thesis holds that individuals have the right not to anticipate their eventual needs. Through a social learning process of trial and error, they may come to realize that a lack of planning can result in indigence, dependency upon others, and loss of freedom for themselves. According to this position, the state has no other function than to guarantee the inviolability of the ownership of the social security savings and the intangibility of contracts. Each person is free to choose whether he saves for his social security or not; and if he chooses to do so, he is also free to dispose of the accumulated resources whenever he wishes, or as allowed by a savings contract freely entered into.

This radical thesis should not be accepted because the community has a right to anticipate that individuals' incontinence in current spending and their lack of planning for their future needs will have adverse effects on the society, considered as a whole. If an individual decided not to plan for his future needs, such as support in old age, he would have no other option but to resort to the aid of others. And there would always be humanitarian persons or groups who would try to provide such aid, for whom the inanition of others is morally and humanely intolerable. On those persons and groups would fall, in a random manner, a burden that could be distributed in a more suitable manner if society as a whole assumed those duties. In addition, the obligation to contribute to their own future support prevents the individuals who would otherwise be dependent upon aid from falling into potential servitude, losing their autonomy and independence.

This reasoning should not be confused with the concept of the welfare state because it does not rely upon the principle of equality and does not impose administration by the state. Instead, it justifies some intervention by the state but does not justify the manner in which state intervention has occurred in socialist and social democratic regimes, which must resort to other arguments.

I have expounded an intermediate position in Valdés-Prieto (1994*b*). My argument there is that the law falsely assumes that *all* workers are unable to plan ahead and that, under that assumption, they must all be forced to surrender the administration of their social security savings to the AFPs. However, compulsory social security savings may be less valuable than voluntary retirement savings because they cannot be used as precautionary saving. In addition, as AFPs are subject to strong regulatory action by the state, such dependence has dangers: the regulations can be increased, and pressure from the governing party may induce regulators to influence the voting decisions of AFPs in shareholder meetings for the purpose of favouring their political supporters or helping party financing.

I have proposed specific rules for exempting individuals from compulsory contributions. To claim an exemption, a worker would have to have made voluntary mandatory contributions, in excess of the mandatory 10 per cent of earnings to his old-age individual account, to any savings programme satisfying two conditions. The first is that the monthly voluntary contribution valid for this purpose must be subject to a ceiling. This maximum could be set at, say, 10 per cent of monthly earnings. The second is that cumulative voluntary contributions must exceed the equivalent of, say, four months of the average monthly earnings over the last ten years. Only an individual who plans ahead (is provident) could meet these requirements. The conditions are tight enough so that no credit company can arbitrage around it, and the programme may be quite attractive to workers over age 35, an age at which credit constraints usually cease to be binding and voluntary saving becomes feasible for many.

Privatization: provision and consumer choice

Regarding the provision of pension services, the 1980 constitution (Article 18) states that 'the action of the State shall be directed to guarantee the access of all the inhabitants to the enjoyment of basic uniform services, be it that these are granted through public *or private* institutions' [emphasis added]. The AFPs have had substantial political impact because they have built themselves into an important pressure group that influences legislation and opinion through selective financial support. The first objective of this important pressure group has been to enhance the legitimacy of the new pension system. In addition, individual AFPs have vied to build a reputation for maximizing the rate of return they offer to pensioners. Their political message is that workers should obtain the highest pensions in exchange for their contributions. This political objective meshes extremely well with their individual commercial interest.

These political implications of privatization exist in all types of privatized pension systems. However, in the reforms implemented in Chile in 1981, the United Kingdom in 1988, Peru in 1993, and Argentina in 1994, there is a second dimension of privatization, which is the privatization in the choice of fund managers. The fact that an AFP has been chosen by its members—not by employers, as in Switzerland beginning in 1985 or Australia beginning in 1986—gives it a sort of mandate to represent their interests in the political arena. Accordingly AFPs have been vocal in all debates about pension reform that have taken place in Chile since 1981.

If AFPs were chosen by state authorities—maybe through a bidding process—they would lack a direct mandate from members, and their political role would be much more limited. That is what happened during the early 1990s in Malaysia, where the employees' provident fund contracted out some fund management services to private firms, with little political effect. It would also happen if the pension system were managed by a private monopoly under price regulation, because the political master would be the authorities who set tariffs, not the customers, who would have no choice.

Vulnerabilities of the new system

The capitalization approach emphasizes individual responsibility and provides incentives and instruments for maximizing individual interests. In it, the individual does not consider himself to be protected by the state from birth to death. Contrary to the rhetoric, however, the state continues to be the paramount force behind the new mandatory capitalization system in Chile. This model therefore remains vulnerable to the political influences that retard political development. If unchecked, those influences could eventually destroy the system.

Pressure groups may buy out politicians in a variety of ways. Politicians may provide weak financial supervision by refusing independence and financial support to tough regulators, and this in turn may allow those pressure groups to pay a lower return to the pension funds than they would to unregulated investors in a competitive environment. In the case of Sweden's AFP system, Pontusson (1984) reports that the big local issuers of securities benefited from tough limits on the purchase of new securities by the ATP pension funds, limits that they controlled themselves.

As a special case of the situation just described, a few incumbent AFPs may decide to buy out politicians or the regulators to assure that the system is subject to regulations that impose hidden barriers to entry. In this scenario, a pressure group favours reforms that limit competition between private providers and blocks reforms that facilitate competition, ensuring that high commission levels can be maintained at the expense of workers and employers. Concern about this possibility has been voiced in Chile, where the four largest AFPs manage 65 per cent of the funds and serve 70 per cent of the members.

A state in which political parties depend upon patronage may use its regulatory powers to force pension-fund managers to vote in favour of party candidates at the shareholder meetings of the companies in which they hold equity. Such a policy may allow political parties to achieve control of private companies and expand the scope of patronage activities.

Populism, presented as a priority of the equality goal, can also materialize if state authorities impose redistributive taxes and transfers on the account balances in the pension system. Such wealth redistributions are hard to justify in a defined-contribution system, but they may still earn electoral approval if presented appropriately and if they benefit a large enough proportion of the voters.

As an example of populism, the state may impose regulations that prohibit fund-management companies from offering discounted commissions to their members, assuring non-discriminatory treatment of all workers. However, those workers who can arrange group contracts and those who are prepared to accept a penalty for quitting the company fund early are prevented from negotiating a discount. This sort of regulation, which exists in Chile, has led fund-management companies to compete on the basis of salespeople rather than on prices, thereby raising administrative costs. Allowing discounted commissions would reduce those costs but might appear to condone price discrimination.

Informal regulatory pressure has been used in another populist scheme, which is to force management companies to reduce their flat administrative charges well below their fixed cost per account. This has made high-income members much more profitable than low-income ones, stimulating expenditure on sales personnel who provide services or even money to attract such members (Valdés-Prieto 1995). The Chilean government has proposed legislative changes that would prohibit members from switching from one management company to another before one year of residence. This approach to the problem does not address the root causes of the high rotation rate.

Either patronage or populism may flourish if political underdevelopment allows a dictator or a single party to require that a majority of the pension funds be invested in government securities that pay low interest rates. In such cases the government may invest the funds in secret projects both at home and abroad. This state of affairs, reminiscent of Singapore, perpetuates political underdevelopment.

A state that is financially strapped may resort to taxing pension funds at abnormal rates. Pension funds are a particularly vulnerable target because they are heavily regulated and their assets are well known. State authorities, for example, can require the funds to hold a certain percentage of their portfolios in special securities, such as housing mortgages or bonds issued by favoured industries, the interest rate of which can be set below market levels. They can also tax pension funds indirectly, by prohibiting the funds from investing abroad, or by limiting the volume of bond and equity issues in the local market and subjecting banks to special reserve requirements on deposits taken by pension funds. The danger of these practices is significant in countries with large fiscal deficits.

The use of the conventional defined-contribution approach opens up the possibility that a string of negative rates of return on investments may induce politicians to nationalize the funds by guaranteeing a fixed return in exchange for control of the existing assets. Legislators can avoid this outcome by adopting a more astute defined-contribution approach that keeps an automatic control over the consequences of such shocks for current pensions. For example, they might introduce a rule prohibiting benefit amounts from falling faster than, say, 5 per cent per year in real terms, so that the funds are used faster if the actual return is much below projections, allowing time for asset values to recover from a large drop. Such schemes have not yet been considered in Chile.

A similar problem can occur if there are predicted or unpredictable increases in life expectancy. Jorge Bravo has pointed out that, as shown in Table 7.1 of this volume, middle-aged men today who will retire in the early 2020s will have an expected retirement life about 20 per cent longer than those who retired in the early 1980s. The older generation will be able to compensate for the longer period they will be dependent upon their pensions by drawing upon the excess capital accumulated during 1981–95, when the real rate of return of the funds was around 13 per cent and the contribution rate was kept at 10 per cent. A related point is that the Chilean system has an automatic safety valve for cases in which longevity increases are not compensated by high returns: the proportion of people who qualify for early pensioning will be much smaller.

In sum, a pension system will always reflect the weakness of the state that gives it life by making contributions mandatory. No system is entirely free from the risk of bad design and political manipulation

Concluding Comments

This chapter has offered an analysis of the political basis of the main pension systems that have been evolving in Chile during the past century, with an emphasis on the new, privately managed and fully funded pension system created in 1981. The main conclusion is that when a country does not acknowledge the true basis of the political competition that governs it, it can adopt a pension system that provides little benefit and can do a lot of harm to its development process.

The time period in which a pension system must operate may be sixty years or more for each individual, which is long enough for a fair share of convulsions and evolutionary change to accumulate in the process of state formation. This long time period argues for a greater reliance in pension matters upon civilian institutions such as private contracts supported by the courts, because they have been shown to be more stable than the political process over the last three hundred years and they have standing going back thousands of years. A complementary option is to maximize the use of another institution that has longer standing than the political process: the family. This requires rolling back mandatory contributions to the bare essentials needed to help improvident citizens.

Policy-makers should demand that a pension system not exacerbate the weaknesses of a state's political system. The Chilean experience may contribute to our understanding of how to achieve this objective. Constitutional rules, legislation that provides automatic inflation adjustments, uniformity of pension regimes, individual ownership, a defined-contribution financial approach, and privatization of both provision and provider selection are tools that emerge from this examination. The reorientation of the redistributive drive towards the really poor is also essential, especially in countries where large groups of workers are outside the formal sector and the state lacks the capacity to force them to contribute.

However, reliance on private institutions does require a significant amount of administrative capabilities from the state, expressed in an ability to regulate financial intermediaries effectively. Moreover, privatization does not guarantee that pensions will be insulated from the political process, for some possibilities for populism and patronage remain. The independence of privatized pension systems from effective regulations has its own danger: the capture of regulators by the private entities that provide social security services. This danger is well known in other privately owned but publicly regulated industries, such as electricity and telecommunications.

Notes

Financial support for the research reported here came from AFP Provida under a 1993–5 research programme on the economics of pensions. I am also grateful for comments by participants at the Seminar on Intergenerational Economic Relations and Demographic Change, especially for comments by Jorge Bravo, and for the references and data he provided for Table 7.1.

1. These contribution rates are the simple sum of employee and employer rates, taken from Wagner (1983: 177, 186). The sum of contributions as a percentage of wage costs rose to 31.2% at EMPART (1947) and to 24.3% at the SSS (1954). The dozen or so *Cajas* formed before 1924 exhibited a variety of contribution rates.
2. This was the simple sum of employers' and workers' contributions (Ffrench-Davis 1973: 342).
3. The dominant model of the political business cycle was created by Nordhaus (1975). See also Weatherford (1988).

4. Jorge Bravo asserts that the military regime raised the mean value of pensions paid to armed-forces retirees from about twice the national mean in 1960 to 3.5 times the national mean in 1980. Even so, his criticism does not deny that the elimination of the special indexing clause for the military prevented the continuation of that trend.
5. Social security contributions for old age are equal to 10% of earnings. Contributions to finance the system of disability and survivorship pensions are paid to insurance companies and are around 0.80% of earnings (Valdés-Prieto and Navarro 1992). The commission charged by private operators is close to 2.2% of gross wages.
6. The defined-benefit approach is far from riskless. It exposes workers to the risk of a low final wage, on which benefits are based, which materializes if their wages do not grow as expected or if they are fired or quit their jobs before pensioning. In addition, in conventional defined-benefit programmes the sponsor retains the right to reduce benefits on the grounds that it cannot be forced to cover benefits of indefinite cost. This provision exposes workers to abuse from sponsors.

8 Pensions and Generational Histories in a Simple Demo-economic Model: The Case of France

Didier Blanchet and Jean-Alain Monfort

This chapter has two goals. The first is to present a simple model describing the future of the French pension system. The model includes simple macroeconomic features that allow us to quantify several variables that are central in the current pension debate in France—namely the consequences of various ways of computing pensions in existing schemes and the effects of developing complementary funded schemes on top of existing schemes, which are almost entirely pay-as-you-go. (Our model also takes into consideration the effects of raising the retirement age, but space limitations preclude our discussing that feature here.) The second goal is to present the results of the model in a generational perspective—that is, to trace the implications of the hypothesized future developments of the pension system for the life courses of both existing and future generations. These two goals are not new, and therefore we start by identifying the specific attributes of the approach we have chosen.

In considering a modelling strategy, we know that the analysis of macro-interactions between economic growth and the functioning of pension systems often relies on applied general-equilibrium models with overlapping generations, initiated by Auerbach and Kotlikoff (1987). Cazes *et al.* (1992) and Chauveau and Loufir (1994, 1995) have applied this modelling approach to France in a series of studies. The model we present here remains several steps behind the current state of the art as represented by those studies. We ignore most of the assumptions of that class of models (full life-cycle behaviour, the inclusion of both labour supply and savings, and long-term perfect foresight). Briefly, our model consists of (1) a demographic projection completed by a description of the various components of the pension system, part of which can lead to some specific capital accumulation; (2) a production function that allows us to assess the effects of changing demographic conditions and capital accumulation on capital intensity and relative remuneration of factors; and (3) a simple labour market equation allowing the existence of either structural or transitory classical unemployment. This simple structure is much less comprehensive than any of the other attempts we have mentioned, but by allowing more systematic explorations of a basic set of parameters, the roles of which can be easily traced out, we believe that this exercise can make its own contribution to the debate.

Our decision to present the results in a generational perspective is motivated by the interest raised by the concept of generational accounting, as introduced by Auerbach, Gokhale, and Kotlikoff (1991). Our approach, however, differs from theirs in two ways.

The first way in which it differs is that we try to present full life-cycle profiles instead of aggregate indicators of net generational transfers. We shall therefore not compute synthetic generational accounts. Nor shall we rely upon other synthetic indicators whose meaning remains unclear, such as cohort measures of internal rates of return on contributions.[1] Of course, there is one cost associated with our decision not to rely upon synthetic cohort indexes: the large quantity of numerical information that must be displayed. We shall show how the systematic use of three-dimensional graphs (Lexis surfaces) already used in other demographic studies can be used to solve this problem.

Given that the legitimacy of current transfers to any existing generation is of little significance if it does not take into account the past experience of that generation, the second way in which our model differs from that of our predecessors is that we try to complement the prospective picture given by the simulation model with some retrospective elements. Most of those elements go back to *circa* 1945–50, which corresponds to the period when the present social security system was established in France. This means that the earliest generations for whom full generational profiles are available are those born between 1925 and 1930.

Those generations correspond precisely to the generations identified in some studies (e.g. Thomson 1989) as 'welfare generations'. They have been given that label because they might have received family benefits when those benefits were generous[2] and might not have had to make large contributions to pension funds or make large health expenditures for their parents (given their parents' relatively short life expectancy, limited pension entitlements, and limited propensity to make use of facilities offered by the health-care system). Those generations are still benefiting from the system because demographic ageing has not yet caused their benefits to be restricted. Two elements outside the welfare system that may also have contributed to their relative advantages have been very low levels of unemployment and negative real interest rates during periods of rapid inflation, which allowed them easy access to home ownership. It is not our purpose to discuss all these aspects of these cohorts' living conditions, but we shall nevertheless try to examine more closely how correct it is to label them as 'welfare generations', bearing in mind that the definition of this term relies on intergenerational comparisons of well-being that are necessarily partial or conventional.

We begin by presenting the structure of the model. Next we shall briefly summarize how we have constructed retrospective data. We shall then present three groups of simulation results: simulation of a 'no reform' scenario, simulation of the 1993 reform within the pure pay-as-you-go (PAYGO) system, and simulation of a transition towards a partially funded scheme.

Projecting the Future

Our model for projecting the future of France's pension system incorporates simplified assumptions about the population's age structure and labour supply, the characteristics of the existing PAYGO pension system, and other components of social protection such as funded pensions and other forms of savings. In addition it takes into consideration wages, the labour market, and net disposable income.

Demographic projections and labour supply

Our demographic projections are derived from those developed in 1994 by the Institute National de la Statistique et des Etudes Economiques (INSEE) (Dinh 1994). They use the same assumptions about mortality trends, which are more optimistic than in the past, when most projections underestimated the increases in life expectancy that have since occurred (Vallin 1992). Average life expectancy is assumed to rise to 90 years for women and 82 years for men by 2050. The total fertility rate is assumed to rise from the 1996 level of 1.7 children per woman to 2.1 during the next twenty years and to remain at that level indefinitely. INSEE's projections included an assumption of positive net in-migration of about 50,000 migrants per year, but we have not included that assumption in our model at this stage. The model treats labour supply as an exogenous variable. Labour-force participation rates, $l(a, t)$, are assumed to be fixed at their initial level in $t_0 = 1990$.

The pension system (PAYGO)

Most of the French pension system is PAYGO, and our description of it assumes a fictitious general scheme already introduced in other studies (Malabouche 1987; Vernière 1990*a*, 1990b). Its rules are a stylization of the rules prevailing in France's basic social security system, the *régime général,* extended to the whole population and to total wages. Those rules consist in computing pension amounts by multiplying the number of years of contributions by an 'annuity rate' and a reference wage that used to be computed as an average of wages obtained over the ten best years of workers' past careers.[3] We shall apply to this fictitious scheme the scenario of future adjustments that were enacted in the pension reform of 1993. They consist mainly of three new provisions: (1) a modification of indexation rules for pensions that are already liquidated, (2) a modification of rules used to compute the reference wage to which the pension is proportional (progressively computed over the twenty-five best years of a worker's career instead of the ten best ones), and (3) a modification of the conditions necessary for a worker to benefit from the normal annuity rate. Our analysis concentrates on the first two provisions. The third one should not have much impact over the medium term, and it relates to the general topic of raising the retirement age (which we do not address here).

Admittedly it is unrealistic to assume that this reform, which applies to the *régime général,* is representative of reforms that might be applied to the entire French system, because we already know that the adaptation of special or complementary schemes may follow different logics or at least proceed at different speeds. Nevertheless we make that assumption here and advise caution in interpreting our results, which are best read as indicating what would happen if all segments of the French pension system were managed in a way similar to the one envisaged for the *régime général.* Having given this caveat, we model the function of the PAYGO segment of the French pension system in the following way:

First, we denote $p(s, a, t)$ as the pension level for persons of gender s and age a at time t.

Second, we compute the pension for persons who were already retired at period $t-1$ by revising the pension level at age $a-1$ and period $t-1$ according to the formula

$$p(s,a,t) = p(s,a-1,t-1)[1 + t_{index}(\bar{w}(t-1)/\bar{w}(t-2) - 1)], \qquad (8.1)$$

where t_{index} measures the degree of indexation of pensions on average net wages $\bar{w}$. A value of 1 implies a full indexation on net wages (lagged one year to preserve a maximum amount of recursivity in the model).[4] A value of zero reproduces the case of indexation limited to prices because the model, working in real prices, neutralizes the inflation rate.

Third, for people entering retirement at time t, we compute the pension according to the following simplified rule:

$$p(s,a,t) = \alpha \sum_{k=1}^{50} l(s,a-k,t-k) \sum_{k=1}^{D} w(s,a-k,t-k)D, \qquad (8.2)$$

where $l(s,a-k,t-k)$ is the sequence of past activity rates, the sum of which gives the average number of years contributed to the system by new pensioners, and where D is the duration over which past sex- and cohort-specific wages, $w(s,a-k,t-k)$, are averaged to compute the reference wage to which the pension is proportional ($D =$ ten years under current conditions and twenty-five years after the reform has fully produced its effects).

This formula is applied separately for each sex, given the differences between men and women in labour-force participation rates and labour earnings. We also differentiate the proportionality coefficient by sex to take into account the existence of non-contributive benefits that either are explicitly directed to women (e.g. bonuses for childrearing years) or accrue more than proportionally to them. This latter type of benefits includes both the consequences of the existence of a minimum pension level and the role of survivor's benefits, the exact modelling of which would have required a specific simulation of the dissolution of couples by death; we have taken them into account in this crude way. In general, under current conditions, we have assumed the annuity rate for men to be 1.4 per cent; that is, one marginal year of contribution entitles a worker to an increase in pension benefits amounting to 1.4 per cent of the reference wage. The same rate for women, estimated according to empirical data on the average level of pensions, amounts to 2.1 per cent.

Once we have computed the pensions, we aggregate them by age and sex at time t. We also compute a uniform contribution rate, θ_r, on gross wages for currently working people by dividing the total amount of pensions by the current total wage bill.

Other components of social protection

Other components of social transfers we model in a preliminary and imperfect way. Here we merely mention them. Like pensions, they are financed by proportional contributions from wages. We classify them as either unemployment benefits or other benefits—mainly health insurance and family benefits. Total unemployment benefits are proportional to the total number of unemployed persons, with a level per unemployed worker that follows an indexation formula similar to the indexation formula used for pensions. We assume the level of indexation on (lagged) net wages to be equal to 1. The aggregate amount of unemployment benefits at time t is therefore computed as:

$$B_u(t) = B_u(t-1) \cdot \frac{\bar{w}(t-1)}{\bar{w}(t-2)} \cdot \frac{L(t) \cdot \bar{u}(t)}{L(t-1) \cdot \bar{u}(t-1)}. \tag{8.3}$$

The formula for the 'other benefits' category is similar, except that the total amount of benefits is assumed to be proportional to the total population. This formula is

$$B_0(t) = B_0(t-1) \cdot \frac{\bar{w}(t-1)}{\bar{w}(t-2)} \cdot \frac{N_{tot}(t)}{N_{tot}(t-1)}. \tag{8.4}$$

These two amounts of benefits allow the determination of two specific contribution rates, θ_u and θ_o, which, combined with the contribution rate to the PAYGO system, θ_r, gives the final relation between gross and net wages as

$$\bar{w}(t) = \bar{w}_{gr}(t)(1 - \theta - \theta_u - \theta_o). \tag{8.5}$$

Funded pensions

In modelling funded pensions, we start from the observation that they can be considered as marginal in the current French system. If we designate $K_f(\mathrm{s}, a, t)$ as the total amount of capital accumulated by persons of gender s and generation $t-a$ in pension funds at age a, we therefore start, at time t_0, with $K_f(s, a, t_) = 0$ for all a. Next we assume that people will start accumulating capital in such funds, the simple hypothesis being that the accumulation by each cohort in the fund will represent a fraction, $\theta_f(t)$, of its current wage, $w(s, a, t)$, net of other social contributions. This fraction is only time-specific, with no age or cohort component; such an approximation is not unrealistic. It is true that generations who are near the end of their economically active lives need a more intensive savings effort to pre-finance a given amount of additional funded pension, but their need for complementary pensions is more limited than that of younger cohorts, who will be leaving activity under less unfavourable conditions. We can assume, as a first approximation, that the two effects cancel each other. As a result, for persons below the retirement age at time t, the model assumes the following simple accumulation equation in the pension fund:

$$k_f(s,a,t) = k_f(s,a-1,t-1)(1+r_t) + \theta_f(t)N(s,a,t)l(s,a,t)(1-u(s,a,t))w(s,a,t), \tag{8.6}$$

where r_t is the net return on capital and $u(s,a,t)$ is the sex- and age-specific unemployment rate.

After retirement, this capital stock is progressively consumed. We assume that pensions distributed by the fund are indexed only on prices and that they are recalibrated each year on the basis of current mortality rather than expected mortality. These two assumptions are not unrealistic. A more disputable (and preliminary) assumption is that pension levels are computed separately for each sex on the basis of its own life expectations.[5] If $\pi(s, a, t)$ is the current survivorship function, the formula for the pension served by the fund is

$$p_f(s,a,t) = \frac{K_f(s,a,t)\pi(s,a,t)}{N(s,a,t)\sum_{a'=a}^{100} e^{-r(t)(a'-a)}\pi(s,a',t)}, \tag{8.7}$$

which implies the following de-accumulation function:

$$K_f(s,a,t) = K_f(s,a-1,t-1)(1+r_t) - p_f(s,a,t)N(s,a,t), \tag{8.8}$$

both equations being applied separately for each sex.

Other forms of savings

Given our assumption that pension funds or equivalent systems are non-existent in France at the start of the projection and may remain so in scenarios where such funds do not develop, the model obviously needs another savings motive to explain capital accumulation. Several possibilities are available. One is to assume that existing savings still obey pure life-cycle motives, even if the savings are not institutionally channelled by pension funds. This assumption does not seem to be especially applicable to the French case: replacement ratios currently offered by PAYGO pension schemes appear quite high by international standards and leave little need for additional pension pre-financing.

Another possibility is to invoke more general precautionary motives, or to assume that, beyond the life-cycle motive, savings are motivated by a desire for intergenerational transmission.[6] This is the assumption made by Chauveau and Loufir (1994, 1995), who have augmented their life-cycle utility function with a bequest factor.

One problem with the last assumption, however, is that we know that the behaviour of intergenerational transmission is highly concentrated (see Kessler, Masson, and Pestieau 1991). This fact suggests a simpler representation of savings for motives other than pension pre-financing, which consists in using a simple Cambridgian two-class framework. The first class will consist of workers for whom we shall assume no bequest motive, and, until now, no need of life-cycle savings, thanks to the high replacement ratios proposed by existing PAYGO schemes. We shall furthermore assume that if this class develops a life-cycle behaviour in the future, it will be exactly the one forced by the eventual pension funds, with no additional retirement savings (either because of individual myopia or because of the cost of entry into capital markets). The second class will be one of so-called 'capitalists'. Given that the economic status of this class is not our primary interest here and that our goal is to keep the model as simple as possible, we describe its behaviour as follows: $K_c(t)$ will be the total amount of capital held by this class at time t. At time t_0, that amount is assumed to be equivalent to the total capital stock, $K(t_0)$. The evolution of this capital will be, at each period, governed by the equation

$$K_c(t) = K_c(t-1)[1 - \delta + \sigma(r_t + \delta)], \tag{8.9}$$

which means that the savings behaviour of this class consists only in reinvesting at a constant rate, σ, the gross revenue of its capital, δ being a depreciation rate. We also assume that savings are a fraction of gross rather than net income to avoid technical problems in the (unlikely) event that economic growth and interest rates became so low that net capital income would be negative.

This representation of savings is crude of course, but it has several advantages that justify its exploration. One is that, although extreme, it is less extreme than the assumption of a uniform population sharing the same dynastic behaviour with perfect foresight. Another is that the dynamics of this kind of model are well known. We know that in this class of model, long-term aggregate capital accumulation is governed only by the behaviour of 'capitalists', so that the only long-term macroeconomic effect of developing the pension fund will be a change in the structure of capital (less K_c and more K_f)—a result that seems realistic and is obtained without requiring any of the assumptions usually needed to justify Ricardian equivalence applied to pension financing. A third advantage of our model is that playing on parameter σ allows us to rederive easily the typical cases considered in debates about pensions. If $\sigma = 1$, this means that all capital income is reinvested and a golden-rule situation prevails that will lead over the long term to identical actuarial returns in PAYGO and funded systems. Therefore we know immediately that funded systems will be more advantageous over the long term only if $\sigma < 1$, which is the situation we shall generally consider, the rewards having to be weighed against the immediate costs of lower consumption by workers.

Wages, the labour market, and net disposable income

Once the two sources of capital accumulation are identified, we can generate a series of total capital stock, $K(t)$. Total labour supply is determined by demographic trends and activity rates. We denote $L(t)$ as the labour force. It will be affected by an average unemployment rate, $\bar{u}(t)$ having two components: an exogenous structural component, $u^*(t)$, and a transitory component resulting from imperfect wage flexibility.

The latter component is modelled in the following way. At time t, we inherit a level of gross wages, $\bar{w}_{gr}(t-1)$. Given the capital stock, $K(t)$, which is the sum of $K_c(t)$ and of $K_f(s, a, t)$ over all ages, and given the production function, which is a function with constant elasticity of substitution (CES) and labour-augmenting technical progress, there is a gross wage rate, $w^*(t)$, that will be compatible with an unemployment rate just equal to the structural unemployment rate. The actual gross wage, $\bar{w}_{gr}(t)$, will then result from an asymmetric adjustment of the productivity-adjusted previous wage to this equilibrium wage:

$$\bar{w}_{gr}(t) = \max\{w^*(t), (1-\mu)[1+g(t)\bar{w}_{gr}(t-1) + \mu w^*(t)]\}. \tag{8.10}$$

This means that wages are perfectly elastic upward and imperfectly inelastic downward, the first assumption being introduced to avoid situations of over-employment.

The system therefore leads to an average level of wages that determines the average unemployment rate at time t. These two average levels are then converted into age-specific wage rates and unemployment rates according to the last-known age distribution of the two variables. A deeper integration of economic and demographic features of the labour market, w, would have required a more satisfactory treatment than this *ad hoc* disaggregation. For instance, a better separation of cohort and period effects on wages would be useful, instead of assuming that the age structure of wages depends upon only a period effect and an age effect. It is also likely that a given increase in the average unemployment rate would not have a uniform effect on the unemployment rates of workers in different age groups; an increasing imbalance between labour supply and demand has a disproportionate effect on unemployment rates at lower ages, in conformity either with insider/outsider or waiting-list models of the labour market, and it generates a higher rate of early retirement by generating unemployment at higher ages. An integration of all these features is beyond the scope of the present exercise, however; we prefer to stick to simple proportionality rules for our first approximation.

Finally, we combine wages, activity rates, and unemployment rates as well as contribution rates to compute indexes of net resources by sex and age. We compute them simply as resources net of contributions for social protection and eventual contributions to the fund, but without taking into account personal income tax, which has not been modelled thus far. We therefore have, for people below the normal retirement age, ($a < a_r$):

$$y(s,a,t) = l(s,a,t)[1 - u(s,a,t)]w(s,a,t)(1 - \theta_f) + l(s,a,t)u(s,a,t)\frac{B_u}{L \cdot \bar{u}}, \qquad (8.11)$$

and for people older than normal retirement age, ($a \geq a_r$):

$$y(s,a,t) = l(s,a,t)[1 - u(s,a,t)]w(s,a,t)(1 - \theta_f) + l(s,a,t)u(s,a,t)\frac{B_u}{L_{\bar{u}}}(1 - l(s,a,t))p_r(s,a,t) + p_f(s,a,t). \qquad (8.12)$$

The first formula is simply the sum of net labour income and unemployment benefits. The second includes the same components (for people still in the labour force), plus social security benefits (for persons no longer in the labour force), and funded pensions. These expressions do not include the 'other' component of social protection benefits which, as a first approximation, we consider rather as simple compensations for specific burdens—e.g. family charges or health costs.

Modelling the Past

Solutions for the retrospective part of the model are still preliminary. Retrospective age structures do not pose any specific problem (Daguet 1995). Our retrospective series of activity rates use reconstitutions made by Guillemot and Bordes (1994) for the post-1962 period and the long series established by Marchand and Thélot (1991) for the previous period. Full series of age- and sex-specific unemployment rates are also available from Guillemot and Bordes (1994) for the period beginning in 1962. For the preceding period only aggregate unemployment rates are available. We use those reconstructed by Villa (1994), disaggregating them by age and sex according to the earliest age- and sex-specific structure available (the one of 1962).

Next we reconstruct the series of average gross wages, normalized to 1 in 1990, using National Accounts and series proposed by Sauvy (1954) for the period from 1920 to 1948. Long series of social expenditures, since 1950, are derived from Social Protection Accounts. Lacking information about the previous period, we assume that expenditures were constant between 1948 and 1950, when the present system was created; and we also assume that social expenditures were negligible before. Dividing these series by the product of gross wages and the employed labour force, we reconstruct apparent contribution rates, which we then deduct from gross wages to compute a long aggregate series of net wages. This series is then disaggregated by age and sex. For the period 1962–90 the disaggregation is based upon actual distributions of labour earnings from *Déclarations Annuelles de Données Sociales*, as compiled by

INSEE. For the earlier period our disaggregation is based upon the earliest distribution (which is once again the one of 1962).

With this information, we are able to provide long series of net resources by age and sex for persons of working age similar to the ones projected by the model with Equation 8.11. For persons of retirement age, who have been combined into a single, non-working group over age 60,[7] we compute PAYGO pensions by spreading total expenditures over that population to derive a ratio of men's to women's average pension of 1.85. The ratio is derived from direct information from recent surveys on pension levels according to gender, but without any differentiation according to age. This is of course an oversimplification: in fact, pension levels decline slightly with age. It is nevertheless those reconstructed pension levels for the most recent generation of pensioners that, after comparing them with the past sequence of wages and activity rates, we have used to compute the apparent annuity rates for men and women, α, that are used in the prospective section: 1.4 and 2.1 per cent, respectively. The higher apparent rate for women illustrates, as mentioned earlier, the greater importance in their case of non-contributory benefits (*minimum vieillesse,* or survivor's benefits, provided as compensation for their childrearing years).[8] Once we have computed individualized pension levels in this way while neglecting other sources of retirement income, we are able to compute living standards for retired persons comparable to the ones to be computed according to Equation 8.12. The way in which our annuity rates are computed ensures continuity between the simulated pensions of new retirees at the onset of the projection and the pensions of the youngest retirees just before the projection starts.

Given all these elements, we see that we have full data for working years starting in 1920 and full pension data starting in 1946. This allows the reconstitution of almost complete generational income profiles starting with the generation born in 1900. We use all or part of this information to analyse the results, depending upon the kind of simulation analysed.

'No Reform' Scenarios

We start by examining a 'no reform' scenario—that is, continuation of the status quo—in which pension financing is entirely PAYGO, there is no change in labour-force participation rates at older ages, ongoing pensions are indexed to net wages, and new pensions are computed according to the current rules (i.e. as a function of the average wages of the ten best years of workers' lifetime wage profiles). These assumptions about the pension system are combined with an economic scenario that assumes a reinvestment rate of 80 per cent for non-pension capital income, an initial capital/output ratio of 2.5, a Cobb–Douglas production function calibrated so that the savings ratio and the K/Y ratio are consistent with an initial equilibrium growth path in which the initial unemployment rate is fixed. Equilibrium unemployment is set at 5 per cent, with a rate of adjustment of wages to their full employment value of 0.2 (coefficient μ of Equation 8.10). Finally, this scenario assumes a rate of labour-augmenting technical progress of 2 per cent per year. This assumption corresponds to the one generally retained for official pension projections (France, Commissariat Général du Plan 1991).

Figure 8.1 graphs the evolution of total net resources per head, for men of ages 20 and above, from both a period and a generational point of view. The period starts in 1950, with three specific generational paths outlined, corresponding respectively to cohorts 1920 (truncated), 1950, and 1980 (full). In this first scenario, the system preserves growing net incomes for both workers and retired persons, given the assumed growth rate. It is noteworthy that, although the cross-sectional profiles indicate moderate declines of retirement incomes with age, the longitudinal profiles show that full indexing of pensions allows those pensioners who reach ages higher than 90 to end up with pension levels higher than the highest of their lifetime wages.

These results show that, if we wish to exhibit significant adverse effects of population ageing on lifetime income paths, we must adopt another perspective, and this can be done in two ways. We can either shift to more pessimistic economic scenarios, or we can construct indicators of living standard that neutralize in one way or another the effect of productivity growth. We shall not

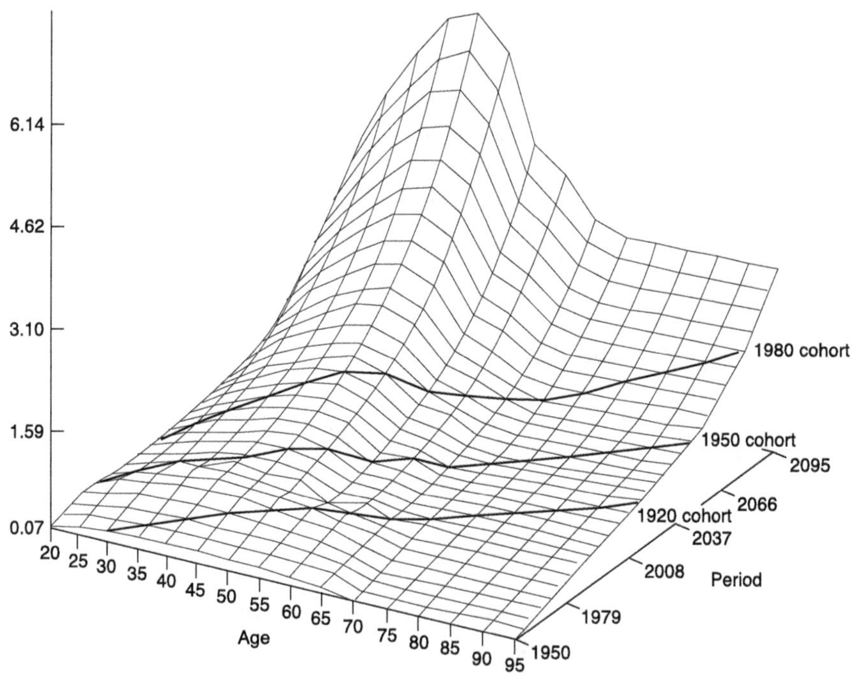

Fig. 8.1. Total net resources in the 'no reform' scenario, by period: France, 1950–2095

present here the results of adopting a pessimistic economic perspective, but rather simply note that assuming that economic growth would stop from now on, combined with the effect of population ageing, would result in new generations being less well-off, in absolute terms, than currently living generations.

Concerning the other option of neutralizing the effect of productivity growth on the living standard, Figures 8.2 and 8.3 present two possibilities. The first, represented by Figure 8.2, is to compute relative measures of income by dividing net resources at age *a* and time *t* by their transversal averages, computed (unweighted) over ages 20 to 95.

This transversal normalization leads to an index that measures how a person of age *a* at time *t* compares with other persons alive at the same time. It first allows us to highlight the decline in the relative income gap between workers and pensioners that occurred between 1950 and 1990. Over-indexation of pensions on net wages during that period led to compensating upward and downward movements of relative living standards above and below age 60.

The decline in the relative income gap stops by assumption around 1990. Its cessation creates a 'welfare generation' effect, with the generation born around 1920 enjoying a better economic situation, in relative terms, than any other generation at the same age. For instance, when retired, their resources are about 85 per cent of those of the entire population, twice as high as those of generations

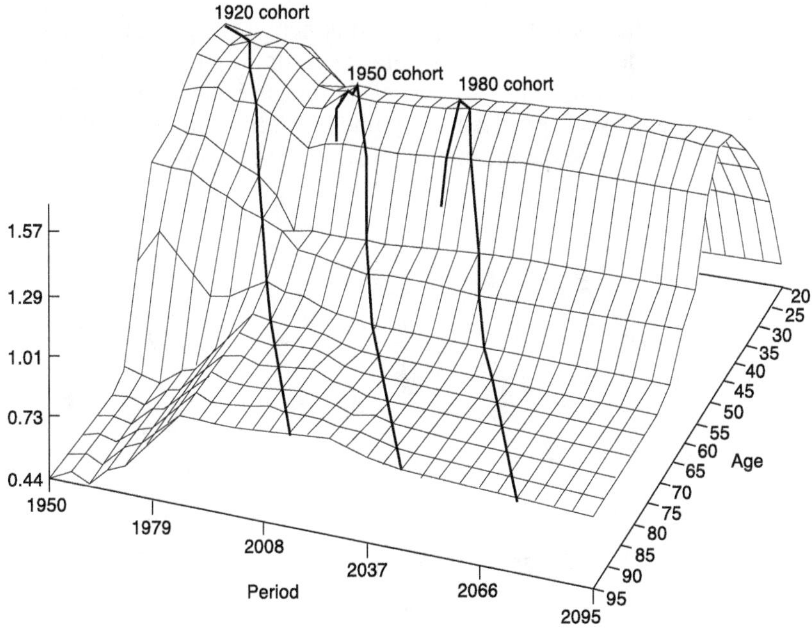

Fig. 8.2. First index of relative well-being: current resources of persons aged *a* at time *t* compared with average resources in the total population during the same period (ratio): France, 1950–2095

who retired during the 1950s, and slightly higher than those expected for post-1920 cohorts when they reach retirement age. This suggests moderate support for the welfare-generation hypothesis—moderate because the support is conditioned by the adoption of a relative-income index.[9]

The second possibility for computing growth-adjusted income indexes is an Easterlinian correction (Easterlin 1973), in which net resources at age *a* for generation *g* are deflated by an index representing the living standard of that generation's parents. The deflator retained is the net resources of persons 45–50 years old when generation *g* was 15–20 years old, the underlying assumption being that consumption habits are formed mainly during adolescence; it is combined with the assumption of a 30–year age gap between children and parents. It measures well-being at age *a* as the gap between realizations at that age and aspirations formed during adolescence. Such an index can be computed for generations as early as 1905 because the retrospective part of the model generates income data for adults starting in 1920. The results are plotted in Figure 8.3, which shows that this other indicator gives another view of what could be called a welfare generation. In the present case it appears that the most favoured generation is not very different from the one shown in Figure 8.2—persons born in 1925 instead of 1920. The result could have been different, however, because the underlying mechanism is entirely different: it is linked to the pattern of economic growth and owes little to the pattern of intergenerational transfers. The most favoured generation here is the one that entered the labour market at the start of the period of rapid economic expansion. The other interesting feature of Figure 8.3 is that its contours are consistent with the idea that younger cohorts experienced a significant decline in relative economic status, whereas in Figure 8.2 the contrast is much less clear.

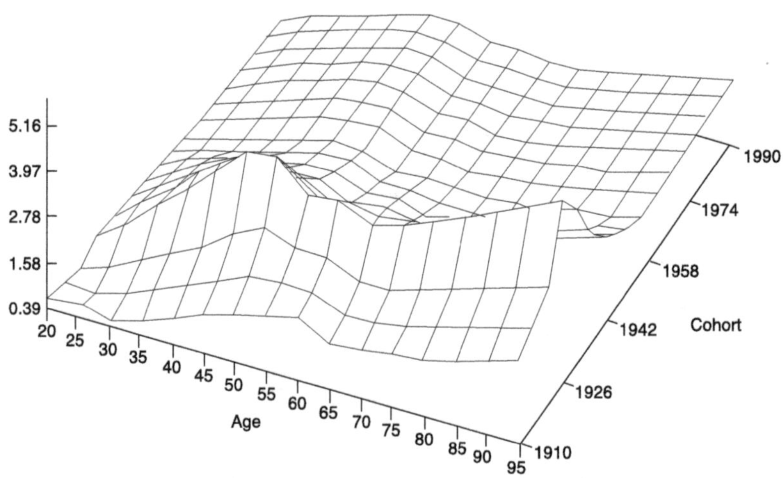

Fig. 8.3. Second index of relative well-being: current resources by age, compared with parent's resources during adolescence (ratio): France, 1950–2095

Reform of the PAYGO System

This first series of results has shown that the concept of advantaged generations is a relative one: our results depend on whether absolute or relative incomes are computed, and they also depend in the first case upon growth assumptions and in the second upon the choice of the formula used to deflate current resources. When the deflating formula assumes that individuals, at each age, are essentially sensitive to the average income of all persons alive at the same period, the relative welfare of cohorts is determined essentially by the organization of transfer schemes (and by seniority rules for relative economic statuses within the labour force). When the deflating formula assumes that individuals judge their income level by comparing it to a previous generation's experience, the acceleration or deceleration of economic growth has a major role.

This distinction illustrates the difficulty of reducing the problem of pensions to one of pure intergenerational equity. The pension problem, therefore, rather lies with the feasibility and the consequences of the large increases in workers' contribution rates, which are implicit in these 'no reform' scenarios. The rise in contribution rates under a 'no reform' scenario is depicted by the thick line in Figure 8.4. In this scenario, the contribution is expected roughly to double between 1990 and 2030. Such an increase presents both a problem of political feasibility and a problem of distortive effects that would be associated with these high levels of taxation.

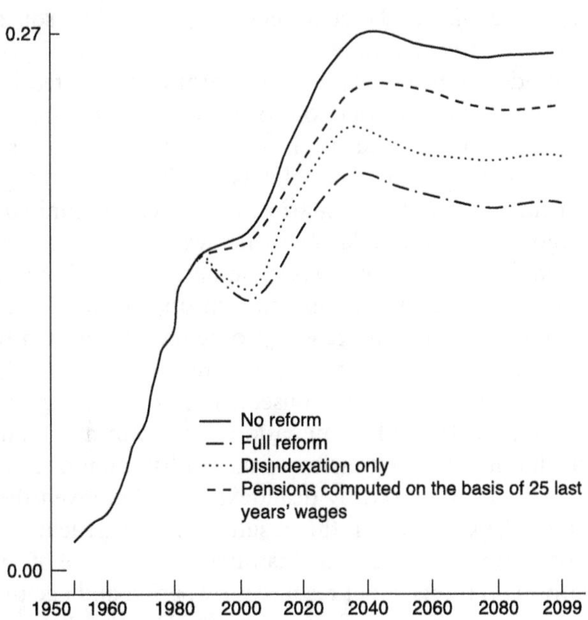

Fig. 8.4. Contribution rates, 'reform' versus 'no reform': France, 1950–2095

It must be admitted that these two questions are themselves controversial. In particular, one interesting feature of the long-term series portrayed in Figure 8.4 is that is puts future evolutions into perspective by recalling that projected increases in contribution rates under the 'no reform' scenario are not larger than the ones that occurred between 1960 and 1990. This observation has been made frequently in debates over France's pension system by those wishing to minimize the importance of population ageing for pensions, since it allows them to argue that the major adjustment of pension systems has already taken place. Their argument has two limitations, however. First, if we believe that contributions to the PAYGO system are equivalent to pure taxes, then taxation theory tells us that shifting from a contribution rate of 15 to 30 per cent has distortive effects on the economy that are much more severe than shifting from zero to 15 per cent. This may not be the major objection, however, for we know that pension contributions are not equivalent to pure taxes, given that they entitle contributors to future benefits that will be more or less proportional to those contributions. The second and more important limitation is one of political feasibility. The juxtaposition of Figures 8.3 and 8.4 makes it clear that the large increases in contribution rates that occurred between 1960 and 1980 applied specifically to the 'favoured' generations in the Easterlinian sense of the word. Increases in contribution rates were therefore easy to obtain because they applied to people who benefited from much better economic conditions than the ones they had expected before entering the labour market. Figure 8.3 shows that such favourable conditions will probably not occur again in the future, even under the relatively optimistic scenario of 2 per cent growth in productivity, and their absence should produce some resistance to future increases in contribution rates.

These two considerations lie behind the reform implemented in 1993, which we described briefly in the introduction to this chapter. Figure 8.4 shows how long this reform should limit the rise in the contribution rate, separating the relative roles of the two main components of the reform by giving results associated with three alternative scenarios: (1) a scenario limited to the disindexation of ongoing pensions relative to net wages; (2) a scenario in which pensions, once liquidated, remain indexed on net wages but their starting level for each successive generation is computed as proportional to the average past wage over a number of years, increasing progressively from ten to twenty-five years; and (3) a scenario approximating full reform (i.e. combining the two preceding ones) but neglecting the consequences of a rising retirement age, which would require a detailed examination. The reform actually reaches its goal of strongly limiting the progression of the contribution rate, with the major and immediate role being played by disindexation. Yet, given the equilibrium condition for the PAYGO system, this result cannot be reached without some losses for retired persons. Figures 8.5 illustrates the structure of those losses by presenting relative variations in net resources by period and age that occur with the 'reform' scenario and the 'no reform' scenario. The graph also underlines the generational profiles of gains or losses for cohorts born in 1920, 1950, and 1980.

We can analyse the effect of reform by distinguishing the consequences of its two components: the lengthening of the period retained for computing the reference wage, and disindexation. Lengthening the period used for computing the reference wage has of course no effect on the cohort of 1920. It plays fully for the cohorts born in 1950 and later, and consists in a loss for everyone around age 60 that is permanent over the remainder of the retirement period. Disindexation, on the other hand, has a negative relative effect on all cohorts currently retired and on subsequent ones, even though it is more limited for the earliest ones. The main point here is that the relative loss is of much greater importance for retired persons when they are at the end of their lives. That is a situation for which there is little justification, especially when one takes into account their needs due to old-age dependency and the absence until now of any significant system of social insurance to address those needs.

Figure 8.5 shows that this latter characteristic of the reform is the one that determines most significantly its global result. It also indicates that reform produces moderate compensation in the form of higher net resources for working people: for full reform, it is about 10 per cent in a steady state, a value that corresponds exactly to the variation in contribution rates shown in Figure 8.4.

Figure 8.6 indicates what the reform implies for the age-period profile of one of the indicators of relative living standard used to evaluate the consequences of the 'no reform' scenario—that is, the index obtained by transversal normalization

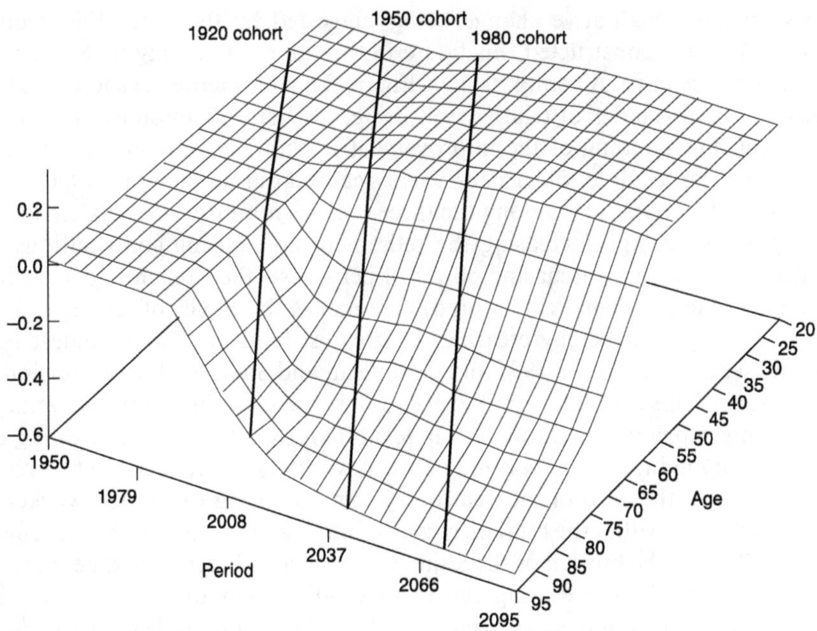

Fig. 8.5. Relative variation in net income, 'reform' versus 'no reform': France, 1950–2095

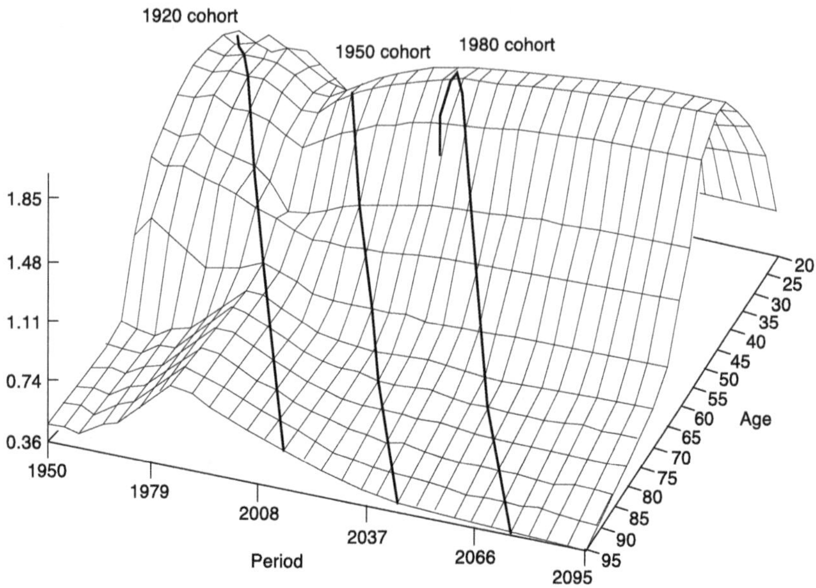

Fig. 8.6. Same index of relative well-being as in Figure 8.2, after 'reform': France, 1950–2095

(no significant qualitative change being suggested by the other Easterlinian index). We have constructed this figure in the same way as Figure 8.2 for the 'no reform' scenario. A comparison of Figure 8.6 with Figure 8.2 shows that, as measured by this index of relative well-being, the 'reform' amounts to a partial but significant undoing of the improvement in the relative living standard of pensioners, especially of older pensioners, realized during the years 1960–80.

This result proves that, among the three options for a PAYGO system facing demographic ageing—increasing the retirement age, raising contributions, or reducing the relative purchasing power of pensions—the French reform as it is described (and somewhat caricatured) here makes the choice of relying heavily on the last option, thereby creating the greatest hardship for the oldest pensioners (see also Hamayon 1995 and Cornilleau and Sterdyniak 1994 for similar discussions). This leads us to make several observations. One of the advantages of reducing expenditures through disindexation is that it avoids aggravating the discontinuity in income that occurs between work and retirement. Yet its result negates one of the aims of the pension system—securing for retired workers a *relative* position within the total hierarchy of incomes throughout the retirement period. Shifting the burden of the adjustment towards older retired people also has the drawback of requiring the relative adjustment to be larger for this population, whose numbers are smaller and whose demographic weight is therefore less than that of other age groups. Furthermore, the gain from disindexation in the form of contribution rates depends upon the rate of productivity growth: if it is zero, which is the case where the pressure against increases in contribution rates would certainly be the greatest, the gain from disindexation would be also zero. Finally, if declines in replacement ratios are to be corrected by the development of complementary funded pensions, the kind of adjustment we discuss next, we know that complementary pensions will have more difficulty compensating for disindexation than for simpler, once-and-for-all declines in the replacement ratio at the beginning of the retirement period, given the limited ability of privately funded systems to offer rents indexed on more than the level of prices. (The latter aim is itself difficult to fulfil when there is a resurgence of inflation.) This likelihood naturally leads us to consider the macro- and microeconomic effects of a policy to supplement reduced PAYGO pensions with privately funded ones.

Funding

We therefore turn to a 'reform plus funding' scenario, which is equivalent to the 'reform' scenario except that, beginning in 1995, working people start contributing to a fund at a rate that increases linearly from 0 to 5 per cent of net wages until 2000 and then stabilizes at that level. We must examine first the macroeconomic consequences of such a change. We did not discuss in detail earlier the macroeconomic mechanisms imbedded in the model because they did not play a major role in the previous simulations. That role was limited to the transitory reabsorption of non-structural unemployment and a moderate capital intensification due to the slowing of labour-force growth; those two phenomena do not make much of a difference in a partial equilibrium simulation in which both unemployment and capital intensity (or gross wages) are kept constant.

Macroeconomic interactions, however, are more important in the funding scenario. Here we raise three questions: How does the return on investment compare with the apparent return of contributions in the PAYGO system, which, in a steady state, is equivalent to the rate of economic growth? How does funding contribute to global accumulation (assuming a favourable situation in which all savings for retirement represent a net addition to total savings)? And to what degree does greater capital intensity resulting from funding have a negative effect on the return? The answers to these questions, as provided by the model, are summarized in Figures 8.7 and 8.8.

Figure 8.7 shows the evolution of the capital stock accumulated by the fund as a fraction of total existing capital at each period. The profile is a sigmoid one with a limit value of about one-third of the total capital stock. The transitory period during which this share of funds in total capital increases is associated with a period of increased capital/labour ratio, as shown by the second trend line of the graph, relative to the time path of the capital/labour ratio under the simple 'reform' scenario. This K/L ratio increases by as much as 10–15 per cent around 2020, but the increase is not permanent. A crowding-out effect occurs,

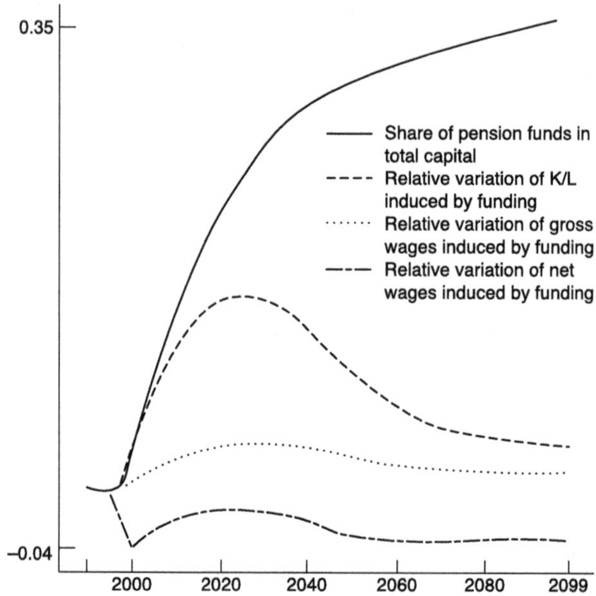

Fig. 8.7. Effect of funding on various macroeconomic variables: France, 1950–2095

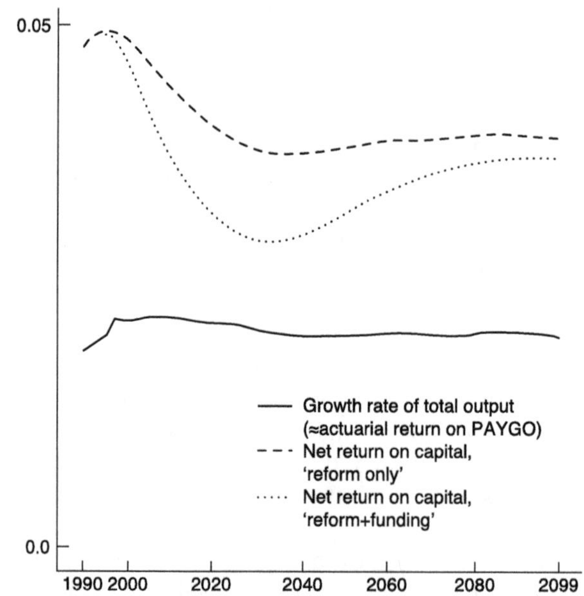

Fig. 8.8. Implicit or explicit returns on contributions, PAYGO and funding: France, 1950–2095

and the *K*/*L* ratio returns to the long-term equilibrium value, which is determined by the non-pension savings rate, σ.[10]

This transitory effect on capital intensity is reflected in the evolution of gross wages, but with a reduced intensity: accumulation for the fund increases gross wages by only about 2 or 3 per cent at most, so that, after taking into account the effect of the contribution to the fund, we have a decline in net wages as compared with the simple 'reform' scenario. This does not allow us, however, to conclude that funding is not useful; the loss during activity has to be compared with the resulting gains during retirement. One key element in this respect is the net return on savings in the fund—that is, capital's net marginal productivity—as compared with the implicit return of the PAYGO system. These elements are displayed in Figure 8.8, which first compares the net returns under the simple 'reform' scenario and the 'reform plus funding' scenario with the performance of the PAYGO system. In the 'no-reform' scenario, the net return that is displayed corresponds to what would be the marginal return of the first franc invested for retirement on top of the PAYGO system.

Given the assumption of a below-golden-rule saving rate, the comparison shows the advantage of funding. But we expect this relative advantage to be reduced by the development of the fund itself. The intermediate curve in Figure 8.8 shows that this is actually the case during the transitory phase when pension funding has a positive effect on *K*/*L*, but not to the point at which the return on funding would be greater than the implicit return on the PAYGO system. In any case, the reduction is only transitory, and in the long run the mixed system is superior to the pure PAYGO one: more pensions are obtained for the same level of contributions, or identical pensions are obtained with lower levels of contributions. Yet we know that this transition has an immediate cost, and we must also see how the system changes the relative statuses, over the long run, of retired people of various ages.

When we take the 'reform only' scenario as our reference point, the result is straightforward. Retired persons are better off once funding has been added to the system. But the proper comparison to be made is between the 'no reform' scenario and the 'reform plus funding' scenario. That is what is done in Figure 8.9, which shows what we finally gain by trying to maintain pensioners' relative living standard within the PAYGO system or with the combination of reduced PAYGO pensions planned by the reform and privately funded pensions.

As far as current workers are concerned, the net effect of the 'reform plus funding' scenario is slightly positive in the long run: they pay less under this scenario than they would have to do under the 'no reform' scenario. They contribute less to the fund than the additional PAYGO contribution they would have been required to make under the 'no reform' scenario. As for pensioners, on the other hand, although the 'reform plus funding' scenario avoids the decline in net resources of young retirees that occurs in the 'reform only' scenario, it does not avoid a large decline in the economic well-being of older retirees. This phenomenon is most pronounced for the 1950 cohort. It is due, as expected, to the limited

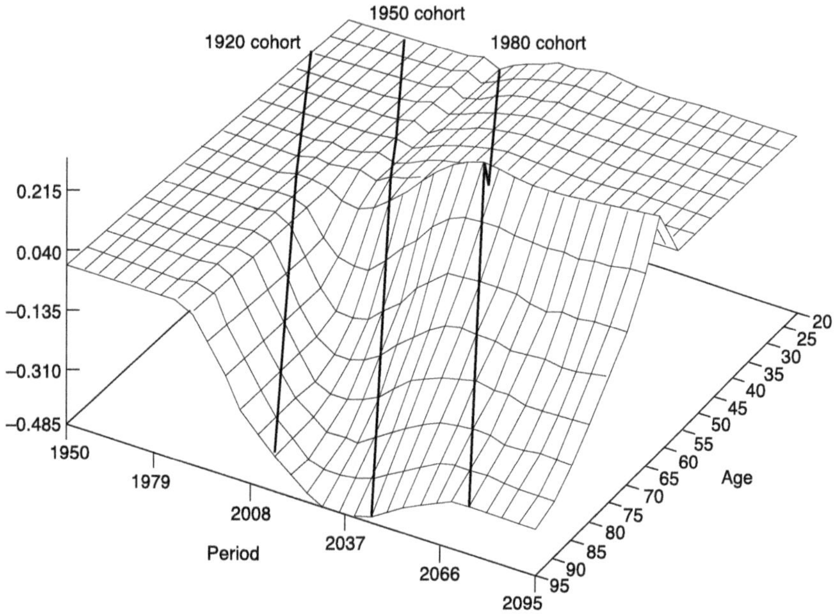

Fig. 8.9. Relative variation in income, 'reform plus funding' versus 'no reform': France, 1950–2095

ability of the funded system to provide indexation on average productivity growth. We therefore observe the following paradox: although the purpose of the 'reform plus funding' scenario is to evolve towards a mixed system that optimizes the complementarity between PAYGO and funded financing, the choice has been made to eliminate from the PAYGO system one of its comparative advantages, the possibility of indexation on wages or productivity growth.

Conclusion

From a methodological perspective, we have presented one way to model the interaction between economic growth and the organization of the pension system in France. Like any model, it is a simplification of reality. The simplification has consisted in adopting a two-class framework that posits two distinct savings motives, a 'capitalist' motive and a 'pension' motive. We have assumed, furthermore, that the second motive is satisfied by a system of mandatory funding, workers being entirely myopic. These crude simplifications may be viewed as one extreme along a spectrum; at the other extreme would be a population of workers with dynastic objectives and perfect or rational foresight. We have chosen this approach not only for its simplicity but also because it is not necessarily far removed from real behaviour.

Other methodological aspects of our analysis are related to debates about intergenerational equity. The first point to be mentioned here is the necessity of complementing prospective cohort profiles by their retrospective components: the solutions we have adopted, because of data limitations, are often *ad hoc* and partial. Second is the necessity of discussing the measures of instantaneous well-being, which are used to compare cohort-specific paths over time: here we have proposed three indexes of well-being that illustrate the relativity of the concept of welfare cohorts. The concept depends on whether well-being is measured in absolute or relative terms and, if in relative terms, relative to what. Last is the difficulty of summarizing cohort-specific paths in a simple way. We have tried to solve this problem by using three-dimensional lexis diagrams allowing a bird's-eye view of age-period-cohort profiles. This approach has its pros and cons. As an exploratory tool, it has enabled us to identify the most interesting cohorts, and it complements classical, two-dimensional representations of specific cohorts.

We have used these tools to evaluate some aspects of the 1993 reform of France's basic social security system, the *régime général.* The most important losses caused by the reform result from new indexation rules and affect older retired persons. Introducing a pension fund on top of the reformed system does not fully correct this problem, whatever positive effect it may eventually have on economic performance. Whether the resulting intergenerational redistribution is fair or unfair must be judged by what the pension system is expected to do for pensioners. Is its purpose to secure an absolute standard of living for all retired workers or instead a relative position for them in the current income distribution of the whole population?

Appendix: List of Notations

α : annuity rate
D : number of years over which past wages are averaged for computing PAYGO pensions
t_{index} : indexation rate for social security pensions
θ : contribution rate for social security pensions
θ_f : contribution rate to the pension fund
θ_u : contribution rate, unemployment insurance
θ_o : contribution rate, 'other' social transfers
p : age and gender-specific pension provided by the PAYGO system
p_f : age and gender-specific pension provided by the fund
B_u : aggregate unemployment benefits
B_0 : aggregate benefits, 'other' social transfers
δ : depreciation rate
g : rate of labour augmenting technical progress
k_f : age and gender-specific amount of capital held by the pension fund
K_c : total non-pension capital
K : total capital
L : labour force
μ : adjustment coefficient of the current gross wages on the equilibrium wage
N : population by age and gender
N_{tot} : total population
r : net return on capital
σ : 'capitalists' savings rate (rate of reinvestment of gross returns on non-pension capital)
l : age and sex specific activity rates
u : age and sex specific unemployment rate
$\bar{u}$: average unemployment rate
u^* : equilibrium unemployment rate
w : age and sex specific net wage
$\bar{w}$: average net wage at time t
$\bar{w}_{gr}$: average gross wage at time t
$\bar{w}^*_{gr}$: equilibrium gross wage

Notes

We thank Ronald Lee and other participants at the Seminar on Intergenerational Economic Relations and Demographic Change for their comments and suggestions. The views expressed here are our own and not necessarily those of our institutions.

1. Future cohorts may have a low rate of return on their social security contributions; but this does not necessarily mean that they will be less well-off than cohorts who benefited from very high rates of return, because this lower rate of return applies to contributions and incomes that benefited from global economic progress. For a more general discussion of the difficulty of finding adequate concepts for comparing the well-being of successive cohorts, see Fleurbaey and Michel (1993) or Kessler and Masson (1995).
2. We might have devoted greater attention in this chapter to the system of family benefits. During the 1950s the system offered benefits affording quite high levels of purchasing power, as compared, for instance, with the average worker's wage. Given their later indexation to prices rather than to wages, this relative advantage to families is no longer as large as it used to be, and the change could be another reason for the thesis of the welfare generation. Yet, given the way family benefits are financed (by contributions on wages), we can also consider that they are largely *intra*generational transfers (they are paid by workers who have responsibility for children), and are neutral with respect to intergenerational redistribution, unless we consider that the benefits accrue to children instead of to their parents. In the latter case, however, the benefiting generation is the one that is currently working, not the one that has retired.
3. The rules of the *régime général* apply only to wages below a specified ceiling (currently 12,000 francs per year). The system is completed by a second group of complementary schemes, the rules of which closely resemble those of actuarially neutral funded schemes: workers' contributions lead to the accumulation of a certain number of 'points', the number of which determines the size of the pension. This two-part structure, furthermore, applies to only 70% of the population. Other schemes apply to persons from the public and para-public sector; those schemes are generally more generous (in compensation for workers' lower wages during their active working lives). The rules are also different for self-employed persons. Taking all this heterogeneity into account should be easier with a microsimulation model, which is currently under construction (Blanchet and Chanut 1995).
4. Indexation of pensions on gross wages used to be the rule before the 1980s and helped to narrow the income gap between workers and retired persons. The only point of consensus about the future of pensions in France is that this mode of indexation does not need to be used anymore, given that the income gap between workers and retirees has now almost disappeared, and given that this mode of indexation implies that the burden of adjustment to future demographic changes falls entirely on workers. This latter point, however, would also apply to the indexing of pensions on prices if adverse demographic conditions, in combination with economic stagnation, implied a decrease in net income per worker over the next century—a development that fortunately appears to be unlikely.
5. Computing a pooled level of benefits complicates the computations because the two sexes are heterogeneous both in their level of mortality risk and in their past contributions (i.e. premium levels).

6. This precautionary motive certainly played a role in the recent increase in French households' savings, which, incidentally, aggravated the recent recession. We do not deal with this kind of short-term negative effect of increased savings in the present model.
7. Although the aggregation does not seem to take into account the changes in the normal retirement age, which was 65 until 1983, those changes are readily incorporated into observed changes in activity rates after age 60.
8. There is of course a contradiction in reintegrating those non-contributory benefits through a proportionality coefficient in a formula that assumes perfect contributivity. This is one among the many approximations in our description of the pension system. In any case, here we do not insist on sex differentials with respect to the pension system; instead we concentrate on series either for men only or for both sexes aggregated.
9. Legris and Lollivier (1996) have created a similar index by using actual survey data for the period between 1970 and 1990. Their result indicates that the 'welfare generation', if there is any, is the 1941–5 cohort. One source of discrepancy between the two studies may be that Legris and Lollivier compute household incomes and divide them by numbers of equivalent adults, whereas we do not introduce a household dimension at this stage. Another difference is that they use actual 1970–90 survey data, whereas we introduce extrapolations before and beyond that limited time period. In any case, the differences between their quantitative results and ours are not large and lead to similar qualitative results: relative well-being is of the same order of magnitude for the cohorts ranging from 1920 to 1941 in both data sets.
10. In equilibrium the equation that determines the total non-pension capital stock per worker, k_c, is

$$\sigma \cdot k_c \cdot (r_{net} + \delta) = (n + g + \delta)k_c.$$

If k denotes the total K/L ratio and $f(k)$ is the per worker production function, this equation immediately determines the equilibrium, k, as the solution of

$$\sigma \cdot f'(k) = n + g + \delta,$$

which will be completely independent of savings behaviour for retirement. Only if all non-pension capital were to be completely crowded out would the previous equation not hold any longer and would equilibrium capital intensity become dependent upon savings for retirement. (For a more complete examination of this scenario, see Blanchet 1988 and 1992. See also a similar model in Blanchet and Kessler 1992.)

9 Demographic Uncertainty and the OASDI Trust Funds of the United States

Shripad Tuljapurkar and Ronald D. Lee

Concern over the future of the US Social Security system is aptly summarized in the title of the book *Can America Afford to Grow Old?* by Aaron, Bosworth, and Burtless (1989). This question lies at the interface of economics, demography, and policy, and it has stimulated studies in each of those disciplines. Support of the elderly retired population depends ultimately on transfers from the population of working age, whether the transfers are organized through the public sector, the family, or the market. The relative numbers of workers and retired persons profoundly affect the terms on which these transfers take place. This is a main reason why the global phenomenon of current and prospective population ageing is so important.

In the case of the US Social Security fund, these issues stand out in projections of the time trajectory of the fund balance, for example those presented by the Board of Trustees of the Old-Age and Survivors Insurance and Disability Insurance (OASDI) Trust Funds (US, Social Security Administration, Board of Trustees 1995). The broad pattern is one of increasing fund balances till about 2010, followed by a decline that makes the funds effectively bankrupt soon after 2025. We should note that bankruptcy is a dramatic term that is frequently used in public debates but is rather misleading, because the main source of revenues from which benefits are paid is not the trust fund, but rather current taxes, and this source of revenues will remain. Furthermore, we expect that remedial action will be taken as the fund balance diminishes, so that it will not actually go to zero.

Here we focus on the effect of population ageing upon the finances of public pension systems. Most such systems are run primarily on a pay-as-you-go basis, with current benefit payments covered by current contributions. Ageing populations will require either reduced benefits or increased contribution rates, neither of which is politically appealing. The long-term finances of these systems depend sensitively upon long-term demographic trends. Demographers are asked to produce forecasts for seventy-five years or a century into the future, and such forecasts are obviously highly uncertain. It is true that all the potential retirees over the next sixty years have already been born, but their survival is not known, so that the future numbers of beneficiaries are uncertain. Moreover, virtually none of the workers whose contributions will pay the benefits of retirees sixty years in the future has yet been born, and so fertility adds another large element of uncertainty. Migration, of course, adds further uncertainty. Non-demographic uncertainty is also important, arising from wage growth, inflation, and interest and disability rates. Public pensions are under pressure to take immediate steps to prepare for the ageing that is implied by the medium forecasts of demographers, but the degree of uncertainty in those forecasts may render such steps problematic.

Unfortunately, conventional methods of demographic forecasting, which are based on high, medium, and low scenarios, are seriously deficient, particularly regarding the age distributions, which are critical for pay-as-you-go pension systems. First, probabilities cannot be attached to outcomes. Second, fertility and mortality are assumed always to follow some specified trajectories, and so fluctuations are ruled out. Third, because high, low, and medium trajectories for fertility or mortality must be bundled together into (typically) three scenarios, arbitrary decisions must be made about how to do this bundling, with decisive implications for the range of each projected age distribution.

For example, the US Census Bureau bundles together high fertility and low mortality to obtain its 'high' forecast, and conversely bundles together low fertility and high mortality to obtain its 'low' forecast. This may give a reasonable range of uncertainty for population size and the growth rate, but it dramatically understates the range of variation in the old-age dependency ratio because high fertility and low mortality have offsetting effects on that ratio, as do low fertility and high mortality. For this reason, the US Social Security Administration, in its forecasts, bundles together high fertility and high mortality, and low fertility and low mortality. There is no reason, however, to expect mortality to be always high or always low, or to be always associated with any particular level of the other vital rate. This explains the failure of the scenario-based method to account for uncertainty in forecasts.

Elsewhere we have developed a method for making stochastic population forecasts with consistent probability distributions for demographic variables such as dependency ratios (R. D. Lee and Tuljapurkar 1994). Here we shall use those forecasts to generate probabilistic forecasts for key aspects of Social Security, the US public pension system. We begin by describing our stochastic population forecasts for the United States, explaining the rationale for such forecasts and the reasons why the stochastic approach is the most useful way of describing forecast uncertainty. Next, we show how the stochastic demographic projection is integrated with the dynamics of the fund, to obtain stochastic projections of the fund's future trajectory. We present results that illustrate the kind of information made available in such an approach, information that is qualitatively and quantitatively different from that obtained by other methods. Finally, we consider various policy issues in the stochastic framework.

The stochastic method described here is the natural framework for policy analyses of the OASDI funds and other problems involving demographic-economic linkages, for three reasons. First, it can be easily extended to include uncertainty about economic variables, an extension that we plan to implement, at least partially. Second, it can accommodate alternative stochastic models of the demographic and economic variables involved. Third, and most important, stochastic analysis allows us to frame policy questions as choices between risky decisions. It allows us to compute explicitly measures of risk based on alternative objectives and costs, and to compare different sets of policies in a meaningful and unified way (see Tuljapurkar 1992).

Stochastic Population Forecasts

Conventional population projections, such as those in the OASDI Board of Trustees 1995 report (US, Social Security Administration, Board of Trustees 1995), or those used by the Census Bureau (US, Bureau of the Census 1989, 1992) use 'high', 'medium', and 'low' scenarios to indicate uncertainty but rarely give probability interpretations. Our method blends mathematical demography and statistical time-series methods to estimate stochastic models of fertility and mortality based on US data going back to 1900, and then uses the theory of random-matrix products to forecast various demographic measures to the year 2065. Using the theory of stochastic demography (see Tuljapurkar 1990), one can generate a fully stochastic forecast with associated prediction intervals. The prediction intervals must be calculated separately for each item of interest: population size, the vital rates, age-group sizes, and age-group ratios, for example. This approach has many advantages. It gives separate forecasts for each vital rate and for any desired population element or ratio. The forecasts and their confidence intervals are probabilistically consistent. Because the vital rates are forecast explicitly and have their own confidence intervals, their paths and intervals can be evaluated independently, drawing upon independent information. Although our current forecasts can deal with both stochastic disturbances to the vital rates and error arising in the estimation of coefficients, they do not deal with specification error or with error arising from historical discontinuities.

In keeping with most demographers, we use a linear model in which births are calculated by applying age-specific fertility rates to the female population, and the sex ratio at birth is assumed to be fixed (at 1.05 males per female in this case). We write the age vector of females at time t as N_t^F and that of males as N_t^M. Let the random-projection matrix for females, containing both fertility and survival rates by age, be X_t^F, and let the random projection matrix for males, containing only survival rates by age, be X_t^M Age-specific net immigration vectors for each sex (I_t^F, I_t^M) are identified similarly. Then the two-sex population recursion is

$$N_t^F = X_t^F N_{t-1}^F + I_t^F,$$
$$N_t^M = X_t^M N_{t-1}^M + I_t^M + B_t. \tag{9.1}$$

Here B_t is a vector with only one entry, representing males born in that period. It is computed from the number of female births and the sex ratio at birth.

We make projections by two methods. One is simply a full Monte Carlo simulation based on the vital rate models and initial conditions summarized below. The other is an analytically derived approximation based on a quadratic perturbation analysis of Equation 9.1. The latter is an accurate and useful method, which allows us to calculate the sensitivity of outcomes to assumptions.

Our stochastic models for fertility and mortality over age and time are based on R. D. Lee and Carter (1992). They represent fertility at age x and time t, $F_{x,t}$, as approximately equal to a pure age-specific term a_x, plus a term expressing the interaction of a period-specific effect, F_t, and an age schedule of fertility changes, b_x,

$$F_{x,t} = a_x + F_t b_x. \tag{9.2}$$

Schedules a_x and b_x are fixed over time, whereas F_t is assumed to vary randomly over time. The level of the age schedule, b_x, is arbitrary, so that it can be normalized to sum to unity; in this case the total fertility rate in year t is just $a + F_t$, where a is the sum of the a_x. For mortality, period variations are described by an index, K_t, in an identical model. Using the procedures described above, we estimated models for US fertility and mortality, based on data from 1917 to 1987 for fertility and from 1933 to 1987 for mortality. Then, in a second stage, we re-estimated the time-varying parameters, F_t and K_t (using the age coefficients a_x and b_x estimated in the first stage), over the expanded periods from 1909 to 1990 and from 1900 to 1989, so that the fitted model predicted exactly the observed number of births and deaths.

We used Box–Jenkins methods to forecast the mortality index, K_t. For fertility we used a Box–Jenkins model of the time series F_t, but with a constrained mean: we constrained the models so that the average value of the total fertility that they yield will converge to a prescribed mean value, which we specify. We used a mean total fertility rate of 2.1, chosen in part because it is close to the ultimate level of the 1992 census projection, and in part because many demographers view such an assumption as appropriate. It is important to consider the possibility that the disturbances in the fertility and mortality processes are associated with one another. We found no such relationship.

Net immigration by age, sex, and time follows the Census Bureau's 1989 ultimate middle migration levels (US, Bureau of the Census 1989: 159). Initial age compositions for males and females are also from the Census Bureau's tabulation (ibid. 40).

A full account of the forecasts is given in R. D. Lee and Tuljapurkar (1994) and is not repeated here. Instead, we focus on features that illustrate the kind of information obtained and the consistency of forecasted measures.

Figure 9.1 displays our analytically derived estimator of total population, $\exp(E \log P_t)$, along with 95 per cent prediction intervals. The curves shown reflect an important feature of the population recursions, that they are multiplicative. In consequence, the total population, P_t, will tend to a lognormal distribution over time. The prediction intervals shown are based on a lognormal

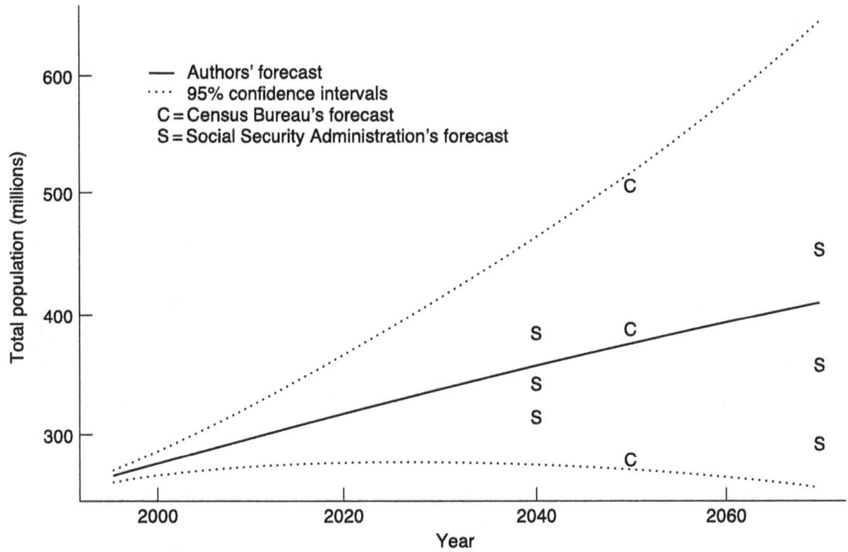

Fig. 9.1. Stochastic forecasts of population size: United States, 1990–2070

distribution of P_t; we first use our quadratic theory to compute the standard deviation, σ_{Lt}, of $\log P_t$, and then define the prediction interval as $\exp(E \log P_t \pm 2\sigma_{Lt})$. Note that the confidence bands are strikingly asymmetric; the distribution of P_t is rather skewed, however, and so there is not much weight in the upper reaches of the fan. A characteristic feature of the confidence bands is that they grow fairly slowly till about 2030 and then start to widen much more rapidly. This accumulation of uncertainty is driven by variance in fertility, as we add random births to random births.

Also displayed in Figure 9.1 are the high, medium, and low estimates from the 1992 census and the 1992 Social Security Administration's forecasts. The trend in the forecasted 'best' location is similar for all three projections through 2050. At that time, our forecast and prediction interval are remarkably similar to those obtained by the Census Bureau, but the Social Security Administration's forecasts have much narrower prediction intervals (possibly because it chooses its high and low scenarios to indicate uncertainty in old-age dependency ratios). At 2070 we have only the Social Security Administration's forecast to compare with our point forecast; and they are substantially different, with a medium predicted population that is only 87 per cent of our forecast. Our forecast is for an overall gain of about 55 per cent in total population by the end of the period. The slowing down of growth that we project at about 2030 is much steeper than in the Social Security Administration's forecast because of our different assumptions about future fertility. The Social Security Administration's projection bands are also much narrower at the end of the period, with a half width of 20 per cent compared with 44 per cent for our forecast.

In 2040 our lower confidence limit is at 77 per cent of our projected population, but the upper confidence limit is at 130 per cent. By the end of the period the lower confidence limit has fallen to 64 per cent of the projected size, but the upper limit has risen to 157 per cent. The Census Bureau's projections show a similar asymmetry, but the Social Security Administration's projections are only slightly asymmetric by comparison.

The uncertainty in our fertility forecast ranged from a total fertility rate of 0.81 to 3.38 children per woman, much larger than that in the scenarios used by either the Census Bureau or the Social Security Administration. Because of the far greater range in our fertility forecast, one might expect the degrees of uncertainty in the forecasts of population size to differ far more than they do. Under the Census Bureau's 'high' assumption, however, fertility is at the upper bound every single year. By contrast, our upper bound on fertility merely states that in any individual year there is a 2.5 per cent chance that fertility might be this high. To generate the population size corresponding to our upper 95 per cent confidence limit in 2065, the total fertility rate would need to average 2.45 or so rather than 3.38. The difference is due to the cancellation of errors: our model anticipates that fertility will be high in some years and low in others (see R. D. Lee 1993).

The upper set of triple lines in Figure 9.2 plots the old-age dependency ratio. This ratio is of particular interest because the payroll tax rate for Social Security and Medicare is roughly proportional to it (subject to some qualifiers). Our point forecast is for the ratio to rise in two steps to a level in 2069 about 2.5 times as high as it is today. The shape and level of the trajectory is very similar to that of the Social Security Administration's forecasts. The Census Bureau's forecasts show an implausibly low level of uncertainty, presumably because their 'high'

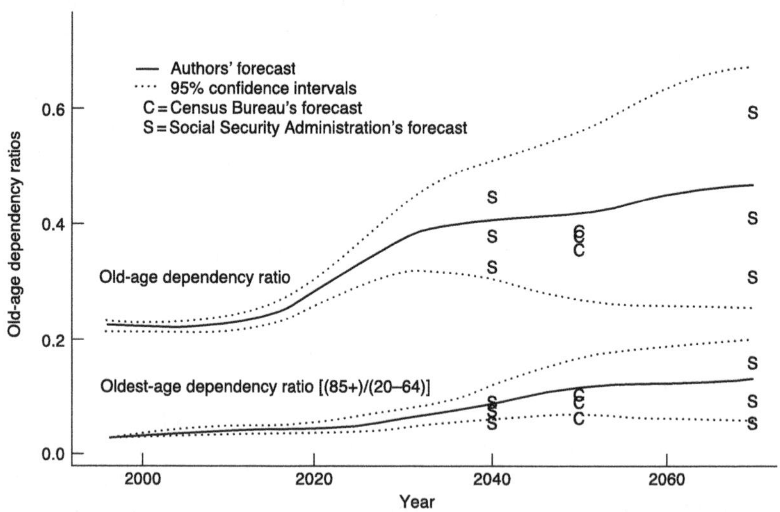

Fig. 9.2. Stochastic forecasts of old-age and oldest-age dependency ratios: United States, 1990–2070

and 'low' scenarios are chosen to indicate uncertainty in population size, and hence combine low mortality with high fertility, unlike the Social Security Administration's forecasts. Until 2010, all the uncertainty is due to mortality, for no persons born in 1990 have yet reached age 20 and the working ages. After 2010, and particularly after 2030, the uncertainty in the forecast increases rapidly, owing to the great uncertainty about fertility, which drives the denominator of the ratio. However, the lower bound of the confidence bracket is about at the level of the dependency ratio of today, no lower; even with a return to high fertility and with a slower mortality decline, the United States is unlikely to avoid population ageing. The upper bound would represent roughly a *tripling* of the dependency ratio. The forecast calls attention to the possibility of an enormous increase in the cost of public-sector pensions.

The Social Security Administration's forecasts are consistent with ours but again have smaller prediction intervals. The interesting feature of the Census Bureau's forecasts is that they have the smallest prediction intervals for the old (and oldest-old) dependency ratios, in contrast to their wide intervals for the numbers in those population segments. This contrast results from the particular fixed pattern of covariation that is built into their fixed trajectories of vital rates. In contrast, the Social Security Administration's forecasts have the opposite feature (higher uncertainty in ratios than in numbers) presumably because they choose combinations of rates that maximize the uncertainty of ratios.

In sum, the comparison of our population-size forecasts and intervals with those prepared by others indicates a high degree of consistency with the latest Census Bureau's forecasts and bounds, and considerable agreement with the bounds derived from *ex post* analysis of the bureau's forecasts by Stoto (1983) and by Census Bureau itself (1989). Our population intervals differ greatly from those of the Social Security Administration, for the reasons noted above.

Why Use Stochastic Forecasts?

An important advantage of the stochastic forecasts is the calculation of probabilistically consistent intervals for population age segments and ratios, which no other method can provide. As compared with our intervals, we find serious inconsistencies in those given for population ratios and components by the Census Bureau and the Social Security Administration. For example, although ours agree quite closely with the Census Bureau's intervals for total population and likewise for numbers under age 20, the census interval for the elderly population (ages 65+) is 2.7 times as broad as ours, and for the 85+ age group it is nearly twice as broad. At the same time, our interval is 2.3 times as wide as theirs for the total dependency ratio, 2.6 times as wide for the youth dependency ratio, and fully 12 times as wide for the elderly dependency ratio.

The stochastic demographic model has certain general features. Because the stochastic disturbances to the rates are approximately additive in each time interval, the uncertainty about population number grows approximately linearly with the forecast span t for about the first twenty-five years. After that, the multiplicative character of the projection starts to take over, and about fifty years into the forecast the forecast variance in population number starts to increase exponentially with time. The variance in population structure, for example in the old-age dependency ratio, has a different character. Here the total population size is scaled out, and the uncertainty propagates in a roughly additive way over time; thus the variance in such ratios grows linearly even for large t.

Finally, there is a natural partition in the sources of uncertainty over time. With a starting (launch) date of 1990, until the year 2010 the working and retired age groups (20+) are subject only to uncertainty in mortality. From 2010 to 2035, the retired age group (65+) is subject only to uncertainty in mortality, while the numbers working become increasingly uncertain owing to uncertainty in fertility. After 2035, fertility works its way into uncertainty in numbers of working and retired persons. It is characteristic of the US data (and of the data of many European countries as well) that the larger source of uncertainty in demographic forecasts is due to fertility.

Modelling the OASDI Fund

We turn now to a model of the OASDI Trust Funds, which we refer to collectively as the OASDI fund. It is not our intention to make a detailed model that captures individual differences within age and sex groups, for example by status as disabled, surviving spouse, early retiree, late retiree, and so on. Rather, we aim to describe the flows into and out of the fund, with the only disaggregation being by age and sex. This involves estimating average distributions of wages, tax rates, and benefit payments by age and sex for workers and beneficiaries. Our estimates have a base (launch) date of 1994, with overall numbers being in agreement with the state of the fund as given in the trustees' 1995 report (US, Social Security Administration, Board of Trustees 1995).

The model of the fund's dynamics can be expressed in a simple form. In year t, let the tax rate (taxes paid into the OASDI fund by age a) be $\tau^F(a)$ and $\tau^M(a)$ respectively for females and males, the benefits (adjusted for taxation) paid by age be $\beta^F(a)$ and $\beta^M(a)$, the fund balance at the start of the year be B_t, the interest earnings on the fund be I_t, and the administrative costs be α_t. Then

$$B_{t+1} = B_t + \sum_a \left[\tau^F(a)N_t^F(a) + \tau^M(a)N_t^M(a)\right] - \sum_a \left[\beta^F(a)N_t^F(a) + \beta^M(a)N_t^M(a)\right] + I_t - \alpha_t B_t. \tag{9.3}$$

Interest earnings are calculated as a product of a time-varying interest rate $r(t)$, with the average fund balance during the year. Administrative costs are described by applying a projected percentage administrative-cost rate to the fund balance each year. Here the population numbers are stochastic quantities generated by our forecast procedure. We present our calculations of the fund balance in constant 1994 dollars.

The demographic assumptions are those described earlier. Other assumptions that are needed in Equation 9.1 include projections of the inflation rate, real interest rate, rate of productivity growth, rates of labour-force participation by sex and age, and estimated administrative costs. For these we follow the assumptions used in the trustees' 1995 report, employing their 'middle' series whenever multiple scenarios are presented. It is a straightforward matter to incorporate stochastic models of some of these factors if such models are available.

The results we present below were obtained by combining simulation results from the demographic projection (Equation 9.1) with Equation 9.3. We are currently using our analytical methods to explore some features of Equation 9.3.

In Figure 9.3 we show stochastic forecasts of the fund's assets through 2025. The solid line indicates the expected value, the inner pair of dashed lines includes 67 per cent of sample paths, and the outer pair of dashed lines includes 95 per cent of sample paths. It is probably a mistake to use a solid line in this figure, for we wish to emphasize that we can forecast only a range with associated probabilities. Note the rapidly increasing dispersion in both bands of sample paths over time.

In our opinion, a limitation of Figure 9.3 is that it does not adequately portray the variability between population trajectories that is characteristic of our projections. To gain an appreciation of this variability, consider Figures 9.4

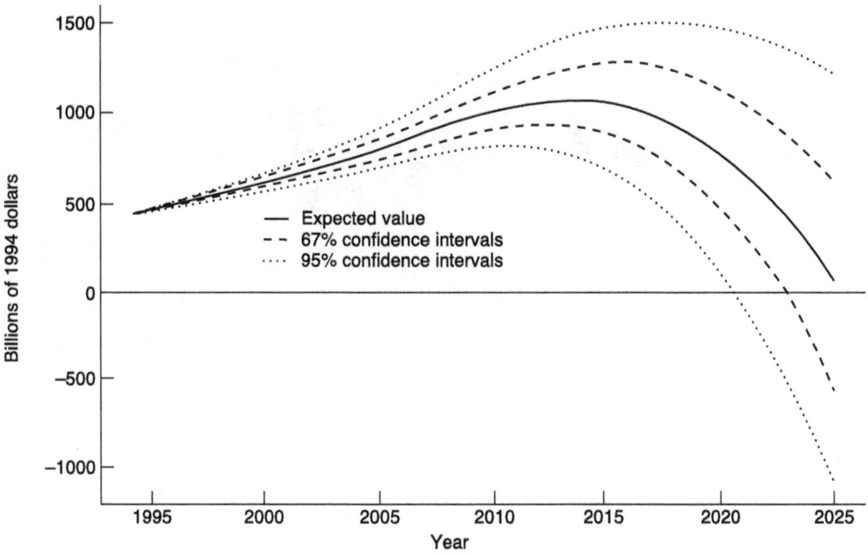

Fig. 9.3. Stochastic forecasts of the OASDI Trust Funds' assets, 1994–2025

to 9.6. In Figure 9.4 we show five sample trajectories of the trust fund's balance. Note that there are cross-overs between trajectories. In Figure 9.5 we display forty sample trajectories. There we have many cross-overs, plus a substantial widening of the downward range. Finally, Figure 9.6 shows ninety trajectories. In this case we see more cross-overs at later times, a widening of the upward

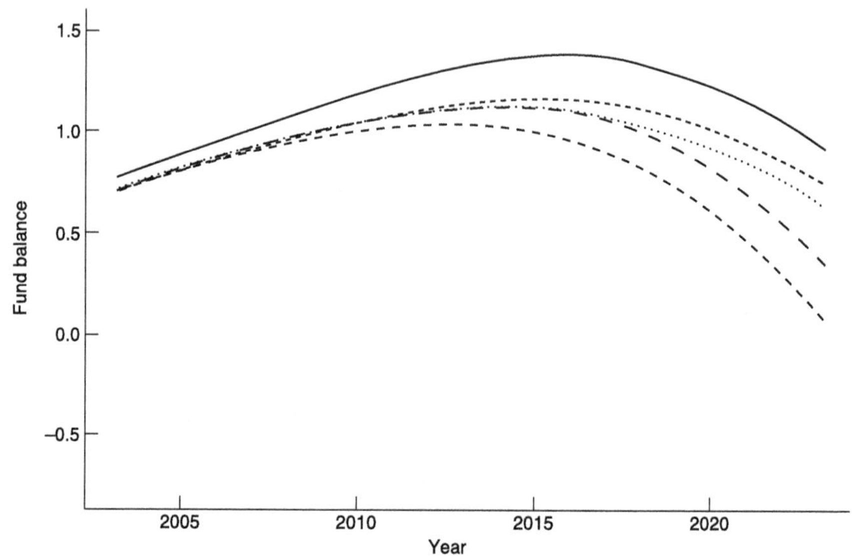

Fig. 9.4. Five trajectories from stochastic simulation of OASDI fund dynamics

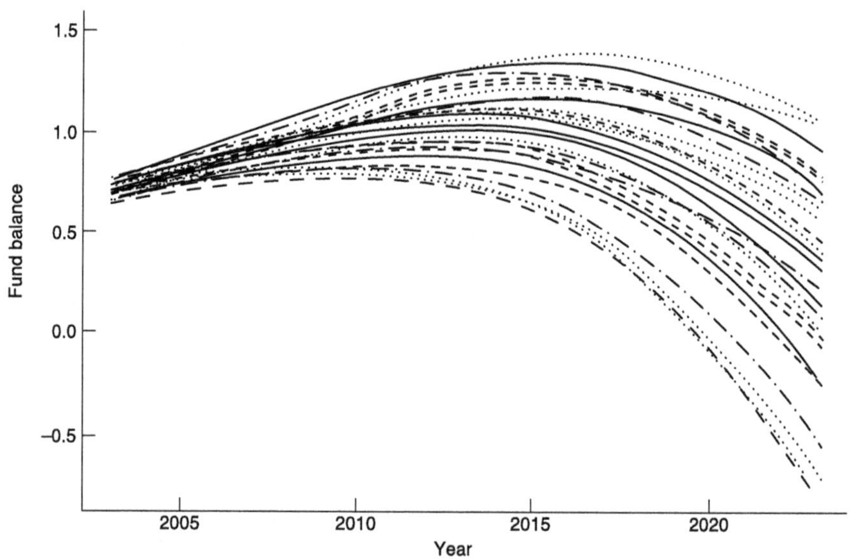

Fig. 9.5. Forty trajectories from stochastic simulation of OASDI fund dynamics

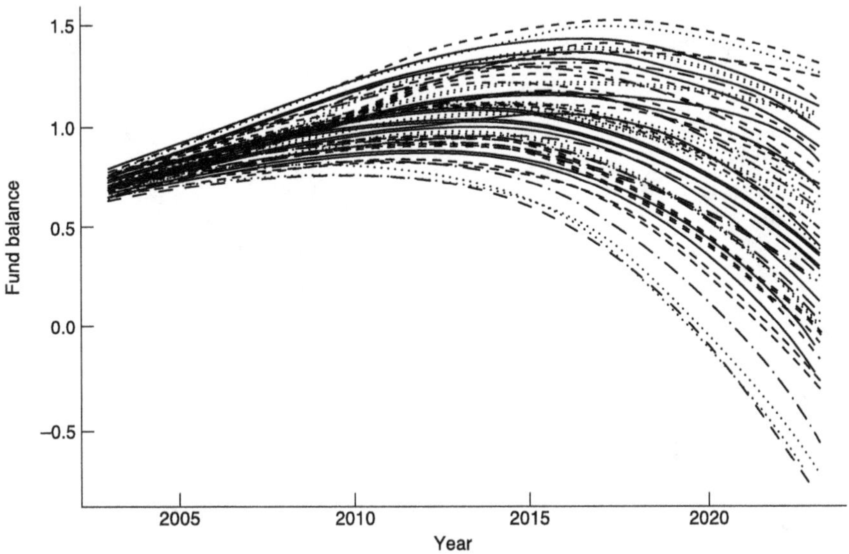

Fig. 9.6. Ninety trajectories from stochastic simulation of OASDI fund dynamics

range, and the appearance of a probability distribution as shown by the clustering of trajectories. Cross-overs between trajectories show that different trajectories may be close together over a period of time but then diverge rapidly. This is not something that one sees in a scenario forecast, and the possibility of divergence is important in examining the effects of policy choices.

The substantial differences between possible future trajectories shown in Figures 9.4 to 9.6 imply that we should think about B_t as a random process, and indeed it has the structure of a random walk with highly autocorrelated steps. To see this, suppose that in Equation 9.2 we used on the right the expected values of the male and female population vectors; the resulting sequence of balances would be some deterministic series, call it b_t. Let the difference between the actual and expected population numbers be $\delta_t(a)$ respectively; for simplicity suppress the superscripts indicating the two sexes. Then the random walk character of the balance is described by

$$B_t - b_t = \sum_a h_t(a)\delta_t(a), \tag{9.4}$$

where the $h_t(a)$ are the appropriate weights from Equation 9.3.

From Equation 9.4 it is clear that the variance in the fund balance B_t is an accumulation of weighted variances in the population vectors. Because the population variance changes linearly with time t at shorter times, and exponentially at longer times, we expect the variance of the fund balance to be an integral (or sum) of this. That is, the variance in B_t will increase quadratically as t^2 in the near future and exponentially over the long term. Figure 9.7 confirms

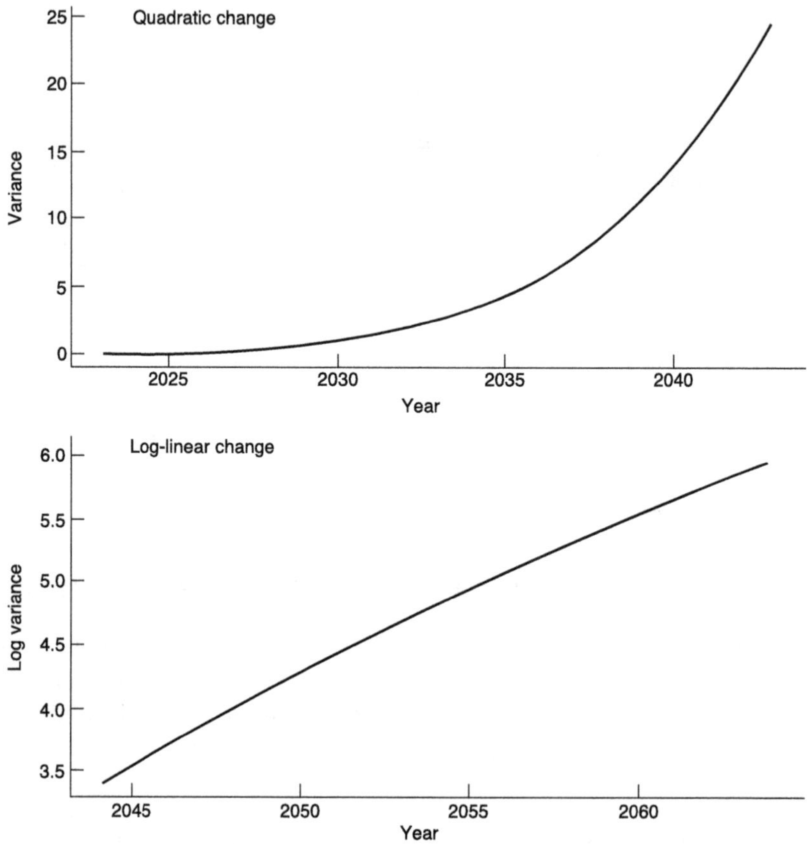

Fig. 9.7. Variance over time of projected OASDI fund balance

these expectations. The upper panel plots the variance of the projected fund balance from 2020 to 2045, growing roughly quadratically. The lower panel shows that the logarithm of this variance grows nearly linearly with t from 2045 to 2070.

Equation 9.4 emphasizes that the dynamics of the fund depend not only upon the structure of the population, e.g. the ratio of retired to working persons, but also upon the total numbers. Thus the uncertainty in B_t reflects the larger uncertainty in total number along with the smaller but still considerable uncertainty in ratios.

The stochastic forecasts here direct attention to the variation between population trajectories. This variation is reflected in the different times at which the trajectories will push the fund balance below zero. The conditional event of bankruptcy over the period of our forecast corresponds to defining the random time T such that $[B_t > 0 \text{ for } t < T, B_t \leq 0 \text{ for } t = T, \text{and } t < 2070]$. A probability distribution of values of T then indicates the distribution of times at

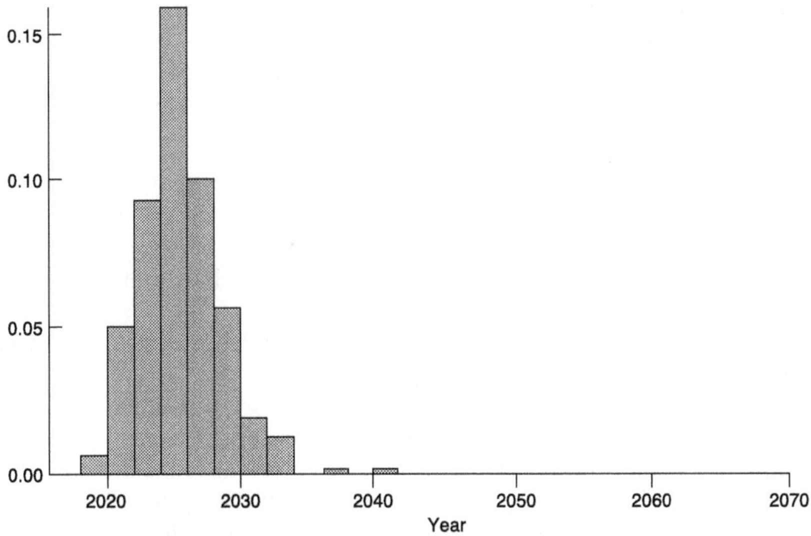

Fig. 9.8. Probability distribution of year in which OASDI fund balance first reaches zero, from simulations

which the fund may go bankrupt in the forecast period. (In stochastic process jargon, this is a density of first passage times to zero.) Figure 9.8 shows this probability distribution of year of bankruptcy. Note the substantial probability of bankruptcy before 2025, as well as the long tail of the distribution. There are some possible, albeit improbable, futures in which the fund balance will remain healthy for much longer times, or indeed over the entire span of the forecast.

Conclusion

Long-term population forecasts are necessary to assess the financial soundness of pay-as-you-go pension programmes, but such forecasts are very uncertain. Unfortunately, conventional scenario-based demographic forecasting methods are intrinsically and seriously deficient in portraying uncertainty: they provide no probabilistic interpretations for their ranges, and the ranges themselves are necessarily highly inconsistent from variable to variable. In this chapter we have used stochastic population forecasts, generated through new methods, to derive stochastic forecasts of the trust fund balance for the US Social Security system. It is equally possible to derive probability distributions for other quantities, such as contribution rates in defined-benefit plans or benefit rates in defined-contribution plans. We have plans to incorporate into these forecasts the uncertainty that arises from economic variables such as interest rates and growth rates of wages. We believe that these probability distributions are a better basis for decisions on pension policy than are the scenario-based deterministic forecasts done by conventional methods.

These stochastic forecasts allow us to examine demographic, economic, and policy alternatives in a unified way and suggest useful directions for future work. Among the possibilities are the following:

- Comparing different stochastic models for the demography, combining models in a Bayesian framework as suggested by Alho (1991), or incorporating stochastic variability in projected immigration streams.
- Using stochastic models for economic variables such as interest rates and rate of productivity growth.
- Evaluating the relative significance of demographic uncertainty and economic uncertainty for projections.
- Employing a stochastic decision-making framework to evaluate policy. For example, the OASDI trustees explore their projections using a criterion of actuarial balance. In the stochastic model one can examine the probability distribution of decision criteria. Examples include the random time at which the average fund balance in a year drops below the expected pay-out for the year and the probability that the fund is bankrupt (in some defined sense) over a specified interval.
- Using stochastic dynamic programming to compare the effects of optimization using alternative strategies (e.g. to maintain solvency of the fund by increasing taxes, reducing benefits, or some combination).
- Distinguishing between the effects of policies on the mean and the variance of the projected balances (there are cost differences between a policy that avoids bankruptcy while increasing the variance and a policy that attempts to control both the mean and the variance).

Finally, the OASDI fund is actually two separate funds, the old-age insurance fund (OASI) and the disability fund (DI). Different demographic factors underlie the dynamics of benefit pay-outs under these funds, especially the possibility of long-term changes in the disability levels and distribution of the elderly population. It may be important to model these funds separately.

Note

Shripad Tuljapurkar thanks Marc Feldman, Jean Doble, and the Morrison Institute for Population and Resource Studies, Stanford University, for encouragement and institutional support; the National Institute for Child Health and Human Development for support through grants HD 16640 and HD 32124; and the Center for the Economics and Demography of Aging, Berkeley, for support. Ronald Lee thanks the National Institute on Aging for support through grant AG 11761. We both thank Tim Miller for useful comments on an earlier draft of this chapter.

Part III

The Family and Intergenerational Transfers

10 Financial Intermediation, Transfers, and Commitment: Do Banks Crowd out Private Insurance Arrangements in Low-Income Rural Areas?

Andrew D. Foster and Mark R. Rosenzweig

An important feature of countries that have not experienced sustained economic development is that a large proportion of their populations participates in informal institutional arrangements to provide services that in developed countries are furnished by formal institutions. One important service is the provision of income insurance. It is also thought that the performance of informal institutions in underdeveloped areas is constrained by the absence of formal contracts and a legal system that could serve to enforce compliance. In particular, the absence of these features of developed environments creates significant barriers to trade across time and states of the world by reducing the ability of parties to commit to certain actions and thus results in inefficient allocations.

The existing empirical evidence suggests that although informal insurance arrangements involving interhousehold transfers do inhibit large fluctuations in consumption in the face of considerable income variability (Rosenzweig 1988; Rosenzweig and Stark 1989), insurance markets are incomplete in rural areas of low-income countries (Morduch 1990; Foster 1994; Townsend 1994). In Foster and Rosenzweig (1995*b*), we have provided further evidence that the presence of commitment problems is one reason why informal transfer arrangements do not, in themselves, provide complete insurance. This evidence suggests that the formation and growth of formal institutions that are part of the development process may lead to the disappearance of informal institutional arrangements.

Little empirical evidence exists on the relationship between the presence or characteristics of formal institutions that improve households' abilities to smooth consumption and informal insurance arrangements. One recent example of such evidence, however, is provided by Rosenzweig and Wolpin (1994), who show that in the United States the public provision of transfers to low-income families reduces family-based transfers only slightly. In this chapter we assess the extent to which the introduction of financial intermediation in the form of formal credit institutions affects informal transfer arrangements among households in poor, rural areas, and test the model with data from two South Asian countries, India and Pakistan. We modify the model of Thomas and

Worrall (1994), which characterizes risk-sharing arrangements under imperfect commitment, by incorporating the possibility that households facing risky incomes can both enter into transfer agreements and make use of liquid assets to smooth consumption. In particular, we assess the welfare gains associated with scenarios characterized by the presence or absence of commitment in transfer arrangements and the degree of asset liquidity, comparing them with autarky and complete asset illiquidity. Simulation results based on the model show that a combination of transfer arrangements and liquid assets appears to be a substantial improvement over liquid assets alone, at least given the limited liquidity being considered, although the additional gain from transfer arrangements, with or without commitment, falls when households gain access to liquid assets. However, the gains from being able to commit to transfer arrangements, which results in greater insurance, are significantly greater in the presence of liquid assets than in cases in which households do not have access to financial institutions. Given that informal insurance arrangements are costly to undertake, these results suggest that the introduction of financial intermediaries in part 'crowds out' private transfer arrangements, but that the arrangements that survive exhibit greater commitment and thus provide on average greater insurance than those that do not survive.

We also use simulations to assess how the behaviour of transfers differs under the various commitment/liquidity scenarios. The purpose is to derive testable implications that can be evaluated using actual data. We find support for the model on the basis of these results, in combination with estimates of transfer- and savings-decision rules from data on Indian and Pakistani households differentiated by whether or not they resided in villages located near formal credit institutions. In particular, we find that savings are significantly greater and contribute more importantly to consumption smoothing in villages closer to banks and that such villages have a reduced incidence of private transfer arrangements. Nonetheless, private transfer arrangements in those villages appear to provide significantly more insurance than do informal arrangements in villages with lesser savings opportunities. Overall, household transfer arrangements appear to enhance the insurance gains from financial intermediation, although not among those households facing high costs of commitment.

Theory

The structure of the model is as follows. We assume that there are two households, $i = 1, 2$. In every period t each household i receives an income, $y_{it} = y_i(s_t)$, where s is the state of nature in period t. The utility function for household i is assumed to be $u_i(c_i)$, where c_i denotes consumption and $u()$ is increasing and concave. Households are assumed to live for T periods, to discount the future with discount factor d, and to maximize expected utility. For each household there is a set, B_i, determined by the extent of financial intermediation available to that household, which dictates the extent to which it can transfer resources across time by borrowing and saving using a riskless asset with per period rate of return of r. For example, in the absence of financial intermediaries, $B = \{0\}$, so that no borrowing or saving is permitted; if, however, households can borrow and sell assets, B may take on the values $\{\Theta, 0, \theta\}$, with Θ setting the ceiling on borrowing and θ setting the ceiling on the amount of resources that can be stored.

Given risk aversion, households will attempt to smooth consumption. With or without the possibility of savings, as long as incomes for any two households are not perfectly correlated, households can benefit through the sharing of resources within each period. In other words, any pair of households is able in principle to devise a mutually beneficial contract dictating flows between the households in different states of the world, thus providing a form of insurance. As with the models of Coate and Ravallion (1993) and Thomas and Worrall (1994), and using the evidence in Foster and Rosenzweig (1995*b*) for households without access to formal credit institutions, we begin with the case in which contracts are not enforceable. Thus enforcement of any contract must rely upon the potential consequences for the two parties of violating the contract. In particular, we assume that if either of the households does not meet the terms of the contract, then the household is excluded from further risk sharing and must consume at autarky levels in subsequent periods.[1] The task is to specify the set of contracts that can be supported in this way.

In general, a risk-sharing contract in the context of this model can be characterized as a transfer function, $t_t(h_t)$, that dictates the (possibly negative) transfer from household 1 to household 2 and asset function $a_{it}(h_t)$ for each household. The asset function specifies the amount of assets that each household should hold, subject to B, if the contract is in force in period t after history h_t, where the latter is defined as the sequence of states up to and including the state realized in period t: $h_t = \{s_1, s_2, \ldots, s_t\}$. (Note that if contracts were fully enforceable, the households would care about the overall level of savings in each state but not about how savings were distributed between the two parties; however, because the autarkic level of utility achieved by the households following a contractual violation will depend in general upon the assets held by the households at that time, the disposition of savings by each party will optimally be specified by the contract.) The transfer and asset functions will depend both upon the extent to which intermediation is available and upon contract enforceability. There are four cases, denoted by superscripts C and I. If $C = 1$, contracts are enforceable in the sense that participants in transfer arrangements can commit to carrying out the plans, and if $C = 0$, contracts are not enforceable. If $I = 1$, the elements in B are not all zero, and if $I = 0$ there is no asset liquidity. Thus letting $U_{it}^{CI}(h_t)$ denote the expected discounted utility, given history h_t under the contract,

$$U_{it}^{CI}(h_t) = E_t \sum_{w=t}^{T} \delta^{j-t} \{u[y_i(s_j) - \tau_w^{CI}(h_w) + R\alpha_{iw}^{CI}(h_w) - \alpha_{iw+1}^{CI}(h_{w+1})]\} \qquad (10.1)$$

When contracts are not enforceable, $C = 0$, the assumption is that a contract is carried out only through the threat of reversion to autarky. This implies that a given contract can be implemented only if for each history h_t the expected discounted utility from the contract is greater than that under autarky; that is, $U_{it}^{0I}(h_t) \geq U_{it}^{AI}(a_{it})$, where $U_{it}^{AI}(a_{it})$, denotes the expected discounted utility under autarky, given financial intermediation regime I, if partner i should renege on the agreement in period t when he holds assets a_{it}. This constraint is known as an implementability constraint.

The solution to this problem is analogous to that for savings under autarky (Deaton 1992), except that instead of applying backwards recursion to the expected discounted utility function for individual i, one applies backwards recursion to the constrained-efficient frontier $W_t(V, h_t, a_{1t}, a_{2t})$, which characterizes in each period t and for each history h_t and household-specific savings a_{it} the maximum level of expected discounted utility achievable by household 1, given the implementability constraints and also given that household 2 receives an expected discounted utility of V. Thus

$$W_t(V, h_t, a_{1t}a_{2t}) = \max_{\tau_w,\, \alpha_{1w},\, \alpha_{2w} \forall w \geq t} U_{1t}^{0I}(h_t) \tag{10.2}$$

such that

$$\begin{aligned} &U_{1w}^{0I}(h_w, a_{1w}, a_{2w}) \geq U_{Iw}^{AI}(a_{1w}),\ \ U_{2w}^{0I}(H_w, a_{1w}) \geq U_{2w}^{AI}(a_{2w}), \text{and} \\ &V = U_{2w}(h_w, a_{1w}, a_{2w}), \end{aligned} \tag{10.3}$$

or equivalently

$$\begin{aligned} W_t(V, h_t, a_{1t}a_{2t}) = \max_{\tau_t,\, c_{1t},\, c_{2t},\, V_{st+1}} & u(c_1 t) + \delta E W_{t+1}[V_{t+1}, h_{t+1}, R(y_{1t} + a_{1t} + \tau_t - c_{1t}), \\ & R(y_{2t} + a_{2t} - \tau_t - c_{2t})] \end{aligned} \tag{10.4}$$

such that

$$\begin{aligned} u(c_{1t}) + {} & \delta E W_{t+1}[V_{t+1}, h_{t+1}, R(y_{1t} + a_{1t} + \tau_t - c_{1t}), \\ & R(y_{2t} + a_{2t} - \tau_t - c_{2t})] \geq U_{1t}^{AI}(a_{1t}) \end{aligned} \tag{10.5}$$

and

$$V = u(c_{2t}) + \delta E V_{st+1} \geq U_{2t}^{AI}(a_{2t}) \cdot \tag{10.6}$$

Simulation

To evaluate the implications of differences in access to financial intermediation for transfer arrangements, as well to derive implications of these differences that may be tested with available data, it is necessary to solve the maximization problems characterized by Equations 10.4 to 10.6. Although analytic solutions are not generally available, for a given set of parametric assumptions it is possible to compute numerically for relatively small T the optimal decision rules.[2]

The specific assumptions used to compute decision rules are as follows. It is assumed that there are four possible states, $s = 1, 2, 3, 4$, characterizing the income realization of a pair of transfer partners. Partner 1 receives an income of 2 in states 1 and 3 and an income of 4 in states 2 and 4; partner 2 receives an income of 2 in states 1 and 2 and an income of 4 in states 3 and 4. It is assumed that the states occur with equal probability so that the incomes of the two partners are independently distributed, with average income for each partner being 3. Note that in this environment, the total income of the two households fluctuates, as does the individual household's income. Thus only with perfect insurance would each household consume an income of 3 in each period. Single-period utility is assumed to exhibit unit-relative risk aversion [$u = ln(c)$], the discount factor (δ) is assumed to be 0.85, and the interest rate $r = 3/17$ so that $R\delta = 1$. This discount rate is sufficiently low that implementability constraints bind, and it is sufficiently high that there remains substantial risk sharing even in the presence of assets. Setting $\delta R = 1$ implies that asset transactions are used primarily for risk accommodation in the sense that no savings would be observed if income was fixed over time.

To examine the implications of the increased availability of financial intermediaries for transfer behaviour in the absence of full insurance, we consider two alternative specifications of the set B of possible asset positions held by each household. In particular, the absence of financial intermediaries is characterized by setting $B = \{0\}$, and the presence of such institutions is characterized by setting $B = \{-0.5, 0, 0.5\}$. Neither of these characterizations should be taken literally, of course. In the absence of financial intermediaries households still have opportunities for transferring resources across time by holding productive assets, storing food stocks, or engaging in informal borrowing and lending. The combinations of savings and borrowing made possible by banks and co-operatives permit households to take on a wide variety of asset positions. Nonetheless, these stylized cases capture a key feature of the distinction between households with access to banks and those without such access: that for those with such access there is an increase in liquidity in the sense that resources may be transferred across time with relative ease or at low cost.[3] For example, although households with land but without access to banks can in principle smooth consumption by buying and selling land, the transaction costs are likely to be higher than in the case in which land can be used as a form of collateral to establish a line of credit with a bank.

In solving the model we find that an important simplification arises from the fact that the history of income shocks, h_t, influences the efficiency frontier, $W_t(V, h_t, a_{1t}, a_{2t})$, only through its effect upon current income and assets. This result, which is a straightforward extension of that provided by Thomas and Worrall (1994) for the case without assets, follows from the fact that expected discounted utility under autarky, and thus the set of implementable transfers, is affected only by the resources available at time *t*, i.e. by the income and assets held by the two parties. Thus, although two different histories resulting in the same income and asset values will generally yield different points on the efficiency frontier, the frontier itself will not be affected. Consequently, the problem of solving for the optimal transfer and savings rules amounts first to determining the efficiency frontier for each set of income and assets in each period *t* and then tracing out the points on the efficiency frontiers that will arise for different initial conditions and income realizations.

Calculation of the efficiency frontier for the specified models proceeds as follows:

Step 1: $W_T(V)$ and U_{iT}^{AI} are calculated for each possible set of asset stocks and income realizations.[4]

Step 2: U_{iT-1}^{AI} and α_{iT-1}^{AI} are determined by choosing the savings decision for each asset position and income that maximizes expected discounted utility in that period.

Step 3: $W_{T-1}(V)$ and $\alpha_{iT-1}^{CI}(V)$ are calculated for discrete values of V by solving the maximization problem characterized by Equations 10.4 to 10.6, conditional upon the expressions obtained for U_{iT-1}^{AI} and W_T.

Step 4: A quadratic spline is used to construct the function $W_{T-1}(V)$ as well as its derivative[5] using the evaluations of $W_{T-1}(V)$.

Step 5: Steps 2–4 are repeated for periods $T-2$ to 1 with $T=4$.

The resulting decision rules are then used to simulate a data set starting from period 1 by taking random initial draws of assets and the utility of partner 2, V, simulating a path of income realizations, and computing the resulting patterns of savings, transfers, and asset stocks under the alternative assumptions about the availability of assets and the presence of commitment problems.[6] In particular, we consider combinations of cases, contrasted with perfect insurance, differentiated by whether there are liquid assets (intermediation) and whether transfers are possible, and, if so, with and without the implementability constraints.

Table 10.1 presents measures of the component of expected discounted utility at period 1 that accrues over the periods 1–3 ($U_{i1}-\delta^3 U_{i4}$, henceforth *net expected discounted utility*).[7] Our assumption is that both partners have initial asset stocks of zero and that the arrangement exhibits symmetry in the sense that average (across first-period states) expected discounted utilities are equal for the two partners. The table shows that access to assets, the ability to make transfers, and the ability to commit (i.e. to avoid the need for implementability constraints) influence the degree to which the partners are insured against income shocks and thus achieve their utility levels. The results also indicate not only that transfers play an important supplemental role in providing insurance, even in the presence of liquid assets, but also that the role of transfers in providing insurance may be enhanced when intermediaries are present.

The first and last rows provide a reasonable metric for evaluating the relative (gross) welfare gains of the various scenarios. The first row shows the net

Table 10.1. Net expected discounted utilities for partner 1 under alternative scenarios

	Utility, by state				Average utility	Relative gain[a]
	yl = 2 y2 = 2	yl = 4 y2 = 2	yl = 2 y2 = 4	yl = 4 y2 = 4		
No liquid assets, autarky	2.541	2.808	2.541	2.809	2.674	0.0
Liquid assets, autarky	2.627	2.892	2.627	2.893	2.760	0.567
No liquid assets, no commitment	2.603	2.907	2.595	2.853	2.740	0.429
Liquid assets, no commitment	2.686	2.992	2.533	2.912	2.781	0.699
No liquid assets, full commitment	2.612	2.773	2.773	2.863	2.756	0.534
Liquid assets, full commitment	2.707	2.821	2.821	2.938	2.822	0.969
Full Insurance	2.826	2.826	2.826	2.826	2.826	1.0

[a] Relative gain is the share of utility gain achieved under full insurance relative to no liquid assets and autarky that is achieved by a specified scenario.
Note: Utility measures are net of discounted utility in final period (period 4). See text.

expected discounted utility in the complete absence of mechanisms for insuring against income shocks—that is, under autarky and in the absence of liquid assets. Note that the net expected discounted utility for partner 1 in period 1 depends importantly upon his income realization in that period and that the average utility across the first-period states is 2.674. The last row shows the net expected discounted utility under full insurance, when each household receives an income of 3 regardless of the state of the world that is realized. Full insurance yields a net expected discounted utility of 2.826 in each state.

Each of the other scenarios provides a net expected discounted utility somewhere between that achieved by these two extremes. The second and third rows of Table 10.1 illustrate the well-known result that assets play a useful but incomplete role in providing insurance. The second row presents the net discounted utility in the presence of assets (financial intermediation) but in the absence of any transfers, showing that even the limited liquidity provided by allowing households to hold a limited set of net asset positions provides substantial insurance relative to the no-assets case: about 57 per cent of the gain associated with full insurance is achieved in this way.[8] However, transfer arrangements, even if implementable only without commitment, provide an additional welfare gain, of 0.021, under intermediation; the gain is 0.062 when there is commitment.

Although transfer arrangements also play a significant role in accommodating risk, they appear less effective as a whole than the ability to use assets, particularly with the expanded asset set considered in note 8. In the absence of liquid assets the full-commitment scenario yields 53 per cent of the gain associated with full insurance, whereas the necessity of relying upon implementability constraints in transfer arrangements yields only 43 per cent. Nonetheless, a combination of transfer arrangements and liquid assets appears to be a substantial improvement over assets alone, at least given the limited liquidity being considered. Transfer arrangements in the absence of commitment but with assets yield 70 per cent of the gain associated with full insurance, as compared with 57 per cent for assets alone. When households can make transfer arrangements without relying upon implementability constraints (with full commitment), and when they also have liquid assets, they can achieve 97 per cent of the benefit from full insurance.

Thus a combination of liquid assets and full-commitment transfers yields a net expected discounted utility that is quite close to that achieved under full insurance. The source of this difference is seen easily by examining the state-specific discounted utility figures: with liquid assets, states 2 and 3 (that is, when the partners have unequal incomes) yield different net discounted utilities because consumption decisions are tied to realizations of their own income. However, with full commitment, consumption decisions depend upon only total income and assets of the partners, and thus net discounted utilities are the same for these two states. Intermediate between these two is the case in which partners cannot commit and must rely upon the implementability constraint.

Comparisons of the combinations of consumption-smoothing mechanisms shown in Table 10.1 indicate how the presence of financial intermediaries affects the incidence and type of transfer arrangements. First, the additional *gross gain* from transfer arrangements, with or without commitment, falls when households have liquid assets rather than autarky. Second, the gains from being able to commit in transfer arrangements are 2.56 times as big in the presence of liquid assets (0.041) as they are when households do not have access to financial institutions (0.016). Apparently the problems associated with implementing a transfer arrangement become greater in the presence of liquid assets, a result that presumably reflects the fact that the presence of liquid assets reduces the benefits from insurance through transfer arrangements.[9]

To use the gross utility gains in Table 10.1 to assess how the introduction of asset liquidity affects the incidence and composition of transfers arrangements, it is necessary to consider why we do not always observe transfer arrangements with commitment, given their greater insurance benefits. Presumably there is heterogeneity in the cost of setting up transfer arrangements of various types. In particular, suppose that individual i must pay a utility cost κ_i^C to establish a transfer arrangement of type $C = \{0, 1\}$ with and without commitment, respectively. Then the individual with asset liquidity determined by $I = \{0, 1\}$ for no intermediation and some intermediation, respectively, will choose the arrangement that yields the highest net utility,

$$\max(U^{1I} - \kappa_i^1, U^{0I} - \kappa_i^0, U^{AI}), \tag{10.7}$$

and the distribution of various types of arrangements in a population will depend upon the joint distribution of the $\{\kappa_i^0, \kappa_i^1\}$.

Suppose, for example, that $\kappa_i^C = \kappa^{-C} + \gamma e_i^C$, where the κ^{-C} are constants, γ is a scalar affecting the variance of the error, and the e_i^I are independent and identically distributed (across individuals and commitment types) extreme-value errors. Then, the probability, $P(C|I)$, that an individual will choose to enter some type of transfer arrangement for a given level of intermediation, I, is given by

$$
\begin{aligned}
P(C|I) &= \frac{\exp[(U^{1I} - \kappa^1)/\delta] + \exp[(U^{0I} - \kappa^0)/\delta]}{\exp[(U^{1I} - \kappa^1)/\delta] + \exp[(U^{0I} - \kappa^0)/\delta] + \exp(U^{AI}/\delta)} \\
&= 1 - \frac{1}{1 + \exp[(U^{1I} - U^{AI} - \kappa^1)/\delta] + \exp[(U^{0I} - U^{AI} - \kappa^0)/\delta]}, \qquad (10.8)
\end{aligned}
$$

which is, not surprisingly, increasing in the utility differences associated with commitment and no commitment transfer arrangements relative to autarky. More significantly, the probability that an individual involved in a transfer arrangement will be under a commitment regime is

$$
\begin{aligned}
P(1|C, I) &= \frac{\exp[(U^{1I} - \kappa^1)/\delta]}{\exp[(U^{1I} - \kappa^1)/\delta] + \exp[(U^{0I} - \kappa^0)/\delta]} \\
&= \frac{1}{1 + \exp[(U^{0I} - U^{1I} + \kappa^0 - \kappa^1)/\delta]}, \qquad (10.9)
\end{aligned}
$$

which is increasing in the difference between the commitment and no commitment utilities, $U^{1I} - U^{0I}$. Thus if, as seen in Table 10.1, the additional utility associated with transfer arrangements with commitment in the presence of financial intermediaries exceeds that arising in the absence of financial intermediaries, then a larger share of transfer arrangements will exhibit commitment if banks are present. Thus areas with financial intermediaries will be characterized by a lower incidence of transfer arrangements, but such arrangements will provide more insurance than exists in areas without intermediaries.

Estimation

The simulation results presented in Table 10.1 establish that transfer arrangements can be complementary with asset liquidity by providing insurance. The results also suggest that although increases in financial intermediation may reduce the incidence of private transfer arrangements as a source of insurance, they alter the types of arrangements so that those that do remain provide increased insurance. These results, which are based upon the model, however, do not indicate how transfer and savings *behaviour* changes as access to financial intermediaries increases and thus do not suggest implications that can be tested with available micro-level data. In particular, we wish to know how we can recognize when transfers are characterized by commitment in scenarios in which assets are either liquid or not liquid.

Given the complexity of the models considered, it is unlikely that formal theoretical predictions can be generated that are themselves testable. Nonetheless, the fact that the model, for a given set of parameter estimates, can be used to simulate a path of transfers and savings for partners involved in these types of arrangements suggests an alternative approach. In particular, a useful way to distinguish among these alternative scenarios, as well as to test the appropriateness of a given scenario, is to compare estimates obtained by applying a given estimation strategy to the actual data with estimates obtained by applying the same approach to simulated data generated according to alternative scenarios.

Given the approach taken, the selection of an estimation strategy is in some sense arbitrary; but it is helpful for interpreting the results to select a strategy in which parameter estimates are at least grounded in the structure of the model. Therefore we focus upon estimates of linear approximations to decision rules for savings and transfers for which the relevant state variables are the history of past transfers and current incomes and assets. We also choose, as a convenient but imperfect measure of history, the sum of past transfers (i.e. the 'stock of transfer assets'). Let τ_{it} denote the net transfers out by household i at time t so that the stock of transfer assets is

$$T_{it} = \sum_{t=0}^{t-1} \tau_{it} \tag{10.10}$$

Then the approximate linear transfer decision rule is

$$\tau_{it} = \beta_0 + \beta_1 T_{it} + \beta_2 y_{it} + \beta_3 y_{-it} + \beta_4 a_{it} + \beta_5 a_{-it}, \tag{10.11}$$

where y_{-it} denotes the income of the household with which i is contracting to provide insurance. The savings-decision rule may be approximated by a similar expression.

The estimation of Equation 10.11 has a number of problems that must be addressed in practice. Most important, certain variables, such as the partner's income and the full history of past transfers, will not usually be available. Some of these difficulties may be addressed in a straightforward fashion.[10] In particular, we assume that income, y_{it} is the sum of a fixed anticipated component and an unanticipated i.i.d. component, $y_{it} = \bar{y}_i + \varepsilon_{it}$. Then we model the correlation between the error terms as $\varepsilon_{-it} = \rho\varepsilon_{it} + \mu_{-it}$ and take the first difference of Equation 10.11 over two consecutive periods to obtain

$$\Delta\tau_{it} = \beta_1 \tau_{it} + \beta_6 \Delta\varepsilon_{it} + \beta_3 \Delta u_{-it} + \beta_4 s_{it} + \beta_5 s_{-it}, \tag{10.12}$$

where Δ denotes a forward first difference, $\beta_6 = \beta_2 + \beta_3 r$, and s_{it} and s_{-it} denote net savings at time t for individual i and his partner. Although this procedure removes the fixed parts of T_{it} and y_{it} from the estimation, there remains an estimation problem even when the own shocks, e_{it}, and savings of both partners are observed because the idiosyncratic part of the shock, u_{-it}, will generally be correlated with the contemporaneous transfer, τ_{it} as well as with own and partner's savings. Thus one must use instruments as well as differences to estimate Equation 10.11. A natural set of instruments consists of period t and $t-1$ shocks, which predict transfers and are, by assumption, independent of u_{-it} and initial values of own and partner's asset stocks.

Table 10.2 presents the results of applying this strategy to data simulated according to the above model. The first six columns (under the heading 'net transfers out') show estimates of the approximate transfer-decision rules applied to data simulated using the model with and without liquid assets and with and without commitment, whereas the next four columns (under the heading 'net savings') show the estimates of approximate savings-decision rules with and without commitment. As there is no possibility of saving under the model of no liquid assets, no savings-decision rule is estimated for that scenario.

The results in the first two columns of Table 10.2 conform to those obtained in Foster and Rosenzweig (1995*b*) and indicate that, in the absence of mechanisms for savings and borrowing, the presence of commitment failures has significant implications for the coefficients on transfer assets (β_1) and income shocks (β_6). In particular, under full commitment the history of past transfers has no effect upon current transfers, and the coefficient on income shocks is 0.5, which corresponds to what might be expected under perfect income pooling and independent incomes.[11] In the absence of perfect commitment, however, transfers are negatively dependent upon past transfers and less responsive to income shocks. Full commitment indicates that there is an extent to which transfers operate as a kind of credit, whereas no commitment indicates that transfer insurance is less than that provided by full income pooling. Our earlier results (ibid.) indicated that in areas without intermediation, transfer behaviour conformed closely to the no-commitment regime.

The model indicates that when assets are liquid, transfer-decision rules incorporate both partners' asset positions. However, because available data sets do not provide information on the transfer partner's assets, we present our results for the transfer-decision rules with liquid assets both with and without controlling for partner's assets. The results indicate that the estimates of the effects of income and own financial asset upon transfers are robust to the exclusion of partner's assets within both commitment regimes. For the no-commitment transfers, moreover, excluding partner's assets does not importantly affect estimates of the transfer-asset effect. The estimate of the transfer-asset effect under the commitment regime, however, has a negative bias. This result is easily seen to be a consequence of omitted-variable bias: the omitted variable in the differenced specification, the partner's savings, is likely to be positively correlated with the level of transfers received by the partner in that period. Thus, except in the case that the partner's assets do not influence the transfer arrangements (either because $\beta_5 = 0$ or because the partners do not have access to liquid

Table 10.2. Estimated savings and transfer decision rules for simulated data, by extent of commitment and access to liquid assets

	Net transfers out						Net savings			
	Without liquid assets		With liquid assets							
	Full commitment	No commitment	Full commitment		No commitment		Full commitment		No commitment	
Own assets			0.451	0.456	0.179	0.143	−0.821	−0.822	−0.839	−0.813
			(13.83)	(12.49)	(8.54)	(5.14)	(45.61)	(45.51)	(48.78)	(37.39)
Partner's assets				−0.663		−0.255		0.162		0.182
				(8.80)		(6.09)		(4.35)		(5.56)
Transfer assets	−0.0170	−0.127	−0.221	0.0586	−0.578	−0.398	0.0870	0.0186	0.0645	−0.00645
	(0.50)	(2.30)	(7.31)	(1.02)	(4.83)	(2.53)	(5.21)	(0.65)	(0.66)	(0.52)
Income	0.506	0.272	0.517	0.514	0.198	0.194	0.193	0.193	0.334	0.336
	(40.44)	(40.38)	(44.76)	(39.91)	(39.57)	(36.70)	(30.21)	(30.29)	(81.44)	(81.25)
Constant	0.0109	0.00367	−0.0125	−0.00185	−0.00178	0.00236	0.0324	0.0298	0.0510	0.0480
	(0.90)	(0.54)	(1.08)	(0.142)	(0.34)	(0.41)	(5.07)	(4.61)	(11.89)	(10.54)

Note: Absolute t-ratios are shown in parentheses.

assets), a negative effect of transfer assets upon transfers does not necessarily imply the presence of imperfect commitment, as it does in the case in which there are no liquid assets. Nevertheless, the resulting coefficient may be useful for interpreting estimates when the same procedure is applied to actual data.

When the partner's assets are controlled for, a clear result from Table 10.2 is that, when households have access to liquid assets, transfer behaviour within each commitment regime is quite similar to that in an environment without liquid assets in terms of the resulting coefficients on transfer assets and income: the presence of financial intermediaries does not substantially affect the structure of each type of transfer arrangement, except that financial assets of both partners affect transfer decisions. In particular, whether or not there are liquid assets, under commitment the transfer asset effect is not significantly different from zero and the income coefficient is close to 0.5, whereas in the absence of commitment the transfer asset effect is significant and negative and the income coefficient is substantially less than 0.5. As might be expected, it is also evident that an increase in own financial assets results in an increase in transfers out, whereas an increase in the partner's assets has the opposite effect. Interestingly, the financial-asset effects, like the income effects, are smaller in the absence of commitment than they are under full commitment.

As indicated by the welfare gains shown in Table 10.1, one implication of the model is that the composition of transfer arrangements changes as a result of increased asset liquidity, with more transfer arrangements being carried out with commitment. The results in Table 10.2 (columns two and three) suggest that if this is the case, then on the basis of data without information about the partner's financial assets, income effects upon transfers should be more positive,[12] whereas transfer-asset effects should be more negative in environments with financial intermediation than in areas without liquid assets, given that in the latter environments no-commitment transfers are dominant. These observations are consistent with our earlier findings (Foster and Rosenzweig 1995*b*).

The last four columns of Table 10.2 present estimates of the savings-decision rules with and without commitment. As might be expected, own assets have a significant negative effect upon savings, whether or not the partner's assets are included in the specification. A comparison of the specifications with and without commitment contrasts interestingly with those for the transfer-decision rules. In particular, whereas a unit increase in income is associated with a 0.336 increase in savings in the absence of perfect commitment, the same effect results in a 0.193 increase in savings under full commitment. This presumably reflects the fact that because the insurance provided by transfer arrangements is less complete in the absence of commitment, savings play a more important role in this regard. Finally, the transfer-asset effects upon savings are small. Only in the case of commitment with the partner's assets excluded is a significant coefficient observed on transfer assets, but this reflects the same omitted-variable bias that is evident in the transfer-decision rules.

Data

Examining the role of imperfect commitment in determining transfer behaviour and showing how this role is influenced by financial intermediation, while taking into account heterogeneity among households, place considerable demands upon data: information is needed on asset flows, transfers, and income shocks over at least two consecutive and comparable periods. We use two data sets from South Asia that meet these criteria.

The first data set is from India's Additional Rural Incomes Survey (ARIS), which gathered longitudinal information on asset stocks and flows and on net transfers for 4,118 households from a stratified national probability sample of all rural households for the crop years 1968–9, 1969–70, and 1970–1. The ARIS was conducted by the National Council of Applied Economic Research (NCAER). It provides village-level information on the realization of an adverse shock as reported by an informed village member and on the presence of and distance to financial intermediaries, including banks and co-operative credit institutions. In particular, 2,731, or 67 per cent, of the 4,081 households surveyed for the analysis were located in villages situated within 5 km. of a bank or cooperative.[13] Those households represented 61 per cent of rural Indian households, given the stratification. The ARIS data were augmented with information from the NCAER's 1981–2 Rural Economic and Demographic Survey. This latter survey, which reinterviewed approximately two-thirds of the households interviewed in 1970–1 (those in which the household head had remained the same through 1981), provides information on the assets inherited by the household heads prior to the 1968 round of the ARIS. We use that information to construct instruments to predict τ_{it}, which include the initial-period adverse shock and that shock interacted with the inheritance variables (wet and dry land, animals, and farm equipment). We estimate income shocks from the residuals obtained from the estimates of profit functions reported in Foster and Rosenzweig (1995*c*), which also used these data.

Our second data set is from the longitudinal Pakistan Food Security Survey (PFSS), conducted between 1986 and 1989 by the International Food Policy Research Institute (IFPRI). It not only provides comprehensive information on financial transactions and includes information on bank proximity, but also contains detailed information on production that was collected in sufficiently closely spaced rounds to identify specific crop stages (planting and harvesting) within each of two annual crop cycles (*Rabi* and *Kharif*). The detailed nature of this information permits us to estimate the 'shock' component of income in the presence of credit-market imperfections that have important effects upon the allocation of agricultural inputs and makes it possible to test whether this shock was unanticipated at the time that input decisions were made.[14] As we have noted, estimating the extent to which shocks influence transfers provides evidence on the extent to which transfers act as a form of insurance.

The PFSS data were collected in twelve rounds over the period from July 1986 to September 1989 and cover a sample of 926 households residing in fifty-two villages in three major wheat-growing provinces of Pakistan—Punjab, Sind, and the Northwest Frontier Province. The survey elicited information, in the first and last rounds, on the proximity of each village to a bank; there were no changes in bank locations between the survey rounds.

Because information in the survey (with the exception of consumption information and some other variables) refers to the interval between rounds, only four of the twelve rounds permit a reasonably precise identification of the relevant variables needed to estimate savings-decision rules that account for the seasonal nature of agricultural production.[15] These rounds permit estimates of savings-decision rules for the harvest stage of the *Rabi* season that condition on asset stocks at the beginning of the corresponding planting period and the shock that is realized at the time of the harvest. Limiting the analysis to those households cultivating in the *Rabi* season and for which the relevant data are available yielded 371 households, of which 166 (45 per cent) were located less than 5 km. from a bank.

The two decisions we examine are net financial savings (that is, changes in financial assets, including bank deposits and other financial instruments) and net transfers (that is, net contributions of moneys and food to friends and relatives). Table 10.3 presents means, standard deviations, and prevalence measures for both savings and transfers in the two samples, stratified for each data set by whether or not the village in which a household resided was located within 5 km. of a commercial bank or financial cooperative. All statistics are based upon a three-year period. In both data sets, as expected, the percentage of

Table 10.3. Means, standard deviations, and prevalence of transfers and savings from two South Asian longitudinal data sets

	India, 1968–71		Pakistan, 1985–8	
	Bank ≤ 5 km	Bank >5 km	Bank ≤5 km	Bank >5 km
Percentage of households with non-zero flows for a 3-year period				
Financial savings	34.2	20.2	29.0	15.0
Transfers	6.5	18.9	85.2	84.1
Gross flows for 3–year period (*rupees*)				
Financial savings	227.4	113.1	4,516	4,306
	(1,047)	(507.0)	(21,588)	(23,710)
Transfers	20.6	34.3	5,908	3,518
	(593.6)	(382.6)	(14,602)	(11,444)
Annual agricultural income	2,454	2,065	31,891	31,498
	(2,927)	(2,584)	(31,382)	(26,738)

Note: Figures for the Indian sample are based upon net flows for each of 3 years, whereas those for Pakistan are based upon gross flows. Standard deviations are shown in parentheses.

households with any financial savings over the three-year period is substantially lower in villages located more than 5 km. from a financial intermediary. In India the ratio of savings participation rates was 1.7 to 1 for households in villages near financial intermediaries as compared with households in villages not having access to such intermediaries, and in Pakistan the ratio was almost 2 to 1.

As with the welfare-gain simulations reported in Table 10.1, in the Indian data the proportion (6.5 per cent) of households in villages near a bank that received or provided transfers over the same period is less than 35 per cent of that in the villages with less access to financial institutions. Access to formal financial institutions does appear to reduce the participation of households in transfer arrangements. The difference in transfer participation rates across villages differentiated by asset liquidity is almost non-existent in the Pakistani data. However, transfers in that setting are dominated by remittances flowing from relatives of the sample households residing outside Pakistan and are ubiquitous in the sample, with approximately 85 per cent of the households receiving transfers. Such transfers do not normally reflect insurance considerations. Indeed, average net transfers received are approximately 3,000 *rupees* in the Pakistan sample and are essentially zero *rupees* over the three-year period in the Indian data, as would be expected when such transfers are responsive to income shocks. Because a large part of transfers in the Pakistani setting represent regular income flows, it is not possible to detect the influence of financial intermediaries upon informal insurance arrangements without examining estimates of the transfer-decision rules.

Estimates from the Sample Data

Table 10.4 presents estimates of the transfer and savings-decision rules for the Indian panel. The estimates for financial savings indicate that savings play a role in smoothing consumption, but only in villages near banks. As with estimates from the simulated data, net savings in those villages are greater when shocks are high and are lower when financial assets are large. In villages in which households do not have access to banks, however, there is little evidence that financial savings play any significant role. Thus proximity to banks appears to be important in affecting the ability of households to use savings to smooth consumption.

The estimates also suggest that the presence of financial intermediaries increases the insurance role of transfers. In particular, the estimates of the shock effects upon transfers and of transfer assets in villages in which households do not have access to banks are consistent with a regime in which transfers play an insurance role but partners are unable to commit: positive shocks induce transfers out, but those households who in the past remitted more transfers out reduce their current transfers for a given profit shock. Thus in areas without a bank, implementability constraints evidently influence transfer behaviour, with each additional *rupee* that has been sent out in the past resulting in almost a

Table 10.4. IV fixed-effects estimates of transfer and savings-allocation rules, by bank proximity: national sample of rural Indian households

	Net transfers out		Net financial savings	
	Bank ≤5 km	Bank >5 km	Bank ≤5 km	Bank >5 km
Net transfer assets (*rupees*)	−2.109	−0.948	1.40	−2.16
	(1.61)	(9.07)	(1.28)	(0.51)
Net financial savings (*rupees*)	0.0104	−0.00222	−1.05	0.122
	(0.08)	(0.02)	(9.85)	(0.02)
Value of farm equipment (*rupees*)	−0.00777	0.0321	0.203	−1.555
	(0.04)	(0.49)	(1.31)	(0.59)
Value of animal stocks (*rupees*)	0.00560	−0.0416	0.119	2.91
	(0.01)	(0.15)	(0.27)	(0.25)
Profit shock (*rupees*)	0.0133	0.008345	0.019	−0.0586
	(1.92)	(2.08)	(3.33)	(0.36)
Constant	−28.35	−24.79	1,117.18	600.17
	(0.85)	(1.67)	(4.23)	(1.00)

Notes: Analysis is based upon 4,081 households, of which 2,731 were located near a bank, with three observations per household. All right-side variables except profit shock are treated as endogenous. Instruments include inheritance of land and other assets, adverse shock in initial period, and interactions of initial adverse shock with inheritance variables. Absolute asymptotic *t*-ratios are shown in parentheses.

one-for-one decline in additional transfers out, given the shock. In villages with access to formal credit institutions, however, the positive shock effect upon transfers is substantially larger than in the villages without banks, indicating that transfers play an enhanced insurance role there. The negative effect of transfer assets is also greater in absolute value in those villages. Both of these differences conform to the simulations in Table 10.2 (those excluding partner assets), which suggest that intermediation induces more transfer arrangements with commitment than those without commitment, a result consistent with the theory's implication that the welfare gains from commitment rise substantially when households can use assets to smooth consumption. Also consistent with the simulation estimates are the positive effects of financial assets upon transfers and the effects of transfer assets on financial savings in villages with access to banks; but neither of these estimates is significantly different from zero.

A shortcoming of the Indian panel estimates is that because the data pertain to a calendar year, some of the variation in savings behaviour may have occurred prior to the time when the income shock is realized. As noted, the IFPRI data set for Pakistan provides data with sufficient temporal disaggregation to construct measures of savings and profits for specific stages of agricultural production. An estimated stage-specific profit function may then be used to construct an idiosyncratic shock measure that is relevant to the savings-decision rule specific to the post-harvest period.

Transfer-decision and savings-decision rules for the Pakistani sample are presented in Table 10.5. As for the Indian case, it is evident that rules governing financial savings decisions differ importantly by the presence of financial intermediaries. The effect of income shock upon net savings in the presence of banks is three times the effect in the absence of banks, and the stock of savings has a substantial effect upon savings only in the presence of banks. Thus bank proximity importantly affects the ability of households to use assets to smooth their consumption in both rural Pakistan and India. The estimates of transfer-decision rules in Pakistani villages without banks, as in India, indicate that transfers play an important insurance role and appear to be transacted among

Table 10.5. IV fixed-effects estimates of asset-accumulation decision rules in the post-harvest (*Rabi*) stage, by bank proximity: villages in rural north-west Pakistan

	Net transfers out		Net financial savings	
	Bank ≤ 5 km	Bank >5 km	Bank ≤ 5 km	Bank > 5 km
Planting stage				
Net transfer assets (*rupees*)	−0.307	−0.328	−0.218	0.088
	(1.37)	(4.34)	(1.93)	(1.21)
Savings (*rupees*)	0.063	−0.028	−0.574	−0.023
	(0.56)	(0.42)	(2.85)	(0.38)
Debt (*rupees*)	0.099	0.161	−0.0239	0.192
	(2.08)	(1.57)	(0.59)	(2.03)
Food stocks (*rupees*)	1.45	−0.824	0.0251	−0.786
	(1.93)	(3.19)	(0.03)	(1.47)
Inventory (*rupees*)	0.111	0.099	−0.004	0.014
	(0.88)	(1.10)	(0.05)	(0.27)
Equipment (*rupees*)	0.095	−0.123	0.608	−0.200
	(2.04)	(1.61)	(1.77)	(1.83)
Potential labour income (*rupees*/day)	195	−149	−20.6	−88.2
	(2.07)	(1.45)	(0.21)	(0.81)
Harvest stage				
Production shock (*rupees*)	0.023	0.037	0.090	0.029
	(1.06)	(2.17)	(2.30)	(1.58)
Potential labour income (*rupees*/day)	−339	63.5	3.48	55.1
	(1.90)	(0.44)	(0.03)	(0.39)
$F(9,311)$	3.43		2.05	
P-value	0.000		0.034	

Notes: Analysis is based upon 371 households, of which 166 are located near a bank, with two observations per household. All specifications include village × time dummies (not shown). These control for contemporaneous variation in wages and prices. All right-side variables other than village × time dummies are treated as endogenous. Instruments include initial crop-cycle state variables (other than the production shock), inherited assets, household composition, land ownership, and village × time × land-inheritance interactions. Absolute asymptotic t-ratios are shown in parentheses.

partners who are unable to commit. In those villages, transfer assets have a negative and significant relationship with transfers out, and income shocks have a significant and positive relationship with transfers made to others in conformity to the estimates from the simulated data under the scenario in which there is no commitment and households do not have liquid assets. In particular, the estimates indicate that in those villages a 100 *rupee* increase in the profit shock results in an increase of 3.7 rupees in transfers out. Less consistent with the estimates from the Indian panel, the shock and transfers-asset coefficients are similar among areas differing according to whether there is a bank near by. However, both the profit shock and the transfer asset effects are less precisely measured in the sample of households in villages located near a bank.

Conclusion

In this chapter we have used a model incorporating transfer behaviour, savings, and imperfect commitment, along with two longitudinal data sets, to examine the implications of the presence of financial intermediaries for transfer behaviour in developing countries. We found, as expected, that the introduction of financial intermediaries provides new opportunities for households to smooth income through saving and dissaving. Although this change appears to diminish somewhat the magnitudes and prevalence of transfers, our results indicate that transfer arrangements continue to play an important role in helping agricultural households to smooth income fluctuations even in the presence of financial institutions. Indeed, because the introduction of financial intermediaries increases the value of full-commitment transfer arrangements, which provide more complete insurance than do no-commitment arrangements, the insurance role of transfers actually tends to be higher in the presence of financial intermediation.

The robustness of informal insurance arrangements to the presence of financial intermediaries is easily understood. Saving and borrowing can assist households in smoothing consumption in the face of income shocks, but they do not actually provide insurance. A combination of income pooling through transfer arrangements and savings behaviour thus provides households with less consumption variability than either can alone. Although informal arrangements among family members and other individuals may be importantly altered by the introduction of more formal mechanisms that meet some of the same needs, it appears that the informal arrangements, particularly those that are less vulnerable to problems of imperfect commitment, still have an important role to play.

Notes

The research for this chapter was supported in part by National Institute of Health grants HD30907 and HD28687 and by National Science Foundation grant SBR93-0405.

1. To avoid the unravelling of mutually beneficial behaviour that arises in games of the finite-period, repeated prisoner's-dilemma type, we assume that the contract can provide for a positive pay-off to both parties in period T that is achieved only if neither party violates the contract before that period. As discussed below, the value of the pay-off is set equal to the infinite-horizon discounted utility expected from full risk-sharing, given the stock of assets in period T. It is worth noting that the use of a finite horizon distinguishes this model from that used by Thomas and Worrall but is necessitated by the introduction of savings behaviour into the model. For large T it may be shown that the solution from this problem will approach that in the infinite-horizon case.
2. Note that this contrasts with Thomas and Worrall (1994) and Foster and Rosenzweig (1995*b*), who construct policy functions for symmetric strategies in the context of an infinite-horizon model. The infinite-horizon case is attractive for studying imperfect commitment because of the impossibility of using future benefits from cooperation to induce cooperative behaviour in the finite-horizon, prisoner's dilemma-type games; however, it proved prohibitive to compute the burden associated with extending the approach to the non-symmetric case with assets. We finesse this difficulty by assuming that welfare at period T is dependent upon whether or not the arrangement is still in force at that period. In particular, if the arrangement is still in force, we assume that partners face a utility possibility frontier in the final period $W_T(V)$ equal to that which would arise under full commitment without further changes in asset stocks, whereas if it is not in force they each receive a final period utility U_{iT}^{AI} equal to the expected discounted utility under autarky without further changes in asset stocks.
3. One feature of the presence of financial intermediaries that is not captured by this specification is that the effects may be asymmetric with respect to positive and negative asset positions: households without access to banks can transfer resources across time through the use of buffer stocks but not through borrowing, whereas households with such access can both borrow and save.
4. The explicit dependence of WT upon income and assets has been dropped for notational simplicity.
5. Obtaining explicit expressions for the derivative is helpful because, given asset stocks and income, and for each possible pair of savings decisions, the transfer in period t and the subsequent utility V_{t+1} for partner 2, given period $t+1$ incomes, solve

$$\frac{u'(y_{1t} - \tau_t - S_{1t})}{u'(y_{2t} + \tau_t - S_{2t})} = E_t[W_{t+1}^1(V_{t+1})]$$

   whenever implementation constraints are not binding.
6. We drew initial assets independently for the two partners from the B, assuming that each level had equal probabilities. Initial V was obtained by drawing a random variable, x, from the uniform distribution, computing $V = F(x) =$ cosine $[(16^*x - 0.5)^{\wedge 5} + 0.5]^* pi/2$. Under imperfect commitment when the resulting V was not implementable, we chose the closest implementable V. We did so because it has the property of selecting starting points along the utility possibility frontier that are close to and symmetric about the 45-degree line.

7. Netting out the component of expected discounted utility accruing at period T removes differences in welfare arising directly from the assumptions made about the differences in pay-offs in period T with and without a transfer arrangement. The purpose is to ensure that some risk sharing takes place in the absence of commitment, as discussed in n. 2.
8. Further increasing liquidity by allowing households to hold net asset positions in the range −4 to 4 in 0.02 intervals increases this figure to 90% indicating, not surprisingly, that substantially greater insurance can be obtained with increased liquidity, although this figure still falls short of the figure of 97% that is attained in the presence of transfer arrangements with the limited asset space but full commitment.
9. As we have pointed out in Foster and Rosenzweig (1995*b*), altruism between transfer partners, as might be present among members of the same family, operates to reduce problems of imperfect commitment. A potential implication of this result is thus that, in the presence of financial intermediaries, transfer arrangements are more likely to be based on family ties. Unfortunately, information on the relationship to the transfer partner is not available in the data sets used in this chapter. The data from the International Crop Research Institute for the Semi-Arid Tropics, which we used in Foster and Rosenzweig (1995*b*), do have information on transfer partners, but the small number of villages precludes an analysis of how financial intermediation affects the transfers.
10. The partner's asset stocks are also unlikely to be known. As these variables cannot be treated in the same way as the partner's income, we assume for the moment that such information is available. Later in the chapter we shall explore the implications of the unavailability of the partner's asset information, using simulated data.
11. Under perfect income pooling the transfer is half the difference between the incomes, so that $\beta_2 = -\beta_3 = 0.5$, and under independence $\rho = 0$, so that $\beta_6 = \beta_2 = 0.5$.
12. Note that above we establish only that the share of full commitment transfers among those making transfers increases. In combination with Tables 10.1 and 10.2, this implies that in a heterogeneous population the effect of a shock on transfers among those making transfers increases with intermediation. For reasonable parameter values, however, it may also be shown that the average effect of a shock on transfers (i.e. including those in autarky, under no commitment, and under full commitment according to their proportion in the population) will rise. For example, for $\delta = 0.01$, $\kappa^{-1} = 0.025$, and $\kappa^{-0} = 0$ and using the coefficient estimates in Table 10.2, it may be shown that the average transfer effect increases from 0.330 to 0.441 with the introduction of financial intermediaries.
13. Originally the sample included 4,118 households, but thirty-seven households had to be dropped because of missing data.
14. Behrman, Foster, and Rosenzweig (1997) present details of the computation of the shock, including estimates of the normalized generalized Leontief profit function used to obtain the shocks, and the test establishing that the estimated shock was unanticipated at the time of the planting stage.
15. Behrman, Foster, and Rosenzweig (1996) provide a detailed discussion of the problems that can arise in the estimation of savings decision rules that ignore the seasonal nature of agricultural production.

11 Self-enforcing Family Constitutions: Implications for Saving, Fertility, and Social Security

Alessandro Cigno

The analysis of the economic implications of social security programmes and other forms of public intervention is based largely on the assumption that individuals interact through the market only. Much of the discussion about saving, growth, and generational accounting is based, for example, on some version of Modigliani's life-cycle theory of saving, in which each person is assumed to be selfishly concerned about his or her own lifetime consumption stream only. It has long been realized, however, that various important aspects of reality cannot be explained by that theory.

First, there is the matter of intergenerational transfers. Modigliani (1988*b*) argues that unintentional transfers in the form of accidental bequests can be accommodated within a life-cycle framework by allowing for uncertainty about the length of life, medical expenses in old age, and other vicissitudes. Uncertainty, however, cannot account for *inter-vivos* transfers, which are obviously intentional. Second, there is the demand for children. Given that reproduction is normally the outcome of voluntary activity, and that raising children is costly, why should people who are interested in only their own consumption choose to have children and even make voluntary transfers to them? An expanded theory of intertemporal choice and intrafamily interactions is clearly needed to answer these questions. The search for such a theory has moved in two main directions: one based on the assumption of some form of intergenerational altruism, the other on what might be called strategic self-interest.

Barro (1974) has provided the best-known example of policy analysis based on the first of these approaches. By assuming descending intergenerational altruism, he shows that voluntary transfers from parents to children will undo any government-engineered transfer in the opposite direction. Becker and Barro (1988) take this approach further by making fertility a decision variable and assuming that the number of children, as well as their well-being, enters positively into the utility function of parents. Descending altruism thus explains a demand for children and voluntary transfers to them, but it does not explain why parents make those transfers in the form of bequests, when *inter-vivos* gifts are more tax-efficient. Nishimura and Zhang (1992) also take fertility as a decision variable, but they reverse the sign of intergenerational altruism: from children to parents rather than parents to children. Children are thus demanded as a good in the Barro–Becker world, as an asset in that of Nishimura and Zhang. In either case, however, intergenerational transfers are free gifts, not part of a deal. Precisely because they are gifts, transfers are unidirectional.

Without reciprocity of sentiments, therefore, an altruistic model cannot explain two-way flows between generations. Furthermore, it does not guarantee an efficient allocation of consumption across generations and over the life cycle of each generation. If income is growing, for example, it may be efficient for grown-up children to support their elderly parents. That, however, cannot happen in a model with descending altruism: if the family founders drew up a dynastic plan involving transfers from children to parents, their successors would simply ignore it. Conversely, in the absence of regulation, parental transfers to young children will never be higher than subsistence if altruism is ascending. Unless we assume that children can borrow from the market the moment they are born, therefore, it is highly unlikely that the life-cycle allocation of consumption generated by ascending altruism will be efficient. Mutual altruism, on the other hand, can explain two-way flows, but it is still no guarantee of efficiency. As Stark (1993) has shown, reciprocity of sentiments does not rule out conflict, and it can lead to inefficiency. Efficiency in a framework of mutual altruism requires unanimity. As I have pointed out elsewhere (Cigno 1991: ch. 9), this requirement imposes much stronger restrictions on individual preferences and expectations than time consistency in the usual sense: every member (present and future) of the same dynasty would have to maximize literally the same family welfare function, subject to the same intertemporal budget constraint.

The other line of explanation starts from the assumption that individuals are interested in only their own lifetime consumption, as in life-cycle theory; but it allows for the possibility that some coalitions of individuals smaller than the market, such as extended families, may be better off reallocating resources through internal deals than trading in the open market. Individuals entering such coalitions make transfers to fellow members, not for altruistic reasons, but because it is in their interest to do so. Kotlikoff and Spivak (1981) move along these lines by characterizing the family as a provider of insurance against the risk of running out of income in old age because of higher than average longevity. In Bernheim, Shleifer, and Summers (1985), parents use the threat of disinheritance as a means to induce their children to look after them. In both of these approaches, the promise of a bequest is traded against a current flow of income or services from children to parents. By this route, grown-up family members can improve the balance between present and old-age consumption. Neither of these approaches explains, however, why self-interested parents should voluntarily make above-subsistence transfers to their young children. Elsewhere (Cigno 1991: ch. 9) I have characterized the family as an institution that co-ordinates the borrowing and saving decisions of individuals at various stages of the life cycle. Above-subsistence transfers from working-age parents to young children are viewed as loans, and transfers from working age children to retired parents are viewed as loan repayments. Children are demanded, according to this approach, because of the opportunities for intertemporal trade that they create.

Unlike intergenerational altruism, strategic self-interest is consistent with evidence of two-way traffic in the flow of transfers between parents and children. On the other hand, it raises questions about the enforcement of (typically implicit) intrafamily contracts, which obviously do not arise in an altruistic framework. Kotlikoff and Spivak (1981) side-step the issue by assuming mutual trust and honesty among relatives. Bernheim *et al.* (1985) similarly elude it by assuming that parents can make unalterable testaments. I have tackled it by looking for conditions, such that a family constitution prescribing transfers from the middle-aged to both the young and the old would be self-enforcing, in the sense of supporting a sub-game-perfect Nash equilibrium (Cigno 1993). In this chapter I show that the explicit introduction of self-enforceability conditions changes the behaviour of the model. I also argue that a family constitution is negotiation-proof if it is designed to generate an intertemporally efficient allocation of consumption; this blurs the difference between enlightened altruism and strategic self-interest.

I start by reformulating and extending the model in Cigno (1991, 1993) in the way indicated. The responses of the model economy to a number of policy packages consistent with the government budget constraint are then derived and compared with those of life-cycle theory and of models (suitably reformulated and extended to make the comparison possible) that assume some form or other of intergenerational altruism. The policy implications of strategic self-interest turn out to be strikingly different not only from those of non-strategic self-interest (i.e. of life-cycle theory), but also from those of intergenerational altruism (ascending or descending, with or without endogenous fertility). Finally, I discuss the results in the light of the available evidence.

Basic Assumptions

Each individual lives three periods, conventionally named 'youth', 'middle age', and 'old age'. The lifetime utility of a person born at date t is given by

$$U(C_1^t, C_2^t, C_3^t) = u_1(C_1^t) + u_2(C_2^t) + u_3(C_3^t), \tag{11.1}$$

where C_j^t denotes consumption in the j-th period ($j = 1, 2, 3$) of that person's life (the assumption of additive separability simplifies the exposition without affecting the conclusions). The functions $u_j(.)$ are increasing and concave, with $u_j = 0$ and $u_j' = \infty$ for C_j^t equal to its subsistence level, s_j.

There are three institutions: the government, the market, and the extended family. At any date, t, the government taxes the middle-aged by a certain amount, T^t, pays the old a certain amount, P^t, and subsidizes parents of young children at the rate B^t. The market offers a wage, Y^t, and an interest rate $(r^t - 1)$. The young and the old can neither work nor borrow. Extended families, which at any date include three generations at various points of the life cycle, are mutual-benefit societies concerned, among other things, with the co-ordination of intergenerational transfers.

The reason for assuming that the young cannot borrow from the market is that minors cannot enter into legal commitments; more generally, one could assume that it is difficult to obtain credit for future labour incomes. The market, therefore, allows consumption to be reallocated from the middle period of life to the last, but not (or not enough) to the first. I shall argue that the extended family can succeed, under certain circumstances, where the market fails.

Each family will have its own constitution, specifying the rights and duties of each member. For example, a constitution might prescribe that, at any date, t, (i) middle-aged parents must transfer some specified amount, $I^t > 0$, to each of their young children, and (ii) each middle-aged child must transfer some specified amount, $D^t > 0$, to each of his or her elderly parents, subject to the proviso that (ii) does not apply if the beneficiary did not obey the rules of his or her own family of origin a period earlier. Notice that this clause exempts a child from supporting a parent if the latter unjustly failed to support a grandparent, but not if the parent justly punished a grandparent for disobeying the rules. I will show that such a constitution may be self-enforcing.

The Decision Framework

The couple is taken as the basic decision unit. Because the analysis focuses on intergenerational transactions, I do not enquire as to why the couple was formed or stays together. I simply assume that individuals marry in middle age, and that consumption is equally distributed between the partners. At any date, t, a couple born at date $(t - 1)$ can choose how many children to have, $2N^t$, and how much wealth to save (lend to the market), $2S^t$, subject to

$$0 \leq N^t \leq m \text{ and } 0 \leq S^t, \tag{11.2}$$

where m is a positive constant (a physiological ceiling).

We now examine the strategies open, at date t, to a couple born at $t - 1$, given the economic environment, $E^t = (Y^t, B^t, T^t, P^{t+1})$, and family constitutions prescribing $F^t = (I^t, D^t, D^{t+1})$. For simplicity, I assume that the partners have the same income and originate from extended families with identical constitutions (a 'marriage of likes' assumption). We can then consider 'the' extended family, and 'the' constitution, as if there were only one for each couple. This simplifying assumption does not affect any of the substantive points at issue in this chapter; all it does is to rule out the possibility that a couple might find it advantageous to, for example, obey the husband's extended family rules, and not the wife's, or vice versa.

The go-it-alone strategy

One of the options open to the partners at date t is not to obey the family constitution, and to use the capital market if they want to shift consumption to period $t+1$. I shall call this the go-it-alone strategy and denote it by $\mathcal{A}^t$. A couple adopting such a strategy will pay nothing to their own parents. If the lowest net cost of raising a child,

$$z^t = s_1 - B^t, \tag{11.3}$$

is positive, go-it-aloners will have no children. Otherwise, they will have as many children as possible, $2m$, and spend no more than is strictly necessary for each child. Whichever is the case, the partners will save (lend to the market) to the point where the marginal rate of substitution of old-age for middle-age consumption equals r^t. The pay-off to each partner of playing $\mathcal{A}^t$ given by

$$V(E^t) = \max_{NS} u_2(Y^t - z^t N^t - T^t - S^t) + u_3(P^{t+1} + S^t r^t), \text{subject to (11.2)}. \tag{11.4}$$

The comply strategy

An alternative to going it alone is to obey the rules of the extended family. I call this the comply strategy and denote it by $\mathcal{C}^t$.

Consider, first, the case in which the couple's parents complied with the rules, and the couple's children will do the same in their turn. This implies that each of the partners will get D^{t+1}, during the next period, from each child whom they choose to put into the world in this period at a cost of

$$z^{*t} = z^t + I^t. \tag{11.5}$$

It also implies, however, that each of the partners will have to pay his or her own parents D^t in the current period, irrespective of the choice of N^t. Given this fixed cost, the couple will play $\mathcal{C}^t$ only if they intend to use children as a vehicle for shifting consumption from the current period to the next period.

The couple will then bear children to the point at which the marginal rate of substitution of old-age consumption for middle-age consumption equals the marginal benefit of having children,

$$r^{*t} = D^{t+1}/z^{*t}, \tag{11.6}$$

or, if that violates the upper bound on fertility, to the physiological maximum, m (the latter would certainly be the case if z^{*t} happened to be negative). In the first case, the couple will save nothing. In the second, they will supplement the expected intrafamily transfers by saving to the point at which the marginal rate of substitution of old-age consumption for middle-age consumption equals r^t. The pay-off to this strategy is

$$V^*(E^t, F^t) = \max_{NS} u_2(Y^t - z^{*t}N^t - T^t - D^t - S^t) + u_3(p^{t+1} + S^t r^t + D^{t+1}N^t), \text{subject to (11.2)}. \tag{11.7}$$

Depending upon the economic environment and upon the family constitution, the pay-off of C^t may be larger or smaller than that of A^t. Given the fixed cost associated with the comply strategy, a necessary but not sufficient condition for V^* to be at least as large as V is that

$$r^t < r^{*t}. \tag{11.8}$$

That is why a couple playing the comply strategy will use the capital market only if fertility is held at its physiological ceiling.[1] Given that ceiling, however, (11.8) does not guarantee that the couple will choose to play C^t, because they may not be able to bear children in sufficient number to recover the fixed cost.

What if the couple's immediate predecessors or successors do not toe the family line? If any one of their parents disobeyed the rules, the couple owe that person nothing. In that case, the pay-off to playing C is greater than V^*, because the fixed cost of the strategy is then less than D^t. By contrast, the pay-off will be less than V^* if any of the couple's children fail to pay their dues.

Self-enforcing Family Constitutions

I now argue that a family constitution is self-enforcing if the prescribed transfers, F^t, satisfy

$$V(E^t) = V^*(E^t, F^t), \tag{11.9}$$

in the given environment, E^t, and the consumption stream generated by C^t satisfies

$$u_2'(C_2^t)/u_3'(C_3^t) = u_1'(C_1^{t+1})/u_2'(C_2^{t+1}), \tag{11.10}$$

for each t. Condition (11.9) stipulates that a middle-aged couple must be at least as well off complying with the existing family rules as going it alone in the market. Condition (11.10) states that the intertemporal allocation of consumption generated by (E^t, F^t) must be Pareto-optimal (over the life cycle of each generation and across generations).

If (11.9) is satisfied, C^t constitutes the couple's best response to their children playing C^{t+1}. The set $\{c^t\}$ is thus a Nash equilibrium. The clause that exempts a grown-up child from supporting a disobedient parent further ensures that this equilibrium is sub-game-perfect because it is clearly in any person's interest not to pay, if that can be done with impunity. The threat implicit in the comply strategy (not to support an ageing parent, if he or she did not obey the relevant family rules when middle aged) is thus credible. Of course, since nobody disobeys the rules in the equilibrium, the threat is never actually carried out.

The question now arises: is it possible to amend a constitution in such a way that it will still support a sub-game-perfect Nash equilibrium in the given economic environment but make the amenders better off? Suppose that, at some date t, a middle-aged couple calculate that they would be better off transferring to their parents less than the amount prescribed by the existing family constitution, even if that should require offering their own children a similar discount. The couple then write a new constitution, consistent with conditions (11.9) and (11.10), looking like the old one in every way except in that it prescribes lower (but still positive) values of D^t and D^{t+1}. At date $t+1$, however, their children would pay the couple absolutely nothing, because the old constitution entitles them to do so. The same would apply if the couple reduced I^t. Therefore, any attempt at constitutional change that involves a reduction of current transfers will not work.

Let me now try a different line of attack. If z^t is positive, it is cheaper for parents to shift any desired amount of consumption from middle to old age by making large transfers to a small number of children, rather than small transfers to a large number of children. Were it possible to raise I^t and D^{t+1}, and to lower r^{*t} (i.e. raise the size of the 'loan' made to each child but lower the implicit interest rate at which young children 'borrow' from their parents), in such a way that both the parents and the children would gain, it would be in the interest of the former to amend the constitution, and of latter to uphold it. Conditions (11.9) and (11.10) rule out the possibility of any such mutually advantageous intergenerational deal.

Given a sequence of economic environments, if there is a sequence of intergenerational transfers (not necessarily unique) that satisfies (11.9) and (11.10), a constitution prescribing those transfers will then be self-enforcing, not only in the sense that it supports a sub-game-perfect Nash equilibrium, but also in the stronger sense that it is negotiation-proof.

In the special case of a stationary economic environment ($E^t = E$ for all t), a self-enforcing family constitution, if one exists, would prescribe the same levels of transfers to each generation ($I^t = I$ and $D^t = D$, for all t). If children are costly, and the upper bound on fertility is never binding, compliers would then save nothing and choose a constant fertility level, $N = r^*$. The number of compliers would then grow steadily at the rate $(r^* - 1)$.

Having established that a self-enforcing family constitution may exist leaves us with two questions: how does a constitution come into force in the first place, and will it ever be changed or abandoned? To answer the first question, suppose that the sequence of economic environments is such that a self-enforcing constitution exists from a certain date only, say from $t = 1$ onwards. For all $t < 1$, couples will have then played $\mathcal{A}^t$ (if the family is not extinct at date 1, this implies $z^t < 0$ for $t < 1$). At date 1, it is in the interest of each middle-aged couple to introduce a self-enforcing constitution. If there is more than one, the constitution actually chosen will be that which maximizes $V^*(E^1, I^1, 0, D^2)$. To answer the second question, suppose that a constitution is in force at date 0. At date 1, however, the economic environment unexpectedly turns out to be such that the existing constitution is no longer self-enforcing (for example, because r^1 is unexpectedly higher than r^{*1}). If the constitution can be made self-enforcing again by changing the prescribed levels of transfer, the middle-aged of the day will play $\mathcal{C}^1$ in accordance with the amended rules; otherwise, they will play $\mathcal{A}^1$. Notice that such an event would have to be unforeseen. Were it known all along that no constitution would be self-enforcing at date 1, none would have been self-enforcing at earlier dates (in order to guard against the expected non-compliance of the next generation, the middle-aged of the day would have played $\mathcal{A}^0$ at $t = 0$, $\mathcal{A}^{-1}$ at $t = -1$, etc.). Had it been known in advance, by contrast, that a feasible amendment would be required at date 1, the original constitution would have been written so as to make the amendment unnecessary.

The fact that a self-enforcing constitution generates an efficient allocation of consumption across generations, and over the life cycle of each generation, blurs the conceptual distinction between altruism and self-interest. As I pointed out at the beginning of the chapter, unidirectional altruism does not guarantee intertemporal efficiency, while mutual altruism is not exempt from conflict and may be inefficient. Therefore, it may be argued that, if it is possible to design a self-enforcing constitution, an altruistic couple will endow their descendants with just such a constitution.[2] This argument, notice, is the opposite of the 'folk theorem': it is not that self-interested individuals behave as if they were altruists in a repeated game, but rather that altruists behave as if they were self-interested in a game played only once.

The possible existence of self-enforcing family constitutions is consistent with the observation of two-way *inter-vivos* flows, from middle-aged parents to young children and from middle-aged children to elderly parents (typically in the form of personal services, rather than cash). Bequests can be easily accommodated in such a scheme by introducing a durable asset with high transaction costs or user value. A perfect example of such an asset is the house, which in many countries is characterized by a sharp difference between the purchase price and the sale price (because of high taxes and legal fees) and by high search costs, and which also generates a flow of residential services without perfect substitutes in the rental market.

Suppose, then, that a person acquired an asset with the said characteristics during middle age. In the next period, the asset holder could choose to sell the asset in order to help finance his or her old-age consumption. Alternatively, it may be in the mutual interest of the asset holder and of his or her middle-aged children to trade a flow of transfers during the current period, for the promise of a bequest at the end of it. Any such arrangement may, of course, run up against enforcement problems (e.g. unknown to his or her children, the old person could promise the same asset to other people, maybe outside the family, in exchange for additional transfers), but these problems are typically less severe than those associated with the intergenerational transactions I have been discussing in this chapter, where the creditor cannot back out of the deal.

Effects of Changes in the Economic Environment

A change in any of the policy variables may affect behaviour in two ways: by altering the optimal choice of decision variables associated with each possible strategy, and by altering the pay-offs of alternative strategies and thus, at the margin, the choice of strategy. The effects on aggregate saving and aggregate fertility will thus reflect two sets of changes: in the optimal choice of S^t and N^t dictated by each strategy, and in the number of couples adopting each strategy. Nothing of substance is lost, and the exposition is considerably simplified, if we make the common assumption that children are always costly ($z^t > 0$), and that the physiological ceiling on fertility is never binding, so that go-it-aloners will have no children and compliers will not save. Time superscripts are inessential in the present context and will be dropped throughout this section (T will represent the tax paid, and D and P the intrafamily transfer and pension received, by those who are currently middle-aged).

Effects on go-it-aloners

Writing U_j for the value of $u_j'(C_j)$, and U_{jj} for that of $u_j''(C_j)$, at the go-it-aloner's choice of C_j, it is possible to state the comparative-statics effects of policy changes on the saving decisions of a couple adopting strategy $\mathcal{A}$ as

$$S_T = -U_{22}H^{-1} < 0, \tag{11.11}$$

$$S_B = 0, \tag{11.12}$$

and

$$S_P = -r^t U_{33}H^{-1} < 0, \tag{11.13}$$

where S_i denotes the partial derivative of S to the variable i, and

$$H = U_{22} + r^2 U_{33} < 0 \tag{11.14}$$

is the relevant Hessian determinant (negative for the second-order conditions). The effects on the pay-off of $\mathcal{A}^t$ are:

$$V_T = -U_2 < 0, \tag{11.15}$$

$$V_B = 0, \tag{11.16}$$

and

$$V_P = U_3 > 0. \tag{11.17}$$

Effects on compliers

Similarly, writing U_j^* for the value of $u_j'(C_j)$, and U_{jj}^* for that of $u_j''(C_j)$, at the complier's choice of C_j, we can express the effects of policy changes on the fertility decisions of someone playing $\mathcal{C}$ as

$$N_T = -z^* U_{22}^*(H^*)^{-1} < 0, \tag{11.18}$$

$$N_B = -(U_2^* - z^* N U_{22}^*)(H^*)^{-1} > 0, \tag{11.19}$$

and

$$N_P = -D U_{33}^*(H^*)^{-1} < 0, \tag{11.20}$$

where

$$H^* = (z^*)^2 U_{22}^* + D^2 U_{33}^* < 0. \tag{11.21}$$

The effects on the pay-off of C are

$$V_T^* = -U_2^* < 0, \tag{11.22}$$

$$V_B^* = N U_2^* > 0, \tag{11.23}$$

and

$$V_P^* = U_3^* > 0. \tag{11.24}$$

Effects on aggregate behaviour

Let us now assume that couples are differentiated by some characteristic, such as income, preferences, or natural fecundity. For any given state of the environment, different couples may thus get different pay-offs from the same strategy. Let n denote the proportion of compliers in the active population. Reinterpreting N as the mean number of children born to couples playing C we can then express aggregate fertility (per active woman or couple) as

$$N = nN. \tag{11.25}$$

Similarly, reinterpreting S as the mean saving of individuals playing $\mathcal{A}$ we can express aggregate saving (per active person) as

$$S = (1 - n)S. \tag{11.26}$$

Assuming a continuum of players, we can take n to be an increasing function, $n = g(V^* - V)$, of the pay-off differential for the marginal player (i.e. for the couple with $V^* = V$). Notice that, in view of (11.8), playing C would entail the choice of a lower value of C_2, and of a higher value of C_3, than playing $\mathcal{A}$. For any given $V^* = V$, U_2^* will then be higher than U_2, and U_3^* lower than U_3. Hence,

$$n_T = -(U_2^* - U_2)g'(0) < 0, \tag{11.27}$$

$$n_B = N U_2^* g'(0) > 0, \tag{11.28}$$

and

$$n_p = (U_3^* - U_3)g'(0) < 0. \tag{11.29}$$

In words, an increase in the child-benefit rate would raise the number of compliers relative to the number of go-it-aloners. An increase in the tax or in the pension would do the opposite.

The comparative statics of aggregate saving and fertility are then

$$S_T = -S_Y = -Sn_T + (1-n)S_T, \tag{11.30}$$

$$N_T = -N_Y = n_T N + nN_T < 0, \tag{11.31}$$

$$S_B = -Sn_B + (1-n)S_B < 0, \tag{11.32}$$

$$N_B = n_B N + nN_B > 0, \tag{11.33}$$

$$S_P = -Sn_P + (1-n)S_P, \tag{11.34}$$

and

$$N_P = Nn_P + nN_P < 0. \tag{11.35}$$

All the effects on aggregate fertility are thus unambiguously signed: positive that of the child-benefit rate, negative those of the tax and of the pension. By contrast, of the effects on aggregate saving, only that of the child-benefit rate is unambiguously negative. A rise in either of the other policy variables would in fact increase the number of potential savers but reduce the amount saved by each of them.

Feasible policy changes

The comparative-statics exercises of the last section do not take account of the government budget constraint. We now examine the total effects of some feasible policy changes, by which I mean changes in more than one policy variable at a time, satisfying the government's intertemporal budget constraint. I shall retain, however, the assumption that incomes are exogenously given. (A more general equilibrium stance, taking into account the effects of the policies on income growth, will be taken in the concluding section.)

The predictions are compared with those of life-cycle theory and of altruistic models. A life cycler behaves qualitatively like a go-it-aloner in every way (except in that N is not necessarily 0 or m). A descending altruist derives utility from that of his or her children, an ascending altruist from that of his or her parents. The predictions of these models, with and without the assumption of endogenous fertility, are derived in the Appendix. A summary of the results is given in Tables 11.1 and 11.2 (in which the strategic self-interest model discussed here is simply labelled 'self-interest' and the life-cycle model is labelled 'self-interest, taking fertility as exogenous').

Table 11.1. Total effects of feasible policy manœuvres on saving and fertility under alternative hypotheses

	Self-interest			Descending altruism			Ascending altruism		
	N	*S*	*S**	*N*	*S*	*S**	*N*	*S*	*S**
Child benefits	?	?	0	+	?	0	+	−	0
Public debt	+	?	+	−	?	+	0	+	+
Old-age security									
Fully funded	−	?	−	0	−	−	0	−	−
Pay-as-you-go	−	?	−	−	?	0	0	−	−

N = aggregate fertility; S = aggregate saving; * Taking fertility as exogenous.

Table 11.2. Total effects of feasible policy manœuvres on the welfare of parents and children under alternative hypotheses

	Self-interest				Descending altruism				Ascending altruism			
	V	*U*	*V**	*U**	*V*	*U*	*V**	*U**	*V*	*U*	*V**	*U**
Child benefits	?	0	0	0	−	−	0	0	−	0	0	0
Public debt	+	−	+	−	−	?	0	0	+	−	+	−
Old-age security												
Fully funded	−	0	0	0	0	0	0	0	0	0	0	0
Pay-as-you-go[a]	+	−	+	−	−	?	0	0	+	−	+	−

V = utility of parents; U = utility of children; * Taking fertility as exogenous; [a] Temporary increase in coverage.

Subsidizing couples with children

We start by considering the effects of an increase in the child-benefit rate, financed by a contemporaneous rise in the tax, such that $N^t dB^t + B^t dN^t - dT^t = 0$. This constitutes a redistribution of income in favour of couples with children (i.e. from go-it-aloners to compliers). Given that $dN_t = N_B dB^t + N_T dT^t$, the trade-off between the benefit and the tax is given by

$$dT^t/dB^t = N^t + B^t(dN^t/dB^t)$$
$$= N^t[1 + e(N^t, B^t)]/[1 + e(N^t, Y^t)b^t] > 0, \tag{11.36}$$

where $e(N, Y)$ and $e(N, B)$ are the elasticities of aggregate fertility to, respectively, aggregate income and the child-benefit rate, both positive in view of Equations 11.31 and 11.33, and b is the ratio of benefits to income.

The total effects of the manœuvre on fertility and saving,

$$dN^t/dB^t = N_B + N_T(dT^t/dB^t) \tag{11.37}$$

and

$$dS^t/dB^t = S_B + S_T(dT^t/dB^t), \tag{11.38}$$

are both ambiguous in view of (11.30)–(11.36). This contrasts with the prediction of all the exogenous fertility models, that the manœuvre would have no effect on saving; with the prediction of the endogenous fertility models with descending altruism, that it would definitely encourage fertility; and with the prediction of the endogenous fertility model with ascending altruism, that it would raise fertility and lower saving.

Depending on whether aggregate fertility responds positively or negatively to the policy, the tax increase required to pay for an extra dollar on the child-benefit rate will be larger or smaller than N^t. Because children are costly, the welfare of a taxpayer with the average number of children may consequently fall or rise. Child welfare will not be affected in any case because the levels of the transfers from parents to children are fixed by the family constitutions. By contrast, the policy will not affect the welfare of a taxpayer with the average number of children if fertility is exogenous, but it will definitely reduce the taxpayer's welfare in an endogenous fertility model with either descending or ascending altruism, in which case aggregate fertility will definitely rise. Paradoxically, if altruism runs from parents to children, and fertility is a choice variable, the policy will also leave each child worse off because it will induce parents to make smaller transfers to each of their children. As it lowers the cost of having an extra child relative to that of raising the quality of life for existing children, the policy induces parents to substitute quantity for quality.

Fully Funded Social Security

Next, we look at the effects of a fully funded increase in pensions, such that $dP^{t+1} = r^t dT^t$. Because

$$dT^t/dP^{t+1} = (1/r^t), \tag{11.39}$$

the present value of the future pension rise is equal to the current tax rise. The total effect on aggregate fertility is negative. From (11.31) and (11.35),

$$dN^t/dP^{t+1} = N_P + N_T(1/r^t) < 0, \tag{11.40}$$

while the total effect on aggregate saving,

$$dS^t/P^{t+1} = S_P + S_T(1/r^t), \tag{11.41}$$

is ambiguous in view of (11.30) and (11.34). The first of these results conflicts with that of Becker and Barro (1988), in whose model fully funded social security has no effect on fertility because it does not involve a net transfer between generations. The second result contradicts the prediction of all alternatives to the present model, that fully funded social security would crowd out voluntary saving.

Given that the public pension system offers the same return as the capital market, the policy has obviously no effect on the welfare of go-it-aloners. In view of (11.8), however, it reduces the welfare of compliers because it obliges them to contribute more to a scheme that offers a lower return than the family transfer system to which they subscribe. In my own model, therefore, the policy is welfare-reducing for the average taxpayer. There are no welfare effects in any of the alternative models considered.

Debt financing

A net transfer in favour of current taxpayers can be engineered by means of a debt-financed tax cut at date t, such that $N^t dT^{t+1} + T^{t+1} dN^t + r^t dT^t = 0$. Since T^{t+1} does not affect the behaviour of current taxpayers, the trade-off associated with this manœuvre is

$$\begin{aligned} -(dT^{t+1}/dT^t) &= (1/N^t)[r^t + T^{t+1}(dN^t/dT^t)] \\ &= (r^t/N^t)[1 - e(N^t, Y^t)f^t], \end{aligned} \tag{11.42}$$

where f is the debt/income ratio. The present value of the future tax rise is then smaller than the current tax cut. The reason is, of course, that the tax cut raises current fertility and therefore the number of future taxpayers. Indeed, if $e(N, Y)$ were larger than $(1/f^t)$, it would then be possible to reduce T^t without raising T^{t+1}.

Whichever is the case, as generation $(t-1)$ does not care about the level of the tax to be paid by generation t, the total effects of the policy on S^t and N^t are equal to the partial effects of a cut in T^t, respectively ambiguous and positive, shown in (11.30) and (11.31). The utility of current taxpayers obviously rises, that of their children obviously falls.

These predictions contrast with those of all the other models considered. In life-cycle theory and in the models with ascending altruism, wherein current taxpayers are not concerned about the size of the future tax rise, saving definitely rises irrespectively of whether fertility is endogenous or not. By contrast, the predictions of models with descending altruism depend crucially on whether parents can or cannot choose the number of children. If fertility is exogenous, the wealth of current taxpayers is not affected by the policy because the present value of the future tax rise is equal to the current tax cut. If that is the case, parents exactly compensate their children for the future tax rise, the utility of parents and children remains unaltered, and saving rises. If fertility is endogenous, by contrast, parents substitute quality for number of children (the direction of the substitution is the opposite of that induced by a tax-financed increase in child subsidies). As fertility falls, the present value of the future tax rise is larger than the current tax cut. The utility of current taxpayers will then fall. Saving, and the utility of each child, may rise or fall.

It should be noted that if fertility is endogenous in a model with descending altruism, the future tax increase raises the cost of having an extra child, relative to the marginal cost of improving the quality of life of existing children. Depending on the relative size of the cross-substitution and income effects, the level of parental transfer to each child (and thus the well-being of each child) may then rise or fall. Saving, too, may rise or fall, depending upon the relative elasticities of parental demand for quantity of children, quality (of life) of children, and the parents' own consumption in old age.

Pay-as-you-go increase in pension coverage

Finally, let us consider a pension rise financed by a contemporaneous increase in the tax, so that $dP^{t+1} - N^t dT^{t+1} - T^{t+1} dN^t = 0$, as in a pay-as-you-go social security system. Such a manœuvre is often assumed to be the equivalent of a debt-financed tax cut (e.g. in Becker and Barro 1988; Wildasin 1990). As we shall see, however, that is not true in general. In any case, it is useful to separate the effects of a self-financing increase in pension coverage from those of an increase in the public debt. The effects of a debt-financed increase in pensions can then be obtained by adding the effects of a debt-financed tax cut to those of a budget-balancing increase in pensions and taxes.

If the policy in question is a one-off measure,

$$\begin{aligned} dT^{t+1}/dP^{t+1} &= (1/N^t)[1 - T^{t+1}(dN^t/dP^{t+1})] \\ &= (1/N^t)[1 - e(N^t, P^{t+1})/g^{t+1}] > (1/Nt), \end{aligned} \tag{11.43}$$

where $e(N, P)$ is the elasticity of aggregate fertility to the pension, negative for (11.35), and g is the share of the tax revenue absorbed by pensions. Since T^{t+1} must rise, generation t will obviously lose out. Not being affected by T^{t+1}, generation $(t - 1)$ will gain. For the same reason, the total effects of the policy on S^t and N^t are equal to the partial effects of P^{t+1}, respectively ambiguous and negative, shown in (11.34) and (11.35).

These predictions contradict all the other models considered. Life-cycle theory, and the models with ascending altruism (with or without endogenous fertility), predict that saving will definitely fall. The models with descending altruism predict that nothing will change if fertility is exogenous, or that current taxpayers will be made worse off, and their children possibly better off, if fertility is endogenous.

If the policy is sustained, all generations from t onwards receive higher pensions and pay higher taxes. Therefore, in a steady state,

$$\begin{aligned} dT/dP &= (1/N)[(1 - T(dN/dP) \\ &= (1/N)[1 - e(N, P)g]/[1 - e(N, Y)h] > (1/N), \end{aligned} \tag{11.44}$$

where h is the tax/income ratio (obviously less than unity). Notice that, here as in the case of a temporary pension increase, the tax has to rise by more than the old-age dependency ratio $(1/N)$. Therefore, any permanent increase in coverage will be achieved at the price of a permanent reduction in the rate of return to participating in the public pension system. The effect on welfare is obviously negative if N is allowed to fall below r. It will be ambiguous otherwise, because the rise in the quota of old-age consumption financed by the pension will leave some compliers (those with r^* greater than N) worse off, but could make everyone else better off. Something similar applies also to the endogenous fertility model with descending altruism, but not to models in which fertility is either exogenous or not affected by the policy (as in the case of ascending altruism).

The signs of the steady-state effects on aggregate fertility and household saving,

$$dN/dP = N_P + N_T(dT/dP) \tag{11.45}$$

and

$$dS/dP = S_P + S_T(dT/dP), \tag{11.46}$$

are the same (respectively, negative and ambiguous) as those of a temporary increase in pension coverage.

Empirical Evidence

Survey evidence on the nature and extent of intrafamily transfers suggests that such transfers are substantial (see e.g. Kotlikoff, Spivak, and Summers 1981; Lampman and Smeeding 1983; Greenwood and Wolff 1992) and unlikely to be altruistically motivated (see e.g. Cox 1987; Altonji, Hayashi, and Kotlikoff 1992 and in the present volume). Indeed, Bhaumik and Nugent in the present volume report evidence for Peru of transfers from grown-up children to elderly parents, apparently as repayment for educational investment, that could be explained by the particular version of the non-altruistic model advocated in this chapter.

Indirect evidence to the same effect comes from a series of papers by Cigno and Rosati (1992, 1996, 1997). Using time-series data relating to post-war Germany, Italy, Japan, the UK, and the USA, we regress, separately for each country, fertility and household saving on a vector of exogenous variables, including the child-benefit rate, various measures of public pension coverage, the social security deficit, household disposable income, and relative prices (male–female wage-rate differential, interest rate). This pair of equations may be interpreted as the reduced form of a model of the simultaneous determination of household saving and fertility. As the social security deficit is controlled for, the regression coefficients of the child-benefit rate and of public pension coverage may be taken as estimates of the effects of balanced-budget changes in the variables in question. Conversely, since the pension and child-benefit rate are controlled for, the regression coefficients of the social security deficit may be interpreted as the effects of a change in the public debt, originating from a change of opposite sign in the social security tax.

For each of the countries considered, the signs of the estimated coefficients are consistent with the predictions of the non-altruistic model with endogenous fertility developed in the present chapter, and contradict all the alternatives taken into consideration. In particular, Rosati and I estimate that a balanced-budget increase in the child-benefit rate would encourage fertility and have no significant effect on saving, whereas a balanced-budget increase in pension coverage would reduce fertility and generally raise household saving. The only exception is Germany, where the effect of old-age security is not significantly different from zero. (Notice that the scenario of a balanced-budget increase in pension coverage is consistent with our model irrespective of whether the public pension system is fully funded or pay-as-you-go.) An increase in the social security deficit, by contrast, would have no significant effect on fertility, but it would generally reduce household saving everywhere except in the USA, where the effect of the deficit is not significant.

The finding of a negative effect of old-age security on fertility confirms existing results (see e.g. Hohm 1975; Entwisle and Winegarden 1984). By contrast, the positive effect on household saving conflicts with the well-known finding of Feldstein (1974, 1980) and others that old-age security discourages voluntary saving. (Leimar and Lesnoy (1982) show, however, that the negative effect of old-age security on saving, reported in Feldstein (1974), is due only to a computational error. Graham (1987) gets ambiguous results.) Nevertheless, none of those authors controls for the deficit. That should not make any difference to fertility, but it could well make a difference to saving, which Rosati and I have found to be negatively affected by the deficit. Given that the emergence of deficits has accompanied, worldwide, the expansion of pay-as-you-go social security, what Feldstein and others have picked up could thus be the effect of the deficit, rather than of coverage *per se*.

Furthermore, Feldstein and the others use the ratio of children to workers as a regressor in the saving equation, thereby implicitly assuming that fertility is exogenous. If fertility is actually endogenous, however, the regression coefficient of old-age security will show the effect of this variable only on household saving, holding fertility constant. To that, one must add the product between the effect of old-age security on fertility, estimated by Rosati and me and by many others to be negative, and the effect of fertility on saving, estimated by Feldstein to be also negative. As this product is positive, the true effect of old-age security on saving (allowing for the simultaneous fertility adjustment) could then have any sign.

On the one hand, because the estimated elasticity of household saving to pension coverage is generally positive, and that of fertility is universally negative, an increase in old-age security would stimulate economic growth, rather than slow it down as is often assumed. On the other, as I have already pointed out, any increase in pension coverage would cause a decline in aggregate fertility and thus, if the system is run on a pay-as-you-go basis, a fall in the implicit rate of return. Indeed, the deficits that have accompanied the expansion of pay-as-you-go social security programmes throughout the world could well be explained as the result of political resistance to such a fall.

For each of the countries considered, the estimated income elasticity of fertility is positive but well below unity. In view of (11.42), this reassures us that the tax policies conducted by those countries are intergenerationally efficient (i.e. that there are no unexploited opportunities for cutting taxes on one generation, without raising it on a subsequent one). It also tells us, however, that even if the public debt is as large as income, and the rate of population growth no higher than the real interest rate, the budget-balancing rise in the future tax is smaller (about half in Italy and smaller still in low-debt countries such as Japan and the USA) than the cut in the current tax. The temptation for a government to engage in some intergenerational substitution to the benefit of its electors must therefore be strong.

Finally, the negative sign of the coefficient of the deficit in the household saving equation tells us that the expansion of old-age security will exercise a stronger stimulus on household saving if the system does not run at a loss. The stimulus to growth will be positive anyway, however, because the deficit has no significant effect on fertility and, everywhere except in Germany, saving has a much larger elasticity with respect to pension coverage than with respect to the deficit.[3] The stimulus to growth would be even greater if the expansion were 'fully funded'—that is, if the present value of future commitments had to be matched by the value of present assets and the tax increase thus had to come *before* any pension increase.[4] In that case the policy would generate real capital formation not only indirectly, by encouraging household saving, but also directly, through the investment of social security taxes.

Concluding Remarks

We have found that the possible presence of extended-family networks (conceived as mutual-benefit societies and governed by self-enforcing constitutions) has strong implications for social security and public intervention generally. We have also seen that the available empirical evidence is consistent with the presence of such networks and appears to reject the alternative hypotheses that individuals make altruistically motivated intergenerational transfers or, at the opposite extreme, that they interact only through the market.

Among other things, the theory developed in this chapter makes sense of the empirical finding that a self-financing expansion in public pension coverage could raise household saving. Combined with the theoretical prediction and empirical evidence of a negative effect on fertility, this tells us that old-age security is likely to be a stimulus, rather than a hindrance, to economic growth. If, on the other hand, the public pension system is pay-as-you-go, a permanent increase in coverage would permanently reduce the return to participation in it. If incomes were constant, as in the analysis of feasible policy changes, the policy could then reduce welfare. If the positive effect on income growth is taken into account, however, it may well be that the policy would turn out to increase welfare.

Either way, allowing for the possibility of self-enforcing intrafamily deals makes a considerable difference to the outcome of policy. My analysis has shown, for example, that a debt-financed tax cut would raise fertility and could lower household saving in the presence of such deals, while the opposite would be true if all intrafamily transfers were gifts or if individuals interacted through the market only. This conclusion points towards a generalized second-best approach to policy design, wherein welfare maximization is constrained by individual behaviour not only in the market, but also within family networks.

Appendix

Model with descending altruism

This is a reformulation of the model underlying Barro (1974), Becker and Barro (1988), and Wildasin (1990). The basic assumption is that $U^t = U(C_0^t, C_1^t, C_2^t, U^{t+1}, N^{t+1})$. Nothing of substance is lost, and much is gained in simplicity, if we take the generation born at t to be the last. Following Cigno (1986), we can then write the minimum cost of providing a child born at t with the level of utility U^t as

$$Z(U^{t+2}, T^{t+2}, p^{t+3}) = \min C_0^{t+1} + (C_1^{t+1} - Y^{t+2} + T^{t+2})r^{-1}$$
$$+ (C_2^{t+1} - p^{t+3})r^{-2},$$

$$\text{subject to } U(C_0^{t+1}, C_1^{t+1}, C^{2t+1}) = U^{t+1}. \tag{11A.1}$$

The compensated demand for C_0^{t+1} generated by this problem, $I^t = I(U^t, T^{t+1}, p^{t+2})$, gives us the level of parental transfer (over and above the subsistence level of consumption) to a young child born at t.

If the number of children is a choice variable, as in Becker and Barro (1988) or Wildasin (1990), a couple born at date $(t - 1)$ will choose $(C_1^{t-1}, C_2^{t-1}, U^t, N^t)$, so as to maximize

$$V(C_1^{t-1}, C_2^{t-1}, U^t, N^t) = U(C_0^{t-1}, C_1^{t-1}, C_2^{t-1}, U^t, N^t), \tag{11.A2}$$

subject to (11.2) and

$$C_1^{t-1} + [c - B^t + Z(U^t, T^{t+1}, P^{t+2})]N^t + (C_2^{t-1} - P^{t+1})r^{-1} = Y^t - T^t. \tag{11.A3}$$

Each partner will then save $S^t = Y^t - T^t - C_1^{t-1} - z^{*t}N^t$, where $z^{*t} = c - B^t + I^t$.

Let $S_{jj} = \lambda H_{jj}/H < 0, s_{jk} = \lambda H_{jk}/H > 0$ and $i_j = H_{5j}/H < 0$

(where λ is the Lagrange multiplier, H is the bordered Hessian determinant, and H_{jj}, H_{jk}, etc., are the signed minors associated with the constrained maximum) denote, respectively, the substitution, cross-substitution, and income effects of a change in the marginal cost of the jth argument of $V(.)$. At an interior solution,

$$\partial N^t/\partial B^t = -(s_{44} + N^t i_4) > 0, \tag{11.A4}$$

$$\partial S^t/\partial B^t = (1 + I_1 + N^t I_U i_3 + i_4)N^t + S_{41} + N^t I_U S_{43} + z^{*t} S_{44}$$
$$= ?, \tag{11.A5}$$

$$\partial U^t/\partial B^t = -(s_{43} + N^t i_3) = ?, \tag{11.A6}$$

$$\partial N^t/\partial T^t = i_4 < 0, \tag{11.A7}$$

$$\partial S^t/\partial T^t = -(1 + I_1 + N^t I_U i_3 + z^{*t} i_4) < 0, \tag{11.A8}$$

$$\partial U^t/\partial T^t = i_3 < 0, \tag{11.A9}$$

$$\partial N^t/\partial P^{t+1} = -i_4 r^{-1} > 0, \tag{11.A10}$$

$$\partial S^t/\partial P^{t+1} = (I_1 + N^t I_U i_3 + z^{*t} i_4) r^{-1} < 0, \tag{11.A11}$$

$$\partial U^t/\partial P^{t+1} = -i_3 r^{-1} > 0, \tag{11.A12}$$

$$\partial N^t/\partial T^{t+1} = (s_{44} + N^t i_4) < 0, \tag{11.A13}$$

$$\partial S^t/\partial T^{t+1} = -[s_{41} + N^t i_1 + N^t I_U(s_{43} + N^t i_3) + z^{*t}(s_{44} + N^t i_4)] r^{-1}, \tag{11.A14}$$

and

$$\partial U^t/\partial T^{t+1} = (s_{43} + N^t i_3) r^{-1}. \tag{11.A15}$$

If fertility is exogenous, as in Barro (1974), s_{j4}, s_{4k} and I_4 vanish. Then (11.A5), (11.A6), and (11.A14) become positive, while (11.A15) becomes negative.

The total effects of the policy packages discussed in the main text are as follows:

(i) A tax-financed increase in child benefits, such that $N^t dB^t + B^t dN^t = 0$.

$$dN^t/dB^t = (\partial N^t/\partial B^t) + (\partial N^t/\partial T^t)(dT^t/dB^t)$$
$$= -s_{44}/(1 - B^t i_4) > 0, \tag{11.A16}$$

$$dSt/dBt = (\partial St/\partial Bt) + (\partial St/\partial Tt)(dTt/dBt) = ?$$
$$= 0 \text{ for } N^t \text{ exogenous}, \tag{11.A17}$$

$$dU^t/dB^t = (\partial U^t/\partial B^t) + (\partial U^t/\partial T^t)(dT^t/dB^t)$$
$$= -[s_{43} + B^t i_3 s_{44}/(1 - B^t i_4)] > 0$$
$$= 0 \text{ for } N^t \text{ exogenous}. \tag{11.A18}$$

(ii) A fully funded pension rise, such that $dP^{t+1} - rdT^t = 0$.

$$dN^t/dP^{t+1} = (\partial N^t/\partial P^{t+1})(\partial N^t/\partial T^t)(dT^t/dP^{t+1}) = 0, \tag{11.A19}$$

$$dS^t/dP^{t+1} = (\partial S^t/\partial P^{t+1}) + (\partial S^t/\partial T^t)(dT^t/dP^{t+1})$$
$$= -r^{-1} < 0, \quad (11.A20)$$

$$dU^t/dP^{t+1} = 0. \quad (11.A21)$$

(iii) A debt-financed tax cut, such that $N^t dT^{t+1} + T^{t+1} dN^t + r dT^t = 0$.

$$-dN^t/dT^t = -(\partial N^t/\partial T^t) - (\partial N^t/\partial T^{t+1})(dT^{t+1}/dT^t)$$
$$= S_{44}/\left[N^t + (S_{44} + N^t i_4)T^{t+1} r^{-1}\right] < 0, \quad (11.A22)$$

$$-dS^t/dT^t = -(\partial S^t/\partial T^t) - (\partial S^t/\partial T^{t+1})(dT^{t+1}/dT^t) = ?$$
$$= 1 \text{ for } N^t \text{ exogenous}, \quad (11.A23)$$

$$-dUt/dTt = -(\partial Ut/\partial Tt) - (\partial Ut/\partial Tt + 1)(dT + 1/dTt)$$
$$= \left[(s_{43} i_4 - s_{44} i_3)T^{t+1} + r s_{43}\right] / \left[N^t + (N^t i_4 - s_{44})T^{t+1}\right] = ?$$
$$= 0 \text{ for } N^t \text{ exogenous}. \quad (11.A24)$$

(iv) A pay-as-you-go pension rise, such that $dP^{t+1} N^t dT^{t+1} - T^{t+1} dN^t = 0$.

$$dN^t/dP^{t+1} = (\partial N^t/\partial P^{t+1}) + (\partial N^t/\partial T^{t+1})(dT^{t+1}/dP^{t+1})$$
$$= s_{44}/\left[rN^t + (s_{44} + N^t i_4)T^{t+1})\right] < 0, \quad (11.A25)$$

$$dS^t/dP^{t+1} = (\partial S^t/\partial P^{t+1}) + (\partial S^t/\partial T^{t+1})(dT^{t+1}/dP^{t+1}) = ?$$
$$= 0 \text{ for } N^t \text{ exogenous}, \quad (11.A26)$$

$$dU^t/dP^{t+1} = (\partial U^t/\partial P^{t+1}) + (\partial U^t/\partial T^{t+1})(dT^{t+1}/dP^{t+1}) = ?$$
$$= 0 \text{ for } N^t \text{ exogenous}. \quad (11.A27)$$

Model with ascending altruism

This is a generalization of Veall (1986) and Nishimura and Zhang (1992), as modified by Cigno (1995). The basic assumptions are that $U^t = U(C_0^t, C_1^t, C_2^t, U^{t-1})$, and that parents make their decisions, taking as parameters the transfers made by their children. If fertility is endogenous, as in Nishimura and Zhang (1992) or Cigno (1995), the demand for children at t is determined by the portfolio condition $r = (D^{t+1}/z^t)$, where $z^t = c - B^t$ is the net marginal cost of a child, and $c = C'(N^t)$ is an increasing function of N^t. Therefore if saving and fertility are both positive, $N^t = N(B^t)$, and $N'(B^t) = c^{-1} > 0$.

At date t, generation $(t-1)$ chooses $(C_1^{t-1}, S^t, N^t, D^t)$ so as to maximize

$$V\left(C_1^{t-1}, rS^t + P^{t+1} + N^t D^{t+1}, rS^{t-1} + P^t + N^{t-1} D^t\right)$$
$$= U\left(C_0^{t-1}, C_1^{t-1}, rS^t + P^{t+1} + N^t D^{t+1}, U^{t-2}\right), \quad (11.B1)$$

subject to (11.2) and

$$C_1^{t-1} + S^t + D^t = Y^t - T^t + B^t N^t - C(N^t). \tag{11.B2}$$

At an interior solution,

$$\partial S^t / \partial B^t = -(N^t - z^t c^{-1}) i_2 = ?, \tag{11.B3}$$

$$\partial S^t / \partial T^t = i_2 < 0, \tag{11.B4}$$

$$\partial S^t / \partial P^{t+1} = -(V_{12} s_{12} + r V_{22} s_{22} + N^{t-1} V_{32} s_{32}) < 0. \tag{11.B5}$$

If fertility is exogenous, as in Veall (1986), the asset demand for children vanishes, and (B3) becomes unequivocally positive.

There follow the total effects of the policy packages under consideration.

(i) A tax-financed increase in child benefits, such that $N^t dB^t + B^t dN^t = 0$.

$$dN^t / dB^t = N'(B^t) > 0, \tag{11.B6}$$

$$dS^t / dB^t = (\partial S^t / \partial B^t) + (\partial S^t / \partial T^t)(dT^t / dB^t) = I_2 < 0,$$
$$= 0 \text{ for } Nt \text{ exogenous.} \tag{11.B7}$$

U^t is not affected by the policy.

(ii) A fully funded pension rise, such that $dP^{t+1} - r dT^t = 0$.

$$dS^t / dP^{t+1} = (\partial S^t / \partial P^{t+1}) + (\partial S^t / \partial T^t)(dT^t / dP^{t+1})$$
$$= -(V_{12} s_{12} + r V_{22} s_{22} + N^{t+1} s_{32} - r i_2) < 0. \tag{11.B8}$$

N^t and U^t are not affected.

(iii) A debt-financed tax cut, such that $N^t dT^{t+1} + T^{t+1} dN^t + r dT^t = 0$.

$$-dS^t / dT^t = -\partial S^t / \partial T^t > 0. \tag{11.B9}$$

N^t is not affected, and U^t falls.

(iv) A pay-as-you-go pension rise, such that $dP^{t+1} N^t dT^{t+1} - T^{t+1} dN^t = 0$.

$$dS^t / dP^{t+1} = (\partial S^t / \partial P^{t+1}) < 0. \tag{11.B10}$$

N^t is not affected, and U^t falls.

Notes

Useful comments by Bob Willis are gratefully acknowledged. The project of which this chapter is one of the results is supported in part by the Italian National Research Council (CNR).

1. Risk considerations, however, may induce the player to use the capital market even before hitting that ceiling (Rosati 1996).
2. There is a difference, however, between a constitution designed by an altruistic couple and one designed by a selfish one: while the latter would maximize the transfer due to the legislators, the former would not.
3. In Germany, as already mentioned, the effect of pension coverage on household saving is not significantly different from zero. On the one hand, a debt-financed expansion of old-age security could thus reduce household saving (by up to about one-tenth of the percentage increase in coverage if the latter were totally debt-financed). On the other, as Germany has a much larger elasticity of fertility to old-age security than the other countries (−0.9, as compared with −0.3 to −0.6), the effect on growth would be just as strong.
4. A pension system governed by such a principle is not to be confused with a deficit-free pay-as-you-go pension system, which merely balances current payments and current receipts period by period.

12 Wealth Accumulation, Fertility, and Transfers to Elderly Household Heads in Peru

Sumon Kumar Bhaumik and Jeffrey B. Nugent

Much of the rapidly growing literature on interhousehold transfers has focused upon the basic motivation for such transfers, be it altruism, exchange, or some other motive (Barro 1974; Becker 1974; Kotlikoff and Spivak 1981; Bernheim, Shleifer, and Summers 1985; Cox 1987; Cox and Rank 1992; Cox and Jimenez 1992, 1993; Lee, Parish, and Willis 1994). For this reason, much of it has concentrated upon bequests and *inter-vivos* transfers from older to younger persons and family members. Initially at least, those transfers seemed hard to explain without recourse to altruism. The literature has given considerably less attention to transfers from young to old that are of importance to the quality of life in old age, especially in rural areas of developing countries, where reliable alternatives to children as sources of old-age security are often lacking. It is in such circumstances that old-age security is often said to be one of the major reasons or even the major reason for having children, and indeed for having many children (Leibenstein 1957, 1975; Cain 1981, 1985, 1986; Nugent 1985).

Until the last several years, most of the studies on transfers to the elderly have generally been confined to one or the other of two distinct types of economies: those with fully developed alternative support systems, found in the more developed countries (Bernheim and Stark 1988; Altonji, Hayashi, and Kotlikoff 1992 and Chapter 14 in this volume; Kendig, Hashimoto, and Coppock 1992; Bengston and Achenbaum 1993; Cox and Jakubson 1995; McGarry and Schoeni 1995*a*, 1995*b*); and those in 'traditional' rural areas of developing countries in Africa or Asia. The latter are characterized by the absence of alternative systems of old-age support, by well-developed social norms underpinning family-based support systems, and by the dominance of the family among institutions and the ability of families to inculcate altruism and enforce social norms (Vlassoff and Vlassoff 1980; Lucas and Stark 1985; Benda-Beckmann *et al.* 1988; Ravallion and Dearden 1988; Hoddinott 1992; Goldstein and Ku 1993; and Y.-J. Lee in Chapter 13 of this volume.). As a result, both types of studies are about societies characterized by more or less stable equilibrium with respect to old-age support systems.

Much more relevant for long-term policy in developing countries, however, would seem to be the experience of societies making the transition from traditional to modern. It is in such societies where it becomes possible to examine such issues as the extent to which the alternative sources 'crowd out' the seemingly informal sources of support (largely children) and to investigate the identity and effectiveness of strategies that parents use in trying to secure support for old age in the face of modernizing influences, which tend to undermine traditional social norms. Latin American countries are good candidates for this type of study for several reasons: they have been subject to many modernizing influences, including European immigration; they have had semi-developed alternative sources of old-age support (such as social security) in place for some time; as a result of high degrees of commercialization and financial development, they have a wide variety of alternatives for accumulating assets; they are highly dualistic or pluralistic societies, with rural–urban, formal–informal, and rich and poor differences such that the importance of support from children to the elderly may vary substantially across groups within a population; and they are in the beginning of a process of population ageing that is proceeding more rapidly than elsewhere in the world.

Within Latin America, Peru represents a particularly interesting case. It has a huge old-age security problem looming on the horizon, and yet it also has formal programmes of social security that, although already somewhat developed, are unlikely to become universal in the foreseeable future despite their recent radical restructuring and privatization.[1] The obstacles to the more widespread coverage of Peru's population within its social security system seem to have resulted from two different but interdependent phenomena, the first being recurring substantial deficits in both Peru's social security system itself and the government's overall budget, and the second being the flight of much of the regular economy into the informal sector in which there is no social security system. In urban areas the informal sector is estimated to have risen from 35 per cent of urban employment in 1981 to 49 per cent in 1985 and is widely believed to have increased further since then (de Soto 1989; Thomas 1992 and the sources therein). Prior to restructuring, most of the contributions to the social security system came from employers. The problem of recurring deficits is attributable in part to decapitalization of the system as a result of the negative real rates of return earned on social security funds, economic stagnation since the late 1970s, the evasion of payments by employers, and exceptionally high administrative costs (as much as 52 per cent of total expenditures in 1986). As in much of the world, it is also due to population ageing, combined with rather low retirement ages—60 for men and 55 for women (Mesa-Lago 1985, 1994; World Bank 1994: table A.4).

Although Peru's fiscal situation has improved recently as a result of a sharp reduction in government expenditures and the restructuring of its social security system, the overall outlook is dampened by its large and growing debt-service burden. Debt service as a percentage of exports in 1993 was reported to be the third highest in the world, behind Uganda and Algeria (World Bank 1995: table 23). Hence, even with a certain degree of privatization, it seems unlikely that the formal social security system will be able to expand its coverage substantially in the foreseeable future. Yet, as a result of rapid population ageing, over the sixty-year period between 1990 and 2050 the importance of old-age dependence is likely to grow sharply. According to World Bank estimates, the percentage of Peru's population over 60 years of age is expected to increase by more than 3.7 times, from 5.8 per cent to 21.5 per cent during that period (World Bank 1994: table A.2). Such a rate of growth is far greater than any experienced by countries outside Latin America and is well above the average for Latin America.

This chapter explores the determinants of transfers from children to elderly parents in both urban and rural areas of Peru where alternative sources of support are semi-developed but vary considerably in development level from place to place and from group to group, and where social norms and the family are no longer as strong as they once were.[2] In view of the apparently dim prospect for universal social security coverage, we shall place considerable emphasis upon the role of savings and wealth accumulation and its effects upon transfers and household structure.

For this purpose we develop a simple model of transfers from adult children to their elderly parents on the basis of strategic as well as altruistic interaction between parents and their adult children. The equilibrium solution to the model shows that, under the conditions assumed, the transfers would be affected by characteristics of the elderly parents (marital status and age), by the parents' accumulation and fertility strategies as reflected in their wealth and the number and education of their children, and by various characteristics of their children, especially the children's residence in relation to that of their parents. In view of the apparently split verdict from the empirical evidence on the relative importance of altruism and strategic exchange, we allow for both altruistic and strategic-exchange motives in our hypotheses. The purpose is to provide the basis for empirical assessments of the effectiveness of various strategies that household heads may follow to encourage transfers from their children in a country like Peru. Because complete data on transfers are available by gender for only donors in the data set used in this study, we deliberately ignore some interesting gender issues related to transfers received from and given to children (including the equity-efficiency trade-offs treated by Quisumbing 1994).

The model represents an attempt to assess the effects of various factors upon transfers from children. Some of those factors would have been under the influence or control of the household head at one time or another in the life cycle, and others are entirely exogenous. In view of the relevance of the strategic-accumulation and fertility behaviour to such transfers (Bernheim *et al.* 1985; Lucas and Stark 1985; Hoddinott 1993), we place considerable emphasis upon age, diverse forms of wealth accumulation, the number of children in a family and their location and education, and the interactions of these variables.

The Conceptual Framework

The conceptual framework adopted here is one in which decisions to make transfers to and from children are determined by factors and actions on both the parents' side and the children's side. Nevertheless, rather than assuming them all to be simultaneously determined, we treat only several of the key choices of each party as being made simultaneously; the rest we treat as being made separately at quite different times (typically a generation apart). In particular, the parents make their key decisions about old-age support during their young adulthood by choosing how much to invest in children (the number and education of children, including transfers to children early in life) and how much to invest in other assets. They do so partly on the basis of their assessment of the way children will behave during the parents' old age in response to the various accumulation strategies the parents have adopted. Then, during the parents' old age, the children decide whether or not and how much to transfer to their parents, given the parents' accumulation of bequeathable assets, the age and needs of the parents, their own education and location (and hence earning potential), and the number of their siblings. In other words, we assume that parents are the leaders whose behaviour is known to the children and incorporated into their own choice strategies. Yet, in equilibrium, the two reaction functions must be consistent with each another.

Each person in the economy lives for three periods: the first, $t-1$, as a child, and the second and third, t and $t+1$, as parents. To focus upon the strategic–altruistic interaction between parents and children, we are concerned here with the latter two periods in the lives of representative parents. In period t, parents have to make two strategic choices: how much to save (S_t) for their old age (i.e. for period $t+1$), and how many children to have (N). Their income is determined by such factors as their education and macroeconomic conditions, which in turn can be assumed to be either predetermined or exogenous to their strategic choices. The parents also spend on the education of their children, E_t, an investment that is both for the future of their children (an altruistic motive) and for the expected value of future transfers from the children (a selfish exchange motive). They discount the future at the rate ρ.

In making their strategic choices, the parents are assumed to maximize their utility (U_p), defined in terms of their own consumption in periods t and $t+1$ and the utility of their children (V_k) in period $t+1$. Consumption in period t is defined as that income (I_t) that remains after we subtract the chosen amount of saving and the educational expenditures on children. The level of educational expenditures is assumed to be dependent upon their income level (I) and the number of children they choose (N).[3] Consumption in period $t+1$ depends upon the rate-of-return-augmented value of savings, $(1+r)S_t$, and expected transfers from children, T_k, less what they leave in the form of bequests to their children, B. The latter we assume to be a function of S_t, the number of children (N) and T_k. The utility they eventually derive from the welfare of their children,

V_k, depends upon the investments they make in them during period t (which may also affect the transfers the children provide them in period $t+1$). As a result, the model is characterized by both reciprocal altruism (in that each generation cares about the utility of the other) and strategic exchange. The fact that in each period the transfers go both upward and downward is consistent with at least a certain degree of self-enforcement which, as suggested by Alessandro Cigno in Chapter 11 of this volume, may make 'intrafamily deals' an efficient means of maximizing utility over time in the face of incomplete and imperfect markets for credit and insurance.

Thus the parents' problem is to maximize their own utility:

$$\begin{aligned} U_p = {} & I_t - S_t - E_t(I_t, N) + [1/(1+\rho)]((1+r)S_t + T_k(E_t, N) \\ & - B[S_t, N, T_k(E_t, N)] + V_k[E_t(I_t, N), T_k(E_t, N)]) \end{aligned} \tag{12.1}$$

with respect to S_t and N, subject to the aforementioned budget constraint. The first-order conditions derived from this problem can be used to solve for $\partial B/\partial S_t$ and $\partial B/\partial T_k$ as follows:

$$\partial B/\partial S_t = r - \rho. \tag{12.2}$$

$$\begin{aligned} \partial B/\partial T_k = {} & \{\partial E_t/\partial N[\partial V_k/\partial E_t + \partial T_k/\partial E_t - (1+\rho)] + \partial T_k/\partial N \\ & - \partial B/\partial N\}/[(\partial T_k/\partial E_t)(\partial E_t/\partial N) + (\partial T_k/\partial N)] + (\partial V_k/\partial T_k). \end{aligned} \tag{12.3}$$

Equation 12.2 provides the intuitively plausible implication that the effect of a given change in S_t on that of B_{t+1} would depend critically upon the relation between r and ρ. As long as altruism exists, the effect of the last term (the altruistic motive) upon $\partial B/\partial T_k$ in Equation 12.3 is clearly positive. The direction of the effect of the other (strategic-exchange) component, however, clearly depends upon the relative magnitude of a number of terms, such as the effects of changes in E_t on those of T_k and V_k and of $\partial T_k/\partial N$ (an implication of the strategic-bequest motive). The larger are $\partial V_k/\partial E_t$, $\partial T_k/\partial E_t$, and $\partial T_k/\partial N$ relative to $(1+\rho)$, the more likely the strategic-exchange component of the determination of $\partial B/\partial T_k$ will be positive and large. The separate introduction of these various terms facilitates distinctions and quantification of the relative importance of these various determinants of transfers.

The child faces a problem that is similar to that of the parent. He (she) knows how parents generally react (in the matter of bequests) to the transfer behaviour of children and takes that into consideration in deciding how much to transfer to his (her) parents in period $t+1(T_k)$.

Let the income of the child in period $t+1$ be I_k. Also, let $\theta \in (0,1)$ be a parameter that determines the extent to which the child values his share of the expected bequest from his parents. The value of θ will be high for a child who happens to reside in the household of the parent but low for one who does not, especially if there are other adult children residing in the parental household.

Finally, V_p is the altruistic utility that the child derives from the well-being of his parents. Hence, the child's utility function can be expressed as

$$U_k = f_1(I_k - T_k) + \theta f_2[B(T_k)] + V_p(T_k), \tag{12.4}$$

where f_1 and f_2 are functional transformations with the usual neoclassical assumptions.

Maximizing Equation 12.4 with respect to T_k yields a first-order condition implying

$$\partial B/\partial T_k = [(\partial f_1/\partial T_k) - (\partial V_p/\partial T_k)]/\theta(\partial f_2/\partial B). \tag{12.5}$$

In equilibrium, of course, the terms $\partial B/\partial T_k$ (the bequest-transfer reaction functions) on the left-hand side of Equation 12.3 from the parent's problem must be equal to that on the left-hand side of Equation 12.5 from the child's problem. Hence, the right-hand sides of the two equations must also be equal to each other. Let us assume the following functional forms for the variables E_t, V_k, T_k, B, f_1, f_2 and V_p, respectively:

$$E_t = \alpha_1 I_t - \alpha_2 N \tag{12.6}$$

$$V_k = \alpha_3 E_t - \alpha_4 E_t^2 - \alpha_5 T_k. \tag{12.7}$$

$$T_k = [E_t(.)]^\sigma + \alpha_6 N - \alpha_7 N^2. \tag{12.8}$$

$$B = \alpha_8 N + \alpha_9 S_t + \alpha_{10} T_k(.). \tag{12.9}$$

$$f_1 = (I_k - T_k)^\eta. \tag{12.10}$$

$$f_2 = B^\mu. \tag{12.11}$$

$$V_p = T_k^\psi. \tag{12.12}$$

Assume further that the functional forms are quasi-concave and reflect diminishing marginal returns and that $\eta < 1$ and $\psi, \mu > 1$. The latter assumption may be justified in the context of semi-traditional developing countries because bequests from parents and transfers to parents generally increase utility in two ways: by increasing present or future consumption and, because of partly internalized social norms, by increasing prestige. These assumptions plus the equilibrium condition between Equation 12.3 and Equation 12.5 yield the following transfer function:

$$\begin{aligned} T_k = & \{[(\theta\mu B^{\mu-1}/\psi)][\gamma + 2\alpha_2\alpha_4 E_t - \alpha_2\alpha_{10}\sigma E_t^{\sigma-1} + 2\alpha_7 N\{1 - (\alpha_5 + \alpha_{10})\} \\ & /(\alpha_6 - 2\alpha_7 N)]\}^{1/(\psi-1)}, \end{aligned} \tag{12.13}$$

where γ is some constant determined by a combination of other parameter values.

Equation 12.13 shows that the volume of transfers is an increasing function of both θ and (given the assumption about the value of μ) B. Because in our model B emerges from accumulated savings (as suggested in Equations 12.2 and 12.9), the expected bequest B in turn depends positively on savings, S. Moreover, because in practice the credibility of any potential bequest to non-resident children resulting from accumulated savings is likely to vary from one form of such accumulation to another and to depend upon whether or not any adult children reside in the parent's household, from Equations 12.4, 12.5, and hence 12.13, the value of θ and hence the transfer-inducing effect of savings should vary from one form of savings to another and depend on whether or not adult children reside in the parent's household.

Bernheim *et al.* (1985) have argued that in a developed-country context, cash and other highly liquid wealth is of lower strategic value to parents in inducing support because it is less credible as inheritance than other less liquid forms of wealth. Hence, the accumulation of less liquid assets such as land, a residence, or a business would be more credible as potential bequest and hence more capable of inducing T_k than more liquid forms. In a developing-country context, however, in which one adult child may reside in the home of his (her) elderly parent, the transfer-inducing power of any such asset may be quite different. In particular, a residence or a private business owned by a parent may be far less useful to a child living outside the parent's household than more liquid assets like money, other financial assets, and transportable durable goods. From an altruistic perspective, however, greater wealth would reduce the need for transfers to parents irrespective of the form it takes.

Let us now consider the other determinants of T_k in greater detail, beginning with the effect of investments in human capital (E). The effect upon T_k of investment in E clearly depends upon the relative magnitude of various parameters, such as α_2, α_4, σ, and α_{10} appearing in Equations 12.6–12.9, respectively. Hence, both the magnitude and even the direction of the effect would have to be determined by empirical analysis. It seems highly likely, however, that the effect will be positive as long as E_t raises the earning potential of the children and induces children to repay their parents for the sacrifices they made as young parents in period t (and even possibly in period $t+1$) as suggested by the two-way and self-enforcing character of transfers in any period (see Chapter 11 by Alessandro Cigno in this volume). The same expectation would be supported from an altruism perspective: namely, the higher the investment in education of children, the lower the savings for old age of the parents (and hence the greater their need), and at the same time the higher the expected incomes of adult children and therefore the greater their ability to demand altruistic pleasure in seeing their parents made better off by transfers.

Next, let us consider the effect of the number of siblings (N) upon T_k. There are clearly two effects of N upon a child's willingness to send transfers to his (her) parents. On the one hand, the more children there are, the less any given child has to provide to assure the elderly parents the same level of living. As this would be the primary effect in the case of pure altruism, rapidly diminishing returns in transfers to the number of children would be the expected outcome of such a model. In the absence of pure altruism, and where there are at best imperfect means of disciplining children for evading their responsibilities, a child with a larger number of siblings may have an incentive to evade these responsibilities by free-riding on the others, thereby providing less support individually and possibly also collectively. On the other hand, from the strategic-bequest point of view (Bernheim *et al.* 1985), larger N may increase the credibility of a threat of disinheritance and hence the incentive of each child to compete for inheritance by providing parents with larger transfers. Hence, the effect of N upon the amount that any child may transfer can be quite different, depending upon the relative importance of the various motives for transfers. As in Equation 12.8, the relationship between N and T_k is expected to be non-linear.

What about the effects of the parent's age and marital status? Other things being equal, from the strategic-bequest perspective, the older the parent, the more the child may be induced to provide additional support because the present value of such transfers will be lower (relative to the expected value of the bequest, which may also be higher due to a higher θ) than if the parent were younger. The same inference can also be drawn about the altruism perspective because the older the parent, the less likely is he (she) to provide adequately for his (her) own welfare. If the parent is married, from the strategic-bequest perspective, the child can be expected to provide less in transfers to the parent because there is both one more alternative potential heir and additional time to wait until inheritance can come to the child (i.e. a lower θ). From the point of view of altruism, however, the effect of the parent's being married (we assume the parent to be a head of household) could either increase or decrease the child's willingness to provide a transfer, depending upon whether or not the parent's spouse would be a net provider to, or net claimant upon, that parent's resources.

What about the effect of the location of other children, in relation to the parent's residence, upon a transfer by an individual non-resident child? As mentioned above, this effect could be captured by the parameter θ. Once again, it may be useful to distinguish between the strategic-exchange and altruism motives for transfers from adult children to their elderly parents. Because an adult child who resides with his (her) elderly parents is generally in a much better position to assist the parents in ways that are most needed and because that child's income is likely to be added to the income of the parents, from the exchange perspective such a child can be expected to receive a larger portion of the inheritance than any non-resident child. For this reason, the presence of another child within the household can be expected to lower θ, and hence lower the amount of transfers that a non-resident adult child provides to his (her) elderly parents. From an altruistic point of view, however, the effect of a child's residing in the parental household is less clear. Although the presence (and presumably help) of such a person in the household may reduce parental needs, if altruism for parents is combined with either a sharing ethic or altruism also for one's siblings, it may also increase the likelihood that a non-resident child will also feel pressure, or will desire, to help.

Although we do not formally introduce social security into the model, we could use the model to derive conclusions about social security. Several effects are possible. On the one hand, social security may add to bequeathable wealth and hence induce more transfers. On the other hand, it may lower μ, ψ, or both and thereby (as shown in Equation 12.13) lower T_k.

Although some of these details are not captured in the model, they are tractable empirically. For this reason, at the empirical level, we deem it important to distinguish among (1) the accumulation of different kinds of assets, such as home ownership, a business, financial assets, and durable goods; (2) the age and marital status of the parent; (3) the number and location of the children; and (4) other characteristics of the parent that could indicate specific needs (such as female headship and sickness).

Data and Empirical Specification of the Model

The data used in this study are from the Peruvian Living Standards Survey (PLSS), conducted in 1985–6. The survey included detailed questions about household composition, income, and expenditures, including transfers (both in and out). It canvassed a national sample of 5,109 households (approximately 27,000 persons) in both urban and rural areas. About one-third of the households in the sample reported receiving private transfers and another third reported having given transfers in the three months immediately preceding the survey. On the receipts side, the transfers received constituted more than 15 per cent of income. A smaller survey of the same sort was repeated in 1990 but was confined to Lima and had other limitations as well.[4] That survey was based upon an entirely different sample and therefore affords no possibility for a panel component.

The urban portion of the PLSS sample was used to advantage by Cox and Jimenez (1992) to measure the extent to which public transfers crowded out private transfers to parents of ages 45 and over. Using a two-stage analysis, they showed that both the transfers given and those received would have been significantly higher had the recipient households not received social security and medical care. Although pure altruism would suggest that the reduction in intrafamilial transfers due to tax-financed social security payments should be one-to-one, the reduction in private transfers was found to be much less than one-to-one. Hence, the crowding out was only partial. Cox and Jimenez based this conclusion in part on the observed effects of public transfers upon private transfers received and in part on the effects of taxes upon the incomes of those giving transfers and hence also on the amount of transfers given. Given the relative importance of the younger elderly in their sample, among whom social security was more common than among the older elderly, it is by no means clear from that study that the significant finding of crowding out would apply in situations in which parents were more elderly (in most countries and studies the elderly are defined as those of ages 60 and over).

Because of our focus on transfers in old age, we concentrate here upon transfers to and from those households headed by persons of ages 60 and over. Yet, to increase the variation in environmental conditions (including modernization), accumulation possibilities, the strength of social norms, and the relative dependence upon children for old-age support, in contrast to Cox and Jimenez we use households from both the rural and urban samples. Also in contrast to Cox and Jimenez, we distinguish between children living inside and those living outside the household. As in their model, however, we include a few interaction terms involving children and various forms of wealth. To mitigate (though certainly not eliminate) the problem of joint determination that results from the inclusion of various income terms that may depend upon transfers, we rely almost exclusively upon the use of wealth rather than current income as explanatory variables.

Our 1985 data are not without shortcomings. One important shortcoming is that the information on children living outside the households of elderly heads is scanty and hence cannot be used. Another shortcoming is that some observations on certain variables are reported as missing and some observations recorded as zeros may in fact not be zero. Despite these drawbacks, and especially in view of the dearth of other suitable data sets for transition countries like Peru, the data set does contain a fairly sizeable number of observations on most of the relevant variables and generally seems highly suitable for testing some of the implications of the model.

Table 12.1 lists various measures of the characteristics of the elderly households and of their children from the 1985–6 survey deemed relevant to operationalizing the conceptual framework outlined above. First are the measures of transfers to the household from non-resident children, which are to be explained in the analysis. There are three such measures—the receipt during the previous three months of a transfer from any adult child living outside the household (CHGIVE), the value of the gross receipts of transfers from non-resident children (GROSREC), and the value of net transfers received from non-resident children (NETREC). As can be seen from the first three entries in the first column of the table, for the full sample of 1,105 households headed by persons of ages 60 and over, 31.3 per cent of them had received some transfer from non-resident children in the ninety days preceding the survey, and 430 and 246 intis were the average values received of gross and net transfers, respectively. (US$1 equals 14 intis.) The former amount represents almost 10 per cent of household income over the equivalent period of time. Clearly, therefore, for those who receive them, transfers from children represent on average a substantial portion (about 30 per cent) of income.

Table 12.1. Means of transfers received and related variables for elderly household heads (ages 60 and older), by various characteristics: Peru, 1985–6

Variable	Full sample (1,105)		Heads without social security (835)	Heads with social security (270)	Heads without children in household (409)	Heads with children in household (696)
	Mean	S.D.				
CHGIVE	0.313	0.460	0.329	0.263	0.386	0.272
GROSREC	430.000	1,918.000	448.000	373.000	735.000	252.400
NETREC	246.000	2,276.000	296.000	92.000	580.000	51.300
CONTRSS	8.000	48.000	0.000	32.000	4.500	9.900
SOCSEC	868.000	2,650.000	0.000	3,554.000	1,111.100	728.900
WEALTH	5,374.000	16,960.000	5,296.000	5,614.000	4,692.100	5,986.100
BUSINESS	0.458	0.498	0.449	0.435	0.359	0.529
HOMEOWN	0.802	0.398	0.836	0.700	0.803	0.802
URBAN	0.616	0.487	0.523	0.900	0.560	0.650
SECH	0.181	0.385	0.112	0.393	0.138	0.207
AGE	68.600	7.110	68.500	69.200	70.600	67.400
FEMHEAD	0.284	0.451	0.299	0.237	0.354	0.241
MARRIED	0.500	0.500	0.466	0.604	0.386	0.568
ACHOUT	1.474	1.187	1.577	1.158	2.580	1.910
ACHIN	1.515	1.742	1.444	1.733	0.000	1.320
FSICK	1.613	0.681	1.637	1.537	1.528	1.640

Notes: Sample sizes are in parentheses. Monetary values are expressed in Peruvian intis (14 intis equalled approximately US$1 in 1985–6).

Definitions: CHGIVE = 1 if household received a transfer from a non-resident child in the last three months; 0 otherwise; GROSREC = gross receipts of transfers from non-resident children in the last three months; NETREC = net receipts of transfers from non-resident children in the last three months; CONTRSS = payments into social security system in the last year; SOCSEC = gross receipts from the social security system in the last year; WEALTH = estimated market value of durable goods, financial assets and land; BUSINESS = 1 if someone in the household owns a business; 0 otherwise; HOMEOWN = 1 if someone in the household owns a home; 0 otherwise; URBAN = 1 if household is located in the urban area; 0 otherwise; SECH = 1 if household head has secondary or higher education; 0 otherwise; AGE = age of the head (>= 60); FEMHEAD = 1 if household head is female; MARRIED = 1 if household head is married; ACHOUT = number of adult children living outside the household of the elderly head; ACHIN = number of adult children living inside the household of the elderly head; FSICK = number who reported having an illness in the last four weeks.

Source: Peruvian Living Standards Survey.

The next two variables are measures of participation in social security programmes providing pension benefits. CONTRSS is the amount that any household headed by an elderly person contributed to the social security system during the previous year. The average value of such payments among members of this sample was only 8 intis. SOCSEC, on the other hand, is the amount of social security transfers received in the previous year. This value was 868 intis, which may seem large in relation to the gross transfers from children (GROSREC) of 430 intis, especially in view of the fact that few rural residents qualify for social security. SOCSEC, however, pertains to twelve months, whereas each of the measures of transfers from children pertains to only the previous three months; and therefore on a monthly basis gross transfers from children were actually twice as large as social security transfers. As anyone paying into the social security system or already receiving something from the system could expect to receive payments from it in the future, the two variables can be considered reasonable proxies for participation in social security.

The interpretation of the effects of these social security participation measures is rendered somewhat ambiguous by the fact that someone other than the household head may have made or received the payments. Nevertheless, especially in households without other adult relatives, it would seem highly likely that the household head is the participant. Even if non-heads are participants, there is still a chance that the heads might also be. Moreover, even if the only participant is not the head, similar effects might be expected, especially in the case of strategic exchange. Hence, from the point of view of altruism, participation in social security is an alternative source of supporting parents in old age and therefore may be expected to have a negative effect upon private transfers from children. From the strategic-exchange point of view, however, it is by no means obvious that social security transfers would have any such effect. Indeed, it is entirely possible that a parent's receipt of social security funds would enhance the credibility of existing assets for bequest purposes and hence induce more transfers, at least in the case in which more than one adult child is living outside the household. Overall, however, in view of Cox and Jimenez's aforementioned finding that social security transfers crowded out transfers from children in urban areas of Peru, the effects of social security measures on transfers from children can be expected to be negative.

The next several variables represent various forms and measures of wealth of the elderly households. Specifically, WEALTH is the value in the survey year of the bequeathable assets of land, durable goods, and financial assets. BUSINESS is a dummy variable for having a business, and HOMEOWN a dummy variable for owning one's own house or apartment. As shown in the previous section, each of these forms of wealth can be expected to have differing effects upon transfers from children (T_k), depending upon whether the exchange motive dominates the altruism motive or vice versa. Given that urban areas of Peru have better access than rural areas to public infrastructure such as schools, hospitals, and financial institutions and also have higher wage rates (thereby allowing their children, who almost invariably also live in urban areas, to earn higher incomes), another wealth-like variable is the dummy variable for urban residence (URBAN). The bequeathability of this form of wealth is ambiguous. On the one hand, an urban residence is heritable in the sense that the children of any parent living in an urban area are also likely to be living in an urban area, thereby raising the probability that such a bequest would improve their circumstances. On the other hand, because that form of wealth is likely to be transmitted to children whether or not the children contribute transfers to their parents, its bequeathability provides no incentive for transfers from the children to the parents.

Another form of wealth is the human capital of the elderly head. For a measure of the head's human capital, we use a dummy variable for whether or not the head has at least a secondary level of education (SECH). As indicated in the first column of Table 12.1, 18 per cent of the elderly heads had educational attainment levels of secondary schooling or higher. As SECH is non-bequeathable, unlike the other forms of wealth, from the strategic-exchange perspective, no effect would be expected. From an altruistic perspective, however, a higher value of SECH can be expected to raise the ability of elderly heads to provide for themselves and thereby lower the need for transfers from children. However, given the incompleteness of data on the educational level of non-resident children and the finding in many studies of a positive correlation between the educational levels of members of different generations within the same family, SECH could also be serving as a proxy for children's education, which we would expect to have a positive effect upon transfers made from both altruistic and exchange motives.

The remaining variables listed in Table 12.1 are all designed to capture various demographic characteristics of the household. AGE represents the age of the household head. FEMHEAD is a dummy variable that assumes a value of 1.0 if the head is female, and MARRIED takes the value of 1.0 if the head is married. ACHOUT represents the number of adult children living outside the household of the elderly head and ACHIN, the number of such children living inside the household. Finally, FSICK is the number of household members who were reported to have been ill (without regard to the seriousness of the illness) at any time during the four weeks preceding the survey, relative to the number of adult equivalents in the household. The average was greater than 1.0. This ratio may be regarded as a measure of the extent of special needs of the parental household.

Table 12.1 reveals that the average age of the heads 60 or older in the sample was 68.8, that 28 per cent of such heads were female, that exactly half were married, and that the heads reported an average of about three living children, virtually evenly split between those living in the household and those living outside the household. Finally, the number of adult equivalents reported ill during the four weeks preceding the survey averaged a little more than 1.6.

The third and fourth columns Table 12.1 present the corresponding means of the same variables as for the 835 elderly households without social security (households that reported neither paying into nor receiving from the social security system in the last year) and the 270 elderly heads for whom at least one of the social security measures had a positive value. From the entries for the measures of transfers from children (CHGIVE, GROSREC, and NETREC) it can be seen that, on average, all three measures were lower for the sample with social security than for that without social security. These results seem to confirm the possibility that social security participation reduces transfers from children. Household heads with social security differed from those without social security in other important ways. In particular, they were wealthier, more urban, more educated, more likely to be married and male, and also more likely to have adult children living in the household but fewer children living outside the household. As a result, it is at least possible that the overall differences in transfers between those with and those without social security were due to these other differences between the two samples.

The remaining columns of Table 12.1 present the corresponding means for samples with and without children living inside the household. The transfers from children were significantly higher for heads with no adult children living in the household. Those with co-resident adult children were more likely to be wealthier, own their own a business, live in an urban area, have more education, and be a married male. Although an elderly parent's need for help could be an important reason for an adult child to live in the household of his (her) elderly parents—the value of FSICK was only slightly higher for the group with adult children in the home than for those without them—the data seem to suggest that, *ceteris paribus*, more well-to-do parents may be better able to hold onto (or attract) their children than less well-to-do ones, and thus obtain the actual or potential support that resident adult children can provide.

Table 12.2 provides similar information for the sample divided into several wealth groups. Elderly heads of 194 households reported having zero wealth. It is highly uncertain that their reports of having no wealth were accurate inasmuch as quite a few of them were affiliated with social security, access to which is generally believed to be limited to better-off households (Mesa-Lago 1994; Cruz-Saco 1995) and some owned their own business or home and had education at the secondary or higher level. For all the other wealth groups the means of most variables vary in predictable ways by wealth. For example, the social security variables (CONTRSS and SOCSEC), URBAN, SECH, and MARRIED all rise with wealth whereas FEMHEAD falls with wealth. Neither HOMEOWN nor BUSINESS appears to rise with reported wealth, however. The reasons may be that many urban residents live in very poor dwellings in squatter settlements, which nevertheless are considered owner-occupied, and that many owned businesses are in the informal sector and generate only low levels of income. Given the suggestion of the model and the above descriptive statistics that adult children living outside the household provide more support

Table 12.2. Means of transfers received and related variables for elderly household heads, by wealth group: Peru, 1985–6

Variable	WEALTH = 0 (194)	Poorest 25% > 0 (82)	Next poorest 25% (276)	Next highest 25% (276)	Highest 25% (277)
CHGIVE	0.376	0.329	0.326	0.275	0.289
GROSREC	563.000	191.000	216.000	360.000	690.000
NETREC	526.000	166.000	88.000	137.000	340.000
CONTRSS	4.000	2.000	8.000	14.000	6.000
SOCSEC	413.000	769.000	519.000	963.000	1,488.000
WEALTH	0.000	46.000	519.000	2,294.000	18,622.000
BUSINESS	0.345	0.610	0.518	0.460	0.430
HOMEOWN	0.799	0.805	0.813	0.768	0.830
URBAN	0.560	0.667	0.587	0.620	0.664
SECH	0.113	0.073	0.116	0.156	0.350
AGE	70.600	67.900	69.200	68.000	67.400
FEMHEAD	0.423	0.329	0.268	0.293	0.181
MARRIED	0.240	0.451	0.511	0.507	0.606
ACHOUT	1.868	1.325	1.456	1.310	1.425
ACHIN	0.897	1.756	1.695	1.866	1.346
FSICK	1.560	5.854	1.632	1.586	1.609

Note: Sample sizes are in parentheses. For definitions, see Table 12.1.

Source: Peruvian Living Standards Survey.

to their parents if no adult children live in the household, and given also the dubious quality of the reports of zero financial and durable good wealth, we deem it important in the subsequent analysis to distinguish between those households with and without co-resident children and between the various wealth groups, including the group claiming to have no wealth.

Empirical Estimates

As noted at the outset, in developing countries like Peru it is often said that an important reason for having children is for support during old age and that co-resident adult children are an important source of that support. Likewise, the need to help elderly parents may be an important reason for adult children to remain in the parental household. We have seen that transfers to parents by non-resident adult children vary significantly according to whether other adult children live with the elderly parents and possibly also according to whether bequeathable forms of wealth belong to the parents. For these reasons we use a two-stage switching regression model for our empirical estimation. In the first stage we estimate a probit maximum-likelihood function for the presence of adult children resident in the household (ACHIND). Then, for each of the three alternative transfer measures (CHGIVE, GROSREC, and NETREC) defined above, we estimate the parameters of the transfer functions corresponding to the theoretical model and the empirical versions thereof, depending upon the presence or absence of resident children in the elderly household. As shown by Maddala (1993: 223–34), the resulting parameter estimates are consistent, though the standard errors have to be adjusted because of heteroscedasticity.

Table 12.3 presents the probit maximum likelihood estimates of the first-stage equation for ACHIND, using all the variables defined above and described in Tables 12.1 and 12.2, except for the following differences. First, the total number of living children (NCHILD) is substituted for the separate numbers of

Table 12.3. Probit analysis of whether elderly household heads have an adult child in the household (ACHIN): Peru, 1985–6

Variable	Coefficient	Chi squared	Significance level
Intercept	13.17000	13.736	0.00
Social security variables			
CONTRSS	0.00180	2.660	0.10
SOCSEC	−0.00003	3.670	0.05
Income and wealth variables			
SELFINC	0.00005	22.770	0.00
WEALTH0	−0.65050	25.570	0.00
WEALTH2	−0.04490	0.150	0.70
WEALTH3	−0.35060	8.460	0.00
BUSINESS	0.21820	5.670	0.02
HOMEOWN	0.05120	0.210	0.65
URBAN	0.16110	2.530	0.11
SECH	0.33730	0.510	0.47
Demographic variables			
AGE	−0.38300	15.006	0.00
AGE2	0.00250	13.140	0.00
FEMHEAD	0.15330	1.710	0.19
MARRIED	0.34670	10.380	0.00
FSICK	0.08620	1.850	0.17
NCHILD	0.40860	38.900	0.00
Interaction term			
NCHILD*SECH	−0.04910	0.080	0.78
Log likelihood: −590.718			
$N = 1.103$			

Definitions: SELFINC = own income of this household head; AGE2 = age squared; NCHILD = number of living children above 20 years of age; WEALTH0 = 1 if reported value of wealth = 0; 0 otherwise; WEALTH2 = 1 if the reported value of wealth is in the second third of the distribution; WEALTH3 = 1 if the reported value of wealth is in the top third of the distribution; For other definitions, see Table 12.1.

Source: Peruvian Living Standards Survey.

those inside and outside the household (ACHIN and ACHOUT). Second, own income (SELFINC) is added. Third, in view of the aforementioned issue about the dubious validity of the zero wealth observations, the influence of wealth is captured by a series of dummy variables (WEALTH0 for WEALTH = 0 and WEALTH2 and WEALTH3 for each of the upper two-thirds in the distribution of the continuous variable WEALTH). Fourth, the square of age (AGE2) is introduced to capture possible non-linearities in the effect of age. Fifth, given that an educated head is more likely than an uneducated head to have educated children, and given that data on the education of children are incomplete, we add an interaction term, NCHILD*SECH, to distinguish the direct effect of the head's education from the indirect effect coming through its influence upon the education of children. Because more-educated children have less need than less-educated children to remain in the parental household and also a higher opportunity cost of doing so, the effect of NCHILD*SECH should be negative.

For reasons given above, the effect of social security variables on ACHIND can be either positive or negative, depending in part upon the relative importance of the altruism and exchange motives for transfers. As can be seen, one of those variables (CONTRSS) has a positive effect whereas the other (SOCSEC) has a negative one, though only the latter effect is significant, at the 0.05 level. SELFINC has a highly significant, though rather small, positive effect. The dummy variables of WEALTH0, WEALTH2, and WEALTH3 have negative and in most cases significant effects upon ACHIN, indicating that financial wealth is not an attraction in itself for children to remain in the household of their elderly parents. In contrast, wealth in the form of owning a business or a home has a positive influence (perhaps because those forms of wealth are more credibly bequeathable to a child residing in the parental household). Only the effect of BUSINESS, however, is statistically significant at the 0.05 level. The other wealth-like variables, namely, URBAN and SECH, exert positive but not significant influences on ACHIND. The effect of age upon ACHIND turns out to be highly non-linear, and as expected the effects of FEMHEAD and FSICK are positive (but not significant at the 0.05 level). Not surprisingly, there is a strong positive effect of NCHILD upon ACHIND. The more living children the parents have, the more likely at least one of them will remain in the household. The coefficient of the interaction term NCHILD*SECH is, as expected, negative but not significant.

The incompleteness of data on the characteristics of children outside the household (those over age 30 being missing) limits the strength of the conclusions that can be derived from these results. In several respects at least, the results would seem more supportive of the exchange motive for living together and making transfers to parents than of the altruism motive. For altruism one would not expect the effects of SELFINC or any of the various forms of wealth to be positive. As is consistent with the strategic-bequest hypothesis, having an adult child reside with the elderly parents is related more positively to assets that are more credibly bequeathable to such a child than to those that are less bequeathable. The fact that one of the social security variables is positively related to ACHIN also seems inconsistent with the altruism motive, as does the effect of MARRIED. Likewise, the results support the connection between the number of children and the likelihood of support from children during their old age.

Next we proceed to the second stage of the analysis, the transfer behaviour of children living outside the household. As noted above, the second stage is contingent upon the results of the first. We estimate the transfers-from-children functions separately for household heads with and without adult children living in the household. In each case, we estimate three such functions: using first a probit model to determine the dummy variable for the elderly parent reporting having received any transfer from his or her children in the previous three months (CHGIVE), then a Tobit function for the level of gross transfers (GROSREC), and finally an ordinary least-squares regression for net transfers from children (NETREC), in each case correcting the standard errors as suggested by Maddala (1983).

The results for the samples of the 696 households with adult children in the household and the 409 households without adult children in the household are given in Tables 12.4 and 12.5, respectively. To test more completely for the empirical relevance of the strategic-bequest motive, which makes the transfer-inducing effects of heritable wealth dependent upon the number of children, in principle it would have been desirable to introduce a whole set of interaction terms between ACHOUT and the various forms of wealth. Given the aforementioned measurement problems requiring instead of WEALTH a set of dummy variables, given too the revealed lack of variation in HOMEOWN and the fact that the resulting interaction terms involve the same also highly correlated dummy variables, in practice few such interaction terms can be introduced without subjecting the estimates to severe multi-collinearity problems. Indeed, for the smaller data set of 407 heads without adult children in the household (Table 12.5), we deem it prudent to introduce only one such interaction term. In each case the probit results for CHGIVE are summarized in the first column, the Tobit estimates for GROSREC in the second column, and the OLS estimates of NETREC in the last column.

Turning first to the results for the three measures of transfers from children to parents with resident adult children in Table 12.4 and looking at the results of all three equations at the same time but taking the right-hand-side variables in order, we see that, just as in Table 12.3, the effects of the social security participation variables are much more mixed than would have been expected on the basis of altruism and the study by Cox and Jimenez (1992). None of the coefficients of the social security variables is statistically significant, and in two cases (CONTRSS in the equations for GROSREC and NETREC) the signs are unexpectedly positive.

As expected, the effects of the wealth variables upon transfers vary considerably from one form of wealth to another. They also vary somewhat from one

Table 12.4. Regression results for a sample of elderly household heads with one or more adult children resident in the household: Peru, 1985–6 (sample size = 694)

Variable	CHGIVE probit	GROSREC Tobit	NETREC OLSQ
Intercept	−0.939	−2,800.600**	−1,092.500
MILLS1	0.427*	469.300	118.700
Social security variables			
CONTRSS	−0.00010	1.340	1.401
SOCSEC	−0.00002	−0.030	−0.011
Income and wealth variables			
WEALTH0	−0.519**	−606.600*	48.900
WEALTH23	−0.170	27.900	−18.000
BUSINESS	−0.040	−38.400	−71.300
HOMEOWN	0.071	135.900	−194.400
URBAN	0.402**	846.600***	185.200
SECH	−0.432**	−370.900*	−426.700**
Demographic variables			
AGE	−0.002	4.293	8.175
FEMHEAD	0.456**	1,096.100***	658.300***
MARRIED	0.295***	675.400***	618.300***
FSICK	−0.041	188.300	114.100
ACHOUTD	0.089	−255.600	−45.500
Interaction terms			
ACHOUTD*WEALTH23	−0.051	−92.109	−30.700
ACHOUTD*SECH	1.142	2,973.800**	1,839.900*
Log likelihood	−388.3	−1,912.7	
R^2			0.041

* $p < 0.10$.
** $p < 0.05$.
*** $p < 0.01$.

Definitions: WEALTH23 = 1 if the value of reported wealth is in the top two thirds of the distribution; 0 otherwise; MILL1 = Value of Mills ratio; For other definitions, see Tables 12.1 and 12.3.

Source: Peruvian Living Standards Survey.

measure of transfers to parents to another. The least bequeathable wealth form, SECH, has a consistently negative and generally significant effect upon all three transfer measures. Even the more credibly bequeathable forms, such as BUSINESS and to a lesser extent the various WEALTH dummies, have generally negative, though not always significant, effects upon the transfer variables. These findings are quite consistent with the altruism motive, suggesting that wealthier parents with resident children have less need than poorer ones for support from non-resident children. The finding that what may be a more bequeathable wealth form (URBAN) has positive and sometimes significant effects seems to support the strategic-exchange motive. Because the children of

Table 12.5. Regression results for a sample of elderly household heads without adult children resident in the household: Peru, 1985–6 (sample size = 407)

Variable	CHGIVE probit	GROSREC Tobit	NETREC OLSQ
Intercept	−7.241	−30,377.000	1,820.700
MILLS1	−1.247***	−6,027.500**	−1,460.100*
Social security variables			
CONTRSS	−0.00081	−1.781	0.909
SOCSEC	−0.00005**	−0.306**	−0.127**
Income and wealth variables			
WEALTH0	−0.175	−1,088.900	−171.800
WEALTH23	−0.347	−2,052.800	−562.600
BUSINESS	0.229	736.400	−1.995
HOMEOWN	0.042	−530.000	−425.200
URBAN	0.205	1,540.230**	770.300**
SECH	−0.313	−533.800	194.700
Demographic variables			
AGE	0.006	−29.123	−23.100
FEMHEAD	0.958***	3,494.800***	736.100
MARRIED	0.790***	2,887.100***	307.200
FSICK	0.106	820.800**	344.700
ACHOUTD	6.675	30,914.600	582.300
Interaction terms			
ACHOUTD*WEALTH23	0.405*	2,792.900**	968.800*
Log likelihood	−235	−1,669.9	
R^2			0.052

For definitions, see Tables 12.1, 12.3, and 12.4.

Source: Peruvian Living Standards Survey.

heads living in urban areas can be expected to have greater access to higher-paying jobs than those of heads living in rural areas, URBAN may also be a reflection of a more favourable earning environment for adult children. The effect of the interaction term between two or more adult children outside the household (ACHOUTD*WEALTH23) is consistently negative, an implication opposite to that of the strategic-exchange hypothesis.

In the case of the demographic variables, the effects of AGE and FSICK are small, insignificant, and sensitive in both direction and magnitude to the particular choice of the dependent variable. The effects of FEMHEAD and MARRIED are strongly and consistently positive, though once again the implications for the choice between altruism and strategic-exchange motives for transfers are mixed and unclear. The positive effect of FEMHEAD is consistent with both altruism and strategic bequest, whereas the expected effect of MARRIED is ambiguous by both motives.

The indirect effect of the parent's education by way of that of children living outside the household (captured by the ACHOUTD*SECH interaction term) is positive and generally significant. However, in strong contrast to the old-age security theory of fertility, the number of children does not have a significantly positive effect upon either the likelihood of receiving a transfer (CHGIVE) or the gross or net amounts of such transfers, implying that more wealth does not induce more transfers from non-resident children when one or more adult children reside within the parental household. This finding directly contradicts an important implication of the strategic-bequest hypothesis.

From the large number of insignificant variables and the extremely low value of the explained variation (R^2) in Table 12.4, it can be seen that for the sample of elderly heads with adult children in the household, the model does not perform very well. Only the demographic variables FEMHEAD and MARRIED and the interaction of ACHOUT and SECH and the human-capital measure SECH itself have statistically significant effects.

What about transfers from children to elderly households with no resident adult children? In the result of the theoretical model given in Equation 12.13 this would be reflected in a higher value of θ and hence a higher transfer to parents. The reader will recall from Table 12.1 that transfers from children outside the household are, on average, significantly larger for this group than for elderly heads who have adult children living in the household. Is there also evidence that the behavioural responses of transfers to their determinants are also different from those of the sample with children in the household, analysed in Table 12.4? To seek answers to these questions, we turn to Table 12.5.

Beginning again with the social security variables, we see for this sample that the effects of SOCSEC upon the transfer measures are consistently negative and significant. Indeed, in the case of GROSREC, each hundred intis of income from social security has the effect of crowding out gross transfers from non-resident children by approximately 30 intis. This behaviour is quite different from that of the sample of elderly heads with resident children revealed in Table 12.4.

Likewise, in the case of the wealth variables, the results in Table 12.5 are quite different from those in Table 12.4. Whereas the sign of the URBAN dummy variable is again positive, the magnitudes of the coefficients are uniformly higher. This result is consistent with both major motives for transfers. Yet, whereas in Table 12.4 the effect of SECH is negative and significant, thereby favouring the altruism hypothesis over the strategic-exchange one, in this case the signs are inconsistent and statistically insignificant, hence no longer supportive of the altruism hypothesis. Both the BUSINESS and HOMEOWN dummy variables also have inconsistent and statistically insignificant effects upon the transfer variables, again suggesting that in the Peruvian context these variables may be poor measures of wealth. The negative effects of the WEALTH dummy variables are still insignificant, though somewhat stronger than in Table 12.4.

Similarly, with respect to the demographic variables, the effects of FEMHEAD, MARRIED, and FSICK are all much larger and generally more significant than in the comparable equations of Table 12.4. Of even greater relevance, however, is that the effects of both the dummy variable for two or more adult children living outside the household (ACHOUT) and its interaction with the high-wealth dummy (WEALTH23) have large and, at least in some cases, significant positive effects upon transfers. The latter transfer-inducing effect of a large amount of wealth—which, without adult children in the household, is more credibly bequeathable—more than offsets the direct negative effect of WEALTH23 upon GROSREC.[5]

Conclusions

An important reason for undertaking this Peruvian case study is that Peru is one of the few Latin American countries with appropriate microdata for studying the behaviour of transfers from children to parents. This is important because Peru, even more so than most Latin American countries, is undergoing a transition from a 'traditional' society in which children are virtually the only external source of old-age support to a 'modern' one in which a variety of other sources, such as financial savings and social security, exist. In addition, its population will be ageing quickly over the next several decades. Nonetheless, because its ability to extend formal social security programmes seems to be rather limited despite recent reforms in those programmes, Peruvian policymakers charged with the design of social and economic policy need to pay more attention to household living arrangements between children and their elderly parents, as well as to private transfers to elderly parents. The simple eclectic model developed here is an attempt to show how such transfers are determined and to do so in a way that facilitates empirical testing.

The basic hypotheses of the eclectic model are (1) that both altruism and strategic exchange may serve as important motives for transfers from children to parents and (2) that the propensity to transfer depends upon various parameters reflecting the marital status of elderly parents, how much wealth they have and in what forms, and whether or not they have adult children living within the household. Because adult children within the parental household are almost invariably a major source of help, and the transfer behaviour of non-resident children is strongly influenced by the presence of resident children within the household, determining whether adult children reside within the parental household is a major step in the analysis. At this stage of the analysis the empirical results indicate the relevance of both altruistic and strategic-exchange motives for transfers to the parents. Many of the explanatory variables are highly significant, and the model's explanatory power is substantial. The results also show that a larger number of children raises the likelihood that one or more children will remain in the parental household.

The results of the empirical analysis of transfers from non-resident children are admittedly much more mixed. The models have lower explanatory power and fewer of the explanatory variables have significant effects. Nevertheless, the Peruvian results support several of the basic features and hypotheses derived from the eclectic-transfer model. Once again, some of the results seem to support the altruism motive over the strategic-exchange model. For example, this seems to be the case for the effect of SECH in Table 12.4, SOCSEC in Table 12.5, and some of the dummy variables for wealth in Table 12.5. In other results, however, the strategic-exchange motive seems to dominate, as in the case of MARRIED and the ACHOUTD*WEALTH23 interaction term in Table 12.5. The latter effects support the hypothesized resource-allocation strategies employed by both heads and their adult children at different stages in their life cycles. A major finding is the substantial difference between elderly households with adult children and those without adult children in both the level of transfers to parents by non-resident children and the sensitivity of such transfers to the determinants. In particular, the presence of adult children in the household seems to be a major deterrent to transfers from non-resident children, rendering the transfers much less sensitive to the determinants than when there are no adult children in the households of the elderly. In the theoretical model, the case of no adult children resident within the household is reflected in a higher value of θ and hence larger transfers, an implication strongly supported by the results.

Despite the significance of some of these effects—especially those presented in Tables 12.3 and 12.5, the results of which are considerably stronger than those in Table 12.4—the conclusions of the present study have to be treated with caution because the data on the characteristics of non-resident children are incomplete, there is a persistent problem of multi-collinearity, and the possibility of specification error remains. (For example, according to the model the various wealth variables are the result of earlier accumulation strategies, but we assume them to be predetermined in the present study.)

It would appear, in the Peruvian context at least, that the best way for parents to ensure old-age support from their children is to provide the kind of home and environment that will induce some of the children to remain in the parental household. Having more children is another strategy for raising the likelihood that some children will remain in the household, thereby increasing transfers in old age. Another way may be to have few but well-educated children, although the incompleteness of the PLSS data on education of adult children living outside the household made it impossible to test for this implication in the present study. Evidence of this exists in other countries (e.g. Knodel 1993 for Thailand; Nugent and Hu 1994 for rural China). Still another way may be to accumulate bequeathable assets capable of inducing transfers from non-resident children—though these effects seem to be rather weak, especially in the case in which children already reside in the household.

We have found little evidence that heads with especially unfavourable characteristics are able to attract significant amounts of support. For example, in only one of the tables (Table 12.5) and only one of the transfer measures (GROSREC) is a transfer from children significantly raised by either the age of the head or the index of ill health (FSICK). The characteristic of female headship (FEMHEAD) is something of an exception. Although the FEMHEAD dummy variable increases the likelihood of having an adult child in the household only slightly and insignificantly (Table 12.3), it increases the likelihood of a transfer (CHGIVE) in both Tables 12.4 and 12.5 substantially, and also the levels of gross and net transfers very substantially, especially in the case in which there are no resident adult children. The latter results may be taken as evidence of the widespread cultural phenomenon that it is mainly women who serve as the focal point for the maintenance of strong intergenerational relationships. Because of the various factors contributing to the prospect of an extensive period of widowhood among once-married women (Nugent 1985), this finding is also consistent with the implication of the old-age security motive that the incentive to cultivate support from children is likely to be especially strong among females.

Other than that, however, elderly heads have limited power to ensure transfers from children through the strategic use of bequeathable wealth. This finding suggests a potential problem: the support for such transfers seems to depend largely upon reinforcing social norms that could be expected to break down under modernization and market influences. Because such influences are clearly stronger in urban than in rural areas, in the future they may act as an important offset to the strong positive effect of URBAN upon transfers arising from higher incomes and increased educational opportunities that exist in urban areas. If this should be the case, it would suggest the importance of policies designed especially to preserve the strength of traditional norms (Nugent and Hu 1994). Otherwise, if the system of support from children cannot be preserved, it suggests the need for either strengthening the incentives for and efficiency of private savings as a substitute for support from children or developing new public programmes. As there will always be some families who are unsuccessful in accumulating savings for old age or having children capable of supporting them, there will always be a need for at least a bare-bones public system (Treas and Logue 1986).

Yet, would not new public programmes hasten the disintegration of the traditional system? As we have noted, Cox and Jimenez (1992) provide evidence from Peru's urban households showing that they generally do. Our own evidence corroborates this finding, but only in the case in which there are no children resident within the elderly household.[6] Even if further analyses reveal additional evidence of the partial crowding out of private transfers by public ones, it is certainly possible to redesign formal old-age support systems to reduce the extent of such substitution behaviour. Conceivably, public or other interventions might even be designed in such a way as to 'crowd in' private transfers. Indeed, some of the recent reforms in Peru's system seem to provide stronger incentives for private transfers, for example by requiring the families of those who receive medical services to provide more in the way of help.

The present study corroborates quite a few of the findings from studies of other countries, especially findings of the importance of co-residence with adult children to the well-being of parents, and of the high incidence of joint living arrangements between parents and their adult children. Like other studies, it does not make clear which motives for transfers dominate, although among non-resident children whose parents live alone old-age security concerns and strategic-bequest motives seem to be somewhat more important than in other studies. One of the strongest implications of the present study, with respect to both the level of transfers and the sensitivity of transfers to the various determinants, is the importance of distinguishing between households with and those without adult children present.

It would be useful and desirable to extend the study in a number of directions. On the theoretical side, the model could be broadened to constitute an overlapping-generations model and thereby to integrate more fully the transfer decisions of children and parents. This would allow transfers to parents' own parents to be included in the analysis of the parents' problem, which was not possible in the present analysis. Another important extension might be to make the model more dynamic. On the empirical side, the most important extension would be to include human-capital investments in children and to see to what extent they enhance support from children during parents' old age. To what extent is having fewer and better-educated children a more successful strategy for old-age support than having more but less-educated ones? How does the education of children affect the influence of other important determinants of transfers? How does the birth-order, gender, and educational mix of children affect the propensity to make transfers to parents? (see Chapter 13, by Yean-Ju Lee, in this volume). Another desirable extension of the Peruvian analysis would be to examine a somewhat more normal and prosperous economic period in that country because the PLSS was conducted in near-crisis conditions, leaving open the question of whether transfer behaviour would be different under more normal conditions. Finally, it would be interesting to determine whether any form of collective or community old-age support may have been emerging in the chaotic financial, social, and political conditions of Peru over the last decade and, if so, to what extent.

Notes

We express our gratitude to Emmanuel Jimenez, the World Bank, and the Government of Peru for permission to use data from the Peruvian Living Standards Survey and to World Bank staff for their help in answering our many queries about the data. We are also grateful to Donald Cox, Andrew Foster, Yean-Ju Lee, Alessandro Cigno, and other participants at the Seminar on Intergenerational Economic Relations and Demographic Changes, Honolulu, and to participants at the Western Economic Association's Sixty-ninth International Conference of 1994, Vancouver, for their comments on an earlier draft of this chapter. We are grateful to the editors of this volume for the opportunity to participate in the Honolulu seminar.

1. The restructuring and privatization of Peru's social security system of 1991–3, which was implemented largely by Presidential decree while the country was under martial law, was based upon the Chilean model (Mesa-Lago 1994; Cruz-Saco 1995). Prior to the restructuring and privatization the main programme for old-age support was a public pension scheme that was based largely upon employer contributions and required a minimum of fifteen years of contributions. The percentage of Peru's labour force covered by social security fell from 37% in 1980 to 32% in 1985–8, approximately the average for Latin American countries (Mesa-Lago 1994: table 2.3).
2. In the 1960s Peru had one of the most unequal distributions of income in the world, and the inequality was by no means confined to income (Jain 1975). Although the inequalities seem to have declined between then and the mid-1980s (Glewwe 1988), this occurred to a large extent at the expense of growth. Real gross domestic product per capita declined by 30% between 1980 and 1990. Between 1985 and 1990 both inequality and poverty rose sharply, and inequalities of income, expenditures, and various kinds of access remained high (Glewwe and Hall 1992).
3. We exclude transfers to and from their own parents because we assumed that such transfers would have been determined in a previous optimization between themselves and their parents. Otherwise, the model would be one of the overlapping-generations variety and more difficult to solve. Another reason for avoiding this complication is that no retrospective data on transfers to survey respondents' own parents at an earlier period of time are available in our data set.
4. Peru experienced dire economic conditions in 1990, and therefore the period of the survey was hardly a normal one for observing transfer behaviour. The survey was collected over a period of months during which the rate of inflation was extremely high (as much as 5% a day), thereby making the results sensitive to the price indexes and problems of recall about the timing of receipts and payments of transfers, neither of which is regarded as very reliable. It did not identify the source or destination of the transfers (i.e. did not designate whether they were to or from children or to or from other persons, but simply indicated the total amounts transferred. Finally, as a result of increased urban terrorism in 1990, the survey had a lower response rate than the earlier survey, especially among wealthier households; hence the representativeness of the sample is more dubious.
5. Because of the smaller size of the sample and the aforementioned collinearity problem, the results for this sample are more sensitive to changes in the specification. Nevertheless, the result obtained by keeping WEALTH2 and WEALTH3 as separate variables does not change the results appreciably.
6. The reasons for this difference in the results of the two studies are (1) the emphasis on the more clearly predetermined wealth variables in our study as opposed to income variables in the earlier study, (2) our decision to model separately parental households with and without adult children, (3) our distinction between children living inside and outside the household, (4) our introduction of one or more important interaction terms involving wealthlike variables, and (5) the difference in the choice of samples (ages 60 and older in the entire national sample in our study as opposed to ages 45 and older in the urban sample in the earlier study).

13 Support between Rural Parents and Migrant Children in a Rapidly Industrializing Society: South Korea

Yean-Ju Lee

Although some observers (e.g. Caldwell 1976; Cowgill 1986) have predicted that a breakdown in the function of the family as a production unit and rising individualism would significantly reduce resource exchanges between parents and their grown children, many recent studies in East and South-East Asian countries where rapid industrialization has been under way have found adult children continuing to support their elderly parents. A majority of elderly parents in those countries still co-reside with one or more of their adult children, and a majority of both co-residing and non-co-residing adult children provide material and financial assistance to their parents (Martin 1991; Eu 1992; Hermalin, Ofstedal, and Lee 1992; Knodel, Chayovan, and Siriboon 1992; Martin and Kinsella 1994; Rhee 1994). This chapter explores the family dynamics underlying adult children's continuing support for elderly parents in the Republic of Korea, focusing on families in which grown children have migrated from their rural places of origin. Implications of the findings for the future of intergenerational support are also discussed.

I begin with the premise that intergenerational transfers between adult children and elderly parents persist during the process of industrialization because such transfers are economically beneficial to both generations. One type of intergenerational transfer is 'mutual aid', as the exchange models describe. For example, the older generation provides adult children with services, such as childcare and help with housework, and in return the younger generation provides financial assistance (Morgan and Hiroshima 1983; Y.-J. Lee and Xiao 1994). For such mutual aid to take place, however, the two generations must share a home or at least live near each other, but that is not a practical arrangement for a majority of family members in an industrializing society. This type of exchange is expected to become less common as incomes rise and market services become more affordable.

In the corporate group model, parents plan long-term transactions with their children to maximize the extended family's wealth (Y.-J. Lee, Parish, and Willis 1994). During the process of rapid economic growth the demand for skilled labour increases and the rate of returns to education is typically high. In such a context, parents with limited resources who care about their children's future income and have concerns about their own old-age support are likely to invest their resources in developing the children's human capital. The parents plan to receive some of children's earnings when the parents reach old age or their health deteriorates. Provided that the children comply with the parents' long-term plan, the family maximizes its wealth and achieves a balanced distribution. If the parents cannot assume that the children will repay the investment, they may not make a sufficient investment to raise the children's income. To ensure that children comply with their plan, the parents attempt to instil in their children such values as filial piety, respect for elders, and a felt obligation to support the parents in old age. This model predicts that parents' earlier investment in children, elderly parents' needs, and children's sense of obligation to repay the parental investment will influence adult children's provision of financial and material support for their elderly parents.

The pattern of inheritance in another industrializing society, Taiwan, is consistent with the corporate group model. In Taiwan a majority of Taiwanese people aged 60 or older, regardless of their economic status, have already transferred part or all of their property to their children (Li, Xie, and Lin 1993). These transfers, considered as inheritance, differ from bequests, which consist of the remains of parents' lifetime consumption that are given to children upon the parents' death. Taiwanese parents seem to assume the extended family will abide as an economic unit and expect to share their children's resources in old age. Acting in accordance with that expectation, a majority of adult children in Taiwan provide financial support to their elderly parents. Furthermore, adult children who have received a share of their parents' property give more assistance to their parents than do adult children who have not received any inheritance; this is so even after one controls for income level (Hermalin *et al.* 1992; Y.-J. Lee *et al.* 1994; Mason and Miller, Chapter 3 in this volume).

Although I shall also discuss alternative hypotheses, the data I analyse here are consistent with the hypothesis that the family takes advantage of rapid economic growth through long-term intergenerational transactions of resources. Like previous studies by my colleagues and me in Taiwan and China (Y.-J. Lee and Xiao 1994; Y.-J. Lee *et al.* 1994), this study does not find any support for strategic exchange models based on self-interest. The current study highlights how the family achieves long-term corporate relations between generations.

Factors Hypothesized to Affect Transfers

To test the corporate group model, I examine variations in intergenerational support both within and among families. Survey data containing information on all surviving children of elderly respondents make it possible to perform analyses at two levels, that of the family and that of the individual child. The implications for society of parents investing in their children's future economic status are enormous, and adult children's assistance is an important determinant of the economic well-being of the elderly in many developing countries. The analysis focuses on adult children's transfer behaviour, but the findings from the two-level analyses also provide insight into parents' allocation of resources among their children. I begin with the hypotheses.

Parents' investment in children

Where neither public subsidies nor loans from the financial market for education are readily available, the parental investment that contributes most to the maximization of family wealth is education. For investment decisions, parents consider wage differentials in the labour market as well as the direct cost of education. The educational wage pattern affects how much education parents want their children to receive. For example, if the rate of return to, say, a college education is unusually high,[1] then given their resources, parents may decide to have one or more of their children receive a college education while investing less in the rest. In making that decision, parents will also consider gender differences in wages and even the patterns of educational assortative mating in the marriage market (Parish and Willis 1993; Brinton, Lee, and Parish 1995).

Within families, parents allocate resources among their children for the best outcome of the extended family. Parents may assume various kinds of transaction contracts with their children, and those contracts may be affected by the children's birth order, gender, and marital status. Whatever its determining factors are, parents' differential investment in children will affect the children's repayment behaviour. Adult children who have received more education than their siblings are more likely to provide financial assistance to their elderly parents. One reason is that children with higher education will earn more than less educated children and thus have more disposable income to transfer to the parents. Parents may adopt a strategy to guarantee repayment from their heavily invested children. For example, they may select children for higher education who are most likely to repay the investment, or they may socialize the children to do so by imparting a sense of obligation. Therefore one should find a positive relationship between parental investment and the incidence of children's financial transfers even after controlling for children's earnings.

The amount invested and the patterns of parental socialization vary among families as well as among siblings within families. Between-family differences may be due to differences in family resources or to some unobserved factors, such as the values parents place on children, education, or intergenerational ties.

Rural parents who care about their children's economic status may decide to finance their children's migration in search of a better job or higher education in urban areas. I hypothesize that the same relationship between parents' investment and children's transfers to parents that obtains in the case of education holds for migration. In the case of migration, however, I do not assume that it always involves parents' investment. Rather, I hypothesize that among migrant children, only those children who have received parental support for their migration will be more likely to provide the parents with old-age support.

Children's positions within the family: gender, marital status, and birth order

The ideals of the Korean family traditionally consisted of a strict division of roles and positions, defined by such demographic traits as gender, generation, birth order, and marital status (Martin 1990; Suh 1992; Brinton *et al.* 1995). Daughters were regarded as family members only until their marriage, when they became members of their husbands' families. Social and economic contacts between married daughters and their parents were minimal. Sons, especially first sons, assumed primary responsibility for supporting elderly parents. Although the traditional division of positions and roles within the family has weakened with the massive transformation of the Korean society since the 1960s, it continues to influence many aspects of family life.

Several studies have described the economic roles of unmarried working daughters during the early stages of industrialization in East Asia, for example in Taiwan, Hong Kong, and South Korea (Salaff 1981; Greenhalgh 1985; Thornton and Lin 1994). Typically, early-born daughters of farmers or of low-income urban families would quit school after completing primary or middle school and begin working outside the home or were married out. Either way, through their income from work or by marrying and thus reducing the family's consumption, these daughters contributed to the family economy and helped later-born sons and daughters to receive a higher education (Parish and Willis 1993).

Once married, the daughters made only a limited contribution to their family of orientation. An increase in a wife's control over household income, mainly through her own employment outside the home, would increase the incidence and amount of support that she gave to her parents (Coward and Dwyer 1990; Chiappori 1992). Increasing rates of labour-force participation among married women in South Korea, especially among highly educated married women in the recent past, suggest that support from married daughters to their parents may be increasing (Noh *et al.* 1992; Brinton *et al.* 1995).

Elderly parents' needs and resources

Children's responses to parents' resources and needs provide clues to the children's motives in making financial transfers to the parents. The altruism model postulates that people provide gifts or loans to needy relatives out of concern for the recipients' well-being. In contrast, the exchange model assumes that monetary or service transfers among relatives are made out of an expectation of rewards. Thus the altruism model predicts that needier relatives will receive more transfers than wealthier ones, whereas the exchange model predicts that people will receive more monetary or service transfers from their relatives if they have more resources with which to reciprocate (Becker 1981; Lucas and Stark 1985; Cox 1987; Altonji, Hayashi, and Kotlikoff 1992; Cox and Rank 1992).

The notion of children's altruism towards parents is compatible with the hypothesis that parents plan for long-term exchanges with their children. Parents who care about the well-being of family members are likely to make a long-term plan to maximize the family's wealth, and children who comply with the plan eventually reciprocate the parents' investment in them. According to the exchange model, parents will give more monetary assistance to wealthier children than to less well-off children as a reward for the children's services because the opportunity cost of the wealthier children's time is greater. The exchange model also predicts that parents who have more properties to bequeath will receive more gifts and time services from their children than will parents with modest resources. However, children's exchange motives may be more clearly observed from their service transfers than from their monetary transfers to parents, as service transfers have greater utility to wealthy parents than do monetary gifts (Bernheim, Shleifer, and Summers 1985; Cox 1987).

Empirical studies of children's transfers to elderly parents have so far shown more support for the altruism model than for the exchange model (e.g. Y.-J. Lee and Aytac 1993; Y.-J. Lee and Xiao 1994; Y.-J. Lee *et al.* 1994; McGarry and Schoeni 1995*a*). Aggregate statistics showing a lower prevalence of upward transfers in wealthier countries than in low-income countries also run counter to the hypothesis of bequest motives. In rapidly growing economies, adult children tend to be wealthier than their parents, and elderly parents in those societies do not have as much property to attract children's transfers as do elderly parents in wealthier countries.

Observed and unobserved family effects

If children's transfers to their elderly parents are part of a parental plan, as the corporate group model assumes, one can expect to observe some family effects in children's transfer behaviour due to the unique attributes of those parental plans. Such family effects may include children's aggregate characteristics, such as the number of siblings and the children's average levels of education and income, which are outcomes of parents' earlier decisions. Family effects may also include unobserved values and attitudes common to family members, which may have been shaped by parents' socialization. (See Dunn 1993*b* and McGarry and Schoeni 1995*a* for a discussion of such unobserved effects in parents' transfers to adult children.) Some parents, for example in southern areas of South Korea, may place more emphasis than others on the traditional values of filial piety and respect for elders.

Family factors other than parents' socio-economic characteristics are less likely to be observed if children's transfers to parents are motivated by self-interested exchanges. In such exchange models, no parental plan is involved and the values and attitudes of parents or siblings will be less relevant to individual children's transfer decisions.

The Korean context: industrialization, urbanization, and the rural elderly

South Korea has experienced remarkable economic growth during the past few decades, providing a good case for testing long-term exchanges between parents and children. Rapid growth causes wide gaps in socio-economic status, including education and income, between older and younger generations. Between 1970 and 1990 South Korea's per capita real gross national product increased almost fourfold, from slightly less than 1,700 dollars to approximately 6,600 dollars (expressed in international prices, base year 1985). Per capita national savings rose at even higher rates, from 265 dollars in 1970 to approximately 2,400 dollars in 1990 (Bank of Korea 1983, 1988, 1993; Summers and Heston 1991; Heston *et al.* 1995).

The early expansion of the economy during the 1960s and 1970s was due to the development of urban-based, labour-intensive manufacturing industries, which provided unprecedented opportunities for employment for young women and men with less than a high-school education. Many of those young workers migrated from rural areas, and their contribution to rural household incomes was considerable. During the late 1970s and the 1980s the Korean economy shifted in emphasis from the light to heavy manufacturing industries, and the service sector expanded. The transformation of the economy coincided with a rapid rise in educational attainment among workers. The proportion of men in the 25–9 age group who graduated from high school or received more education grew from 38 per cent in 1970 to 83 per cent in 1990. The increase was even greater among women of the same ages, from 17 to 74 per cent (ROK, Economic Planning Board 1973; ROK, Statistical Office 1993).

Along with the growth of the secondary and tertiary sectors, South Korea experienced a rapid decline in the relative size of its agricultural labour force. In 1966 more than half of the labour force participated in agriculture, but by 1990 only 18 per cent did so (Korea National Agricultural Cooperative Federation 1981, 1991). The population living in rural areas shrank by one-third, from 60 to 28 per cent, between 1970 and 1990 (ROK, Korea Economic Planning Board 1973; ROK, Statistical Office 1993). Although industrialization of the labour force and urbanization of the population occurred in all age groups, the rates of change were greatest in the younger age groups. As a result of selective rural-to-urban migration among young adults that began in the 1960s, today's working-age Koreans are much less likely to live in rural areas than are older people. The age differences in rural–urban residence were clear by 1970 and have widened since then (Figure 13.1). By 1990 about 45 per cent of Koreans aged 60 or older were living in rural areas, compared with only about 20 per cent of those in their twenties and thirties. One consequence of this age difference in urbanization has been a rapid decline in extended-family living arrangements

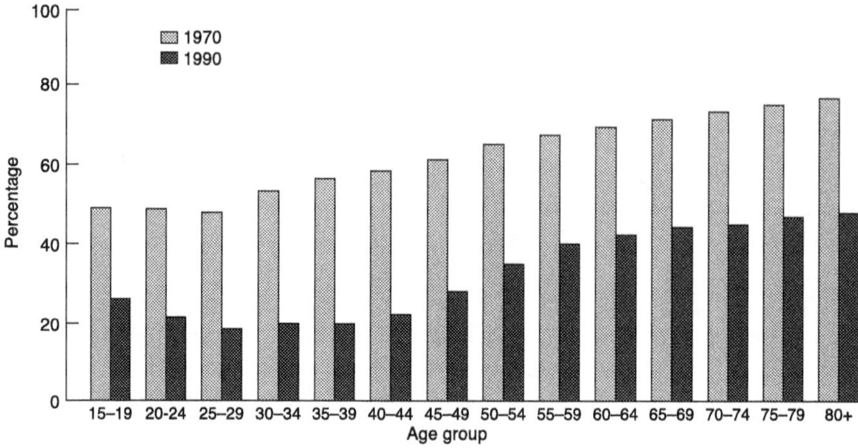

Fig. 13.1. Percentages of the population living in rural areas, by age group: South Korea, 1970 and 1990

among the rural elderly. According to an analysis of Korean census data, whereas about 75 per cent of rural residents aged 60 or older lived in extended families in 1970, a decade later that proportion was only about 60 per cent—lower even than the ratio among urban elderly, among whom the incidence of extended families remained stable (DeVos and Lee 1993).

Owing to a low level of income and savings during their working ages, the rural elderly have minimal incomes from public or private pension programmes, and their income from savings is also almost non-existent (Kim *et al.* 1993; Rhee 1994). The traditional expectation that their children would support them in old age may have encouraged them to invest whatever resources they had in their children. The family is thus a significant source of support for rural elderly who are no longer working. Assistance from migrant children has become more important to rural elderly parents with the shift from co-residence by grown children. One indication is that between 1975 and 1990, transfer income from public and private sources rose from 7 to 17 per cent of total household income in rural areas (Korea National Agricultural Cooperative Federation 1981, 1991). Among elderly households, the percentages may have been even larger.

In 1988 the Korean government established a national pension programme to secure the income of retirees. As this is a fully funded system, however, retirees will not begin to receive any significant amount of benefits before 2000. Initially participation in the programme was compulsory only among workers in firms with ten or more employees, where it applied to those between ages 18 and 60. The programme expanded its coverage to workers in firms with five or more employees in 1992, and on a voluntary basis to farmers and fishermen in 1995. Thus it is not certain that the rural elderly will have income security even after the national pension system has matured in a decade or two (Nam, Min, and Chang 1990; ROK, Economic Planning Board 1994; Moon 1995).

In the late 1980s Korea also established a universal health insurance programme. Like the national pension programme, the health programme gradually expanded its coverage from urban paid employees to rural and urban self-employed workers. By late 1993 virtually all Koreans were participating in the national health insurance programme; the relatively few who did not were extremely poor people, who nevertheless received free services. The quality of the programme's services varies greatly from region to region and between rural and urban areas, however, because the programme is managed separately by hundreds of local units. In rural areas, where income levels and hence premium levels are low, the programme's resources are not sufficient to provide quality services (Kwon and Yang 1990; ROK, Economic Planning Board 1994; ROK, Health and Social Affairs Ministry 1994).

It is obvious that the rapid economic changes that South Korea has experienced during the past few decades have created both challenges and opportunities for the family to protect its welfare. In the following sections of this chapter I explore the assumption that in the absence of major public programmes for redistributing income, families have had to adopt strategies for maximizing their incomes and redistributing those incomes among family members. In particular, I propose to test four hypotheses involving families with adult migrant children. First, parents' investment in children in earlier stages of the life cycle increases the probability of migrant children's financial assistance to elderly parents. Within families, the larger the parents' investment in one child compared with their investment in the child's siblings, the more likely is that child to provide assistance to the parents in their old age. Children's schooling and parental support for migration are the measures of parental investment. Second, migrant children's position within the family—that is, their gender, birth order, and marital status—affects whether they provide financial assistance to their elderly parents. Third, needy elderly parents are more likely to receive financial assistance from their migrant children than are wealthier parents. Elderly parents who have lower incomes, poor health, and no children residing with them are more likely to receive financial assistance from their children than are parents with higher incomes, good health, and co-residing children. Fourth, aggregate family characteristics, such as average levels of income and education among the children, affect the probability of migrant children's financial assistance to parents independently of individual characteristics. Unobserved family characteristics also affect the probability of migrant children's financial assistance to elderly parents.

The Survey Data and Variables Used in the Analysis

My data are from the Survey of Family Structure and Support Systems in Rural Areas, which the Korea Institute for Health and Social Affairs (KIHASA) conducted in 1993 (Kim *et al.* 1993). KIHASA selected households using a multi-stage cluster sampling method. Clusters were chosen purposively, to include villages with diverse geographic and economic characteristics. Of nine provinces (called *do*) in South Korea, the investigators selected three; within each province they chose one or two counties (*gun*); and within each county they selected two or three villages (*ri*). Altogether they chose sixteen villages, surveying all households in each village. Among the 1,093 households interviewed, 590 had at least one member aged 60 or older. My analysis is based on those 590 households.

For the main part of the questionnaire, which included a roster of the extended family and exchanges between the reference person (any family member over age 59) and his or her children (co-residing and non-co-residing), the respondent was the household head or the spouse of the head. Thus in households in which a reference person lived with an adult child, the respondent was the adult child or his or her spouse. In households with no co-resident adult children, an elderly resident (usually the husband) was asked to provide the roster of family members and exchanges. Afterwards, all of the elderly persons in the household were interviewed about their economic and health status. Some reference persons were younger than 60 but had a spouse 60 or older. For my analysis I have excluded eighteen such cases. The analysis focuses on 527 elderly persons (the elderly sample) who had at least one adult child who was living elsewhere and was not a student, and on their 2,217 children who lived elsewhere and were not students (the migrant children sample). I use the term 'migrant children' interchangeably with 'non-co-residing children' because the great majority (92 per cent) of non-co-residing children were not living in the same village.

The elderly respondents were asked if they had received financial assistance from any of their children during the twelve months prior to the survey. If they had, they were asked who the children were and whether the support from each child had been regular or occasional. Respondents were asked the same questions about assistance that they had given to their children. The survey did not ask about the amounts of support.

For the multivariate analyses of the determinants of the probability of children's financial assistance to elderly parents, I have selected as explanatory variables both individual and family characteristics. Adult children's years of education measure parents' investment. Information on non-co-residing children's income is not available from the survey. I therefore impute children's income from data on their years of education, age, occupation, gender, and marital status. For married daughters I also impute their husbands' incomes. My earnings equation is from Yoon (1991: 108), which is based on data from the 1989 Occupational Wage Survey. For both schooling and income, I calculate averages among all siblings and create two dummy variables, one indicating whether a child's schooling was higher than average, the other whether his or her income was above average. Another measure of parents' investment in their children is whether the parents were involved in the children's migration decision. Variables representing adult children's position within the family include their gender by marital status (four categories), age, and the number of migrant children within the family (including the respondent), by gender.

I use geographic distance between children and their elderly parents as a control variable. Although adult children can send money to their parents without visiting them, I assume that the frequency of visits is highly correlated with the provision of gifts or loans, which, in turn, is facilitated by geographic proximity. However, I do not control for the number of visits because I suspect that it and the provision of financial assistance are determined jointly. The variables measuring elderly parents' needs and resources include their health status, education, couple income, and number of co-residing children. The analysis also takes into consideration elderly parents' demographic characteristics, such as gender, marital status, and age.

Analysis and Results

In my analysis I obtain descriptive statistics from both the elderly sample and the migrant-children sample. Information on characteristics of the elderly parents and their children and on exchanges between the two generations is aggregated at the family level in the elderly sample. Using the elderly sample, I calculate the distribution of the elderly respondents by the number of migrant children and the number who provide assistance in order to gain an understanding of the gaps between the two sets of descriptive statistics representing the children's and the elderly parents' perspectives.

The multivariate analyses of the determinants of children's financial transfers are based on the migrant-children sample. I use both binomial and multinomial logit models, the latter distinguishing regular and occasional assistance from no assistance. The explanatory variables include individual children's characteristics, aggregate characteristics of siblings, and parents' characteristics. I also estimate a fixed-effects logit model, which controls for both observed and unobserved family characteristics by assuming a separate intercept for each family (Greene 1993, 1995).[2] As my ordinary logit model controls for observed family-level variables, I ascribe the differences between the results of the ordinary and the fixed-effects logit models to the unobserved family factors.

Likelihood of giving and receiving financial assistance: children's perspective

The descriptive statistics in Tables 13.1 to 13.3 shed light on intergenerational assistance as seen from the migrant children's and the elderly parents'

Table 13.1. Percentages of migrant children exchanging financial support with elderly parents during the past year: South Korea, 1993

Gave to parents	Received from parents			
	Regularly	Irregularly	Never	Total
Sons and daughters ($n = 2,217$)				
Regularly	0.3	0.4	4.7	5.4
Irregularly	1.1	6.0	48.5	55.6
Never	0.6	4.1	34.3	39.0
Total	2.0	10.5	87.5	100.0
Sons ($n = 1,088$)				
Regularly	0.6	0.7	7.2	8.5
Irregularly	2.0	7.8	49.4	59.2
Never	0.8	4.9	26.6	32.3
Total	3.4	13.4	83.2	100.0
Daughters ($n = 1,129$)				
Regularly	0.0	0.2	2.3	2.5
Irregularly	0.3	4.2	47.7	52.2
Never	0.3	3.3	41.7	45.3
Total	0.6	7.7	91.7	100.0

Source: Survey of Family Structure and Support Systems in Rural Areas.

perspectives. Table 13.1, which presents percentages of migrant children who exchanged financial assistance with their rural elderly parents during the year preceding the survey, indicates that the dominant flow of assistance was upward. About 5.4 per cent of the children gave regular support and 55.6 per cent gave occasional support to their parents during the year. Only 2.0 per cent of the children received regular financial support and 10.5 per cent of them received occasional support from their parents.

Migrant sons' and daughters' behaviours differed more in the exchanges of regular financial support than in the exchanges of irregular support with their rural parents (bottom two panels of Table 13.1). On the one hand, the likelihood of both giving and receiving regular assistance was about three times higher for sons than for daughters, although in neither case was the probability large: 8.5 per cent of sons gave regular assistance to their parents, compared with 2.5 per cent of daughters; and 3.4 per cent of sons received regular assistance from their parents, whereas only 0.6 per cent of daughters received such support. On the other hand, 59.2 and 52.2 per cent of migrant sons and daughters, respectively, provided occasional assistance to their parents, and 13.4 and 7.7 per cent of sons and daughters, respectively, received occasional support from their parents.

Table 13.2 indicates a very weak negative relationship between migrant children's provision of financial assistance to their parents and the number of

Table 13.2. Percentages of migrant children providing financial support to elderly parents, by number of migrant siblings: South Korea, 1993

No. of migrant siblings[a]	Financial support to parents			
	Regular	Irregular	Regular/irregular	(No.)
1	7.3	51.2	58.5	(41)
2	5.2	56.9	62.1	(116)
3	5.0	60.9	65.9	(261)
4	4.5	57.9	62.4	(420)
5	5.9	56.0	61.9	(580)
6	7.5	58.2	65.7	(414)
7	3.9	50.7	54.7	(203)
8	3.1	40.6	43.8	(128)
9	3.7	42.6	46.3	(54)
Total	5.4	55.6	61.0	(2,217)

[a] Including respondent.

Source: Survey of Family Structure and Support Systems in Rural Areas.

migrant siblings in the family. This finding contrasts with findings from earlier studies in other Asian countries (e.g. Knodel *et al.* 1992), in which the relationship between migrants' propensity to give assistance and the number of siblings was clearly negative, suggesting that declining fertility did not affect the amount of support elderly parents received from adult children provided that they had at least one child. In Table 13.2, a substantial decline in the propensity of providing financial assistance can be seen only when the number of migrant siblings rises from six (65.7 per cent) to seven (54.7 per cent). This result suggests that some elderly parents who have only one or two migrant children may not receive any financial support from those children, whereas those who have many migrant children may receive support from several children. Table 13.2, however, is based on the cross-family sample of migrant children and does not disaggregate differences within and between families.

Likelihood of receiving financial assistance: elderly parents' perspective

Table 13.3 presents the incidence of children's financial assistance, based on the sample of elderly parents. The vertical axis indicates the total number of migrant children, and each row shows a percentage distribution of families by the number of migrant children who provided either regular or irregular financial support to their elderly parents during the year preceding the survey. The marginal distribution in the last row shows that 81.6 per of the rural elderly received financial support from at least one child. Rather surprisingly, about half of these elderly parents received support from all their migrant children, totalling 41.6 per cent of all elderly parents (cells in the diagonal line). The

Table 13.3. Percentage distribution of elderly parents by number of migrant children providing financial support: South Korea, 1993

Total no. of migrant children	No. of migrant children providing financial support to elderly parents									
	0	1	2	3	4	5	6	7	8	Total
1	41.5	58.5								100.0
	(17)	(24)								(41)
2	27.6	20.7	51.7							100.0
	(16)	(12)	(30)							(58)
3	17.2	17.2	16.1	49.4						100.0
	(15)	(15)	(14)	(43)						(87)
4	19.0	10.5	14.3	14.3	41.9					100.0
	(20)	(11)	(15)	(15)	(44)					(105)
5	14.7	12.1	9.5	12.1	16.4	35.3				100.0
	(17)	(14)	(11)	(14)	(19)	(41)				(116)
6	7.3	17.4	4.3	5.8	11.6	17.4	36.2			100.0
	(5)	(12)	(3)	(4)	(8)	(12)	(25)			(69)
7	20.7	6.9	13.8	6.9	3.4	6.9	10.3	31.0		100.0
	(6)	(2)	(4)	(2)	(1)	(2)	(3)	(9)		(29)
8–9	4.5	13.6	22.7	18.2	4.5	9.1	13.6	0.0	13.6	100.0
	(1)	(3)	(5)	(4)	(1)	(2)	(3)	(0)	(3)	(22)
Total	18.4	17.6	15.6	15.6	13.8	10.8	5.9	1.7	0.6	100.0
	(97)	(93)	(82)	(82)	(73)	(57)	(31)	(9)	(3)	(527)

Notes: Percentages may not sum exactly to 100.0 because of rounding. Numbers in parentheses represent the number of cases.
Source: Survey of Family Structure and Support Systems in Rural Areas.

transfer from all migrant children is less likely as the number of migrant children increases, but among parents with seven or fewer children the decrease is not large, about 5 per cent with each child added. In sum, 63.9 per cent of the elderly parents received support from two or more children, and approximately 19.0 per cent received support from five or more children.

Two inferences can be drawn from these results. The first, which is consistent with Table 13.2, is that having a large number of children ensures that elderly parents will receive financial support from at least some of them. Among the current cohort of rural elderly Koreans, who have on average a larger number of surviving children than any other cohort, receiving financial support from their children is commonplace. It is possible, however, that the amount of assistance given per child declines as the number of children increases; our data do not contain information on amounts received. The second inference is that, given the large proportions of parents who receive assistance from all their children, there may be some family-level effects that lead to the same behavioural patterns among children from the same family. I use multivariate analyses to explore those family effects.

Determinants of children's financial assistance

The multivariate analyses of the determinants of migrant children's financial transfers to parents are based on the sample of children across the families. Siblings of migrant children had completed, on average, 9.8 years of education (Table 13.4). For about a third of the migrant children, the parents had participated in their migration decision, either supporting the children's decision or making the decision themselves. Two-thirds of the migrant children had made the migration decision alone. As expected, among elderly parents the largest group comprised widowed mothers (42 per cent) and widowed fathers were the smallest group (6 per cent). The elderly parents had, on average, five migrant children (2.4 sons and 2.6 daughters). Eleven per cent of the parents had severe difficulty in undertaking daily activities, and 65 per cent had some difficulty.

In Table 13.5, which presents results from the logit analyses, the first pair of columns presents the binomial logit equation, contrasting any type of support with no support, and the last two pairs of columns show the multinomial logit results for regular and irregular support as two separate choices. Although the probability of regular support is very low, I believe that regular support is more important for the well-being of elderly parents than occasional support because it is more dependable. Given the degree of commitment represented by regular support, it is also likely to be a greater amount over a year's time than occasional support.

As expected, even when children's education and income are controlled, their financial assistance to elderly parents is highly contingent upon the children's gender and marital status. In accordance with traditional norms, sons are more likely than daughters to provide financial assistance to their parents, but this is true only for married sons. Unmarried daughters are almost as likely as married sons to provide financial assistance to parents; they are particularly likely to provide regular support. Unmarried sons and married daughters are less likely than either married sons or unmarried daughters to provide financial support to their elderly parents. The overall probability of regular assistance is only about one-tenth of the probability of irregular assistance (0.05 versus 0.56), but the high likelihood of regular assistance from unmarried daughters confirms evidence from previous studies (e.g. Salaff 1981; Greenhalgh 1985) that migrant daughters are an important source of income among rural households.

The descriptive statistics showed no clear negative relationship between the number of siblings and the children's financial transfers to elderly parents, although having more siblings suggests the availability of other sources of support for parents. In the multivariate analysis the number of sisters decreases the likelihood of a child's financial assistance to parents, but the number of brothers does not. Further analyses (not shown) reveal an interaction effect between the number of brothers and average sibling education; the number of brothers has a negative effect on children's transfers to parents when average sibling education is at its mean, but that effect disappears as average sibling education goes up.

Table 13.4. Characteristics of migrant children and their elderly parents: South Korea, 1993

Characteristics	Mean/proportion
Migrant children's characteristics	
Mean income, imputed (10,000 won)	64.4
Education	
Mean years (all siblings)	9.8
Relative to sibling average	
(Equal to/less than average)	0.70
More than average	0.30
Decision maker(s) of migration	
(Child alone)	0.68
Parents and child/parents alone	0.32
Mean age	37.7
Gender and marital status	
(Married daughter)	0.48
Unmarried daughter	0.03
Married son	0.42
Unmarried son	0.07
Distance from parent	
(Walking distance)	0.05
Less than 3 hours by car	0.59
More than 3 hours by car	0.34
Missing/abroad	0.02
Elderly parents' or family's characteristics	
Gender and marital status	
(Married female)	0.23
Widowed/divorced female	0.42
Married male	0.29
Widowed/divorced male	0.06
Mean age	68.5
Mean number of co-residing children	0.56
No. of migrant sons	2.4
No. of migrant daughters	2.6
Education	
(Primary school or less)	0.64
Middle school	0.33
High school or more	0.03
Couple's mean income (10,000 won)	25.5
Couple's income missing	0.09
Ability to conduct daily activities	
(No difficulty)	0.24
Some difficulty	0.65
Severe difficulty	0.11
County 1	0.21
County 2	0.12
County 3	0.19
County 4	0.24
County 5	0.24
No. of cases	2,217

Note: Characteristics in parentheses are reference categories.

Source: Survey of Family Structure and Support Systems in Rural Areas.

Table 13.5. Determinants of migrant children's providing financial support to elderly parents: South Korea, 1993

Determinant	Binomial logit, regular or irregular support		Multinomial logit			
			Regular support		Irregular support	
	beta	s.e.	beta	s.e.	beta	s.e.
Migrant children's characteristics						
Income, imputed	0.011**	(0.003)	0.020**	(0.006)	0.010**	(0.003)
Education						
Mean years (all siblings)	0.067*	(0.026)	0.148*	(0.060)	0.061*	(0.026)
Relative to sibling average						
(Equal to/less than average)						
More than average	−0.140	(0.115)	−0.089	(0.253)	−0.144	(0.117)
Decision maker(s) of migration						
(Child alone)						
Parents and child/parents alone	0.280*	(0.111)	0.174	(0.252)	0.293**	(0.112)
Age	0.003	(0.008)	0.003	(0.018)	0.003	(0.008)
Gender and marital status						
(Married daughter)						
Unmarried daughter	0.691*	(0.340)	2.802**	(0.677)	0.488	(0.362)
Married son	0.830**	(0.125)	2.371**	(0.314)	0.722**	(0.127)
Unmarried son	−0.175	(0.244)	1.395*	(0.578)	−0.277	(0.249)
Distance from parent						
(Walking distance)						
Less than 3 hours by car	0.012	(0.206)	−0.617	(0.426)	0.054	(0.209)
More than 3 hours by car	−0.042	(0.217)	−1.023*	(0.458)	0.032	(0.220)
Missing/abroad	−1.58**	(0.451)	−1.185	(0.817)	−1.68**	(0.481)
Elderly parents' or family's characteristics						
Gender and marital status						
(Married female)						
Unmarried female	0.087	(0.132)	0.056	(0.294)	0.089	(0.133)
Married male	−0.274	(0.148)	−1.035*	(0.333)	−0.219	(0.150)
Unmarried male	0.229	(0.237)	0.381	(0.491)	0.204	(0.241)
Age: 60	0.056*	(0.027)	0.149*	(0.068)	0.049	(0.027)
Age: 60 squared	−0.002	(0.001)	−0.005	(0.003)	−0.001	(0.001)
No. of coresiding children	−0.161*	(0.078)	−0.857**	(0.210)	−0.116	(0.079)
No of migrant sons	0.018	(0.041)	−0.114	(0.093)	0.027	(0.042)
No of migrant daughters	−0.084*	(0.036)	0.048	(0.084)	−0.094*	(0.037)
Education						
(Primary school or less)						
Middle school	0.587**	(0.128)	1.521**	(0.284)	0.513**	(0.129)
High school or more	0.152	(0.337)	1.505*	(0.561)	−0.004	(0.346)
Couple's income	−0.004**	(0.001)	−0.014**	(0.004)	−0.003*	(0.001)
Couple's income missing	0.754**	(0.185)	−0.973	(0.764)	0.821**	(0.186)
Ability to conduct daily activities						
(No difficulty)						
Some difficulty	−0.022	(0.119)	0.268	(0.272)	−0.050	(0.120)
Severe difficulty	−0.647**	(0.179)	−0.416	(0.432)	−0.678**	(0.182)
Constant	−1.092*	(0.509)	−7.15**	(1.18)	−1.110*	(0.521)
Mean of dependent variables	0.610		0.054		0.556	
No. of cases	2,217		2,217			
Log-likelihood	−1,315		−1,645			

* $p < 0.05$, ** $p < 0.01$.

Note: The equations include four community dummy variables. Characteristics in parentheses are reference categories.

Source: Survey of Family Structure and Support Systems in Rural Areas.

The analysis also explores how parents' investment in their children and children's resources affect the probability of children's financial transfers to parents when the parents become old. Table 13.5 shows that the mean number of years of education among all siblings has a positive effect on the probability of transfers from a migrant child to elderly parents, and that the migrant child's relative educational status among siblings does not have any additional effect on such transfers. Children's own income has a significant positive effect on the incidence of financial transfers to elderly parents.

Further analysis, presented in Table 13.6, confirms that parents' investment, represented by children's education, and children's resources (income) show different patterns of variation within and between families. The table presents five binomial logit models in which the children's income and education variables are specified differently while all other variables are held constant like those in Table 13.5. When children's own income is controlled, their relative income status among siblings does not have any additional effect (Model 1). When children's relative income status and the average income among siblings are considered together, the sibling average does not have a significant effect on the incidence of financial transfers to parents, whereas higher than average status has a positive effect (Model 2). Children's education displays

Table 13.6. Five binomial logit models for the effects of children's education and income on the provision of financial support to elderly parents: South Korea, 1993

Income/education	Change income variables		Change education variables		
	Model 1, beta (s.e.)	Model 2, beta (s.e.)	Model 3, beta (s.e.)	Model 4, beta (s.e.)	Model 5, beta (s.e.)
Income					
Own income	0.011** (0.003)	—	0.011** (0.003)	0.011** (0.003)	0.011** (0.003)
Average income (all siblings)	—	0.007 (0.032)	—	—	—
Relative to sibling average					
(Equal to/less than average)					
More than average	0.009 (0.031)	0.219* (0.109)	—	—	—
Education					
Own years of schooling	—	—	0.020 (0.021)	−0.021 (0.026)	0.042 (0.023)
Average years (all siblings)	0.066* (0.026)	0.079* (0.032)	—	0.087** (0.032)	—
Relative to sibling average					
(Equal to/less than average)					
More than the average	−0.150 (0.118)	−0.085 (0.117)	—	—	−0.279* (0.129)
Log-likelihood	−1,315	−1,320	−1,320	−1,316	−1,317

* $p < 0.05$, ** $p < 0.01$.

Note: The explanatory variables other than child's income and education are the same as in Table 13.5.

Source: Survey of Family Structure and Support Systems in Rural Areas.

a quite different result. Contrary to expectation, after income is controlled, children's own years of schooling have no significant effect on the incidence of financial transfers to parents (Model 3). If not controlled for income, children's own years of schooling have a positive effect, reflecting their income (results not shown). A surprising result is that, as shown in Table 13.5, the average number of years of schooling among siblings has an important effect on individual children's provision of financial assistance to parents (Model 4). Because the sibling average is important but children's own years of schooling are not, when one examines children's own educational status with an indicator of their relative status among siblings, having a higher than average educational status is negatively related to providing financial assistance to elderly parents (Model 5). The reason for this result is that when children's own education is held constant, the sibling averages among children with higher relative status are lower than the sibling averages among those with lower relative status.

In sum, for both children's income and education, relative status among siblings does not have any *net* effect on children's provision of financial assistance to their elderly parents. Adult children's education displays a significant family effect, whereas children's income does not. Although individual years of schooling make up sibling averages, those averages influence children's behaviour independently of individual schooling. It is possible that the effect of schooling on transfer behaviour results from knowledge or attitudes acquired in the course of formal education; but this interpretation is not very plausible because individual schooling does not have any significant effect on the provision of support—only sibling averages do. Sibling averages may reflect parents' target levels of education for their children, whereas variations among siblings result from differences in ability or values. Thus the results seem to suggest that parental socialization has effects on children's propensity to provide support, lending credence to the hypothesis that parents plan for long-term transactions, and that a long-term arrangement of parents' investment and children's repayment operates collectively among family members.

Children are more likely to provide financial assistance to elderly parents who were involved in the children's decision to migrate than to parents who were not. Parents' involvement in children's migration decisions implies their help with the migration process. The result of the multinomial analysis suggests that adult children who receive such help repay it in the form of old-age support.

The analysis also considers parents' characteristics. A corollary of the hypothesis that parents invest in their children, expecting repayment in old age, is that adult children will give more support if their parents are needy. The results in Table 13.5 generally support this assumption. Both regular and irregular financial assistance from children is negatively related to parents' income. Moreover, migrant children are significantly less likely to provide support to rural parents who co-reside with a larger number of children than to those who live alone or with a smaller number of children. Parents' greater age increases the probability of financial assistance from migrant children.

Parents' education and health status, however, show unexpected results. Adult children are more likely to give support to parents with a middle-school education than to parents with a primary-school or less education, and they are more likely to give support to healthy parents than to parents who have severe difficulty in conducting daily activities. These results may suggest that self-interest motivates children's financial transfers to parents, causing them to give less to parents who have not the resources to reciprocate. In rural areas, however, where family farming is the main industry, elderly parents' education may not necessarily indicate their level of wealth or permanent income. It may indicate instead their ability to adopt a strategy for maximizing the family's well-being and to plan corporate relations between generations. Similarly, more educated parents may be more effective in instilling in their children a sense of obligation to support the parents in old age.[3]

Compared with the other results that confirm the hypothesis of need-based support, the negative effect of parents' poor health on children's financial support is rather puzzling. However, some studies have found that self-reported health is endogenous to the social and economic well-being of respondents: those who are better off tend to report more health problems than those who are less well off.

Another possibility is that the result is related to the national health insurance programme that South Korea adopted in the late 1980s. Owing to a government subsidy for rural areas, premiums for rural households are very low, about US$7 a month (ROK, Economic Planning Board 1994), and the insurance pays up to 80 per cent of the cost of out-patient care for rural residents. The monetary needs of the rural elderly with poor health may therefore not be great, although the quality of medical services is generally lower in rural than in urban areas. Parents in poor health are probably not able to provide as much help in the form of services to their children as can healthy parents and may therefore receive less financial assistance from them in return. It is therefore possible that parents in poor health maintain support exchanges with only a few of their children, who may provide a larger amount of assistance. This interpretation is consistent with another finding, from the multivariate analysis of the elderly-parents sample, that elderly parents' poor health does not affect the likelihood of assistance from some migrant children but that it has a substantial negative effect on the likelihood of assistance from *all* migrant children (results not shown). In sum, the results based on parents' health status lend support for the mutual aid model rather than the self-interested exchange model and are therefore compatible with the hypothesis of need-based transfers.

Controlling for unobserved family factors: fixed-effects logit model

The results from both the descriptive and the multivariate analyses suggest that family-level characteristics influence migrant children's decisions to provide support for elderly parents. We have seen that various parental characteristics

Table 13.7. Fixed-effects model for determinants of migrant children's providing financial support to elderly parents: South Korea, 1993

Determinant	Binomial logit[a]		Fixed effects, binomial logit	
	beta	s.e.	beta	s.e.
Migrant children's characteristics				
Income, imputed	0.011**	(0.003)	0.027**	(0.005)
Education				
Mean years (all siblings)	0.067*	(0.026)	—	—
Relative to sibling average				
(Equal to/less than average)				
More than average	−0.140	(0.115)	−0.081	(0.199)
Decision maker(s) of migration				
(Child alone)				
Parents and child/parents alone	0.280*	(0.111)	−0.036	(0.222)
Age	0.003	(0.008)	0.024	(0.013)
Gender and marital status				
(Married daughter)				
Unmarried daughter	0.691*	(0.340)	1.643**	(0.560)
Married son	0.830**	(0.125)	1.336**	(0.199)
Unmarried son	−0.175	(0.244)	0.277	(0.395)
Distance from parent				
(Walking distance)				
Less than 3 hours by car	0.012	(0.206)	−0.503	(0.324)
More than 3 hours by car	−0.042	(0.217)	−0.927**	(0.357)
Missing/abroad	−1.58**	(0.451)	−3.58**	(0.865)
Elderly parents' or family's characteristics				
Gender and marital status				
(Married female)				
Unmarried female	0.087	(0.132)		
Married male	−0.274	(0.148)		
Unmarried male	0.229	(0.237)		
Age: 60	0.056*	(0.027)		
Age: 60 squared	−0.002	(0.001)		
No. of co-residing children	−0.161*	(0.078)		
No. of migrant sons	0.018	(0.041)		
No. of migrant daughters	−0.084*	(0.036)		
Education				
(Primary school or less)				
Middle school	0.587**	(0.128)		
High school or more	0.152	(0.337)		
Couple income	−0.004**	(0.001)		
Couple income missing	0.754**	(0.185)		
Ability to conduct daily activities				
(No difficulty)				
Some difficulty	−0.022	(0.119)		
Severe difficulty	−0.647**	(0.179)		
Constant	−1.092*	(0.509)		
Mean of dependent variables	0.610		0.610	
No. of cases (families)	2,217		2,176 (486)[b]	
Log-likelihood	−1,315		−343	

* $p < 0.05$, ** $p < 0.01$.

[a] The equation is the same as in Table 13.5.

[b] The fixed-effects analysis excludes one-child families.

Note: Characteristics in parentheses are reference categories.

Source: Survey of Family Structure and Support Systems in Rural Areas.

affect children's financial transfers and that the mean educational level of all adult children in the family is positively related to individual children's financial transfers. In addition to those observed family characteristics, the analysis explores whether any unobserved family factors influence children's transfer decisions. The fixed-effects model controls for both observed and unobserved family factors by assuming a separate intercept for each family. The equation upon which Table 13.7 is based therefore excludes family-level variables, and the coefficients show variations among siblings within families. The fixed-effects model is estimated only for the binomial logit.

The differences between the fixed-effects model and those in the first column of Table 13.7 are due to unobserved family effects. Some of those differences are important. First, the effect of parents' involvement in children's migration decision becomes non-significant in the fixed-effects model. This result indicates that some unobserved family traits, such as parents' preferences—not individual children's traits—explain parents' help with children's migration, children's repayment of parents' investment, or both. Relative educational status among siblings remains non-significant. On the other hand, the effects of migrant children's income, gender, marital status, age, and distance from parents all become stronger in the fixed-effects model. That is, those characteristics are more important within families, but some unobserved family traits operate across families, neutralizing the effects of those characteristics in the cross-family sample. Moreover, the pattern of sub-group differences in the fixed-effects model is similar to that in the regular-assistance equation in Table 13.5, suggesting that those neutralizing unobserved family traits operate mainly for irregular financial assistance. This result is plausible because the majority of adult children provide irregular assistance and in many cases the assistance from all siblings is irregular. Only a small number of adult children provide regular assistance, and that fact distinguishes them from their siblings within families.

Discussion and Conclusion

This chapter has examined the determinants of adult children's financial assistance to their elderly parents in rural areas of South Korea and explored the hypothesis that during a period of rapid economic growth families maximize their well-being by engaging in long-term exchanges between generations. Contrary to the modernization hypothesis, which posits that the transformation of an economy based on family farming into one based on industry weakens the economic relationship between generations, studies in many newly industrializing Asian countries report high levels of intergenerational financial support. Lingering traditional values alone do not seem to explain the persistence of intergenerational support.

Data from KIHASA's 1993 Survey of Family Structure and Support Systems in Rural Areas support the corporate group model, which hypothesizes that adult children's financial assistance to elderly parents is a repayment of parents' earlier investment in them. Parents' support for children's schooling and their help with children's migration increase the likelihood of adult children's financial assistance to elderly parents, after income is controlled. The model assumes that parents plan such long-term exchanges to maximize the well-being of both generations; that is, while investing in their children's future financial success, parents may also be instilling in them a sense of obligation to repay that investment. The KIHASA data indicate that more schooling among all children in a family has a positive effect on individual children's provision of financial assistance to elderly parents, but an individual child's own years of schooling does not have such an effect. I interpret this positive effect of sibling education to be a reflection of the values that parents who invested in their children instilled in them. The effects of parental socialization should be common to all children within the family, unlike knowledge or attitudes acquired through formal education, the effects of which should be limited to the individual. The positive effect of average sibling education on assistance to elderly parents is consistent with the hypothesis that parents plan for a long-term exchange with their children.

The findings on the effect of parental involvement in children's migration also supports the importance of parents' long-term planning. A comparison of the ordinary and fixed-effects logit results has shown that a positive relationship between parents' help with migration and children's financial assistance exists between families but not within families. This finding suggests some unobserved family-level effects of parents' decisions to help their children migrate or to enforce the children's repayment of such help. Siblings' relative status in education or in parental help with migration does not affect a child's likelihood of providing financial assistance to the parents.

Although these exchanges of parental investment and children's repayment take place mostly at the family level, some demographic characteristics of children are responsible for differences within the family. In particular, adult children's gender and marital status, which have traditionally defined positions within the Korean family, are still important determinants of financial assistance to elderly parents even after differences among the children in parents' investment and in the children's earnings are taken into consideration. Married sons and unmarried daughters are providers of financial assistance, especially regular assistance, to their elderly parents. This result confirms gender differences in contracts of intergenerational exchange: parents expect quick returns from daughters before the daughters join their husbands' families. However, the result obtains after the analysis controls for the income of married daughters and their husbands, which is substantially higher than that of unmarried daughters. The gross effect of daughters' marital status is not significant.

A majority of elderly parents in rural South Korea receive financial assistance from their migrant children. During the year preceding the survey, 82 per cent of the respondents aged 60 or older who had at least one migrant child received regular or irregular financial assistance from their migrant children, and about one-half of those elderly recipients received assistance from all of their migrant children. As expected, parents who had lower income, were older, and did not live with their children were more likely to receive financial assistance from their migrant children than were those who had higher income, were younger, and lived with their children.

Economic growth in South Korea during the past few decades has been remarkable. For example, between 1970 and 1990, per capita GNP increased almost fourfold, savings increased even more, and the proportion of the labour force participating in agriculture decreased from 48 to 18 per cent. In that context, even parents with meagre resources placed the highest priority on investing in their children, such as providing for their education and professional training or subsidizing their migration to urban areas for better employment opportunities, to maximize the earnings of the extended family. The analysis has revealed that parents who invest heavily in their children are more likely than those who do not to receive support from them in old age.

The data also show that although parental investment pays dividends in the form of children's support in old age, this investment-repayment linkage is not automatic. The strong family effects in children's repayment suggest that parents who invest more in their children than others also inculcate in their children a sense of obligation to support the parents in old age. In other words, the long-term exchange of resources between generations takes place in a particular context, one combining rapid economic expansion and the traditional value of filial piety. The inverse relationship between children's geographic distance from parents and their likelihood of providing financial assistance to the parents suggests that such assistance is determined not only by parental investment or by children's positions within the family, but also by other factors.

This type of intergenerational economic exchange may be short-lived. On the one hand, in a society undergoing rapid economic expansion, the economic status of the elderly population may improve and their needs for support may decrease in a short time. On the other, a slowdown of economic growth rates means lower returns to parents' investment in their children. As families achieve some level of affluence, the interest of both generations in maximizing the earnings of the extended family may have less importance than their desire for independence. The erosion of traditional Confucian values will accelerate this change. Emerging public programmes, such as a national pension plan and health insurance, will make intergenerational economic ties less necessary. Nevertheless, as long as wage differentials between urban and rural areas persist and cohort gaps in socio-economic status remain, some intergenerational exchange will continue, especially between rural elderly and their migrant children.

Elderly parents in rural South Korea during the 1990s seem to be situated in an exemplary context for receiving support from their migrant children, although migration has made co-residence with adult children less common than heretofore. Moreover, today's elderly Korean parents have the largest number of surviving children ever recorded because of high fertility several decades ago and declining mortality since then. This study has found that having a large number of migrant children does not necessarily weaken the long-term exchange relationship between generations.

Notes

I thank Eung-Suk Kim, Sae-Kwon Kong, and Seung-Kwon Kim of the Korea Institute for Health and Social Affairs for providing me with the survey data for this research and for their encouragement. I also thank my colleagues at the East-West Center's Program on Population and the participants of the Seminar on Intergenerational Economic Relations and Demographic Change, especially Jeffrey Nugent, for their helpful comments on earlier drafts of this chapter.

1. e.g. educational wage differentials are much larger in South Korea than in Western countries or in Japan. Among workers in Korean firms with ten or more employees, the wages of college graduates were twice as high as those of high-school graduates throughout the 1970s and 1980s. In contrast, the ratio was 1.3 in Japan in 1986 (Yoon 1991).
2. The equation of the fixed-effects logit model is of the form $\ln(\frac{p_{it}}{1-p_{it}}) = a_i + bx_{it}$, where subscript i represents family and t represents the individual child. Thus p_{it} is the probability that child t of family i provides financial assistance to her parent, and x_{it} is a vector of the child's characteristics. The only difference from an ordinary logit model is that a separate intercept, a_i, is assumed for members in family i. However, a_i's are not of any interest and not obtained in the actual estimation.
3. A model (not shown) with interaction terms between parents' education and income shows that the main effect of parents' having at least a high-school education is positive; but the 'high-school or more' education category is highly responsive to income, showing a significant negative effect of income. When interaction terms are not included, the 'high-school or more' category does not show a significant positive effect on children's propensity to provide old-age support.

14 The Effects of Income and Wealth on Time and Money Transfers between Parents and Children

Joseph G. Altonji, Fumio Hayashi, and Laurence Kotlikoff

In this chapter we examine the effects of income and wealth on transfers of money and time between individuals and their parents and in-laws, using US data. Our purpose is to contribute to a growing body of evidence on the effects of differences in income, assets, and current income relative to permanent income on the direction and quantity of transfers. (See Hill and Soldo (1993) and Shoeni (1993*c*) for recent surveys of the literature on transfers and Hill, Morgan, and Heroz (1993) for a descriptive analysis of transfer data from the Panel Study of Income Dynamics.) We estimate the effects of siblings' incomes on the amounts received from and given to parents. We provide the first estimates of the effects of a married person's parents' income, relative to the income of the person's parents in-law, on the amounts given to and received from the two sets of parents. Also considered is how the relative incomes of divorced parents influence transfers to and from adult children. Finally, we examine the interrelationship between time transfers and money transfers and also the effects of distance on the two types of transfers. Our results have a number of implications for alternative theories of transfers.

Our analysis is based on the 1968–88 waves of the Panel Study of Income Dynamics (PSID), conducted by the Institute for Social Research at the University of Michigan in Ann Arbor, Michigan. We use data on a special survey about family transfers that was conducted as part of the 1988 wave of the PSID, along with panel data on the income, wealth, health status, employment outcomes, and household composition of a matched set of parents and their adult children. We are also able to match data on siblings. The 1988 PSID transfer supplement provides information on time and money transfers to and from the parents of the household head and spouse (if a spouse was present). Furthermore, the respondents provided information on the income, wealth, and health status of both sets of parents even if one or both sets of parents were not PSID sample members.

These data items make the PSID an unusually attractive data set for examining family transfers, for several reasons. First, most theoretical models of family economic exchange suggest that the incomes of all immediate relatives should affect transfer patterns, but few data sets contain information on the income of most family members. Second, the fact that the PSID data include several years of income data for many sample members and their parents enables us to obtain more precise measures of permanent income measures than are available in most other data sets.[1] The panel data on income permit a sharper distinction to be made between current income and permanent income than is usually possible and enable us to examine the response of transfers to shocks, such as unemployment. Third, information in the PSID about transfers of time as well as money permits us to examine more directly the issue of whether money transfers from parents to children are driven by altruism or exchange motives. The data set also contains some information on 'help from relatives' in years prior to 1988, as well as information on bequests received and expectations about future bequests.[2]

In the following sections we review the theoretical arguments about the relationship between income and transfers of time and money, discuss the sample and some potential problems with the transfer data, present descriptive statistics on differences between householders who do and do not receive transfers of money and time, and present a multivariate analysis of the effects of income, wealth and distance on transfers between parents and children. We also consider how other family members influence who gives and who receives, focusing on the relative incomes of siblings, differences in the incomes of parents and in-laws, and differences in the incomes of divorced parents.

We have six main results. First, parental income has a positive effect on the probability and the amount of money transfers from the parents to the child and a negative effect on transfers of money from the child to the parents. The child's income reduces the probability and amount of money transfers from the parents to the child and raises the probability and amount of money transfers from the child to the parents. Second, the magnitudes of the income effects on the size of the transfer are much smaller than the magnitudes implied by the basic altruism model. Third, children whose current income is low relative to their permanent income are less likely to give and more likely to receive monetary transfers, a finding that provides support for the view that liquidity constraints and insurance influence the timing of monetary transfers. Fourth, the links between the parents' and the child's incomes and time transfers are relatively weak in both directions. The parents' permanent income is negatively related to the number of hours that children spend helping parents, which seems inconsistent with the view that time and money transfers are best viewed as exchange. Fifth, we find that geographic distance from the parents has a strong negative effect on time transfers to or from the parents but not on money transfers. We argue that this pattern is inconsistent with a simple exchange model of money transfers. Finally, our fixed-effects analyses of the relative incomes of siblings, parents and parents-in-law, and divorced parents all confirm that money transfers flow from rich to poor within the family, while the direction of time transfers is only weakly related to income differences. They also confirm that time transfers decline with geographic distance but money transfers do not.

Theoretical Background

To provide a context for our empirical analysis, it is useful to review briefly the theoretical arguments on the relationship between time and money transfers and current income, permanent income, wages, and assets. (For a comprehensive survey of the theoretical literature, see Cigno 1991.) Transfers between a parent's and a child's household should be influenced by the resources and needs of the child's siblings, in-laws (if the child is married), and other relatives. We explore these interdependencies in our empirical work, using relatively straightforward econometric methods. Exchange models imply that a decline in time transfers as physical distance from parents increases are associated with a decline in money transfers, whereas in an altruism model money transfers may be unrelated to distance.

Models of transfers based on altruism and exchange

We estimate equations of the following form:

$$P(R_j < 0) = P^{Rj}(Y_p, Y_k, Y_s, Y_{pt}, Y_{kt}; X) \tag{14.1}$$

$$R_j = R^j(Y_p, Y_k, Y_s, Y_{pt}, Y_{kt}; X, u) \tag{14.2}$$

$$P(S_j > 0) = P^{Sj}(Y_p, Y_k, Y_s, Y_{pt}, Y_{kt}; X) \tag{14.3}$$

$$S_j = S^j(Y_p, Y_k, Y_s, Y_{pt}, Y_{kt}; X, u) \tag{14.4}$$

The variables R and S denote time and money transfers, respectively, in a particular year (1987 in our case). The subscript j has the value p when the transfer is from the parent to the child and k when the transfer is in the opposite direction. $P(R_j > 0)$ is the probability that a money transfer occurs, and R_j is the amount if R_j is positive. $P(S_j > 0)$ and S_j have similar definitions. Y_p and Y_k are measures of the permanent endowment of the parent and the child, such as permanent income or earnings. In some specifications we include the difference between current and permanent income (Y_{jt}), and in others we also include measures of the permanent income of other relatives (such as siblings), denoted here by Y_s. The vector X contains a set of control variables and u is an error component.

The literature on transfers has emphasized six motives for time and money transfers. The first is altruism, by which we mean that the parents' utility depends upon the utility of their children. In the two-sided case, the child's utility depends on the utility of the parents. The second motive is exchange. In this case, the parents 'buy' time help (that is, help requiring an investment of time), attention, respect, visits, etc., from indifferent children, paying with money or perhaps time help. The third, fourth, and fifth motives fall into the categories of both altruism and exchange and have implications for how transitory variation in income affects money transfers. Insurance, the third motive, serves as a hedge against income variation. The fourth motive is access to credit: the family may act as a substitute for credit markets and provide money transfers when the current income of one of its members falls below expected future income and the family does not have assets. The fifth motive, for time transfers, is comparative advantage among the family members. In an exchange model, family members will pay for time transfers with money; but in an altruism model, comparative advantage will influence time transfers even though time donors will not necessarily be compensated with time or money. The sixth motive is 'warm glow' (Andreoni 1989). Parents may receive utility from helping their children with time or money that may be partially independent of the needs of the children.

Empirical implications of alternative transfer models

Initially, we assume that our measures of endowment (Y_k, Y_p, Y_s) are independent of the market value of time or that the market value of time is held constant. Our purpose is to observe the effects of differences in wage rates on transfer patterns. First we consider the effects of Y_k and Y_p on $P(R_p > 0)$ and on R_p.

Altruism models imply that money transfers flow from rich to poor. Consequently, they imply that $\partial P(R_p > 0)/\partial Y_p > 0, \partial P(R_p > 0)/\partial Y_k < 0$, and the opposite sign pattern for $P(R_k > 0)$. Simple exchange models such as that of Cox (1987) also imply this pattern. The 'warm glow' model implies that $\partial P(R_p > 0)/\partial Y_p > 0$, assuming that utility from the act of giving transfers is a normal good. It does not have clear implications for the sign of $\partial P(R_p > 0)/\partial Y_k$. Next we consider the effects of Y_k and Y_p on the level of R_p. With everything else held constant, in the altruism regime the child's income, Y_k, has a negative effect on the level of R_p, given $R_p > 0$, as well as a negative effect on $P(R_p > 0)$. In the exchange regime, however, Y_k may have a positive, a negative, or no effect on the level of R_p when R_p is greater than 0. Cox's (1987) analysis implies that the sign depends upon the responsiveness of the parents' demand for services to the implicit price of services. The intuition is that the larger Y_k, the larger is the 'bribe' that is necessary for the parent to induce the child to provide services. Cox uses the potential difference in the implications of the two models as the basis for testing altruism versus exchange models. In his empirical work he focuses on R_p and finds that Y_k reduces $P(R_p > 0)$ and increases $E(R_p \mid R_p > 0)$. He interprets the latter result as support for the exchange model of transfers (see also Cox and Rank 1992). However, in Altonji, Hayashi, and Kotlikoff (1995) we show that if one does not control for heterogeneity in preferences (represented by u in the above equations), then Y_k may have a positive sign even if transfers are motivated by altruism.[3] The warm-glow motive seems consistent with $\partial R_p/\partial Y_p > 0$ if we assume that giving transfers is a normal good.

Next we consider the effects of other relatives' income. Altruism leads to gifts from the least needy to the most needy. The income of a child's siblings should increase the probability and size of parental transfers of money to that child and should reduce money transfers from that child to the parent. Consequently, altruism models imply that Y_s will reduce R_k, where s refers to a sibling. We are also interested in learning whether the relative incomes of parents and parents-in-law affect which set of parents gives to or receives money transfers from a married couple, and whether the effect is the same when the parents are divorced. The analysis of parents and parents-in-law raises the question of whether, for example, the parents of the wife are indirectly supporting the parents of the husband. This can happen if some of the money given to the wife is passed on to the husband's parents. Similar issues arise for divorced parents. The theory is less clear on how the availability of resources from other relatives influences the link between money and transfers.

A third issue concerns the effects of income and wealth on time transfers. In a model with one-sided altruism (from the parents to the child) and exogenous endowments that are unrelated to the market price of time, Cox (1987) shows that the effects of parents' income and the child's income on S_k are equal in sign and magnitude but may be positive or negative. (Cox makes clear that S_k in his model is time use that does not have close market substitutes.) In his model parents cannot obtain a positive value of S_k when R_p is zero because the child's utility depends negatively on S_k. If children are altruistic towards their parents, the children's utility may depend positively on S_k over some range. In this case children may choose to provide a positive level of S_k even though R_p is zero. We find this to be very common in the data. We suspect (but have not shown) that there are no clear predictions from the altruism model in the more realistic case of two-way altruism once corner solutions in money transfers are taken into account. We conjecture that Cox's result that Y_k and Y_p have identical effects continues to hold if there are operative money transfers in either direction, but that there are no restrictions on the effects of Y_k and Y_p when money transfers are zero.

Exchange models of the type discussed in Bernheim, Shleifer, and Summers (1985) and Cox (1987) imply that services from a child to his or her parents will be positively related to the parents' wealth and income and negatively related to the income and wealth of the child. The intuition is that the increase in Y_k raises the price of services to the parent, whereas Y_p has a positive income effect and S_k is a normal good from the parents' perspective. This suggests that the probability and the amount of a time transfer from the parents to the child will be positively related to Y_p and negatively related to Y_k. However, both studies view 'services' that parents desire from children, such as affection, phone calls, or family visits, as services for which there are not good market substitutes.

To the extent that good market substitutes exist for the time help reported in the PSID, and that the demand for services with good market substitutes is more income-elastic than the demand for services without market substitutes, wealthier parents may place less value on time help from children. This weakens the negative relationship between Y_k and S_k even if the market wages of both the parents and the child are held constant.[4] If we assume that market wage rates are not related to the components of S that do not have good market substitutes, in both the exchange and the altruism regimes a simultaneous increase in the wages of the child and the parents should induce substitution away from the provision of time for services that have good market substitutes.

Our analysis considers the effects of market wages on transfers. Differences in market wages may lead to exchanges of money for time help based on comparative advantage, even if one controls for permanent income. One might expect the difference in wages between the parent and the child to be positively related to money transfers and negatively related to time transfers. In our analysis we investigate this possibility, using models that control for wealth. Unfortunately, it is difficult to distinguish the substitution effects of wages from the income effects.

A fourth issue that we examine is the interrelationship among transfers. To the extent that differences exist among extended families in the strength of altruism, one might expect a positive correlation between time transfers from parent to child and from child to parent and also a positive correlation between time transfers and a flow of money, regardless of the direction of the money flow. In close-knit families, time will flow in both directions and money will flow from the least to the most financially needy. To the extent that a household's marginal utility of income is positively correlated with the marginal utility of services received from relatives, time and money flows may go in the same direction.

Exchange models are also consistent with a positive correlation in time flows from parents to children and from children to parents, since parents may use both money and time to 'buy' services. In the exchange model, however, one would expect money from parents to be positively correlated with time transfers from children, with parents buying time transfers from their children. By the same token, money transfers from the children might be used to buy time transfers from the parents (for example, babysitting), leading to a positive correlation between money transfers from children and time transfers from parents.

Our analysis attempts to distinguish between the two models by using siblings to analyse how relative dependence of money flows from parents to children and time flows from children to parents depends on distance from the parents. Time transfers should decline with distance in either the altruism model or the exchange model because distance raises the costs of such transfers. Our idea is that if money flows are an implicit payment for services, then money flows should also decline with distance from the parent. (Although one might object that distance from parents is endogenous and related to the strength of the altruistic link between particular parents and children, it is not clear why a correlation between distance and preferences would influence time transfers more than money transfers.)

Fifth, the presence of siblings and other dependants of the parents can affect transfers in both positive and negative ways. Parental resources per child are negatively related to the number of children This suggests that the odds of receiving parental time and money transfers and the size of the transfers will be negatively related to number of siblings, regardless of the motive for transfers. Less clear are the effects of the number of siblings on total transfers provided by the parents. They would seem to depend upon the way in which the number of children enters the utility function of the parents. Moreover, heterogeneity in preferences that influence fertility choices may be related to heterogeneity in preferences that influence aid to independent children.

The number of potential donors to the parents increases with the number of children. This suggests that the probability and the size of a time and money transfer from a particular child to the parents will be negatively related to the number of children if one controls for parental income and needs. In an exchange framework with one-sided altruism we would also expect a negative relationship between the number of children and the odds that a particular child will make a time transfer, although this hypothesis may be sensitive to the form of the parent's utility function and to how the number of children affects bargaining between parents and children.

The needs of the child's grandparents for market and non-market help and their ability to supply such help to the parents or the child will influence flows of time and money from the parents to the child, just as competition from siblings should influence these flows. Our analysis investigates this hypothesis.

The PSID Data

Our data are from the 1988 PSID. We work with two sub-samples. The first, which we call the 'matched' sample, contains the records of parents and children from 1968 PSID families who were heads of household or wives of household heads at the time of the 1988 study. The second, referred to as the 'full' sample, consists of the records of all respondents who reported having living parents or in-laws.

For the matched sample we have annual information on the income, labour market activity, and family composition of the households containing matched parents. We also have information on their assets, health status, income, and other variables that was collected in years before 1988. Households in 1988 containing heads or wives who were children in the 1968 households are matched to the households of their parents. An observation consists of one such matched pair. Given that a child's mother and father may live in separate households, each child may appear in one or two records. Parents with more than one child appear in as many records as they have respondent children. The distribution of parent household records by the number of children is summarized as follows:

No. of children per household	1	2	3	4	5	6	7	8	9	10
No. of observations	607	480	263	154	80	32	20	11	1	1

That is, 607 parent households have been matched to only one child, 480 have been matched to two children, etc. The sample contains 3,326 children who are matched to one-parent households and 235 children who are matched to two-parent households; they account for 3,796 of the 3,811 households in the matched sample.[5]

Only 1.6 per cent of the children who were heads of household and 0.7 per cent of the children who were wives in 1988 were students at the time of the survey. Among those who received parental transfers the percentages were 2.9 and 0.6. Only 4 per cent of the heads and 2 per cent of the wives were students in one or more years between 1986 and 1988. Thus parental transfers for schooling have little effect on our analysis.

Information about the full sample comes from the reports of the grown children in the 1988 transfer supplement. Each child can have up to four records (if both his own parents and his spouse's parents live in separate households). Because the parents in these records are not necessarily sample members, the information on their assets, income, labour market activity, and family composition is much more limited than in the matched sample. This sample is useful for testing hypotheses about the relationships of people who are related solely through the marriage of their children. It provides a larger sample of divorced or separated parents than does the matched sample (approximately 1,500 cases versus 238 cases).

Data on transfers between parents and children were gathered as a supplement to the 1988 PSID. Respondents were asked about time and money they had given to other individuals. Six questions were used to construct R_k, $R_k > 0$, S_k, $S_k > 0$, R_p, $R_p > 0$, and S_p, $S_p > 0$. They were asked in the order shown here but were not asked consecutively.

1. *In 1987, did (you/your family living there) give any money towards the support of anyone who was not living with you at the time? What is that person's name? What is his/her relationship to you? How much money was it?* [R_k, $R_k > 0$]
2. *Let's start by talking about help in the form of time, either in an emergency or with everyday activities such as errands, housework, small repairs to a car, or babysitting. In 1987, did (you/ your family living there) spend a lot of time helping your parents? About how many hours in 1987 did you or your family living there spend helping them?* [S_k, $S_k > 0$]
3. *How about time they spent helping you? In 1987, did your parents spend a lot of time helping you or your family living there? About how many hours did they spend helping (you/your family living there)?* [S_p, $S_p > 0$]
4. *During 1987, did (you/your family living there) receive any loans, gifts, or support worth $100 or more from your parents? About how much were those loans, gifts, or support worth altogether in 1987?* [R_p, $R_p > 0$]

5. *During 1987, did (you/your family living there) receive any loans, or support worth $100 or more from a friend or relative, besides parents, who was not living with you at the time?* [Respondents were then asked, 'From how many people did you receive help?' They were asked the name and the relationship of each person and 'About how much were (his/her) loans, gifts, or support worth altogether in 1987?']

6. *About help in the form of time, either in an emergency or with everyday activities such as errands, housework, small repairs to a car, or babysitting: in 1987 did (you/your family living there) spend a lot of time helping a friend or relative, besides parents, who was not living with you then? About how many hours in 1987 did you or your family living there spend helping them?*

Several points about these questions deserve mention. Question 1 and questions 5 and 6 are open ended about the relationship between the respondent and the donor or recipient, whereas 2, 3, and 4 single out the parents. The 'support received' questions (4 and 5) ask about loans, gifts, or support worth more than $100. Question 1 asks only about money. We argue in Appendix A that these differences may be partly responsible for the fact that the percentage of individuals who reported giving monetary support to their parents (2.3 per cent) was much lower than the percentage who reported giving time (29.5 per cent) or receiving either time or money (28.6 and 19.4 per cent, respectively). This conclusion is based on a comparison of information on R_p and S_p, which is based on the responses by the children to questions 4 and 3, with the responses of the parents to questions 5 and 6, and also on a comparison of the information based on the above questions with information on income received from relatives that is based on another set of questions in the PSID.

We rely on the children's reports of transfers. However, we believe that money transfers from children to parents may be understated relative to money transfers from parents to children and time transfers in both directions. One must therefore be careful in comparing the magnitudes of coefficients in the equations for money transfers to and from parents. A thorough study of the pattern of responses to the various questions about transfers deserves a high research priority.

A key variable used in our analysis is the permanent household income of individuals. This requires a history of family incomes and as such is available only for members of PSID sample households. Thus we use this measure only in the matched sample. To construct this variable, we estimated gender-specific regressions of log family income against a fourth-order polynomial in age, a set of marital-status dummies, year dummies, and counts of the number of children. We computed the mean of the residuals from the regression for each person and added that to the prediction from the regression for a person of age 40 who was married and had no children. We included all years of data in which persons were a head of household or the wife of the head. Consequently, in the case of divorce the data for women include information from the years in which they were married as well as the later years, but the regressions control for marital status. We experiment with a variety of alternatives in constructing these measures, but a measure that is independent of marital status and other family demographics is a good place to start.[6] We call the permanent income Y_p in the case of parents and Y_k in the case of children. In Altonji *et al.* (1995) we experiment with a third-order auto-regressive model to form an index of permanent income, obtaining similar results.

Family income may reflect the asset income from past transfers, and therefore we also experiment with measures of permanent labour earnings of the husband and wife and with measures of their permanent wage rates. We defer a discussion of those variables to the results section.

Descriptive Statistics on Transfers

Because the 1988 PSID transfer supplement is a new data set, we begin our analysis with detailed descriptive statistics on transfers and their determinants, considering first the univariate distribution of transfers. We approximate a representative sample of independent children with one or more living parents by using the 1988 person weights presented in Tables 14.1 to 14.5. Statistics reported here are based on unweighted samples unless we explicitly indicate otherwise. The multivariate analyses are unweighted.[7]

Tables 14.1 and 14.2 report the mean probability of a transfer and the mean, median, standard deviation, and the fifth, twenty-fifth, seventy-fifth, and ninety-fifth percentiles of the distribution of positive transfers. They also present corresponding statistics for R_p and R_k divided by parental income in 1988 and by the income of the child in 1988. In Table 14.1 the results are based on the matched sample, and the parents are either the parents of the husband or the parents of the wife, depending upon whether the husband or the wife was a child in the original 1968 PSID sample. Table 14.2 presents results from the sample of PSID household heads and wives who indicated that they had living parents, regardless of whether those parents were members of the PSID sample. In both tables we aggregate transfers received from and given to parents living separately, so that each person with living parents appears only once in the sample used to compute the tables. (In practice, this makes little difference.)[8]

As shown in Table 14.1 for the matched sample, only 1.7 per cent of children give money to the parental household ($R_k > 0$). The unweighted fraction of parents who receive a transfer from at least one child is 0.043. The mean of R_k is \$22.6, whereas the mean and median of the R_k when $R_k > 0$ are \$1,325 and \$500, respectively. When $R_k > 0$, the median and ninety-fifth percentile of the ratio of R_k to current income of the parents are, respectively, 0.039 and 1.019. The median and ninety-fifth percentile of the ratio of R_k to the child's income are 0.016 and 0.148. Because R_k is positive for only 1.7 per cent of the child-parent pairs, the data on R_k suggest that few children have much of an effect on the current income of their parents.

Table 14.1. Distribution of positive transfers, matched sample: United States, 1987

Type of transfer/ratio	Fraction > 0	Mean	Mean > 0	Std. dev. > 0	Percentile					
					5th	25th	50th	75th	95th	100th
	(1)	(2)	(3)	(4)	(5)	(6)	(7)	(8)	(9)	(10)
Money transfers ($s), parent to child	0.240	444.06	1,851	5,153	100	200	500	1,200	6,000	50,000
Ratio to current income										
Child		0.020	0.081	0.218	0.000	0.006	0.018	0.051	0.372	2.314
Parent		0.012	0.051	0.185	0.000	0.004	0.013	0.035	0.189	3.084
Ratio to permanent income										
Child		0.009	0.038	0.099	0.000	0.004	0.009	0.023	0.157	0.957
Parent		0.006	0.024	0.062	0.000	0.003	0.007	0.017	0.089	0.659
Money transfers ($s), child to parent	0.017	22.64	1,325	1,920	150	200	500	1,500	7,000	10,000
Ratio to current income										
Child		0.001	0.039	0.060	0.000	0.007	0.016	0.034	0.148	0.331
Parent		0.003	0.171	0.309	0.000	0.018	0.039	0.125	1.019	1.269
Ratio to permanent income										
Child		0.000	0.023	0.036	0.000	0.004	0.010	0.023	0.106	0.191
Parent		0.001	0.033	0.053	0.000	0.007	0.013	0.030	0.178	0.407
Time transfers (hours)										
Parent to child	0.302	84.74	281	510	10	40	100	260	1,105	4,000
Child to parent	0.273	66.14	242	383	15	48	100	250	1,040	4,000

Note: Estimates are weighted, using the person weights of the children.

Source: PSID 1988.

Table 14.2. **Distribution of positive transfers, full sample: United States, 1987**

Type of transfer/ratio	Fraction > 0	Mean	Mean > 0	Std. dev. > 0	Percentile					
					5th	25th	50th	75th	95th	100th
	(1)	(2)	(3)	(4)	(5)	(6)	(7)	(8)	(9)	(10)
Money transfers ($s), parent to child	0.203	375.78	1,848	5,007	100	240	500	1,200	6,000	50,000
Ratio to current income										
Child		0.014	0.070	0.203	0.000	0.004	0.014	0.041	0.333	2.765
Parent		0.013	0.050	0.186	0.000	0.004	0.013	0.035	0.182	3.084
Ratio to permanent income										
Child		0.007	0.034	0.093	0.000	0.003	0.008	0.021	0.142	0.957
Parent		0.006	0.023	0.061	0.000	0.003	0.007	0.017	0.085	0.659
Money transfers ($s), child to parent	0.028	48.93	1,779	3,509	100	280	600	1,800	7,000	24,000
Ratio to current income										
Child		0.001	0.028	0.046	0.000	0.005	0.012	0.027	0.142	0.267
Parent		0.003	0.160	0.301	0.000	0.012	0.036	0.125	1.019	1.269
Ratio to permanent income										
Child		0.001	0.022	0.047	0.000	0.003	0.009	0.021	0.091	0.369
Parent		0.001	0.031	0.052	0.000	0.005	0.010	0.030	0.178	0.407
Time transfers (hours)										
Parent to child	0.235	66.38	282	503	10	40	100	260	1,161	4,000
Child to parent	0.273	80.18	293	493	15	50	104	300	1,095	4,000

Note: Estimates are weighted, using the person weights of the children.

Source: PSID 1988.

Twenty-four per cent of the children received money transfers from their parents. The overall mean transfer is \$444. The mean and median of the positive transfers are \$1,851 and \$500. When R_p is positive, the median and ninety-fifth percentile of the ratio of R_p to the child's 1988 income are 0.018 and 0.372 for the sample with positive income. Thus relatively few adult children are dependent upon their parents for a substantial part of their income.

In the full sample (Table 14.2), 2.8 per cent of the parent-child pairs report money transfers from the child to the parent, and 20.3 per cent of the parent-child pairs involve money transfers from parents to children. The difference in the ages between the children and their parents in the two samples may partly explain the difference in these percentages.

Help in the form of time is common in both directions. In the matched sample (Table 14.1), 27.3 per cent of the children report that they help their parents ($S_k > 0$). The mean of S_k is 66.1 hours. The mean and median among the positive cases are 242 and 100, respectively. The respondents report receiving help from their parents in 30.2 per cent of the cases ($S_p > 0$). The mean of S_p is 84.7 hours and the mean and median of the positive cases are 281 and 100 hours, respectively. Thus time help is quite substantial.

Table 14.3 presents weighted estimates, for the matched sample, of the probability of transfers and the mean amount given a positive transfer, by the permanent income decile of the parent. In column 2 the probability of a transfer from the parent to the child rises from 0.107 for the lowest decile to 0.225 in the fifth decile to 0.342 in the highest decile. The mean amount of the transfers also rises with parental income, from \$452 in the lowest decile to \$3,206 in the highest. In column 4 the probability of transfers from the child to the parent is much lower for parents above the sixth income decile than for parents below it: 0.011 and 0.005 for parents in the two highest deciles and 0.030 and 0.043 for children with parents in the two lowest deciles. However, the size of the amount, given a positive transfer, tends to be higher for parents in the highest income decile (column 5). (It should be noted that some parents who are estimated to have very high permanent incomes may have experienced negative income changes in the years just prior to the 1988 survey. Moreover, in many cases the means are based on only a few observations, given the low probability of a money transfer from the child to the parent.) Column 6 shows only a weak, negative relationship between parental income and the odds that children receive time help from their parents. Time transfers from children to parents drop from a probability of 0.380 with a mean of 303 hours in the lowest decile to 0.221 with a mean of 154 hours in the top decile (columns 8 and 9). Taken at face value, these simple tabulations do not support an 'exchange' interpretation in which money transfers from parents to children implicitly buy time transfers from children to parents.

Table 14.4 breaks out transfers by the income decile of the child's household using the weighted matched sample. Columns 2 and 3 show that the probability of a money transfer from the parent to the child changes little with the child's

Table 14.3. Probability of transfers and mean transfer amount by permanent income of the parent, based on weighted estimates from matched sample: United States, 1987

Permanent income decile of the parent	Average income ($s) (1)	Probability of money transfer, parent to child (2)	Av. money transfer, parent to child if > 0 ($s) (3)	Probability of money transfer, child to parent (4)	Av. money transfer, child to parent if > 0 ($s) (5)	Probability of time transfer, parent to child (6)	Av. time transfer, parent to child if > 0 (hours) (7)	Probability of time transfer, child to parent (8)	Av. time transfer, child to parent if > 0 (hours) (9)
Lowest	22,764	0.107	452	0.030	871	0.314	255	0.380	303
Second	32,686	0.137	645	0.043	1,060	0.273	435	0.311	361
Third	39,556	0.189	1,986	0.024	3,006	0.301	313	0.238	313
Fourth	45,907	0.191	1,007	0.024	525	0.348	333	0.285	241
Fifth	51,922	0.225	1,541	0.018	2,288	0.351	417	0.266	238
Sixth	58,112	0.239	1,285	0.010	979	0.293	337	0.268	227
Seventh	65,081	0.289	718	0.003	500	0.281	174	0.262	139
Eighth	74,284	0.303	2,242	0.007	491	0.273	188	0.228	206
Ninth	86,699	0.337	2,767	0.011	1,371	0.339	195	0.253	200
Highest	127,674	0.342	3,206	0.005	1,500	0.265	160	0.221	154
Total	62,584	0.240	1,851	0.017	1,324	0.302	281	0.273	242

Note: Permanent income deciles of the parent are constructed by using person weights of the parent household, but average income and probabilities are calculated by using the person weights of the child.

Source: PSID 1988.

Table 14.4. **Probability of transfers and mean transfer amount by permanent income of the child, based on weighted estimates from matched sample: United States, 1987**

Permanent income decile of the parent	Average income ($s) (1)	Probability of money transfer, parent to child (2)	Av. money transfer, parent to child if > 0 ($s) (3)	Probability of money transfer, child to parent (4)	Av. money transfer, child to parent if > 0 ($s) (5)	Probability of time transfer, parent to child (6)	Av. time transfer, parent to child if > 0 (hours) (7)	Probability of time transfer, child to parent (8)	Av. time transfer, child to parent if > 0 (hours) (9)
Lowest	18,456	0.258	1,295	0.009	345	0.354	426	0.368	455
Second	29,186	0.270	1,055	0.014	351	0.309	305	0.285	228
Third	35,936	0.200	1,159	0.014	1,920	0.298	286	0.313	206
Fourth	42,193	0.269	1,600	0.019	414	0.265	404	0.303	164
Fifth	47,266	0.246	3,499	0.006	1,858	0.312	318	0.258	219
Sixth	52,218	0.190	2,507	0.010	689	0.339	226	0.263	182
Seventh	58,373	0.212	1,569	0.022	1,434	0.310	223	0.286	207
Eighth	65,851	0.230	1,392	0.021	3,618	0.257	239	0.217	302
Ninth	76,302	0.236	2,066	0.018	1,136	0.307	189	0.258	172
Highest	103,508	0.290	2,350	0.037	979	0.270	174	0.185	233
Total	52,926	0.240	1,851	0.017	1,324	0.302	281	0.273	242

Note: Permanent income deciles of the child as well as all averages and probabilities are constructed using the person weights of the child.

Source: PSID 1988.

income, although it is noteworthy that children in the highest income decile have the highest probability of receiving a transfer (0.290). The amount of the transfers tends to increase with the child's income. This simple tabulation is consistent with Cox's (1987) finding of a positive relationship between the size of parental transfers and the child's income in a multivariate analysis. However, as we pointed out in the theoretical background section, pure altruism models are consistent with a positive association between the mean and the variance of parental transfers (conditional on a positive value) and the child's income if the marginal utility of income is decreasing and there is heterogeneity in preferences.

Columns 4 and 5 of Table 14.4 show that the probability and amount of money transfers from children to parents rise with the child's income. Columns 8 and 9 indicate that the odds of a time transfer from children to parents declines from 0.368 for children in the lowest decile to 0.185 for children in the highest decile and that the mean value of the transfers also drops substantially, from 455 to 233 hours. The pattern is similar to the relationship between parental income and time transfers from children to parents. Time transfers from the parent to the child drop with the child's income, although less sharply than the odds of a time transfer from the child to the parent (columns 6 and 7). The average amount of the transfers shows a similar pattern for the time transfers from child to parent.

Table 14.5 presents the transfer probabilities and average transfer amounts by income quintile of the parent (rows) and income quintile of the child (columns). To save space we report only the first, third, and fifth quintiles. The first panel shows that $P(R_p > 0)$ is negatively related to Y_k, holding the parental income quintile constant, although, as we saw in Table 14.4, there is a weak positive correlation if the parent's income quintile is not held constant. The amounts show little relationship to the child's income when the parent's income is held constant, rising at first and then declining, in contrast to Table 14.3 and 14.4, which show a fairly strong positive link between Y_k and R_p. Panel 1 of Table 14.5 also shows that parental income has a strong positive relationship to the transfer probability and to the transfer amount in the event of a positive transfer. Not controlling for the child's income makes less of a difference, which reflects the finding that the direct effect of the child's income on the transfer probability and amount is less than the effect of parental income.

The second panel of Table 14.5 shows that the probability and the mean positive transfer from the child to the parent (R_k) rises with Y_k when Y_p is held constant. The relationship between $P(R_k > 0)$ and Y_k is very strong for parents in the lowest income quintile and relatively weak for parents in the third and fifth quintiles. Y_p has a strong negative relationship to the transfer probability. The relationship between Y_p and the size of R_k with Y_k held constant is unclear. The evidence suggests that children give help to parents when the disparity between their resources is large in the children's favour.

Panel 3 shows that the probability and amount of time help from parents to children (S_p) falls with Y_k. The probability does not have a clear relationship to

Table 14.5. Probability of transfers, mean transfer amount, and sample size, by parent's and child's permanent income quintile: United States, 1987

Type of transfer and parent's permanent income quintile	Child's permanent income quintile		
	Lowest	Third	Highest
Money transfers from parent to child			
Lowest quintile			
Probability	0.140	0.113	0.177
Average amount ($s)	474	1,144	780
Sample size	545	169	60
Third quintile			
Probability	0.277	0.231	0.187
Average amount ($s)	693	2,123	1,685
Sample size	176	143	111
Highest quintile			
Probability	0.499	0.322	0.350
Average amount ($s)	2,612	4,003	3,372
Sample size	66	104	185
Money transfers from child to parent			
Lowest quintile			
Probability	0.016	0.050	0.156
Average amount ($s)	399	1,172	963
Sample size	545	169	60
Third quintile			
Probability	0.009	0.000	0.035
Average amount ($s)	500	u	1,094
Sample size	176	143	111
Highest quintile			
Probability	0.000	0.001	0.019
Average amount ($s)	u	300	1,425
Sample size	66	104	185
Time transfers from parent to child			
Lowest quintile			
Probability	0.309	0.310	0.279
Average amount (hours)	336	415	272
Sample size	545	169	60
Third quintile			
Probability	0.339	0.329	0.255
Average amount (hours)	617	201	182
Sample size	176	143	111
Highest quintile			
Probability	0.399	0.260	0.296
Average amount (hours)	324	239	125
Sample size	66	104	185
Time transfers from child to parent			
Lowest quintile			
Probability	0.349	0.344	0.290
Average amount (hours)	387	245	0.215
Sample size	545	169	60
Third quintile			
Probability	0.269	0.256	0.164
Average amount (hours)	356	195	280
Sample size	176	143	111
Highest quintile			
Probability	0.388	0.217	0.196
Average amount (hours)	337	116	141
Sample size	66	104	185

u: data are unavailable because no positive transfers were observed.

Source: PSID 1988.

parental income, and the amounts fall with parental income when Y_k is in the third or fifth quintile. Panel 4 shows that the probability and amount of time transfers from children to parents (S_k) tend to decline as parents' income rises. The probabilities and amounts also fall with Y_k when Y_p is held constant.

In sum, the simple cross-tabulations show that richer parents are more likely than poorer parents to give transfers to their children and less likely to receive transfers from them. Likewise, richer children are more likely than poorer children to give and less likely to receive transfers. The connections between income and time transfers from parents to children and from children to parents, however, are weak.

The Effects of Income and Wealth on Transfers between Parents and Children

Turning to multivariate analysis, we estimate the effects of the income and wealth of parents and children on the probability and amount of transfers, using linear probability, probit, and Tobit models. We begin with an analysis of money transfers and time transfers, then consider Tobit results and other experiments.

The probability of money transfers from parents to children

All equations in Tables 14.6 to 14.9, which estimate the probability of money transfers, control for marital status by gender and race of the child, number of young children in the household of the adult child, an interaction between marital status and number of young children in the child's household, cubics in the age of the child and his or her parent, and whether the parent in the parental household is the father or the mother interacted with marital status. (The marital-status categories are divorced and not remarried, divorced and remarried, widowed and not remarried, widowed and remarried. Parents who are still married are the reference category.) The equations also control for whether the parent and the child live in the same residence, the child's report of distance in miles from the parental household,[9] and the inverse of 1 plus the number of siblings that the child reports. They also control for whether the parent is in a nursing home, whether the parent lives with another relative, and the health status of the child and the parent at the survey date.[10] In Appendix Table 14B.1 we present the means of a large set of variables broken out by whether R_p, R_k, S_p, and S_k are greater than zero. In Appendix Tables 14B.2 and 14B.3 we summarize the effects of the specific variables just mentioned on the probability and amount of the transfers relative to a base case.

Column 1 of Table 14.6 reports probit estimates, for the matched sample, of the effects of the child's and parent's permanent incomes on the probability that the child receives money from the parent. Rows 1 and 2 report the probit coefficient and standard error on the log permanent income of the child (Yk)

Table 14.6. Effects of permanent income and earnings on the transfer probability: probit estimates

Income measure (dependent variable)		Log of permanent family income				Log of permanent family earnings			
		Money transfer, parent to child (1)	Money transfer, child to parent (2)	Time transfer, parent to child (3)	Time transfer, child to parent (4)	Money transfer, parent to child (5)	Money transfer, child to parent (6)	Time transfer, parent to child (7)	Time transfer, child to parent (8)
Child's income									
Linear effect	(1)	−0.181	0.608	−0.068	−0.089	−0.164	0.424	−0.060	−0.029
Standard error	(2)	0.057	0.122	0.052	0.053	0.049	0.106	0.046	0.046
Derivative at median	(3)	−0.063	0.005	−0.013	−0.021	−0.058	0.003	−0.022	−0.027
Probability of transfer									
At median	(4)	0.161	0.005	0.248	0.253	0.151	0.002	0.222	0.239
At 20th percentile	(5)	0.188	0.002	0.256	0.255	0.179	0.001	0.234	0.246
At 80th percentile	(6)	0.137	0.007	0.243	0.238	0.127	0.004	0.214	0.224
Parent's income									
Linear effect	(7)	0.665	−0.627	0.016	−0.136	0.439	−0.237	0.006	−0.049
Standard error	(8)	0.065	0.128	0.059	0.058	0.051	0.075	0.040	0.039
Derivative at median	(9)	0.182	−0.010	−0.006	−0.022	0.086	−0.003	−0.012	−0.027
Probability of transfer									
At median	(10)	0.161	0.005	0.248	0.253	0.151	0.002	0.222	0.239
At 20th percentile	(11)	0.096	0.012	0.248	0.275	0.104	0.005	0.225	0.251
At 80th percentile	(12)	0.254	0.002	0.245	0.249	0.196	0.001	0.214	0.223

Notes: Other variables in the models include the following (definitions are given in Table 14B.1): ksinfem, ksinmal, kmarfem, knkid88, ksinkids, fathdsin, fathdrem, fathwsin, fathwrem, mothdsin, mothdrem, mothwsin, mothwrem, krplvapt, nonwhite, pinhous pinnh, pinorh, khlth88, phlth88, kuemph88, kuem1000, puemph88, puem1000, krpdist, invnkid, and a cubic in kage and page. Linear effect comes from a model in which only linear income terms are included. All other models include a cubic in the income measures. A cubic in both child's and parent's wealth is included in those models in which permanent earnings are the measure of parental income. Probabilities are evaluated at the mean of the included variables and the median of the income and wealth variables.

Source: PSID 1988.

for a model in which only the linear terms for the log permanent incomes of the child and the parent are entered. The coefficient and standard errors are −0.181 and 0.057. The corresponding coefficient and standard error on parent's income (Y_p) is 0.665 and 0.065 (rows 7 and 8). Thus $P(R_p > 0)$ rises with Y_p and falls with Y_k. However, the probability is much more sensitive to Y_p than to Y_k.

To provide a sense of how the probabilities vary with income, we estimated a model with cubics in Y_k and Y_p. We used this model to evaluate the probability of a transfer at the twentieth percentile, median, and eightieth percentile of Y_k, the median of Y_p, and the mean of all other variables. The probability is 0.161 at the median, 0.188 at the twentieth percentile, and 0.137 at the eightieth percentile (rows 4 through 6). The probability is 0.096 at the twentieth percentile of Y_p (and the mean of everything else) and 0.254 at the eightieth percentile (rows 11 and 12). These effects are large, given that the probability at the median is only 0.161 (row 10).[11]

In column 5 of Table 14.6 we report estimates after substituting permanent log earnings for family income and adding cubic specifications for net assets of the parent and the child (measured in 1984). Variation among individuals in the

Table 14.7. Effects of wealth on the transfer probability: probit estimates

		Money transfer		Time transfer	
		Parent to child (1)	Child to parent (2)	Parent to child (3)	Child to parent (4)
Child's wealth ($000s)					
Derivative at median	(1)	−0.18	−0.01	0.05	0.74
Probability of transfer					
At median	(2)	0.152	0.002	0.222	0.239
At 20th percentile	(3)	0.152	0.002	0.222	0.234
At 80th percentile	(4)	0.147	0.002	0.224	0.259
Parent's wealth ($000s)					
Derivative at median	(5)	0.92	−0.07	0.55	0.22
Probability of transfer					
At median	(6)	0.152	0.002	0.222	0.239
At 20th percentile	(7)	0.115	0.008	0.199	0.239
At 80th percentile	(8)	0.222	0.000	0.262	0.252

Notes: Other variables in the models include ksinfem, ksinmal, kmarfem, knkid88, ksinkids, fathdsin, fathdrem, fathwsin, fathwrem, mothdsin, mothdrem, mothwsin, mothwrem, krplvapt, nonwhite, pinhous pinnh, pinorh, khlth88, phlth88, kuemph88, kuem1000, puemph88, puem1000, krpdist, invnkid, a cubic in kage and page, and a cubic in the log of permanent earnings. Definitions are given in Table 14B.1. The models include a cubic in the parent's wealth and the child's wealth. Probabilities are evaluated at the mean of the included variables and the median of the income and wealth variables.

Source: PSID 1988.

age of retirement may weaken the link between earnings and permanent income for the parents. The probit coefficients on the earnings variables are a bit below the corresponding coefficients on the family income. The twentieth to eightieth percentile differentials in the probability of a transfer are not sensitive to the measure of Y_k but are lower when earnings are used as the measure of Y_p.

Column 1 of Table 14.7 reports the effects of assets. The child's assets have little effect, although the sign is negative. The negative sign for assets is qualitatively consistent with the effect of Y_k and earnings. Because the child's assets, particularly early in the life cycle, may be heavily influenced by previous transfers, this coefficient is probably biased upward in the likely event that unobserved, serially correlated factors influence transfers. The parent's assets have a substantial positive effect. The coefficient on the parent's assets may be biased upward to the extent that parents accumulate assets in anticipation of providing transfers to their children.

The probability of money transfers from children to parents

Column 2 of Table 14.6 reports probit results for $P(R_k > 0)$. The probit coefficient on Y_k is positive and approximately equal to and opposite in sign from the coefficient on Y_p. Using the equation with cubics in the income terms, we find that the twentieth to eightieth percentile differentials in $P(R_k > 0)$ are 0.005 for Y_k (row 3) and -0.01 for Y_p (row 9). These differentials are small in an absolute sense but are very large relative to the transfer probability evaluated at the median of the income variables and the mean of everything else, which is only 0.005. When earnings are used with controls for assets, the effects are reduced, though not relative to the probability of a transfer at the median earnings levels. We obtained qualitatively similar but numerically larger results using linear probability models. This suggests that effects of income evaluated at the means are smaller than the mean effect of income.

In column 2 of Table 14.7 we find that the odds of a transfer from the child to the parent decline with parental assets but do not change with child's assets. These results, combined with the results for income from Table 14.6, are consistent with a two-sided altruism hypothesis. Our main finding is that the child's resources increase the odds of a money transfer to the parent and that the parent's resources lower the odds of such a money transfer. The effects of changes in the relative income and assets of parents and children are small in absolute terms but large in relation to the probability of a transfer from children to parents evaluated at the means. It is likely that the absolute magnitudes are understated in relation to the coefficients on transfers from parents to children because of the difference in survey questions discussed earlier.

The probability of time transfers

Table 14.6, column 3, shows that Y_k and Y_p have a statistically and economically insignificant relationship with time transfers from parent to child (S_p). We draw a similar conclusion when earnings are used (column 7). In Table 14.7, column 4, we report that the difference in parental assets between the twentieth and the eightieth percentiles is associated with an increase in time transfers of 0.06. The child's assets have essentially no effect (Table 14.7, column 3).

The corresponding results for time transfers from the child to the parent (Table 14.6, column 4) indicate that both the child's income and parental income have a weak negative relationship to the transfer probability. Using the cubic income specification, we find that the difference between the twentieth and eightieth percentiles in the probability is –0.026 for parental income and –0.017 for child's income. The results for parental income seem inconsistent with a strategic exchange motive, in which money transfers from the parent to the child buy time transfers from the child to the parent. Using the model with both earnings and assets (Table 14.7, column 4), we find that parental assets raise time transfers, but so do the child's assets.

Tobit results

Tables 14.8 and 14.9 use Tobit models to analyse the effects of the parent's and child's income and wealth on the magnitude of transfers.[12] For both the child's and the parent's income the tables report the Tobit index coefficients and standard errors for Y_k and Y_p, based on a linear specification. The sign patterns and relative magnitudes of the effects of Y_k and Y_p are similar to those in the probit models (as they almost have to be). The *signs* of the derivatives of the Tobit index for R_p and R_k, with respect to Y_k and Y_p, are consistent with altruism in the sense that transfers flow from the rich to the poor. However, as we have pointed out in Altonji *et al.* (1995), the difference between those derivatives is only about one-tenth as large as the value of 1 implied by the basic altruism model, in which households care about their own consumption and the utility of others.

Using the equation with cubics in the income terms, we find that the twentieth to eightieth percentile differential in R_k (including zero transfers) is –103 for Y_k. This differential is large relative to the conditional mean of R_k evaluated at the median of Y_k, which is \$343. The corresponding twentieth to eightieth percentile differential in R_k is \$360 for Y_p. It is noteworthy that the income and wealth variables have trivial effects on estimated transfers from children to parents but substantial effects on the size of a transfer if one occurs. The other main result is that the effects of Y_p and Y_k on time transfers are small in relation to the mean values for those variables.

Ionnides and Kan (1993) and to a lessor extent Shoeni (1993*c*) use the 1988 transfer supplement to examine the effects of parents' and children's income and wealth on money and time transfers from parents to children and from children to parents. Shelton and Sueyoshi (1994) present a somewhat similar analysis using the panel data on help from relatives and a matched sample of parents and children. The results of those studies indicate that parental income has a positive

Table 14.8. Effects of permanent income and earnings on transfer amounts: Tobit estimates

Income measure (dependent variable)		Log of permanent family income				Log of permanent family earnings			
		Money transfer, parent to child ($s) (1)	Money transfer, child to parent ($s) (2)	Time transfer, parent to child (hours) (3)	Time transfer, child to parent (hours) (4)	Money transfer, parent to child ($s) (5)	Money transfer, child to parent ($s) (6)	Time transfer, parent to child (hours) (7)	Time transfer, child to parent (hours) (8)
Child's income									
Linear Tobit coefficient	(1)	−799	1,539	−41	−62	−857	1,096	−31	−31
Standard error	(2)	302	331	35	28	267	284	31	24
Derivative of transfer									
At median	(3)	−128	6	−4	−9	−163	2	−8	−13
Estimated transfer									
At median	(4)	343	4	92	69	309	2	81	64
At 20th percentile	(5)	393	2	93	73	388	1	84	69
At 80th percentile	(6)	290	7	89	65	244	3	78	58
Derivative of transfer if > 0									
At median	(7)	−183	99	−4	−10	−246	79	−8	−15
Estimated transfer if > 0									
At median	(8)	2,655	783	412	329	2,597	717	398	319
At 20th percentile	(9)	2,724	724	413	333	2,709	684	402	324
At 80th percentile	(10)	2,575	820	409	325	2,493	756	394	312

Parent's income									
Linear Tobit coefficient	(11)	3,658	−1,473	−44	−82	2,326	−550	−26	−18
Standard error	(12)	354	341	40	32	280	197	27	21
Derivative of transfer									
At median	(13)	375	−8	−21	−15	177	−3	−17	−11
Estimated transfer									
At median	(14)	343	4	92	69	309	2	81	64
At 20th percentile	(15)	212	11	97	78	232	4	88	69
At 80th percentile	(16)	572	2	82	64	428	1	71	58
Derivative of transfer if > 0									
At median	(17)	535	−138	−22	−16	267	−88	−19	−12
Estimated transfer if > 0									
At median	(18)	2,655	783	412	329	2,597	717	398	319
At 20th percentile	(19)	2,443	859	418	339	2,473	771	406	324
At 80th percentile	(20)	2,939	735	401	324	2,763	680	387	312

Notes: Other variables in the models include ksinfem, ksinmal, kmarfem, knkid88, ksinkids, fathdsin, fathdrem, fathwsin, fathwrem, mothdsin, mothdrem, mothwsin, mothwrem, krplvapt, nonwhite, pinhous pinnh, pinorh, khlth88, phlth88, kuemph88, kuem1000, puemon88, puem1000, krpdist, invnkid, a cubic in kage and page, and a cubic in the log of permanent family earnings. Definitions are given in Table 14B.1. Linear effect comes from a model in which only linear wealth terms are included. All other models include a cubic in the wealth measures. Estimated transfers are evaluated at the mean of the included variables and the median of the income and wealth variables.

Source: PSID 1988.

Table 14.9. Effects of wealth on transfer amounts: Tobit estimates

Income measures (dependent variables)		Money transfer ($s)		Time transfer (hours)	
		Parent to child (1)	Child to parent (2)	Parent to child (3)	Child to parent (4)
Child's wealth ($000s)					
Derivative of transfer					
At median	(1)	1,795	17	118	209
Estimated transfer					
At median	(2)	309	2	81	64
At 20th percentile	(3)	297	2	82	63
At 80th percentile	(4)	337	2	78	70
Derivative of transfer if > 0					
At median	(5)	2,705	579	−128	227
Estimated transfer if > 0					
At median	(6)	2,597	717	398	318
At 20th percentile	(7)	2,579	713	399	317
At 80th percentile	(8)	2,668	738	395	324
Parent's wealth ($000s)					
Derivative of transfer					
At median	(9)	2,975	−55	201	46
Estimated transfer					
At median	(10)	309	2	81	64
At 20th percentile	(11)	198	7	73	62
At 80th percentile	(12)	558	0	96	67
Derivative of transfer if > 0					
At median	(13)	4,483	−182	218	50
Estimated transfer if > 0					
At median	(14)	2,597	717	398	318
At 20th percentile	(15)	2,410	809	389	316
At 80th percentile	(16)	2,917	623	413	322

Notes: Other variables in the models include ksinfem, ksinmal, kmarfem, knkid88, ksinkids, fathdsin, fathdrem, fathwsin, fathwrem, mothdsin, mothdrem, mothwsin, mothwrem, krplvapt, nonwhite, pinhous pinnh, pinorh, khlth88, phlth88, kuemph88, kueml000, puemph, pueml000, krpdist, invnkid, a cubic in kage and page, and a cubic in the log of permanent family earnings. Definitions are given in Table 14B.1. Linear effect comes from a model in which only linear wealth terms are included. All other models include a cubic in the wealth measures. Estimated transfers are evaluated at the mean of the included variables and the median of the income and wealth variables.

Source: PSID 1988.

Table 14.10. Effects of current and permanent income on transfers: probit models (standard errors in parentheses)

Effects of current and permanent income		Money transfers	
		Child to parent (1)	Parent to child (2)
Effects of child's current income			
Probit coefficient, linear specification	(1)	0.0084	−0.0044
Standard error		(0.0036)	(0.0021)
Mean of derivatives	(2)	0.0003	−0.0021
Probability of transfer			
At median	(3)	0.0019	0.145
At 20th percentile	(4)	0.0013	0.176
At 80th percentile	(5)	0.0029	0.116
Effects of parents' current income			
Probit coefficient, linear specification	(6)	−0.0044	0.0036
Standard error		(0.0047)	(0.0011)
Mean of derivatives	(7)	−0.0013	0.0014
Probability of transfer			
At median	(8)	0.0019	0.145
At 20th percentile	(9)	0.0051	0.127
At 80th percentile	(10)	0.0013	0.183
Effects of child's permanent income			
Probit coefficient, linear specification	(11)	0.0056	−0.0021
Standard error		(0.0030)	(0.0016)
Mean of derivatives	(12)	0.0004	−0.0003
Probability of transfer			
At median	(13)	0.0019	0.145
At 20th percentile	(14)	0.0008	0.152
At 80th percentile	(15)	0.0031	0.139
Effects of parents' permanent income			
Probit coefficient, linear specification	(16)	−0.0079	0.0075
Standard error		(0.0035)	(0.0013)
Mean of derivatives	(17)	−0.0002	0.0024
Probability of transfer			
At median	(18)	0.0019	0.145
At 20th percentile	(19)	0.0032	0.096
At 80th percentile	(20)	0.0006	0.197

Notes: Conventional probit and Tobit asymptotic standard errors are shown in parentheses in Tables 14.10 and 14.11. They do not correct for correlations among observations involving separate parental households and the same child or among siblings. Other variables in the models include ksinfem, ksinmal, kmarfem, knkid88, ksinkids, fathdsin, fathdrem, fathwsin, fathwrem, mothdsin, mothdrem, mothwsin, mothwrem, krplvapt, nonwhite, pinhous, pinorh, khlth88, phlth88, krpdist, invnkid, a cubic in kage and page, and a cubic in wealth of the parent and child. Definitions are given in Table 14B.1. Wealth controls are also included (see n. 3). Cubics in the wealth of the parent and the child are also included. Probit and Tobit coefficients and standard errors for the linear specification come from models that contain only linear income (and wealth and current income) terms (rows 1, 6, 11, and 16 in Table 14.8 and rows 1, 5, 9, and 13 in Table 14.9). All other results are based on models that include a cubic in the income (and wealth) measures and an interaction between the level income terms.

Probabilities and transfer amounts are evaluated at the mean of the included variables and the median of the income and wealth variables. Derivatives for income or earnings are the change in transfer for one dollar of change in income.

Source: PSID 1988.

effect on the probability and the amount of transfers from parents to children and a negative effect on transfers of money from children to parents. The studies also show that children's income reduces the probability and the amount of money transfers from parents to children and raises the probability and amount of money transfers from children to parents.

Other experiments

With permanent income controlled, current income of the child or the parent may matter if family money transfers are used to smooth household income over time. It may play this role if access to credit markets is limited. In Table 14.10 we add current non-asset income to probit models that include permanent income and assets. Rows 1 and 6 report the coefficients on the current income of the child and the parent, respectively, from an equation that includes only the linear terms in current income, permanent income, and assets. In the equation for $P(R_p > 0)$ we obtain a positive, statistically significant effect of Y_{kt}. The probit coefficient is -0.0044 (0.0021). This coefficient is about double the effect of permanent income, with current income held fixed, although one would combine the coefficients to obtain the total effect of a shift in permanent income. The results in rows 2 to 5 and 7 to 10 are based on a non-linear specification that includes cubics in Y_{kt} and Y_{pt} as well as the product of Y_{kt} and Y_{pt}. They imply that an increase in Y_{kt} from the twentieth to the eightieth percentile would shift the probability of a transfer from 0.176 to 0.116.

In the linear specification, Y_{pt} has a coefficient of 0.0036 (0.0011), which is less than half of the coefficient on Y_p. The Tobit coefficients for the linear specification in Table 14.11 also show that the ratio of the coefficients on Y_{kt} and Y_k is 2.3, while the ratio of the coefficients on Y_{pt} and Y_p is 0.2. The finding that current income of the child plays a more important role than does permanent income, whereas the opposite is true for Y_p and Y_{pt}, is consistent with the view that liquidity constraints are more important for younger than for older persons.

We now turn to the effects of Y_{kt} and Y_{pt} on money transfers from child to parent. As shown in row 1 of Table 14.10, the coefficient on the Y_{kt} is 0.0084 (0.0036). The coefficient on Y_{pt} is -0.0044 (0.0047), which is not significantly different from zero (row 6). The results in rows 2 to 5 and 7 to 10 are based on a non-linear specification that includes cubics in Y_{kt} and Y_{pt} as well as the product of Y_{kt} and Y_{pt}. They suggest that a shift in Y_{kt} from the twentieth to the eightieth percentile has a small positive effect on the transfer probability, holding Y_k and A_k. A corresponding increase in Y_{pt} has a small negative effect on the probability of a transfer. The Tobit estimates in Table 14.11 also point to a small, statistically significant positive effect of the Y_{kt} on R_k and a smaller, statistically insignificant negative effect of Y_{kt}.

The fact that Y_{kt} has an important role in the equation for R_p provides some evidence that transfers play a role in smoothing income, as one may expect if

Table 14.11. Effects of income and wealth on transfer amounts: Tobit estimates (standard errors in parentheses)

Effects of income and wealth		Money transfers	
		Child to parent (1)	Parent to child (2)
Effects of child's current income			
Linear Tobit coefficient	(1)	0.0220	−0.023
Standard error		(0.0096)	(0.011)
Average derivative of			
Tobit index	(2)	0.0213	−0.0716
Transfer	(3)	0.0006	−0.0113
Transfer if > 0	(4)	0.0022	−0.0140
Effects of parent's current income			
Linear Tobit coefficient	(5)	−0.0115	0.009
Standard error		(0.0122)	(0.003)
Average derivative of			
Tobit index	(6)	−0.0718	0.0243
Transfer	(7)	−0.0019	0.0037
Transfer if > 0	(8)	−0.0051	0.0047
Effects of child's permanent income			
Linear Tobit coefficient	(9)	0.0157	−0.010
Standard error		(0.0080)	(0.008)
Average derivative of			
Tobit index	(10)	0.0218	0.0091
Transfer	(11)	0.0004	0.0017
Transfer if > 0	(12)	0.0020	0.0019
Effects of parent's permanent income			
Linear Tobit coefficient	(13)	−0.0189	0.046
Standard error		(0.0095)	(0.006)
Average derivative of			
Tobit index	(14)	−0.0103	0.0538
Transfer	(15)	−0.0002	0.0071
Transfer if > 0	(16)	−0.0012	0.0098

Note: See notes in Table 14.10.

Source: PSID 1988.

liquidity constraints or intertemporal risk-sharing are important.[13] One would need a model of how our current income and permanent income measures are related to future income expectations to provide a full interpretation of these coefficients.[14] It is possible, for example, that children with high current income relative to Y_k, which is based on incomes in 1988 and prior years, have unusually high lifetime incomes and receive lower transfers as a result. Rosenzweig and Wolpin (1993, 1994) and Dunn (1993*a*) provide evidence that current income of the child is negatively related to money transfers; they do so by using a fixed-effects methodology to control for permanent income of the child and the parents. They do not find a role for current income of the parents, in contrast to our results here. We cannot include fixed effects for individuals because we lack panel data on transfers from parent to child, but one could used fixed effects in an analysis of the 'help from relatives' data.

In some models we excluded the current income term and added hours of unemployment and a dummy for whether hours of unemployment exceeded 1,000. We found that the variables did not have a significant effect in the probit or the Tobit model for R_k and R_p (see Appendix Tables 14B.2 and 14.B.3). More generally, one could examine whether the family responds differentially to particular components of permanent income and shocks to income over time, and whether those responses are influenced by social-insurance programmes. Shoeni (1993*a*, 1993*b*) addresses the issue of whether public transfers crowd out private transfers.

Finally, we investigated the issue of liquidity constraints by adding two dummy variables to our linear probability model of $P(R_p > 0)$ containing the other variables in our basic specification. They were whether the child had moved from rental housing to home ownership (1) between the 1986 and 1987 surveys or (2) between the 1987 and 1988 surveys, along with a control for home ownership at the survey date in 1988. The probability of receiving a transfer is actually 0.062 lower (with a t value of 1.75) for persons who moved from rental housing to home ownership between 1986 and 1987 than for those who did not. The coefficient on the dummy for whether the person became a homeowner between 1987 and 1988 is essentially zero, with a standard error of 0.032. This result, that transfers from parents to children do not tend to coincide with moves from rental housing to home ownership, is surprising. It would seem to contradict casual observations suggesting that parents play an important role in the financing of their children's first home.

Wage rates

Various models suggest that the value of time, as measured by the wage rate, will be negatively related to time transfers if one holds the marginal utility of household income constant. The models suggest that time transfers should be positively related to the price of time of the recipient household. In Table 14.12 we add the current log wage of the head and that of the wife in the child's household, as well as dummy variables for whether the head worked positive hours and whether the wife worked positive hours, to probit models for $P(S_k > 0)$, $P(R_k > 0)$, and $P(R_p > 0)$. The models also contain detailed controls for other characteristics of the child's and the parent's household. The head's wage-term and work-hour dummy variables are set at zero if the head did not work. The wife's wage-term and work-hour dummy variables are set at zero if the child was not married. We also added similar wage-term and work-hour

Table 14.12. Probit estimates of the effects of wage rates on the probability of time and money transfers (derivatives of the transfer probability evaluated at the mean probability, with standard errors in parentheses)

Independent variable	$P(R_p > 0)$ (1)	$P(R_k > 0)$ (2)	$P(S_k > 0)$ (3)
Child's family			
Head worked	0.0248	−0.0004	0.1048
	(0.0366)	(0.0111)	(0.0422)
Log wage of head	−0.0208	0.0126	−0.0544
	(0.0121)	(0.0031)	(0.0149)
Wife worked if present	0.0078	−0.0097	−0.0194
	(0.0383)	(0.0095)	(0.0462)
Log wage of wife	−0.0045	0.0027	0.0051
	(0.0159)	(0.0040)	(0.0198)
Parents' family			
Head worked	−0.0331	0.0008	0.0227
	(0.0284)	(0.0067)	(0.0337)
Log wage of head	0.0490	−0.0007	−0.0049
	(0.0111)	(0.0031)	(0.014)
Wife worked if present	−0.1128	0.0209	0.0571
	(0.0425)	(0.0113)	(0.0493)
Log wage of wife	0.0711	0.0203	−0.0174
	(0.0195)	(0.0081)	(0.0234)

Note: The probit models also include the control variables listed in the footnotes to Table 14.6, with the exception of permanent income and indicators for unemployment. Detailed controls for the marital status of both the child's and the parent's household are included, so that the dummy variable on whether the wife worked is the extra effect of working, conditional upon the wife's presence.

Source: PSID 1988.

dummies for the parent (for either the father or the mother when only one parent was present and for the father when both were present) and for the mother (zeros if the mother did not work or if the mother and father were not living together). The equations contain detailed controls for the marital status of the child and the parents, and so the coefficient on whether the wife works is the effect of working, with a control for whether the wife is present. It should be kept in mind, however, that the wage coefficients combine income and substitution effects, which complicate their interpretation. We are not holding the marginal utility of income constant.

Table 14.12 reports the derivatives of $P(S_k > 0)$ evaluated at the unconditional probability of $(S_k > 0)$. Because the coefficient on whether the wife worked is −0.0194 and the coefficient on the log of the wife's wage is 0.0051, the results imply that a woman with a log wage rate of less than $0.0194/0.0051 = 3.804$, or a wage rate of \$44.9 per hour, provides less help if she works. However, the point estimate of the effect of working is trivial for a woman earning \$10.00 per hour [$-0.0194 + 0.0051^* \log(10) = 0.0073$]; and the coefficient on the wife's wage has the wrong sign from the point of view of models of time transfers that are based on comparative advantage in an altruism framework or selfish exchange. Nevertheless, the coefficient on whether the head works is 0.1048 (0.0422), and the coefficient on the log wage of the head is −0.0544 (0.0149). Although these effects are substantial and the wage coefficient has the right sign, they imply that the transfer probability is 0.020 higher for a head who works and earns \$10.00 per hour than for a head who does not work. A 50 per cent increase in the wage—which is large relative to most estimates of the return to four years of college for the PSID sample—lowers the time transfer probability by only 0.022. (We also estimated models using wages and a work dummy for the heads of the parent's and child's households and for the spouse of the parent's and child's households, set to zero if the spouse was not present, with qualitatively similar results.) The parents' wage rates do not have statistically significant effects on $P(S_k > 0)$.

To summarize, we have three main findings in this section. First, money transfer flows tend to flow from rich to poor family members. Parental income has a positive effect on the probability and the amount of money transfers from parents to children and a negative effect on transfers of money from children to parents.[15] With permanent income controlled, parental assets are positively related to money transfers from parent to child and negatively related to money transfers from child to parent. The child's income reduces the probability and amount of money transfers from parents to children and raises the probability and amount of transfers from children to parents. The sensitivity of the transfer amounts to differences in incomes is not large. Second, time transfers to and from the parents are only weakly related to incomes and assets of the parents and child. The finding that parents' permanent income is negatively related to the number of hours that children spend helping parents seems inconsistent with the view that time and money transfers are best viewed as exchange.[16] Third, children whose current income is low relative to their permanent income are less likely to give and more likely to receive money transfers, suggesting that insurance needs and liquidity constraints affecting the child influence the timing of transfers.[17] The current income of the parents is much less important.

Competition and Coordination among Siblings

Table 14.13 reports linear probability models with a fixed effect included for each parental household in 1988. The models control for all additive factors that are common to the parent, including the parent's average income and the average needs of his or her children. The coefficient on Y_k rises in absolute magnitude relative to what one obtains by estimating the linear probability model with fixed effects excluded. This result can be expected if parents use transfers to equalize

Table 14.13. Effects of income and distance from parents on the transfer probability (linear probability models with fixed effects for each parent household)

Independent variable	$P(R_p > 0)$	$P(R_k > 0)$	$P(S_p > 0)$	$P(S_k > 0)$
Y_k	−0.057	0.0270	−0.0177	−0.0473
	(0.018)	(0.0061)	(0.0214)	(0.0215)
Distance	−0.004	−0.0001	−0.046	−0.0048
(hundreds of miles)	(0.004)	(0.0015)	(0.005)	(0.0051)

Note: This table uses the full sample. Standard errors do not correct for heteroskedasticity or for correlation across observations involving the children of parents living in separate households (e.g. divorced parents). The sample size and the number of fixed effects included are respectively 5,257 and 3,003 in the case of R_p, 5,056 and 2,932 in the case of R_k, 5,059 and 2,934 in the case of S_k, and 5,056 and 2,932 in the case of S_p. Controls for other characteristics of the child's household are not shown.

Source: PSID 1988.

Table 14.14. Conditional logit estimates of the effects of Y_k and $Y_{kt} - Y_k$ on $\log\{P(R_p > 0)/[1 - P(R_p > 0)]\}$ (standard errors in parentheses)

Independent variable	Model 1	Model 2
Y_k	−0.686	−0.606
	(0.172)	(0.183)
$Y_{kt} - Y_k$		−0.687
		(0.174)

Note: Controls for other characteristics of child's household not shown.

income and if the more well-to-do children assume a larger share of support for a parent. Dunn (1993*a*) estimates fixed-effects Tobit models using Honore's (1992) procedure and obtains findings that are qualitatively consistent with ours.

Our findings for *inter-vivos* transfers contrast with the findings of Menchik (1980) and Wilhelm (1996), which indicate that bequests are typically divided equally. Several interesting explanations can be suggested for why parents may treat *inter-vivos* transfers differently from bequests. In particular, bequests are public whereas *inter-vivos* transfers are not. Nevertheless, the relatively small size of the coefficient on Y_k and Y_{kt} in the Tobit models that also include the mean of Y_k across siblings suggests that parents perform only a modest redistribution of income among siblings (calculations not reported).

Because the fixed-effects linear probability model has well-known problems, we estimated a conditional logit model of $P(R_p > 0)$ (from Chamberlain 1984) that controls for family effects common to siblings.[18] The results are reported in Table 14.14.

The coefficients are in the log-odds metric, which is hard to interpret. They indicate, however, that both the relative permanent incomes of siblings and the relative differences between the current incomes and the permanent incomes of siblings are negatively associated with the relative probabilities that the siblings will receive a transfer.

We have also added the average permanent incomes of siblings to the linear probability models and probit models of the transfer probabilities on the subset of children who have at least one sibling in the matched sample. Using a linear probability model containing controls similar to those used in Tables 14.6 and 14.7, we obtain coefficients of –0.057 (0.015) on Y_k, 0.166 (0.017) on Y_p, and 0.042 (0.018) on the average of Y_k across siblings. For the same specification and sample, the coefficients on Y_k and Y_p are –0.044 (0.171) when we exclude the average. The change in the coefficients illustrates the potential for bias in analyses of family transfers when the resources of some members of the extended family are not held constant. We obtain the same pattern using a probit specification with only linear terms in Y_p, Y_k, and the average of Y_k across siblings included. In a Tobit model the coefficients on Y_k, Y_p, and the sibling average are −885, 3,517, and 598; but the last variable has a *p*-value of only 0.156. These results are consistent with the fixed-effects results, suggesting that transfer flows between the parent and the child depend on the relative needs and resources of other family members. However, average sibling income is not statistically significant in probit and Tobit equations for R_k, although it does enter with the correct sign.[19]

In Tables 14B.2 and 14B.3 we report estimates of the effect of the number of siblings on the probability of a transfer and the amounts. The tables present the effect of having no siblings and having four siblings relative to having two siblings. The probability of receiving a money transfer from parents is much higher for children with no siblings, and the probability of receiving a time transfer is also higher for such children. The same is true of the amounts, including the zeros. However, the number of siblings has no effect on the probability of a money transfer to the parent, and it has only a weak positive effect on the average time transfer to the parent. Using the mean transfer amount for the base case reported at the top of Table 14B.3, one can compute the effect of the number of children on the total amount of money transfers to and from the parent. The estimates imply that money transfers from the parent rise from \$585 + \$646 for a parent with one child to 5*(\$585 – \$129) = \$2,280 for a parent with five children. Time transfers from the parent rise from 78 + 53 hours to 5*(78 – 11) = 335 hours. The Tobit estimates for S_k and R_k imply that parents with more children receive substantially more time and money than do those with fewer children.

To summarize, the fixed-effects evidence suggests that the relative incomes of siblings influence who receives transfers from and who provides transfers to parents. This view is supported by evidence that the average income of one's siblings increases the probability and amount of money transfers received from parents. The number of living children lowers the odds that a particular child (as opposed to at least one child) receives money or time from the parent, as one would expect given limits on the money and time of the parent. However, the number of living children has little effect on the odds of a transfer from a particular child in the other direction.

The Effects of the Relative Incomes of Parents and In-laws on Transfers

Little is known about whether the relative incomes of parents and parents-in-law affect the level of support provided to and by them. This question underlies the issue of whether the altruistic links between each set of parents and their children lead to indirect links between the parents and the in-laws. In Table 14.15 we report linear probability models of $R_p > 0$, $R_k > 0$, $S_p > 0$, and $S_k > 0$ that account for child-specific fixed effects by differencing across the observations involving the husband's parents and the wife's parents. We work with married couples in the full sample. The couples are included if both the husband and the wife have at least one living parent and if neither the husband nor the wife has parents who live separately. We simply difference the transfer indicators and explanatory variables and estimate by least squares. The incomes of the parents are reported by the children, and so downward bias from measurement error may be a serious problem. Because the correlation between the child's report of parental income and parent's income as reported by the parent is about 0.5, the usual correction of measurement error, under the assumption of independence in the reporting errors and independence in the true incomes, would approximately double the income coefficients. The appropriate correction would be reduced if the measurement errors were positively correlated but would be increased by the fact that the incomes of in-laws have a fairly strong positive correlation (see Altonji and Dunn 1991).[20]

The results in column 1 of Table 14.15 show that the difference in the incomes of the husband's and wife's parents is positively related to the difference in the probabilities that each set of parents receives money transfers from the children. The results in column 2 indicate that differences in the incomes of the two sets of parents are negatively related to the difference in the probability that they provide money transfers. An interesting question for future research is whether part of the income transfer from one set of parents is in effect transferred to the in-laws by the children.

Finally, we find that the income difference has a negative but statistically insignificant relationship to the difference in probability of time transfers (columns 3 and 4 of Table 14.15). This finding is consistent with the results in Tables 14.6 and 14.7 and seems at odds with the selfish-exchange model.

These models also contain the difference in a dummy variable that is 1 for the parents of the husband and zero for the parents of the wife (Δ *PAR_O_S*). A negative coefficient on this variable in the equations for the differences in $P(R_p > 0)$ and $P(S_p > 0)$ would indicate that the parents of the husband are less likely to give transfers than the parents of the wife. A negative coefficient on this variable in the equations for $P(R_k > 0)$ and $P(S_k > 0)$ indicates that couples are more likely to give transfers to the husband's parents than to the wife's parents, everything else being equal. The coefficient on the variable is -0.0715 (0.0133) in the equation for $P(S_p > 0)$, which indicates that the parents of the

Table 14.15. Difference in the probability of transfers to and from the parents of the husband and the wife (OLS regression coefficients, standard errors in parentheses)

Independent variable	Variable name	Dependent variable			
		Δ parent gave child money (1)	Δ child gave parent money (2)	Δ parent gave child time (3)	Δ child gave parent time (4)
Child is male	ΔPAR_O_S	−0.0125 (0.0121)	0.0058 (0.0057)	−0.0715 (0.0133)	−0.0101 (0.0140)
Parental household: widowed, not remarried father	ΔFATHERSIN	−0.0003 (0.0434)	−0.0248 (0.0204)	−0.0128 (0.0477)	0.1136 (0.0501)
Parental household: widowed, remarried father	ΔFATHWREM	−0.0764 (0.0469)	−0.0223 (0.0222)	−0.1402 (0.0516)	−0.1077 (0.0543)
Parental household: widowed, not remarried mother	ΔMOTHWSIN	0.0230 (0.0226)	0.0284 (0.0106)	0.0074 (0.0248)	0.1008 (0.0260)
Parental household: widowed, not married mother	ΔMOTHWREM	0.0180 (0.0430)	0.0267 (0.0200)	−0.0298 (0.0470)	0.0509 (0.0495)
Child's report of parent's age	ΔKRPAGE	−0.0588 (0.0530)	−0.0271 (0.0250)	0.0027 (0.0583)	−0.0375 (0.0613)
Square of child's report of parent's age	ΔKRPAGE2	8.0E-4 (8.0E-4)	4.0E-4 (3.8E-4)	−4.7E-5 (8.9E-4)	4.8E-4 (9.3E-4)
Cube of child's report of parent's age	ΔKRPAGE3	−3.4E-6 (4.1E-6)	−1.8E-6 (1.9E-6)	4.4E-7 (4.5E-6)	−1.8E-6 (4.7E-6)
Child's report of health (1 = excellent, 5 = poor)	ΔKRPHLTH	−0.0127 (0.0080)	0.0078 (0.0038)	−0.0173 (0.0088)	0.0466 (0.0092)
Distance to parent's house (estimated)	ΔKRPDIST	−8.0E-5 (4.9E-5)	−4.8E-5 (2.3E-5)	−4.9E-4 (5.4E-5)	−5.1E-4 (5.7E-5)
Parent resides with child	ΔPINHOUS	−0.0768 (0.1143)	−0.0808 (0.0538)	0.3731 (0.1258)	0.2603 (0.1323)
Parent resides in nursing home	ΔPINNH	−0.0548 (0.0845)	−0.0909 (0.0398)	−0.0232 (0.0930)	0.0201 (0.0978)
Parent resides with another relative	ΔPINORH	0.0486 (0.0625)	0.0225 (0.0289)	−0.1684 (0.0674)	−0.1845 (0.0709)
Log of child's report of parent's income	ΔLKRPINC	0.0458 (0.0116)	−0.0123 (0.0055)	−0.0057 (0.0128)	−0.0171 (0.0134)

Note: The dependent variable and independent variables represent the differences between values for the respondent's parents and the spouse's parents. The sample consists of married couples in the full sample. The couples are included if both the husband and the wife have one or more living parents and if neither the husband nor the wife has parents who live separately. Sample sizes range from 1,351 to 1,368 observations.

husband are substantially more likely to provide time help. (Recall that the unconditional probability of receiving time help is about 0.30.) The variable is small and statistically insignificant in the equations for the other transfer measures, including S_k. We would have expected the children to provide more time help to the wife's parents, everything else being equal.[21]

The coefficient on $\Delta KRPDIST$ indicates that parents who live farther from the child have a slightly lower probability of giving money than do those who live near by. The difference in $P(R_p > 0)$ between one set of parents living 300 miles away and the other living 1 mile away is -0.024 (0.015). The corresponding differences in $P(S_p > 0)$ and in $P(S_k > 0)$ are much larger: -0.147 (0.016) and -0.153 (0.017), respectively. If time transfers are made in exchange for money, then one would expect a sharper drop in $P(R_p > 0)$ as distance makes time transfers more difficult. Although it is logically possible to argue that the monetary value of the time transfers does not vary with distance despite the steep drop-off in transfer incidence and transfer hours, this seems improbable, especially given other results (discussed in the next section) indicating that time transfers to the parents have little connection to money transfers from the parents.

We have also used the conditional logit model as an alternative approach to controlling for unobserved error components and the resources of the household and as a check on the sign pattern and statistical significance of the linear probability model results. We obtain the same sign pattern, and the *t*-statistics are also very similar to what we obtain with the linear probability models. The results are omitted to save space.

In sum, our examination of the effects of differences in the incomes of the husband's parents and the wife's parents on the relative probability of transfers to and from them has produced four main findings. First, the difference in the incomes of the husband's and wife's parents is positively related to the difference in the probability that they receive money transfers from the children. Second, the difference in the incomes of the two sets of parents is negatively related to the difference in the probability that they provide money transfers to the children. Third, the income difference has a negative but insignificant relationship to the difference in the probability of giving time transfers. Fourth, the set of parents who live closer to the children are more likely to give and receive time transfers but are only slightly more likely to give money.

The Effects of Relative Incomes of Divorced Parents on Transfers

The linear probability models in Table 14.16 relate differences between divorced fathers and mothers in the probability of giving or receiving a transfer to the characteristics of the parents. The analysis yields three main results. First, all four transfers are much more likely to involve mothers than fathers. The difference is particularly large for $P(S_k > 0)$ if the mother has not remarried.

Table 14.16. Difference in the probability of transfers to and from divorced parents (OLS regression coefficients, standard errors in parentheses)

Independent variable	Label	Δ parent gave child money (1)	Δ child gave parent money (2)	Δ parent gave child time (3)	Δ child gave parent time (4)
Parental household: divorced, remarried father	ΔFATHDREM	0.0258	−0.0030	0.0024	0.0096
		(0.0370)	(0.0148)	(0.0405)	(0.0396)
Parental household: divorced, not remarried mother	ΔMOTHDSIN	0.0705	0.0267	0.1509	0.2647
		(0.0342)	(0.0137)	(0.0373)	(0.0366)
Parental household: divorced, remarried mother	ΔMOTHDREM	0.0727	0.0177	0.1543	0.1235
		(0.0367)	(0.0146)	(0.0400)	(0.0392)
Child's report of parent's age	ΔKRPAGE	0.1874	−0.1096	−0.3059	−0.1536
		(0.1260)	(0.0507)	(0.1379)	(0.1351)
Square of child's report of parent's age	ΔKRPAGE2	−0.0038	0.0019	0.0049	0.0027
		(0.0022)	(0.0009)	(0.0024)	(0.0024)
Cube of child's report of parent's age	ΔKRPAGE3	2.5E-5	−1.1E-5	−2.5E-5	−1.5E-5
		(1.2E-5)	(5.1E-6)	(1.4E-5)	(1.4E-5)
Child's report of health (1 = excellent, 5 = poor)	ΔKRPHLTH	−0.0327	0.0100	−0.0138	0.0164
		(0.0131)	(0.0053)	(0.0144)	(0.0141)
Distance to parent's house (estimated)	ΔKRPDIST	−7.9E-5	7.6E-6	−4.7E-4	−4.7E-4
		(7.2E-5)	(2.9E-5)	(8.0E-5)	(7.8E-5)
Parent resides with child	ΔPINHOUS	0.1029	−0.0266	0.1051	0.1728
		(0.0915)	(0.0370)	(0.1003)	(0.0982)
Parent resides in nursing home	ΔPINNH	−0.0930	−0.0114	−0.0412	0.2161
		(0.1283)	(0.0519)	(0.1406)	(0.1377)
Parent resides with another relative	ΔPINORH	−0.0382	0.0024	0.0501	−0.0264
		(0.0587)	(0.0235)	(0.0644)	(0.0630)
Log of child's report of parent's income	ΔLKRPINC	0.0164	−0.0183	0.0050	0.0009
		(0.0169)	(0.0068)	(0.0184)	(0.0181)

Note: The dependent variable and independent variables represent the differences between values for the respondent's mother and father. The sample consists of respondents in the full sample whose parents are divorced and living.

Source: PSID 1988.

Second, the pattern of the coefficients on distance from parents is similar to the pattern for parents and parents-in-law for married couples in Table 14.15. In particular, there is no evidence that money transfers from the parents buy time transfers from the child. Third, the relative resources of the parents matter. The difference in the current incomes of divorced parents is positively related to the difference in the probability that they provide money to the child (column 1) and negatively related to the difference in the probability that they receive money from the child (column 2). Only the latter effect is statistically significant. The difference in current incomes has a small and statistically insignificant effect on the difference in probabilities of help in the form of time from parents to child or from child to parent (column 3 and 4). These results confirm a main theme of the chapter, which is that money transfers tend to compensate in part for income differences among relatives. We obtain qualitatively similar results using conditional logit models (not shown).

The Interrelationship between Time and Money Transfers

As a crude attempt to look at the links between time and money transfers, we added the dummy variables for ($S_p > 0$) and ($S_k > 0$) to probit and Tobit models of $R_k > 0$, $R_p > 0$, and added $R_k > 0$, $R_p > 0$, and $S_p > 0(S_k > 0)$ to the model for $S_k > 0(S_p > 0)$. The models are otherwise the same as those underlying columns 1 to 4 of Table 14.6 when only the linear terms in Y_p and Y_k are entered. The results are reported in Table 14.17.

The regression produces two strong results. The first is the strong positive association between time transfers received and time transfers given. For example, in the Tobit model for S_p the coefficient on ($S_k > 0$) is 613, and in the

Table 14.17. Interrelationship between time and money transfers

	Probit models: derivatives of the transfer probability (standard errors), dependent variable				Tobit models: Tobit coefficients (standard errors), dependent variable			
	$P(R_p > 0)$	$P(R_k > 0)$	$P(S_p > 0)$	$P(S_k > 0)$	R_p	R_k	S_p	S_k
$R_p > 0$			0.165	0.0022			208	22.4
			(0.024)	(0.0245)			(42)	(35.3)
$R_k > 0$			0.063	0.1546			127	71.4
			(0.067)	(0.0624)			(119)	(88.3)
$S_p > 0$	0.133	0.0053		0.415	2,091	320		508
	(0.019)	(0.0049)		(0.021)	(357)	(257)		(31)
$S_k > 0$	−0.0094	0.0096	0.423		−47.2	575	613	
	(0.0193)	(0.0047)	(0.021)		(369)	(250)	(39)	

Note: See Tables 14.6 and 14.7 for a list of the other variables included in the models. The equations include linear terms in Y_p and Y_k and exclude assets.

Source: PSID 1988.

Tobit model for S_k the coefficient on S_p is 508 (31). This has an altruism interpretation if parents and children receive utility from helping each other or an altruism or exchange interpretation if (1) parents have a comparative advantage over children in certain tasks and (2) market alternatives are a poor substitute for help from family members. The second result is that persons who provide (or receive) money also tend to provide (or receive) time, although the effects are not always statistically significant. Moreover, the effect of R_p on S_p is much stronger than the effect on S_k, and $S_k > 0$ actually has a negative effect on $P(R_p > 0)$ and R_p. One interpretation of these results is that the extent to which parents and children are altruistically linked varies among families. Those with strong links provide time help in both directions and money help from the most needy to the least. An explanation that involves money transfers paying for time transfers is less obvious, given that the time transfers go in both directions and that the coefficient on S_k is negative in the equations for R_p.

One may control for the needs, preferences, and resources of the child by adding $\Delta(S_p > 0)$ and $\Delta(S_k > 0)$ to the differenced linear probability model for money transfers from parents and parents-in-law discussed above. The coefficient on $\Delta(S_p > 0)$ is 0.11 (0.041), indicating that money transfers are much more likely in the presence of time transfers from the same parent. However, the coefficient on $\Delta(S_k > 0)$ is only 0.012 (0.78). These results are fully consistent with those in Table 14.17.

Conclusion

Our analysis indicates that money transfers tend to reduce inequality in household incomes and that time transfers are only weakly related to income differences. Richer siblings give more to parents and receive less. Among parents and parents in-law the richer set of parents is more likely to give money and less likely to receive money. The same is true of divorced parents. In contrast to simple exchange models of transfers, we find little evidence in the cross-sectional analysis or in our analyses of siblings that parental income or wealth increases time transfers from children or that time transfers are exchanged for money transfers. And in neither the cross-section nor among siblings is the strong negative relationship between time transfers and distance from parents associated with a strong negative relationship with either distance or money transfers.

Our results and those of other recent studies suggest several stylized facts about family transfers in the United States. First, money transfers tend to flow from rich to poor within the extended family. Second, the magnitude of the response of transfers to differences in incomes is small. Third, time transfers are common and flow in both directions. Fourth, time flows decline sharply with distance but money flows do not. Fifth, time flows from children do not tend to be accompanied by money flows from their parents, and vice versa. There is some evidence that parents who give money are also likely to give time. Sixth, money transfers are more responsive to the current income of the children than to their permanent incomes. Seventh, the transfers are not generated by unidirectional altruism.

Although our purpose has been to help develop a solid empirical foundation for modelling economic relationships between parents and children rather than to formally test alternative structural models of the family, we close the chapter with a few comments on what the results seem to imply. At first glance, the findings would seem to square fairly well with an altruism model in which households maximize utility functions defined over their own consumption and the utility of others. There is little evidence, at least for the United States, that money transfers are an implicit payment for services. However, in Altonji *et al.* (1995) we point out that the second stylized fact about family transfers is a serious problem for such an altruism model. The responsiveness of transfers to income is an order of magnitude smaller than the prediction of a model in which preferences depend on the consumption of one's own household and the utility of others. A number of possible modifications to the basic altruism model exist that would help square the model with the facts. These include the possibility that parents have little information about the needs of their adult children, possible jealousy or envy on the part of siblings who learn that they have received less money than their siblings, the negative incentive effects of providing too much income security, or the possibility that when there are multiple siblings, bargaining costs lead to inefficient outcomes. We explore some of these modifications in Altonji *et al.* (1995) and conclude that none of them is sufficient to save the basic altruism model. However, we are still in the early stage of developing empirically tractable models of strategic altruism as well as alternative models of family behaviour that share some of the predictions of the altruism model regarding the redistribution of resources and the provision of resources.[22] The challenge is to find a parsimonious model that can fit the facts at each stage of the life cycle.

Appendix A: Comparisons of Alternative Measures of Family Transfers

We used the matched sample to check whether the form of the question about money given affected the responses. Parents and children in our matched sample responded to question 5, which asked whether they had received money from any individual other than their parents and, if so, to identify the donor. Respondents also answered questions 1 and 6, which asked about help they had provided in the form of money and time and who the recipient was. We found that responses to the more general questions were less likely to identify a transfer received or given than were responses to the questions that singled out parents as potential recipients or donors. The parents reported giving money to the child (question 1) in 4.1 per cent of the parent-child matches, whereas the children reported receiving money (question 4) in 19.4 per cent of the matches. The parents reported giving time help to the child (question 6) in 5.5 per cent of the matches, whereas the child reported receiving time help from the parent household in 29.3 per cent of the matches. Only 3.2 of the parents' households reported receiving time help from the child's household (question 5), but children reported giving time to the parental household in 28.6 per cent of the matches.

We also examined the relationship between the 1988 transfer supplement data and responses to questions about income received by the head of household and spouse (if present) in 1987 that was 'help from relatives'. This question was asked in the 1988 survey and many earlier surveys. It did not ask the respondent to identify the specific relationship between the donor and the recipient. The unweighted fraction of the children who reported help from relatives in 1988 is only 6.4 per cent, less than one-third of the fraction who reported help from parents. However, 63.7 per cent of those who reported receiving help from relatives also reported receiving money from parents. Only 2.6 per cent of the parent households reported receiving help from relatives, but the percentage is 18.2 among parents whose children reported giving money to the parental household. It is possible that the help received by the parent came from a different child. Among parental households who reported receiving monetary help from the child, 36.8 per cent also reported receiving financial help from relatives. Overall, the cross-tabulations of the information based on the 'help from relatives' questions and the responses to the 1988 transfer supplement suggest that questions that do not identify the donor or recipient lead to lower response rates, and that the measures of the monetary transfers are approximate.

Appendix B: Other Determinants of Transfers

Table 14B.1 reports weighted means of a wider class of variables for the matched sample, classified by transfer status. Most of the variables are used in the multivariate analyses. Column 1 presents the means for all observations in the matched sample. Columns 2 and 3 contrast the means for parent-child pairs in which the parents either did not or did give money to the child. Columns 4 and 5 contrast the means for children who either did not or did give money to the parents. Columns 6 and 7 contrast the means for pairs in which the parents either did not or did spend time helping the child. Columns 8 and 9 report the means for pairs in which the child either did not or did spend time helping the parents. The table provides weighted means for the subset of variables that are available for the full sample.

Tables 14B.2 and 14B.3 present estimates of the effects of control variables used in our analysis on, respectively, the probability of transfers and the amount of transfers. The estimates in Table 14B.2 are based on a probit model. The estimates in Table 14B.3 are based on the expected value of the transfer amount (including zero transfers) and are derived from Tobit estimates. In both tables the estimates are relative to the transfer probability for a 30-year-old white married male with two siblings, no children, good health, a permanent household income of $45,000, and no unemployment in the previous year, and whose parents are married 60-year-olds in average health with a permanent income of $48,000, live 140 miles away, and are not in a nursing home or living with a relative.

Space precludes a detailed discussion of these tables. However, the parents' marital status and health and the child's gender, age, and distance from the parents all play important roles in the transfer of assistance between generations. See Shoeni (1993*c*) for a discussion of the evidence from the PSID and other studies. See also Cox (1987) and Cox and Raines (1985) for descriptive statistics on the determinants of money transfers, based on the data sets from the President's Commission on Pension Policy; Gale and Sholz (1994) for descriptive statistics on money transfers, from the Survey of Consumer Finances; and Dunn (1993*a*) and Rosenzweig Wolpin (1993, 1994) from the National Longitudinal Surveys of Labor Market Experience.

Table 14B.1. Weighted means by transfer status, matched sample: United States, 1988

Variable name	Label	All transfer categories (1)	No money to child (2)	Money to child (3)	No money to parent (4)	Money to parent (5)	No time to child (6)	Time to child (7)	No time to parent (8)	Time to parent (9)
Transfers										
Parent gave child money	KRMGPKI	0.240	0.000	1.000	0.242	0.108	0.195	0.335	0.227	0.277
Child gave parent money	KRMGKPI	0.017	0.018	0.007	0.000	1.000	0.013	0.018	0.009	0.030
Parent gave child time	KRTGPKI	0.302	0.262	0.425	0.300	0.380	0.000	1.000	0.174	0.645
Child gave parent time	KRTGKPI	0.273	0.260	0.314	0.269	0.560	0.139	0.582	0.000	1.000
Amount of money parent gave child ($s)	KRMGPKA	444.058	0.000	1,850.785	446.545	297.537	369.656	610.748	425.454	507.016
Amount of money child gave parent ($s)	KRMGKPA	22.648	15.225	27.366	0.000	1,323.705	7.465	41.273	5.131	52.268
Amount of time parent gave child (hours)	KRTGPKA	84.747	72.071	124.965	83.274	109.484	0.000	280.629	43.866	194.971
Amount of time child gave parent (hours)	KRTGKPA	66.145	60.187	83.639	64.537	171.571	29.343	148.283	0.000	241.958
Sex and marital status of child										
Child is unmarried female	KSINFEM	0.179	0.166	0.222	0.179	0.217	0.150	0.239	0.164	0.212
Child is unmarried male	KSINMAL	0.152	0.126	0.237	0.152	0.158	0.153	0.148	0.144	0.176
Child is married female	KMARFEM	0.328	0.347	0.256	0.328	0.340	0.320	0.341	0.342	0.284
Child is married male	KMARMAL	0.341	0.361	0.286	0.341	0.285	0.377	0.272	0.349	0.328
Composition of parent's household										
Parent is both mother and father	FATHMOTH	0.594	0.578	0.659	0.601	0.244	0.576	0.651	0.619	0.552
Parent is divorced, not remarried father	FATHDSIN	0.026	0.027	0.021	0.026	0.001	0.028	0.018	0.024	0.027
Parent is divorced, remarried father	FATHDREM	0.032	0.031	0.037	0.032	0.026	0.038	0.020	0.036	0.021
Parent is widowed, not remarried father	FATHWSIN	0.017	0.019	0.010	0.017	0.020	0.021	0.010	0.017	0.018
Parent is widowed, remarried father	FATHWREM	0.017	0.020	0.008	0.018	0.000	0.020	0.014	0.020	0.012
Parent is divorced, not remarried mother	MOTHDSIN	0.074	0.075	0.061	0.073	0.110	0.073	0.067	0.063	0.092
Parent is divorced, remarried mother	MOTHDREM	0.048	0.046	0.046	0.047	0.082	0.049	0.038	0.050	0.033
Parent is widowed, not remarried mother	MOTHWSIN	0.151	0.160	0.124	0.146	0.431	0.156	0.138	0.125	0.213
Parent is widowed, remarried mother	MOTHWREM	0.041	0.044	0.034	0.040	0.086	0.040	0.043	0.045	0.032
Parents are married but live apart	KRPLVAPT	0.006	0.006	0.007	0.006	0.007	0.005	0.007	0.005	0.008
Other demographics										
No. of children in child's HH 0-2	KNKUND2	0.252	0.251	0.251	0.254	0.158	0.207	0.352	0.246	0.264
No. of children in child's HH 3-5	KNK3TO5	0.265	0.286	0.195	0.265	0.264	0.252	0.284	0.263	0.262
No. of children in child's HH 6+	KNKOV6	0.692	0.778	0.441	0.691	0.669	0.736	0.592	0.721	0.608
No. of children in single child's HH	KSINKIDS	0.174	0.173	0.173	0.174	0.156	0.135	0.246	0.153	0.213
Age of child	KAGE	31.110	31.656	29.533	31.068	32.850	31.726	29.691	31.457	30.194
Age of parent	PAGE	59.699	60.080	58.679	59.623	63.512	60.124	58.786	59.852	59.340
No. of parent's children from child's report of sibs	N CHILD	4.392	4.579	3.794	4.392	4.312	4.507	4.089	4.376	4.387
Reports race as not white	NONWHITE CHILD	0.116	0.124	0.082	0.113	0.282	0.113	0.113	0.103	0.144

Location and distance										
Parent resides with child	PINHOUS	0.049	0.041	0.072	0.049	0.023	0.032	0.082	0.030	0.096
Parent resides in nursing home	PINNH	0.002	0.003	0.000	0.002	0.023	0.001	0.003	0.001	0.005
Parent resides with another relative	PINORH	0.012	0.011	0.015	0.012	0.004	0.012	0.012	0.011	0.014
Parent lives less than 1 mile away	PDLT	0.120	0.125	0.107	0.119	0.205	0.092	0.186	0.089	0.201
Parent lives 1–10 miles away	PD1_10	0.280	0.287	0.247	0.282	0.198	0.249	0.341	0.248	0.355
Parent lives 10–100 miles away	PD10_100	0.252	0.253	0.252	0.252	0.226	0.257	0.248	0.260	0.239
Parent lives more than 100 miles away	PD100UP	0.298	0.293	0.321	0.297	0.348	0.370	0.142	0.373	0.107
Health										
Child's HH changed head since 1986	KCHS86	0.168	0.137	0.256	0.168	0.212	0.151	0.204	0.159	0.193
Child's HH head's health excellent in 1986	KHEX	0.300	0.300	0.300	0.302	0.234	0.306	0.284	0.317	0.259
Child's HH head's health very good in 1986	KHVG	0.306	0.320	0.275	0.305	0.371	0.309	0.305	0.305	0.314
Child's HH head's health good in 1986	KHGD	0.174	0.190	0.130	0.175	0.112	0.180	0.164	0.172	0.180
Child's HH head's health fair in 1986	KHFR	0.044	0.045	0.035	0.044	0.052	0.046	0.038	0.040	0.046
Child's HH head's health poor in 1986	KHPR	0.007	0.009	0.004	0.007	0.019	0.008	0.007	0.007	0.009
Parent's HH changed head since 1986	PCHS86	0.039	0.038	0.036	0.038	0.131	0.037	0.035	0.033	0.046
Parent's HH head's health excellent in 1986	PHEX	0.167	0.152	0.220	0.170	0.001	0.167	0.175	0.180	0.141
Parent's HH head's health very good in 1986	PHVG	0.256	0.250	0.271	0.257	0.199	0.254	0.259	0.275	0.206
Parent's HH head's health good in 1986	PHGD	0.286	0.285	0.297	0.286	0.322	0.287	0.290	0.283	0.304
Parent's HH head's health fair in 1986	PHFR	0.176	0.190	0.135	0.175	0.216	0.181	0.168	0.166	0.202
Parent's HH head's health poor in 1986	PHPR	0.075	0.084	0.043	0.074	0.131	0.074	0.074	0.063	0.101
Assets and income										
Log of child's permanent income	KLOGPINC	10.766	10.767	10.768	10.763	10.923	10.782	10.743	10.801	10.687
Log of parent's permanent income	PLOHPINC	10.923	10.871	11.086	10.928	10.608	10.931	10.910	10.956	10.851
Log of child's current income	KLOGINC	10.184	10.229	10.044	10.180	10.402	10.278	9.995	10.289	9.920
Log of parent's current income	PLOGINC	10.061	9.973	10.320	10.072	9.397	10.042	10.129	10.117	9.962
Log of child's permanent earnings	KLPFERN	10.665	10.674	10.645	10.662	10.835	10.683	10.642	10.700	10.589
Log of parent's permanent earnings	PLPFERN	10.732	10.663	10.943	10.737	10.404	10.738	10.729	10.773	10.648
Child's HH head changed head since 84	KCHS84	0.310	0.267	0.431	0.311	0.294	0.280	0.374	0.294	0.352
Child's assets in 1984 if same head ($000s)	KASSET84	26.773	29.119	20.483	26.145	57.389	28.416	23.430	27.870	24.196
Parent's HH head changed head since 84	PCHS84	0.075	0.070	0.081	0.073	0.157	0.073	0.068	0.063	0.091
Parent's assets in 1984 if same head ($000s)	PASSET84	124.798	110.126	169.364	126.311	36.872	124.254	129.610	131.795	112.598
Hours of child's HH head's unemployment	KUEMPH88	73.619	66.090	99.199	72.555	119.576	65.217	91.952	61.982	104.038
Child's HH head unemployed more than 1,000 hours	KUEM1000	0.023	0.021	0.031	0.022	0.064	0.019	0.032	0.017	0.039
Hours of parent HH head's unemployment	PUEMPH88	37.579	42.796	23.429	36.872	82.821	43.351	24.844	40.976	30.663
Parent's HH head unemployed more than 1,000 hours	PUEM1000	0.011	0.013	0.006	0.011	0.028	0.014	0.005	0.014	0.006
No. of observations		3,561	2,774	688	3,476	78	2,432	1,001	2,408	1,046

Note: The number of observations may not be consistent across transfer types because of missing data.

Source: PSID 1988.

Table 14B.2. Effects of the child's and parent's characteristics on the probability of a transfer (results based on probit models)

Child's or parent's characteristic	Money transfer, parent to child (1)	Money transfer, child to parent (2)	Time transfer, parent to child (3)	Time transfer, child to parent (4)
Base case probability	0.2426	0.0038	0.2205	0.2439
Difference from base case				
Child is 22 years old	0.0843‡	0.0033*	0.1005‡	0.0718‡
	(0.0268)	(0.0020)	(0.0236)	(0.0252)
Child is 38 years old	−0.0832‡	0.0011	−0.1018‡	−0.1031‡
	(0.0232)	(0.0015)	(0.0197)	(0.0206)
Parent is 52 years old	0.0093	0.0005	−0.0055	−0.0108
	(0.0155)	(0.0011)	(0.0133)	(0.0141)
Parent is 75 years old	0.0183	0.0046†	0.0629†	0.0948‡
	(0.0339)	(0.0021)	(0.0290)	(0.0301)
Single male	0.0683†	−0.0004	0.0856‡	0.0375
	(0.0297)	(0.0024)	(0.0278)	(0.0291)
Married female	−0.0127	0.0000	0.0676‡	−0.0393*
	(0.0230)	(0.0018)	(0.0201)	(0.0214)
Single female	0.0166	0.0022	0.1319‡	0.0519*
	(0.0322)	(0.0023)	(0.0293)	(0.0307)
1 child in base household	−0.0243†	−0.0010	0.0290‡	0.0051
	(0.0101)	(0.0008)	(0.0086)	(0.0091)
1 child in single male household	0.0698†	−0.0023	0.1069‡	0.0259
	(0.0321)	(0.0025)	(0.0296)	(0.0310)
1 child in single female household	0.0181	0.0003	0.1532‡	0.0403
	(0.0288)	(0.0021)	(0.0260)	(0.0271)
Father is divorced, not remarried	−0.1417†	−0.0484	−0.1957‡	−0.0921*
	(0.0604)	(0.6598)	(0.0558)	(0.0563)
Father is divorced, remarried	−0.0926†	−0.0036	−0.2599‡	−0.2086‡
	(0.0437)	(0.0053)	(0.0504)	(0.0556)
Father is widowed, not remarried	−0.1648‡	−0.0048	−0.1851‡	−0.0454
	(0.0625)	(0.0077)	(0.0535)	(0.0506)
Father is widowed, remarried	−0.1647†	−0.0303	−0.0617	−0.0363
	(0.0766)	(0.8650)	(0.0631)	(0.0708)
Mother is divorced, not remarried	−0.0473	0.0060‡	−0.0448*	0.0910‡
	(0.0319)	(0.0022)	(0.0274)	(0.0283)
Mother is divorced, remarried	−0.0804†	0.0063†	−0.0663*	−0.0364
	(0.0411)	(0.0028)	(0.0371)	(0.0407)
Mother is widowed, not remarried	−0.0592†	0.0095‡	−0.0215	0.1366‡
	(0.0254)	(0.0017)	(0.0214)	(0.0219)
Mother is widowed, remarried	−0.1112*	0.0032	−0.0100	−0.0494
	(0.0578)	(0.0045)	(0.0459)	(0.0519)
Parents are married, live apart	−0.1189*	0.0038	−0.0223	0.0291
	(0.0717)	(0.0040)	(0.0513)	(0.0527)
Non-white	−0.0401*	0.0038†	−0.0582‡	−0.0325*
	(0.0225)	(0.0016)	(0.0190)	(0.0198)
Parent resides with child	0.0204	−0.0096†	0.1844‡	0.1777‡
	(0.0331)	(0.0043)	(0.0289)	(0.0305)
Parent lives 20 miles away	0.0014	−0.0006	0.0581‡	0.0754‡
	(0.0051)	(0.0004)	(0.0051)	(0.0057)
Parent lives 1,000 miles away	−0.0097	0.0043	−0.4161‡	−0.5402‡
	(0.0366)	(0.0026)	(0.0365)	(0.0410)
Parent resides in nursing home	−1.1691	0.0177†	0.0229	0.1789
	(15.68)	(0.0078)	(0.1826)	(0.1647)

Parent resides with other relative	−0.0230	0.0006	−0.0823	−0.0201
	(0.0738)	(0.0041)	(0.0616)	(0.0584)
Child's health is excellent	−0.0119	−0.0002	0.0020	−0.0001
	(0.0097)	(0.0007)	(0.0084)	(0.0089)
Child's health is poor	0.0357	0.0005	−0.0059	0.0004
	(0.0291)	(0.0022)	(0.0251)	(0.0267)
Parent's health is excellent	−0.0096	−0.0006	0.0239	−0.0396‡
	(0.0167)	(0.0013)	(0.0146)	(0.0153)
Parent's health is poor	0.0096	0.0006	−0.0239	0.0396‡
	(0.0167)	(0.0013)	(0.0146)	(0.0153)
Child HH head unemployed 100 hours	0.0057	−0.0004	0.0017	0.0008
	(0.0050)	(0.0004)	(0.0043)	(0.0045)
Child HH head unemployed 1,000 hours	−0.0023	0.0053	0.0222	0.0594
	(0.0480)	(0.0033)	(0.0402)	(0.0415)
Parent HH head unemployed 100 hours	−0.0049	0.0007	−0.0024	−0.0042
	(0.0079)	(0.0004)	(0.0064)	(0.0069)
Parent HH head unemployed 1,000 hours	−0.1722	0.0019	−0.1436*	−0.0674
	(0.1106)	(0.0049)	(0.0822)	(0.0833)
Child has no siblings	0.1996‡	0.0018	0.0887‡	0.0141
	(0.0323)	(0.0023)	(0.0295)	(0.0316)
Child has 4 siblings	−0.0399‡	−0.0004	−0.0177‡	−0.0028
	(0.0065)	(0.0005)	(0.0059)	(0.0063)
Child income is in 10th percentile	0.0435†	−0.0065‡	0.0146	−0.0008
	(0.0215)	(0.0019)	(0.0183)	(0.0195)
Child income is in 25th percentile	0.0275‡	−0.0023‡	0.0056	0.0021
	(0.0106)	(0.0009)	(0.0090)	(0.0096)
Child income is in 75th percentile	−0.0385	−0.0032	0.0015	0.0190
	(0.0258)	(0.0033)	(0.0213)	(0.0228)
Child income is in 90th percentile	−0.0505‡	0.0023†	−0.0045	−0.0279*
	(0.0150)	(0.0012)	(0.0134)	(0.0148)
Parent income is in 10th percentile	−0.1301‡	0.0057‡	−0.0017	0.0419†
	(0.0198)	(0.0013)	(0.0160)	(0.0167)
Parent income is in 25th percentile	−0.0803‡	0.0030‡	0.0015	0.0157*
	(0.0107)	(0.0008)	(0.0091)	(0.0096)
Parent income is in 75th percentile	0.0794‡	−0.0022‡	−0.0034	−0.0046
	(0.0096)	(0.0007)	(0.0083)	(0.0086)
Parent income is in 90th percentile	0.1636‡	−0.0037†	−0.0061	−0.0054
	(0.0184)	(0.0015)	(0.0163)	(0.0172)

* significant at the 10% level.
† significant at the 5% level.
‡ significant at the 1% level.

Notes:

1. Standard errors in parentheses.
2. Variables in the model include ksinfem, kmarfem, knkid88, ksinkids, fathdsin, fathdrem, fathwsin, fathwrem, mothdsin, mothdrem, mothwsin, mothwrem, krplvapt, nonwhite, pinhous, pinnh, pinorh, khlth88, phlth88, kuemph88, kuem1000, puemph88, puem1000, krpdist, invnkid, and a cubic in kage, page, klogpinc, and plogpinc. Definitions are in Table 14B.1.
3. The estimates in Table 14B.2 are the effects on the expected value of the transfer amount (including zero transfers) and are derived from Tobit coefficients. In both tables the estimates are relative to the transfer probability for a 30-year-old white married male with two siblings, no children, good health, a permanent household income of $45,000, and no unemployment, whose parents are 60 years old, married, in average health, with a permanent income of $48,000, a head of household with no unemployment, and who live 140 miles away and are not in a nursing home or living with a relative.
4. Child's permanent income distribution: 10th percentile = $19,843; 25th percentile = $30,019; 75th percentile = $60,681; 90th percentile = $77,997. Parent's permanent income distribution: 10th percentile = $23,806; 25th percentile = $32,792; 75th percentile = $66,601; 90th percentile = $93,429.

Source: PSID 1988.

Table 14B.3. Effects of the child's and parent's characteristics on transfer amounts (estimates derived from Tobit models)

Child's or parent's characteristic	Money transfer, parent to child (1)	Money transfer child to parent (2)	Time transfer, parent to child (3)	Time transfer, child to parent (4)
Base case amount ($s)	585	6	78	58
Difference from base case				
Child is 22 years old	215†	−2.4*	41‡	31‡
	(88)	(1.5)	(10)	(8)
Child is 38 years old	−155†	5.3‡	−46‡	−25‡
	(77)	(1.3)	(9)	(7)
Parent is 52 years old	49	9.2‡	−9	−6
	(51)	(1.0)	(6)	(4)
Parent is 75 years old	53	−23.7‡	23*	21+
	(111)	(2.7)	(13)	(10)
Single male	140	0.7	37‡	14
	(97)	(1.7)	(13)	(9)
Married female	−38	−0.3	34‡	−9
	(76)	(1.3)	(9)	(7)
Single female	−38	1.0	58‡	27‡
	(106)	(1.8)	(13)	(10)
1 child in base household	−71†	0.2	10‡	1
	(33)	(0.5)	(4)	(3)
1 child in single male household	156	0.3	47‡	12
	(105)	(1.8)	(13)	(10)
1 child in single female household	−22	0.6	69‡	25‡
	(95)	(1.6)	(12)	(9)
Father divorced, not remarried	−442†	−0.4	−71‡	−21
	(203)	(3.2)	(26)	(18)
Father divorced, remarried	−303†	0.4	−117‡	−68‡
	(144)	(2.3)	(24)	(19)
Father widowed, not remarried	−490†	−0.4	−74‡	−16
	(212)	(3.9)	(24)	(16)
Father widowed, remarried	−542†	−0.8	−12	−6
	(263)	(4.8)	(28)	(23)
Mother divorced, not remarried	−192*	1.6	−9	22†
	(106)	(1.5)	(12)	(9)
Mother divorced, remarried	−212	1.0	−25	−8
	(135)	(1.9)	(17)	(13)
Mother widowed, not remarried	−185†	1.0	−6	48‡
	(84)	(1.4)	(10)	(7)
Mother widowed, remarried	−352*	0.3	−36*	−18
	(193)	(2.7)	(22)	(17)
Parents married, live apart	−341	0.1	−17	12
	(242)	(3.1)	(23)	(17)
Non-white	−112	1.2	−17†	−3
	(75)	(1.2)	(9)	(6)
Parent resides with child	67	−1.4	82‡	68‡
	(109)	(2.0)	(12)	(9)
Parent lives 20 miles away	7	−0.4	24‡	23‡
	(17)	(0.3)	(2)	(2)
Parent lives 1,000 miles away	−48	2.8	−170‡	−162‡
	(120)	(2.0)	(17)	(14)

Parent resides in nursing home	−3,761	3.7	−16	28
	(50,280)	(8.4)	(87)	(50)
Parent resides with other relative	−53	−1.0	−44	3
	(248)	(3.6)	(28)	(18)
Child's health is excellent	−5	0.1	2	1
	(32)	(0.5)	(4)	(3)
Child's health is poor	15	−0.3	−5	−2
	(97)	(1.6)	(11)	(9)
Parent's health is excellent	−32	−0.2	8	−14‡
	(55)	(0.9)	(7)	(5)
Parent's health is poor	32	0.2	−8	14‡
	(55)	(0.9)	(7)	(5)
Child HH head unemployed 100 hours	19	−0.1	1	2
	(17)	(0.3)	(2)	(1)
Child HH head unemployed 1,000 hours	−4	0.4	15	14
	(159)	(2.6)	(18)	(13)
Parent HH head unemployed 100 hours	−2	0.1	−2	−2
	(26)	(0.4)	(3)	(2)
Parent HH head unemployed 1,000 hours	−162	0.1	−59	0.3
	(335)	(4.1)	(37)	(26)
Child has no siblings	646‡	0.6	53‡	23†
	(105)	(1.8)	(13)	(1)
Child has 4 siblings	−129‡	−0.1	−11‡	−5†
	(21)	(0.4)	(3)	(2)
Child's income is in 10th percentile	91	−1.8	2	5
	(71)	(1.2)	(8)	(6)
Child's income is in 25th percentile	61*	−0.9	1	3
	(35)	(0.6)	(4)	(3)
Child's income is in 75th percentile	−64	1.2	5	3
	(85)	(1.4)	(9)	(7)
Child's income is in 90th percentile	−139‡	1.2	−4	−6
	(49)	(0.8)	(6)	(5)
Parent's income is in 10th percentile	−344‡	1.7*	4	14†
	(67)	(1.0)	(7)	(5)
Parent's income is in 25th percentile	−195‡	0.9	5	6†
	(35)	(0.6)	(4)	(3)
Parent's income is in 75th percentile	211‡	−0.6	−8†	−4
	(32)	(0.5)	(4)	(3)
Parent's income is in 90th percentile	503‡	−1.0	−16†	−7
	(62)	(1.0)	(7)	(6)

Notes: See notes in Table 14B.2.
Source: PSID 1988.

Notes

We are grateful to Daniel Aaronson and especially to Charles Pierret for excellent research assistance and to the National Institute of Aging and the Center for Urban Affairs and Policy Research, Northwestern University, for financial support. We also thank Alessandro Cigno, Thomas Dunn, and Finis Welch, participants in the Seminar on Intergenerational Economic Relations and Demographic Change, and participants in seminars at Duke University, Michigan State University, Northwestern University, Syracuse University, the University of Wisconsin, and the National Bureau of Economic Research for their valuable comments.

1. The original National Longitudinal Survey of Labor Market Experience (NLS) cohorts share a number of advantages of the PSID for the study of transfers. Analysing the NLS cohort data, Rosenzweig and Wolpin (1993,1994) have emphasized tradeoffs between public and private transfers, as well as the effects of movements in current income relative to permanent income on transfers. Dunn (1993*a*) has examined some of the same issues that we explore in this chapter.
2. In addition, the availability of data on food expenditures in years prior to 1988 make it possible to construct proxies for the relative marginal utility of income among households. We have made use of this information to study altruistic links among households and family risk-sharing in Altonji, Hayashi, and Kotlikoff (1992) and Hayashi, Altonji, and Kotlikoff (1996).
3. The finding that R_p has a distribution, even after conditioning on Y_k, Y_p, and observed preference shifters, and the finding that the conditional probability of $R_p > 0$ is neither 1 nor zero indicate that unobserved preference shifters are important empirically. Intuitively, two factors may give rise to a positive association between Y_k and R_P under the null hypothesis of altruism. The first is that the amount of income that will be shifted in response to a given difference in the preferences (needs) of the parents and the child will depend on the level of income of the parents and the child, holding the ratio constant. In this case, the mean and variance of positive transfers could be positively related to the child's income as well as to the parents' income. The mean of a random variable that is truncated from below is positively related to the dispersion of the untruncated distribution in many cases. As a crude check on the empirical significance of this issue, we modified the Tobit models of R_P (reported below) to allow the coefficients and error variance to depend on whether the average of the permanent incomes of the parents and the children was in the top third of the distribution of these averages. The coefficients and the error variance are in fact substantially larger for parent-child pairs with high incomes than for other families. The second factor that may lead to a positive relation between Y_k and R_p is a more conventional problem of selectivity. When parental income is held constant, parents who provide transfers to rich children tend to have weaker preferences for their own consumption, to have children who have strong needs for consumption goods, or to be more altruistic than parents who provide transfers to poorer children. We conclude that the sign of the estimated relationship between Y_k and R_p does not provide a clean test of the altruism model. In fairness, we should point out that Cox (1987) tries to address the problem of selectivity. However, the fact that transfer functions are not additively separable in income and observed and unobserved preference components (the first factor mentioned above) invalidates the conventional methods he uses to deal with the problem, and he relies primarily on OLS regression.

4. As an example, consider house painting. Rich people may have a large demand for high-quality work that can be done only by skilled professionals. Poorer people may demand less expensive, lower-quality work that can be done by either less skilled professional painters or relatives. Yet rich parents and poor parents may place equal value on attention and respect from their adult children, for which there are no market substitutes.
5. Owing to a programming error, nine of the children who are matched to one parent appear in the sample twice, and three of the children who are matched to one parent appear in the sample three times, accounting for fifteen additional observations. The summary statistics in Tables 14.1 through 14.5 are correct.
6. Because marital status is held constant in the definition of permanent income, the coefficients on the marital-status variables in the transfer regressions may be picking up the effects on transfers of variation in marital-status-related differences in permanent income, as well as the effects of variation in need or in the strength of ties between relatives. We do not stress the marriage coefficients in this chapter.
7. It should be kept in mind that the parents and independent children in the matched sample are relatively young. The mean ages of the child and the head of the parental household are 30 and 58, respectively. In the full sample the corresponding means are 35 and 62. Our multivariate analysis (see Appendix 14.B) indicates that transfers from parents to children decline with the child's age and are not very sensitive to the age of the parent in the range between 52 and 75. The probability and the average amount of a money transfer from a child to the parent (including the zero values) is positively related to the age of the child. Time transfers from a parent to the child decline with the age of the child when the parent's age is held constant. Time transfers from a child to the parent tend to decrease with the age of the child when the parent's age is held constant, and to increase with age of the parent when the child's age is held constant. It is worth noting that co-residence with parents is a major source of economic support for young adults and declines with the age of the child (see Rosenzweig and Wolpin 1993, 1994). We should also note that few of the sample members were students.
8. In the full sample, married couples who are original sample members contribute two observations to the weighted estimates, one containing information on transfers from the husband's parents, the other containing information on transfers from the wife's parents. If the husband or the wife married into a PSID family, that person has been assigned a person weight of zero and does not contribute to the weighted sample statistics.
9. Distance is constructed from information on whether the parent lives in the same household, less than 1 mile, 1 to 10 miles, 10 to 100 miles, or more than 100 miles. We obtain similar results for the income terms when we include dummies for the distance categories in place of the linear distance term.
10. In earlier versions of this chapter and in some of the models reported here we used information from the more detailed questionnaire on health status in 1986 to construct health categories. This had little effect on our main results. Because the health-status information from 1986 is available only if the head of household did not change between 1986 and 1988, when we use the 1986 information we include dummies for whether the head of household in the child's household or in the parent's household changed since 1986 and set the health dummies to zero in those cases.

11. We experimented with the use of the level of permanent income rather than the log. Once cubic terms are included, the specifications are very comparable, although the log specification is much better when only linear income terms are included.
12. Elsewhere (Altonji *et al.* 1995) we have noted that the Tobit model is an inappropriate model for transfers, particularly of money, because transfers are unlikely to be additively separable in income and unobserved heterogeneity in preferences and needs. In that paper we use a new estimator that can handle arbitrary non-linearity in the observables and errors and does not require normality. We stick with the Tobit here because it is a standard method, is easy to use, and is adequate for the descriptive multivariate analysis that we provide.
13. We are not making a careful distinction here between myopic Keynesian behaviour and the behaviour of rational, forward-looking consumers who face liquidity constraints. The specifications and samples underlying these linear probability models differ slightly from those in Tables 13.8 and 13.9 owing to missing data on current income in some cases.
14. Rosenzweig and Wolpin (1994) present evidence that declines in earnings of young men increase the odds that they receive a transfer from parents or co-reside with them. Thus far we have largely ignored the issue of co-residence, but the fact that children are not fully surveyed in the PSID until they become household heads or wives in a separate household limits the use of the PSID data for the study of co-residence with parents for young men and women. One can examine the probability of returning to live with parents or elderly parents going to live with independent children.
15. The finding that transfers are relatively small in magnitude but tend to equalize income is qualitatively consistent with Altonji *et al.* (1992). In that article we relate the distribution of household consumption to the distribution of household income among related households and conclude that altruistic links are far from perfect and that the income of relatives has a small positive effect on one's own consumption.
16. Cox (1987) and Bernheim *et al.* (1985) provide models of exchange-motivated transfers and interpret their empirical results as providing support for the exchange model. Pollack (1994) summarizes the literature and presents evidence from the PSID that is consistent with our results.
17. See Cox (1990) for theory and evidence that transfers are motivated by liquidity constraints. Rosenzweig and Wolpin (1993, 1994) find a strong negative relationship between the child's current income and the odds of a monetary transfer in fixed-effect logit models that control implicitly for permanent income. They interpret this as evidence that parents smooth the incomes of their children. They find little evidence that current parental income matters once a fix effect is controlled for. Dunn (1993) obtains similar results with the child's current and permanent income included, but no fixed effect.
18. We thank Lew Segal for providing us with a program to compute the conditional logit model in the presence of various numbers of siblings per family.
19. Although many of the parents in the PSID sample had living parents whom they may have had to support, we found little evidence that time or money transfers between parents and their adult children were affected by whether the grandparents were alive.
20. For the matched sample the coefficient in a regression of the parents' report of income in 1988 on the child's report is 0.48. The correlation of the child's report of

income in 1988 with the parent's permanent income is 0.31. One might be able to devise a correction or IV procedure by exploiting the fact that we have multiple reports on the income of some parents from siblings and the parents' own reports for the matched sample, but we have not done so.

21. Note, however, that these equations do not control for the difference between the parents of the husband and those of the wife in the number and gender composition of children. If we assume that the gender of siblings is approximately independent, the parents of the wife are no more likely to have another daughter who could care for them than are the parents of the husband. The PSID data do not identify whether the time help is provided by the husband or the wife.
22. See e.g. the work on insurance arrangements by Thomas and Worrall (1994) , Urdry (1994), and Foster and Rosenzweig (1995*a*) . Cigno (Ch. 6) discusses a model in which families manage to organize an efficient allocation of resources through an implicit contract, which he calls a 'family constitution'. Cigno's model shares many of the implications of the altruism model. However, the constraint that the contract be incentive-compatible may weaken the strong predictions of the altruism model regarding the magnitude of the response of transfer amounts to relative incomes. Altruism models imply that households will redistribute permanent endowments (such as the rewards to innate ability), as well as pool risks, with the incidence and extent of the redistribution of endowments depending on preferences and the distribution of income and needs across households. Without altruism, it is not clear how family redistribution of the exogenous components of initial endowments of children who have not been born can be contracted on today, either implicitly or otherwise. The results in Altonji *et al.* (1992) suggest that such redistribution is quite limited.

15 Housing Inheritance: An Empirical Analysis of French Data

Anne Laferrère

Home ownership is at the heart of most households' wealth. According to the Enquête Actifs financiers, a recent survey of financial assets among French households, 60 per cent of French households own at least one dwelling. Between 1970 and 1992 the proportion of French households owning a primary home rose from 45 to 54 per cent.[1] Nearly 10 per cent of French households own a second (vacation) home, and 13 per cent own dwellings for rental and investment purposes. Because transaction taxes are high, homes do not change hands often and the housing market tends to be sluggish. Moreover, home owners cannot draw upon housing equity before death—for instance, through a market of reverse annuity mortgages—as easily as they can draw upon other, more liquid assets (Bernheim 1991), and it seems that a majority of elderly people would not want to move from their homes (Venti and Wise 1990). As a result, much of the housing market is fuelled instead by divorce and inheritance, according to the real estate profession. Housing accounts, on average, for 42 per cent of estates' value (Laferrère and Monteil 1994).

What happens to this residential property after the owners die? Does it help members of the younger generation to establish themselves? Does it come too late, after those who inherit it have already purchased a home, so that they decide to sell the inherited property? In that case, does this release of property trigger a fall in housing prices, or does it enhance financial investment and consumption? Alternatively, do the beneficiaries decide to find renters for the inherited property, thus contributing to a growing rental sector? Or do they pass the property along to the next generation? In exploring these questions, this chapter draws upon data from the Enquête Actifs financiers, which surveyed a nationally representative sample of French households on their ownership of assets, inheritance, and gifts received. The survey was conducted in 1991–2 by the Institut National de la Statistique et des Etudes Economiques (INSEE).

Previous Studies

There exists hardly any economic literature on the use of inherited wealth. This should come as no surprise, for most economists make no distinction among assets that are substitutable: whether acquired through saving or from inheritance, wealth is the same—a means of holding value from one period to another for consumption purposes. The presence of positive wealth at the time of death has been ascribed alternatively to the decedent's uncertainty about the timing of death (i.e. to a precautionary motive or having insufficient time to consume the wealth because of an untimely death); to the absence of an annuity market; to the sheer amount of wealth, which cannot be fully consumed in old age because its owner has reached a 'bliss point' of consumption; to the pure pleasure of having wealth *per se*; and to the desire to leave something to one's children, whether for their benefit alone or in the expectation of receiving help and care from them. One may also make gifts to children during one's lifetime in order to solicit their care in gratitude.

The importance of bequests is disputed. Some economists argue that most wealth comes from life-cycle accumulation (Modigliani 1988*a*), whereas others argue that most of it is transmitted from previous generations (Kotlikoff and Summers 1988). A few sociologists (e.g. Gotman 1991) have studied the factors that make an inherited good different from the same good outside the family circle or from its monetary equivalent. Using French estate data and the hypothesis of a permanent regime of intergenerational transmissions, I have estimated that between one-quarter and one-half of household wealth in France is inherited, the proportion depending upon assumptions about prices and interest rates (Laferrère 1989).

In this chapter I address the following related questions. Among households owning a home, how many inherited it and how many bought it with the help (at least in part) of inheritance? Why do parents transfer housing to their children either as a gift or as inheritance? Why do children decide to keep or to sell housing received from parents? And what use is made of the proceeds when an inherited house is sold? (Unless otherwise qualified, I use the term 'inherited' throughout the chapter to describe housing that is either inherited or received as an *inter-vivos* gift.)

Only a few studies have investigated housing inheritance empirically. Other than the INSEE survey, the three studies with which I am familiar focus on Britain (Hamnet, Harmer, and Williams 1990), Canada (Thorns 1994), and France (Massot 1995).

Drawing upon a 1988 national survey of 3,100 adults that included questions about inheritance, Hamnet and his colleagues found that 9 per cent of British households had inherited housing. In 93 per cent of those inheritances the property had been lived in by the deceased, and in 7 per cent it had been rented out. Among the inheriting households, 66 per cent had sold the property, 25 per cent had kept it to live in, and only 5 per cent had kept it as a long-term investment asset. The proceeds from the sale of the inherited property were used for financial investment (in 42 per cent of the cases), consumption (31 per cent), and the purchase or improvement of a home (27 per cent). Hamnet and his colleagues conclude that inherited housing erodes the rental sector but has only a small effect on the housing market. They also found that more than a quarter of all respondents had placed most of the money from the sale of inherited property in a building society. Thus it seems that, at least in Britain, heirs use inherited capital to produce income. Part of the questionnaire for the Enquête Actifs financiers was designed with this British survey in mind.

Thorns (1994), drawing mostly upon the Canadian Family Expenditure Survey, found that in 1986, transfers from parents amounted to 6 per cent of household income. He concludes that a qualitative study is needed to identify the types of gifts and inheritance that are made in Canada and to investigate the family dynamics that surround such transfers.

Focusing on France's rental-housing sector, Massot (1995) examined a sample of 125 estate tax returns that included information on investment housing. He found that 60 per cent of the heirs of family homes and 40 per cent of the heirs of rented houses had sold them immediately. His study does not indicate whether the sold houses were put on the rental market, nor what the heirs did with the proceeds.

The Enquête Actifs Financiers

The Enquête Actifs financiers was conducted in late 1991 and early 1992 with major support from INSEE and additional support from seven other organizations. INSEE canvassed a nationally representative sample of 9,530 French households about their financial assets and, retrospectively, about inheritances and gifts received by both the reference person and his spouse. (The questions are summarized in the Appendix.) Respondents were interviewed in person. For the purpose of focusing on inheritance patterns, my analysis in this chapter is based on responses from households past the formative stage and those in a position to inherit—that is, on those households in which the reference person (normally the husband) was over 30 years of age and, within that group, those in which either the reference person or his spouse had lost at least one parent. Except in Table 15.1, I have also narrowed the sub-sample to 4,632 households having at least one parent who had owned housing at the time of death or had given it to the household earlier as an *inter-vivos* gift.

The sample over-represented households in which the reference person was self-employed or an executive. Because the distribution of wealth is highly skewed, this was done deliberately to ensure the quality of the information about assets owned by the wealthiest households. Except in the econometric models, however, all figures reported here are weighted to represent the French population at large.

Patterns of parents' housing ownership and transfer

In 27 per cent of the households, neither the reference person's parents nor that person's in-laws had ever owned a house, and in 57 per cent at least one of the

Table 15.1. Housing status of surveyed households and of reference persons' parents or in-laws, transfers from parents or in-laws (frequencies), disposition of inherited property, and mean age of reference persons at the time their household purchased or received a home: France, 1991–2

Status	Frequency or age
Housing status of parents or in-laws (%)	
Never owned housing	27.2
Owned housing during reference person's or spouse's youth	57.0
Owned housing at death	61.0
Did not own at death but had given housing as inter vivos gift	0.8
Housing status of surveyed household (%)	
Own housing	60.8
Parents or in-laws also owned	69.2
Parents or in-laws did not own	48.2
Do not own housing	39.2
Transfers from parents or in-laws (%)	
Housing received as gift	8.7
Full property	4.4
Expectant interest or jointly	4.3
Housing inherited	23.6
Housing inherited or received as gift	29.7
Full property	13.5
Expectant interest or jointly	10.1
Parent's or in-laws' primary home	25.4
Parents' or in-laws' second home	3.4
Other property of parents/in-laws	2.5
Disposition of inherited property (%)	
Household kept housing	19.9
Household sold housing	9.8
'Feel we inherited housing'	16.2
'Own and feel we inherited housing'	21.8
Reference person's age	
Upon the household's purchase of a home	
Mean age	39.1
Median age	37
Upon the household's receipt of a home	
Median age	42
First decile	24
Third quartile	53
Ninth decile	62

Note: Sample includes 6,659 households in which the reference person was over 30 years of age and at least one parent was no longer living, weighted to represent the French population.

Source: INSEE, Enquête Actifs financiers, 1991–2.

four parents had owned a house during the youth of the reference person or spouse (Table 15.1). Among nearly two-thirds of the households, however, at least one of the four parents had either owned a house at the time of death (60 per cent) or had given away a home prior to death (nearly 1 per cent). Thus a substantial majority of households in the sample were in a position to inherit a home from parents or to be given one as a gift. About one-third of the households reported actually receiving housing as a gift (9 per cent) or inheritance (24 per cent). Among all French households the proportion of such beneficiaries is lower—22 per cent, which is more than twice the level in England, as reported by Hamnet *et al.* (1989).

Parents can give away their property while keeping a life interest in it. This type of gift is called an 'expectant interest' in the property, and it reduces the value of the property by an amount that depends upon the age of the donor.[2] Among the 9 per cent of respondent households who had received housing as an *inter-vivos* gift, half had been given full ownership. The parents or surviving parent of the other half had kept a life interest in the property. Nearly one-fourth (24 per cent) of the households had inherited housing. Of those, more than half had inherited a full interest in the property, the rest an expectant interest or joint ownership.

The survey included a question specifically intended to elicit respondents' recollection of property received from parents: 'Did your share [gift or inheritance] include housing?' Nearly one-third (30 per cent) responded affirmatively. Among that group, 67 per cent had kept it and 33 per cent had sold it; and among those who had sold it, half had used the proceeds for housing. Hence in eight out of ten cases, gifts of housing were used for housing, directly or indirectly.

Finally respondents were asked: 'Today do you feel you have inherited housing?' Sixteen per cent said yes. Among homeowners, 22 per cent acknowledged having received their housing through inheritance.

I attempted to calculate the proportion of households who, despite probing, failed to mention having received housing as a gift or inheritance because they had sold the property immediately upon receiving it. First, I considered those reference persons who had no siblings and whose parents had owned a house. Among this group 35 per cent did not mention receiving a house. Supposing that in half of those cases the house went to the deceased's surviving spouse, I inferred that the rest of this group, or about 17 per cent, had inherited and sold a house without mentioning it in the survey. The second way I estimated the size of this group was by considering those respondents (for the sake of simplicity, the reference person only) who did not mention inheriting a house but did mention the immediate selling of property upon a parent's death. In such cases I inferred that the property sold was likely to have been a house. Eight per cent of households fell into this category. I therefore concluded that between 8 and 17 per cent of households had received housing that they immediately sold.

Assuming conservatively that the proportion was 10 per cent, I deduced the following estimates: from inherited estates that included some kind of housing,

10 per cent were immediately sold, 49 per cent went to siblings or a surviving parent, and 41 per cent became the property of the surveyed household. Applying these frequencies to all households, I conclude that 30 per cent had ever received housing and that 4 per cent had sold it without mentioning its existence (see Figure 15.1).

It was possible to ascertain the age at which homeowners had purchased their home in 80 per cent of households. Half had bought their house before the age

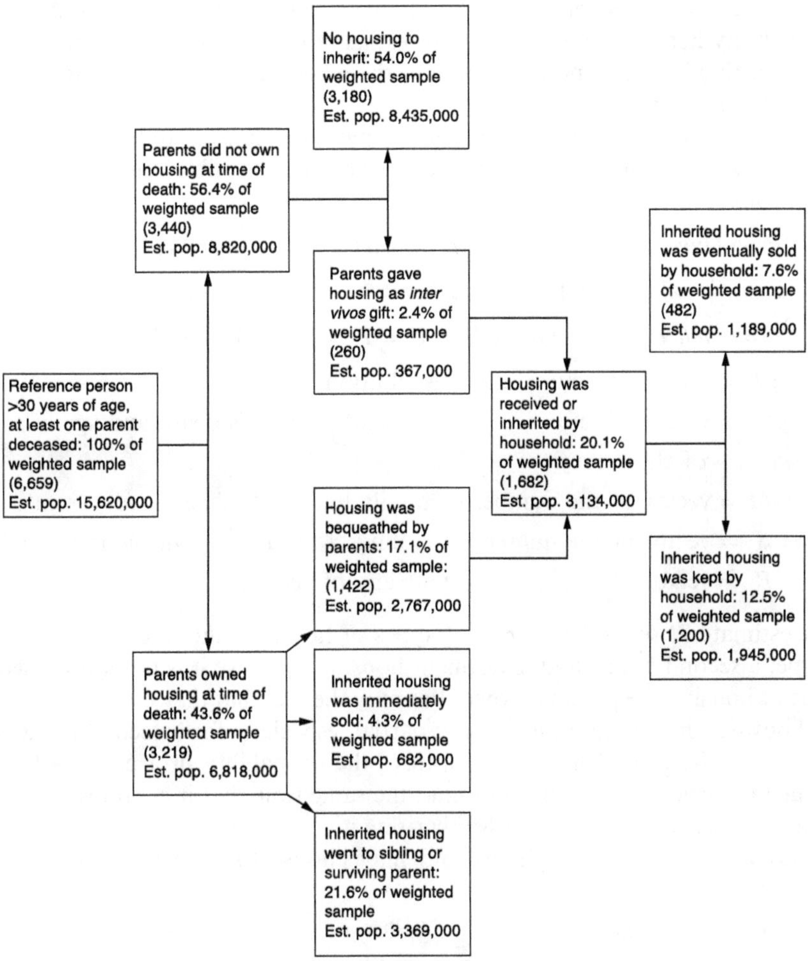

Note: Sample sizes are shown in parentheses except for inherited housing that was immediately sold and inherited housing that went to surviving sibling or parent. Weighted population sizes are also shown.

Source: INSEE, Enquête Actifs financiers, 1991–2.

Fig. 15.1. Estimates of housing inheritance from parents: France, 1991–2

of 37. Most of the others declared that they had not purchased their home, but rather had been living in it since childhood. Thus I again arrive at a figure of 15 to 20 per cent of households who had received (or were going to receive) their home from their parents.

The models

Having inherited a house or having used an inheritance to finance the purchase of one increases the probability of homeownership. I do not estimate this probability here; instead I attempt to estimate logit models of the probability of inheriting housing and of keeping of the inheritance, distinguishing the type of housing received.

For a person to inherit a house from his parents, there has to be a house in the parents' estate. Other factors influence the choice of possible beneficiaries. Thus the probability of inheriting is:

$$Prob\ (inherit) = Prob\ (parents\ owned) * Prob\ (inherit \mid parent\ owned)$$

The conditional probability can be directly modelled as follows:

$$Prob\ (inherit \mid parent\ owned) = \mathrm{H} = F(a\,Q + b\,M + c\,S + d\,R),$$

where F = the logistic cumulative distribution function,

Q = vector of reference person's age at parent's death and age at time of the survey,

M = vector of the number of family lines and of deceased parents,

S = vector of the number of siblings and rank among siblings, and

R = vector of wealth of parents and of recipient.

I estimate H separately for three types of housing inheritance: the parents' home, a second home, and investment housing. Because it is not known which type of housing the parents owned, but only the fact that they owned some type of housing, the conditioning is only partial, especially for a second home and investment housing. The model captures the probability of a parent's having owned a particular type of housing at the same time that it captures the probability of the child's household's inheriting it.

Having received it, the household may choose to keep it or not, with a probability of T.

$$Prob\ (keep \mid inherited) = T = F(s\,\Phi + tA + uI + vO + wG),$$

where Φ = family variables (number of children, type of family),

A = calendar variables (date of death, age at transfer),

I = income and wealth variables,

O = environment (region, location, value, other inherited assets, etc.), and

G = taste variables (family tradition).

Explanatory variables

For the logit analysis I have identified a dozen explanatory variables. They are the number of family lines, the number of deceased parents, the number of siblings in the family of origin, the reference person's or spouse's age rank among the siblings, parents' age at death, the reference person's age at the time of the survey, parents' wealth during the reference person's youth, the recipient household's wealth at the time of receiving the property, the period of the life cycle in which the household receives the gift or inheritance, the existence and number of children of the household, and the household's region of residence.

The number of family lines is defined from the reference household's point of view: a single or divorced person inherits from one line; a married couple or widowed person inherits from two lines. The probability of inheriting becomes greater as the number of lines increases. One line is considered ended when both parents in that line are deceased. A first inheritance (that is, after the death of one parent) is less likely than the second to result in the transference of property, for the reason, mentioned in note 2, that a surviving spouse may retain a life interest in property.

Having to share the parents' estate with siblings reduces the probability of inheriting the parental house.[3] The more numerous the siblings, therefore, the higher are the odds that it will be sold or go to another sibling.

Age rank among siblings (of either the reference person or the spouse) is defined dichotomously as being or not being the eldest. I tested for whether rank had an independent effect on either the probability of inheriting the family home or on the use of the inheritance.

The parents' age at death may influence the transfer of housing to children. Even after controlling for the reference person's age at the time of the survey and the fact that two parents in a line were deceased, it is possible to capture, for the householders who were very young when one or both parents died, the fact that the process of transferring property may have been different from the customary process in such cases. The surviving parent may have remarried, or the property may have been sold immediately upon the parents' death. Another reason for the interest in the parents' ages was that even with a control for the fact that the parents had owned housing, the type of housing they owned at the time of death was likely to be linked to their age—that is, to the stage in their savings life cycle. For example, if they had lived into old age they might have owned more than one house or, alternatively, sold a second home. For the sake of simplicity, however, in the analysis presented here we considered only the reference person's age at the time of the parents' death and introduced dummies for an early, late, or very late death of the parents.

I assumed that the reference person's age at the time of the survey would have the same effect on the probability of inheritance as the number of deceased parents; that is, the older the person was, the more likely the parents were to be deceased. The time that had elapsed since the parents' death might also influence the respondent's answers to the survey questions: he or she was more likely to mention a house as his or her share of the inheritance if more time had elapsed and 'things were settled', the period of joint ownership being over. This remains a tentative interpretation because we do not know exactly what respondents meant by their answers—for instance, whether they felt they had inherited a house when they owned only part of it. There may have also been a cohort effect, older households being more attached to family homes and younger ones more likely to have well-off parents and more likely to inherit.

Parents' wealth, measured in this case by their occupation during the youth of the reference person or that person's spouse, should influence the type of housing they owned at their death through income and saving. I introduced two dummies, one for the parents' ownership of securities at the time of their death, the other for the existence of a very large estate (more than 1 million francs). The dummies act as a proxy for wealth, which eases the process of dividing the estate among siblings (the one who does not inherit the house can be compensated with securities) and makes it likely that the parents owned more than one house.

So much for variables predicting the probability of inheriting housing. Next are those I identified as predicting the probability that a household would keep an inherited house after receiving it.

First is the reference person's age at time of the survey. The probability that the recipient household would keep the housing may be considered a cohort function, for instance because older generations may have had a greater sentimental attachment to the parental home than younger ones. On the other hand, older persons also had longer histories, which increased the probability that the inherited house had changed hands. Given that this variable is linked to parents' age, I did not introduce it separately; from a cross-sectional analysis it is not possible to distinguish cohort and time effects. Instead, I introduced dummies for the length of time elapsed since the parents' death.

The recipient household's wealth at the time the reference person or spouse received the house should have also affected the probability of their keeping it. The richer they were, the more likely they were to be able to buy their siblings' share of a jointly inherited home, take care of additional property in the event that the inherited property was a second home, or manage their affairs without having to sell it for consumption or tax purposes. Because I have no information about the reference household's wealth at the time they inherited a house or received one as a gift, I have used the reference person's occupation *(catégorie sociale)* as a proxy.

I chose the timing of the gift or inheritance—that is, the stage in the life cycle when a house was received—as a predictor for several reasons. If the utility of a house is important to its owners, then its usefulness to the recipients may be greatest early in their adult lives, before they have purchased their own home, and again after their children have grown up, when they may want to help the children establish a household of their own. If, on the other hand, liquidity constraints are considered to be important, then the results could be the reverse: the heirs may be more likely to sell the parents' home when they are young because they need the cash and more likely to keep it when they are older because then they can afford to maintain a second home.

The existence and number of children a couple had (or planned to have) when they received a home as a gift or inheritance should be positively related to the probability of their still owning it as their primary home or second home at the time of the survey. The existence of children, however, increases the likelihood that the household already owned a home, and therefore the effect could be ambiguous.

Finally, the use to which an inherited home is put depends on whether it is the only asset received or one among several. For example, whether the house was the main home of the parents or only one of several properties given to the beneficiaries should affect what they did with it. Other gifts or bequests, such as cash or securities, could also affect the outcome, as could the composition of the beneficiary's wealth at the time he or she received the house, information about which is not available from the survey. The quality of the inherited house is another factor that could influence the decision to keep it or use it as an investment asset.

The same building can be used as a primary home, a second home, or an investment asset at various stages of the life cycle, and this fact made it more difficult to predict what a recipient would do with it and for the recipient to describe what actually happened. The small size of the INSEE sample does not permit the analysis of such detailed effects. The difference between receiving something and keeping it is not as clear-cut as it might seem. In modelling the act of receiving a home, I therefore felt it necessary to introduce some of the beneficiary's characteristics.

Results: The Probability of Inheriting Housing

In analysing the probability of inheriting housing from parents, I considered three types of housing that the parents might own: their primary home, a second home, and investment housing. In each case, I examined both the situation of the parents and the characteristics of the heirs in determining the probability. Table 15.2 presents the raw frequencies of housing transfers by the characteristics of the recipient households. Tables 15.3 and 15.4 show the results of modelling the probability of receiving the parents' primary home. Table 15.5 shows the results of modelling the probability of receiving the parents' second home (first two columns) and investment housing (last two columns).

Parents' primary home

The probability of inheriting the parents' primary home is greater when the heir is older and, more significantly, when both parents in a line are deceased. If both parents of respondents had died, the process of transferring the property was

Table 15.2. Frequencies of receiving housing through inheritance or gift, by characteristic of household: France, 1991–2

Characteristic	Percentage of households receiving		
	Parents' primary home	Parents' second home	Parents' investment housing
All households	41.0	5.5	4.2
Occupation of parents or in-laws			
Farmer	44.0	4.9	3.5
Self-employed[a]	43.0	7.6	6.8
Executive	36.4	15.5	8.4
White-collar worker	41.3	4.1	2.8
Clerical worker[b]	39.4	3.6	2.6
Blue-collar worker	34.3	2.8	2.0
Occupation of reference person			
Farmer	64.7	4.1	4.0
Self-employed[a]	47.9	8.7	7.9
Executive	39.2	10.8	7.5
Other white-collar worker	38.2	7.4	4.5
Clerical worker[b]	35.9	4.0	2.5
Blue-collar worker	35.3	2.2	2.1
No. of siblings in reference person's family of origin			
None	58.4	6.2	5.8
One	44.7	8.0	7.2
Two	42.1	6.1	3.7
Three or more	33.6	3.8	2.5
No. of siblings in spouse's family of origin			
None	56.0	6.5	4.8
One	45.5	8.0	5.4
Two	39.7	6.2	4.2
Three or more	34.5	3.7	3.4
Timing of parents' death			
Early (ref. person's age < 32)	24.1	3.9	2.8
Late (ref. person's age 53–64)	55.4	7.6	5.5
Very late (ref. person's age 65+)	60.5	4.0	4.5
No. of parents and parents-in-law deceased			
One, or one in each family line	20.8	4.9	2.9
Both in one or both family lines	51.6	5.8	4.9
No. of family lines			
One (ref. person single or divorced)	39.3	5.1	4.0
Two (ref. person married or widowed)	41.3	5.6	4.2
Farmer, one family line	77.9	3.8	2.9
Farmer, two family lines	62.3	4.1	4.2
Non-farmer, one line	34.2	5.3	4.2
Non-farmer, two lines	39.0	5.7	4.2
Residence of inheriting household			
Paris	29.3	9.6	4.2
Mediterranean	45.4	8.8	6.0
Other regions (excluding Paris)	43.4	4.7	4.2

[a] Self-employed in a non-farming occupation—e.g. as an entrepreneur.
[b] This category includes clerical and other workers such as police officers, shop attendants, and housemaids.
Note: Sample includes 4,632 households in which the reference person was over 30 years of age, at least one parent was no longer living, and at least one parent had owned housing, weighted to represent the French population.
Source: INSEE, Enquête Actifs financiers, 1991–2.

Table 15.3. Logit analysis of receiving parents' primary home: models 1 and 2

Variable	Model 1		Model 2	
	Parameter estimate	Wald χ^2	Parameter estimate	Wald χ^2
Constant	−2.52†	134.45	−2.13†	57.05
Parents' characteristics				
Occupation (ref. category = clerical worker)				
Farmer	0.51†	20.09	0.04	0.09
Self-employed	0.25*	5.03	0.11	0.84
Executive	0.07	0.16	0.10	0.36
Other white-collar worker	0.01	0.01	0.03	0.08
Blue-collar worker	−0.09	0.39	−0.04	0.09
Owned securities	0.04	0.29	−0.05	0.32
Both deceased in one family line	1.03†	136.78	1.03†	131.91
Large estate (> 1 million francs)	0.71†	8.53	0.71†	8.18
Early death (ref. person's age =< 32)	−0.15	2.34	−0.15	2.21
Late death (ref. person's age = 53–65)	0.07	0.57	0.04	0.18
Very late death (ref. person's age = 65+)	0.13	0.50	0.20	1.19
Beneficiaries' characteristics				
Reference person the eldest child	−0.05	0.36	−0.07	0.71
Spouse the eldest child	−0.09	1.09	−0.09	1.25
No. of reference person's siblings (ref. category = three or more)				
None	1.06†	74.69	1.07†	72.28
One	0.43†	25.01	0.39†	19.59
Two	0.32†	13.33	0.31†	11.93
No. of spouse's siblings (ref. category = three or more)				
None	0.76†	37.59	0.79†	38.76
One	0.43†	20.85	0.44†	21.43
Two	0.29†	9.85	0.28†	8.93
No spouse (one family line)	0.63†	32.03	0.58†	16.56
Age at survey	0.01†	16.55	0.01†	8.62
One child or more	—	—	−0.27†	5.11
Reference person's occupation (ref. category = clerical worker)				
Farmer	—	—	1.11†	65.11
Self-employed	—	—	0.34†	6.58
Executive	—	—	0.37†	6.02
Other white-collar	—	—	0.14	0.91
Blue-collar	—	—	0.08	0.31
Income				
<100,000 francs	—	—	−0.03	0.17
200,000+ francs	—	—	−0.05	0.33
Divorced or stepchild	—	—	−0.32†	9.89
Residence: Paris (Ile de France)	—	—	− 0.46†	16.43

* Significant at 0.10.
† Significant at 0.01.
Notes: Sample includes 4,632 households in which the reference person was over 30 years of age, at least one parent was no longer living, and at least one parent had owned housing. Dependent variable (receiving primary home) = 1 (2,079 households). Model 2 includes some characteristics of beneficiaries not included in model 1. Model 1: −2 log likelihood = 6,372.73; χ^2 = 781.14 with 21 d.f. Model 2: −2 log likelihood = 6,372.73; χ^2 = 957.51 with 31 d.f.

Source: INSEE, Enquête Actifs financiers, 1991–2.

Table 15.4. Logit analysis of receiving parents' primary home: all households and farming households

Variable	All households		Farming households	
	Parameter estimate	Wald χ^2	Parameter estimate	Wald χ^2
Constant	−1.06†	94.22	0.03	0.01
Reference person's parents' characteristics				
Occupation (ref. category = clerical worker)				
Farmer	0.90†	62.17	0.21	0.14
Self-employed	0.62†	28.68	0.14	0.06
Executive	0.33*	4.10	−1.40	0.94
Other white-collar worker	0.11*	0.49	−2.47*	3.91
Blue-collar worker	0.06	0.27	0.22*	0.12
Owned securities	0.15*	3.09	0.02*	0.01
Both deceased	1.23†	62.15	0.20	0.36
Reference person's characteristics				
Eldest child	−0.06	0.71	0.08	0.30
No. of siblings (ref. category = three or more)				
None	1.22†	106.73	1.85†	34.60
Two	0.33†	16.36	0.34*	3.74
No spouse	−0.49†	13.40	0.60*	3.34

* Significant at 0.10.
† Significant at 0.01.
Notes: Sample includes 4,632 households, including 1,075 farming households, in which the reference person was over 30 years of age, at least one parent was no longer living, and at least one parent had owned housing. Dependent variable (receiving primary home) = 1 (all households: 2,079; farming households: 717). Model 1: −2 log likelihood = 6,372.72; χ^2 = 360.50 with 12 d.f. Model 2: −2 log likelihood = 1,368.04; χ^2 = 82.67 with 12 d.f.
Source: INSEE, Enquête Actifs financiers, 1991–2.

regarded as completed and the raw frequency of inheritance more than doubled (from 21 to 52 per cent, as shown in Table 15.2). Respondents were less likely to say they had inherited their parents' home if only one of the parents to whom the house had belonged had died (Table 15.3). This was so even if a respondent legally owned an expectant interest in the house.

Having only one family line from which to inherit decreases the probability of inheriting parents' primary home. I obtained this result by running a logit in which only one spouse variable was introduced, the absence of a spouse in the inheriting household (Table 15.4). The parameter is negative and significant; in other words, a single or divorced person is less likely than a married couple or widowed person to inherit the home.

Running a separate model for farmers, I found the parameter to be positive (significant at the 10 per cent level). This outcome may be a reflection in part of a high celibacy rate among farmers. As I discuss later, being a farmer's child and oneself a farmer makes inheriting the parents' home likely. For a farmer, being unmarried makes this outcome even more likely.

Not surprisingly, the probability of inheriting the parents' primary home is inversely related to the number of siblings that the reference person and his spouse have. This effect is highly significant: when there is housing in the estate, 58 per cent of reference persons with no siblings inherit their parents' primary home, compared with 34 per cent of reference persons with three or more siblings. (It should be borne in mind that the type of housing the parents owned is not known; they may have owned only a second home. It is common for an inherited home to be sold immediately or to go to the surviving parent.) Being the eldest child has no effect *per se*, nor has age at inheritance.

Introducing beneficiaries' characteristics improves the model but does not change the estimates of other parameters—except for the parents' characteristics, which become non-significant (Table 15.3, model 2). A farmer is significantly more likely than a clerical or blue-collar worker to receive the parents' primary home; so is a self-employed person and an executive. Even if a direct comparison cannot be made among beneficiaries within the same family, these results indicate that among reference persons whose parents were farmers, the child who has remained in farming is likely to receive the parents' house, which goes with the farm. The same is true for the entrepreneur's child who becomes self-employed in a non-farming occupation; the advantage of having self-employed parents is evident only for the self-employed child (see Laferrère and McEntee 1995 for a discussion of entrepreneurs and inheritance in France). The positive effect of being an executive, together with the effect of a large estate, is a wealth effect. The house is less likely to be sold immediately for financial reasons, to pay inheritance tax, for example, or to facilitate the division of the estate among the siblings, and therefore the child is more likely to inherit it.

The household's income does not influence the probability of receiving the parents' home. Being childless increases the probability of inheriting, whereas being divorced or remarried with stepchildren decreases it. It may be that households with children are more likely already to own a house at the time of the parents' death and for that reason may decide to let a childless sibling have the parents' home or to sell it immediately. If the beneficiary is divorced or has stepchildren—that is, if either the reference person or his spouse is remarried with children from a prior marriage—this variable may act as a proxy for a less family-oriented 'taste', suggesting greater psychological distance from the family of origin. Finally, inheriting the parents' primary home is less likely if the household lives in Paris rather than elsewhere in France. (Nothing is known of the location of the parents' home.)

Parents' second home

The probability of inheriting the parents' second home is greatest if they were executives and entrepreneurs (that is, self-employed), as compared with other occupational categories (Table 15.5). The logit analysis captures here the effect that, among the parents' generation, owning a second home is a characteristic of

Table 15.5. Logit analysis of receiving parents' second home or investment housing

Variable	Second home		Investment housing	
	Parameter estimate	Wald χ^2	Parameter estimate	Wald χ^2
Constant	−4.27†	81.01	−5.47†	72.78
Parents' characteristics				
Occupation (ref. category = clerical worker)				
Farmer	0.30	1.22	0.51	2.60
Self-employed	0.80†	10.52	0.93†	10.46
Executive	1.31†	20.80	0.77*	4.58
Other white-collar worker	0.05	0.06	−0.38	2.14
Blue-collar worker	−0.19	0.25	0.03	0.01
No spouse	0.24	1.03	0.44	2.48
Both deceased in one family line	0.12	0.46	0.59†	8.31
Early death (ref. person's age =< 32)	0.14	0.50	0.05	0.05
Late death (ref. person's age = 53–64)	−0.10	0.33	0.26	1.94
Very late death (ref. person's age 65+)	−0.82*	3.43	0.26	0.48
Beneficiaries' characteristics				
Age	0.01	0.66	0.01	0.10
Occupation				
(ref. category for second home = other white-collar and clerical workers)				
(ref. category for investment housing = clerical worker)				
Farmer	0.26	1.44	0.72*	3.41
Self-employed	0.17	0.82	0.79*	4.53
Executive	−0.08	0.13	0.68*	3.06
Other white-collar worker	—	—	0.46	1.35
Blue-collar worker	−0.85†	8.55	0.33	0.60
Income				
<100,000 F	−0.07	0.19	−0.82†	16.31
200,000+ F	0.03	0.02	0.13	0.51
No. of reference person's siblings (ref. category = three or more)				
None	0.45*	5.21	0.40*	2.98
One	0.40*	5.69	0.56†	9.01
Two	0.27	2.27	0.44*	4.85
No. of spouse's siblings (ref. category = three or more)				
None	0.53†	6.98	0.30	1.68
One	0.32*	3.09	0.13	0.38
Two	0.35*	3.68	0.44*	4.96
Residence (ref. category = other areas of France)				
Paris (Ile-de-France)	0.40*	4.72	−0.07	0.10
Paris (excluding Ile-de-France) (Bassin Parisien)	−0.28	2.40	—	—
Mediterranean	—	—	0.48*	6.12
Divorced or with stepchild	—	—	−0.47*	3.74

* Significant at 0.10.

† Significant at 0.01.

Notes: Sample includes 4,632 households in which the reference person was over 30 years of age, at least one parent was no longer living, and at least one parent had owned housing. Second home: −2 log likelihood = 2,064.36; χ^2 = 142.17 with 26 d.f. Investment housing: −2 log likelihood = 1,788.06; χ^2 = 212.09 with 28 d.f.

Source: INSEE, Enquête Actifs financiers, 1991–2.

the upper classes. The parents' ownership of securities also has a strong positive effect.

Again the likelihood of inheriting the parents' second home increases when the reference person and the spouse have fewer siblings. However, there is no decisive advantage in being an only child, contrary to the case of inheriting a primary home. The ownership and transfer of a second home seem to be linked to familial values associated with the presence of more than one child in the family of origin. In contrast, the beneficiaries' age does not seem to influence their chances of inheriting a second home. Nor does the timing of the parents' death, except in the case of a very late death, which has a negative effect. The reason may be that very old parents are more likely than younger ones to sell a second home because it proves difficult for them to maintain; or they may turn it into their primary residence when they retire. Neither the number of family lines nor the number of deaths in a line has an effect on the probability of inheriting the parents' second home; one may inherit the second home after the death of just one parent. The surviving parent seems less inclined to keep the second home than to keep the primary one. It may also be that a second home is less often part of the community property, having been itself inherited. Finally, other things being equal, being a blue-collar worker decreases the likelihood of inheriting a second home from the parents. This may be a wealth effect; I suspect it means that the second home is more likely to be sold immediately upon the parents' death for financial reasons.

Parents' investment housing

The probability of inheriting investment housing from parents is greatest for children of entrepreneurs (that is, non-farming, self-employed parents) and executives. Again the probability of owning investment housing is greater for such parents than for those having other occupations (last two columns of Table 15.5). The fact that the parents owned securities increases significantly the likelihood that the children inherit investment property. Self-employed offspring and executives are also more likely to inherit investment property than are clerical or blue-collar workers. Likewise, the reference person's being an only child or having only one or two siblings increases the probability of inheriting. In contrast, having an income of less than 100,000 francs diminishes that probability (this is an endogenous income effect).

People living near the Mediterranean coast are more likely than those living elsewhere in France to inherit an investment home, which is not the case among those inheriting a second home. The rental market may be more active in that region, which is linked with tourism and the presence of retired elderly.

Many self-employed people live in the south of France. Renting out houses is common among this group of people, many of whom regard rental income as a necessary nest egg for retirement because they are less likely than wage earners to have retirement benefits. Unlike retirement benefits, which cannot be transmitted by inheritance, investment assets, including housing, can be passed on to children.

The Probability of Keeping Inherited Housing

Logit analysis is used to learn which predictor variables affect the decision of beneficiaries to keep an inherited house instead of selling it (Table 15.6). In this section the analysis does not take into account the actual use of the house—that is, whether the beneficiaries live in it, rent it out, or leave it empty. That will be considered later.

Keeping the parents' primary home

As might be expected, farmers are the most likely group to keep a primary inherited home, presumably a farmhouse. An inherited primary house that is kept also comes more frequently from the reference person's family line than from that of the spouse. Outside farming, which line the house comes from does not seem to make a significant difference. (These results are from a logit interaction of the 'family line' variables with a farming occupation for the household, not shown here.)

Beneficiaries are less likely to keep the parents' primary home if they inherit later in life, presumably because by then they have already purchased a home. They are also less likely to keep it if they have two or more children, the explanations in this case probably being that couples with larger families are more likely than others to own a home already and that they are less able to move easily, even if they are renters rather than homeowners. The probability of keeping the parents' primary home increases when the beneficiaries also keep other inherited housing, particularly investment housing: the wealthier one is, the more one can afford to keep.

Beneficiaries whose parents had died after 1970 (that is, less than twenty years before the survey) were more likely to own still their parents' primary home than were those whose parents had died before 1950. This finding does not necessarily indicate that older beneficiaries are less attached to a family home, but rather that they have had more time to sell it than have younger beneficiaries. The mere passing of time seems to make it less likely that people keep their parent's primary home.

Keeping the parents' second home

The predictor variables do not do a good job of explaining beneficiaries' decision to keep a second home inherited from parents. The χ^2 is 41.2 for 22 degrees of freedom, indicating a barely acceptable level of significance. For the first time the main predictor variable is the existence of children, and its influence is positive.

Table 15.6. Logit analysis of keeping parents' primary or second home

Variable	Primary home (1,502)[a]		Second home (188)[a]	
	Parameter estimate	Wald χ^2	Parameter estimate	Wald χ^2
Constant	0.19*	0.30	−1.77*	1.79
Characteristics of the home				
From reference person's parents	0.40*	4.84	1.63*	2.08
From spouse's parents	0.28	2.56	1.50	1.79
Beneficiaries' or reference person's characteristics				
Married	−0.61†	8.10	−0.75	1.57
Divorced or with stepchild	−0.51†	9.09	−0.86*	3.19
Number of children				
One	0.01	0.01	1.30*	4.97
Two or more	−0.26*	4.94	−0.16	0.25
Occupation (ref. category = clerical worker)				
Farmer	1.77†	60.74	0.42	0.44
Self-employed	0.35*	2.82	−0.45	0.54
Executive	−0.26	1.29	−0.54	0.69
Other white-collar worker	−0.38*	2.84	− 0.28	0.20
Blue-collar worker	0.27	1.53	−0.01	0.01
Income				
< 100,000 F	−0.14	1.00	−0.14	0.15
200,000+ F	0.15	0.94	0.29	0.53
Residence (ref. category = other regions)				
Paris	—	—	0.39	0.93
Eastern France	0.53†	7.41	—	—
Western France	0.90†	25.93	—	—
South-eastern France	0.94†	26.59	—	—
Timing of parents' death				
Early (ref. person's age =< 32)	0.09	0.29	0.15	0.13
Late (ref. person's age = 53–64)	−0.40*	5.71	−0.59	1.63
Parents' death after 1970	0.39†	6.81	0.48	1.21
Parents' death before 1950	−1.01*	5.36	0.19	0.03
Kept inherited home				
Parents' primary home	—	—	0.76*	3.31
In-laws' primary home	—	—	0.97*	3.55
Second home	0.63*	3.90	—	—
Investment housing	1.17†	11.62	1.64*	4.18
Other housing	0.89†	6.93	−0.30	0.19

* Significant at 0.10.
† Significant at 0.01.
[a] No. in parentheses is the number of beneficiary households who kept the home.
Notes: Sample includes 2,341 households in which the reference person was over 30 years of age, at least one parent was no longer living, and the reference person had received a home from the parents. Of those households, 2,070 had received the parents' primary home and 271 had received the parents' second home. Keeping primary home: −2 log likelihood = 2,432.59; χ^2 = 363.18 with 23 d.f. Keeping second home: −2 log likelihood = 333.92; χ^2 = 41.24 with 22 d.f.

Source: INSEE, Enquête Actifs financiers, 1991–2.

Possibly the second home is useful for family vacations. There is also a hint here of the influence of taste or familial values. Being divorced or remarried with stepchildren has a negative effect on the propensity to keep the second home.

The analysis does not take into account a number of economic and psychological factors that may influence decisions about keeping an inherited second home—for example, the value of the house and the beneficiaries' feelings toward the parents. The 'divorced, stepchild' variable is a poor proxy for psychological distance among family members.

Investment and other housing

The model fit is poor for investment housing (not shown). Other types of housing bequests (e.g. garages and vacant housing) seem to be kept mostly by farming households.

The Use of Inherited Housing

I was also interested in learning what the beneficiaries of inherited housing did with it, and for that purpose considered those households that had received at least one house in their share of parents' property (Table 15.7). Eighty-six per cent of those who inherited housing from their parents received their parents' primary home (73 per cent inheriting only that home, and 13 per cent inheriting other housing property as well), 11 per cent received their parents' second home (in half of the cases that property alone), 9 per cent inherited investment housing, and 8 per cent inherited some other domestic property such as unused farm buildings and garages. Among those who received housing property of any kind, two out of three kept it, or at least part of it, and one out of three sold it. Among those who sold the property, half used the money for housing. Thus, in eight cases out of ten, inherited housing continued to be used for housing, directly or indirectly.

Beneficiaries were more likely to keep investment housing (72 per cent) and both second homes and other non-professional housing (71 per cent) than primary homes (65 per cent). Among those inheriting investment housing, 53 per cent kept it as an investment, 8 per cent used it as a primary home, and 4 per cent used it as a second home. In some cases the parents may have lived in the house earlier and converted it to rental housing towards the end of their lives. Such bequests can bring income to the heir, and its very existence is a sign of a large estate—and of heirs able to afford keeping it. Among the large majority of those who inherited other non-professional housing and kept it, nearly one-fifth used it for professional purposes, 15 per cent made it their primary home, 12 per cent rented it out, and 11 per cent converted it into a second home. I suspect that, except for garages, these were mainly uninhabited dwellings or old farm buildings that the farmers' children converted to other uses.

Table 15.7. Among households receiving housing in their share of inheritance, percentages who kept and who sold the housing: France, 1991–2

Heirs' use of home	Type of housing inherited				
	Primary home	Second home	Investment housing	Other housing	All housing
% of inheriting households	85.5	11.5	8.7	8.4	100.0
Kept home	64.6	71.3	71.8	70.6	67.0
As primary home	36.8	15.7	8.2	15.4	34.9
As second home	12.9	34.3	4.1	11.1	15.4
Rented it out	5.2	12.4	53.1	12.1	9.8
For professional use	1.9	0.0	0.6	18.8	3.1
For children	1.5	1.0	2.0	0.6	1.6
Sold home and used proceeds	35.4	28.7	28.2	29.4	33.0
To buy primary home	14.4	10.2	7.5	10.4	14.4
To buy second home	1.5	0.6	2.2	2.5	1.7
To buy investment housing	0.7	0.2	2.6	0.3	1.1
For professional use	3.8	3.6	1.1	4.8	3.8
To make financial investment	11.9	10.8	6.9	5.2	12.1
To buy children a home	1.9	0.3	0.5	0.5	1.7
For children's education	2.4	0.4	1.7	1.5	2.4
To buy durables	4.0	1.8	2.7	2.1	3.1
For other consumption	8.2	5.4	7.9	4.5	8.1

Notes: Sample includes 2,402 households in which the reference person was over 30 years of age, at least one parent was no longer living, and the household had inherited or been given housing; the sample is weighted to represent the French population. A household may have inherited more than one type of housing and may have used it for more than one purpose. Hence the percentages of inheriting households (first row) exceed 100.00 and the percentages of uses (in the columns) exceed the totals.

Source: INSEE, Enquête Actifs financiers, 1991–2.

Those inheriting a primary home kept it as such in more than a third of the cases, but 13 per cent used it as a second home and 5 per cent rented it out. Likewise, 34 per cent of those inheriting a second home kept it for that purpose; the other main uses were as a primary residence (16 per cent) and rental property (12 per cent). Second homes, many of which were located in scenic areas or near Paris, were more likely to be kept than primary homes, which tended to be located near the parents' workplace. In any case, equal proportions (51 per cent) of those households inheriting primary and second homes kept them for their own or their children's use, but those inheriting a second home were more likely than those inheriting a primary home to turn it into rental property.

In most cases those keeping a primary home were already living in it: only 26 per cent mentioned moving into the house after their parents' death. Farmers (82 per cent) were especially likely to keep their parents' home, but even children of non-farmers kept it in 53 per cent of the cases. In comparison, in Britain only 25 per cent of inherited housing is kept for the family's use (Hamnet *et al.* 1990).

Fewer than 2 per cent of inherited French homes, however, go directly to the grandchildren of the deceased. One reason may be that property owners have no incentive to name grandchildren as heirs because the threshold at which inheritance tax is levied on property is lower for grandchildren than for children (10,000 francs versus 300,000 francs). In another study (Laferrère and Verger 1993), we found that inheritance rarely skips a generation through immediate *inter-vivos* gifts from the inheriting children to their own children.

The Use of Proceeds from the Sale of Inherited Housing

Those who inherited housing property and sold it used the proceeds in most cases to purchase other housing—either a primary or second home for themselves (16 per cent), for their children (2 per cent), or for investment purposes (1 per cent) (see bottom panel of Table 15.7). Other uses were investing in financial securities (12 per cent), in a business or profession (4 per cent), or in children's education (2 per cent) and consumption (11 per cent).

The finding that most people who sell an inherited home use the proceeds to purchase a primary home goes against the widely held view that inheritance 'comes too late in life'. Actually for most of the living generations who have inherited, the age at inheritance may not have risen as much over the past century as is commonly believed. Between 1870 and 1970 average life expectancy in France rose only three years for adult men and six years for women, although during the brief period between 1970 and 1991 it rose by another three years for men and three and a half years for women.[4] According to data on estate duties, mean age at inheritance was 44 in 1987, and mean age at second inheritance was 52 (Laferrère 1994). It is those who have not yet inherited (one may refer to them as the baby boomers) who will inherit at later ages because their parents are expected to live longer, and it will be a while before that phenomenon reaches its peak. The age at which parents have children and the difference in age between spouses in both parents' and children's cohorts also affect the age at inheritance.

How many households can be said to have inherited their home? The answer to that simple question is not straightforward because some respondents to the survey may have forgotten to mention a home they had sold immediately after inheriting it, whereas others mentioned inheriting and keeping a house but not owning it at the time of the survey. The latter type of response was especially common in the case of inherited second homes and investment housing, and it may indicate that some respondents answered the question about their use of an inheritance by considering what they had done with it in the past, whereas at the time of the survey their use of the house had changed. These are some of the difficulties associated with asking biographical questions in retrospective surveys. Respondents were probably less likely to have put an inherited primary home to multiple uses over time than a second home or investment property.

Combining direct and indirect uses of inheritance, I find that 20 per cent of all households in my sub-sample and 27 per cent of current home-owning households owned their homes through inheritance: 15 per cent directly, 7 per cent by selling inherited housing, and 5 per cent by selling other inherited assets such as securities. Thus 12 per cent owed their homeownership to indirect uses of inheritance. This figure does not include those households who had ever received help from their parents in such forms as paying the rent, lending a home, providing collateral when the beneficiaries' home was bought, or giving money for the purchase of a home (that is, unrecorded *inter-vivos* gifts). According to weighted data from the INSEE survey, some 1.3 million homeowners had received such help, although they had not received a home as a gift or inheritance. That means that among homeowners, nearly one out of two (45 per cent) received some sort of help from their parents in acquiring housing.

It is more difficult to assess the importance of inheritance in the case of housing used as a second home because, as mentioned above, some inheriting householders no longer owned the second home at the time of the INSEE survey. About 5 per cent of surveyed households currently owned an inherited second home. It seems that between 23 and 45 per cent of second homes were inherited either directly or indirectly through proceeds from the sale of other inherited property, and in a preponderance of cases (between 19 and 40 per cent of owners of second homes) the inheritance was direct (not shown). These findings bear testimony to the French attachment to family-owned homes.

Some 3 per cent of all households owned investment housing as a consequence of inheritance. The percentage of investment-housing owners who owned it through inheritance ranged between 17 and 22 per cent (not shown).

The role of inheritance in triggering investment housing

Also of interest is the amount of inherited housing that beneficiaries kept and turned into new investment housing. Nationwide, 5 per cent of primary homes (or 207,000 units), were turned into investment housing; corresponding figures for second homes and for other non-professional housing were 12 per cent (66,000 units) and 12 per cent (47,000 units), respectively (top panel of Table 15.7). At the same time 19 per cent of inherited investment housing units (76,000) were kept by the beneficiaries and not rented out. As a result, among households that had received housing property, 244,000 directly released new properties into the rental market. About 68,000 had used the proceeds from the sale of an inherited home or other forms of inheritance to buy investment housing.

It is not known what happened to the houses that were sold. Were they purchased by buyers who intended to occupy them or by those looking for investment property? If the effect of selling the homes is assumed to be neutral, it appears that inheritance has increased the number of households who rent out homes. This is in line with findings by Clanché (1995), who reports a recent increase in privately owned investment housing. I estimate that some 10 per cent of households who own investment housing turned an inherited house into an investment, renting it out to others.

The use of inherited housing for financial investment and consumption

Twelve per cent of households inheriting housing sold the property and used the proceeds for financial investments (bottom panel of Table 15.7). Hamnet *et al.* (1990) have found the proportion to be considerably larger—29 per cent—in Great Britain, where about half of such households invested the proceeds in building societies. Among households responding to INSEE's survey, direct consumption of inheritance, including the purchase of durables such as cars, was of the same order of magnitude as financial investment (10 per cent on average, 11 per cent in households with children, 8 per cent in childless households)—again, less than in Britain. Four per cent (5 per cent of those who had children) used the proceeds from the sale of an inherited house directly for their children, for example to purchase them a home or to pay for their education. An average of 13 per cent of households used the proceeds for their children or for consumption; among households with children the proportion was 14 per cent, and among those without children it was 8 per cent.

Conclusion

Among French households in which the reference person was more than 30 years old and at least one parent or parent-in-law of the reference person had died, about 30 per cent had inherited a house. A household was more likely to have inherited the parents' home after the death of both parents or parents-in-law and if the householder or his wife was an only child or had only one or two siblings; was a farmer, self-employed, or an executive; and was not residing in Paris. Children of self-employed parents and executives were more likely than others to inherit investment housing. Farmers were more likely than householders in other occupations to keep a home inherited from their parents. Beneficiaries were less likely to keep a home if it was inherited late in life, and households with children tended to keep an inherited second home of their parents. Owning a second home was a sign of wealth.

Among inheriting households, 33 per cent sold the property and 49 per cent kept it for their primary or second residence. Only 10 per cent kept it as a long-term investment asset. I found no evidence that beneficiaries transferred property to their own children upon receiving it from their parents.

In most cases the proceeds from the sale of an inherited home were used to purchase a home. Other uses, reported by about equal proportions of beneficiaries, were consumption and financial investment.

Among homeowners occupying their home, 15 per cent had received it directly from their parents, and 12 per cent mentioned using the proceeds of an inheritance to buy or improve their home. Thus 27 per cent of French households in which the householder is over age 30 can be said to have used an inheritance to help them become homeowners. Moreover, a substantial amount of inherited property was released into the rental sector. Contrary to findings from a British study, inheritance does not seem to erode the rental sector in France.

These findings suggest that for those alive today inheritance contributes significantly to homeownership. The future of home inheritance will depend on the behaviour of both children and parents. Compared with the current generation, the next generation of inheritors will be more likely to own a house already, to have fewer siblings, and therefore to inherit more and be more willing to rent out or sell the inherited property. These changes could increase the private ownership of rented houses and exert a negative influence on the price of housing.

Tomorrow's parents may also be in a position to help their children earlier in life, all the more so because those children will be less numerous. On the other hand, longer life expectancy may cause parents to exchange the deed to their home for a guaranteed life income and some amount of immediate cash in order to complement their retirement benefits. Others may decide to sell the family home and move into sheltered housing, thereby reducing the amount of intergenerational housing transfers by consuming part of their home equity.

Appendix: The Survey Questionnaire

All the questions were addressed first to the reference person of the household, then to the spouse. In all currently married households the reference person was the husband. The spouse's characteristics were described not only for currently married couples but also for widowed respondents. In the case of widowed female respondents, I transposed the spouse's and reference person's variables so that 'in-laws' always meant the wife's parents. Most of the questions analysed in this chapter are biographical and retrospective. A summary of the main questions follows.

- *Did your parents ever help you with paying the rent or lend you a house without charging you rent?*
- *Did they ever provide collateral or back a loan for you?*
- [The respondent was asked to recall each death of a parent or parent-in-law, in chronological order.] *At the time of this death and after having made gifts, did your deceased parent own... housing property (including his/her main home) or securities?*
- *After this death and after the payment of inheritance taxes did you personally receive ... housing?*
- [If yes] *In full ownership, with restriction on the ownership (life interest), or with some* [of the housing] *still held jointly?*
- *Before the estate was divided, were some of the deceased's assets immediately sold?*
- *Now we want to take a broader view of the use you made of transfers. Did your share of gifts or inheritance include*

  your parents' primary home?
  a second home of your parents?
  investment housing?
  other housing property? [These might include garages, parking lots, or unused buildings. In most cases such structures were on farms or in the country. Professional buildings were not supposed to be mentioned here.]

[For each type of property the following questions were asked:]

- *Did you keep it?*
- [If so,] *as your primary home, as your second home, as investment property, for your professional activity, as a home for your children or grandchildren, for other purposes?* [Respondents could select up to three of these answers.]
- *Did you sell it?*
- [If so,] *did you use the product of the sale to buy a primary home, to buy a better home, to pay off a real estate loan or mortgage, to improve your home* [these items were grouped under the category of 'buying primary home']; *to buy a second home, to buy investment property, to help your children or grandchildren in buying a home, to extend*

your farm, to start a business, to extend your business [labelled as 'professional' purposes]; *to invest in securities, to put into a savings account, to purchase life insurance, for another investment* [labelled as 'financial investments']; *to buy durables (for example, a car), for your children's or grandchildren's education, for a trip or vacation, for other purposes* ['miscellaneous' categories] *?* [Respondents could select up to three possible answers for the proceeds of the sale.]

- *Today, with the passing of time, and considering the assets you own, do you feel you have inherited some housing property?*

Notes

Thanks are due to the other participants in the Seminar on Intergenerational Demographic Relations and Demographic Changes, especially to Didier Blanchet for his helpful comments. Advice from members of the Research Department at INSEE is also gratefully acknowledged. Any errors, however, are my own.

1. Enquêtes Logement, INSEE (Vanderkerhove, Desmond, and Birot de la Pommeraye 1995). France ranks tenth in the level of homeownership among the twelve European countries, ahead of the Netherlands and Germany; Spain ranks first, at 88% in 1990. The rate for the United Kingdom was 68% in 1986 (Bertrand 1993).
2. No estate duty is assessed on a life interest. Upon the death of the first parent, the surviving spouse and children may share the decedent's real property. The spouse enjoys a life interest in his or her share (typically one-fourth of the estate) while continuing to own one-half of the community property, and the children own an expectant interest in the surviving parent's share.
3. In France parents are free to dispose of only one-quarter of their estate as they wish; the rest must be evenly divided among their offspring. In countries not influenced by the French civil code, equal distribution is not compulsory, but it is the practice in a vast majority of cases (Laferrère 1989).
4. Until the 1950s the decline in mortality affected mainly children (Bourgoin and Nizard 1995).

References

Numbers in square brackets and boldface type after dates of publication represent the chapters in which the referenced works are cited.

Aaron, H. J., Bosworth, B., and Burless, G. (1989). **[9]** *Can America Afford to Grow Old?* (Washington, DC, Brookings Institution).

ADB (Asian Development Bank) (1991). **[3]** *Asian Development Outlook, 1991* (Manila).

Administración Nacional de al Seguridad Social (ANSeS) (1994). **[6]** 'Estadísticas', *Previsión Social* 13: 187–232.

——(1995*a*). **[6]** 'Cuadro estadístico de distribución por AFJP del mes de Marzo de 1995', unpublished report, May 1995 (Buenos Aires).

——(1995*b*). **[6]** 'Tabulado de jubilaciones por edad y sexo', unpublished report, May 1995 (Buenos Aires).

Alho, J. M. (1991). **[9]** 'Stochastic methods in population forecasting', *International Journal of Forecasting* 6: 521–30.

Allende, S. (1972 and 1973). **[7]** *Presidential Message* (Santiago).

Altonji, J. G., Hayashi, F., and Kotlikoff, L. J. (1992). **[11, 12, 13, 14]** 'Is the extended family altruistically linked? Direct evidence using micro data', *American Economic Review* 82(5): 1177–98.

————(1995). **[14]** 'Parental altruism and inter vivos transfers: Theory and evidence', NBER Working Paper 5378 (Cambridge, Mass., National Bureau of Economic Research).

Altonji, J. G., and Dunn, T. (1991). **[14]** 'Relationships among the family incomes and labor market outcomes of relatives', *Research in Labor Economics* 12: 269–310.

Ando, A., and Modigliani, F. (1963). **[4]** 'The "Life Cycle" hypothesis of saving: Aggregate implications and tests', *American Economic Review* 53: 55–84.

Andreoni, J. (1989). **[14]** 'Giving with impure altruism: Applications to charity and Ricardian equivalence', *Journal of Political Economy* 97(6): 1447–58.

Arellano, J. P. (1985). **[7]** *Políticas Sociales y Desarrollo: Chile 1924–84* (Santiago, CIEPLAN).

Arrau, P. (1991). **[5]** ' La reforma previsional chilena y su financiamiento durante la transición', *Collección Estudios (CIEPLAN)* 32 (June): 5–44.

Arthur, B. W., and McNicoll, G. (1978). **[2]** 'Samuelson, population and intergenerational transfers', *International Economic Review* 19(1): 241–6.

Assael, P. (1993). **[7]** 'Ciclos Político- Económicos en Chile: Un Enfoque Oportunista', M.Sc. thesis (Instituto de Economía, P. Universidad Católica de Chile, Santiago).

Auerbach, A. J., and Kotlikoff, L. J. (1987). **[2, 8]** *Dynamic Fiscal Policy* (Cambridge, Cambridge University Press).

——Gokhale, J., and Kotlikoff, L. (1991). **[1, 2, 3, 4, 8]** 'Generational accounts: A meaningful alternative to deficit accounting', in D. Bradford (ed.), *Tax Policy and the Economy*, 5 (Cambridge, Mass., MIT Press for the National Bureau of Economic Research): 55–110.

—— —— and Kotlikoff, L. (1994). **[3, 4]** 'Generational accounting: A meaningful way to evaluate fiscal policy', *Journal of Economic Perspectives* 8(1): 73–94.

—— —— —— and Steigum, E. (1992). **[4]** 'Generational accounting in Norway: Is the nation over-consuming its petroleum wealth?', Working Paper 9305 (Cleveland, Federal Reserve Bank).

Bank of Korea (various years). **[13]** *Economic Statistics Yearbook* (Seoul).

Barclay, G. W. (1954). **[3]** *A Report on Taiwan's Population to the Joint Commission on Rural Reconstruction* (Princeton, Office of Population Research, Princeton University).

Barro, R. J. (1974). **[1, 2, 3, 11, 12]** 'Are government bonds net wealth?', *Journal of Political Economy* 82(6): 1095–117.

Becker, G. S. (1974). **[12]** 'A theory of social interactions', *Journal of Political Economy* 82: 1063–93.

——(1981). **[2, 13]** *A Treatise on the Family* (Cambridge, Mass., Harvard University Press).

——(1988). **[2]** 'Family economics and macro behavior', *American Economic Review* 78(1): 1–13.

——and Barro, R. J. (1988). **[11]** 'A reformulation of the economic theory of fertility', *Quarterly Journal of Economics* 103: 1–26.

Behrman, J., Foster, A. D., and Rosenzweig, M. R. (1997). **[10]** 'Dynamic savings decisions in agricultural environments with incomplete markets', *Journal of Business and Economic Statistics* 15(2): 282–92.

Benda-Beckmann, F. von., Benda-Beckmann, K. von, Casino, E., Hirtz, F., Woodman, G. R., and Zacher, H. F. (eds.) (1988). **[12]** *Between Kinship and the State: Social Security and Law in Developing Countries* (Dordrecht, Foris).

Bengston, V. L., and Achenbaum, W. A. (eds.) (1993). **[12]** *The Changing Contract across Generations* (New York, Aldine de Gruyter).

Bengtsson, T., and Kruse, A. (1992). **[5]** 'Demographic effects on the Swedish pension system', IIASA Working Paper WP–92–35 (Laxenburg, International Institute for Applied Systems Analysis).

Bernheim, B. D. (1991). **[15]** 'How strong are bequest motives? Evidence based on estimates of the demand for life insurance and annuities', *Journal of Political Economy* 99(5): 899–927.

——and Stark, O. (1988). **[12]** 'Altruism within the family reconsidered: Do nice guys finish last?', *American Economic Review* 78: 1034–45.

——Shleifer, A., and Summers, L. H. (1985). **[11, 12, 13, 14]** 'The strategic bequest motive', *Journal of Political Economy* 93: 1045–76.

Bertrand, L. (1993). **[15]** 'Europe: tendance commune vers l'accession à la propriété', in *Données Sociales 1993* (Paris, INSEE).

Beveridge, W. (1942). **[7]** *Social Insurance and Allied Services* (London, HM Stationery Office).

Blanchet, D. (1988). **[8]** 'Retraites par répartition et par capitalisation selon le contexte démographique: quelques résultats comparatifs', *Annales d'Economie et de Statistiques* 18: 63–90.

——(1992). **[8]** 'Retraites et croissance à long terme: un essai de simulation', *Economie et Prévision* 105: 1–16.

——and Chanut, J. M. (1995). **[8]** 'Modèle de micro-simulation destiné à la projection des retraites', Note INSEE 240–G211 (Paris, Institute de Statistique et d'Etudes Economiques).

Blanchet, D. and Kessler, D. (1992). **[8]** 'Optimal Pension Funding with Endogenous Return on Capital', in *Fiscal Implications of Population Ageing*, D. Bös and S. Cnossen (eds.) (Berlin, Springer Verlag).

Bommier, A., and Lee, R. D (1995). **[2]** 'Continuous and dynamic overlapping generations models', manuscript (Department of Demography, University of California, Berkeley).

Bourgoin, N., and Nizard, A. (1995). **[15]** 'La survie des personnes âgées', *Population et Sociétés, Bulletin de l'Institut National d'Etudes Démographiques*, 302.

Bravo, J. (1994) . **[5]** 'Demographic changes and unfunded pension systems: financial aspects', paper presented at the 1994 Annual Meeting of the Population Association of America, Miami.

Brinton, M. C., Lee, Y.-J., and Parish, W. L. (1995). **[13]** 'Married women's employment in East Asia', *American Journal of Sociology* 100: 1099–1130.

Cabello, O., *et al.* (1946). **[7]** 'Tablas de Vida para Chile: 1920,1930 y 1940, Part I', *Revista Chilena de Higiene y Medicina Preventiva* (Santiago) 8: 103–6.

Cain, M. (1981). **[12]** 'Risk and insurance: perspectives on fertility and agrarian change in India and Bangladesh', *Population and Development Review* 7: 435–74.

——(1985). **[12]** 'The fate of the elderly in South Asia: Implications for fertility', in *IUSSP International Population Conference, Florence*, 4 (Liège, International Union for the Scientific Study of Population).

——(1986). **[12]** 'The consequences of reproductive failure: Dependence, mobility and mortality among elderly of rural South Asia', *Population Studies* 40: 375–88.

Caldwell, J. C. (1976). **[1, 2, 13]** 'Toward a restatement of demographic transition theory', *Population and Development Review* 2(3–4): 321–66, repr. as ch. 4 in J. C. Caldwell (1982), *Theory of Fertility Decline* (New York, Academic Press): 113–80.

Cazes, S., Chauveau, T., Le Cacheux, J., and Loufir, R. (1992). **[8]** 'Retraites et évolutions démographiques en France. Première partie: le long- terme', *Observations et Diagnostics Economiques* 39: 93–149.

CELADE [Centro Latinoamericano de Demografía] (1994). **[7]** *Latin America: Life Tables 1950–2025* (Santiago).

Chamberlain, G. (1984). **[14]** 'Panel data', in Z. Griliches and M. D. Intriligator (eds.), *Handbook of Econometrics*, 2 (New York, Elsevier Science Publishers): 1248–1318.

Chang, C. (1959). **[3]** *Chung-kuo jen kou wen ti* (Taipei, Chung-kuo jen kou hsui hui).

Chauveau, T., and Loufir, R. (1994). **[8]** 'L'avenir du régime de retraite français: les enseignements d'un modèle à générations imbriquées', *Revue Economique* 45: 789–804.

————(1995). **[8]** 'L'avenir des régimes publics de retraite dans les pays du G7', *Observations et Diagnostics Economiques* 1: 49–103.

Chayanov, A. V. (1966). **[1, 3]** *The Theory of Peasant Economy*, D. Thorner *et al.*, trans. (University of Wisconsin Press, originally 1925): 53–81.

Chen, C., and Tuan, C.-H. (1951). **[3]** *Population of Taiwan* (Taipei, National Taiwan University).

Cheyre, H. (1991). **[7]** *La Previsión en Chile. Ayer y Hoy* (Santiago, Centro de Estudios Públicos).

Chiappori, P.-A. (1992). **[13]** '"Collective" models of household behavior: The sharing rule approach', paper presented at the International Food Policy Research Institute–World Bank Conference on Intrahousehold Resource Allocation: Policy Issues and Research Methods, Washington, DC.

Chile, Government of (1993). **[7]** *Political Constitution of the Republic of Chile* (Santiago, Editorial Jurídica de Chile).

Cho, L.-J., and Yada, M. (eds.) (1994). **[3]** *Tradition and Change in the Asian Family* (Honolulu, East-West Center, distributed by University of Hawaii Press).

Cifuentes, R. (1994). **[5]** 'Changing retirement ages: The welfare effects', *Revista de Análisis Económico* 9 (1): 35–56.

——(1995). **[5]** 'Reforma de los sistemas previsionales: Aspectos macroeconómicos', *Cuadernos de Economía* 32,(96): 217–50.

Cigno, A. (1986). **[11]** 'Fertility and the tax-benefit system: A reconsideration of the theory of family taxation', *Economic Journal* 96: 1035–51.

——(1991). **[11, 14]** *Economics of the Family* (New York and Oxford, Oxford University Press and Clarendon Press).

——(1993). **[11]** 'Intergenerational transfers without altruism: Family, market and state', *European Journal of Political Economy* 7: 505–18.

——(1995). **[11]** 'Public pensions with endogenous fertility: Comment on Nishimura and Zhang', *Journal of Public Economics* 57: 169–73.

——and Rosati, F. C. (1992). **[11]** 'The effects of financial markets and social security on saving and fertility behaviour in Italy', *Journal of Population Economics* 5: 319–41.

————(1996). **[11]** 'Jointly determined saving and fertility behaviour: Theory, and estimates for Germany, Italy, UK and USA, *European Economic Review* 40: 1561–89.

————(1997). **[11]** 'Rise and fall of the Japanese saving rate: The role of social security and intra-family transfers', *Japan and the World Economy* 9(1): 81–92.

Clanché, F. (1995). **[15]** 'La reprise du locatif privé', *Economie et Statistique*, INSEE, 288/289, (8/9): 77–89.

Coale, A. J., and Demeny, P. (1983). **[2]** *Regional Model Life Tables and Stable Populations* (New York, Academic Press).

Coate, S., and Ravallion, M.(1993). **[10]** 'Reciprocity without commitment: Characterisation and performance of informal insurance arrangements,' *Journal of Development Economics* 40: 1–24.

Cornilleau, G., and Sterdyniak, H. (1994). **[8]** 'Les retraites: des réformes sans plan d'ensemble', *Observations et Diagnostics Economiques* 126: 1–6.

Coward, R. T., and Dwyer, J. W. (1990). **[13]** 'The association of gender, sibling network composition, and patterns of parent care by adult children', *Research on Aging* 12(2): 158–81.

Cowgill, D. O. (1986). **[13]** *Aging around the World* (Belmont, Calif., Wadsworth).

Cox, D. (1987). **[11, 12, 13, 14]** 'Motives for private income transfers', *Journal of Political Economy* 95(3): 508–46.

——(1990). **[14]** 'Intergenerational transfers and liquidity constraints', *Quarterly Journal of Economics* 105: 187–218.

——and Jakubson, G. (1995). **[12]** 'The connection between public transfers and private family transfers', *Journal of Public Economics* 57: 129–67.

——and Jimenez, E. (1992). **[12]** 'Social security and private transfers in developing countries: The case of Peru', *World Bank Economic Review* 6: 155–69.

————(1993). **[12]** 'Private transfers and the effectiveness of public income redistribution in the Philippines' (Washington, DC, World Bank), mimeo.

——and Raines, F. (1985). **[14]** 'Interfamily transfers and income redistribution', in M. David and T. Smeeding (eds.), *Horizontal Equity, Uncertainty, and Measure of Well-being* (Chicago, University of Chicago Press for the National Bureau of Economic Research): 395–421.

Cox, D. and Rank, M. (1992). **[12, 13, 14]** 'Inter-vivos transfers and intergenerational exchange', *Review of Economics and Statistics* 74 (2): 305–14.

Cruz-Saco, M. A. (1995). **[12]** 'The pension system reform in Peru: The economic rationale versus the political will', paper presented at the 1995 Latin American Studies Association International Congress, Washington, DC, Sept. 28–30.

Daguet, F. (1995). **[8]** *Un siècle de demographie française: structure et: évolution de la population de 1901 à 1993*, INSEE Resultats 434–5.

Deaton, A. (1992). **[10]** *Understanding Consumption* (Oxford, Clarendon Press).

——and Muelbauer, J. (1986). **[2]** 'On measuring child costs: With applications to poor countries', *Journal of Political Economy* 94(4): 720–44.

De Soto, H. (1989). **[12]** *The Other Path* (New York, Harper & Row).

DeVos, S., and Lee, Y.-J. (1993). **[13]** 'Change in extended family living among elderly people in South Korea, 1970–1980', *Economic Development and Cultural Change* 41(2): 377–93.

Diamond, P. (1965). **[2, 5]** 'National debt in a neoclassical growth model', *American Economic Review* 55: 1126–50.

——(1977). **[7]** 'A framework for the Analysis of Social Security', *Journal of Public Economics* (North Holland) 8: 275–98.

——(1996). **[7]** 'Government Provision and Regulation of Economic Support in Old Age', in *Annual World Bank Conference on Development Economics, 1995*, M. Bruno and B. Pleskovic (eds.) (Washington, DC, World Bank).

——and Valdés-Prieto, S. (1994). **[7]** 'Social Security Reforms', ch. 6 in B. Bosworth, R. Dornbusch, and R. Labán (eds.), *The Chilean Economy* (Washington, DC, Brookings Institution).

Dinh, Q. C. (1994). **[8]** 'La population de la France à l'horizon 2050', *Economie et Statistique* 274: 7–32.

Dodds, D., Friou, D., and Mason, C. (1996). **[2]** 'Does intergenerational wealth flow upward in lowland tropical America?: A test of Caldwell's hypothesis', paper presented at the 1996 Annual Meeting of the Population Association of America, New Orleans.

Dunn, T. A. (1993*a*). **[14]** 'The distribution of intergenerational income transfers between and within families', manuscript (Syracuse University).

——(1993*b*). **[13]** 'Essays on the economic linkages among family members', Ph.D. dissertation (Department of Economics, Northwestern University, Evanston).

Durand, J. D. (1975). **[2]** *The Labor Force in Economic Development: A Comparison of International Census Statistics: 1946–66* (Princeton, Princeton University Press).

Easterlin, R. (1973). **[8]** 'Relative economic status and the American fertility swing', in *Family Economic Behavior*, E. B. Sheldon (ed.) (Philadelphia, J. B. Lippincott).

Entwisle, B., and Winegarden, C. R. (1984). **[11]** 'Fertility and pension programs in LDCs: A model of mutual reinforcement', *Economic Development and Cultural Change* 32: 331–54.

Ermisch, J. (1989), **[1, 2]** 'Intergenerational transfers in industrialized countries: Effects of age distribution and economic institutions', *Journal of Population Economics* 1: 269–84.

Eu, H. (1992). **[13]** 'Health status and social and demographic determinants of living arrangements among the Korean elderly', *Korea Journal of Population and Development* 21(2): 197–223.

Federal Reserve System , Board of Governors (1963 and 1983). **[4]** *Survey of Consumer Finances* (Washington, DC).

Fehr, H., and Kotlikoff, L. (1995). **[4]** 'Generational accounting in general equilibrium', Working Paper 5090 (Washington, DC, National Bureau of Economic Research).

Feldstein, M. (1974). **[1, 2, 11]** 'Social security, induced retirement, and aggregate capital accumulation', *Journal of Political Economy* 82(5): 905–26.

——(1980). **[11]** 'International differences in social security and saving', *Journal of Public Economics* 14: 225–44.

Ffrench-Davis, R. (1973). **[7]** *Políticas Económicas en Chile 1952–1970* (Santiago, Ediciones Nueva Universidad, Universidad Católica de Chile).

Fleurbaey, M., and Michel, P. (1993). **[8]** 'Quelle justice pour les retraites', *Revue d'Economie Financière* 23: 47–64.

Foster, A. D. (1994). **[10]** 'Prices, credit markets and child growth in low-income rural areas', *Economic Journal* 105: 551–70.

——and Rosenzweig, M. R. (1995*a*). **[14]** 'Does transfer behavior exhibit imperfect commitment? Insurance, the family, and financial institutions in low-income rural areas,' manuscript (Dept. of Economics, University of Pennsylvania, Philadelphia).

————(1995*b*). **[10]** 'Imperfect commitment, altruism, and the family: Evidence from transfer behavior in low-income rural areas', manuscript (Dept. of Economics, University of Pennsylvania, Philadelphia).

————(1995*c*). **[10]** 'Learning by doing and learning from others: Human capital and technical change in agriculture', *Journal of Political Economy* 103(6): 1176–1209.

Foxley, A., Aninat, E., and Arellano, J. P. (1977). **[7]** 'Efectos de la Seguridad Social sobre la Distribución del Ingreso', *Estudios CIEPLAN* 8 (March): 5–44.

France, Commissariat Général du Plan (1991). **[8]** *Livre Blanc sur les Retraites* (Paris, La Documentation Française).

Franco, D., Gokhale, J., Guiso, L., Kotlikoff, L., and Sartor, N. (1994). **[4]** 'Generational accounting: The case of Italy', in A. Ando, L. Guiso, and I. Visco (eds.), *Saving and the Accumulation of Wealth: Essays on Italian Household and Government Saving Behaviour* (Cambridge, Cambridge University Press): 128–60.

Fricke, T. E. (1990). **[2]** 'Darwinian transitions? A comment', *Population and Development Review* 16(1): 107–19.

——Chang, J. S., and Yang, L. S. (1994). **[3]** 'Historical and ethnographic perspectives on the Chinese family,' in A. Thornton and H.-S. Lin (eds.), *Social Change and the Family in Taiwan* (Chicago, University of Chicago Press).

Gale, D. (1973). **[2]** 'Pure exchange equilibrium of dynamic economic models', *Journal of Economic Theory* 6: 12–36.

Gale, W. G., and Scholz, J. K. (1994). **[14]** 'Intergenerational transfers and the accumulation of wealth', *Journal of Economic Perspectives* 8(4): 145–60.

Glewwe, P. 1988. **[12]** 'The distribution of welfare in Peru in 1985–86', World Bank Living Standards Measurement Study Working Paper 42 (Washington, DC, World Bank).

——and Hall, G. (1992). **[12]** 'Poverty and inequality during unorthodox adjustment: The case of Peru, 1985–90', World Bank Livings Standards Measurement Study Working Paper 86 (Washington, DC, World Bank).

Godoy, O., and Valdés-Prieto, S. (1997). **[7]** 'Democracy and Pensions in Chile: Experience with Two Systems,' in S. Valdés-Prieto (ed.), *The Economics of Pensions: Principles, Policies, and International Experience* (Cambridge, Cambridge University Press).

Gokhale, J., Kotlikoff, L., and Sabelhaus, J. (1996). **[4]** 'Understanding the post war decline in United States' saving: A cohort analysis', *Brookings Papers on Economic Activity* 1: 315–407.

Gokhale, J., Raffelhüschen, B., and Walliser, J. 1995. **[4]** 'The burden of German unification: A generational accounting approach', *FinanzArchiv*, Neue Folge, 52/2.

Goldstein, M. C., and Ku, Y. (1993). **[12]** 'Income and family support among rural elderly in Zhejiang Province, China', *Journal of Cross-Cultural Gerontology* 8: 197–223.

Gotman, A. (1991). **[15]** 'L'héritier et le commis voyageur: transmission et héritage de la maison de famille', in M. Ségalen (ed.), *Jeux de Famille* (Paris, Presses du Centre National de la Recherche Scientifique).

Graham, J. W. (1987). **[11]** 'International differences in saving rates and the life cycle hypothesis', *European Economic Review* 31: 1509–29.

Greene, H. W. (1993). **[13]** *Econometric Analysis* (New York, Macmillan).

——(1995). *LIMDEP (Limited Dependent Variable Models) Version 7.0: User's Manual and Reference Guide* (Bellport, NY, Econometric Software, Inc.).

Greenhalgh, S. (1985). **[13]** 'Sexual stratification: The other side of "growth with equity" in East Asia', *Population and Development Review* 11: 265–314.

Greenwood, D. T., and Wolff, E. N. (1992). **[11]** 'Changes in wealth in the United States, 1962–83', *Journal of Population Economics* 5: 261–88.

Guillemot, D., and Bordes, M. M. (1994). **[8]** *Marché du Travail: Séries Longues*, INSEE Résultats 305–6.

Haindl, E., Budinich, E., and Irarrázabal, I. (1989). **[7]** *Gasto Social Efectivo: Un Instrumento Que Asegura la Superación Definitiva de la Pobreza Crítica* (Santiago, ODEPLAN and Facultad de Ciencias Económicas y Administrativas, Universidad de Chile).

Hamayon, S. (1995). **[8]** 'Perspectives du système de retraite en France', in *Les Retraites: Genèse, Acteurs, Enjeux*, B. Cochemé and F. Legros (eds.) (Paris, Armand Colin).

Hamnet, C., Harmer, M., and Williams, P. (1990) **[15]** *Safe As Houses: Housing Inheritance in Britain* (London, Paul Chapman).

Hayashi, F., Altonji, J., and Kotlikoff, L. (1996). **[14]** 'Risk sharing between and within families', *Econometrica* 64(2): 261–94.

Hermalin, A. I., Ofstedal, M. B., and Lee, M.-L. (1992). **[13]** *Characteristics of Children and Intergenerational Transfers*, Comparative Study of the Elderly in Asia Research Reports, 92–21 (Ann Arbor, Population Studies Center, University of Michigan).

Heston, A., Summers, R., Nuxoll, D. A., and Aten, B. (1995). **[13]** 'Penn World Table (Mark 5.6*a*)', computer diskette (Cambridge, Mass., National Bureau of Economic Research).

Hill, M. S., and Soldo, B. (1993). **[14]** 'Intergenerational transfers: economic, demographic and social perspectives', manuscript (Institute for Social Research, University of Michigan, Ann Arbor).

——Morgan, J. N., and Herzog, R. (1993). **[14]** 'Intergenerational aspects of inter-family help patterns', manuscript (Institute for Social Research, University of Michigan, Ann Arbor).

Hoddinott, J. (1992). **[12]** 'Rotten kids or manipulative parents: Are children old age security in western Kenya?', *Economic Development and Cultural Change* 40: 545–65.

Hohm, C. H. (1975). **[11]** 'Social security and fertility: An international perspective', *Demography* 12: 629–44.

Honore, B. E. (1992). **[14]** 'Trimmed LAD and least squares estimation of truncated and censored regression models with fixed effects', *Econometrica* 60(3): 533–66.

INDEC [Instituto Nacional de Estadísticas y Censos] (1994). **[6]** *Estimaciones y Proyecciones de Población.Total del País 1950–2050*, Estudios INDEC 23 (Buenos Aires, INDEC-CELADE [Centro Latinoamericano de Demografía]).

Ioannides, Y. M., and Kan, K. (1993). **[14]** 'The nature of two-directional intergenerational transfers of money and time: An empirical analysis', manuscript (Virginia Polytechnic Institute and State University, Blacksbury).

Jain, S. (1975). **[12]** *The Size Distribution of Income: A Compilation of Data.* (Washington, DC, World Bank).

Johnson, A. (1975). **[2]** 'Time allocation in a Machiguenga community', *Ethnology* 14: 301–10.

Kaplan, H. (1994) **[2]** 'Evolutionary and wealth flows theories of fertility: empirical tests and new models', *Population and Development Review* 20(4): 753–91.

Kendig, H. L., Hashimoto, A., and Coppard, L. C. (eds.) (1992). **[12]** *Family Support for the Elderly: The International Experience* (Oxford, Oxford University Press).

Kessler, D., and Masson, A. (1995). **[8]** 'Redistribution et politiques sociales: la double dimension de l'âge et de la génération', in *Les Retraites: Genèse, Acteurs, Enjeux*, B. Cochemé and F. Legros (eds.), (Paris, Armand Colin).

—— —— and Pestieau, P. (1991). **[8]** 'Trois vues sur l'héritage: la famille, la propriété, l'Etat', *Economie et Prévision* 100–101: 1–29.

Keyfitz, N. (1985). **[5]** 'The demographics of unfunded pensions', *European Journal of Population* 1(1): 5–30.

Kim, E.-S., Lee, S.-H., Kim, S.-K., and Yu, S.-E. (1993). **[13]** *Structural Characteristics of Rural Households and Family Support System*, Publication 93–12 (Seoul, Korea Institute for Health and Social Affairs). In Korean.

Klein-Saks Commission (1957). **[7]** *Informe de la Comisión Klein-Saks* (Santiago).

Knodel, J. (1993). **[12]** *Using Qualitative Data for Understanding Old Age Security and Fertility*, Population Studies Center Research Report 93–299 (Ann Arbor, University of Michigan).

—— Chayovan, N., and Siriboon, S. (1992). **[13]** 'The impact of fertility decline on familial support for the elderly: An illustration from Thailand', *Population and Development Review* 18(1): 79–103.

Korea National Agricultural Cooperative Federation (various years). **[13]** *Agricultural Cooperative Yearbook* (Seoul). In Korean.

Kotlikoff, L. J. (1987). **[7]** 'Justifying Public Provision of Social Security', *Journal of Policy Analysis and Management* 6(4): 674–89.

—— (1992). **[1, 4]** *Generational Accounting: Knowing Who Pays, and When, for What We Spend* (New York, Free Press).

—— and Spivak, A. (1981). **[11, 12]** 'The family as an incomplete annuities market', *Journal of Political Economy* 89: 372–91.

—— and Summers, L. H. (1981). **[2]** 'The role of intergenerational transfers in aggregate capital accumulation', *Journal of Political Economy* 89: 706–32.

—— —— (1988). **[2, 15]** 'The contribution of intergenerational transfers to total wealth: A reply', in D. Kessler and A. Masson (eds.), *Modeling the Accumulation and Distribution of* Wealth (Oxford, Oxford University (Clarendon) Press): 53–67.

—— —— and Summers, L. (1981). **[11]** 'The role of intergenerational transfers in aggregate capital accumulation', *Journal of Political Economy* 89: 706–32.

Kwon, S., and Yang, B. (1990). **[13]** *Policies for Improving the National Health Insurance Program* (Seoul, Korea Development Institute). In Korean.

Laferrère, A. (1989). **[15]** 'La part héritée de la fortune entre le quart et la moitié', *in Les Ménages: Mélanges en l'Honneur de Jacques Desabie* (Paris, INSEE).

Laferrère, A. (1994). **[15]** 'Le rôle de la transmission du patrimoine au sein de la famille', *Gérontologie et Société* 68: 45–54.

——and McEntee, P. (1995). **[15]** 'Self-employment and intergenerational transfers: An empirical analysis on French data', *Economic and Social Review* 27: 43–53.

——and Monteil, P. (1994). **[15]** *Le patrimoine à la fin de la vie*, INSEE Première, 344.

——and Verger, D. (1993). **[15]** 'La transmission du patrimoine entre les générations', in *Données Sociales, 1993* (Paris, INSEE).

Lampman, R. J., and Smeeding, T. M. (1983). **[11]** 'Interfamily transfers as alternatives to government transfers to persons', *Review of Income and Wealth* 29: 45–66.

Lapkoff, S. (1985). **[5]** 'Pay-as-you-go retirement systems in nonstable populations', Dept. of Demography Working Paper (Berkeley, University of California).

——(1991). **[5]** 'A research note on Keyfitz's "The demographics of unfunded pensions"', *European Journal of Population* 7(2): 159–69.

Lazear, E. P., and Michael, R. T. (1988). **[2]** *Allocation of Income within the Household* (Chicago and London, University of Chicago Press).

Lee, R. D (1985). **[2]** 'Population growth and intergenerational transfers in a household setting', Working Paper 20, Graduate Group in Demography, University of California, Berkeley.

——(1990). **[2]** 'Population Policy and Externalities to Childbearing', *Annals of the American Academy of Political and Social Science* 510 (July): 17–32, special issue edited by S. Preston, *World Population: Approaching the Year 2000*.

——(1991). **[2]** 'Evaluating externalities to childbearing in developing countries: The case of India', in G. Tapinos, D. Blanchet, and D. E. Horlacher (eds.), *Consequences of Rapid Population Growth in Developing Countries* (New York, Taylor & Francis): 297–342.

——(1993). **[9]** 'Modeling and forecasting the time series of U.S. fertility: Age distribution, range and ultimate level', *International Journal of Forecasting* 9: 187–202.

——(1994*a*). **[2]** 'The formal demography of population aging, transfers, and the economic life cycle', in L. G. Martin and S. Preston (eds.), *The Demography of Aging* (Washington, DC, National Academy Press): 8–49.

——(1994*b*). **[2]** 'Population age structure, intergenerational transfers, and wealth: A new approach, with applications to the US', with the assistance of T. Miller; *Journal of Human Resources* 29(4): 1027–63, special issue edited by P. Gertler, *The Family and Intergenerational Relations*.

——(1994*c*). **[5]** 'Race-ethnicity and social security transfers: Who gains and who loses?', paper presented at the 1994 Annual Meeting of the Population Association of America, Miami.

——and Carter, L. (1992). **[9]** 'Modeling and forecasting the time series of U.S. mortality', *Journal of the American Statistical Association* 87: 659–71.

——and Lapkoff, S. (1988). **[2]** 'Intergenerational flows of time and goods: Consequences of slowing population growth', *Journal of Political Economy* 96: 618–51.

——and Miller, T. (1990). **[2]** 'Population growth, externalities to childbearing, and fertility policy in the Third World', *Proceedings of the World Bank Annual Conference on Development Economics*, Supplement to *World Bank Economic Review* and to *World Bank Research Observer*: 275–304.

————(1995). **[2]** 'Interage resource flows in the US: A descriptive account', paper presented at the 1995 Annual Meeting of the Population Association of America, San Francisco.

——and Tuljapurkar, S. (1994). **[9]** 'Stochastic population forecasts of the United States: Beyond high, medium, and low', *Journal of the American Statistical Association* 89: 1175–89.

Lee, T. (1968). **[3]** *A Study on Social Increase of Population in Taiwan* (Taiwan [city not identified], Taiwan Population Studies Center, Taiwan Provincial Department of Health).

Lee, Y.-J., and Aytac, I. A. (1993). **[13]** 'Intergenerational financial support among Whites, Blacks, and Hispanics', paper presented at the Annual Meeting of the Population Association of America, Pittsburgh.

——and Xiao, Z. (1994). **[13]** 'Public and familial support for the elderly in China', paper presented at the Annual Meeting of the Population Association of America, Miami.

——Parish, W. L., and Willis, R. J. (1994). **[12, 13]** 'Sons, daughters, and intergenerational support in Taiwan', *American Journal of Sociology* 99(4): 1010–41.

Legris, B., and Lollivier, S. (1996). **[8]** 'Le niveau de vie par génération', *INSEE Première*, 423 (Paris, Institut de Statistique et d'Etudes Economiques).

Leibenstein, H. (1957). **[12]** *Economic Backwardness and Economic Growth* (New York, Wiley).

——(1975). **[12]** 'The economic theory of fertility decline', *Quarterly Journal of Economics* 89: 1–31.

Leimar, R. D., and Lesnoy, S. D. (1982). **[11]** 'Social security and private saving: New time-series evidence', *Journal of Political Economy* 90: 606–29.

Li, R. M., Xie, Y., and Lin, H. S. (1993). **[13]** 'Division of family property in Taiwan', *Journal of Cross-cultural Gerontology* 8: 49–69.

Lucas, R. E. B., and Stark, O. (1985). **[12, 13]** 'Motivations to remit: Evidence from Botswana', *Journal of Political Economy* 93: 901–18.

McGarry, K., and Schoeni, R. F.(1995*a*). **[12, 13]** 'Transfer behavior in the Health and Retirement Study: Measurement and the redistribution of resources within the family', *Journal of Human Resources* 30 (Suppl.): S184–S226.

————(1995*b*). **[12]** 'Transfer behaviour within the family: Results from the Asset and Health Dynamics Survey', unpublished working paper, RAND Corporation, Santa Monica.

Maddala, G. S. (1983). **[12]** *Limited-Dependent and Qualitative Variables in Econometrics* (Cambridge, Cambridge University Press).

Malabouche, G. (1987). **[8]** 'L'évolution à long terme du système de retraites: une nouvelle méthode de projection', *Population* 42: 9–38.

Marchand, O., and Thélot, C. (1991). **[8]** *Deux Siècles de Travail en France*, INSEE-Etudes (Paris, Institut National de Statistique et d'Etudes Economiques).

Martin, L. G. (1990). **[13]** 'Changing intergenerational family relations in East Asia', *Annals of the American Academy of Political and Social Science* 510: 102–14.

——(1991). **[13]** 'Population aging policies in East Asia and the United States', *Science* 251(1): 527–31.

——and Kinsella, K. (1994). **[13]** 'Research on the demography of aging in developing countries', in L. G. Martin and S. H. Preston (eds.), *Demography of Aging* (Washington, DC, National Academy Press for the Committee on Population, Commission on Behavioral and Social Sciences and Education, National Research Council): 356–404.

Mason, A. (1987). **[2]** 'National savings rates and population growth: A new model and new evidence', in D. G. Johnson and R. D. Lee (eds.), *Population Growth and*

Economic Development: Issues and Evidence (Madison, University of Wisconsin Press): 523–60.

——and Martin, L. G. (1982). **[3]** 'Intergenerational differences in income: An analysis of Japan', *Population Development and Review* 8 (Suppl.): 179–91.

——and Miller, T. (1995). **[3]** 'Living arrangements, intergenerational transfers, and dynastic income: Aggregate change in Taiwan, 1976–1991', paper presented at the 1995 Annual Meeting of the Population Association of America, San Francisco.

Massot, A. (1995). **[15]** 'Fiscalité successorale et patrimoines locatifs', *L'Observatoire de l'Immobilier* 31: 60–63.

Menchik, P. L., (1980). **[14]** 'Primogeniture, equal sharing, and the U.S. distribution of wealth', *Quarterly Journal of Economics* 94(2): 299–316.

Méndez, J. C. (ed.) (1992). **[7]** *El Ladrillo* (Santiago, Centro de Estudios Públicos).

Mesa-Lago, C. (1978). **[6, 12]** *Social Security in Latin America: Pressure Groups, Stratification, and Inequality* (Pittsburgh, University of Pittsburgh Press).

——(1989). **[6]** *Ascent to Bankruptcy: Financing Social Security in Latin America* (Pittsburgh, University of Pittsburgh Press).

——(1994). **[6, 12]** *Changing Social Security in Latin America.* (Boulder, Colo., Lynne Rienner).

Modigliani, F. (1966). **[1]** 'The life cycle hypothesis of savings, the demand for wealth and the supply of capital', *Social Research* (Summer): 160–217.

——(1988*a*). **[2, 15]** 'Measuring the contribution of intergenerational transfers to total wealth: Conceptual issues and empirical findings', in D. Kessler and A. Masson (eds.), *Modeling the Accumulation and Distribution of Wealth* (Oxford, Clarendon Press): 21–52.

——(1988*b*). **[1, 11]** 'The role of intergenerational transfers and life-cycle saving in the accumulation of wealth', *Journal of Economic Perspectives* 2(2): 15–40.

——and Brumberg, R. (1954). **[1]** 'Utility analysis and the consumption function: An interpretation of cross-section data', in K. Kurihara (ed.), *Post-Keynesian Economics* (Princeton, Princeton University Press).

Moon, H.-K. (1995). **[13]** *Financing the Pension Programs in Korea* (Seoul, Korea Development Institute). In Korean.

Morduch, J. (1990). **[10]** 'Risk, production and savings: Theory and evidence from Indian households', manuscript (Dept. of Economics, Harvard University, Cambridge, Mass.).

Morgan, S. P., and Hiroshima, K. (1983). **[13]** 'The persistence of extended family residence in Japan', *American Sociological Review* 48: 269–81.

Mueller, E. (1976). **[2]** 'The economic value of children in peasant agriculture', in R. Ridker (ed.), *Population and Development: The Search for Interventions* (Baltimore, Johns Hopkins Press): 98–153.

Nam, S., Min, J., and Chang, C. (1990). **[13]** *Policy Alternatives in Financing the National Pension Program* (Seoul, Korea Development Institute). In Korean.

Nishimura, K., and Zhang, J. (1992). **[11]** 'Pay-as-you-go public pensions with endogenous fertility', *Journal of Public Economics* 48: 239–58.

Noh, M.-H., Kim, T.-H., Kim, Y.-O., Yang, S.-J., and Moon, Y.-K. (1992). **[13]** *Preliminary Report on the 1992 Women's Employment Survey* (Seoul, Korea Women's Development Institute). In Korean.

Nordhaus, W. (1975). **[7]** 'The Political Business Cycle', *Review of Economic Studies* 42: 169–90.

Nugent, J. B. (1985). **[12]** 'The Old Age Security Motive for Fertility', *Population and Development Review* 11: 75–97.

——and Hu, W. (1994). **[12]** 'Changing generations and actual and expected support from children: The case of rural China', paper presented at Sixty-ninth Meeting of the Western Economic Association, Vancouver, July.

Oreopoulos, P. (1995). **[4]** 'A generational accounting approach to Canadian public policy', manuscript (Western Ontario, University of Western Ontario, Huron College).

Orloff, A. (1992). **[7]** *The Politics of Pensions: A Comparative Analysis of Britain, Canada and the United States, 1880–1940* (Madison, University of Wisconsin Press).

Parish, W. L., and Willis, R. J. (1993). **[13]** 'Daughters, education, and family budgets: Taiwan experiences', *Journal of Human Resources* 28(4): 863–98.

Pollak, H. (1994). **[14]** 'Informal transfers within families', Ph.D. dissertation (Harvard University).

Pontusson, J. (1984). **[7]** *Public Pension Funds and the Politics of Capital Formation in Sweden.* (Göteborg, Arbetslivscentrum, Tryckt av Graphic Systems AB).

Prat, J. (1962). **[7]** *La Legislación Previsional. Comentarios y Proyectos de Reforma* (Santiago, Universidad Católica de Chile.)

Prat Commission [Comisión de Estudios de la Seguridad Social] (1961). **[7]** 'Deterioro de las Pensiones', Report 8 of *Informe sobre la Reforma de la Seguridad Social Chilena* [Prat Report] (Santiago, Editorial Jurídica de Chile).

——(1959–62). **[7]** *Informe sobre la Reforma de la Seguridad Social Chilena* (Santiago, Editorial Jurídica de Chile).

Quisumbing, A. R. (1994). **[12]** 'Intergenerational transfers in Philippine rice villages: Gender differences in traditional inheritance customs', *Journal of Development Economics* 43: 167–95.

Ravallion, M., and Dearden, L.(1988). **[12]** 'Social security in a moral economy: An empirical analysis of Java', *Review of Economics and Statistics* 70: 36–44.

Rofman, R. (1993). **[5]** 'Social security and income distribution: Mortality and equity in pension plans', Ph.D. dissertation (Berkeley, Department of Demography, University of California).

Rhee, K.-O. (1994). **[13]** *Development of Comprehensive National Policies on Ageing: Life-long Preparatory Measures Including Social Security* (Seoul, Korea Institute for Health And Social Affairs).

ROK [Republic of Korea], Economic Planning Board. (1973). **[13]** *The 1970 Census Report*, 1, *Whole Country* (Seoul).

——(1994). **[13]** *Summary Report on the Korean Economy: 1994* (Seoul). In Korean.

——Health and Social Affairs Ministry (1994). **[13]** *Summary Report on Health and Social Affairs in Korea: 1994* (Seoul). In Korean.

——Statistical Office (1993). **[13]** *The 1990 Census Report*, 1, *Whole Country* (Seoul).

Rosati, F. C. (1996). **[11]** ' Social security in a non-altruistic model with uncertainty and endogenous fertility', *Journal of Public Economics* 60: 283–94.

Rosenzweig, M. R. (1988). **[10]** 'Risk, implicit contracts and the family in rural areas of low-income countries', *Economic Journal* 98: 1148–70.

——and Stark, O. (1989). **[10]** 'Consumption smoothing, migration and marriage: Evidence from rural India', *Journal of Political Economy* 97: 905–26.

——and Wolpin, K. I. (1993). **[14]** 'Intergenerational support and the life-cycle incomes of young men and their parents: human capital investments, co-residence, and inter-household transfers', *Journal of Labor Economics* 11(1): 84–112.

Rosenzweig, M. R. and Wolpin, K. I. (1994). **[10, 14]** 'Parental and public transfers to young women and their children', *American Economic Review* 84(5): 1195–1212.

Sackett, R. D. (1989). **[2]** 'Cross-cultural variation in time allocation: Do activity patterns scale with socio-ecological complexity?', paper presented at the Symposium on Time Allocation in Cross-cultural Perspectives, Annual Meeting of the American Ethnological Society, Santa Fe.

Salaff, J. W. (1981). **[13]** *Working Daughters of Hong Kong*, Arnold and Caroline Rose Monograph Series of the American Sociological Association (Cambridge, Cambridge University Press).

Samuelson, P. (1958). **[1, 2, 5]** 'An exact consumption-loan model of interest with or without the social contrivance of money', *Journal of Political Economy* 66(6): 467–82.

——(1975). **[2]** 'The optimum growth rate for population', *International Economic Review* 16(3): 531–8.

Sauvy, A. (1954). **[8]** 'Rapport sur le revenu national: avis et rapports du Conseil Economique, *Journal Officiel*, 7 Avril (repr. in INSEE *Annuaire statistique de la France, Résume Rétrospectif*, 1966).

Shelton, J., and Sueyoshi, G. T. (1994). **[14]** 'Intra- family transfers and relative household income', manuscript (Dept. of Economics, University of California at San Diego, La Jolla).

Shoeni, R. F. (1993*a*). **[14]** 'Does aid to families with dependent children displace family assistance?', manuscript (RAND Corporation, Santa Monica).

——(1993*b*). **[14]** 'Does unemployment insurance displace familial assistance?', manuscript (RAND Corporation, Santa Monica).

——(1993*c*). **[14]** 'Private interhousehold transfers of money and time: New empirical evidence', Labor and Population Program Working Paper 93–26 (Santa Monica, RAND Corporation).

Simmons, L. (1945). **[2]** *The Role of the Aged in Primitive Society* (New Haven, Yale University Press).

Stark, O. (1993). **[11]** 'Non-market transfers and altruism', *European Economic Review* 37: 1413–24.

Stecklov, G. (1995). **[2]** 'Intergenerational Resource Flows in Côte d'Ivoire: An Empirical Analysis', paper presented at the 1995 Annual Meeting of the Population Association of America, San Francisco.

Stoto, M. (1983). **[9]** 'The accuracy of population projections', *Journal of the American Statistical Association* 78: 13–20.

Suh, M.-K. (1992). **[13]** 'The elderly population in Korea: Their health status and kin-based social support', *Korea Journal of Population and Development* 21(2): 197–223.

Summers, R., and Heston, A. (1991). **[1, 13]** 'The Penn World Table (Mark 5): An expanded set of international comparisons, 1950–1988', *Quarterly Journal of Economics* 106: 327–68.

Taiwan, DGBAS [Directorate-General of Budget, Accounting and Statistics], Executive Yuan, Republic of China. (various years). **[3]** *Report on the Survey of Personal Income Distribution in Taiwan Area, Republic of China* (Taipei).

Teng, S. (1964). **[3]** *Tai Wan Jen K'ou Wen T'I* (Taichung, Teng Shan-chang).

Thayer, W., and Fernández, E. (1981). **[7]** *El Nuevo Régimen Previsional y de* Cotizaciones (Santiago, Editorial Jurídica de Chile).

Thomas, J. J. (1992). **[12]** *Informal Economic Activity* (Ann Arbor, University of Michigan Press).

Thomas, J. P., and Worrall, T. (1994). **[10, 14]** 'Informal insurance arrangements in village economies', manuscript (Dept. of Economics, University of Warwick).

Thomson, D. (1989). **[8]** 'The welfare state and generation conflict: Winners and losers', in *Workers versus Pensioners: Intergenerational Justice in an Ageing World*, P. Johnson, C. Conrad, and D. Thomson (eds.) (Manchester, Centre for Economic Policy Research/Manchester University Press).

Thorns, D. C. (1994). **[15]** 'The role of housing inheritance in selected owner-occupied societies (Britain, New Zealand, Canada)', *Housing Studies* 9(4): 473–92.

Thornton, A., and Lin, H.-S. (1994). **[3, 13]** *Social Change and the Family in Taiwan* (Chicago, University of Chicago Press).

Townsend, R. (1994). **[10]** 'Risk and insurance in village India', *Econometrica* 62(3): 539–91.

Treas, J., and Logue, B. (1986). **[12]** 'Economic development and the older population', *Population and Development Review* 12: 645–73.

Tuljapurkar, S. D. (1990). **[9]** *Population Dynamics in Variable Environments* (New York, Springer-Verlag).

——(1992). **[9]** 'Stochastic population forecasts and their uses', *International Journal of Forecasting* 8: 385–91.

Turke, P. W. (1989). **[2]** 'Evolution and the Demand for Children', *Population and Development Review* 15(1): 61–90.

Udry, C. (1994). **[14]** 'Risk and insurance in a rural credit market: An empirical investigation in northern Nigeria', *Review of Economic Studies* 61: 495–526.

UN [United Nations], DESA [Department of Economic and Social Affairs] (1962). **[2]** *Demographic Aspects of Manpower: Sex and Age Patterns of Participation in Economic Activities*. Population Studies, 33.

——Population Division (1994). **[6]** *World Population Prospects: The 1994 Revision* (New York, Dept. for Economic and Social Information and Policy Analysis of the United Nations Secretariat).

——Bureau of the Census (1989). **[9]** *Current Population Reports*, Series P-25, 1018, *Projections for the Population of the United States, by Age, Sex, and Race: 1988 to 2080*, by G. Spencer (Washington, DC, US Government Printing Office).

——Bureau of the Census (various years). **[4]** *Current Population Survey* (Washington, DC, US Government Printing Office).

——(1990). **[2]** *Statistical Abstract of the United States: 1990*, 110th edition (Washington, DC).

——(1992). **[9]** *Current Population Reports Series*, P25–1092, *Population Projections of the United States, by Age, Sex, Race, and Hispanic Origin: 1992 to 2050*, by J. C. Day (Washington, DC, US Government Printing Office).

——(various years). **[4]** *Survey of Income and Program Participation* (Washington, DC, US Government Printing Office).

——Bureau of the Census for the Bureau of Labor Statistics (1993). **[2]** *Current Population Survey*, March, on CD ROM (Washington, DC).

——Department of Commerce, Bureau of Economic Analysis (various years). **[4]** *Survey of Current Business* (Washington, DC, US Government Printing Office).

——Federal Reserve System, Board of Governors (1994). **[4]** *Balance Sheets of the U.S. Economy, 1945–1993, Flow of Funds* (Washington, DC, US Government Printing Office).

UN [United Nations], Social Security Administration (various years). **[4]** *Annual Statistical Supplement to the Social Security Bulletin* (Washington, DC, US Government Printing Office).

——Social Security Administration, Board of Trustees (1995). **[9]** *1995 Annual Report of the Board of Trustees of the Federal Old-Age and Survivors Insurance and Disability Trust Funds* (DC, US Government Printing Office).

——Social Security Administration, Office of Research and Statistics (1994). **[2]** *Social Security Bulletin, Annual Statistical Supplement* (Washington DC, Government Printing Office).

——Social Security Administration, Office of the Actuary (1992). **[9]** *Social Security Area Population Projections 1991*, Actuarial Study 106 (SSA Pub. No. 11–11553), by A. Wade (Washington, DC, US Government Printing Office).

Valdes-Prieto, S. (1994*a*). **[6]** 'Distributive concerns when substituting a pay-as-you-go by a fully funded pension system', *Revista de Análisis Económic*, 3(1): 77–103.

——(1994*b*). **[7]** 'The mandate to contribute: a solvable mistake', *Administración y Economía U.C.* (Santiago), 16.

——(1995). **[7]** 'Vendedores de AFP: Producto del mercado o de regulaciones ineficientes?', Working Paper 178 (Santiago, Instituto de Economía, P. Universidad Católica de Chile).

——and Navarro, E. (1992). **[7]** 'Subsidios cruzados en el seguro de invalidez y sobrevivencia del Nuevo Sistema Previsional Chileno', *Cuadernos de Economía* 29(88): 409–42.

Vallin, J. (1992). **[8]** 'Quelles hypothèses peut-on faire sur l'évolution future de la mortalité?', in *La France dans Deux Générations*, G. Tapinos (ed.), (Paris, Fayard).

Vanderkerkhove, L., Desmond, N., and Birot de la Pommeraye G. (1995). **[15]** 'Habitat et occupation du parc de logement', *INSEE Résultat 392/393.*

Veall, M. R. (1986). **[11]** 'Public pensions as optimal social contracts', *Journal of Public Economics* 31: 237–51.

Venti, F., and Wise, D. A. (1990). **[15]** 'But they don't want to reduce housing equity', in D. A. Wise (ed.), *Issues in the Economics of Aging*, National Bureau of Economic Research Project Report (Chicago and London, University of Chicago Press): 13–32.

Vernière, L. (1990*a*). **[8]** 'Les retraites pourront-elles être payées après l'an 2000', *Economie et Statistique* 233: 19–27.

——(1990*b*). **[8]** 'Retraites: l'urgence d'une réforme', *Economie et Statistique* 233: 29–38.

Villa, P. (1994). **[8]** *Un Siècle de Données Macro-économiques*, INSEE Résultats 303–4.

Vlassoff, M., and Vlassoff, C. (1980). **[12]** 'Old age security and the utility of children in rural India', *Population Studies* 34: 487–99.

Wallich, C. (1983). **[7]** 'Savings Mobilization through Social Security: The experience of Chile during 1916–77'. World Bank Staff Working Paper 553 (Washington, DC, World Bank).

Wagner, G. (1991). **[7]** 'La Seguridad Social y el Programa de Pensión Mínima Garantizada', *Estudios de Economía* 18 (June): 35–91.

——(1983) **[7]** *Antiguo Sistema 1925–1980*, Vol. 2 of *Estudio de la Reforma Previsional* (Santiago, Instituto de Economía, P. Universidad Católica de Chile).

Weatherford, S. (1988). **[7]** 'Political Business Cycles and the Process of Policymaking', *American Politics Quarterly* 16 (Jan.): 99–136.

Weinstein M., Sun, T. H., Chang, M. C., and Freedman, R. (1994). **[3]** 'Co-residence and other ties linking couples and their parents,' in A. Thornton and H.-S. Lin (eds.), *Social Change and the Family in Taiwan* (Chicago: University of Chicago Press).

Wildasin, D. E. (1990). **[11]** 'Non-neutrality of debt with endogenous fertility', *Oxford Economic Papers* 42: 414–28.

Wilhelm, M. (1996). **[14]** 'Bequest behavior and the effect of heirs' earnings: Testing the altruistic model of bequests', *American Economic Review* 86(4): 874–92.

Willis, R. (1987). **[2]** 'Externalities and population', in D. G. Johnson and R. D. Lee (eds.), *Population Growth and Economic Development: Issues and Evidence* (Madison, University of Wisconsin Press): 661–702.

——(1988). **[2]** 'Life cycles, institutions and population growth: A theory of the equilibrium interest rate in an overlapping-generations model', in R. D. Lee, W. B. A., and G. Rodgers (eds.), *Economics of Changing Age Distributions in Developed Countries* (Oxford, Oxford University Press): 106–38.

——(1994). **[2]** 'Economic analysis of fertility: Micro-foundations and aggregate implications', in K. L. Kiessling and H. Landberg (eds.), *Population, Economic Development, and the Environment* (Oxford, Oxford University Press): 139–72.

World Bank (1994). **[6, 12]** *Averting the Old Age Crisis: Policies to Protect the Old and Promote Growth* (Washington, DC, Oxford University Press).

——(1995). **[12]** *World Development Report 1995: Workers in an Integrating World* (Oxford, Oxford University Press).

Yoon, D.-S. (1991). **[13]** 'The eVect of employer size on wage rates in Korea', Ph.D. dissertation (Manoa, Department of Economics, University of Hawaii).

Index

Page numbers in bold refer to figures, and those in italic to tables.

The manufacturer's authorised representative in the EU for product safety is Oxford University Press España S.A. of el Parque Empresarial San Fernando de Henares, Avenida de Castilla, 2 – 28830 Madrid (www.oup.es/en or product.safety@oup.com). OUP España S.A. also acts as importer into Spain of products made by the manufacturer.

www.ingramcontent.com/pod-product-compliance
Lightning Source LLC
Chambersburg PA
CBHW071352220926
51613CB00008B/137
9780198296201